an
introduction
to
modern
philosophy

an introduction to modern philosophy

THIRD EDITION

in eight philosophical problems

by Alburey Castell

macmillan publishing co., inc.
New York
collier macmillan publishers
London

MACMILLAN PUBLISHING CO., INC.
866 Third Avenue, New York, New York 10022

COLLIER MACMILLAN CANADA, LTD.

Library of Congress Cataloging in Publication Data

Castell, Alburey, (date)
  An introduction to modern philosophy in eight philosophical problems.

  First ed. published in 1943 under title: An introduc-
tion to modern philosophy in six philosophical problems.
  Includes index.
  1. Philosophy, Modern. I. Title.
B791.C3 1976   190   74-25600
ISBN 0-02-320070-7

Printing: 1 2 3 4 5 6 7 8   Year: 6 7 8 9 0 1 2

acknowledgments

Acknowledgment is made to the authors and publishers cited below for permission to quote from the
following copyrighted works:
Miracles by C. S. Lewis, reprinted by permission of Macmillan Publishing Co., Inc., New York, and Collins
Publishers, London.

"Existentialism Is a Humanism" by Jean Paul Sartre, translated by B. Frechtman. Copyright 1947 by
Philosophical Library, Inc.

*To my friend
and colleague,*
JOSEPH WARREN BEACH

There is nothing more wholesome for us than to find problems that quite transcend our powers.

Charles Peirce to William James, 1905

a note on the third edition

The major change in this (third) edition is the inclusion of an eighth topic, "The Nature of Man." It has been inserted between what are now the first and third topics, between "The Existence of God" and "Right and Wrong." More than any other, this topic has been suggested as a needed addition by those who have used or considered using this book. Aside from the materials from Holbach, James, Sartre, Ducasse, and Ryle, added to form this new topic, some new authors have been added to the topics carried over from the second edition. Thus, in Topic One, C. S. Lewis's counterattack on naturalism has been added. Because of the character of Lewis's argument, that naturalism cannot give a satisfactory account of man, this section provides a stepping-stone from Topic One ("The Existence of God") to Topic Two ("The Nature of Man"). In Topic Three ("Right and Wrong") a new concluding section has been added: Brand Blanshard's paper criticizing what he called the new subjectivism. Topic Four ("The State and Law") carries Rousseau and Marx from the second edition, and adds sections from Austin, Mill, and Hart. To make room for these additions, some sections have been dropped from topics carried forward from the second edition. These deletions have involved hard decisions. They have been a stiff price to pay for the new materials. Each section in each topic now carries a feature ("Suggestions for Independent Study") intended to enable a student to work on his own with assignments that will introduce him to useful secondary sources, particularly articles in the *Encyclopedia of Philosophy*, edited by Paul Edwards.

Alburey Castell

contents

xi

topic **three**   **right and wrong**   195

topic **four**   **state and law**   276

topic **five**   **history and historical thinking**   372

topic **six**   **art and feeling**   457

topic **seven**   **traditional metaphysics**   514

topic **eight**   **experience and knowledge**   572

index

introduction
an account of this book

This book now (in its third edition) contains readings and comments on eight standing topics in modern philosophy:

1. The existence of God.
2. The nature of man.
3. Right and wrong.
4. The state and law.
5. History and historical thinking.
6. Art and feeling.
7. Traditional metaphysics.
8. Experience and knowledge.

These topics do not form an entirely miscellaneous set. We find ourselves in a world that we did not make and do not sustain. It is there; and, in some sense, we are "in" it. Can we say anything about ourselves in relation to the world, the Cosmos, the "natural" order in which we find ourselves? We know enough about the natural sciences (e.g., astronomy, physics, chemistry, physiology, and so on) to know that by reasoning validly from sufficient relevant data we have gotten to know a considerable amount about the world, and can get to know more. With this large-scale fact "in mind" we sometimes say that the world is, or contains, a rational order, an order you can increasingly find out about the more you reason validly about it from sufficient relevant data. That is one sense in which we use the term *rational* and apply it to the world, or anything in the world: by reasoning about it, you can get to know about it. In this sense we might refer to the solar system as a rational order. This sense of *rational* we are increasingly inclined to ascribe to our world and everything in it. But there is a second sense of *rational* that we are increasingly reluctant to apply to our world and most things in it: the sense in which we say that man is a rational animal, meaning that he can reason and be reasoned with. These two senses of *rational* are distinct: the sense in which the solar system is rational, and the sense in which an astronomer is rational. The more confident we are that our world, or something in our world, is rational in Sense One, the more confident we had *better* be that we are rational in Sense Two, because it takes investigative activity, performed by an animal that is rational in Sense Two, to discover and identify processes that are rational in Sense One.

From the fact that natural science exists, we can say that nature is rational in Sense One and that scientists are rational in Sense Two. This is an argument from the existence of natural science to the existence of rational animals who produced the science. That will give you anthropology, but it will not give you theology. From the existence of a world which is rational in Sense One can you argue to the existence of a Producer of that world who is rational in Sense Two? If not, why not? Can you use what you know about the world to infer anything about a Power, not ourselves, who produced the world? If so, what? If not, why not? The selections in the first topic, "The Existence of God," from Pascal, Hume, Mill, Huxley, James, and Lewis deal with that question.

Corresponding to our two senses of *rational,* there are at least two modes of behavior in the world. There is behavior that is rational in Sense One, e.g., the investigated behavior of chemicals. And there is behavior that is rational in Sense Two, e.g., the investigative behavior of the chemist. Wherever you distinguish between nature and natural scientists, e.g., between the solar system and astronomers, you encounter these two modes of behavior. In what way do processes rational in Sense One differ from activities rational in Sense Two? What is the relation between these two modes of behavior, e.g., between the investigative activities of a chemist and the processes (perhaps chemical) that are going on in his brain and nervous system? That is a way of asking, "What is the relation between man and nature?" The selections in the second topic, "The Nature of

Man," from Descartes, Holbach, James, Sartre, Ducasse, and Ryle deal with aspects of this general question.

In the case of man considered as a rational animal, his rationality, in Sense Two ("he can reason and can be reasoned with"), is expressed when he performs the activity called getting-to-know. But is this cognitive activity the only behavior in which his rationality, in Sense Two, is expressed? Take the behavior in which he is doing what is right, or refraining from doing what is wrong. Such behavior is traditionally called moral. How does such behavior differ from the behavior of a chemical or of a planet revolving on its axis? If you do something because, and only because, it is right, is your behavior rational in Sense Two? If not, why not? The selections in the third topic, "Right and Wrong," from Paley, Kant, Mill, Nietzsche, Ayer, and Blanshard deal with this question.

Man is sometimes called a "political" animal. This means that he is, characteristically, a member of a *polis*, a community committed to the legislative way of life, committed to the regulation of some human behavior by man-made laws. Is his ratonality, in Sense Two, expressed in his behavior as a political animal? If not, why not? The selections in the fourth topic, "The State and Law," from Rousseau, Mill, Marx, and Hart deal with this question.

Man is sometimes called a "historical" animal. This means not only that he has a past, but that he has an indefinitely increasable knowledge of the past, including his own past, and that he bases much, if not all, of his behavior in the present on a knowledge of the past, including his own past. This is characteristically human. Is part of, or an aspect of, man's rationality in Sense Two—a mode of rationality that is not present in the behavior of a planet or a chemical—expressed in his behavior as a historical animal? If not, why not? The selections in the fifth topic, "History and Historical Thinking," from Kant, Hegel, Engels, Spengler, and Collingwood deal with this question.

Man is sometimes called an emotional animal. He "has" emotions or feelings, e.g., anger, sorrow, joy, fear, and so on. At first glance it seems that emotions are something that "happen" to you; that is, they are not something you "do," not activities you perform. If this is so, then having them happen to you is importantly different from, say, getting-to-know. Emotions or their "happening" would be rational in Sense One, but not in Sense Two. They would be "psychological processes" but not "rational activities." They would "happen" to an animal rational in Sense Two, perhaps because he is an animal rational in Sense Two, but would themselves be rational in Sense One. Many persons have given this account of their emotions, and they have gone on to give an account of an activity that they claim to perform with reference to their emotions. They claim to have written poems, composed tunes, painted pictures, and so on, intended to "express," or even to "communicate" their emotions. Such artifacts they call "works of art"; that is, "emotive" symbols, symbols expressing emotions. Reflection upon the activity whereby an artist produces a work of art, when such reflection is triggered by philosophical questions, is called aesthetics. The selections in the sixth topic, "Art and Feeling," from Véron, Tolstoy, Collingwood, Hospers, and Weitz deal with this matter.

Man is a scientific, science-producing animal. This activity marks him as rational in Sense Two, and his world as rational in Sense One. If, as has been claimed, science has presuppositions, and if, as has also been claimed, these presuppositions are productive of but not produced by science, then what are we to say of them? They are metascientific; they come before science, making science possible, but are not the outcome of scientific activity. If you use the term *physics* to stand for all natural science, then they would be *metaphysics*. One of the oldest and "simplest" positions in metaphysics is *materialism,* the presupposition that if anything is real then it is made of matter; and that matter is what physics says it is. Materialism is not the only position in metaphysics. Not all metaphysicians agree that if anything is real then it is made of matter. So they dispute among themselves, producing criticisms and alternatives. The selections in the seventh topic, "Traditional Metaphysics," from Hobbes, Berkeley, Schopenhauer, and Comte provide access to argumentation, claim and counterclaim, in reference to this aspect of the cognitive life of rational animals.

The eighth and last topic is an extension of Topic Seven. It is one thing to claim, for example, that if X is known, then X is real; and that if X is real, then X is matter. That will put you in business as a metaphysician, a rational animal with a claim about knowledge in relation to reality. It is, however, another thing to claim that if X is known, then X has been experienced; that if you have had no experience of X, then you have no knowledge of X; that "all knowledge comes from experience." The traditional term for this *sort* of claim is not *metaphysics* but *epistemology.* The claim that all getting-to-know originates, and must not transcend, experiencing is the epistemological thesis traditionally designated *empiricism.* Empiricism is not the only theory about getting-to-know, but as with materialism in metaphysics, it is a good point at which to start. The selections in the final, eighth, topic, "Experience and Knowledge," from Hume, Kant, Ayer, and Collingwood introduce you to one major issue, one center of claim and counterclaim, in reference to this aspect of the cognitive life of rational animals.

topic **one**
the existence of God

THE PROBLEM STATED

The existence of "natural" science—e.g., astronomy, physics, chemistry, physiology, and geology, and so on—is *prima facie* evidence that nature, or much of nature, is rational in Sense One. If you reason validly from sufficient relevant data you can find out about nature, or much of nature. If nature, or no part of nature, is rational in Sense One, it becomes difficult to account for the existence, the production, of natural sciences. But that is not all. You can go on to say that the existence of natural science is also *prima facie* evidence that natural scientists, producers of natural science, are rational in Sense Two. If scientists are not rational in Sense Two, if they can neither reason nor be reasoned with, it becomes difficult to account for the existence, the production, of natural sciences.

In addition to natural science, it is customary to speak of natural theology: knowledge, or beliefs, about God based on knowledge, or beliefs, about nature. So conceived, natural theology would be a worked-out, reasoned-out, rationally arrived-at knowledge or belief about God. Given the question, "Can you use what you know about nature to justify what you believe about God?" natural theology   5 would propose the answer "yes." It is clear that natural theology goes beyond natural science. Given the question, "Can you use what you know about nature to justify what you believe about nature?" natural science proposes the answer "yes." This would get you from nature to natural science, but it is a step beyond that to get from nature, or even from natural science, to natural theology. If you set out from nature, hoping to reason your way from, or through, nature to God, will you end up in atheism, or skepticism, or theism? The answer to this question is going to depend, in part, on what you know about nature and in part on what you believe about God.

Atheism is the claim that, given what most people *mean* when they use the term *God*, there is no God. The proviso is important. If, by the term *God*, you mean simply that nature, the whole of nature, is through and through rational in Sense One, and nothing more than this, then it is possible that you may not have a run-in with the atheist. But natural theology has traditionally claimed more than this. It has claimed that God created, produced, and sustains nature; and achieves specifiable purposes in so doing. For natural theology what you *mean* by *God* has never been simply equivalent to what you *mean* by *nature*. God, in one way or another, has been claimed as something *more* than nature; and more, in a different and further way than natural science, or even a natural scientist, is more than nature. It is this "more" that atheism denies. That nature exists, that nature is rational in Sense One, that natural science exists, that men are rational in Sense Two—none of these facts, says atheism, requires us to claim that God exists.

On this point it is important to distinguish between atheism and skepticism. Many people who claim to be atheists turn out to be skeptics. Their claim is "I do not know. We do not know." This is a more modest claim than that of atheism. It is one thing to claim that you do not know whether it is possible to reason validly from nature to God. It is more ambitious to claim that it is not possible to reason validly from nature to God. This is traditional atheism. It is even more ambitious to claim that it is possible to reason validly from nature to the nonexistence of God. Most atheists do not sponsor this last claim.

The authors brought together in the present topic (Pascal, Hume, Mill, Huxley, James, and Lewis) invite your attention to the central question in natural theology: "Can you use what you know about nature to justify what you believe about God?" From the fact that all of them answer this question with a "no," you cannot infer that any of them is an atheist. Pascal was a devout seventeenth-century French Catholic: no room for atheism there. Hume was a convinced skeptic: he insists that if you put the question in those terms, you ensure the triumph of skepticism. Mill insists that unless you radically scale down what you *mean* by the term *God,* then you cannot use what you know about nature to justify what you believe about God. Huxley's agnosticism comes out close to Hume's skepticism. Huxley's term *agnosticism* contains a moral note which is not present in Hume's skepticism. Agnosticism is a second-order claim. It is that if you cannot use what you know to justify what you believe, then your belief, he would say, is a "stolen" belief, a belief that it is immoral to hold. James, like Pascal, was a committed believer, but, also like Pascal, he was convinced that our knowledge of nature does not justify us in what we believe about God. He insisted that if you believe in God, you are exercising the *will to believe;* that is, you are allowing your will to believe to outrun your capacity to produce objective, justifying, evidence. Finally, C. S. Lewis proposes a counterattack against atheism and skepticism in theology. His counterattack forms part of his attempt to rehabilitate the case for miracles. His claim is that the existence of God is presupposed by the existence not of nature, but of natural science.

In Topic One you are to read selected passages from Pascal, Hume, Mill, Huxley, James, and Lewis. Each will deal directly or indirectly with the overall question, "Can you use what you know about nature as evidence for what you believe about God?" If you are to learn from your authors, what they think and why they think it, it is imperative that you make an effort to discover what *you* think and why *you* think it. If you do not know your own mind on a given question, you are more or less at the mercy of your authors. How do you find out *what* you think and *why* you think it, on such a question as your authors are dealing with? How can you trigger your own mind about a large and complex question? This is an important part of learning to read, write, and talk philosophy. Here are a dozen questions to put to yourself as a preparatory exercise, a "warm-up," before moving on to your authors. For each question, once you are satisfied that you understand the question, find out what you think, and, equally important, why you think it. The question asks, "What do you think on this matter?" It may be that you do not know precisely *what* you think. Pester your mind until you find out. That is half the job. A more demanding question remains: "*Why* do you think whatever it is you think on this matter?" The *why* here asks for your *reason.*

TRIGGER QUESTIONS

1. If you were an atheist, your claim would be that God does not exist. How would you defend your claim?

2. If you were an agnostic, your claim would be that neither His existence nor His nonexistence can be known. How would you defend your claim?
3. If you claim that God is good, should you therefore also claim that He cares more about our goodness than He does about our happiness?
4. If a person claims that God is dead, what question is he open to?
5. What is it to *create*?
6. Are there any miracles?
7. Why is there any evil and misery in the world?
8. A historian, it seems, may address himself without undue misgivings to the question "Did the Crucifixion and the Reformation happen?" However, what about the question "Did the Incarnation and the Ascension happen?"
9. Voltaire claimed that if God did not exist, it would be necessary for us to invent Him. Why, would you say?
10. Claims answer questions, and then give rise to questions. Illustrate from theology.
11. Is it ever the part of wisdom to let belief outrun evidence?
12. Is there any form of life higher than human life?
13. Compare these two questions: (a) Can you use what you know about nature as evidence for what you believe about God? (b) As evidence for what you believe about man?
14. If it were possible for you to ask God one question, what would the question be? Having asked the question, what two points could you be sure of?

SECTION 1. BLAISE PASCAL: THE RELIGIOUS WAGER

Biographical Note.   Pascal was born in 1623 and died in 1662 at the age of thirty-nine. He was educated at home. His parents, especially his father, were devout Catholics, pious but stern. Blaise early displayed a remarkable precocity in physics and mathematics; at the age of fifteen he was producing monographs on conic sections which were thought important enough to be read to "the most learned and scientific men in Paris." He was counted one of the outstanding physicists and mathematicians of his time. His discoveries were made during the years when most scientists are still mastering the known facts of their field.

The elder Pascal died in 1650, leaving a patrimony to Blaise and his sister Jacqueline. Jacqueline entered a convent; Blaise went off to Paris. During the next four years he lived among scholars, scientists, wits, and the nobility. On November 23, 1654, he had what is termed a mystical experience. That he had this experience, there is no reason to doubt; that it meant what he interpreted it to mean is perhaps open to debate.

That hour, described for posterity in a note which was found sewn into the coat he was wearing at the time of his death, wrought a change in Pascal's life. Austerity, self-denial, almsgiving, obedience to his spiritual director replaced his routine of scientist and man-about-town. He threw himself into the defense of the Cistercian abbey of Port Royal des Champs, which was being persecuted by the hierarchy for a number of real or supposed heresies. The case for the Port Royalists was stated by Pascal in his celebrated *Letters to a Provincial*. The closing years of his life were given to planning and sketching in what was to have been, had he lived to complete it, an apologia for the Christian faith addressed to persons of unbelief and indifference. The book was never finished. It consists of hundreds of loosely grouped fragments, aphorisms, jottings. It has been known, in French, by the title *Pensées;* in English, by the title *Thoughts.* The passages which follow are quoted, abridged, or paraphrased from this unfinished defense of Pascal's religious beliefs.

The passages given below do not trace the argument of Pascal's entire book. Much of that volume deals with special topics, for example, the relation of other religions to Christianity, the significance of miracles, prophecy, revelation, and so on. With these we are not concerned. Our interest is limited to the question "Can a man, by the use of his reason, infer the existence of God from the existence of nature?" Can you use what you know about nature to justify what you believe about God? To this question, Pascal, a devout Christian and Catholic, answers in the negative. The movement of his thought is as follows: Some persons are skeptical or indifferent in matters of religious belief. Such persons are to be pitied and scorned. But no appeal to reason, no natural theology, will avail to dissolve their doubts, denials, indifference. This for two reasons: they are too hardened; and in any case, human reason is unequal to the task of elaborating a rational theology. Pascal soliloquizes at some length on the littleness of man and the impotence of reason. If not through his rational powers, then through what can the doubting and indifferent soul be brought to a belief in God? Pascal's answer is this: through his emotions. In a famous line he remarks: "The heart hath its reasons, which the reason knows not of." The utmost that reason can do is to pose and defend what Pascal describes as a "wager," that is, a bet that God exists. Man must see for himself that his happiness lies in belief in and love of God. When he has seen this fact, his skepticism and indifference will be replaced by faith and happiness and true goodness.

He begins with those who have doubts about the existence of God and are not particularly worried over it:

Before entering on the proofs of the Christian religion, I find it necessary to set forth the unfairness of men who are indifferent to the search for truth in a matter which is so important to them and which touches them so nearly. Among all their errors, this most proves them to be fools and blind.

We know well enough how men of this temper behave. They believe they have made a great effort after their instruction when they have spent a few hours reading some book of Scripture and putting a few questions to some ecclesiastic. Whereupon they boast that they have "in vain consulted books and men." Such carelessness is intolerable.

Among unbelievers I make a vast distinction. I can have nothing but compassion for all who sincerely lament their doubt, who look upon it as the worst of evils, who spare no pains to escape it, who make these matters their chief and most serious occupation. But those who pass their lives without thinking of this ultimate end of existence, who neglect to examine whether these are matters which people receive through credulous simplicity or have a solid and impregnable basis, such persons I regard in a wholly different manner. Their negligence irritates me much more than it excites my pity. It astonishes and overwhelms me; it is for me something monstrous.

There are but three classes of persons: those who have found God and serve Him; those who have not found God, but do diligently seek Him; and those who have not found God, and live without seeking Him. The first are happy and wise. The second are unhappy, but wise. The third are unhappy and fools.

It is a sorry evil to be in doubt. It is an indispensable duty to seek when we are in doubt. Therefore he who doubts and neglects to seek to dispel these doubts, is at once in a sorry plight and guilty of great perversity. If he is calm and contented in his doubt, if he frankly avows it, if he boasts of it, if he makes it the subject of vanity and delight, I can find no terms with which to describe him.

How do men come by these sentiments? What delight is there in such things? What is there to be proud of in beholding ourselves in the midst of impenetrable darkness? How can any rational man reason in this way: "I know not who has put me in the world, nor what the world is, nor what I am myself. I am in terrible ignorance of all these things. I view the awful spaces of the universe that surround me, I find myself fixed to a corner of this vast extent, I see nothing but infinities on every side enclosing me like an atom. All that I know is that I must soon die. Such is my state—full of misery, weakness, obscurity. And from this I conclude that I ought to pass all the days of my life without thinking of what is to happen to me hereafter. It may be that I could find some answers to my doubts; but I am unwilling to take the trouble."?

Who would desire to have for a friend a man who discourses in such a fashion? Who would select such a person to be the confidant of his affairs? Who would have recourse to such a one in his afflictions? In fine, for what use in life could such a man be destined? It is the glory of religion to have such irrational men for its enemies. Such strange insensibility for the greatest things is something monstrous. It is an incomprehensible delusion.

There must be a strange revulsion in the nature of man, to make him glory in such a state. Most of those who are thus involved are people who have heard that fine worldly manners consist in what they call "throwing off the yoke." This they try to imitate. But, what good does it do us to hear a man say that he has "thrown off the yoke," that he does not believe there is a God, that he is answerable in his conduct to none but himself? Is this a thing to be said gaily? On the contrary, is it not a thing to be said with sadness, as of all things the saddest? It requires all the love of the religion which they despise, not to despise such persons and abandon them in their folly.

So much for perverse doubts and callous indifference. Pascal knows that there is a long tradition of rational theologizing which, in its heyday, triumphed easily over such skepticism and infidelity. But that day had passed. Since then, Montaigne had written. Doubt had taken too firm a hold to be dislodged by appeals to man's reason in support of religious belief. To what point, he seems to ask, such intellectual circumgyrations as the argument from design, or the argument from first cause, when a man has really ceased to believe in God?

I wonder at the boldness of those who undertake to speak of God to the irreligious. Their first chapter is to prove the existence of God by reference to the works of nature. I should not be astonished if they addressed their argument to those who already believe; for those who have a lively faith in their heart see at once that all that exists is none other than the handiwork of God. But for those who are destitute of faith—to tell them that they need only look at nature around them in order to see God unveiled, to give them the course of the sun and the moon as the sole proof of this important matter, to imagine with such an argument we have proved anything, is only to give grounds for believing that the proofs of our religion are very feeble. Indeed, I see by reason and experience that nothing is more fitted to excite contempt.

This is what I see, and what troubles me. I look on all sides, and see nothing but obscurity; nature offers me nothing but matter for doubt. If I saw nothing in nature which marked a Divinity, I should decide not to believe in Him. If I saw everywhere the marks of a Creator, I should rest peacefully in faith. But I see too much to deny, and too little to affirm; so my state is pitiful. A hundred times I have wished that God would mark His presence in nature unequivocally, if He upholds nature; or that nature would wholly suppress the signs which she gives of God, if those signs are fallacious; that she would either say all or say nothing, so I might see what part I should take. While in my present state, ignorant of what I am and of what I ought to do, I know neither my condition nor my duty.

The metaphysical proofs of God are so far apart from man's reason, and so complicated, that they are but little striking. If they are of use to any, it is only during the moment that the demonstration is before them. An hour afterwards they fear they have been mistaken. Therefore I do not here undertake to prove by natural reason the existence of God. I do not feel myself strong enough to find in nature proofs to convince hardened atheists. All who seek God in nature find no light to satisfy them. They fall either into atheism or into deism, two things which the Christian religion almost equally abhors.

What then? Revealed theology, as Pascal well knows, is a dead horse when one is chasing doubters and deniers. Rational theology, in the sense of a reasoned appeal from nature to God, he has himself rejected as barren and unconvincing if a man does not already feel God in his heart. His answer, worked out in the fragments of his unfinished *Thoughts,* comes to this: The strongest proof for the existence of God is the great need felt by the human soul for the sustaining presence of such a Being in an otherwise empty universe.

He begins this step in his argument by drawing attention to the immensity of the spatio-temporal universe in which man finds himself:

Let a man contemplate nature in her full majesty. Let him extend his view beyond the objects which surround him. Let him regard the sun. Let him consider the earth whereon he lives as a point in comparison with the vast orbit described by the sun. Let him learn that this vast orbit is but a point compared with that embraced by the stars which roll in the firmament. Let his imagination pass beyond. All this visible cosmos is but a point in the ample bosom of nature. In vain we extend our conceptions beyond imaginable spaces: We bring forth but atoms in comparison with the reality of things. For the universe is an infinite sphere whose center is everywhere and whose circumference is nowhere.

From the vastness of things, he passes to the other extreme. Compared to the whole of nature, man may be a mere speck. But compared to the infinitely small particles which compose the material world, he is a colossus.

There is another aspect, equally astonishing. Let a man seek things the most minute. Let him consider a mite, in the exceeding smallness of its body: parts incomparably smaller, limbs with joints, veins in those limbs, blood in those veins, humors in this blood, globules in these humors, gases in the globules. Let him divide these globules. Let him exhaust his powers of conception. He will think perhaps that he has arrived at the minutest atom of nature. I will show him therein a new abyss. I will picture to him the inconceivable immensity of nature in the compass of this abbreviation of an atom. Let him view therein an infinity of worlds, each with its own firmament, its planets, its earth, in the same proportion as the visible world. Let him lose himself in these wonders, as astonishing in their littleness as the others in their magnitude. His body, which just before was imperceptible in the universe, is now a colossus in comparison with the infinitely small at which it is possible to arrive.

With this contrast in mind, Pascal pauses to ask: What is man, amid all this? He could have used the words of the Psalmist, "What is man that Thou art mindful of him?" But at this point, that would be begging the question: it is that "Thou" that is in question.

What is man, in the midst of these two infinities? A nothing compared with the infinitely large, all compared with the infinitely small. A mean between all and nothing, infinitely far from comprehending the extremes. Let us, then, know our range. Such is our true state. This is what renders us incapable, alike of absolute knowledge and absolute ignorance.

Nature confounds the skeptics, and reason confounds the dogmatists. What will become of you, O man, who would search out your true condition by your natural reason? You can avoid neither skepticism nor dogmatism; but, alas, you can live with neither!

Our intelligence holds the same position as our body, in the vast extent of nature. This middle state between two extremes is common to all our weaknesses: our senses can perceive no extreme; too much noise deafens us, too much light blinds us, too far or too near interferes with our vision, too much brevity or too much prolixity obscures our understanding, too much truth overwhelms us, too much pleasure cloys on us, too many benefits annoy us, we feel neither extreme heat nor extreme cold, too much and too little teaching hinder our minds—in a word, all extremes are for us as though they were not. They escape us or we escape them.

Man is a creature full of natural error. Nothing shows him the truth, everything deceives him. His reason and his senses deceive each other. The senses trick the reason by false appearances; reason in turn avenges herself and deceives the senses. His emotions trouble his senses and make false impressions on him. Reason, senses, emotions, lie and deceive, outdoing each other.

What a chimera is man! Strange and monstrous! A chaos, a contradiction, a prodigy. Judge of all things, yet a weak earthworm. Depository of truth, yet a cesspool of uncertainty and error; the glory and the scrapings of the universe.

Who will unravel such a tangle? Is it beyond the power of dogmatism, of skepticism, of philosophy. Man is incomprehensible by man. We grant that to the skeptics. Truth is not within our reach, nor to our taste; her home is not on earth.

We sail on a vast expanse of being, ever uncertain, ever drifting, ever hurried from one goal to another. If we seek to attach ourselves to any one point, it totters and fails us; if we follow, it eludes our grasp, vanishing forever. Nothing stays for us. This is our natural condition. Yet, it is the condition most contrary to our inclination; for we burn with desire to find a steadfast place and a fixed basis whereon we may build. But our whole foundation breaks up, and the abysses open before us.

When I consider the short duration of my life, swallowed up in an eternity before and after, the small space I fill engulfed in the infinite immensity of spaces whereof I know nothing, and which know nothing of me, I am terrified. The eternal silence of these infinite spaces alarms me. I wonder why I am here, rather than there, now rather than then. Who has set me here? By whose order and design have this place and time been destined for me?

When I see the blindness and misery of man; when I survey the whole dumb universe; when I see man left to himself without a light unto his path, lost in this corner of the cosmos, ignorant of who placed him here, of what he has come here to do, of what will overtake him when he dies, I fall into terror. And my terror is like that of a man who should awake upon a terrible desert island with no means of escape. And I wonder why men do not fall into despair. I see others around me, of like nature. I ask if they are better informed than I am; and they say they are not.

We may not, then, look for certainty or stability. Our reason is always deceived by changing shows. It matters not that man should have a trifle more knowledge of the universe; if he has it, he but begins a little higher; but he is always infinitely distant from the end. In regard to the infinities, all finites are equal, and I see no reason why we should fix our imagination on one more than on another.

Who would not think, when we declare that man consists of mind and matter, that we really understood this combination? Yet—it is the one thing we least understand. Nothing is more obscure than just this mixture of spirit and clay. Man is, to himself, the most marvelous object in nature, for he cannot conceive what matter is, nor what mind is, nor how a material body should be united to an immaterial mind. This is the crown of all his difficulties; yet it is his very being.

These are some of the causes which render man so totally unable to know nature. For nature has a twofold infinity, while he is finite. Nature is permanent, while he is fleeting and mortal. All things change and fail; he sees them only as they pass. All things have their beginning and their end; he sees neither the one nor the other. Things are simple and homogenous. He is complex and composed of two different elements.

Not from space must I see my dignity. I should have no more if I possessed whole worlds. By space the universe encompasses and swallows me as an atom. Man is but a reed, weakest in nature, but a reed which thinks. A thinking reed. It needs not that the whole universe should arm to crush him. A vapor, a drop of water is enough to kill him. But were the universe to kill him, man would still be more noble than that which has slain him, because he knows that he dies, and that the universe has the better of him. The universe knows nothing of this.

Know then, proud Man, how great a paradox thou art to thyself. Bow down thyself, impotent reason; be silent, thou foolish human nature. Learn that man is altogether incomprehensible by man.

Let man now estimate his value. Let him love himself, because he has a nature capable of good. But let him not love the vileness which exists in that nature. He has in himself the capacity of knowledge and happiness, yet he finds no last truth or satisfaction. I would lead him to desire it; to be freed from passions, to know how his passions obscure his knowledge and his achievement of happiness. I would have him hate in himself the desires which bias his judgment, that they might neither blind him in choosing nor obstruct him when he has chosen.

The net result is that man is ignorant and helpless and alone. The blind forces of nature offer him no haven. The universe at large cares as little for his living as for his dying. In his quest for happiness and goodness, he is confronted by an alien, indifferent, even hostile world. Pascal might have let it go at that. Many have; for example, Schopenhauer and Thomas Hardy and Bertrand Russell. Not so Pascal. In such a plight, his soul could find no peace and rest. So he picks up the argument again, reminding man that the conquest of true happiness is at stake:

All men seek happiness. To this there is no exception. Our will makes no step, except toward this object. This is the motive of every action of every man. And yet, after so many years no one has arrived, without faith, at the point to which all eyes are turned. All complain, rulers and ruled, nobles and commons, old and young, strong and weak, learned and ignorant, sound and sick, of all countries, all times, all ages, and all conditions.

A trial so long, so constant, so uniform, should have convinced us of our inability to arrive at our complete happiness by our own strength. But example teaches us little. We expect that our efforts will not be foiled on this occasion, as before. Thus while the present never satisfies us, experience never teaches us; and from misfortune to misfortune we are led on to death, the eternal crown of our sorrows.

This desire, and this weakness, cry aloud to us that there is an empty space in man which he seeks vainly to fill from all that surrounds him, seeks vainly to find in things absent the happiness which he finds not in things present.

Peace of mind, happiness of soul, are nowhere within reach so long as these are sought for among the things of this world. Who can deny that? But who is prepared to let it go at that? Not Pascal, at any rate. It is at this point that his argument becomes a record of his personal findings:

Man finds his lasting happiness only in God. Without Him, there is nothing in nature which will take His place; neither the stars, nor heaven, nor earth, nor the elements; not plants, cabbages, animals, insects, calves, serpents, fever, pestilence, war, famine, vices, adultery, incest. Since man has lost track of his true happiness, all things appear equally good to him, even his own destruction, though so contrary to God, to right reason, and to the whole course of nature.

There is no good without knowledge of God. Only as we approach Him are we happy; and our ultimate good is to know Him certainly. We are unhappy, in proportion as we are removed from Him; and the greatest evil would be the certainty of being cut off from Him.

These reflections bring Pascal to the terms of his famous religious wager. It may be well to restate his position before proceeding: Some men doubt God's existence, and are indifferent to their doubts. For them Pascal has nothing to say. But others doubt, and are concerned. Like the man in the New Testament they cry, paradoxically: "Lord, I believe, help Thou my unbelief!" To those who feel this cry, Pascal addresses himself. They must recognize the futility of attempting a "rational" solution to their doubts: Renaissance skepticism, personified in Montaigne, has blown up that bridge. It remains to face squarely the utter loneliness and littleness of man. Left to himself, his hopes and joys and values and aspirations are doomed to extinction. In God alone, if there be a God, can he hope to find a friend and protector. But, good skeptic that he is, Pascal knows that there is a gap between the fact of our need for God and God's inferred existence to fill that need. Hence his intellectual honesty. He is himself satisfied to argue from our need for God to the existence of God. But he does not ask his reader to follow him in that inference. He proposes a wager:

> If there be a God, He is infinitely incomprehensible, since, having neither parts nor limits, He has no relation to us. We are, then, incapable of knowing either that He is or what He is.
>
> Let us examine this point: "Either God is, or is not," we can say. But to which side shall we incline? Reason cannot help us. There is an infinite gulf fixed between creature and creator. What will you wager? It is like a game in which heads or tails may turn up. There is no reason for backing either the one possibility or the other. You cannot reasonably argue in favor of either.
>
> If you know nothing either way, it might be urged, the true course is not to wager at all. But you must wager; that does not depend on your will. You are embarked in this business. Which will you choose?
>
> Let us see. Since you must choose, your reason is no more affronted in choosing one way than the other. That point is clear. But what of your happiness? Let us weigh the gain and the loss in wagering that God does exist. If you wager that He does, and He does, you gain all; if you wager that He does, and He does not, you lose nothing. If you win, you take all; if you lose, you lose nothing. This is demonstrable, and if men are capable of any truths, this is one. Wager then, unhesitatingly, that He does exist.
>
> If we ought to do nothing except on a certainty, we ought to do nothing for religion, because it is not a matter of certainty. But it is false to say, "We ought to do nothing except on a certainty." In a voyage at sea, in a battle, we act on uncertainties. If it be the case that we ought to do nothing except on a certainty, then we ought to do nothing at all, for nothing is certain.
>
> You may object: "My hands are tied, my mouth is gagged. I am forced to wager, I am not free. But, despite this, I am so made that I cannot believe. What then would you have me do?"
>
> I would have you understand your incapacity to believe. Labor to convince yourself, not by more "proofs" of God's existence, but by disciplining your passions and wayward emotions. You would arrive at faith, but know not the way. You would heal yourself of unbelief, yet know not the remedies. I answer: Learn of those who have been bound as you are. These are they who know the way you would follow, who have been cured of a disease you would be cured of. Follow the way by which they began, by making believe what they believed. Thus you will come to believe.
>
> Now, what will happen to you if you take this side in the religious

wager? You will be trustworthy, honorable, humble, grateful, generous, friendly, sincere, and true. You will no longer have those poisoned pleasures, glory and luxury; but you will have other pleasures. I tell you that you will gain this life; at each step you will see so much certainty of gain, so much nothingness in what you stake, that you will know at last that you have wagered on a certainty, an infinity, for which you have risked nothing.

If my words please you, and seem to you cogent, know that they are the words of one who has thrown himself on his knees before and after to pray to that infinite Being to whom he submits all; know too that you also would submit to Him your all for your own good and His glory, and that this strength may be in accord with this weakness.

Thus Pascal, seventeenth-century religiously minded skeptic. Does he leave more to be said on the question of natural theology? Hume, in the eighteenth century, only articulates more delicately the case against "reason" in these matters. Mill, in the nineteenth century, advances a claim designed to save men from the emotionalism of Pascal and the skepticism of Hume. James, in the twentieth century, comes full circle back to Pascal in a pragmatic approach to this perennial question.

Note on Sources. The Pascal material in this section is quoted, abridged, or paraphrased from his book *Thoughts.* That book consists of 923 numbered items. The following items have been used in this chapter: Numbers 194, 195, 205, 206, 229, 233, 347, 348, 434, 437—and a few here and there among the remaining items.

Reading References. Aldous Huxley, the English novelist, has written what amounts to a small book on Pascal. It is to be found in his volume of essays *Do What You Will.* In this study, Huxley attempts to "take Pascal to pieces" to see precisely what it is that "makes the wheels go round." The result is catastrophic—for Huxley, if you agree with Pascal; for Pascal, if you agree with Huxley. Such highly seasoned and partisan treatment should be balanced by something more conventional and appreciative. Several first-rate monographs exist. Among these are *Pascal* by Jacques Chevalier and *Pascal—the Life of Genius* by Morris Bishop. Bishop's volume is more suited to those who come to the study of Pascal from Anglo-American traditions.

READING QUESTIONS

1. As a first step toward his wager, Pascal classifies people into three groups. To which group will he address his wager? Why not to the other groups?

2. His second step is to undermine natural or rational theology. How this prepares for the wager.
3. He argues against theology, first from the side of nature and then from the side of man. Which argument you consider most incisive in each of these two lines of attack.
4. His third step is to insist that man seeks happiness but to deny that he will find it in either nature or himself. How this prepares for the wager.
5. Why you do or do not agree with Pascal that man cannot find true happiness in either nature or himself.
6. At this point he proposes his wager. State it.
7. Sense in which doubt, not belief, is a premise of the wager.
8. If you cannot believe, then make believe. Why? What good will come of it?
9. Pascal's point in each of the following:
   a. Too much to deny, too little to affirm.
   b. Nature confounds the skeptics and reason confounds the dogmatists.
   c. Nothing is more obscure than just this mixture.
   d. Not from space must I seek my dignity.
   e. The two infinities.
10. What do you know of the seventeenth century that makes Pascal a plausible figure?
11. Wherein you find Pascal (a) most convincing, (b) least convincing.

INDEPENDENT STUDY

1. Read the article on Pascal by R. H. Popkin in the *Encyclopedia of Philosophy*, Volume 6, and the article by W. F. Cobb in the *Encyclopedia of Religion and Ethics*, Volume 9. Supplement these two articles by the materials in this chapter. Use all three sources to compose a paper on the life and thought of Pascal.
2. Consult the card catalogue in your library under *Pascal*. Examine books published in the last forty years (1935–1975). Select the volume that seems to you the most promising, e.g., Bishop's *Pascal: The Life of Genius*, or Mesnard's *Pascal: His Life and Works*. Read as much of the book you select as needed to provide you with material for a paper on a Pascal theme of your own choosing.
3. Consult a volume of Pascal's writings, e.g., *Living Thoughts of Pascal*, edited by François Mauriac, or *Pensées*, with an introduction by T. S. Eliot. Use either or both of these volumes to work out a paper on a Pascal topic of your own choosing.

SECTION 2. DAVID HUME: DOUBTS ABOUT
NATURAL THEOLOGY

From Pascal to Hume.   The problem of natural theology continued to command attention. We have seen repudiation by Pascal; a repudiation, however, that left no bitter taste in the devout reader's mouth, since Pascal strove earnestly to restore with one hand what he swept aside with the other. By the middle of the eighteenth century times and tempers had changed. The "Age of Reason" had set in. The French Revolution was drawing nearer. The natural sciences, from their small beginnings with Galileo and Bacon and Harvey in the seventeenth century, had come to exercise considerable dominion over the imaginations of the intellectual classes. It was in this somewhat more chilly climate of opinion that David Hume turned his critical attention to natural theology.

Biographical Note.   Hume was born in Scotland in 1711 and died in 1776 at the age of sixty-five. Although he was destined, along with Immanuel Kant, to mark the opening of an as yet unclosed chapter in the history of philosophy, his early life was passed in obscurity, and his fame, among his contemporaries, was based principally upon his writings in the field of political history.

He was intended by his father for the law, and to that end was educated in Edinburgh. However, he abandoned the study of law and tried his hand in a Bristol counting-house. This, too, proved uncongenial. He went to France, where he proceeded to write one of the epoch-making books in modern philosophy, his *Treatise of Human Nature.* The theme of this philosophical masterpiece is simply stated in the form of a question: How much of human knowledge, human emotional preferences and aversions, human morality, is what it is for no better reason than the fact that human nature is what it is? The suggestion, that once you have taken the "human" out of these things there is nothing left over, was too much for his generation to entertain. It contained too many skeptical implications. The *Treatise* fell, as though stillborn, from the press.

Hume now set about to find employment that would put him in a position of independence. He applied, without success, for the chair of moral philosophy in the University of Edinburgh. For two years he tutored an almost insane Scottish marquis. He accompanied a diplomatic expedition to France. He applied, again without success, for the chair of logic at the University of Glasgow. At last he secured the position of Keeper of the Advocates' Library in Edinburgh. The access to books and original authorities that this gave him suggested the idea of writing a work on history. This he proceeded to do and, between 1754 and 1762, produced his famous *History of England,* which ranked, in that century, with Gibbon's *Decline and Fall of the Roman Empire.*

In the lean years before he became Keeper and turned historian, Hume continued reworking and expanding the ideas of his original philosophical treatise. These were published in a series of short monographs and collections of essays. In this form they gained a gradual acceptance. But it was still the historian who overshadowed the philosopher in the minds of his generation. He retired from active life in 1769, on a combined income and pension of £1,000 a year. He spent the remainder of his days, the recognized head of the intellectual and literary society in Edinburgh, admired by those who read his *History* and his miscellaneous essays, distrusted or misunderstood by those who tried their hand at his philosophy.

The Argument of the Passages.   The selections that follow provide a skeptical examination of natural theology. They are, for the most part, from Hume's essay "On Miracles" and from *Dialogues Concerning Natural Religion.* They presuppose, as a starting point, that the reader is familiar with the stock arguments for the existence of God.

The position finally occupied by Hume is somewhat complex. We may imagine him saying,

Either we have knowledge of God's existence and nature, or we do not. If we do not possess such knowledge, there is no call for a skeptical examination. If, however, we do possess, or claim to possess, such knowledge, then it must rest on some sort of evidence. What is this evidence? It is formulated, usually, in three "arguments." There is the argument from miracles, the argument from design, and the argument from first cause. A skeptical examination of the claims of natural theology will include a skeptical examination of these three arguments. We shall advance two lines of criticism with respect to each: first, that the argument itself is questionable; second, that even if it were accepted without question, it does not prove what it claims to prove.

It is well to remember the limitations of the task which Hume sets himself. He is not attempting to prove that God does not exist; that is, he is not stating the case for atheism. Nor is he seeking to discredit all belief in God. His claim is the more modest one, namely, that such belief, whether true or false is not susceptible of the traditional argumentative justification; that no "appeal to reason," can be made in support of the claims of natural theology.

Belief in God has, in times past, been supported by what is called the *argument from miracles.* It is to this effect: Miracles, violations of natural laws, occur from time to time. An explanation of such events must therefore refer to something outside or beyond nature. That is, miracles point to a miracle-worker, namely, God. Hence Hume's interest in the question of miracles. His approach is indirect. He does not deny that miracles ever happen. He directs attention to the nature of the evidence upon which we believe that miracles happen and claims that the evidence in question is not strong enough to support the belief:

> I flatter myself I have discovered an argument which will be an everlasting check to all kinds of superstitious delusion, all accounts of miracles and prodigies sacred and profane.
> A miracle is a violation of the laws of nature. Now, as a firm and unalterable experience has established our belief in those laws, the proof against miracles, from the very nature of the case, is as entire as any argument from experience can possibly be imagined. There must be a uniform experience against any miracle; otherwise it would not be so described. Now, as a uniform experience amounts to a proof, there is here a full proof against the occurrence of any miracle. Nor can such a proof against any miracle be weakened or destroyed, except by an opposite proof which would be superior to it.
> The plain consequence is this: No testimony is sufficient to establish a miracle unless the testimony be of such a kind that its falsehood would be as miraculous as, or more miraculous than, the fact which it endeavors to establish. Even in that case there is a mutual destruction of arguments; and the superior only gives us an assurance suitable to that degree of evidential force which remains after deducting the inferior.
> A man tells me he saw one dead restored to life. I ask myself: Is it more probable that he should deceive or be deceived, or that the fact which he relates should really have happened? I weigh one miracle against the other, and reject the greater. If the falsehood of his testimony would be more miraculous than the event which he relates, then (but not until then) can he command my belief.

There are two parts to Hume's criticism of the evidence for believing that miracles happen. The first, and most incisive, has been given already: Miracles purport to be violations of the laws of nature. Our evidence for believing in the uniformity of nature is so great that no evidence for doubting it could be strong enough, since it would have to be stronger than the evidence for believing in nature's uniformity and this latter includes practically all our experience. He moves on to a second criticism:

> We have supposed in the foregoing that the evidence for a miracle may be so strong that its falsehood would itself be a miracle. But it is easy to show that we have been a great deal too liberal in our concessions, and that no miracle has ever been established on so full an evidence.

First: There is not to be found in all history any miracle attested by a sufficient number of men of such unquestioned good sense, education, and learning, as to secure us against all delusion in themselves; of such undoubted integrity as to place them beyond all suspicion of any design to deceive others; of such credit and reputation as to have a great deal to lose in case of being detected in any falsehood; and, at the same time, attesting facts in such a manner and in so celebrated a place as to render that detection unavoidable.

Second: The many instances of mistaken or fraudulent miracles which have been detected show that mankind have a strong propensity to believe in the extraordinary and marvelous. This fact ought reasonably to beget a suspicion against all narratives concerning such matters.

Third: Reports of miracles abound chiefly among ignorant and barbarous peoples; or if such reports have been admitted by civilized and educated peoples they will be found to have received them from ignorant and barbarous peoples who transmitted them with that sanction and authority which, among such peoples, attends received opinions. This fact constitutes a strong presumption against all accounts of miracles.

Fourth: There is no *a priori* case in favor of the miracles peculiar to any one religion. The miracles of all religions stand on the same footing. If any such should be mutually incompatible, they simply cancel each other out. Nor is there any *a priori* case in favor of religious over secular miracles.

Fifth: The records of miracles in ancient times are not to be placed on an equal level with the records of nonmiraculous events in ancient times. Because some human testimony has the utmost force and authority in some cases, as when it relates to the battle of Philippi or Pharsalia, the assassination of Caesar or the execution of Socrates, it is not therefore reasonable that all kinds of testimony must, in all cases, have equal force and authority.

It appears, then, that no testimony for any kind of miracle has ever amounted to a probability, much less a proof. Experience only gives authority to human testimony, and it is experience which assures us of the laws of nature. When, therefore, these two kinds of experiences are contrary, we can only subtract the one from the other and embrace the opinion with that assurance which arises from the remainder. But, according to the measures of probability above established, this subtraction amounts to entire annihilation. Therefore no human testimony can have such force as to prove a miracle and make it a just foundation for any system of religion.

Mere reason is not sufficient to convince us of the miracles of the Christian religion. Whoever is moved by faith to assent to it, is conscious of a continued miracle in his own person, which subverts all the principles of his understanding and gives him a determination to believe what is most contrary to custom and experience.

The net result thus far: Belief in God rests in part on belief in miracles. Belief in miracles rests on questionable grounds. Belief in God, therefore, insofar as it rests on belief in miracles, rests on questionable grounds. Hume's case against the argument from miracles ends at that point. He might have rounded out his argument with greater force. This was done by T. H. Huxley, Hume's biographer, in the next century. Huxley's argument proceeded along this line: Suppose the evidence for believing in miracles is left unquestioned. Suppose we admit without argument, that miracles do take place. What follows? Belief in the Deity described by orthodox Christian theology? It would seem not. For miracles are an equivocal kind of evidence. They point frequently to a Deity who befriends some people at the expense of others. Consider, for example, the Old Testament miracle of the taking of Jericho. What kind of evidence would this be, in the eyes of a citizen of Jericho? Or consider the miracle of the Gadarene swine recorded in the New Testament. What kind of evidence would this be, in the eyes of the unfortunate individual who owned those swine, or (to stretch a point) in the eyes of the still more unfortunate swine? These, and similar miracles, are equivocal testimony to the Deity's universal benevolence. Moreover, if miracles are evidence of His benevolence, why do they fail to occur in so many cases where benevolence would seem to be in order, for example, when a vessel is sinking in a storm at sea? The point does not need elaboration: miracles, even if not disputed, do not provide us with decisive evidence one way or the other about God. And, when evidence is ambiguous, it is wiser to omit it.

Hume proceeds, in his examination of natural theology, to a statement and refutation of the *argument from design*. This is one of his most famous pieces of destructive criticism.

The chief argument for divine existence is derived from the order of nature. Where there appear marks of intelligence and design, you think it extravagant to assign for its cause either chance or the blind unguided force of matter. This is an argument from effects to causes. From the order of the work, you infer there must have been project and forethought in the workman.

Look around the world. Contemplate the whole and every part of it. You will find it to be nothing but one great machine, subdivided into an infinite number of lesser machines, which again admit of subdivisions to a degree beyond what human senses can trace and explain.

All these various machines, and even their most minute parts, are adjusted to each other with an accuracy which ravishes into admiration all men who have ever contemplated them. The curious adapting of means to ends, throughout all nature, resembles exactly, though it much exceeds, the productions of human contrivance, human design, human thought, wisdom, intelligence.

Anatomize the eye. Survey its structure and contrivance. Does not the idea of contriver immediately flow in upon you with the force like that of a sensation? Behold the male and female of each species, their instincts, their passions, the whole course of their life before and after generation. Millions of such instances present themselves through every part of the universe. Can language convey a more intelligible, more irresistible meaning than the curious adjustment of means to ends in nature?

Since the effects (natural productions and human productions) resemble each other, you are led to infer, by analogy, that the causes also resemble; that the author of nature is somewhat similar to the mind of man, though possessed of larger powers, proportioned to the grandeur of the work He has created.

You compare the universe to productions of human intelligence, to houses, ships, furniture, machines, and so forth. Since both terms of the comparison exhibit adaptation and design, you argue that the cause of the one must resemble the cause of the other.

The argument from design, he says, is an argument from analogy: We examine a watch, a house, or a ship, and we conclude that such things were produced by beings possessing intelligence and controlled by purposes. We can, if we wish, verify this inference by acquainting ourselves with watchmakers, architects, and shipwrights. We examine the universe, or parts of it, and conclude that it too must have been produced by a being possessing intelligence and controlled by purposes. Our reason for drawing this inference is that we find the universe, or parts of it, intelligible and answering to our needs and purposes. That is, we draw the analogy watch-watchmaker and universe-Deity. From the intelligibility and utility of a watch, we infer intelligence and purposiveness in the watchmaker. By analogy, from the intelligibility and utility of nature we infer intelligence and purposiveness in the author of nature. Hume's criticisms are directed toward undermining the strength of the proposed analogy between human product–human producer, on the one hand, and nature–author of nature on the other: "Is the analogy entire and perfect?" he asks and proceeds to show in what respects he thinks it is weak:

When two things (human intelligence and the products of human intelligence) have been observed to be conjoined, you can infer, by custom, from the one to the other. This I call an *argument from experience.* But how this argument can have place in the present case, may be difficult to explain. If you see a house, you can conclude it had an architect or builder because such effects, you have experienced, proceed from such causes.

But does the universe resemble a house so closely that we can with the same certainty infer a similar cause? Is the analogy entire and perfect? Can you pretend here to more than a guess, a conjecture, a presumption, concerning a similar cause? To ascertain such reasoning, it were necessary that you have had experience in the origin of the world. Have worlds ever been formed under your eye? Have you experienced the generation of the universe as you have experienced the building of a house?

If you survey a ship, you form an exalted idea of the ingenuity of the builder. You find him a stupid mechanic who imitated others, who copied an art which through a long succession of ages, after multiplied mistakes, corrections, deliberations, and controversies has been gradually improving. On your argument, then, many worlds might have been botched and bungled ere this one was arrived at; much labor lost; many fruitless trials made; a slow improvement during infinite ages in the art of world-making.

When you read a book, you enter into the mind and intention of the author, and have an immediate feeling and conception of those ideas which revolved in his imagination while employed in that composition. Is it thus when you read the book of nature?

By this argument from analogy, how prove the unity of Deity? Many men join in building a house or ship or city or commonwealth. Why may not several deities have combined in framing a world? This is only so much greater similarity to human affairs, to the operation of human intelligence. By dividing thus the work among several, you would get rid of that extensive power and knowledge which must be supposed in one deity.

Were one deity, who possessed every attribute necessary to the production of the universe, and not many deities, proved by this argument from analogy, it would be needless to suppose any other deity. But while it is still an open question whether all these attributes are united in one deity or dispersed among several independent deities, by what phenomena in nature can you pretend to decide the controversy? On this kind of argument from nature, polytheism and monotheism are on a like footing. Neither has any advantage over the other.

By this method of reasoning from analogy you renounce all claim to perfection in any of the attributes of the Deity. Imperfections in human productions you ascribe to imperfections in human producers. There are many inexplicable difficulties in the work of nature. Are you to ascribe these to the imperfections of the author of nature?

By representing Deity as so intelligible and comprehensible, so similar to a human mind, you make ourselves the model. Is this reasonable? The sentiments of the human mind include gratitude and resentment, love and hate, friendship and enmity, blame and approval, pity and scorn, admiration and envy. Do you propose to transfer such sentiments to a Supreme Being? Or suppose Him actuated by them? Do you propose to ascribe to Him only knowledge and power but no virtues?

The preceding passages bring out several difficulties in the proposed analogy which, Hume thinks, lies at the heart of the argument from design. The criticism continues, the point of attack being shifted slightly. From the nature of the product, you infer certain characteristics in the producer; from a man's handiwork you infer that the man is of such and such character. Hume has no objection to this. His next point is merely that we should extend the same reasoning to the world and the maker of the world. What sort of place is this world, anyway? Is it such that we are obliged to argue that its author must have possessed the benevolent and providential attributes ascribed to him by traditional theology?

Can any man, by a simple denial, hope to bear down the united testimony of mankind? The whole earth is cursed and polluted. A perpetual war is kindled among all living creatures. Necessity, hunger, want, stimulate the strong and courageous; fear, anxiety, terror, agitate the weak and the infirm. The first entrance into life gives anguish to the newborn infant and to parent. Weakness, impotence, distress, attend each stage of many lives which are finished at last in agony and horror.

Is it not thus in nature? Observe the curious artifices of nature to embitter the life of living beings. The stronger prey upon the weaker, and keep them in perpetual terror and misery. The weaker, too, often prey upon the stronger. Consider those species of insects which are bred on the body of animals, or flying about, infix their stings into them. These insects have others, still more minute, which torment them. On every hand animals are surrounded with enemies which cause their misery and seek their destruction.

Why should man pretend to be exempted from the lot which befalls all other animals? Man is the greatest enemy of man. Oppression, injustice, contempt, slander, violence, sedition, war—by these men torment each other. The external ills of humanity, from the elements, from other animals, from men themselves, form a frightful catalogue of woes; but they are nothing compared with those that arise from conditions within. How many lie under the lingering torment of disease? How many suffer remorse, shame, anguish, rage, disappointment, fear, despair? How many suffer those deep disorders of mind, insanity, idiocy, madness? Who has passed through life without cruel inroads from these tormentors?

Were a stranger to drop into this world, I would show him, as a specimen of its ills, a hospital full of diseases, a prison crowded with malefactors, a battlefield strewn with carcasses, a fleet floundering in the ocean, a nation languishing under tyranny, famine, or pestilence. Labor and poverty are the certain lot of the far greater number, while the few who enjoy riches and ease never reach contentment or true felicity. All the good things of life taken together make a man very wretched indeed.

You ascribe an author to nature, and a purpose to the author of nature. What, I beseech you, is the object fulfilled by these matters to which attention has been drawn? Our sense of music, harmony, beauty, has some purpose. But what of gout, gravels, megrims, toothaches, rheumatisms? How does divine benevolence and purpose display itself here? Why argue for the power and knowledge of the Deity while His moral qualities are in doubt?

You say: But this world is only a point in comparison of the universe; this life is but a moment in comparison of eternity. Present evils are rectified in other regions and future times. And the eyes of men, being then opened to large views of things see the whole connection of general laws, and trace with adoration the benevolence and wisdom of the Deity through all the mazes and intricacies of his providence.

I answer: The only method of supporting divine benevolence is for you to say to me, "Your representations are exaggerated; your melancholy views are mostly fictitious; your inferences are contrary to fact and experience; health is more common than sickness; pleasure, than pain; happiness, than misery; for one vexation we meet, we attain a hundred enjoyments."

I add: Can such apologetics be admitted? Even allowing your claim that human happiness exceeds human misery, yet it proves nothing. For an excess of happiness over misery is not what we expect from infinite power coupled with infinite wisdom and infinite goodness.

The questions asked by Epicurus, of old, are yet unanswered. Is Deity willing to prevent evil, but not able? Then He is not omnipotent. Is He able, but not willing? Then He is malevolent. Is He both able and willing? Then whence cometh evil? Is He neither able nor willing? Then why call Him Deity?

Evil and unhappiness are the rocks upon which all arguments for Deity must finally come to wreck. Why is there any misery and wickedness at all in the world? Not by chance, surely. From some purpose or cause then? Is it from the intention of the Deity? But He is perfectly benevolent. Is it contrary to his intention? But He is almighty. Nothing can shake the solidity of this reasoning, so short, so clear, so decisive; unless we agree that these matters lie beyond human capacity, that our human reason is not applicable to them. This is the counsel of skepticism that I have all along insisted on.

In the preceding passages Hume has been making capital out of the problem of evil. He has, by this time, made his two principal criticisms of the argument from design: The analogy upon which it rests cannot be admitted; and even if it were admitted, it would come to grief over the problem of evil. However, he cannot let it go at that. The next seven passages give a different line of criticism. The point they make is sufficiently evident to require little comment. From God as Designer, he turns to God as Soul, of the world.

You have argued, thus far, on the principle that like effects have like causes. But there is another you might try, based no less on experience: Where several known parts are observed to be similar, the unknown parts will also be found similar. Thus, if you see the limbs of a human body, you conclude that it is attended with a human head, though hid from you. If you see a small part of the sun, through a chink in the wall, you conclude that, were the wall removed, you should see the rest. Within the limits of experience, this method of reasoning is obvious and reliable.

Now I say, if you survey the universe, so far as it falls under your knowledge, it bears a great resemblance to an animal, or organized body, and seems actuated by a like principle of life and motion. A continual circulation of matter produces no disorder. A continual waste in every part is incessantly repaired. Each part, in performing its proper offices, operates both to its own preservation and that of the whole. From all this, why not infer that the world is an organism, an animal, and that Deity is the soul of the world, actuating it and being actuated by it?

If it be legitimate to argue thus by analogy from part to whole, I affirm that other parts of the world bear a greater resemblance to the structure of the world than do matters of human invention; and, therefore, should afford a better conjecture concerning the origin and nature of the whole. These parts are animals and vegetables. The world resembles more an organism than a clock or a knitting loom. Its cause, therefore, more probably resembles the cause of the former, namely, generation.

As a tree sheds its seed into neighboring fields, so the great system of the world produces certain seeds which, being scattered into the surrounding chaos, grow into new worlds. A comet, for instance, may be taken as such a seed. After it has been fully ripened, by passing from sun to sun and star to star, it is at last tossed into the unformed elements which surround this universe, and sprouts into a new system.

Or, for variety (for I see no other advantage), suppose this world to be an animal instead of a vegetable. A comet then would be an egg. And, in like manner as an ostrich lays its egg in the sand, which without any further care hatches the egg, so. . . .

You protest: What wild, arbitrary suppositions are these? What data have I for such extraordinary conclusions? Is the slight resemblance of the world to a vegetable or animal sufficient basis for an argument as to further resemblances? You are right. This is what I have been insisting on, all along. We have no data, or insufficient data, for any such speculations. Our experience, from which alone we can argue safely, is so limited in extent and duration as to afford us no probable conjecture concerning the whole of things.

If you agree that our limited experience is an unequal standard by which to judge of the unlimited extent of nature, a too narrow stretch upon which to erect hypotheses concerning so vast a matter, you entirely abandon your case, and must admit of the absolute incomprehensibility of the author of nature.

The whole matter is summarized in the two following passages:

In a word, a man who follows this kind of argument from analogy, where one of the terms of the analogy lies beyond his experience, may perhaps be able to conjecture that the universe arose from something like design. But beyond that he cannot go, except by the utmost license of thought.

On this argument, for all you know to the contrary, this world may be a very faulty and imperfect copy compared to a superior standard; only the first rude essay of some infant deity who afterwards abandoned it, ashamed of his lame performance; only the work of some dependent, inferior deity, the object of derision to his superiors; only the product of old age and dotage in some superannuated deity, and ever since his death running on at adventures from the first impulse it received from him.

Thus far, the argument from miracles and the argument from design. The argument from the analogy of human producers led one to deny or left one unable to account for the facts of evil and misery, and led one to admit or left one unable to deny the absurd speculations which he suggested regarding the organic nature and origin of the world. If these arguments from miracles and from design presented so many difficulties, would one fare better with the argument from first cause? By this argument could one prove the infinity, the unity, and the perfection, of the author of nature? Hume states this argument as follows:

The argument from first cause is this. Whatever exists must have a cause of its existence. Nothing can produce itself. In mounting up, therefore, from effects to causes, we must go on tracing an infinite regression without any ultimate cause, or must finally have recourse to an ultimate cause. Now, it is insisted, the conception of an infinite regression, of utterly no beginning cause to which all others can be traced, is absurd. We must, therefore, have recourse to a necessarily existent being, the first cause of all things, who carries the reason of His existence in Himself, and whom we cannot suppose not to exist without embracing an absurdity. Such a being is the Deity.

His criticism is brief and to the point:

Wherein do we find the absurdity of an infinite regression? It leads us beyond our powers of conceiving? So also does the conception of an infinite deity.

Let us admit its absurdity. Let us admit the necessity of a first cause. Shall we then ask for a cause of this cause? If not, then may we not argue a material first cause of this material universe? If not, may we ascribe to the spiritual first cause the origin of evil and misery and waste which we noted in our analysis of the argument from analogy? If not, to what cause then are they to be traced? If so, wherein do we fare better with the argument from the necessity of a first cause than from the probability of an intelligent designer?

His conclusion to the whole business is a plea for skepticism in natural theology:

All religious systems are subject to insuperable difficulties. Each disputant triumphs in his turn, exposing the absurdities, barbarities, and pernicious tenets of his antagonist. But all of them prepare a complete triumph for the skeptic who tells them no system ought ever to be embraced with regard to such questions. A total suspense of judgment is here our only reasonable recourse.

The upshot of Hume's critique of natural theology is skepticism. Its historical importance is along several lines. In the first place, it was a nemesis visited upon the Age of Reason; for what Hume showed was the helplessness of reason to cope with the problems of natural theology. In some minds this work has never been undone. For them, Hume administered a deathblow to the speculations at which he directed his attention. Rational theology, in the grand manner has never been completely restored to its former intellectual respectability. In the second place, Hume's handling of these questions led to an interesting attempt, by John Stuart Mill in the following century, to introduce into theology the conception of a finite God; in the twentieth century, to the pragmatic approach to these matters in the writings of the American, William James.

Note on Sources.   The Hume material in this section is quoted, abridged, or paraphrased from the short essay "On Miracles" in his book *An Enquiry Concerning Human Understanding;* and from his small book *Dialogues Concerning Natural Religion.* The *Dialogues* is divided into twelve Parts. The present section is based on Parts 2, 3, 4, 5, 6, 7, 8, 9, and 10.

Reading References.   Hume's skeptical examination of natural theology forms only one part of his general philosophy. He cultivated comparable doubts in other fields. The reading from Hume given in the eighth chapter of this book, the chapter dealing with epistemology, provides the premises from which he approached problems. These will be looked at at that point.

READING QUESTIONS

1. Why Hume is interested in a criticism of belief in miracles.
2. Where we get our evidence for believing in the uniformity of nature. Why, then, the proof against miracles is "as strong as any argument from experience could be."
3. Five reasons for saying that the evidence for belief in miracles cannot be so strong that its falsity would be a miracle.
4. Why the Christian who believes in miracles is conscious of a miracle in himself. Does Hume use the term *miracle* in the same sense each time here?
5. What addition to Hume's criticism is contained in Huxley's criticism?
6. In what way the Jericho episode and the Gadarene episode are equivocal as evidence.
7. Distinguish between criticizing the evidence *for* miracles, and criticizing miracles *as* evidence. Which of these two, if valid, would be the more devastating?
8. Why Hume does well to criticize the evidence for belief in miracles rather than to try to prove that miracles do not happen.
9. Which: (a) You believe that God exists because you believe that miracles happen; or (b) you believe that miracles happen because you believe that God exists.

10. Hume defines a miracle as a violation of the laws of nature. How about this? Need it be so defined?
11. State the analogical argument to which Hume reduces the so-called design argument.
12. His primary criticism of the analogy is contained in the paragraphs "When two" and "But does." State this criticism.
13. He then makes four supplementary criticisms: (a) On this argument many worlds might have been botched and bungled. (b) On this argument how prove the unity of the Deity? (c) On this argument how prove the perfection of the Deity? (d) On this argument you make ourselves the model. Bring out his point in each case.
14. He then has a long aside on the ills of nature, society, and man. Why this gloomy review?
15. What come-back ("you say") a reader might make. Hume's come-back to such a come-back. ("I answer." "I add.")
16. Set of questions he ascribes to the Greek philosopher Epicurus. Hume's point here.
17. Restate the following in the form of a dilemma: Why is there any misery and wickedness in the world? Is it from the intention of the Deity? But He is perfectly benevolent. Is it contrary to His intention? But He is almighty.
18. Having considered and rejected the argument which would make God the designer of the world, he then considers the argument that would make Him the soul of the world. On what grounds he rejects it also.
19. His two criticisms of the argument that says that the world must have a first cause and that the first cause is God.
20. Wherein you find Hume (a) most, (b) least convincing.

INDEPENDENT STUDY

1. Read "Miracles" by A. Flew; "Evil, The Problem of," by J. Hick; and "Teleological Argument for the Existence of God" by W. P. Alston; all three are articles in *The Encyclopedia of Philosophy.* Use these three articles to work out a paper in which you *either* criticize *or* extend Hume's treatment of natural theology in this chapter.
2. Write a paper on A. E. Taylor as critic of David Hume in theology. Base your paper on at least these items by Professor Taylor; (a) *David Hume and the Miraculous,* originally published as a booklet, and subsequently republished in Taylor's volume of

essays *Philosophical Studies.* (b) Taylor's article "Theism," in Hastings's *Encyclopedia of Religion and Ethics.* You might find use for Chapter 6, Volume Two, of Sir Leslie Stephen's *English Thought in the Eighteenth Century.*
3. Read any three parts in Hume's *Dialogues Concerning Natural Religion.* If the parts are consecutive and connected, give a coherent account of what Hume is talking about, what he says about it, and why he says it. Include criticism only if you desire to do so.

SECTION 3. JOHN STUART MILL: A FINITE GOD

From Hume to Mill. Thus far we have examined Pascal and Hume on the question: "Can you use what you know about nature to support what you believe about God?" Pascal gave reasons for answering: "No. There is no sound argument from nature to God. If you are unable or unwilling to accept revelation, you had better settle for a wager." Hume gave reasons for rejecting any argument from miracles, or design, or causation, in nature to the proof of anything like the orthodox Christian beliefs about God. This brings matters close to the end of the eighteenth century. In the century that followed, interesting variations were proposed. Not least among these was John Stuart Mill's celebrated attempt to save natural theology from skepticism by advancing the claim that an appeal to reason, based on what we know about nature, might be made in support of belief in a finite or limited God.

Biographical Note. John Stuart Mill was born in England in 1806 and died in 1873 at the age of sixty-seven. Lord Morley, in a review of Mill's life and work, referred to him as "the saint of Victorian rationalism." He might well have added "and of Victorian liberalism." For a great portion of Mill's contribution to modern liberalism is summed up in two propositions: that human reason applied to human experience is the only source of human knowledge; and that a maximum of individual liberty of thought and action is the surest means of extending knowledge and increasing happiness. In the elaboration and defense of these claims he wrote books and essays that came, in time, to form the staples of British liberalism in the nineteenth century. That all knowledge comes from experience is the thesis of his *System of Logic.* That the distribution of wealth is the fundamental problem in economics is the thesis of his *Principles of Political Economy.* That freedom of thought and action is the safest gurantee of individual and social well-being is the thesis of his essay *On Liberty.* That an act is right if, and only if, it produces more happiness than any other act possible, is the thesis of his *Utili-*

tarianism. That government by elected representatives is preferable to either constitutional monarchy or an enlightened aristocracy is the thesis of his *Considerations on Representative Government.* That women have as much right to votes and careers as men, is the thesis of *The Subjection of Women.* That the evils of a capitalistic economy give some point to the doctrines of socialists is the thesis of his *Socialism.* And that only so much as can be grounded in experience should be retained in a living theology is the thesis of *Three Essays on Religion.* For further biographical material, see pp. 222 and 312 ff.

The Argument of the Passages. Mill seeks to establish (1) that Deity is a Being of "great but limited power"; (2) that He is a Being of "great and perhaps unlimited knowledge and intelligence"; (3) that benevolence but not justice is one of His attributes; (4) and that a theology centering in this conception has several things to recommend it over the more traditional views. The selections are from his essay on theism. The argument opens as follows:

The most important quality of an opinion on any momentous subject is its truth or falsity. It is indispensable that the subject of religion should be reviewed from time to time, and that its questions should be tested by the same methods, and on the same principles as any of the speculative conclusions drawn by physical science.

From this introductory remark, Mill passes to a consideration of the argument from design. He prefers it because it "is grounded wholly on our experience of the appearances of the universe"; that is, we can see order and harmony and adaptation of some sort by merely observing the nature of things, whereas we have no experience whatever of such things as first causes and unmoved movers.

Whatever ground there is to believe in an author of nature is derived from the appearances of the universe. The argument from design is grounded wholly on our experience of the appearances of the universe. It is, therefore, a far more important argument for theism than any other.

Mill's formulation of the argument from design, given in the next six passages, is more elaborate than we have met hitherto. His words bear close attention:

The order of nature exhibits certain qualities that are found to be characteristic of such things as are made by an intelligent mind for a purpose. We are entitled from this great similarity in the effects to infer similarity in the cause, and to believe that things which it is beyond the power of man to make, but which resemble the works of man in all but power, must also have been made by intelligence armed with a power greater than human.

The argument from design is not drawn from mere resemblances in nature to the works of human intelligence, but from the special character of those resemblances. The circumstances in which it is alleged that the world resembles the works of man are not circumstances taken at random, but are particular instances of a circumstance which experience shows to have a real connection with an intelligent origin; the fact, namely, of conspiring to an end or purpose.

To show this, it will be convenient to handle, not the argument from design as a whole, but some one of the most impressive cases of it, such as the structure of the eye or the ear. It is maintained that the structure of the eye proves a designing mind. The argument may be analyzed as follows:

1. The parts of which the eye is composed, and the arrangement of these parts, resemble one another in this very remarkable respect, that they all conduce to enabling the animal to see. These parts and their arrangement being as they are, the animal sees. This is the only marked resemblance we can trace among the different parts of the eye; beyond the general likeness in composition which exists among all other parts of the animal.

2. Now, the combination of the parts of the eye had a beginning in time and must therefore have been brought together by a cause or causes. The number of instances (of such parts being brought together to enable organisms to see) is immensely greater than is required to exclude the possibility of a random or chance concurrence of independent causes. We are therefore warranted in concluding that what has brought all these parts together was some cause common to them all. And, since the parts agree in the single respect of combining to produce sight, there must be some connection between the cause which brought the parts together, and the fact of sight.

3. Now sight, being a fact which follows the putting together of the parts of the eye, can only be connected with the production of the eye as a final cause, not an efficient cause; since all efficient causes precede their effects. But a final cause is a purpose, and at once marks the origin of the eye as proceeding from an intelligent will.

At this point we should expect Mill to proceed with his evaluation of the design argument. But he proposes, instead, to develop an alternative explanation covering the type of facts which would be explained by the hypothesis of God's existence if that hypothesis were accepted. This alternative to "creative forethought," or "intelligent will," is the hypothesis of "natural selection" suggested by Mill's contemporary, Charles Darwin. The important point to notice is the way in which natural selection, if granted as an hypothesis, would account for the type of fact which seems to demand explanation in terms of intelligent will.

Of what value is this argument? Is intelligent will, or creative forethought, the only hypothesis that will account for the facts? I regret to say that it is not. Creative forethought is not the only link by which the origin of the mechanism of the eye may be connected with the fact of sight. There is another connecting link on which attention has been greatly fixed by recent speculation. This is the principle of natural selection, of "the survival of the fittest."

This principle of the survival of the fittest does not pretend to account for the origin of sensation, or of animal or vegetable life. It assumes the existence of some one or more very low forms of organic life, in which there are no complex adaptations. It next assumes, as experience warrants us in doing, that many small variations from those simple types would be thrown out, which would be transmissible by inheritance, some of which would be advantageous to the creature in its struggle for existence and others disadvantageous. The forms which are advantageous would always tend to survive; and those which are disadvantageous, to perish. Thus there would be a constant, though slow, general improvement of the type as it branched out into many different varieties, until it might attain to the most advanced examples which now exist.

It must be acknowledged that there is something very startling, and *prima facie* improbable in this hypothetical history of nature.

With reference to the eye, for example, it would require us to suppose that the primeval animal could not see, and had at most such slight preparation for seeing as might be constituted by some chemical action of light upon its cellular structure; that an accidental variation (mutation) would produce a variety that could see in some imperfect manner; that this peculiarity would be transmitted by inheritance while other variations continued to take place in other directions; that a number of races would thus be produced who, by the power of even imperfect sight, would have a great advantage over all other races which could not see and would in time extirpate them from all places except perhaps from a few very peculiar situations underground. Fresh variations would give rise to races with better and better seeing powers until we might at last reach as extraordinary a combination of structures and functions as are seen in the eye of man and of the more important animals.

Of this theory, when pushed to this extreme point, all that can now be said is that it is not so absurd as it looks; and that the analogies which have been discovered in experience, favorable to its possibility, far exceed what anyone could have supposed beforehand. Whether it will ever be possible to say more than this is at present uncertain.

Leaving this remarkable speculation to whatever fate the progress of discovery may have in store for it, I think it must be allowed that, in the present state of our knowledge, the adaptions in nature afford a large balance of probability in favor of creation by intelligence. It is equally certain that this is no more than a probability.

Having noted these two hypotheses, creative forethought and natural selection, and rejected the latter as less probable, Mill turns to the question of the nature of the being whose creative forethought is under consideration:

The question of the existence of a Deity standing thus, it is next to be considered what sort of Deity the indications point to. What attributes are we warranted, by the evidence which nature accords of a creative mind, in assigning to that mind?

The first attribute is great but limited power:

It needs no showing that the power, if not the intelligence, must be so far superior to that of man as to surpass all human estimate. But from this to omnipotence and omniscience there is a wide interval. And the distinction is of immense importance.

For I shall argue that the net result of natural theology, on the question of the divine attributes is this: a Being of great but limited power; how, or by what, limited we cannot even conjecture; of great, perhaps unlimited intelligence; who desires and pays some regard to the happiness of His creatures but who seems to have other motives of action for which He cares more, and who can hardly be supposed to have created the universe for that purpose alone.

Then follow passages in which this claim is supported by a series of ingenious arguments:

Every indication of design in the cosmos is so much evidence against the omnipotence of the designer. For what is meant by *design?* Contrivance, the adaptation of means to end. But the necessity for contrivance, the need of employing "means" to achieve an "end," is a consequence of the limitation of power.

Who would have recourse to means, to attain his end, if his mere wish or word was enough? The very idea of *means* implies that the means have an efficacy which the direct action of the being who employs them has not. Otherwise, they are not means but an encumbrance.

A man does not use machinery to move his arms; unless he is paralyzed, i.e., has not the power to do so directly by his volition.

But, if the use of contrivance is a sign of limited power, how much more so is the careful and skillful choice of contrivance? Could we speak of "wisdom in the selection of means," if he who selects them could, by his mere will, have achieved the same results without them, or by any other means? Wisdom and contrivance are shown in overcoming difficulties, and there is no room for difficulties, and so no room for wisdom or contrivance, in an omnipotent being.

Any evidences of design in nature, therefore, distinctly imply that the author of nature worked under limitations; that he was obliged to adapt himself to conditions independent of his will and to attain his ends by such arrangements as those conditions admitted of.

On this hypothesis, the Deity had to work out His ends by combining materials of given nature and properties. This required skill and contrivance; and the means by which it is effected are often such as justly excite our wonder and admiration. But, exactly because it requires wisdom, skill, contrivance, it implies limitation of power.

It may be said: An omnipotent Creator, though under no necessity of employing contrivances such as man must use, thought fit to do so in order to leave traces by which man might recognize his Creator's hand.

The answer is: This equally supposes a limit to the Deity's omnipotence, for it is a contrivance to achieve an end. Moreover, if it was His will that man should know that they and the world are His work, He, being omnipotent, had only to will that they should be aware of it.

From the question of God's power, Mill turns to the question of His knowledge and wisdom. The claim here is that there are probably no grounds for ascribing infinite knowledge or intelligence to Deity:

Omnipotence, therefore, cannot be predicated of the Creator on the evidences of design in nature. But what of omniscience? If we suppose limitation of power, must we also suppose limitation of knowledge and wisdom?

To argue that Deity possesses only limited power does not preclude us from ascribing unlimited knowledge and wisdom to Him. But there is nothing to prove it. The knowledge and wisdom necessary to planning and arranging the cosmos are, no doubt, as much in excess of human knowledge as the power implied is in excess of human power. But nothing obliges us to suppose that either the knowledge or the skill is infinite.

We are not even obliged to suppose that the contrivances and arrangements were always the best possible. If we judge them as we judge the work of human artificers, we find abundant defects. The human body, for example, is one of the most striking instances of artful and ingenious contrivance which nature offers. But we may well ask whether so complicated a machine could not have been made to last longer, and not get out of order so easily and frequently.

We may ask why the human race should have been so constituted as to grovel in wretchedness and degradation for countless ages before a small portion of it was enabled to lift itself into the very imperfect state of intelligence, goodness, and happiness which we enjoy.

If, however, Deity, like a human ruler, had to adapt Himself to a set of conditions which He did not make, it is as unphilosophical as it is presumptuous in us to call Him to account for any imperfections in His work; to complain that he left anything in it contrary to what (if indications of design prove anything) He must have intended.

Great but limited power. Great, perhaps unlimited, knowledge and intelligence. What moral attributes? To settle this question Mill suggests a consideration of the probable purposes of the author of nature. The idea here is that one's moral qualities will be embodied in, and therefore inferable from, whatever one devotes time and forethought to making or doing. The only conclusion Mill is able to reach is "some benevolence but no justice." The argument is as follows:

Assuming then, that while we confine ourselves to the evidences of design in nature, there is no ground for ascribing infinite power, and probably no grounds for ascribing infinite knowledge or intelligence to Deity, the question arises as to the same evidence afforded with regard to His moral attributes. What indications does nature give of the purposes of its author?

This question bears a very different aspect to us from what it bears to those who are encumbered with the doctrine of the omnipotence of Deity. We do not have to attempt the impossible problem of reconciling infinite benevolence and justice with infinite power and knowledge in such a world as this. The attempt to do so involves a contradiction, and exhibits to excess the revolting spectacle of a jesuitical defense of enormities.

To what purpose, then, do the expedients and contrivances in the construction of animals and vegetables appear to tend? These are the "adaptations" which most excite our admiration. If they afford evidence of design, of purpose, in nature, we can best hope to be enlightened by examining such parts of nature.

There is no blinking the fact that these animal and vegetable adaptations tend principally to no more exalted object than to make the structure remain in life and in working order for a certain time: the individual for a few years, the species for a longer but still limited period.

The greater part of the design or adaptation in nature, however wonderful its mechanism, is, therefore, no evidence of any moral attributes in the author of nature; because the end to which it is directed is not a moral end: it is not the good of any creature but the qualified permanence, for a limited period of the work itself.

The only inference that can be drawn from most of nature, respecting the character of the author of nature, is that He does not wish His work to perish as soon as created. He wills it to have a certain duration.

In addition to the great number of adaptations which have no apparent object but to keep the organism going, there are a certain number of provisions for giving pleasure and a certain number for giving pain. These, perhaps, should be included among the contrivances for keeping the creature or its species in existence; for both the pleasures and the pains are generally so disposed as to attract to the things which maintain existence and deter from the things which would destroy it.

When these matters are considered, a vast deduction must be made from the facts usually cited as evidence of the benevolence of the Creator; so vast, indeed, that some may doubt whether any remains.

Yet, viewing the matter impartially, it does appear that there is a preponderance of evidence that the Creator desired the pleasure of His creatures. This is indicated by the fact, which cannot itself be denied, that pleasure of one description or another, is afforded by almost all of the powers, mental and physical, possessed by the creature.

The author of these pleasure-giving and pain-preventing adaptations is no doubt accountable for having made the creature susceptible of pain. But this may have been a necessary condition of its susceptibility to pleasure: a supposition which avails nothing on the theory of an omnipotent creator., but is extremely probable in the case of a limited creator.

There is, therefore, much evidence that the creature's pleasure is agreeable to the Creator; while there is very little if any evidence that its pain is so. There is, then, justification for inferring that benevolence is one of the attributes of the Creator.

But to jump from this to the inference that his sole or chief purposes are those of benevolence, and that the single end and aim of creation was the happiness of his creatures, is not only not justified by any evidence but is a conclusion in opposition to such evidence as we have.

If the motive of the Deity for creating sentient beings was the happiness of those beings, His purpose, in our corner of the universe at least, must be pronounced to have been thus far an ignominious failure. If God had no purpose but our happiness, and that of other living creatures, it is incredible that He would have called them into existence with the prospect of being so completely baffled.

If man had not the power, by the exercise of his own energies, to improve himself and his circumstances, to do for himself and other creatures vastly more than God had in the first instance done, then He [God] would deserve something very different from thanks at his [man's] hands.

Of course, it may be said that this very capacity to improve himself was given to man by God, and that the changes which man will be able ultimately to effect will be worth purchasing by the sufferings and wasted lives.

This may be so; but to suppose that God could not have procured these blessings for man at a less frightful cost is to make a very strange supposition concerning the Deity. It is to suppose that God could not, in the first instance, create anything better than a primitive savage, and was yet able to endow this primitive savage with the power of raising himself into a Newton or a Fénelon. We do not know the nature of the barriers which limit the divine omnipotence; but it is a very odd notion of them that they enable the Deity to confer on a primitive savage the power of producing what God Himself had no other means of creating.

Such are the indications respecting the divine benevolence. If we look for any other moral attribute, for example, justice, we find a total blank. There is no evidence whatever in nature of divine justice, whatever standard of justice we may hold. There is no shadow of justice in the general arrangements of nature. Whatever justice exists in human society is the work of man himself, struggling upwards against immense natural difficulties into civilization, and making to himself a second, and far better and more unselfish nature than he was created with.

Looking back, Mill summarizes his findings:

These, then, are the net results of natural theology on the question of the divine attributes. A Being of great but limited power, how or by what limited we cannot even conjecture; of great and perhaps unlimited intelligence; who desires, and pays some regard to the happiness of His creatures, but who seems to have other motives of action which He cares more for, and who can hardly be supposed to have created the universe for that purpose alone.

Such is the Deity whom natural religion points to; and any idea of God more captivating than this comes only from human wishes, or from the teaching of either real or imaginary revelation.

Mill goes on to note that there are several considerations in favor of this hypothesis of a finite Deity. It eliminates the problem of evil and the problem of free will. These problems, it will be recalled,

were raised by the claim that Deity combines in Himself the two attributes of omnipotence and complete benevolence. It keeps close to
what experience actually tells us about the world we live in. And, by
way of conclusion, it gives meaning to the notion of helping or working with God:

> This religious idea admits of one elevated feeling, which is not open to
> those who believe in the omnipotence of the good principle in the universe,
> the feeling of helping God—of requiting the good He has given by a volun-
> tary cooperation which He, not being omnipotent, really needs, and by
> which a somewhat nearer approach may be made to the fulfillment of His
> purposes. This is the most invigorating thought which can inspire a human
> creature.

A contemporary of Mill had argued "that even if the investigation
of the concept of God as the absolute, infinite, all-powerful, all-good
Being, leads to self-contradiction, yet we must believe in such a
Being, since neither human logic nor human ethics are applicable to
such a being." To this Mill replied:

> Convince me that the world is ruled by a being whose attributes are infi-
> nite, but what they are we cannot learn (except that the highest human mo-
> rality which we are capable of conceiving does not sanction them) and I will
> bear my fate as I may. But when I am told that I must believe this, and at the
> same time call this being names that affirm the highest human morality, I say
> in plain terms that I will not. Whatever power such a being may have over
> me, there is one thing which he shall not do; he shall not compel me to
> worship him. I will call no being good who is not what I mean when I apply
> that epithet to my fellow creatures; and if such a being can sentence me to
> hell for not so calling him, to hell I will go.

Note on Sources. The Mill material in this section is quoted,
abridged, or paraphrased from the essay "Theism," in his book *Three
Essays on Religion.* That essay is divided into five Parts. Part I is itself divided into an Introduction and six brief chapters. The present
section is based on Part I, especially the Introduction and Chapter 6;
and Part II, entitled "Attributes." The concluding ("to hell I will
go") paragraph is from Mill's book *An Examination of Sir William
Hamilton's Philosophy.*

Reading References. There are not many valuable commentaries
on Mill's handling of this particular theological problem. The notion
of a finite or limited deity did not originate with Mill; indeed, it is to
be found as far back as Plato's *Republic* in the fourth century B.C.[1]

[1] Plato, *Republic, Book II:* "Then God, if he be good, is not the author of all
things, as the many assert, but he is the cause of a few things only, and not of most

But Mill did set himself more deliberately to argue the case than any of his predecessors had done. Since his day, it has passed into the writings of William James and has been used by H. G. Wells as the theme of his little book *God the Invisible King.*

When J. S. Mill was still exercising a great influence in England, his work was subjected to considerable critical overhauling by one of his fellow countrymen, F. H. Bradley. In the course of many years' study and writing Bradley declared himself upon most of the major themes in Mill's general philosophy. In *Essays on Truth and Reality* he has a chapter, "On God and the Absolute," which contains some suggestive remarks on the conception of a limited God. It is instructive to watch another philosopher at work on the idea. Moreover, in the concluding sentences, Bradley raises a point which forms, so to speak, a beginning for William James's pragmatic approach to this question. Says Bradley:

There is a fundamental inconsistency in religion. For, in any but an imperfect religion, God must be perfect. God must be at once the complete satisfaction of all finite aspiration, and yet on the other hand must stand in relation to my will. Religion (at least in my view) is practical, and on the other hand in the highest religion its object is supreme goodness and power. We have a perfect real will, and we have my will, and the practical relation of these wills is what we mean by religion. And yet, if perfection is actually realized, what becomes of my will which is set over against the complete good will? While, on the other hand, if there is no such will, what becomes of God? The inconsistency seems irremovable. . . .

An obvious method of escape is to reject the perfection of God. God will remain good, but in a limited sense. He will be reduced to a person who does the best that is in Him with limited knowledge and power. Sufficiently superior to ourselves to be worshipped, God will nevertheless be imperfect, and, with this admitted imperfection, it will be said, our religion is saved. . . .

Now certainly on such terms religion still can persist, for there is practical devotion to an object which is taken to be at a level far above our own. Such a religion even in one sense, with the lowering of the Deity, may be said to have been heightened. To help a God in His struggle, more or less doubtful and blind, with resisting evil, is no inferior task. And if the issue were taken as uncertain, or if even further the end were known to be God's indubitable defeat and our inevitable disaster, our religion would have risen thereby and would have attained to the extreme of heroism.

But on the other hand, if religion is considered as a whole and not simply from one side, it is not true that with the lowering of God religion tends to grow higher. A principal part of religion is the assured satisfaction of our good will, the joy and peace in that assurance, and the added strength which

---

things that occur to men. For few are the goods of human life, and many are the evils, and the good is to be attributed to God alone; of the evils, the causes are to be sought elsewhere, and not in him."

in the majority of men can come perhaps from no other source. To sacrifice altogether or in part this aspect means on the whole to set religion down to a lower level. And it is an illusion to suppose that imperfection, once admitted into the Deity, can be stopped precisely at that convenient limit which happens to suit our ideas. The assertor of an imperfect God is, whether he knows it or not, face to face with a desperate task or a forlorn alternative. He must try to show (how, I cannot tell) that the entire rest of the universe, outside his limited God, is known to be still weaker and more limited. Or he must appeal to us to follow our Leader blindly and, for all we know, to a common and overwhelming defeat. In either case, the prospect offered entails, I should say, to the religious mind, an unquestionable loss to religion.

And yet it will be urged that we have ourselves agreed that all other ways of escape are closed. For, if God is perfect, we saw that religion must contain inconsistency, and it was by seeking consistency that we were driven to a limited God. But our assumption here, I reply, is precisely that which we should have questioned from the first. Is there any need for our attempt to avoid self-contradiction? Has religion really got to be consistent theoretically? Is ultimate theoretical consistency a thing which is attainable anywhere? And, at all events, is it a thing attainable in life and in practice? That is the fundamental question upon which the whole issue depends. And I need not pause here to ask whether it is quite certain that, when God is limited, the universe becomes theoretically consistent. . . .

Viewed thus, the question as to what may be called religious ideas is seriously changed. To insist upon ultimate theoretical consistency, which in no case can we reach, becomes once for all ridiculous. The main question is as to the real nature and end of religion, and as to the respective importance of those aspects which belong to it. The ideas which best express our highest religious needs and their satisfaction, must certainly be true. Ultimate truth they do not possess, and exactly what in the end it would take to make them perfect we cannot know.

READING QUESTIONS

1. Why Mill prefers the design-argument in theology.
2. He says, "It is maintained that the structure of the eye proves a designing mind." In what way does it do this?
3. Why Mill considers the hypothesis of natural selection in nature. Why he does not adopt it.
4. The lines along which he revises the traditional conception of God.
5. Why evidence *for* design in nature is evidence *against* the omnipotence of the author of nature.
6. Why he thinks it is not necessary to infer that the Deity is either all-knowing or all-wise.

7. Why he is unwilling to ascribe unlimited benevolence to the Deity.

8. On what grounds he would be willing to ascribe limited benevolence.

9. The two claims about the Deity which pose an impossible problem, involve a contradiction, lead to jesuitical defense of enormities.

10. The claim about the Deity which would force you to infer that He had failed ignominiously and was completely baffled.

11. What bearing Mill's limited theism might have on the problem of evil and the problem of free will in theology.

12. The elevated feeling, the invigorating thought, which he derives from his limited theism.

13. What would lead him to say "to hell I will go."

14. Where you find Mill (a) most, (b) least convincing.

15. What Bradley has to say (a) for, (b) against the notion of a finite Deity.

16. Bradley's handling of limited theism turns on the question of whether there is any need to avoid self-contradiction in religion. Is there, would you say?

INDEPENDENT STUDY

1. Begin by reading W. L. Davidson's article "Mill, James and John Stuart," in Hastings's *Encyclopedia of Religion and Ethics.* This will give you a sense of who Mill was, and what matters he wrote about. Then secure a copy of Mill's book *Three Essays on Religion.* The third of these three essays is the basis of this chapter in this book. Either or both of the other two are worth your reading time, and will supply a topic for independent study. Perhaps the essay "Nature" is the best to begin with. As you will see, it is closely connected with Mill's ideas about God and religion, and about right and wrong. If you can write a paper giving an account of what Mill is talking about, why he is talking about it, what he says about it, and why he says it, you will have worked out a modest addition to your own liberal education.

2. Consult the *Index* volume of the *Encyclopedia of Philosophy*, under the index entry "God." You will find three columns of God references. Work from these columns to the articles in the volumes, limiting your search to items relevant to J. S. Mill's limited theism. What other *authors* shared his theological position? Are their lines of support the same as his? What other *topics* are indexed that Mill could well have included?

SECTION 4. T. H. HUXLEY: AGNOSTICISM

From Mill to Huxley. Two famous books, both published in 1859, entered into popular discussion of our question. The first was Charles Darwin's *Origin of Species;* the second, John Stuart Mill's *On Liberty.* Our question has been: Can you use what you know about nature to justify what you believe about God? Both books bore on that question.

Darwin's book caused many persons to revise their conception of nature, thus causing them to question their conception of God. The book pictured plants and animals engaged in a ruthless and life-long struggle for existence. In one way or another they must eat or be eaten, kill or be killed. Tennyson's phrase "Nature red in tooth and claw" expressed the point. Under the pressure of this struggle for existence some species were eliminated and some survived. This was "natural selection": nature "selected" the fit and eliminated the unfit. If nature is created and sustained by God, then this natural selection is Divine Selection: God, through the struggle for existence, selects the fit and eliminates the unfit; in so doing, He brings about an evolution from the lowest beginnings of life up to the present stage of the higher animals and man. Suppose this is what we know about nature. Can we use this knowledge to justify what we believe about God? Can we, as one writer asked, proceed "through nature to God"?

Mill's book, especially in its famous second chapter, argued for the right of the individual to think for himself. It provided the classic plea for "the right to pro and con," on all questions, no matter how important or sacred or long established. Darwin's "downgrading" of nature, particularly if you thought about God as the author of nature, produced a crisis in public discussion of these matters. Mill's chapter was a timely warning against obscurantism and intolerance.

That was in 1859. In 1877 William Kingdon Clifford published a paper, *The Ethics of Belief,* in which he argued that ethics as well as logic has something to say on the justification of belief: if you are not logically entitled to hold a particular belief, then you are not morally entitled to hold that belief. Clifford included religious beliefs in this winnowing demand. The result was something of a paradox for many of his readers: they were familiar with the claim that in these matters doubt or disbelief was a sin, and here was Clifford insisting that in the absence of logical justification belief was immoral and sinful.

Thomas Henry Huxley's *Agnosticism,* which repeated and extended Clifford's thesis, became a symbol for the state of mind in which many found themselves. Huxley commanded a wider hearing, spoke with greater authority, and ranged over a wider field. The papers in which he stated and applied his agnosticism provided Victorian England with one of its liveliest controversies. Since Clifford's paper expressed so much of what Huxley meant by agnosticism, we shall begin by looking at what he had to say:

A shipowner was about to send to sea an emigrant ship. He knew that she was old, not overwell built, and often had needed repairs. It had been suggested to him that possibly she was not seaworthy. He thought that perhaps he ought to have her overhauled and refitted, even though this should put him to great expense.

Before the ship sailed, however, he said to himself that she had gone safely through so many voyages and weathered so many storms, that it was idle to suppose that she would not come safely home from this trip also. He would put his trust in Providence, which could hardly fail to protect all these unhappy families that were leaving their fatherland to seek for better times elsewhere. He would dismiss ungenerous suspicions about the honesty of builders and contractors. In such ways he acquired a sincere and comfortable conviction that his vessel was safe and seaworthy; he watched her departure with a light heart, and benevolent wishes for the success of the exiles in their new home; and he got his insurance money when she went down in mid-ocean and told no tales.

What shall we say of him? Surely that he was guilty of the death of those men. He sincerely believed in the soundness of his ship; but the sincerity of his conviction can in nowise help him, because he had no *right* to believe on such evidence as was before him. He had acquired his belief not by honestly earning it in patient investigation, but by stifling his doubts.

Let us alter the case a little, and suppose that the ship was not unsound after all; that she made her voyage safely, and many others after it. Will that diminish the guilt of her owner? Not one jot. The man would not have been innocent; he would only have been not found out. The question of right or wrong has to do not with whether his belief turned out to be true or false, but whether he had a *right* to believe on such evidence as was before him.

Although he had sincerely and "conscientiously" believed, yet he had no *right* to believe on such evidence as was before him. His sincere convictions, instead of being honestly earned, were stolen. The question is not whether his belief was true or false, but whether he entertained it on wrong grounds.

If he chose to examine himself *in foro conscientiae*, he would know that he had acquired and nourished a belief, when he had no *right* to believe on such evidence as was before him; and therein he would know that he had done a wrong thing.

No real belief, however trifling and fragmentary it may seem, is ever truly insignificant; it prepares us to receive more of its like, confirms those which resembled it before, and weakens others; and so gradually lays a stealthy train in our inmost thoughts, which may some day explode into overt action, and leave its stamp upon our character forever.

It is wrong to believe on insufficient evidence, or to nourish belief by suppressing doubts and avoiding investigation. Since no belief, however seemingly trivial, and however obscure the believer, is ever actually insignificant or without its effect, we have no choice but to extend our judgment to all cases of belief whatever. Belief, that sacred faculty, which prompts the decisions of our will, and knits into harmonious working all the energies of our being, is ours not for ourselves but for humanity. It is *rightly* used on truths which have been established by long tradition and waiting toil, and which have stood in the fierce light of free and fearless questioning. It is desecrated when given to unproved and unquestioned statements, for the solace and private pleasure of the believer; to add a tinsel splendor to the plain straight road of our life and display a bright mirage beyond it; or even to drown the common sorrows of our kind by a self-deception which allows them not only to cast down, but also to degrade us. Whoso would deserve well of his fellows in this matter will guard the purity of his belief with a very fanaticism of jealous care, lest at any time it should rest on an unworthy object, and catch a stain which can never be wiped away.

It is not only the leader of men, statesman, philosopher, or poet, that has this duty to mankind. Every rustic who delivers in the village alehouse his slow infrequent sentences, may help to kill or keep alive the fatal superstitions which clog his race. No simplicity of mind, no obscurity of station, can escape the universal *duty* of questioning all that we believe.

It is the sense of power attached to a sense of knowledge that makes men desirous of believing, and afraid of doubting. This sense of power is the highest and best of pleasures when the belief on which it is founded has been fairly earned. But if the belief has been accepted on insufficient evidence, the pleasure is a *stolen* one. Not only does it deceive ourselves by giving us a sense of power which we do not really possess, but it is *sinful*, because it is *stolen* in defiance of our *duty*. That *duty* is to guard ourselves from such beliefs as from a pestilence, which may shortly master our own body and then spread to the rest of the town. What would be thought of one who, for the sake of a sweet fruit, should deliberately run the risk of bringing a plague upon his family and his neighbors?

Every time we let ourselves believe for unworthy reasons, we weaken our powers of self-control, of doubting, of judicially and fairly weighing evidence. We all suffer severely enough from the maintenance of false beliefs and the fatally wrong actions which they lead to. The evil born when one such belief is entertained is great and wide. But a greater and wider evil arises when the credulous character is maintained, when a habit of believing for unworthy reasons is fostered and made permanent.

It is *wrong* always, everywhere, and for any one, to believe anything upon insufficient evidence. Habitual want of care about what I believe leads to habitual want of care in others about the truth of what is told to me. The credulous man is father to the liar and the cheat.

If a man, holding a belief which he was taught in childhood or persuaded of afterwards, keeps down doubts which arise about it in his mind, purposely avoids the reading of books and the company of men that call in question or discuss it, and regards as impious those questions which cannot easily be asked without disturbing it; the life of that man is one long *sin* against mankind.

If this judgment seems harsh when applied to those simple souls who have never known better, who have been brought up with a horror of doubt, and taught that their eternal welfare depends on *what* they believe; then it leads to the very serious question, *Who hath made Israel to sin?*

Inquiry into the evidence of a doctrine is not to be made once for all, and then taken as finally settled. It is never *lawful* to stifle a doubt; for either it can be honestly answered by means of the inquiry already made, or else it proves that the inquiry was not complete.

"But," says one, "I am a busy man; I have no time for the long course of study which would be necessary to make me in any degree a competent judge of certain questions, or even able to understand the nature of the arguments." Then he should have no time to believe.

The beliefs about right and wrong which guide our actions in dealing with men in society, and the beliefs about physical nature which guide our actions in dealing with animate and inanimate bodies, these never suffer from investigation; they can take care of themselves, without being propped up by "acts of faith," the clamor of paid advocates, or the suppression of contrary evidence.

Since it is not enough to say, "It is wrong to believe on unworthy evidence," without saying also what evidence is worthy, we shall now go on to inquire under what circumstances it is lawful to believe on the testimony of others; and more generally when and why we may believe that which goes beyond our own experience, or even beyond the experience of mankind.

The Argument in Huxley.   In reading Huxley on these matters it is well to keep Mill and Darwin and Clifford in mind. In what follows there are five extended quotations from Huxley. In the *first* he tells how he arrived at the position that he calls agnosticism, and why he coined that word as a name for it. In the *second* he gives a statement of the essential ideas he wants held together by the term *agnosticism*. To put it briefly, agnosticism is the claim that if you cannot use what you know to justify what you believe, then it is immoral to go on believing. Suppose a man asks himself "Am I *morally* entitled to entertain a certain belief of mine?" Agnosticism asks him: "Are you *logically* entitled to entertain the belief to which you refer?" If the answer is "No," then agnosticism says to him: "Then you are not *morally* entitled to entertain the belief. You have no *moral* right to a belief which you cannot justify logically." In the *third* set of quotations Huxley presents three examples of the winnowing results of insisting that what you *believe* shall rest on, be justified by, what you *know*: (a) Are the Gospel records a historically reliable source for the narrative which they set forth? (b) Given what we know about evolution in nature, what are we entitled to believe about the Author of nature? (c) Given what we know about nature, are we entitled to argue that an act is right if and only if it is according to nature? Can we say that "nature's ways," the "cosmic process," provide us with any model of the good for man?

1

Looking back nearly fifty years, I see myself as a boy, whose education has been interrupted, and who intellectually, was left, for some years, altogether to his own devices. At that time, I was a voracious and omnivorous reader; a dreamer and speculator, endowed with that courage in attacking any and every subject, which is the blessed compensation of youth and inexperience. Among the books and essays, on all sorts of topics from metaphysics to heraldry, which I read at this time, two left indelible impressions on my mind. One was Guizot's "History of Civilization," the other was Sir William Hamilton's essay "On the Philosophy of the Unconditioned." The latter was strange reading for a boy, and I could not possibly have understood a great deal of it; nevertheless, I devoured it with avidity, and it stamped upon my mind the strong conviction that, on even the most solemn and important of questions, men are apt to take cunning phrases for answers; and that the limitation of our faculties, in a great number of cases, renders real answers to such questions, not merely actually impossible, but theoretically inconceivable.

When I reached intellectual maturity and began to ask myself whether I was an atheist, a theist, or a pantheist; a materialist or an idealist; a Christian or a freethinker; I found that the more I learned and reflected, the less ready was the answer; until, at last, I came to the conclusion that I had neither art nor part with any of these denominations, except the last. The one thing in which most of these good people were agreed was the one thing in which I differed from them. They were quite sure they had attained a certain "gnosis,"—had, more or less successfully, solved the problem of existence; while I was quite sure I had not, and had a pretty strong conviction that the problem was insoluble. And, with Hume and Kant on my side, I could not think myself presumptuous in holding fast by that opinion.

This was my situation when I had the good fortune to find a place among the members of that remarkable confraternity of antagonists, long since deceased, but of green and pious memory, the Metaphysical Society. Every variety of philosophical and theological opinion was represented there, and expressed itself with entire openness; most of my colleagues were -*ists* of one sort or another; and, however kind and friendly they might be, I, the man without a rag of label to cover himself with, could not fail to have some of the uneasy feelings which must have beset the historical fox when, after leaving the trap in which his tail remained, he presented himself to his normally elongated companions. So I took thought, and invented what I conceived to be the appropriate title of "agnostic." It came into my head as suggestively antithetic to the "gnostic" of Church history, who professed to know so much about the very things of which I was ignorant; and I took the earliest opportunity of parading it at our Society, to show that I, too, had a tail, like the other foxes. To my great satisfaction, the term took; and when the *Spectator* had stood godfather to it, any suspicion in the minds of respectable people, that a knowledge of its parentage might have awakened was, of course, completely lulled.

That is the history of the origin of the terms "agnostic" and "agnosticism."

2

Agnosticism is properly described as a creed in so far as it expresses absolute faith in the validity of a principle which is as much ethical as intellectual. This principle may be stated in various ways, but they all amount to this: that it is wrong for a man to say that he is certain of the objective truth of any proposition unless he can produce evidence which logically justifies that certainty. This is what agnosticism asserts; and, in my opinion, it is all that is essential to agnosticism.

That which agnostics deny and repudiate as immoral is that there are propositions which men ought to believe, without logically satisfactory evidence; and that reprobation ought to attach to the profession of disbelief in such inadequately supported propositions. The justification of the agnostic principle lies in the success which follows upon its application, in natural or in civil history; and in the fact that, so far as these topics are concerned, no sane man thinks of denying its validity.

Agnosticism is a creed, in so far as its general principle is concerned. The application of that principle results in the denial of, or the suspension of judgment concerning, a number of propositions respecting which contemporary "gnostics" profess entire certainty.

The extent of the region of the uncertain, the number of the problems the investigation of which ends in a verdict of not proven will vary according to the knowledge and the intellectual habits of the individual agnostic. What I am sure about is that there are many topics about which I know nothing, and which, so far as I can see, are out of reach of my faculties. Relatively to myself, I am quite sure that the region of uncertainty is far more extensive than I could wish. Materialism and idealism; theism and atheism; the doctrine of the soul and its mortality or immortality—appear in the history of philosophy like the shades of Scandinavian heroes, eternally slaying one another and eternally coming to life again. It is getting on for twenty-five centuries, at least, since mankind began seriously to give their minds to these topics. Generation after generation, philosophy has been doomed to roll the stone up hill; and, just as all the world swore it was at the top, down it has rolled to the bottom again. All this is written in innumerable books; and he who will toil through them will discover that the stone is just where it was when the work began. Hume saw this; Kant saw it; since their time, more and more eyes have been cleansed of the films which prevented them from seeing it; until now the weight and number has begun to tell in practical life.

Between agnosticism and clericalism, there can be neither peace nor truce. The cleric asserts that it is morally wrong not to believe certain propositions, whatever the results of a strict scientific investigation of the evidence of these propositions. He tells us that "religious error is, in itself, of an immoral nature." He declares that he has prejudged certain conclusions, and looks upon those who show cause for arrest of judgment as emissaries of

Satan. It necessarily follows that, for him, the attainment of faith, not the ascertainment of truth, is the highest aim of mental life. And, on analysis, it will be found to be the "power of saying you believe things which are incredible." Now I, and many other agnostics, believe that faith in this sense is an abomination; and we feel that the disagreement between ourselves and those who hold this doctrine is even more moral than intellectual. It is desirable there should be an end of any mistakes on this topic.

Those who appreciate our position will see that when any one declares that we ought to believe this, that, and the other, and are wicked if we don't, it is impossible for us to give any answer but this: We have not the slightest objection to believe anything you like, if you will give us good grounds for belief; but, if you can not, we must respectfully refuse, even if that refusal should wreck morality and insure our own damnation several times over.

3(a)

I find, in the second Gospel (chap. v.), a statement, to all appearance intended to have the same evidential value as any other contained in that history. It is the story of the devils who were cast out of a man, and ordered, or permitted to enter into a herd of swine, to the loss and damage of the innocent Gadarene pig owners. There can be no doubt that the narrator intends to convey his conviction that this casting out and entering in were effected by the agency of Jesus of Nazareth; that, by speech and action, Jesus enforced this conviction; nor does any inkling of the legal and moral difficulties of the case manifest itself.

On the other hand, everything that I know of physiological and pathological science leads me to entertain a very strong conviction that the phenomena ascribed to [demoniacal] possession are as purely natural as those which constitute smallpox; everything that I know of anthropology leads me to think that the belief in demons and demoniacal possession is a mere survival of a once universal superstition, and that its persistence, at the present time, is pretty much in the inverse ratio of the general instruction, intelligence, and sound judgment of the population among whom it prevails. Everything that I know of law and justice convinces me that the wanton destruction of other people's property is a misdemeanor of evil example. Again, the study of history, and especially of that of the fifteenth, sixteenth, and seventeenth centuries, leaves no shadow of doubt on my mind that the belief in the reality of possession and of witchcraft, justly based, alike by Catholics and Protestants, upon this and innumerable other passages in both the Old and New Testaments, gave rise, through the special influence of Christian ecclesiastics, to the most horrible persecutions and judicial murders of thousands upon thousands of innocent men, women, and children.

If the testimony of the Gospel, is sufficient to do away with all rational doubt as to a matter of fact of the utmost practical and speculative importance—belief or disbelief in which may affect, and has affected, men's lives and their conduct towards other men, in the most serious way—then I am bound to believe that Jesus implicitly affirmed himself to possess a "knowledge of the unseen world," which afforded full confirmation of the belief in demons and possession current among his contemporaries. If the story is true, the medieval theory of the invisible world may be, and probably is, quite correct; and the witch-finders, from Sprenger to Hopkins and Mather, are much-maligned men.

On the other hand, humanity, noting the frightful consequences of this belief; common sense, observing the futility of the evidence on which it is based, in all cases that have been properly investigated; science, more and more seeing its way to inclose all the phenomena of so-called "possession" within the domain of pathology—all these powerful influences concur in warning us, at our peril, against accepting the belief without the most careful scrutiny of the authority on which it rests.

I can discern no escape from this dilemma: either Jesus said what he is reported to have said, or he did not. In the former case, his authority on matters connected with the "unseen world" should be roughly shaken; in the latter, the blow falls upon the authority of the Gospels. If their report on a matter of such stupendous and far-reaching practical import as this is untrustworthy, how can we be sure of its trustworthiness in other cases?

The choice then lies between discrediting those who compiled the Gospel biographies and disbelieving the Master, whom they, simple souls, thought to honor by preserving such traditions of the exercise of his authority over Satan's invisible world. This is the dilemma. No deep scholarship, nothing but a knowledge of the revised version (on which it is to be supposed all that mere scholarship can do has been done), with the application thereto of the commonest canons of common sense, is needful to enable us to make a choice between its alternatives.

I am not aware that I have been influenced by any more bias in regard to the Gadarene story than I have been in dealing with other cases of like kind the investigation of which has interested me. I was brought up in the strictest school of evangelical orthodoxy; and when I was old enough to think for myself, I started upon my journey of inquiry with little doubt about the general truth of what I had been taught; and with that feeling of the unpleasantness of being called an "infidel" which, we are told, is so right and proper. Near my journey's end, I find myself in a condition of something more than mere doubt about these matters.

3(b)

The vast and varied procession of events, which we call Nature, affords a sublime spectacle and an inexhaustible wealth of attractive problems to the speculative observer. If we confine our attention to that aspect which engages the attention of the intellect, nature appears a beautiful and harmonious whole, the incarnation of a faultless logical process, from certain premises in the past to an inevitable conclusion in the future. But if it be regarded from a less elevated, though more human, point of view; if our moral sympathies are allowed to influence our judgment, and we permit ourselves to criticize our great mother as we criticize one another; then our verdict, at least so far as sentient nature is concerned, can hardly be so favorable.

In sober truth, to those who have made a study of the phenomena of life as they are exhibited by the higher forms of the animal world, the optimistic dogma, that this is the best of all possible worlds, will seem little better than a libel upon possibility. It is really only another instance to be added to the many extant, of the audacity of *a priori* speculators who, having created God in their own image, find no difficulty in assuming that the Almighty must have been actuated by the same motives as themselves. They are quite sure that, had any other course been practicable, He would no more have made infinite suffering a necessary ingredient of His handiwork than a respectable philosopher would have done the like.

But even the modified optimism of the time-honored thesis of physico-theology, that the sentient world is, on the whole, regulated by principles of benevolence, does but ill stand the test of impartial confrontation with the facts of the case. No doubt it is quite true that sentient nature affords hosts of examples of subtle contrivances directed towards the production of pleasure or the avoidance of pain; and it may be proper to say that these are evidences of benevolence. But if so, why is it not equally proper to say of the equally numerous arrangements, the no less necessary result of which is the production of pain, that they are evidences of malevolence?

If a vast amount of that which, in a piece of human workmanship, we should call skill, is visible in those parts of the organization of a deer to which it owes its ability to escape from beasts of prey, there is at least equal skill displayed in that bodily mechanism of the wolf which enables him to track, and sooner or later to bring down, the deer. Viewed under the dry light of science, deer and wolf are alike admirable; and, if both were non-sentient automata, there would be nothing to qualify our admiration of the action of the one on the other. But the fact that the deer suffers, while the wolf inflicts suffering, engages our moral sympathies. We should call men like the deer innocent and good, men such as the wolf malignant and bad; we should call those who defended the deer and aided him to escape brave and compassionate, and those who helped the wolf in his bloody work base and cruel. Surely, if we transfer these judgments to nature outside the world of man at all, we must do so impartially. In that case, the goodness of the right hand which helps the deer, and the wickedness of the left hand which eggs on the wolf, will neutralize one another: and the course of nature will appear to be neither moral nor immoral, but non-moral.

This conclusion is thrust upon us by analogous facts in every part of the sentient world; yet, inasmuch as it not only jars upon prevalent prejudices, but arouses the natural dislike to that which is painful, much ingenuity has been exercised in devising an escape from it.

From the theological side, we are told that this is a state of probation, and that the seeming injustices and immoralities of nature will be compensated by and by. But how this compensation is to be effected, in the case of the great majority of sentient things, is not clear. I apprehend that no one is seriously prepared to maintain that the ghosts of all the myriads of generations of herbivorous animals which lived during the millions of years of the earth's duration, before the appearance of man, and which have all that time been tormented and devoured by carnivores, are to be compensated by a perennial existence in clover; while the ghosts of carnivores are to go to some kennel where there is neither a pan of water nor a bone with any meat on it. Besides, from the point of view of morality, the last stage of things would be worse than the first. For the carnivores, however brutal and sanguinary, have only done that which, if there is any evidence of contrivance in the world, they were expressly constructed to do. Moreover, carnivores and herbivores alike have been subject to all the miseries incidental to old age, disease, and overmultiplication, and both might well put in a claim for "compensation" on this score.

On the evolutionist side, on the other hand, we are told to take comfort from the reflection that the terrible struggle for existence tends to final good, and that the suffering of the ancestor is paid for by the increased perfection of the progeny. There would be something in this argument if, in Chinese fashion, the present generation could pay its debts to its ancestors; otherwise it is not clear what compensation the *Eohippus* gets for his sorrows in the fact that, some millions of years afterwards, one of his descendants wins the Derby. And, again, it is an error to imagine that evolution signifies a constant tendency to increased perfection. That process undoubtedly involves a constant remodeling of the organism in adaptation to new conditions; but it depends on the nature of these conditions whether the direction of the modifications effected shall be upward or downward. Retrogressive is as practicable as progressive metamorphosis. If what the physical philosophers tell us, that our globe has been in a state of fusion, and, like the sun, is gradually cooling down, is true; then the time must come when evolution will mean adaptation to an universal winter, and all forms of life will die out, except such low and simple organisms as the Diatom of the arctic and antarctic ice and the Protococcus of the red snow. If our globe is proceeding from a condition in which it was too hot to support any but the lowest living thing to a condition in which it will be too cold to permit the existence of any others, the course of life upon its surface must describe a trajectory like that of a ball fired from a mortar; and the sinking half of that course is as much a part of the general process of evolution as the rising.

From the point of view of the moralist the animal world is on about the same level as a gladiator's show. The creatures are fairly well treated, and set to fight—whereby the strongest, the swiftest, and the cunningest live to fight another day. The spectator has no need to turn his thumbs down, as no quarter is given. He must admit that the skill and training displayed are wonderful. But he must shut his eyes if he would not see that more or less enduring suffering is the meed of both vanquished and victor. And since the great game is going on in every corner of the world, thousands of times a minute it seems to follow that, if the world is governed by benevolence, it must be a different sort of benevolence from that of John Howard.

If the optimism of Leibnitz is a foolish though pleasant dream, the pessimism of Schopenhauer is a nightmare, the more foolish because of its hideousness. Error which is not pleasant is surely the worst form of wrong.

This may not be the best of all possible worlds, but to say that it is the worst is mere petulant nonsense. A worn-out voluptuary may find nothing good under the sun, or a vain and inexperienced youth, who cannot get the moon he cries for, may vent his irritation in pessimistic moanings; but there can be no doubt in the mind of any reasonable person that mankind could, would, and in fact do, get on fairly well with vastly less happiness and far more misery than find their way into the lives of nine people out of ten. If each and all of us had been visited by an attack of neuralgia, or of extreme

mental depression, for one hour in every twenty-four—a supposition which
many tolerably vigorous people know, to their cost, is not extravagant—the
burden of life would have been immensely increased without much practical
hindrance to its general course. Men with any manhood in them find life
quite worth living under worse conditions than these.

There is another sufficiently obvious fact, which renders the hypothesis
that the course of sentient nature is dictated by malevolence quite untenable. A vast multitude of pleasures, and these among the purest and the
best, are superfluities, bits of good which are to all appearances unnecessary
as inducements to live, and are, so to speak, thrown into the bargain of life.
To those who experience them, few delights can be more entrancing than
such as are afforded by natural beauty, or by the arts, and especially by
music; but they are products of, rather than factors in, evolution, and it is
probable that they are known, in any considerable degree, to but a very
small proportion of mankind.

The conclusion of the whole matter seems to be that pessimism is as
little consonant with the facts of sentient existence as optimism. If we desire
to represent the course of nature in terms of human thought, and assume that
it was intended to be that which it is, we must say that its governing principle is intellectual and not moral; that it is a materialized logical process, accompanied by pleasures and pains, the incidence of which, in the majority of
cases, has not the slightest reference to moral desert. That the rain falls alike
upon the just and the unjust, and that those upon whom the Tower of Siloam
fell were no worse than their neighbors, seem to be Oriental modes of expressing the same conclusion.

We are more than sufficiently familiar with modern pessimism, at least as
a speculation; for I cannot call to mind that any of its present votaries have
sealed their faith by assuming the rags and the bowl of the mendicant
Bhikku, or the wallet of the Cynic. We also know modern speculative optimism, with its perfectability of the species, reign of peace, and lion and
lamb transformation scenes; but one does not hear so much of it as one did
forty years ago; indeed, I imagine it is to be met with more commonly at the
tables of the healthy and wealthy, than in the congregations of the wise. The
majority of us, I apprehend, profess neither pessimism nor optimism. We
hold that the world is neither so good, nor so bad, as it conceivably might be;
and, as most of us have reason, now and again, to discover that it can be.
Those who have failed to experience the joys that make life worth living are,
probably, in as small a minority as those who have never known the griefs
that rob existence of its savor and turn its richest fruits into mere dust and
ashes.

3(c)

There is a fallacy which appears to me to pervade the so-called "ethics of
evolution." It is the notion that because, on the whole, animals and plants
have advanced in perfection of organization by means of the struggle for existence and the consequent "survival of the fittest"; therefore men in society,
men as ethical beings, must look to the same process to help them towards
perfection. I suspect that this fallacy has arisen out of the unfortunate ambi-

guity of the phrase "survival of the fittest." "Fittest" has a connotation of "best"; and about "best" there hangs a moral flavor. In cosmic nature, however, what is "fittest" depends upon the conditions. Long since, I ventured to point out that if our hemisphere were to cool again, the survival of the fittest might bring about, in the vegetable kindgom, a population of more and more stunted and humbler and humbler organisms, until the "fittest" that survived might be nothing but lichens, diatoms, and such microscopic organisms as those which give red snow its color; while, if it became hotter, the pleasant valleys of the Thames and Isis might be uninhabitable by any animated beings save those that flourish in a tropical jungle. They, as the fittest, the best adapted to the changed conditions, would survive.

Men in society are undoubtedly subject to the cosmic process. But the influence of the cosmic process on the evolution of society is the greater the more rudimentary its civilization. Social progress means a checking of the cosmic process at every step and the substitution for it of another, which may be called the ethical process; the end of which is not the survival of those who may happen to be the fittest, in respect of the whole of the conditions which obtain, but of those who are ethically the best.

The practice of that which is ethically best—what we call goodness or virtue—involves a course of conduct which, in all respects, is opposed to that which leads to success in the cosmic struggle for existence. In place of ruthless self-assertion it demands self-restraint; in place of thrusting aside, or treading down, all competitors, it requires that the individual shall not merely respect, but shall help his fellows; its influence is directed, not so much to the survival of the fittest as to the fitting of as many as possible to survive. It repudiates the gladiatorial theory of existence. It demands that each man who enters into the enjoyment of the advantages of a polity shall be mindful of his debt to those who have laboriously constructed it; and shall take heed that no act of his weakens the fabric in which he has been permitted to live. Laws and moral precepts are directed to the end of curbing the cosmic process and reminding the individual of his duty to the community, to the protection and influence of which he owes, if not existence itself, at least the life of something better than a brutal savage.

Let us understand, once for all, that the ethical progress of society depends not on imitating the cosmic process, still less in running away from it, but in combating it. It may seem an audacious proposal thus to pit the microcosm against the macrocosm and to set man to subdue nature to his higher ends; but I venture to think that the great intellectual difference between the ancient times and our day, lies in the solid foundation we have acquired for the hope that such an enterprise may meet with a certain measure of success.

The history of civilization details the steps by which men have succeeded in building up an artificial world within the cosmos. Fragile reed as he may be, man, as Pascal says, is a thinking reed: there lies within him a fund of energy operating intelligently and so far akin to that which pervades the universe, that it is competent to influence and modify the cosmic process. In virtue of his intelligence, the dwarf bends the Titan to his will. In every family, in every polity that has been established, the cosmic process in many has been restrained and otherwise modified by law and custom.

Note on Sources. The Clifford material in this section is quoted or abridged from his essay "The Ethics of Belief." The Huxley material is quoted from his essays "Agnosticism," "Agnosticism and Christianity," "The Struggle for Existence in Human Society," and "Prolegomena to Evolution and Ethics."

Reading References. Huxley is eminently readable. Almost any collection or selection of his essays will be found worth reading. The essays and parts of essays brought together in the Huxley volume in the Crofts Classics series make a good starter.

People have written interesting books and essays on Huxley. The following are examples: Clarence Ayres, *Huxley;* Houston Peterson, *Huxley—Prophet of Science;* William Irvine, *Apes, Angels and Victorians;* T. H. Huxley and Julian Huxley, *Touchstone for Ethics 1893–1943;* John Fiske, *Through Nature to God,* Chap. 2; Leonard Huxley, *Life and Letters of T. H. Huxley.*

READING QUESTIONS

1. Imagine that Pascal and Hume have read Darwin's book. Why might they have found it interesting?
2. What is the point of the title of Clifford's essay? Of his parable of the shipowner?
3. How both logic *and* ethics enter into what Clifford wants to say about belief.
4. How Huxley came to invent the term *agnostic.*
5. His point here: "I too had a tail like the other foxes."
6. What agnosticism asserts. What it denies and repudiates.
7. What was the episode of the Gadarene swine?
8. What physiology and pathology, anthropology, law and justice, and history suggest about such an episode.
9. "I can discern no escape from this dilemma. . . . This is the dilemma." Namely.
10. What is meant by "evolution by natural selection."
11. He says nature can be looked at from two points of view. Namely.
12. Why men felt called upon to explain away the gladiatorial aspect of nature.
13. Name and formulate the two arguments by which they tried to do that.
14. Give Huxley's most incisive criticism of each.
15. His thesis about the behavior of "ethical man" and the "cosmic

process." Bearing of this on the theological problem examined in this Topic I.

16. Wherein you find Huxley (a) most, (b) least convincing.

INDEPENDENT STUDY

1. Secure a copy of John Fiske's little volume *Through Nature to God*. Do not be put off by the fact that it is "dated." At one time it was quite alive. Even today it may not be as dead as you think. In any case, it will acquaint you with the writings of a young American who, toward the end of the last century, had read and thought about John Stuart Mill and T. H. Huxley in reference to natural theology. Fiske's book contains three essays. Concentrate on the first two. They can be read rapidly, once you get started. Work out a paper on those two essays, with reference to matters you have been reading in Pascal, Hume, Mill, and Huxley, especially the last two.

2. Read the article on T. H. Huxley by T. A. Goudge in the *Encyclopedia of Philosophy*. Use it to track down relevant essays or chapters in Huxley's own writings. Write an account of Huxley's ideas in philosophy in *general*, centering your account in his philosophy of religion.

SECTION 5. WILLIAM JAMES: THE WILL TO BELIEVE

From Huxley to James.   It will be recalled that Pascal, writing in the seventeenth century, repudiated the possibility of rational theology but clung to orthodox convictions. He rejected the appeal to reason in theology, but he retained the theology. John Stuart Mill, writing two centuries later, reversed the procedure. He clung to the idea of a rational theology, but repudiated the orthodox convictions. He rejected the orthodox theology, but he retained the appeal to reason. The most man can rationally justify, he argued, is the belief in a finite God. William James, writing in America toward the close of the nineteenth and in the opening years of the twentieth centuries, stands at the end of a line of rational theologians stretching back to Pascal and beyond. He was familiar with Pascal, Hume, Mill, and Huxley. Dispassionate consideration convinced him that the appeal to reason in theology was bankrupt. No one had ever properly answered Hume on his own grounds. But James found himself believing wholeheartedly in the existence of God. That, he could not shake off. Accordingly, he sought to combine the two compromises offered by Pascal and Mill, respectively: an appeal to what he called "the will to believe" in support of the belief in a finite God.

On the face of it, James's "will to believe," later his pragmatism, is closely related, historically, to Huxley's agnosticism. That is apparent on reading James's essay. Huxley had said that if you couldn't logically justify what you believe, then it was immoral to believe. Such belief would be "stolen." It is this note of moral censure in Huxley's agnosticism that caught James's attention. His argument is that among Huxley's own beliefs are some which he (Huxley) could not justify "logically," "intellectually"; but which he (Huxley) nevertheless will not abandon. Such beliefs embody "the will to believe." Beliefs that are *appropriate* objects of the will to believe are not open to the moral criticism proposed by Huxley's agnosticism.

Biographical Note. William James was born in 1842 and died in 1910 at the age of sixty-eight. He was educated at Harvard and in Europe. He was appointed to the teaching staff of Harvard in the department of physiology. From physiology he moved later to psychology, writing his brilliant and epoch-making *Principles of Psychology* and *Varieties of Religious Experience*. From psychology he moved on to philosophy. His best-known and most controversial books were written during his years as professor of philosophy. He gathered about him, at Harvard, what was perhaps the most brilliant group of teachers and writers in philosophy ever assembled at any one time in any university in this country. These philosophical colleagues included Josiah Royce, George Herbert Palmer, George Santayana, and (in psychology) Hugo Münsterberg.

Although James was trained as physiologist, he had many of the interests of a moralist and theologian. His robust assurance that the good life, in the long run, provides the deepest and most lasting satisfaction; his passionately felt need for a "Friend" sustaining the universe and reaching out to man in his struggle for righteousness and truth, are convictions that pervade many of his writings. His three books, *The Will to Believe and Other Essays, The Varieties of Religious Experience*, and *Pragmatism*, contain popular presentation of these views.

The Argument of the Passages. The passages quoted or abridged hereunder are, for the most part, from James's essay "The Will to Believe." He states somewhere that it might better have been called "The Right to Believe." His aim is to point out that, in certain cases, where the evidence is insufficient to justify belief on "rational" grounds, there may nevertheless be other grounds. In a word, sufficient evidence is not the only thing that justifies belief, is not the only thing that gives us a "right to believe." Agnosticism may not be the last word here. In such cases upon what does our right to believe rest? Where the evidence is insufficient, is it necessary to say, with agnosticism, that belief is everywhere and always immoral?

That is the central problem of the essay. James begins by a few remarks on hypotheses in general. The purpose of these remarks is to explain what he means by a "genuine option" between rival hypotheses. Where we are faced with a genuine option between rival hypotheses, neither of which is backed by sufficient evidence, upon what principle may we legitimately exercise our will to believe? James then formulates the principle that, he thinks, justifies belief under such circumstances. The question now is: Are there any beliefs which present themselves for acceptance on this principle? James notes that moral judgments are of this nature. If this is so, then the moral judgments proposed by agnosticism, or moral principles embodied in such judgments, would be important exceptions to the rule laid down by agnosticism. However, and more important, the "religious hypothesis" is of this nature. He then states the terms of this hypothesis. In what follows, he deals with two possible lines of criticism that, he knows, will be directed against his position. The first of these is the objection of the agnostic, namely, that where evidence is insufficient to justify belief, we have no right to believe. The second objection is to the effect that once you set up any principle designed to justify belief on insufficient grounds, you have (in principle) obliterated the distinction between intelligent belief and any but the wildest superstition. Finally, in a few passages, we note his acceptance of Mill's limited theism.

James begins:

Let us give the name of *hypothesis* to anything that may be proposed to our belief. And, just as electricians speak of live and dead wires, let us speak of an hypothesis as either live or dead. A live hypothesis is one which appeals as a real possibility to him to whom it is proposed.

Next, let us call the decision between hypotheses an *option*. Options may be of several kinds. They may be living or dead, forced or avoidable, momentous or trivial.

A living option is one in which both hypotheses are live. If I say to you: "Be a theosophist or be a Mohammedan," it is probably a dead option, because for you neither hypothesis is likely to be live. But if I say: "Be an agnostic or be a Christian," it is otherwise. Trained as you are, each hypothesis makes some appeal, however small, to your belief.

A forced option is one which arises when there is no standing outside of the alternative hypotheses. If I say to you: "Choose between going out with your umbrella or without it," I do not offer you a forced option. You can easily avoid it by not going out at all. But if I say: "Either accept this truth or go without it," I put on you a forced option, for there is no third alternative and no standing outside of these two alternatives.

A momentous option is one that is presented when the opportunity is unique, when the stake is significant, or when the decision is irreversible if it later prove unwise. If I were Dr. Nansen and proposed to you to join my North Pole expedition, your option would be momentous; for this would probably be your only opportunity, and your choice now would either exclude you from the North Pole sort of immortality altogether, or put at least the chance of it into your hands. *Per contra,* the option is trivial when the opportunity is not unique, when the stake is insignificant, or when the decision is reversible if it later prove unwise.

An option is genuine when it is of the living, forced, momentous kind.

So much for hypotheses and options. Suppose, now, that a man is confronted by a pair of rival beliefs, neither of which can be said to rest on sufficient evidence to justify belief. What is he to do? Upon what principle can he justify himself in accepting the one or the other? It is the following:

The thesis I defend is this: Our passional [emotional] nature not only lawfully may, but must, decide an option between propositions, whenever it is a genuine option that cannot by its nature be decided on intellectual grounds.

The essence of the matter is contained in this principle. We are curious to know where, among our beliefs, we shall find some which call for acceptance on this principle. One example would be our moral beliefs: that it is better to do this than that, better to be this sort of man than that, and so on.

The question arises: Are there any such forced options in our speculative opinions? Are there some options between opinions in which this passional influence must be regarded both as an inevitable and as a lawful determinant of our choice?

Moral questions immediately present themselves. A moral question is a question not of what exists, but of what is good, or would be good if it did exist.

Science can tell us what exists; but to compare the worths, both of what exists and what does not exist, we must consult not science, but what Pascal calls our "heart," i.e., our passional nature. Science, herself, consults her heart when she lays it down that the infinite ascertainment of fact and correction of false belief are the supreme goods for man. Challenge the statement, and science can only repeat it oracularly, or else prove it by showing that such ascertainment and correction bring man all sorts of other goods which man's heart in turn declares desirable.

Moral beliefs. Is that all? What about religious beliefs? Are they appropriate objects of our sheer "will to believe"?

Let us pass to the question of religious faith. What do we mean by the religious hypothesis? Broadly it is this: Science says things are: morality says some things are better than other things: religion says that the best things are the more eternal things, the things in the universe that throw the last stone, so to speak, and say the final word: and that we are better off, even now, if we believe her first affirmation to be true.

Now let us consider what the logical elements of this situation are in case the religious hypothesis in both its branches be really true. We must admit that possibility at the outset.

We see, first, that religion offers itself as a momentous option. We are supposed to gain, even now, by our belief, and to lose by our nonbelief, a certain vital good.

We see, second, that religion is a forced option so far as that vital good is concerned. We cannot escape the issue by remaining skeptical, because although we do avoid error in that way if religion be untrue, we lose the good, if it be true. Skepticism, then, is not an avoidance of the option.

In these matters, the skeptic's position is this: Better risk the loss of truth than the chance of error. But in this he is actively playing his stake as much as the believer is. He is backing the field against the religious hypothesis, just as the believer is backing the religious hypothesis against the field.

Now, to most of us, religion comes in a still further way. What I mean is this. The more perfect and more eternal aspect of the universe is represented in our religions as having a personal form. The universe is no longer a mere It, but a Thou, if we are religious; and any relation that may be possible from person to person might be possible here. We feel, too, as if the appeal of religion were made to our own active good will, as if evidence for its truth might be forever withheld from us unless we met the hypothesis halfway.

This feeling, forced on us we know not whence, that by obstinately believing that there are gods we are doing the universe the deepest service we can, seems part of the living essence of the religious hypothesis.

God is the natural appellation, for us Christians at least, for the supreme reality, so I will call this higher part of the universe by the name of God. We and God have business with each other; and in opening ourselves to His influence our deepest destiny is fulfilled. The universe, at those parts of it which our personal being constitutes, takes a turn genuinely for the worse or for the better in proportion as each one of us fulfills or evades God's demands.

God's existence is the guarantee of an ideal order that shall be permanently preserved. This world may indeed some day burn up or freeze up; but if it is part of His order, the old ideals are sure to be brought elsewhere to fruition, so that where God is, tragedy is only provisional and partial, and shipwreck and dissolution are not the absolutely final things.

Only when this farther step of faith concerning God is taken, and remote objective consequences are predicted, does religion, as it seems to me, get wholly free from subjective experience, and bring a real hypothesis into play.

What is this but to say that religion, in her fullest exercise of function, is a postulator of new facts? The world interpreted religiously is not the materialistic world over again, with an altered expression. It must have, over and above the altered expression, a natural constitution different at some point from that which a materialistic world would have. It must be such that different events can be expected in it, different conduct must be required.

All this on the supposition that our passional nature may be prophetic and right: and that the religious hypothesis is a live hypothesis which may be true.

We are now in possession of the essentials of James's position. We know what he means by a genuine option between rival hypotheses. We know the principle by which he would justify belief in such circumstances. We know that he considers the religious hypothesis a case in point. We know, finally, what he means by this religious hypothesis. His defense of the whole position is still to be made. He deals first with the skeptic. The point here is this: It may be all very well to talk about the demands of our "passional nature," but, as a matter of fact, why is it not just as legitimate to refuse to believe either hypothesis when neither is backed by sufficient evidence? Why may an agnostic not take the stand, in all conscience, that under the circumstances stipulated by James, the proper attitude is one of suspended judgment? Let us hear, through James, the agnostic's statement of the case:

It does seem preposterous on the very face of it, to talk of our opinions being modifiable at will. Can our will either help or hinder our intellect in its perceptions of truth? . . . Indeed, the talk of believing by our volition seems from one point of view, simply silly. From another point of view it is worse than silly, it is vile. When one turns to the magnificent edifice of the physical sciences, and sees how it was reared, what thousands of disinterested moral lives of men lie buried in its mere foundations; what patience and postponement, what choking down of preference, what submission to icy laws of outer fact are wrought into its very stones and mortar; how absolutely impersonal it stands in its vast augustness—then how besotted and contemptible seems every little sentimentalist who comes blowing his voluntary smoke wreaths! Can we wonder if those bred in the rugged and manly school of science should feel like spewing such subjectivism out of their mouths? The whole system of loyalties which grow up in the schools of science go dead against its toleration; so that it is only natural that those who have caught the scientific fever should pass over to the opposite extreme and write sometimes as if the incorruptibly truthful intellect ought positively to prefer bitterness and unacceptableness to the heart in its cup.

Clough sings:

It fortifies my soul to know
That, though I perish, Truth is so

while Huxley exclaims: "My only consolation lies in the reflection that, however bad our posterity may become, so far as they hold by the plain rule of not pretending to believe what they have no reason to believe, because it may be to their advantage so to pretend, they will not have reached the lowest depth of immorality."

And that delicious *enfant terrible*, Clifford, writes: "Belief is desecrated when given to unproved and unquestioned statements for the solace and private pleasure of the believer. Whoso would deserve well of his fellows in this matter will guard the purity of his belief with a very fanaticism of jealous care, lest at any time it should rest on an unworthy object, and catch a stain which can never be wiped away. If a belief has been accepted on insufficient evidence, even though the belief be true, the pleasure is a stolen one. It is sinful because it is stolen in defiance of our duty to mankind. That duty is to guard ourselves from such beliefs as from a pestilence which may shortly master our body and then spread to the rest of the town. It is wrong, always, everywhere, and for everyone, to believe anything upon insufficient evidence."

Now, all of this strikes one as healthy, even when expressed by Clifford with somewhat too much of robustious pathos in the voice. Willing and wishing do seem, in the matter of our beliefs, to be only fifth wheels to the coach.

How shall this indictment be answered? It will be noticed that James has been fair to the agnostic in admitting the genuine possibility here of a moral issue. The agnostic's claim is not, at its best, that we are merely foolish to believe on insufficient evidence. It is the more serious claim that we *ought* not to believe on insufficient evidence; that belief, in such cases, is immoral. That is the point which agnosticism adds to skepticism. That is the charge with which James is faced. The first move in his defense is to note that in this unique case of the religious hypothesis doubt is the equivalent of denial; and, the point is, denial is not suspended judgment. (It may be necessary to reread James's wording of the religious hypothesis, especially its *second* part, to follow his argument here.)

To preach skepticism in these matters is tantamount to telling us, when in the presence of the religious hypothesis, that to yield to our fear of its being false is wiser and better than to yield to our hope that it may be true.

As James points out, this puts a slightly different face on the matter. Why is it "wiser and better" to refrain from belief on all occasions where the evidence is insufficient?

This is not a case of "intellect" against "passion." It is only intellect, with one passion—the dread or horror of believing what may be false—laying down its law—never to believe what may be false when there is no evidence that it may be true.

And by what, forsooth, is the supreme wisdom of this passion warranted? Dupery for dupery, what proof is there that dupery through hope is so much worse than dupery through fear? I, for one, can see no proof; and I simply refuse to imitate the skeptic's option in a case where my own stake is important enough to give me the right to choose my own form of risk.

And what it comes down to is this:

We may regard the case for truth as paramount, and the avoidance of error as secondary; or we may treat the avoidance of error as more imperative, and let truth take its chance. Clifford exhorts us to the latter course. Believe nothing, he tells us, keep your mind in suspense forever, rather than, by closing on insufficient evidence, incur the awful risk of believing lies. You, on the other hand, may think that the risk of being in error is a very small matter when compared with the blessings of real knowledge, and be ready to be duped many times rather than postpone indefinitely the chance of guessing true.

This being so, he knows where he stands:

For my own part, I have also a horror of being duped. But I can believe that worse things than being duped may happen to a man in this world. So Clifford's exhortation has to my ears a thoroughly fantastic sound. Our errors are surely not such awfully solemn things. In a world where we are so sure to incur them, a certain lightness of heart seems healthier than this excessive nervousness on their behalf.

If the religious hypothesis be true, and the evidence for it still insufficient, I do not wish, by putting a skeptical extinguisher upon my nature, to forfeit my sole chance of getting upon the winning side; that chance depending, of course, on my willingness to run the risk of acting as if my passional need of taking the world religiously might be prophetic and right.

When I look at the religious hypothesis, as it really puts itself to men, and when I think of all the possibilities which it involves, then the skeptical command to put a stopper on our heart and wait—acting meanwhile more or less as if religion were not true—wait till doomsday, or till such time as our intellect and senses may have raked in enough evidence—this command, I say, seems to me the queerest idol ever manufactured in the philosophic cave.

If the religious hypothesis were true, then pure intellectualism, with its veto on our willingness to make advances, would be an absurdity; and some participation of our sympathetic nature would be logically required. I, therefore, for one, cannot see my way to accepting the agnostic rules for truth-seeking (never to believe any hypothesis when there is no evidence or insufficient evidence) or to willfully agree to keep my willing nature out of the game.

I cannot do so for this plain reason: A rule of thinking which would prevent me from acknowledging certain kinds of truth if those kinds of truths were really there, would be an irrational rule. That, for me, is the long and short of the logic of the situation.

The great empiricists are only empiricists on reflection; left to their instincts, they dogmatize like infallible popes. When the Cliffords tell us how sinful it is to be Christians on such "insufficient evidence," insufficiency is really the last thing they have in mind. For them the evidence is absolutely sufficient, only it makes the other way. They believe so completely in an anti-Christian order of the universe that there is no living option: Christianity, for them, is a dead hypothesis from the start.

As a kind of Parthian shot, James throws a question at the skeptics themselves:

Our belief in truth itself, for instance, that there is a truth and that our minds and it are made for each other—what is it but a passionate affirmation of desire in which our social system backs us up? We want to have a truth; we want to believe that our experiments and studies and discussions must put us in a continually better and better position toward it; and on this line we agree to fight out our thinking lives.

But if a skeptic asks us how we know all this, can our logic find a reply? It cannot. It is just one volition against another; we are willing to go in for life upon a trust or assumption which he, for his part, does not care to make. As a rule we disbelieve all facts and theories for which we have no use. Clifford's cosmic emotions find no use for Christian feelings. Huxley belabors the bishops because there is no use for sacerdotalism in his scheme of life. But Newman goes over to Romanism, and finds all sorts of reasons good for staying there, because a priestly system is for him an organic need and delight.

So Clifford notwithstanding, our nonintellectual nature evidently does influence our convictions. The state of things is far from simple, and pure insight and pure logic, whatever they may do ideally, are not the only things that really do produce our creeds.

If we had an infallible intellect, with its objective certitudes, we might feel ourselves disloyal to such a perfect organ of knowledge in not trusting to it exclusively, in not waiting for its releasing word. But if we believe that no bell in us tolls to let us know for certain when truth is in our grasp, then it seems a piece of idle fantasticality to preach so solemnly of our duty of waiting for the bell.

James has still to deal with another sort of critic, no less hostile. The charge this time is not that where evidence is lacking it is wiser and better to suspend judgment. It is, rather, this: If you start justifying belief on this basis, where and how are you going to draw the line? The justification is not, by its nature, the peculiar property of the man who desires to believe in God. It would seem to be equally available, as a principle of justification, for other beliefs as well, some of which might be incompatible with those beliefs which James used it to defend. A man who advances a principle that would justify incompatible beliefs has some explaining to do. James knew this. Although convinced that his argument was sound, he knew that others would not be. Thus:

I confess I do not see how this logic can be escaped. But sad experience makes me fear that some of you may still shrink from saying with me that we have the right to believe at our own risk any hypothesis that is live enough to tempt our will.

If this is so, however, I suspect it is because you have got away from the logical point of view altogether, and are thinking of some particular religious hypothesis which for you is dead. The freedom to "believe what we will" you apply to the case of some patent superstition; and the faith you think of is the faith defined by the schoolboy when he said: "Faith is when you believe something that you know ain't true."

I can only repeat that this is a misapprehension of my position. The freedom to "believe what we will," for which I have been arguing, can only cover living options which the intellect by itself cannot resolve; and living options never seem absurd or superstitious to him who has them to consider.

Where there is no such forced option, the dispassionately judicial intellect with no pet hypothesis, saving us, as it does, from dupery, at any rate, ought to be our ideal.

It would appear that James has only restated his difficulty. It is still open to anyone to point out: "Yes, what you have said, you have said. The point is, however, that what you have not said, you have not said. What about the man whose passional nature inclines him to embrace, as true, a proposition that is incompatible with one that your passional nature has inclined you to embrace? As between two passional natures having divergent inclinations, how do you decide?" A glance through the published letters of William James shows that he was bothered by this point. Writing to his brother Henry, the novelist, he protests:

When I *say* that, *other things being equal,* the view of things that seems more satisfactory morally will legitimately be treated by men as truer than the view that seems less so, *they quote me as saying* that anything morally satisfactory can be treated as true, no matter how unsatisfactory it may be from the point of view of its consistency with what we already know or believe to be true about physical or natural facts, which is rot!!

James has drawn a two-edged sword. To vary the metaphor, his principle may be used to reinforce either theism or atheism, or for the matter of that, some third alternative equally removed from either, say skepticism or polytheism. In the last analysis he merely reinforces the most deeply congenial belief; he does not state which belief is or ought to be the most congenial. However, he is not done protesting. Writing to an English philosopher, he has much the same thing to say:

Would to God I had never thought of that unhappy title for my essay. What I meant by the title was the state of mind of the man who finds an impulse in him toward a believing attitude, and who resolves not to quench it simply because doubts of its truth are possible. Its opposite would be the maxim: Believe in nothing which you can possibly doubt.

My essay hedged the license to indulge in private overbeliefs with so many restrictions and sign boards of danger that the outlet was narrow enough. It made of tolerance the essence of the situation. It defined the permissible cases. It treated the faith attitude as a necessity for individuals, because the total "evidence" which only the race can draw includes their experiments among its data. It tended to show only that faith cannot be absolutely *vetoed*, as certain champions of "science" had claimed it ought to be.

I cry to heaven to tell me of what insane root my "leading contemporaries" have eaten, that they are so smitten with blindness as to the meaning of printed texts.

In my essay the evil shape was a vision of "Science" in the form of abstraction, priggishness and sawdust, lording it over all. Take the sterilest scientific prig and cad you know, compare him with the richest religious intellect you know, and you would not, any more than I would, give the former the exclusive right of way.

There are two parts to a man's exposition of his ideas concerning God. In the first place, he should make clear why he believes that God exists. In the second, he should make clear what he conceives God's nature to be. So far as God's existence goes, we know where James stands in this essay. "Why do I believe in God? Is it because I have experienced his presence? No; rather because I need that it be true." Before quitting James, it is worth noting that he used his principle to justify his belief in God's finiteness. Like Mill, and other recent and contemporary theologians, James repudiated the celebrated "omni's" of traditional theology.

I simply refuse to accept the idea of there being no purpose in the objective world. On the other hand, I cannot represent the existence of purpose except as based in a mind. The "not-me," therefore, so far as it contains purpose, must spring from a mind; but not necessarily a *One and Only* mind.

In saying God exists, all I imply is that my purposes are cared for by a mind so powerful as on the whole to control the drift of the universe. That is . . . merely a practical emotional faith.

The only difficulties of theism are the moral difficulties and meanness; and they have always seemed to me to flow from the gratuitous dogma of God being the all-inclusive reality. Once think possible a pluralism of which He may be one member, and piety forthwith ceases to be incompatible with manliness, and religious faith with intellectual rectitude.

In short, the only theism I defend is that of simple unphilosophic mankind. God, in the religious life of ordinary men is the name, not of the whole of things, heaven forbid, but only of the ideal tendency in things. . . . He works in an external environment, has limits, and has enemies. . . . If there be a God, how the devil can we know what difficulties he may have had to contend with? Possible difficulties! They save everything. But what are they if not limitations to the all-inclusiveness of any single being!

Having an environment, being in time, and working out a history just like ourselves, He escapes from the foreignness from all that is human, of the static, timeless, perfect absolute.

My God, being part of a pluralistic system, is responsible only for such things as He knows enough and has enough power to have accomplished. The "omniscient" and "omnipotent" God of theology I regard as a disease of the philosophy shop.

The line of least resistance, as it seems to me, both in theology and in philosophy, is to accept, along with the Superhuman Consciousness, the notion that It is not all embracing; the notion, in other words, that there is a God, but that He is finite, either in power or in knowledge, or in both at once.

Note on Sources.   The James material in this section is quoted or abridged from his essay "The Will to Believe." The concluding passages (pp. 67–68 of this book) are from the chapters entitled "Conclusion" and "Postscript" in his book *Varieties of Religious Experience.*

Reading References.   The best thing to do with William James is to read him. In many respects, he is his own best commentary. The volume, *The Will to Believe and Other Essays,* from which this chapter has been largely drawn, is a delightful collection. (See also *Essays in Pragmatism,* edited by the present writer.) But one may desire to know what other people think about an author whom one has read. A useful book here is Julius Bixler's *Religion in the Philosophy of William James.* The most complete account of James's life and times is to be found in R. B. Perry's two monumental volumes, *The Life and Thought of William James.* The chapter in which Perry gives an account of "The Will to Believe" will repay perusal.

READING QUESTIONS

1. What James means by (a) a hypothesis, (b) a live hypothesis, (c) an option, (d) a genuine option.
2. He distinguishes between genuine options that can be decided on intellectual grounds and genuine options that cannot be so decided. Give an example of the first sort. What he would have us do about genuine options of the first sort.
3. State his thesis about genuine options of the second sort, i.e., those that cannot be decided on intellectual grounds.

4. Give three examples—your own, not James's—of genuine options which cannot be decided on intellectual grounds.

5. When you decide a genuine option that cannot be decided on intellectual grounds, you exercise the "will to believe." By "will" here, do you understand simply "desire" or "wish"? Is the "will to believe" simply another name for "wishful thinking"?

6. James says that moral questions present genuine options that cannot be decided on intellectual grounds. (a) Give an example of his point here. (b) Why, looking forward to Clifford and Huxley, he does well to include moral questions at this point.

7. He says that the religious hypothesis has two parts to it, both necessary: (a) A personal God exists, over and above nature. (b) We are better off, even now, if we believe that. If that is the religious hypothesis, do you find it, in James's sense, "live"? If that is the religious hypothesis, how would you state the religious option? Would it be, in James's sense, a genuine option? Of the second sort?

8. A genuine option that cannot be decided on intellectual grounds might be called an "open" question that you see no intellectually defensible way of "closing." The skeptic advises suspended judgment: on grounds of prudence such options should be avoided, such questions be left "open." James's rejoinder to him.

9. The agnostic (Clifford, Huxley) goes further. He says that it is *immoral* to exercise the will to believe in the case of genuine options that cannot be decided on intellectual grounds. James's rejoinder to him.

10. The atheist goes further than either the skeptic or the agnostic. Suggest what James would say to him.

11. If you decide a genuine option that cannot be decided on intellectual grounds, you exercise the "will to believe." What is the "two-edged sword" objection?

12. State James's "piece-meal" supernaturalism. His reasons for adhering to it.

13. Wherein James invites comparison with Pascal and Mill, but contrast with Hume.

14. Wherein you find James (a) most, (b) least convincing.

INDEPENDENT STUDY

1. In addition to his paper "The Will to Believe," James wrote three others dealing with the same question: "Is it ever the part of wis-

dom to let belief outrun evidence?" where *evidence* is used in the sense of empirically known facts requiring the belief in question. The earliest of these essays on the rationale of "overbeliefs" is perhaps his paper "The Sentiment of Rationality." Then came "The Will to Believe," then "Philosophical Conceptions and Practical Results," then Chapter Two ("What Pragmatism Means") of his book *Pragmatism.* All four of these essays are lively and readable. Taken as a set, they provide usable material for a paper.

2. Consider the claim that every event has a cause. By consulting Topic Eight in this book, you will find Hume and Kant and Collingwood dealing with the question, "In *what* sense do we know, or *why* are we justified in believing that every event has a cause?" Compare what they say with what James would say.

3. In *The Will to Believe* James is concerned primarily with religious belief. Read his chapter "The Conscious-Automaton Theory" (*Principles of Psychology,* Volume One), his essay "The Dilemma of Determinism," his essay "The Moral Philosopher and the Moral Life," and his Ingersoll Lecture "Human Immortality." What question is he concerned with in each of these papers? Can you see the "will to believe" at work in each?

4. Read the article on James by W. J. Earle in the *Encyclopedia of Philosophy.* Base further reading in James's essays and chapters on Earle's article. Work out a paper on James's positions in philosophy *in general.* Center your paper on James's position in philosophy of religion.

The following are two lists of books containing popular (i.e., not technical) discussions of questions in theology. There is no reason that only professional theologians should write and read books about God. If you have found Pascal, Hume, Mill, Huxley, and James worth reading, then you should extend your holdings. If your thinking runs with Pascal and Mill and James, you will perhaps prefer to browse in the first list; if, however, with Hume and Huxley, then the second list.

LIST I

Chesterton, G. K. *Orthodoxy, The Everlasting Man.*
Eddington, Sir Arthur. *Science and the Unseen World.*
Hocking, W. E. *Science and the Idea of God.*
Joad, C. E. M. *God and Evil.*
More, Paul Elmer. *The Skeptical Approach to Religion.*
Paton, H. J. *The Modern Predicament.*

Shaw, Bernard. *Infidel Half Century.* (Preface to *Back to Methuse-
lah.*)
Stace, W. T. *Time and Eternity* and *Religion and the Modern Mind.*

LIST II

Bury, J. B. *History of Freedom of Thought.*
Dewey, John. *A Common Faith.*
Freud, Sigmund. *The Future of an Illusion.*
Mencken, H. L. *Treatise on the Gods.*
Paine, T. *The Age of Reason,* Part I.
Russell, Bertrand. *Religion and Science.*
Santayana, George. *Reason in Religion.*
Stephen, Sir Leslie. *An Agnostic's Apology* and *Freethinking and
Plain Speaking.*

SECTION 6. C. S. LEWIS: COUNTERATTACK

From James to Lewis. The authors whom you have been reading
thus far (Pascal, Hume, Mill, Huxley, James) have been examined
with reference to the question, "Can you use what you know about
nature to justify what you believe about God?" Pascal, Hume, and
Huxley said "no." Mill offered a qualified "perhaps," depending on
what you believe about God. If you believe that He is finite, then
perhaps "yes." James pointed out that if your are a scientist, or an author of moral judgments, or a practitioner of religion, you will at
some crucial point exercise the "will to believe"; he did not see that
scientists alone were entitled to do this on behalf of their investigative activities.

In the case of our final author the question needs to be stated this
way: "Can you use what you know about *human* nature, to justify
what you believe about God?" Is there anything about man, in contrast to nature, from which one would be entitled to infer the existence of God? I have used the term *counterattack* in the case of
Lewis because he writes out of a somewhat belligerent opposition to
skeptics, agnostics, atheists, materialists, evolutionary naturalists,
and so on; and because in his four lively books on these matters he
defends what many of his contemporaries regard as "impossible"
positions. Thus, in *The Problem of Pain,* he denies that orthodox
Christianity is bankrupted by the problem of evil in the world. In the
Abolition of Man he claims that if you construe man as an object in
nature you simply abolish the distinctively human. In *Miracles* he
argues that miracles are not impossible unless you subscribe to a

hard-nosed naturalism, and that if you do subscribe to such a natural-ism you would be better advised to defend your own position than to use it as a basis for simply rejecting miracles and whatever supernat-uralism they may require. In *Mere Christianity* he draws attention to points in Christian belief that are not as "mere" as its critics and disowners would have you suppose.

Biographical Note. C. S. Lewis was born in 1898 and died in 1963 at the age of sixty-five. He was a Fellow and Tutor of Magdalen College, Oxford, from 1925 to 1954. In 1954 he became professor of Medieval and Renaissance English at Cambridge University. His au-tobiography, *Surprised by Joy,* gives an account of his early atheism and subsequent conversion (or reconversion) to Anglican Chris-tianity. His great years as "defender of the faith" include the fifteen years between 1937–1938 and 1952–1953. The four books mentioned were published as follows: *The Problem of Pain,* 1940; *The Abolition of Man,* 1944; *Miracles,* 1947; and *Mere Christianity,* 1952. He wrote three "interplanetary" novels, which he regarded as exercises in Christian myth making: *Out of the Silent Planet,* 1938; *Perelandra,* 1943; and *That Hideous Strength,* 1945. His first book to become something of an international best seller, *The Screwtape Letters,* was published in 1942. It was a wry and ironic effort to give substance and plausibility to the Christian conception of a power in the world, not ourselves, making for all unrighteousness. A similar fable, *The Great Divorce,* published in 1945, presented an imaginary concep-tion of hell.

The Argument of the Selections. Mr. Lewis begins with a defi-nition of the term *miracle;* an event in nature caused to happen by the intervention of a power above, beyond, "super," with respect to nature. If there is nothing "super" with respect to nature, then no events are miraculous. Some persons take up the position that nature is all that there is, a self-sufficient whole; that there is nothing super-natural. "I call these people Naturalists," says Lewis, "and their po-sition, naturalism." Unless Mr. Lewis can show grounds for rejecting naturalism, he cannot make out a case for miracles. His argument is that if you use what you know about human nature, you can show grounds for rejecting naturalism. There is nothing in nature, as natu-ralism conceives of nature, that corresponds at all closely to the power of rational thinking and moral judgment in man. If this is so, then even the human is, in these two respects, supernatural. This much Mr. Lewis regards as a necessary, though not sufficient, case for claiming some events as miracles. If man is above nature, then miracles are not to be rejected on the grounds that there is nothing above nature. If man is above nature, then naturalism is in no position to claim that there is nothing above man. For all that naturalism has to say about it, miracles are possible and may be actual. Who is to say that there is nothing in the world superior to man as man is superior to nature?

The following material is from Chapters 2, 3, and 5 of C. S. Lewis's book *Miracles*. In Chapter 2 he distinguishes between the naturalist and the supernaturalist, between naturalism and supernaturalism. His defense of belief in miracles takes off from this distinction because the naturalist, or naturalism, denies that there are any miracles as Lewis defines that term. In Chapter 3 he advances one criticism of the naturalist's position, based on the character of thinking that is rational in Sense Two. In Chapter 5 he advances a second criticism of the naturalist's position, based on the character of morality, activity performed because believed to be right. His overall claim is that, given his position, the naturalist cannot produce a finally satisfactory account of either rational thinking or moral conduct. His overall claim is not that if naturalism is false or supernaturalism is true, then a belief in miracles is true. It is rather this: unless naturalism is false, unless supernaturalism is true, a belief in miracles could not be true. He begins by distinguishing the two positions. The numbers here assigned to his first three paragraphs do not occur in the original.

1. I use the word *Miracle* to mean an interference with Nature by supernatural power. Unless there exists, in addition to Nature, something else which we may call the supernatural, there can be no miracles. Some people believe that nothing exists except Nature; I call these people *Naturalists*. Others think that, besides Nature, there exists something else: I call them *Supernaturalists*. Our first question, therefore, is whether the Naturalists or the Supernaturalists are right.

2. What the Naturalist believes is that the ultimate Fact, the thing you can't go behind, is a vast process in space and time which is *going on of its own accord*. Inside that total system every particular event (such as your sitting reading this book) happens because some other event has happened; in the long run, because the Total Event is happening. Each particular thing (such as this page) is what it is because other things are what they are; and so, eventually, because the whole system is what it is. All the things and events are so completely interlocked that no one of them can claim the slightest independence from "the whole show." None of them exists "on its own" or "goes on of its own accord" except in the sense that it exhibits, at some particular place and time, that general "existence on its own" or "behavior of its own accord" which belongs to "Nature" (the great total interlocked event) as a whole. Thus no thoroughgoing Naturalist believes in free will: for free will would mean that human beings have the power of independent action, the power of doing something more or other than what was involved by the total series of events. And any such separate power of originating events is what the Naturalist denies. Spontaneity, originality, ac-

tion "on its own," is a privilege reserved for "the whole show," which he calls *Nature*.

3. The Supernaturalist agrees with the Naturalist that there must be something which exists in its own right; some basic Fact whose existence it would be nonsensical to try to explain because this Fact is itself the ground or starting-point of all explanations. But he does not identify this Fact with "the whole show." He thinks that things fall into two classes. In the first class we find either things or (more probably) One Thing which is basic and original, which exists on its own. In the second we find things which are merely derivative from that One Thing. The one basic Thing has caused all the other things to be. It exists on its own; they exist because it exists. They will cease to exist if it ever ceases to maintain them in existence; they will be altered if it ever alters them.

Having formulated these two positions, Lewis goes on to contrast them. He does this at some length because he wants the reader to see that if the first is presupposed, then the question of miracles does not arise; whereas if the second is presupposed, there is at least some point to the question. So:

The difference between the two views might be expressed by saying that Naturalism gives us a democratic, Supernaturalism a monarchical, picture of reality. The Naturalist thinks that the privelege of "being on its own" resides in the total mass of things, just as in a democracy sovereignty resides in the whole mass of the people. The Supernaturalist thinks that this privilege belongs to some things or (more probably) One Thing and not to others—just as, in a real monarchy, the king has sovereignty and the people have not. And just as, in a democracy, all the citizens are equal, so for the Naturalist one thing or event is as good as another, in the sense that they are all equally dependent on the total system of things. Indeed each of them is only the way in which the character of that total system exhibits itself at a particular point in space and time. The Supernaturalist, on the other hand, believes that the one original or self-existent thing is on a different level from, and more important than all other things.

At this point a suspicion may occur that Supernaturalism first arose from reading into the universe the structure of monarchical societies. But then of course it may with equal reason be suspected that Naturalism has arisen from reading into it the structure of modern democracies. The two suspicions thus cancel out and give us no help in deciding which theory is more likely to be true. They do indeed remind us that Supernaturalism is the characteristic philosophy of a monarchical age and Naturalism of a democratic, in the sense that Supernaturalism, even if false, would have been believed by the great mass of unthinking people four hundred years ago, just as Naturalism, even if false, will be believed by the great mass of unthinking people to-day.

The difference between Naturalism and Supernaturalism is not exactly the same as the difference between belief in a God and disbelief. Naturalism, without ceasing to be itself, could admit a certain kind of God. The great interlocking event called Nature might be such as to produce at some stage a great cosmic consciousness, an indwelling "God" arising from the whole process as human mind arises (according to the Naturalists) from human organisms. A Naturalist would not object to that sort of God. The reason is this. Such a God would not stand outside Nature or the total system, would not be existing "on his own." It would still be "the whole show" which was the basic Fact, and such a God would merely be one of the things (even if he were the most interesting) which the basic Fact contained. What Naturalism cannot accept is the idea of a God who stands outside Nature and made it.

We are now in a position to state the difference between the Naturalist and the Supernaturalist despite the fact that they do not mean the same by the word Nature. The Naturalist believes that a great process, or "becoming," exists "on its own" in space and time, and that nothing else exists—what we call particular things and events being only the parts into which we analyse the great process or the shapes which that process takes at given moments and given points in space. This single, total reality he calls Nature. The Supernaturalist believes that one Thing exists on its own and has produced the framework of space and time and the procession of systematically connected events which fill them. This framework, and this filling, he calls Nature. It may, or may not, be the only reality which the one Primary Thing has produced. There might be other systems in addition to the one we call Nature.

Before moving to his two criticisms of naturalism, Lewis again reminds the reader that presupposing supernaturalism will not of itself guarantee that belief in miracles is true:

All this is, at present, purely speculative. It by no means follows from Supernaturalism that Miracles of any sort do in fact occur. God (the primary thing) may never in fact interfere with the natural system He has created. If He has created more natural systems than one, He may never cause them to impinge on one another.

But that is a question for further consideration. If we decide that Nature is not the only thing there is, then we cannot say in advance whether she is safe from miracles or not. There are things outside her: we do not yet know whether they can get in. The gates may be barred, or they may not. But if Naturalism is true, then we do know in advance that miracles are impossible: nothing can come into Nature from the outside because there is nothing outside to come in, Nature being everything. No doubt, events which we in our ignorance should mistake for miracles might occur: but they would in reality be (just like the commonest events) an inevitable result of the character of the whole system.

Our first choice, therefore, must be between Naturalism and Supernaturalism.

How is this choice to be made? Lewis's strategy is to point out two difficulties in the naturalist's position. His first difficulty might be put this way: If naturalism is the whole truth about nature, then, although it may well be that everything in nature is rational in Sense One, nothing is rational in Sense Two. There are "natural processes." There are no "rational activities." The investigated behavior of chemicals, for example, belongs in the naturalist's picture of nature, but the investigative behavior of the chemist does not. This would be a serious objection to naturalism, if conceded. It would amount to the claim that if you are a naturalist, then you cannot see how natural science is possible. Lewis spells his point out at some length:

If naturalism is true, every finite thing or event must be (in principle) explicable in terms of the Total System. I say "explicable *in principle*" because of course we are not going to demand that naturalists, at any given moment, should have found the detailed explanation of every phenomenon. Obviously many things will only be explained when the sciences have made further progress. But if Naturalism is to be accepted we have a right to demand that every single thing should be such that we see, in general, how it could be explained in terms of the Total System. If any one thing exists which is of such a kind that we see in advance the impossibility of ever giving it *that kind* of explanation, then Naturalism would be in ruins. If necessities of thought force us to allow to any one thing any degree of independence from the Total System—if any one thing makes good a claim to be on its own, to be something more than an expression of the character of Nature as a whole—then we have abandoned Naturalism we mean the doctrine that only Nature—the whole interlocked system—exists. And if that were true, every thing and event would, if we knew enough, be explicable without remainder (no *heel-taps*) as a necessary product of the system. The whole system being what it is, it ought to be a contradiction in terms if you were not reading this book at the moment; and, conversely, the only cause why you are reading it ought to be that the whole system, at such a place and hour, was bound to take that course.

One threat against strict Naturalism has recently been launched on which I myself will base no argument, but which it will be well to notice. The older scientists believed that the smallest particles of matter moved according to strict laws: in other words, that the movements of each particle were "interlocked" with the total system of Nature. Some modern scientists seem to think—if I understand them—that this is not so. They seem to think that the individual unit of matter (it would be rash to call it any longer a "particle") moves in an indeterminate or random fashion; moves, in fact, "on its own" or "of its own accord." The regularity which we observe in the movements of the smallest visible bodies is explained by the fact that each of these contains millions of units and that the law of averages therefore levels out the idiosyncrasies of the individual unit's behaviour. The movement of one unit is incalculable, just as the result of tossing a coin once is incalculable: the majority movement of a billion units can however be predicted, just as, if you tossed a coin a billion times, you could predict a nearly equal number of heads and tails. Now it will be noticed that if this theory is true we have really admitted something other than Nature. If the movements of the individual units are events "on their own," events which do not interlock with all other events, then these movements are not part of Nature. It would be, indeed, too great a shock to our habits to describe them as *super*-natural. I think we should have to call them *sub*-natural. But all our confidence that Nature has no doors, and no reality outside herself for doors to open on, would have disappeared. There is apparently *something* outside her, the Subnatural; it is indeed from this Subnatural that all events and all "bodies" are, as it were, fed into her. And clearly if she thus has a back door opening on the Subnatural, it is quite on the cards that she may also have a front door opening on the Supernatural—and events might be fed into her at that door too.

I have mentioned this theory because it puts in a fairly vivid light certain conceptions which we shall have to use later on. But I am not, for my own part, assuming its truth. Those who (like myself) have had a philosophical rather than a scientific education find it almost impossible to believe that the scientists really mean what they seem to be saying. I cannot help thinking they mean no more than that the movements of individual units are permanently incalculable *to us*, not that they are in themselves random and lawless. And even if they mean the latter, a layman can hardly feel any certainty that some new scientific development may not to-morrow abolish this whole idea of a lawless Subnature. For it is the glory of science to progress.

It is clear that everything we know, beyond our own immediate sensations, is inferred from those sensations. I do not mean that we begin as children, by regarding our sensations as "evidence" and thence arguing consciously to the existence of space, matter, and other people. I mean that if, after we are old enough to understand the question, our confidence in the existence of anything else (say, the solar system or the Spanish Armada) is challenged, our argument in defence of it will have to take the form of inferences from our immediate sensations. Put in its most general form the inference would run, "Since I am presented with colours, sounds, shapes, pleasures and pains which I cannot perfectly predict or control, and since the more I investigate them the more regular their behaviour appears, therefore there must exist something other than myself and it must be systematic." Inside this very general inference, all sorts of special trains of inference lead us to more detailed conclusions. We infer Evolution from fossils: we infer the existence of our own brains from what we find inside the skulls of other creatures like ourselves in the dissecting room.

All possible knowledge, then, depends on the validity of reasoning. If the feeling of certainty which we express by words like *must be* and *therefore* and *since* is a real perception of how things outside our own minds really "must" be, well and good. But if this certainty is merely a feeling *in* our own minds and not a genuine insight into realities beyond them—if it merely represents the way our minds happen to work—then we can have no knowledge. Unless human reasoning is valid no science can be true.

It follows that no account of the universe can be true unless that account leaves it possible for our thinking to be a real insight. A theory which explained everything else in the whole universe but which made it impossible to believe that our thinking was valid, would be utterly out of court. For that theory would itself have been reached by thinking, and if thinking is not valid that theory would, of course, be itself demolished. It would have destroyed its own credentials. It would be an argument which proved that no argument was sound—a proof that there are no such things as proofs—which is nonsense.

We must believe in the validity of rational thought, and we must not believe in anything inconsistent with its validity. But we can believe in the validity of thought only under certain conditions. Consider the following sentences. (1) "He thinks that dog dangerous because he has often seen it muzzled and he has noticed that messengers always try to avoid going to that house." (2) "He thinks that dog dangerous because it is black and ever since he was bitten by a black dog in childhood he has always been afraid of black dogs."

Both sentences explain *why* the man thinks as he does. But the one explanation substantiates the value of his thought, the other wholly discredits it. Why is it that to discover the cause of a thought sometimes damages its credit and sometimes reinforces it? Because the one cause is a good cause and the other a bad cause? But the man's complex about black dogs is not a bad cause in the sense of being a weak or inefficient one. If the man is in a sufficiently pathological condition, it may be quite irresistible and, in that sense, as good a cause for his belief as the Earth's revolution is for day and night. The real difference is that in the first instance the man's belief is caused by something rational (by argument from observed facts) while in the other it is caused by something irrational (association of ideas).

We may in fact state it as a rule that *no thought is valid if it can be fully explained as the result of irrational causes.* Every reader of this book applies this rule automatically all day long. When a sober man tells you that the house is full of rats or snakes, you attend to him: if you know that his belief in the rats and snakes is due to *delirium tremens* you do not even bother to look for them. If you even *suspect* an irrational cause, you begin to pay less attention to a man's beliefs; your friend's pessimistic view of the European situation alarms you less when you discover that he is suffering from a bad liver attack. Conversely, when we discover a belief to be false we then first look about for irrational causes ("I was tired"—"I was in a hurry"—"I wanted to believe it"). The whole disruptive power of Marxism and Freudianism against traditional beliefs has lain in their claim to expose irrational causes for them. If any Marxist is reading these lines at this moment, he is murmuring to himself, "All this argument really results from the fact that the author is a bourgeois"—in fact he is applying the rule I have just stated. Because he thinks that my thoughts result from an irrational cause he therefore discounts them. All thoughts which are so caused are valueless. We never, in our ordinary thinking, admit any exceptions to this rule.

Now it would clearly be preposterous to apply this rule to each particular thought as we come to it and yet not to apply it to all thoughts taken collectively, that is, to human reason as a whole. Each particular thought is valueless if it is the result of irrational causes. Obviously, then, the whole process of human thought, what we call Reason, is equally valueless if it is the result of irrational causes. Hence every theory of the universe which makes the human mind a result of irrational causes is inadmissible, for it would be a proof that there are no such things as proofs. Which is nonsense.

But Naturalism, as commonly held, is precisely a theory of this sort. The mind, like every other particular thing or event, is supposed to be simply the product of the Total System. It is supposed to be that and nothing more, to have no power whatever of "going on of its own accord." And the Total System is not supposed to be rational. All thoughts whatever are therefore the results of irrational causes, and nothing more than that. The finest piece of scientific reasoning is caused in just the same irrational way as the thoughts a man has because a bit of bone is pressing on his brain. If we continue to apply our Rule, both are equally valueless. And if we stop applying our Rule we are no better off. For then the Naturalist will have to admit that thoughts produced by lunacy or alcohol or by the mere wish to disbelieve in Naturalism are just as valid as his own thoughts. What is sauce for the goose is sauce for the gander. The Naturalist cannot condemn other people's thoughts because they have irrational causes and continue to believe his own which have (if Naturalism is true) equally irrational causes.

The shortest and simplest form of this argument is that given by Professor J. B. S. Haldane in *Possible Worlds* (p. 209). He writes, "If my mental processes are determined wholly by the motions of atoms in my brain, I have no reason to suppose that my beliefs are true . . . and hence I have no reason for supposing my brain to be composed of atoms." If I have avoided this form of the argument, this is because I do not wish to have on our hands at this stage so difficult a concept as Matter. The trouble about atoms is not that they are material (whatever that may mean) but that they are, presumably, irrational. Or even if they were rational they do not produce my beliefs by honestly arguing with me and proving their point but by compelling me to think in a certain way. I am still subject to brute force: my beliefs have irrational causes.

An attempt to get out of the difficulty might be made along the following lines. Even if thoughts are produced by irrational causes, still it might happen by mere accident that some of them were true—just as the black dog might, after all, have been really dangerous though the man's reason for thinking it so was worthless. Now individuals whose thoughts happened, in this accidental way, to be truer than other people's would have an advantage in the struggle for existence. And if habits of thought can be inherited, natural selection would gradually eliminate or weed out the people who have the less useful types of thought. It might therefore have come about by now that the present type of human mind—the sort of thought that has survived—was tolerably reliable.

But it won't do. In the first place, this argument works only if there are such things as heredity, the struggle for existence, and elimination. But we know about these things—certainly about their existence in the past—only by inference. Unless, therefore, you start by assuming inference to be valid, you cannot know about them. You have to assume that inference is valid before you can even begin your argument for its validity. And a proof which sets out by assuming the thing you have to prove, is rubbish. But waive that point. Let heredity and the rest be granted. Even then you cannot show that our processes of thought yield truth unless you are allowed to argue "Because a thought is useful, therefore it must be (at least partly) true." But this is itself an inference. If you trust it, you are once more assuming that very validity which you set out to prove.

In order to avoid endless waste of time we must recognise once and for all that this will happen to any argument whatever which attempts to prove or disprove the validity of thought. By trusting to argument at all you have assumed the point at issue. All arguments about the validity of thought make a tacit, and illegitimate, exception in favour of the bit of thought you are doing at that moment. It has to be left outside the discussion and simply believed in, in the simple old-fashioned way. Thus the Freudian proves that all thoughts are merely due to complexes except the thoughts which consti- tute this proof itself. The Marxist proves that all thoughts result from class conditioning—except the thought he is thinking while he says this. It is therefore always impossible to begin with any other data whatever and from them to find out whether thought is valid. You must do exactly the op- posite—must begin by admitting the self-evidence of logical thought and then believe all other things only in so far as they agree with that. The valid- ity of thought is central: all other things have to be fitted in round it as best they can.

Some Naturalists whom I have met attempt to escape by saying that there *is* no ground for believing our thoughts to be valid and that this does not worry them in the least. "We find that they work," it is said, "and we admit that we cannot argue from this that they give us a true account of any exter- nal reality. But we don't mind. We are not interested in truth. Our habits of thought seem to enable humanity to keep alive and that is all we care about." One is tempted to reply that every free man wants truth as well as life: that a mere life-addict is no more respectable than a cocaine addict. But opinions may differ on that point. The real answer is that unless the Natural- ists put forward Naturalism as a true theory, we have of course no dispute with them. You can argue with a man who says, "Rice is unwholesome": but you neither can nor need argue with a man who says, "Rice is unwholesome, but I'm not saying this is true." I feel also that this surrender of the claim to truth has all the air of an expedient adopted at the last moment. If the Natu- ralists do not claim to know any truths, ought they not to have warned us rather earlier of the fact? For really from all the books they have written, in which the behaviour of the remotest nebula, the shyest photon and the most prehistoric man are described, one would have got the idea that they were claiming to give a true account of real things. The fact surely is that they nearly always are claiming to do so. The claim is surrendered only when the question discussed in this chapter is pressed; and when the crisis is over the claim is tacitly resumed.

If naturalism is presupposed, then it may be that nature is through and through rational in Sense One, consists of "natural pro- cesses" but not "rational activities." If, however, man is, in some of his behavior, an agent who performs activities, then it will follow that, to the extent that man is rational in Sense Two, he is not a part of nature. What then is the relation between man, to the extent that

he is rational in Sense Two, and an order of nature that is only rational in Sense One? Lewis must face up to this difficult question. He
does this before introducing his second criticism of the naturalist
position:

If our argument has been sound, rational thought or Reason is not interlocked with the great interlocking system of irrational events which we
call Nature. I am not maintaining that consciousness as a whole must necessarily be put in the same position. Pleasures, pains, fears, hopes, affections
and mental images need not. No absurdity would follow from regarding
them as parts of Nature. The distinction we have to make is not one between
"mind" and "matter," much less between "soul" and "body" (hard words,
all four of them) but between Reason and Nature: the frontier coming not
where the "outer world" ends and what I should ordinarily call "myself"
begins, but between Reason and the whole mass of irrational events whether
physical or psychological.

At that frontier we find a great deal of traffic but it is all one-way traffic. It
is a matter of daily experience that Rational thoughts induce and enable us
to alter the course of Nature—of physical nature when we use mathematics
to build bridges, or of psychological nature when we apply arguments to
alter our own emotions. We succeed in modifying physical nature more often
and more completely than we succeed in modifying psychological nature,
but we do at least a little to both. On the other hand, Nature is quite powerless to produce Rational thought: not that she never modifies our thinking
but that the moment she does so, it ceases (for that very reason) to be rational. For, as we have seen, a train of thought loses all rational credentials as
soon as it can be shown to be wholly the result of irrational causes. When
Nature, so to speak, attempts to do things to Rational thoughts she only
succeeds in killing them. That is the peculiar state of affairs at the frontier.
Nature can only raid Reason to kill; but Reason can invade Nature to take
prisoners and even to colonise. Every object you see before you at this
moment—the walls, ceiling, and furniture, the book, your own washed hands
and cut finger-nails, bears witness to the colonisation of Nature by Reason:
for none of this matter would have been in these states if Nature had had her
way. And if you are attending to my argument as closely as I hope, that attention also results from habits which Reason has imposed on the natural ram-
blings of consciousness. If, on the other hand, a toothache or an anxiety is at
this very moment preventing you from attending, then Nature is indeed interfering with your consciousness: but not to produce some new variety of
reasoning, only (as far as in her lies) to suspend Reason altogether.

In other words the relation between Reason and Nature is what some
people call an Unsymmetrical Relation. Brotherhood is a symmetrical relation because if A is the brother of B, B is the brother of A. Father-and-Son is
an unsymmetrical relation because if A is the father of B, B is *not* the father
of A. The relation between Reason and Nature is of this kind. Reason is not
related to Nature as Nature is related to Reason.

I am only too well aware how shocking those who have been brought up
to Naturalism will find the picture which begins to show itself. It is, frankly,
a picture in which Nature (at any rate on the surface of our own planet) is

perforated or pock-marked all over by little orifices at each of which something of a different kind from herself—namely a Reason—can do things to her. I can only beg you, before you throw the book away, to consider seriously whether your instinctive repugnance to such a conception is really rational, or whether it is only emotional or aesthetic. I know that the hankering for a universe which is all of a piece, and in which everything is the same sort of thing as everything else—a continuity, a seamless web, a democratic universe—is very deep-seated in the modern heart: in mine, no less than in yours. But have we any real assurance that things are like that? Are we mistaking for an intrinsic probability what is really a human desire for tidiness and harmony? Bacon warned us long ago that "the human understanding is of its own nature prone to suppose the existence of more order and regularity in the world than it finds. And though there be many things which are singular and unmatched, yet it devises for them parallels and conjugates and relatives which do not exist. Hence the fiction that all celestial bodies move in perfect circles" (*Novum Organum*, I. 45). I think Bacon was right. Science itself has already made reality appear less homogeneous than we expected it to be: Newtonian atomism was much more the sort of thing we expected (and desired) than Quantum physics.

If you can, even for the moment, endure the suggested picture of Nature, let us now consider the other factor—the Reasons, or instances of Reason, which attack her. We have seen that rational thought is not part of the system of Nature. Within each man there must be an area (however small) of activity which is outside or independent of her. In relation to Nature, rational thought goes on "of its own accord" or exists "on its own."

Mr. Lewis has a second string to his bow. It is possible for a human being to incur an obligation. Suppose he borrows a thousand dollars from a poor but trusting friend, promising to repay it within six months. He thereby incurs an obligation. We sometimes express this by saying that he ought to repay the money he has borrowed, that it is his duty to do so, that it would be wrong of him not to do so. Here are four terms (*obligation, ought, duty, wrong*) that have wide application to human behavior. Are we to say that no person ever has any obligations to anyone, not even to himself? Or that he never ought to live up to them? Or that doing so is never a duty? Or that it is never wrong to flout them? We can express this by saying that man is a moral animal. This may or may not be included in the claim that he is a rational animal. It will make no difference to Mr. Lewis's second point in reference to what the naturalist means by nature, because, of course, nothing in nature, as the naturalist conceives of nature, has any obligations, any oughts, any duties, or can do anything either immoral or wrong. Run over the subject matters of the natural sciences: solar systems, electrons and protons, chemicals, light waves and sound waves, electricity and magnetism, rocks and minerals, cells, and so on. Where, in the order of nature as conceived by Mr. Lewis's naturalist, do you encounter an obligation, an ought, a duty, an immorality, or a wrong? Nature, in the naturalist's sense, is closed to such realities. If nature is nonrational, in the sense that it can neither reason nor be reasoned with, and nonmoral, in the sense that she is neither moral nor immoral, then in what sense is man, in these essential respects, an integral part of nature, nothing but a "natural object"? It is possible for a normal human being to reason and to be reasoned with; to be under obligations to others and for others to be under obligations to him. The naturalist makes no provision for any such matters in his conception of nature. What then? Will he revise his conception of nature? Or will he revise his conception of man's relation to nature?

Some people regard logical thinking as the deadest and driest of our activities and may therefore be repelled by the privileged position I gave it in the last chapter. But logical thinking—Reasoning—had to be the pivot of the argument because, of all the claims which the human mind puts forward, the claim of Reasoning to be valid is the only one which the Naturalist cannot deny without (philosophically speaking) cutting his own throat. You cannot, as we saw, prove that there are no proofs. But you can if you wish regard all human ideals as illusions and all human loves as biological by-products. That is, you can do so without running into flat self-contradiction and nonsense. Whether you can do so without extreme unplausibility—without accepting a picture of things which no one really believes—is another matter.

Besides reasoning about matters of fact, men also make moral judgments—"I ought to do this"—"I ought not to do that"—"This is good"—"That is evil." Two views have been held about moral judgments. Some people think that when we make them we are not using our Reason, but are employing some different power. Other people think that we make them by our Reason. I myself hold this second view. That is, I believe that the primary moral principles on which all others depend are rationally perceived. We "just see" that there is no reason why my neighbour's happiness should be sacrificed to my own, as we "just see" that things which are equal to the same thing are equal to one another. If we cannot prove either axiom, that is not because they are irrational but because they are self-evident and all proofs depend on them. Their intrinsic reasonableness shines by its own light. It is because all morality is based on such self-evident principles that we say to a man, when we would recall him to right conduct, "Be reasonable."

But this is by the way. For our present purpose it does not matter which of these two views you adopt. The important point is to notice that Moral Judgments raise the same sort of difficulty for Naturalism as any other thoughts. We always assume in discussions about morality, as in all other discussions, that the other man's views are worthless if they can be fully accounted for by some non-moral and non-rational cause. When two men differ about good and evil we soon hear this principle being brought into play: "He believes in the sanctity of property because he's a millionaire"—"He believes in Pacifism because he's a coward"—"He approves of corporal punishment because he's a sadist." Such taunts may often be untrue: but the mere fact that they are made by the one side, and hotly rebutted by the other, shows clearly what principle is being used. Neither side doubts that if they were true they would be decisive. No one (in real life) pays attention to any moral judgment which can be shown to spring from non-moral and non-rational causes. The Freudian and the Marxist attack traditional morality precisely on this ground—and with wide success. All men accept the principle.

But, of course, what discredits particular moral judgments must equally discredit moral judgment as a whole. If the fact that men have such ideas as *ought* and *ought not* at all can be fully explained by irrational and non-moral causes, then those ideas are an illusion. The Naturalist is ready to explain how the illusion arose. Chemical conditions produce life. Life, under the influence of natural selection, produces consciousness. Conscious organisms which behave in one way live longer than those which behave in another. Living longer, they are more likely to have offspring. Inheritance, and sometimes teaching as well, pass on their mode of behaviour to their young. Thus in every species a pattern of behaviour is built up. In the human species conscious teaching plays a larger part in building it up, and the tribe further strengthens it by killing individuals who don't conform. They also invent gods who are said to punish departures from it. Thus, in time, there comes to exist a strong human impulse to conform. But since this impulse is often at variance with the other impulses, a mental conflict arises, and the man expresses it by saying "I want to do A but I ought to do B."

This account may (or may not) explain why men do in fact make moral judgments. It does not explain how they could be right in making them. It excludes, indeed, the very possibility of their being right. For when men say "I ought" they certainly think they are saying something, and something true, about the nature of the proposed action, and not merely about their own feelings. But if Naturalism is true, "I ought" is the same sort of statement as "I itch" or "I'm going to be sick." In real life when a man says "I ought" we may reply, "Yes. You're right. That *is* what you ought to do," or else, "No. I think you're mistaken." But in a world of Naturalists (if Naturalists really remembered their philosophy out of school) the only sensible reply would be, "Oh, are you?" All moral judgments would be statements about the speaker's feelings, mistaken by him for statements about something else (the real moral quality of actions) which does not exist.

Such a doctrine, I have admitted, is not flatly self-contradictory. The Naturalist can, if he chooses, brazen it out. He can say. "Yes. I quite agree that there is no such thing as wrong and right. I admit that no moral judgment can be 'true' or 'correct' and, consequently, that no one system of morality can be better or worse than another. All ideas of good and evil are hallucinations—shadows cast on the outer world by the impulses which we have been conditioned to feel." Indeed many Naturalists are delighted to say this.

But then they must stick to it; and fortunately (though inconsistently) most real Naturalists do not. A moment after they have admitted that good and evil are illusions, you will find them exhorting us to work for posterity, to educate, revolutionise, liquidate, live and die for the good of the human race. A Naturalist like Mr. H. G. Wells has spent a long life doing so with passionate eloquence and zeal. But surely this is very odd? Just as all the books about spiral nebulae, atoms and cave men would really have led you to suppose that the Naturalists claimed to be able to know something, so all the books in which Naturalists tell us what we ought to do would really make you believe that they thought some ideas of good (their own, for example) to be somehow preferable to others. For they write with indignation like men proclaiming what is good in itself and denouncing what is evil in itself, and not at all like men recording that they personally like mild beer but some people prefer bitter. Yet if the "oughts" of Mr. Wells and, say, Franco are both equally the impulses which Nature has conditioned each to have and both tell us nothing about any objective right or wrong, whence is all the fervour? Do they remember while they are writing thus that when they tell us we "ought to make a better world" the words "ought" and "better" must, on their own showing, refer to an irrationally conditioned impulse which cannot be true or false any more than a vomit or a yawn?

My idea is that sometimes they do forget. That is their glory. Holding a philosophy which excludes humanity, they yet remain human. At the sight of injustice they throw all their Naturalism to the winds and speak like men and like men of genius. They know far better than they think they know. But at other times, I suspect, they are trusting in a supposed way of escape from their difficulty.

It works—or *seems* to work—like this. They say to themselves, "Ah, yes. Morality"—or "bourgeois morality" or "conventional morality" or "traditional morality" or some such addition—"Morality *is* an illusion. But we have found out what modes of behaviour will in fact preserve the human race alive. That is the behaviour we are pressing you to adopt. Pray don't mistake us for moralists. We are under an entirely new management" . . . just as if this would help. It would help only if we grant, firstly, that life is better than death and, secondly, that we ought to care for the lives of our descendants as much as, or more than, for our own. And both these are moral judgments which have, like all others, been explained away by Naturalism. Of course, having been conditioned by Nature in a certain way, we do feel thus about life and about posterity. But the Naturalists have cured us of mistaking these feelings for insights into what we once called "real value." Now that I know that my impulse to serve posterity is just the same kind of thing as my fondness for cheese—now that its transcendental pretensions have been exposed for a sham—do you think I shall pay much attention to it? When it happens to be strong (and it has grown considerably weaker since you explained to me its real nature) I suppose I shall obey it. When it is weak, I shall put my money into cheese. There can be no reason for trying to whip up and encourage the one impulse rather than the other. Not now that I know what they both are. The Naturalists must not destroy all my reverence for conscience on Monday and expect to find me still venerating it on Tuesday.

There is no escape along those lines. If we are to continue to make moral judgments (and whatever we say we shall in fact continue) then we must believe that the conscience of man is not a product of Nature. It can be valid only if it is an offshoot of some absolute moral wisdom, a moral wisdom which exists absolutely "on its own" and is not a product of non-moral, non-rational Nature. As the argument of the last chapter led us to acknowledge a supernatural source for rational thought, so the argument of this leads us to acknowledge a supernatural source for our ideas of good and evil.

The materials in this section occur in connection with Lewis's defense of belief in miracles. In the book from which they are quoted that is his principal concern. However, he begins by acknowledging that if the position called *naturalism* is conceded, then any defense of miracle is lost before it begins. If that ism is presupposed, and the term *miracle* is used as Lewis proposes to use it—"an interference with nature on the part of a supernatural power"—then there are no miracles. It is for this reason that he works out a two-front critique of naturalism. The removal of naturalism will not guarantee that some events are miraculous, but it would open the way toward a consideration of supernaturalism; and that is important because, unless some form of supernaturalism is validly entertainable, there is no point to asking whether miracles are even possible. At the conclusion of his two criticisms of naturalism Lewis reminds the reader of the rationale of his procedure. Thus:

It must be clearly understood that the argument so far leads to no conception of "souls" or "spirits" (words I have avoided) floating about in the realm of Nature with no relation to their environment. Hence we do not deny— indeed we must welcome—certain considerations which are often regarded as proofs of Naturalism. We can admit, and even insist, that Rational Thinking can be shown to be conditioned in its exercise by a natural object (the brain). It is temporarily impaired by alcohol or a blow on the head. It wanes as the brain decays and vanishes when the brain ceases to function. In the same way the moral outlook of a community can be shown to be closely connected with its history, geographical environment, economic structure, and so forth. The moral ideas of the individual are equally related to his general situation: it is no accident that parents and schoolmasters so often tell us that they can stand any vice rather than lying, the lie being the only defensive weapon of the child. All this, far from presenting us with a difficulty, is exactly what we should expect.

The rational and moral element in each human mind is a point of force from the Supernatural working its way into Nature, exploiting at each point those conditions which Nature offers, repulsed where the conditions are hopeless and impeded when they are unfavourable. A man's Rational thinking is *just so much* of his share in eternal Reason as the state of his brain allows to become operative: it represents, so to speak, the bargain struck or the frontier fixed between Reason and Nature at that particular point. A nation's moral outlook is just so much of its share in eternal Moral Wisdom as its history, economics etc. lets through. In the same way the voice of the Announcer is just so much of a human voice as the receiving set lets through. Of course it varies with the state of the receiving set, and deteriorates as the set wears out and vanishes altogether if I throw a brick at it. It is conditioned by the apparatus but not originated by it. If it were—if we knew that there was no human being at the microphone—we should not attend to the news. The various and complex conditions under which Reason and Morality appear are the twists and turns of the frontier between Nature and Supernature. That is why, if you wish, you can always ignore Supernature and treat the phenomena purely from the Natural side; just as a man studying on a map the boundaries of Cornwall and Devonshire can always say, "What you call a bulge in Devonshire is really a dent in Cornwall." And in a sense you can't refute him. What we call a bulge in Devonshire always *is* a dent in Cornwall. What we call rational thought in a man always involves a state of the brain, in the long run a relation of atoms. But Devonshire is none the less something more than "where Cornwall ends," and Reason is something more than cerebral bio-chemistry.

When you are looking at a garden from a room upstairs it is obvious (once you think about it) that you are looking through a window. But if it is the garden that interests you, you may look at it for a long time without thinking of the window. When you are reading a book it is obvious (once you attend to it) that you are using your eyes: but unless your eyes begin to hurt you, or the book is a text book on optics, you may read all evening without once thinking of eyes. When we talk we are obviously using language and grammar: and when we try to talk a foreign language we may be painfully aware of the fact. But when we are talking English we don't notice it. When you shout from the top of the stairs, "I'm coming in half a moment," you are not usually conscious that you have made the singular *am* agree with the singular *I*. There is indeed a story told about a Redskin who, having learned several other languages, was asked to write a grammar of the language used by his own tribe. He replied, after some thought, that it had no grammar. The grammar he had used all his life had escaped his notice all his life. He knew it (in one sense) so well that (in another sense) he did not know it existed.

All these instances show that the fact which is in one respect the most obvious and primary fact, and through which alone you have access to all the other facts, may be precisely the one that is most easily forgotten—forgotten not because it is so remote or abstruse but because it is so near and so obvious. And that is exactly how the Supernatural has been forgotten. The Naturalists have been engaged in thinking about Nature. They have not attended to the fact that they were *thinking*. The moment one attends to this it is obvious that one's own thinking cannot be merely a natural event, and that therefore something other than Nature exists. The Supernatural is not remote and abstruse: it is a matter of daily and hourly experience, as intimate as breathing. Denial of it depends on a certain absent-mindedness. But this absent-mindedness is in no way surprising. You do not need—indeed you do not wish—to be always thinking about windows when you are looking at gardens or always thinking about eyes when you are reading. In the same way the proper procedure for all limited and particular inquiries is to ignore the fact of your own thinking, and concentrate on the object. It is only when you stand back from particular inquiries and try to form a complete philosophy that you must take it into account. For a complete philosophy must get in *all* the facts. In it you turn away from specialised or truncated thought to total thought: and one of the facts total thought must think about is Thinking itself. There is thus a tendency in the study of Nature to make us forget the most obvious fact of all. And since the Sixteenth Century, when Science was born, the minds of men have been increasingly turned outward, to know Nature and to master her. They have been increasingly engaged on those specialised inquiries for which truncated thought is the correct method. It is therefore not in the least astonishing that they should have forgotten the evidence for the Supernatural. The deeply ingrained habit of truncated thought—what we call the "scientific" habit of mind—was indeed certain to lead to Naturalism, unless this tendency were continually corrected from some other source. But no other source was at hand, for during the same period men of science were coming to be metaphysically and theologically uneducated.

That brings me to the second consideration. The state of affairs in which ordinary people can discover the Supernatural only by abstruse reasoning is recent and, by historical standards, abnormal. All over the world, until quite modern times the direct insight of the mystics and the reasonings of the philosophers percolated to the mass of the people by authority and tradition; they could be received by those who were no great reasoners themselves in the concrete form of myth and ritual and the whole pattern of life. In the conditions produced by a century or so of Naturalism, plain men are being forced to bear burdens which plain men were ever expected to bear before. We must get the truth for ourselves or go without it. There may be two explanations for this. It might be that humanity, in rebelling against tradition and authority, have made a ghastly mistake; a mistake which will not be the less fatal because the corruptions of those in authority rendered it very excusable. On the other hand, it may be that the Power which rules our species is at this moment carrying out a daring experiment. Could it be intended that the whole mass of the people should now move forward and occupy for themselves those heights which were once reserved only for the sages? Is the distinction between wise and simple to disappear because all are now expected to become wise? If so, our present blunderings would be but growing pains. But let us make no mistake about our necessities. If we are content to go back and become humble plain men obeying a tradition, well. If we are ready to climb and struggle on till we become sages ourselves, better still. But the man who will neither obey wisdom in others nor adventure for her himself is fatal. A society where the simple many obey the few seers can live: a society where all were seers could live even more fully. But a society where the mass is still simple and the seers are no longer attended to can achieve only superficiality, baseness, ugliness, and in the end extinction. On or back we must go; to stay here is death.

Mr. Lewis began by formulating what naturalists claim about nature. He then pointed out that, granted their conception of nature, naturalists must ignore or deny rational thinking and moral judging. If neither rational thinking nor moral judging are to be encountered anywhere in nature as conceived by the naturalist, then one must go beyond nature, or above nature, to encounter them. In that sense, rational thinking and moral judging would be supernatural. In that sense, there is something supernatural about man, at least in respect to two activities that he characteristically performs.

Perhaps Mr. Lewis's position thus far could be paraphrased as follows: We use the term *rational* in two senses. In the first sense we use it to mean, "Can be discovered, can be found out about, by reasoning validly from sufficient relevant data." In this sense we might say of the solar system that it has a rational order. Get sufficient relevant data, and reason validly from those data, and you can find out about the solar system. In *this* sense of *rational*, there is nothing irrational about the solar system. If you claim that there is, then your claim is not based on sufficient relevant data, or it was not arrived at by a sufficient amount of valid reasoning. In this sense (Sense One), the naturalist would say, nature is through and through rational; there are no ultimate mysteries, no dead ends, nothing irrational.

We also use the term *rational* in a second sense, to mean, "Can reason and can be reasoned with." In this sense we sometimes say that man is a rational animal, meaning that he can reason and be reasoned with. In *this* sense (Sense Two) we would *not* say that the solar system is a rational order. It cannot reason or be reasoned with. If it could, it might have produced some astronomy; but it takes an astronomer, rational in Sense Two, to do that. If you can neither reason nor be reasoned with, you may get by as a solar system, but *not* as an astronomer. In this sense the naturalist does not claim that nature is "through and through rational." Nature may be wholly rational in Sense One, but not at all rational in Sense Two. Man's body, considered as subject matter for physics, chemistry, physiology, may be wholly rational in Sense One, but not at all rational in Sense Two.

But unless *something* is rational in Sense Two ("Can reason and can be reasoned with"), then we would have no knowledge of nature. There would be no natural sciences, and no naturalists claiming that their naturalism is the final truth about nature. If a naturalist denies that he can either reason or be reasoned with, what has he done to his naturalism? He may face a dilemma at this point. Mr. Lewis claims that the naturalist does indeed face a dilemma. If the naturalist insists that nature is only rational in Sense One, and that there is nothing that is not "reducible" to nature so conceived, then what account is the naturalist to give of naturalism and the natural sciences? If he admits that naturalists and natural scientists are rational in Sense Two ("Can reason and can be reasoned with"), then how can he insist that they are integral parts of nature, that there is nothing about them that is "super" with respect to nature?

Of course, Mr. Lewis wants more than nature (rational in Sense

One) and man (rational in Sense Two). He also wants God, because he is writing a book on miracles and has defined a miracle as something produced by the intervention of a supernatural power. If man is the *only* supernatural being in or related to the world, Mr. Lewis will not have a miracle worker in the traditional sense of the word. Mr. Lewis has breached the wall that naturalism throws around man in relation to nature. Can he now argue from man as supernatural to God as supernatural? At this point Mr. Lewis is no longer arguing with the naturalist. Now he is arguing with the atheist, because an atheist would (or could) admit that man is supernatural, but deny that there is any form of life higher than the human. If the atheist can prove that man is the highest form of life in the world or related to the world, then Mr. Lewis cannot have his supernatural power that could intervene in nature and perform a miracle.

Reading References. The passages quoted in this section are from the early chapters of Mr. Lewis's book *Miracles.* If you are interested in pursuing the argument any further, secure a copy of that book and read as much as you care to. The book on miracles was published in 1947. It had been preceded by two others, which are part of Mr. Lewis's counterattack on naturalism: *The Abolition of Man* in 1944, in which "scientizing the human" is brought under a considerably more sustained criticism; and *The Problem of Pain* in 1940, in which Mr. Lewis argues that the existence of misery and wickedness in the world is not incompatible with a belief in the existence of God. All three books are short and readable. The same can be said of *Mere Christianity,* published in 1952.

READING QUESTIONS

1. Why, in a book in defense of belief in miracles, does Lewis begin by an attack on naturalism? How does he define that ism?
2. Make clear that Lewis is shifting from the question, "Can you use what you know about nature as evidence for what you believe about God?" to the question, "Can you use what you know about nature as evidence for what you believe about man?"
3. Is Lewis trying to show that if naturalism is false, then belief in miracles is true? If not, then what?
4. Jot down two senses in which we sometimes use the term *rational*. Indicate Lewis's stake in this.
5. Elucidate: "If you are a naturalist, then you cannot see how natural science is possible." Therefore what?

6. Lewis's first criticism of naturalism depends on the notion of man as a rational animal; his second, on the notion of man as a moral animal. Sketch out this second criticism.
7. Which of Mr. Lewis's two criticisms do you find most incisive? Give your reason for your answer.
8. Retake on questions 5 and 6: "Granted their conception of nature, naturalists must ignore or deny rational thinking and moral judgment." (a) How so? (b) Therefore what?
9. "An atheist could admit that man is supernatural, but deny that there is any form of life higher than the human." (a) How so? (b) Therefore what, for Lewis?
10. Wherein you find Lewis (a) most convincing, (b) least convincing.

INDEPENDENT STUDY

Some persons are "turned off," not to say intellectually scandalized and outraged by Lewis's exposition and defense of Christian supernaturalism. They do not relish the spectacle of his abilities being put to such ends. For persons of this persuasion the best thing to do with Lewis is to let him go unread, or to set him up for criticism and refutation.
1. Begin by brushing up on Hume and Huxley in this book. Supplement Hume and Huxley by reading John Hick's article "Evil, the Problem of" and Antony Flew's article "Miracles," both in the *Encyclopedia of Philosophy*. Then give a careful reading to either Lewis's book *The Problem of Pain* or his book *Miracles*.
2. Read B. F. Skinner's *Walden Two* and *Beyond Freedom and Dignity*. Then read Joseph Wood Krutch's *The Measure of Man* and Abraham Maslow's *The Psychology of Science*. Use what you get from those four to assess Lewis's *The Abolition of Man*.
3. Compare or contrast G. K. Chesterton's *Orthodoxy* with Lewis's *Mere Christianity*.
4. Line up Huxley's *Brave New World* and Orwell's *Nineteen Eighty-four* and Skinner's *Walden Two*. With these in mind, read Lewis's *That Hideous Strength* and *The Abolition of Man*.

topic **two**
the nature of man

THE PROBLEM STATED

It is often claimed that man is "a part of nature." The claim is an obscure one. What does it mean for man to be "a part of nature"? What would be good evidence in support of the claim? Why do some persons want to believe this? If *nature* is taken widely enough (e.g., as meaning "all that there is"), then, no doubt, since man is indeed a part of all that there is, you can say that man is a part of nature; but, by parity of reasoning, you could also say that God, provided that He exists, is also a part of nature. But those who say that man is a part of nature do not usually have in mind to go on and say that God, too, is a part of nature. The claim, applied to man, is intended to indicate, at least indirectly, something that man is not; e.g., that he is not "a child of God," that he is not a "creature" in the sense of "one created," that he does not have free will, that he does not survive the death of his body, that, indeed, he is not "more than" his body, and so on. These would be typical of claims ruled out, or intended to be ruled out, by the claim that man is part of nature.

In the preceding topic we examined half a dozen authors who addressed themselves to the question "Can you use what you know about nature to justify what you believe about God?" We saw that even so devout a Catholic as Pascal was led to conclude emphatically not. Was this, perhaps, a consequence of the fact that Pascal did not know, or even claim to know, that God is a part of nature? If God is not part of nature, then perhaps we should not expect to use what we know about nature to justify what we believe about God. If a hypotenuse is not a part of a right-angled triangle, then why should we expect to use what we know about right-angled triangles to justify what we believe about a hypotenuse? Suppose, however, that man *is* "a part of nature." Does that have any bearing on the question, "Can you use what you know about nature to justify what you believe about man?" The answer to that question is going to depend in part on what you know about nature, or what you mean by *nature*, and in part on what you believe, or want to believe, about man.

It is not easy to arrive at a clear and precise answer to the question, "What do we know about nature? or "What do we mean by *nature*"? If you equate *nature* with *the subject matter of the natural sciences* and go on to claim that man is a part of nature, you are committing yourself to the claim that man is, and is only, what the natural sciences are in a position to say he is. There is an element of "legislation" in equating nature with the subject matter of the natural sciences. Anything that turns out *not* to form part of the subject matter of the natural sciences thereby turns out not to be part of nature. Who knows enough to say that? Or who knows enough to say, "If anything does not form part of nature, in the sense of not forming part of the subject matter of the natural sciences, then it does not exist"? What is a person trying to fend off who talks this way about himself and other people? Is he trying to protect the claim that man, and everything about him, is through and through rational in *Sense One?* The claim is worth protecting, but the cost of the "protection" comes high if you must first buy the claim that only when you are thinking in a natural science are you reasoning validly from sufficient relevant data. What proposition in natural science says that only propositions in natural science are reasonable, and can reasonably be said to be true? Let us go around once more. When it is claimed that man is a part of nature is this a way of claiming that man is not rational in *Sense Two*, that, like a plant or a planet or a chemical, he can neither reason nor be reasoned with? Is this claim worth protecting? What makes it worth protecting? What do you need to know in order to protect it? How would you use what you know, in order to protect it? If man can neither reason nor be reasoned with, then no reason can be given or accepted on behalf of the claim that he is a part of nature, or that he is *not* rational in Sense Two.

The authors in this topic are interested in the question, "What is man?" Or, "What is a man?" Or, "What is it to be human?" They are therefore interested in the further questions, "Is man a part of nature?" and, "Can you use what you know about nature to justify what you believe about man?" In this Topic Two, what would be the analogue of atheism in Topic One? Or of skepticism?

TRIGGER QUESTIONS

In Topic Two you are to read selected passages from Descartes, Holbach, James, Sartre, Ducasse, and Ryle. Each will deal directly or indirectly with the overall question, or some phase of the overall question, "Can you use what you know about nature as evidence for what you believe about man?" If you are to profit from reading these authors on this question, it is well to be clear, or to make an effort to become clear, what you think about this question, and why you think it. Here are some questions to put to yourself. For each question, what do *you* think? Why do *you* think it?

1. Does a person have a free will?
2. Is any human behavior intentional?
3. Could there be any evidence that behavior is not predictable?
4. How do you distinguish between behavior and misbehavior?
5. Why does a science never propose criticism of the behavior it studies?
6. We have abnormal psychology. Why don't we have abnormal physics?
7. We encounter dead bodies. Why do we never encounter dead minds?
8. Would you get a bigger jolt from discovering that you do or do not survive the death of your body?
9. Is there any difference between response to a stimulus and response to a challenge? Between causing and causing intentionally?
10. If I were a planet or a computer would I discover that some of my behavior is rational in Sense Two?
11. Can you define the term *fact* without *any* reference, implicit or explicit, to the term *person* or any synonym or derivative of the term *person*?
12. Use the distinction between measles and diagnosing measles to illustrate the distinction between *rational* in Sense One and *rational* in Sense Two.
13. If you are *sure* that some behavior is rational in Sense One, why had you better be sure that you are rational in Sense Two?

14. Reason aloud into a tape recorder. Play the tape back. Does it do any reasoning? Did it do any learning?
15. If you personify a thing, you speak in metaphor. If you thingify a person, do you also speak in metaphor?

SECTION 1. RENÉ DESCARTES: RES COGITANS VERSUS RES EXTENSA

Philosophical interest in the nature of man begins for many persons with certain writings by René Descartes in the middle span of the seventeenth century. As a French Catholic, Descartes was raised to believe that a person, a referent of personal pronouns, is a created spiritual substance, obscurely related to a body and the world of matter, rational, active, free, and immortal. Such a conception of man is far removed from the claim that he is simply a part of nature. The story of Descartes' century—"the century of genius"—is a lively chapter in the history of modern "scientizing" of nature. Once this "scientizing" of nature has been pushed to include, at least as a hoped-for outcome, the scientizing of the human, the stage is set for the question "Is man a part of nature?" And if so, what does that make of him? Or, what does it do to our conception of him? When you revise your conception of something, you discard your former belief, which has turned out to be doubtful or false, and replace it by a belief that promises to hold up as more probable or true. If you do this enough times over a wide enough range, you may, in the manner of Descartes, begin to wonder whether anything of what you or anyone else once learned will survive the "scientizing" that has been increasing, indeed accelerating.

Descartes' reasoning takes off from his realization that an increasing number and range of his beliefs are either doubtful or false. This triggered the question of whether *any* of his beliefs is neither doubtful nor false. To settle this he asked whether any of his beliefs is indubitable, not doubtable. *Not doubtable* is a stronger term than *not doubtful*. If a claim is not doubtable, then there is no way to show by reasoning validly from relevant data that it is doubtful. If you cannot show that it is doubtful, then have you any reason to believe that it is false?

Well, if, like Descartes, you are harassed by doubts and denials, and if doubting and denying are modes of thinking, then there is no doubt that, there is no doubting that, it is not doubtable that you do think. There is, under the conditions of such harassment, no such question as, "Do you perform the activity that is normally called *thinking?*" You cannot cast reasonable doubt on the claim that you think, that you are, as Descartes says of himself, a *res cogitans*, a thinking thing. And further, if to think, you must exist, then the indubitable character of "I think" carries over to "I am." As he says, "I think, therefore I am; *cogito, ergo sum*." Granted that he is, indubitably, a *res cogitans*, and therefore an existing thing, are there any other claims he can make about himself? He is a *res cogitans*. Is he anything else? That is one line along which he worked.

A second and related line took off from the question, "What is it to think?" "What is the nature, the defining character, of the activity which a thinker, a rational animal, typically performs?" Hence such titles as *Rules for the Direction of the Understanding*, and, *Discourse on the Method of Rightly Conducting One's Reason and Seeking Truth in the Sciences*. A third line took off from the contrast between an activity and a passivity. This is not the contrast between an agent and an activity. For Descartes an agent is not the activity that he performs. This third concern centers on the contrast between what I *do* and what *happens* to me, between activities that I perform and processes that "go on" in me, in the sense of in my mind. What sort of event happens to you because you are a rational animal, a *res cogitans*, which does not happen to a stone or a plant? Descartes' treatise on these matters, published in 1649, the year before he died, is called *The Passions of the Soul*, meaning the modes of passivity to which the souls, the psyches, of rational animals are liable. It dealt with sensations and emotions and related modes of passivity.

In respect to modern interest in the nature of man, Descartes is something of a *Caput Nili*, a source of the Nile. When he is working at the question of the nature of the *I* in *I think*, the outcome is a contribution to metaphysics. When he is working at the question of the nature of the thinking activity performed by the *I*, the outcome is a contribution to logic and epistemology. When he is working at the question of the nature of the conscious (or, later, subconscious) processes that occur in or to the psyches of rational animals, the outcome is a contribution to philosophical psychology. As with Plato among the ancients, Descartes among the moderns is an excellent introduction to the philosophical study of the nature of man.

Biographical Note. Descartes was born in France in 1596 and died in Sweden in 1650 at the age of fifty-four. His formal education, from eight to sixteen, was received at the Jesuit college of La Flèche. Here he acquired the essentials of a "gentleman's education," which he subsequently devoted much time to erasing. Before he had turned seventeen he put aside his books and after a few lessons in fencing and horsemanship went to "the great world of Paris." Here he remained for about five years, living at first the usual life of gaiety and gambling, but retiring after a while to the quiet and seclusion of an obscure lodging house. His thoughtful temper reasserted itself. Habits of reflection acquired at La Flêche, and roused once more by a Catholic friend, one Father Mersenne, took possession of him again.

In 1618 Descartes left Paris, determined to see the world. He became a soldier, serving in three different European armies, in the Netherlands, in Bavaria, and in Hungary. It was a life which gave him much time for thought during the months of idleness in winter quarters. He stuck to soldiering for three or four years, then resolved "no longer to carry a musket." Army days over, he continued his travels for five or six years more, visiting Switzerland and Italy, until, in 1628, he decided that he had read enough in the "great book of the world."

In 1629, his mind crowded with ideas demanding to be written down, he settled in Holland. He was seeking quiet and seclusion once more. His European retirement, as he called it, lasted twenty years. These were the years of fruitful production. Book followed book. His reputation spread. He had the intellectuals of his generation for his readers, and its rulers for his patrons and friends. In rapid succession he wrote his *Quest for Truth*, his *Rules for the Direction of the Mind*, his *Discourse on Method*, his *Meditations on First Philosophy*, his *Principles of Philosophy*, his *Treatise on the Passions*, and many other volumes that soon became stock in trade for the philosophically minded of his day. In 1649 he was invited by Queen Christina of Sweden to visit her at Stockholm and expound the principles of the "new philosophy." After much hesitation, and against the advice of his friends, he agreed to go. It cost him his life, for he caught a cold in his lungs that brought about his death.

The Argument of the Passages. Most of the following passages are quoted, abridged, or paraphrased from Descartes' little book *Meditations on First Philosophy*. The thought of these six short soliloquies might be paraphrased as follows: I was given the usual gentlemen's education in my youth. Presently I became skeptical of most of what had been taught me. Accordingly, I determined to abandon all my learning and begin again with a clean slate upon which no one but myself should write, and upon which nothing should be written that was not clear and distinct. I needed, as a starting point, something that could stand against skepticism, something not doubtable. To that end I set about the cultivation of doubt. My doubts were brought to an end by the fact of my own existence. The fact that I was doubting entailed necessarily my own existence as a doubter. From this *indubitandum* my reconstruction must proceed. Could I use the fact of my own existence to prove the existence of anything else? Two great steps were in order: to demonstrate the existence of

God and the existence of the material world. The steps by which I moved from doubts about things taught me at school, to the demonstrated existence of myself, God, and the external world, constitute the theme of these *Meditations*.

The first passages supply some autobiographical facts:

I had been nourished on letters since my childhood, and since I was given to believe that by their means a clear and certain knowledge could be obtained of all that is useful in life, I had an extreme desire to acquire instruction.

But as soon as I had achieved the entire course of study at the close of which one is usually received into the ranks of the learned, I entirely changed my opinion. I found myself embarrassed with so many doubts and errors that it seemed to me that the effort to instruct myself had no effect other than the increasing discovery of my own ignorance. And yet I was studying at one of the most celebrated schools in Europe, where I thought there must be men of learning if such were to be found anywhere in the world.

I learned there all that others had learned. Moreover, not being satisfied with the sciences that we were taught, I even read through all books which fell into my hands, treating of what is considered most curious and rare. Along with this, I knew the judgments which others had formed of me, and I did not feel that I was esteemed inferior to my fellow students. And finally, our century seemed to me as flourishing, and as fertile in great minds, as any which had preceded it.

These reflections combined to make me take the liberty of judging all others by myself, and of coming to the conclusion that there was no learning in the world such as I had formerly believed it to be.

That is why, as soon as age permitted me to emerge from the control of my tutors, I entirely quitted the study of letters. I resolved to seek no other knowledge than that which could be found in myself, or at least in the great book of the world. I employed the rest of my youth in travel, in seeing courts and armies, in intercourse with men of diverse temperaments and conditions, in collecting varied experiences, in testing myself in the various predicaments in which I was placed by fortune. In all circumstances I sought to bring my mind to bear on the things that came before it so that I might derive some profit from my experience.

For nine years I did nothing but roam hither and thither, trying to be a spectator rather than an actor in all the comedies which the world displays. Especially did I ask myself, in each matter that came before me, whether anything could make it subject to suspicion or doubt.

I considered the manners and customs of other men, and found nothing to give me settled convictions. I remarked in them almost as much diversity as I had formerly seen in the opinions of philosophers. So much was this so, that I learned to believe nothing too certainly of which I had been convinced only by example and custom.

I thus concluded that it is much more custom and example that persuade us than any certain knowledge. And this despite the fact that the voice of the majority affords no proof of any value in matters a little difficult to discover. Such truths are like to have been discovered by one man, more than by a nation. But I could not, however, put my finger on a single person whose opinions seemed preferable to those of others.

I found I was constrained, so to speak, to undertake the direction of my own inquiries.

As regards all the opinions which, up to that time, I had embraced, I thought I could not do better than try once for all to sweep them completely away. Later on they might be replaced, either by others which were better, or by the same when I had made them conform to the uniformity of a rational scheme. I firmly believed that by this means I should succeed much better than if I had built on foundations and principles of which I had allowed myself to be persuaded in youth without having inquired into their truth. My design has never extended beyond trying to reform my own opinions and to build on a foundation which is entirely my own.

I was not seeking to imitate the skeptics, who only doubt for the sake of doubting and pretend always to be uncertain. On the contrary, my design was only to provide myself with good ground for assurance, to reject the quicksand and the mud in order to find the rock or clay.

These remarks give us the terms of his self-imposed task: on the one hand, to work himself free from the opinion which he had accepted as part of a normal education; on the other, to avoid mere skepticism. The execution of this design called for a definite procedure. This Descartes outlines:

Like one who walks alone and in the twilight, I resolved to go slowly, to use so much circumspection that even if my advance was very small at least I guarded myself from falling. I did not wish to reject any opinion finally until I had planned out the task I had undertaken, and until I had sought out the true method of arriving at a knowledge of the things of which my mind was capable.

In my younger days I had studied logic and geometry and algebra—three sciences which, it seemed, ought to contribute something to the design I had in view.

But, in examining them, I observed in respect to logic, that syllogisms and the rest served better to explain those things which one already knows than to learn something new. As to geometry and algebra, they embrace only the most abstract matters, such as appear to have no actual use. This made me feel that some other method must be found exempt from their fault. So, in place of the many precepts of which logic is composed, and the many rules and formulae of which mathematics is composed, I settled on four rules for the direction of the understanding.

My first rule was to accept nothing as true which I did not clearly recognize to be so; to accept nothing more than what was presented to my mind so clearly and distinctly that I could have no occasion to doubt it. The second rule was to divide each problem or difficulty into as many parts as possible. The third rule was to commence my reflections with objects which were the simplest and easiest to understand, and rise thence, little by little, to knowledge of the most complex. The fourth rule was to make enumerations so complete, and reviews so general, that I should be certain to have omitted nothing.

Those long chains of reasoning which geometricians make had caused me to imagine that all parts of human knowledge might be mutually related in the same fashion; and that, provided we abstain from receiving anything as true which is not so, and always deduce one conclusion from some other, there can be nothing so remote that we cannot reach it, nor so recondite that we cannot discover it.

But what pleased me most, in this method which I was determined to follow, was that I was certain by its means to exercise my reason in all things; if not perfectly, at least as well as was in my power. I felt that, in making use of it, my mind would gradually accustom itself to think about its objects more accurate and distinctly.

The first of the above rules is perhaps the important one: to accept nothing as true that he did not clearly recognize to be so. It is one thing to lay this rule down. It is another to abide by it. The difficulty is in knowing where to start searching for one indubitable fact. But the search is under way.

. . . it is necessary for me to reject as false everything as to which I can imagine the least ground of doubt, in order to see if anything remains that is entirely certain. So I set myself seriously and freely to the general upheaval of all my former opinions.

To that end it is not requisite that I examine each opinion in particular. That would be an endless undertaking. Owing, however, to the fact that the destruction of the foundations brings with it the downfall of the rest of the edifice, I shall only attack those principles upon which all my former opinions rested.

All that up to the present time I have accepted as most true and certain I have learned either from the senses or through the senses. But it is sometimes proved to me that these senses are deceptive. And it is wiser not to trust entirely to anything by which we have once been deceived.

But it may be objected that, although the senses sometimes deceive us concerning things which are hardly perceptible or are very far away, there are yet many things as to which we cannot reasonably have any doubt although we recognize them by their means. For example, there is the fact that I am here, seated by the fire, attired in a dressing gown, having this paper in my hand. And how could I deny that these hands and this body are mine?

At the same time I must remember that I am in the habit of sleeping, and in my dreams representing to myself the same things. How often has it happened that I dreamt I was in this particular place, dressed and seated near the fire, while in reality I was lying undressed in bed. On many occasions I have in sleep been deceived by similar illusions. In thinking carefully about this fact, I see that there are manifestly no certain indications by which we may clearly distinguish wakefulness from sleep.

Suppose we assume, then, that we are asleep; that all these particulars, e.g., opening our eyes, shaking our head, extending our hand, are but false delusions; that possibly neither our hands nor our body are such as they appear to us to be.

There is a point, however, which we must not overlook. We must admit that the things which are represented to us in sleep are like painted representations which can only have been formed as the counterparts of something real and true, i.e., not illusory. It would follow from this admission that those general things at least, i.e., eyes, head, hands, body, are not imaginary things but things really existent.

We are bound, at the same time, to confess that there are some objects yet more simple and universal than eyes, a head, a body, etc., namely, colors, shapes, size, number, etc., which are real and true. For, whether I am awake or asleep, red is not blue, two and three make five, squares have only four sides, and so on. It does not seem possible that truths so clear can be suspected of any falsity.

Nevertheless, I have long had fixed in my mind the belief that an all-powerful God existed by whom I have been created such as I am. But how do I know that He has not brought it to pass that there is no earth, no heaven, no extended body, no magnitude, no place; and that, nonetheless, I possess perceptions of all these things which seem to me to exist just exactly as I now see them?

It might be urged against this suggestion that God has not desired that I should be thus deceived. For is He not said to be supremely good? However, if it is contrary to His goodness to have made me such that I am constantly deceived, it would also seem to be contrary to His goodness to permit me to be sometimes deceived; and yet it cannot be denied that He does permit this.

There may indeed be those who, rather than believe that all other things are uncertain, would prefer to deny the existence of a God so powerful. Let us not oppose them. Let us suppose, then, not that God (who is supremely good and the fountain of truth) but some evil genius not less powerful than deceitful, has employed his whole energies in deceiving me.

I shall suppose, then, that some evil genius not less powerful than deceitful is employing His whole energies to deceive me. I shall consider that the heavens, the earth, colors, shapes, sounds, and all other external things, are nothing but illusions and dreams by which this evil genius has laid traps for my credulity. I shall consider myself as having no hands, no eyes, no flesh, no blood, nor any senses; yet falsely believing myself to possess all these things. I shall remain obstinately attached to this idea. If, by this means, it is not in my power to arrive at the knowledge of any truth, I may at least do what is in my power, namely, suspend judgment, and thus avoid belief in anything false and avoid being imposed upon by this arch deceiver, however powerful and deceptive he may be.

Determined to "doubt everything," until doubt becomes impossible of being pushed further, Descartes has had recourse to heroic measures. The senses have been discredited, and with them the credibility of the external world revealed by the senses. This, one might have thought, would have sufficed. But assurance must be made doubly sure. Hence the hypothesis of a malignant genius who deceives him. At this point the eagerly sought *indubitandum* begins to appear.

I suppose, then, that all the things that I see are false. I persuade myself that nothing has ever existed of all that my fallacious memory represents to me. I consider that I possess no senses. I imagine that body, figure, extension, motion, and place are but the fictions of my mind. What, then, can be esteemed as true? Perhaps nothing at all, unless that there is nothing in the world that is certain.

But immediately I notice that while I wish to think all things false, it is nonetheless absolutely essential that I, who wish to think this, should truly exist. There is a powerful and cunning deceiver who employs his ingenuity in misleading me? Let it be granted. It follows the more that I exist, if he deceives me. If I did not exist, he could not deceive me. This truth, "I think, therefore I am; *cogito, ergo sum,*" is so certain, so assured, that all the most extravagant scepticism is incapable of shaking it. This truth, "I am, I exist," I can receive without scruple as the first principle of the philosophy for which I am seeking.

I think, therefore I am. But what am I? I do not yet know; and hence I must be careful lest I imprudently take some other object in place of myself and thus go astray in respect of this knowledge which I hold to be the most certain of all that I formerly believed.

What then did I formerly believe myself to be? I considered myself as having a face, hands, arms, and all that system of members which I designate by the name of body. In addition to this, I considered that I was nourished, that I walked, that I felt, and that I thought.

But what am I, now that I assume that there is an evil and malicious genius who employs all his powers to deceive me? Can I affirm, with as much certainty as I can affirm my existence, that I possess any of the least of all those things which I have just now ascribed to myself? I pause to consider. I resolve all these things in my mind. I find none of the bodily attributes which I can ascribe to myself.

What of thinking? I find that thought alone is an attribute which cannot be separated from me. I am, I exist; that is certain. But this certainty reposes on the "I think" which preceded. I am trying here not to admit anything which is not necessarily true. To speak thus strictly, I am nothing more than a thing which thinks, that is, to say, a mind, an understanding. I am a real thing. I really exist. But what am I? I have answered: a thing which thinks.

I am a thing which thinks. And what more? What is a thing which thinks? It is a thing which doubts, understands, conceives, affirms, denies, wills, refuses, imagines, feels. Certainly it is no small matter if all these things pertain to my nature.

But why should they not so pertain? Am I not that being who now doubts nearly everything, who nevertheless understands certain things, who affirms that only one thing is true, who denies all other things, who desires to know more, who is averse from being deceived, who imagines many things, who perceives many things? Is there, in all this, anything which is less certain than that I exist? Indeed, it is so evident that it is I who doubt, who understand, who desire, and so on, that there is no reason here to add anything to explain it. From this time I begin to know what I am with a little more clearness and distinctness than before.

Doubt has been explored and exploited. Self has been isolated as the single indubitable fact. The nature of self, a thinking thing, has been noted. Can this be used as a steppingstone? Does the fact of himself and his thoughts imply any other fact?

I shall now close my eyes; I shall stop my ears. I shall call away all my senses. I shall efface from my thoughts all images of material things—or, since that is hardly possible—I shall esteem them as vain and false. Thus holding converse only with my self, and considering my own nature, I shall try to reach a better knowledge of what I am.

I am a thing which thinks; that is to say, that doubts, affirms, denies, knows, is ignorant, wills, desires, imagines, perceives. For, as I remarked before, although the things which I perceive and imagine are perhaps nothing apart from me, yet the perceptions and imaginings certainly reside in me. And in the little that I have just said, I think I have summed up all that I really know, or was hitherto aware that I knew. To extend my knowledge further, I shall look around more carefully and see whether I cannot still discover in myself some other things which I have not hitherto perceived.

I am certain that I am a thing which thinks. But if I am indeed certain of this I must know what is requisite to render me certain of anything. I must possess a standard of certainty. In this first knowledge which I have gained, what is there that assures me of its truth? Nothing except the clear and distinct perception of what I state. This, indeed, would not suffice to assure me that what I state is true if it could ever happen that I should clearly and distinctly perceive to be true something which was in fact false. Accordingly, I can establish as a general rule that all things which I perceive very clearly and very distinctly are true.

All things which I perceive very clearly and very distinctly, are true. If I have heretofore judged that such matters could be doubted, it was because it came into my mind that perhaps a God might have endowed me with such a nature that I might have been deceived even concerning things which seemed to me most manifest. I see no reason to believe that there is a God who is a deceiver; however, as yet I have not satisfied myself that there is a God at all.

I must inquire whether there is a God. And, if I find that there is a God, I must also inquire whether He may be a deceiver. For, without a knowledge of these two truths, I do not see that I can ever be certain of anything.

Now, it is obvious that there must be at least as much reality in any cause as in its effect. For whence could the effect derive its reality, if not from its cause? From this it follows that something cannot proceed from nothing; and that the more or the greater cannot proceed from the less.

The longer and more carefully I investigate these matters, the more clearly and distinctly do I perceive their truth. But what may I conclude from it all, finally? It is this: If I have any idea which I myself cannot be the cause of, it follows of necessity that I am not alone in the world, that there is some other being which exists as the cause of this idea. Have I any such idea?

There is the idea of God. Is this idea something that could have originated in, been caused by, me? By the name *God* I understand a being that is infinite, eternal, immutable, independent, all-knowing, all-powerful, by which I myself and everything else (if anything else does exist) have been created.

Now, all these qualities are such that the more diligently I attend to them, the less do they appear capable of originating in me alone. Hence, from what was premised above, we must conclude that God necessarily exists as the origin of this idea I have of Him. For, to consider but one point, the idea of a being or a substance is within me owing to the fact that I am myself a being or substance; nevertheless, I would not have the idea of an infinite being, since I am myself finite, unless it had proceeded from some being who was infinite.

I see nothing in all that I have just said which, by the light of nature, is not manifest to anyone who desires to think attentively on the subject. It only remains to examine into the manner in which I have acquired this idea from God.

I have not received it through the senses; nor is it a fiction of my mind, for it is not in my power to take from or add to it. The only alternative is that it is innate in me, just as the idea of myself is innate in me.

It is not strange that God, in creating me, placed this idea within me to be like the mark of the workman imprinted on his work. For, from the fact that God created me it is most probable that He has placed His image and similitude upon me. The whole strength of the argument which I have here used to prove the existence of God consists in this: It is not possible that my nature should be what it is, and that I should have in myself the idea of a God, if God did not exist. God, whose idea is in me, possesses all those supreme perfections of which our mind may have some idea but without understanding them all; is liable to no errors or defects, and has none of those marks which denote imperfection. From this it is manifest that He cannot be a deceiver, since fraud and deception proceed from some defect.

Before I pass on to the consideration of other truths which may be derived from this one, it seems to me right to pause for a while to contemplate God Himself, to ponder at leisure His marvelous attributes, to consider and to admire and to adore the beauty of His light. Faith teaches us that supreme felicity of the life to come consists in this contemplation of the Divine Majesty. Even so we continue to learn by experience that a similar meditation, though less perfect, causes us to enjoy the greatest satisfaction of which we are capable in this life.

Disillusionment. Systematic doubt. Existence of self as a thinking thing. Existence of God, no longer the deceiving genius of the early part of the argument. There remains only the external world, revealed by the senses. Can this be reinstated? Can its existence be shown to be part of the network, inextricably bound up with his own and Deity's nature and existence?

And so I see that the certainty and truth of all knowledge depends alone upon the knowledge of the true God. Before I knew Him, I could not have a perfect knowledge of any other thing. Now that I know Him I have the means of acquiring a perfect knowledge of an infinitude of things.

Nothing further now remains but to inquire whether material things exist. And first of all I shall recall those matters which I hitherto held to be true, as having perceived them through the senses; in the next place I shall examine the reasons which have since obliged me to place them in doubt; and in the last place I shall consider which of them I must now believe.

First of all, I perceived that I had a head, hands, feet, and all other members of which this body is composed. Further, I was sensible that this body was placed amid many others. In them, in addition to extension, figure, and motion, I remarked hardness, heat, light, color, scents, sounds, and so forth.

Considering the ideas of all these qualities which presented themselves to my mind, it was not without reason that I believed myself to perceive objects quite different from my thought, to wit, bodies from which those ideas proceeded. For I found by experience that these ideas of all these qualities presented themselves to me without my consent being needed. Thus, I could not perceive any object unless it were present to the organs of sense; nor could I help but perceive it, when it was present.

Furthermore, because these ideas which I received through my senses were clearer, more lively, more distinct, than any ideas I could myself frame in meditation or find in memory, it appeared as though they could not have proceeded from my mind. So, therefore, I concluded that they must have been produced in me by some other things. And, since I had no knowledge of these objects except the knowledge which the ideas themselves gave me, nothing was more likely to occur to my mind than that the objects themselves were similar to the ideas which were caused.

But afterwards many experiences destroyed, little by little, all the faith which I had rested in my senses. For example, I observed that towers, which from afar appeared to me to be round, seemed square when more closely observed; that colossal statues seemed quite tiny when viewed from a distance; that persons whose legs or arms had been cut off seemed to feel pain in the part which had been amputated; that my dreams, which could not be caused by outside objects, closely resembled my waking moments; and so on.

Now, however, that I begin to know myself better ("I am a thing which thinks") and to discover more clearly the author of my being, I do not think I should rashly admit all the things which the senses seem to teach me, nor do I think that I should doubt them all universally.

This much is certain, i.e., clear and distinct: There is in me the capacity to receive and recognize the ideas of sensible things. The active cause of these ideas which I passively receive cannot be in me, since those ideas are often produced in me without my contributing in any way to the same, often even against my will. It follows that the power which produces these ideas resides in some substance different from me. This substance is either a material object of God or some other creature.

But, I have argued already, God is no deceiver. He has given me a very great inclination to believe that my ideas of sensible objects are sent or conveyed to me by external material objects. I do not see how He could be defended from the accusation of deceit if these ideas were produced in me by any cause other than material objects. Hence we must allow that material objects exist.

Descartes' meditations have brought him full circle. It is well to remember that he wrote in the seventeenth century, and to appreciate the gesture of impatience and sincerity with which he seeks to abandon old traditions and to start over again. The full weight of tradition was pressing upon him from the past. The new sciences and new world were beckoning toward the future. A clean break with the past seemed required. The *Meditations* were an attempt to see what ideas of the past must be allowed for by the future.

Note on Sources. The Descartes material in this section is quoted, abridged, or paraphrased from his *Discourse on Method* and his *Meditations.* The autobiographical account and the statement of the rules is from the *Discourse*, Parts I, II, III. The rest is from *Meditations* I, II, III, and VI.

Reading References. There is little point in trying to read an entire book on Descartes at this stage. One does best to concentrate on the ideas presented in the little books from which the passages in this chapter were taken, his *Meditations* and his *Discourse on Method.* These are still readable and valuable. An old volume by a German historian of philosophy, Kuno Fischer, translated into English under the title *Descartes and His School,* is lively and interesting. In T. H. Huxley's volume of essays *Method and Results* there is a good study of Descartes as a thinker.

READING QUESTIONS

It cannot be repeated too often: Descartes repays study. Become familiar with him, and you are in a fair way to proceed to other thinkers. Study his way of thinking. It is typical of many others.

1. What realization on Descartes' part touched off the reflections that led him to the *Cogito?*

2. In these reflections he "was not seeking to imitate the skeptics." Wherein he differs from them.
3. To guide him in these reflections he laid down four rules. Namely. Why the first rule is the most important.
4. Show that his first rule required him to track down an *indubitandum,* something not doubtable.
5. Why, in this search for an *indubitandum,* he did not examine each of his particular beliefs separately.
6. His motive and his reason for deciding to doubt his senses.
7. Why he sets up his hypothesis of an evil genius who systematically deceives him.
8. How he arrives finally at the *Cogito* as an *indubitandum.*
9. Why the *indubitandum* has to be a *res cogitans* and not a *res extensa.*
10. Why, having arrived at the *Cogito,* he then tackles the question of God's existence. Argument by which he seeks to prove His existence.
11. Why at this point Descartes could not have made use of the design argument for the existence of God.
12. Having established his own existence and God's existence he turns to establish the existence of material things. His argument here.
13. Wherein you find Descartes (a) most, (b) least convincing.

INDEPENDENT STUDY

1. Read the *Descartes* article by B. Williams in the *Encyclopedia of Philosophy,* and by E. S. Haldane in *The Encyclopedia of Religion and Ethics.* Write a paper on Descartes' general position in philosophy. The result may be more extensive than intensive. For a first run at Descartes' position, or positions, there is no harm in that.
2. Read the "Mind–Body Problem" article by J. Shaffer in the *Encyclopedia of Philosophy.* What is this "mind–body problem"? Where does Descartes stand on it? What is his reason for his stand? What "awkward questions" does his stand give rise to? You take it from there, going as far as you are inclined to. Notice Professor Shaffer's bibliography on this problem.
3. Read the article *"Cogito Ergo Sum"* by A. J. Ayer in Volume 14 (1953) of the journal *Analysis;* and the article *"Cogito Ergo Sum:* Inference or Performance?" by J. Hintikka in Volume 71 (1962) of the *Philosophical Review.* What is each author's main point? Which article does the most for you? Why?

SECTION 2. HOLBACH: THE ILLUSION OF FREE WILL

There is a prominent feature of some human behavior that has been made the occasion for claim and counterclaim, argument and counterargument. The issue is sometimes referred to as free will versus determinism. Suppose you have an examination tomorrow and someone asks you to forgo studying and spend the evening on the town. He does not urge or threaten or coerce. He says, "You decide. It's your choice what you do. It's strictly up to you. Nobody and nothing is going to make you do whatever you do. What you do, you do freely, voluntarily, of your own free will." There are more words and phrases he might use, but the point would be the same: you are responsible for what you do—stay in or go out. This is a prominent feature of some human behavior. In respect to this feature—being expressive of free choice—not all human behavior is the same. Suppose you are standing near the edge of the roof of a fifteen-story building, when a gust of wind topples you over the edge. You fall to the street below, sustaining a broken back. Teetering off the edge, falling to the ground, breaking your back all lack what was a prominent feature of your behavior in respect to "stay in and study, or go out." Words or phrases that make sense in the one case, do not in the other case. Of slipping and falling it makes no sense to say, "You decided. You chose to fall off and fall down. It was strictly up to you. Nobody and nothing made you do it. It was all free will and voluntary on your part." One has only to experience living through behavior of each sort to realize that, in respect to this feature, they differ essentially and radically. If, having taken the night off, you next morning took the test "cold" and failed it, you would be at least *open* to the rebuke: "You have only yourself to blame. You should have stayed in and studied." But having been toppled off the roof by the wind, fallen to the street, and broken your back, you would *not* be open to the rebuke: "You have only yourself to blame. You should not have toppled, and gone on to fall, and broken your back." The argument between free will and determinism, after the dust has been blown off it, is about human behavior in respect to this feature, which is noticeably present in the one case and absent in the other. One editor's title for the following selection from Holbach, "The Illusion of Free Will," expresses the point clearly enough: there was no more free will, real choice, in going out when you might better have stayed in, than there was when you toppled, fell, and broke your back. In each case the behavior was *necessitated.* In the roof case you were under no illusion. You realized clearly that your behavior was being caused by forces over which you had no control. In

the going-out case you were under an illusion; you did *not* realize
that your behavior was being caused by forces over which you have
no control.

Biographical Note on Holbach.　Holbach was born in 1723 and
died in 1789, aged sixty-six. His name was originally Paul Heinrich
Dietrich. He was born in Germany, educated in the then natural
sciences at the University of Leiden, and came to Paris in 1749. He
became a French subject and in 1753 inherited from his uncle the
title of Baron D'Holbach and properties that made him financially independent for the rest of his life. He established a "circle" that included such Frenchmen as Diderot, Helvetius, D'Alembert, Rousseau, Condillac, Turgot, and Condorcet and such foreigners as
Hume, Gibbon, Adam Smith, Priestly, Walpole, Garrick, Sterne, Bec-
caria, and Franklin. He contributed some four hundred articles to
Diderot's *Encyclopedia.* He propagandized and translated on behalf
of materialism, atheism, revolution, and republicanism. Perhaps his
best-known book, *Le Système de la nature* (*The System of Nature*),
was published anonymously in respect to nature, and of the claim
that man is a part of nature. Since there is no free will anywhere in
the behavior of matter, there is none in nature and none in man. Holbach's determinism as a doctrine about man is a corollary of his materialism as a doctrine about nature.

The Arguments of the Selections.　Holbach's claim called *determinism* or *necessitarianism,* is an answer to this question, "Does anyone ever determine any of his behavior for himself? Is anyone ever
responsible for *any* of his behavior? He being who *he* is, the circumstances being what *they* are, can he ever do anything other
than he does do?" Holbach's answer to that question is a categorical,
unqualified no. Your thoughts and actions are the effects of
causes over which you have no control. If you think you could have
done otherwise, you are mistaken.

Suppose a person protests that his *experience* of acting, at the
moment of action, does not bear out Holbach's claim. Thus: "When I
perform a voluntary act, I have no *experience* of this necessity. My
experience is that what I do, I do freely, voluntarily, choosing between alternatives. Holbach's point about illusion refers to any such
"appeal to experience" against his determinism. Thus (1) If you
think you could have done otherwise, you are mistaken. This is the
illusion of alternatives. There are no alternatives, ever. (2) If you
think any of your acts are voluntary, you are mistaken. This is the
illusion of voluntariness. There are no voluntary acts, in the sense
that you mean, ever. (3) If you think that in acting you freely chose
one possibility from among two or more that confronted you, and ac-

tualized it, you are mistaken. This is the illusion of possibilities. There are no possibilities, ever. There are only necessities and impossibilities. And he would go on: "You cannot appeal to experience against determinism. You cannot appeal to experience in support of these illusions. Such an appeal is disallowed in advance. Such an experience would be illusory, like the experience of a man, far gone in his cups, who sees pink snakes and green elephants. No such experience as you mention would be veridical. However, it should be noted that the experience of involuntariness is always veridical, never illusory." He would continue: "Experience confirms determinism provided it is the experience of involuntariness. Experience can never disconfirm determinism: the experience of voluntariness and similar experiences are always illusory, and so have no power to disconfirm. However, the experience of involuntariness is always veridical, and always confirms determinism. Determinism has no quarrel with experience, so long as experience backs it up." And he would conclude: "Determinism cannot be criticized empirically, inductively: negative instances, contrary instances, counterinstances are illusory. Nor can it be criticized deductively: there is no wider or firmer truth from which you could deduce that determinism is false. Is there any third way? If not, then it is immune to criticism, not open to significant debate, not falsifiable not testable."

The following paragraphs are quoted from the eleventh chapter of Holbach's historically important book *The System of Nature.* The title indicates that Holbach is a clear example of what, in the preceding topic, C. S. Lewis meant by the terms *naturalist* and *naturalism.* Nature, the title says, is a vast interlocked system in which every event is caused, necessitated, determined by all the other events that make up the total system. Many would grant this claim without argument when it is made of physical nature, nature taken as the subject matter of physics; but some demur when this claim is extended to include human nature and human behavior. They hold out for the possibility that some human behavior expresses a will that acts autonomously, is constrained neither by nature nor by events in nature. Holbach's chapter was written to deny any such claim.

Let us begin by reading half a dozen paragraphs in each of which he reiterates his central claim. Each paragraph is here assigned a number so that it may be referred to for purposes of discussion. Also, the central claim ("No human behavior expresses free will"), no matter how worded, has here been printed in italic. Neither the numbers nor the italic occur in the original.

1. *In whatever manner man is considered, he is connected to universal nature, and submitted to the necessary and immutable laws that she imposes on all the beings she contains,* according to their peculiar essences or

to the respective properties with which, without consulting them, she endows each particular species. Man's life is a line that nature commands him to describe upon the surface of the earth, without his ever being able to swerve from it, even for an instant. He is born without his own consent; his organization does in nowise depend upon himself; his ideas come to him involuntarily; his habits are in the power of those who cause him to contract them; he is unceasingly modified by causes, whether visible or concealed, over which he has no control, which necessarily regulate his mode of existence, give the hue to his way of thinking, and determine his manner of acting. He is good or bad, happy or miserable, wise or foolish, reasonable or irrational, without his will being for anything in these various states.

2. The will, as we have elsewhere said, is a modification of the brain, by which it is disposed to action, or prepared to give play to the organs. This will is necessarily determined by the qualities, good or bad, agreeable or painful, of the object or the motive that acts upon his senses, or of which the idea remains with him, and is resuscitated by his memory. In consequence, he acts necessarily, his action is the result of the impulse he receives either from the motive, from the object, or from the idea which has modified his brain, or disposed his will. When he does not act according to this impulse, it is because there comes some new cause, some new motive, some new idea, which modifies his brain in a different manner, gives him a new impulse, determines his will in another way, by which the action of the former impulse is suspended: thus, the sight of an agreeable object, or its idea, determines his will to set him in action to procure it; but if a new object or a new idea more powerfully attracts him, it gives a new direction to his will, annihilates the effect of the former, and prevents the action by which it was to be procured. This is the mode in which reflection, experience, reason, necessarily arrests or suspends the action of man's will: without this he would of necessity have followed the anterior impulse which carried him towards a then desirable object. In all this *he always acts according to necessary laws from which he has no means of emancipating himself.*

3. This will, or rather the brain, finds itself in the same situation as a bowl, which, although it has received an impulse that drives it forward in a straight line, is deranged in its course whenever a force superior to the first obliges it to change its direction. The man who drinks the poisoned water appears a madman; but the actions of fools are as necessary as those of the most prudent individuals. The motives that determine the voluptuary and the debauchee to risk their health, are as powerful, and their actions are as necessary, as those which decide the wise man to manage his. But, it will be insisted, the debauchee may be prevailed on to change his conduct: this does not imply that he is a free agent; but that motives may be found sufficiently powerful to annihilate the effect of those that previously acted upon him; *then these new motives determine his will to the new mode of conduct he may adopt as necessarily as the former did to the old mode.*

4. *Man, then, is not a free agent in any one instant of his life;* he is necessarily guided in each step by those advantages, whether real or fictitious, that he attaches to the objects by which his passions are roused: these passions themselves are necessary in a being who unceasingly tends towards his own happiness; their energy is necessary, since that depends on his tem-

perament; his temperament is necessary, because it depends on the physical elements which enter into his composition; the modification of this temperament is necessary, as it is the infallible and inevitable consequence of the impulse he receives from the incessant action of moral and physical beings.

5. *There is, in point of fact, no difference between the man that is cast out of the window by another, and the man who throws himself out of it,* except that the impulse in the first instance comes immediately from without whilst that which determines the fall in the second case, springs from within his own peculiar machine, having its more remote cause also exterior. When Mutius Scaevola held his hand in the fire, he was as much acting under the influence of necessity (caused by interior motives) that urged him to this strange action, as if his arm had been held by strong men: pride, despair, the desire of braving his enemy, a wish to astonish him, and anxiety to intimidate him, etc., were the invisible chains that held his hand bound to the fire.

6. He may be compared to a heavy body that finds itself arrested in its descent by any obstacle whatever: take away this obstacle, it will gravitate or continue to fall; but who shall say this dense body is free to fall or not? Is not its descent the necessary effect of its own specific gravity? The virtuous Socrates submitted to the laws of his country, although they were unjust; and though the doors of his jail were left open to him, he would not save himself; *but in this he did not act as a free agent:* the *invisible chains* of opinion, the secret love of decorum, the inward respect for the laws, even when they were iniquitous, the fear of tarnishing his glory, *kept him in his prison;* they were motives sufficiently powerful with this enthusiast for virtue, to induce him to wait death with tranquility.

Holbach's claim is now clear: human behavior is never expressive of free will because there is no free will. Man, he might syllogize, is a part of nature; there is no free will in nature; there is, therefore, no free will in man. However, Holbach knew from many discussions in his weekly philosophical salon, that it is one thing to deny free will in man and another thing to secure agreement with this denial. For example, a person might admit to the involuntary, unfree, patently "necessitate" character of some behavior. If you slip and fall, your fall is not an expression of your free will. If you are blown off the roof of a building, your fall is not an expression of your free will. In many instances your behavior *feels* directly and undeniably "necessitated," unfree, and so on. But, the person might insist, in some behavior you directly *experience* yourself "freely deciding, and freely acting." Why must it be the case that the experience of involuntariness, of necessitated behavior, is always veridical, whereas the experience of voluntariness, of freely choosing, is never veridical, but always illusory? Why is the appeal to experience in some cases ruled in and in other cases ruled out? In the following five paragraphs Holbach grudgingly acknowledges this point, but refuses to concede the claim based on it. Of course people have the "feeling," the "experience" of acting freely; but the experience is illusory, based upon their ignorance of the many and complex causes. Thus:

> Man believes he acts as a free agent, every time he does not see any thing that places obstacles to his actions; he does not perceive that the motive which causes him to will, is always necessary and independent of himself.
>
> From whence it may be seen, that the same necessity which regulates the physical, also regulates the moral world, in which every thing is in consequence submitted to fatality. Man, in running over, frequently without his own knowledge, often in spite of himself, the route which nature has marked out for him, resembles a swimmer who is obliged to follow the current that carries him along: he believes himself a free agent, because he sometimes consents, sometimes does not consent, to glide with the stream, which, notwithstanding, always hurries him forward; he believes himself the master of his condition, because he is obliged to use his arms under the fear of sinking.
>
> It is, then, for want of recurring to the causes that move him; for want of being able to analyze, from not being competent to decompose the complicated motion of his machine, that man believes himself a free agent: it is only upon his own ignorance that he founds the profound yet deceitful notion he has of his free agency; that he builds those opinions which he brings forward as a striking proof of his pretended freedom of action. If, for a short time, each man was willing to examine his own peculiar actions, search out their true motives to discover their concatenation, he would remain convinced that the sentiment he has of his natural free agency, is a chimera that must speedily be destroyed by experience.
>
> It is the great complication of motion in man, it is the variety of his action, it is the multiplicity of causes that move him, whether simultaneously or in continual succession, that persuades him he is a free agent: if all his motions were simple, if the causes that move him did not confound themselves with each other, if they were distinct, if his machine were less complicated, he would perceive that all his actions were necessary, because he would be enabled to recur instantly to the cause that made him act.
>
> The errors of philosophers on the free agency of man, have arisen from their regarding his will as the *primum mobile*, the original motive of his actions; for want of recurring back, they have not perceived the multiplied, the complicated causes which, independently of him, give motion to the will itself; or which dispose and modify his brain, whilst he himself is purely passive in the motion he receives.

Holbach is not done with this objection yet. Someone will object: "If you propose to a person that he raise his hand or walk over and close the window, and if he is not drugged or under hypnosis or any in any other way deprived of his normal modes of self-control, and if *he* decides to oblige you, and does so, is this *no* evidence of "free agency" on his part? What would count as evidence against Holbach's determinism? It seems that nothing would. If you cannot find a necessitating cause that is no evidence that there is none. It is evidence that you are not a good enough "cause-finder."

In spite of these proofs of the want of free agency in man, so clear to unprejudiced minds, it will perhaps be insisted upon with no small feeling of triumph, that if it be proposed to any one, to move or not to move his hand, an action in the number of those called indifferent, he evidently appears to be the master of choosing; from which it is concluded that evidence has been offered of free agency. The reply is, this example is perfectly simple; man in performing some action which he is resolved on doing, does not by any means prove his free agency: the very desire of displaying this quality, excited by the dispute, becomes a necessary motive, which decides his will either for the one or the other of these actions: What deludes him in this instance, or that which persuades him he is a free agent at this moment, is, that he does not discern the true motive which sets him in action, namely, the desire of convincing his opponent: if in the heat of the dispute he insists and asks, "Am I not the master of throwing myself out of the window?" I shall answer him, no: if, notwithstanding this, to prove he is a free agent, he should actually precipitate himself from the window, it would not be a sufficient warranty to conclude he acted freely, but rather that it was the violence of his temperament which spurred him on to this folly.

To be undeceived on the system of his free agency, man has simply to recur to the motive by which his will is determined; he will always find this motive is out of his own control. It is said: that in consequence of an idea to which the mind gives birth, man acts freely if he encounters no obstacle. But the question is, what gives birth to this idea in his brain? was he the master either to prevent it from presenting itself, or from renewing itself in his brain? Does not this idea depend either upon objects that strike him exteriorly and in despite of himself, or upon causes, that without his knowledge, act within himself and modify his brain?

When it is said, that man is not a free agent, it is not pretended to compare him to a body moved by a simple impulsive cause: he contains within himself causes inherent to his existence; he is moved by an interior organ, which has its own peculiar laws, and is itself necessarily determined in consequence of ideas formed from perception resulting from sensation which it receives from exterior objects. As the mechanism of these sensations, of these perceptions, and the manner they engrave ideas on the brain of man, are not known to him; because he is unable to unravel all these motions; because he cannot perceive the chain of operations in his soul, or the motive principle that acts within him, he supposes himself a free agent; which literally translated, signifies, that he moves himself by himself; that he determines himself without cause: when he rather ought to say, that he is ignorant how or why he acts in the manner he does.

Nevertheless it must be acknowledged that the multiplicity and diversity of the causes which continually act upon man, frequently without even his knowledge, render it impossible, or at least extremely difficult for him to recur to the true principles of his own peculiar actions, much less the action of others: they frequently depend upon causes so fugitive, so remote from their effects, and which, superficially examined, appear to have so little analogy, so slender a relation with them, that it requires singular sagacity to bring them into light.

Some persons, thinking of themselves as spokesmen for religion and for society, refuse to admit Holbach's claim that no human behavior expresses free will because, they say, if that were so neither religion nor society could hold anyone responsible for his actions, and therefore, under assignable circumstances, there could be no proper recipients of reward or punishment. If I read him correctly, Holbach rejects this as a presentation of contrary *evidence,* and dismisses it as a piece of rationalizing. Thus:

Nevertheless, in spite of the shackles by which he is bound, it is pretended he is a free agent, or that independent of the causes by which he is moved, he determines his own will, and regulates his own condition.

However slender the foundation of this opinion, of which everything ought to point out to him the error, it is current at this day and passes for an incontestable truth with a great number of people, otherwise extremely enlightened; it is the basis of religion, which, supposing relations between man and the unknown being she has placed above nature, has been incapable of imagining how man could merit reward or deserve punishment from this being, if he was not a free agent. Society has been believed interested in this system; because an idea has gone abroad, that if all the actions of man were to be contemplated as necessary, the right of punishing those who injure their associates would no longer exist. At length human vanity accommodated itself to a hypothesis which, unquestionably, appears to distinguish man from all other physical beings, by assigning to him the special privilege of a total independence of all other causes, but of which a very little reflection would have shown him the impossibility.

By way of concluding these selections from the eleventh chapter of Holbach's *System of Nature,* I propose to quote half a dozen paragraphs in which he moves from abstract formulation of his determinism to some concrete applications of it. The passage is clear-cut and vivid. He imagines himself summoning an ambitious man, a miserly man, a voluptuary man, a choleric or bad-tempered man, and a zealous man, and letting each in turn testify to the truth of Holbach's claim:

The *ambitious man* cries out: you will have me resist my passion; but have they not unceasingly repeated to me that rank, honours, power, are the most desirable advantages in life? Have I not seen my fellow citizens envy them, the nobles of my country sacrifice every thing to obtain them? In the society in which I live, am I not obliged to feel, that if I am deprived of these advantages, I must expect to languish in contempt; to cringe under the rod of oppression?

The *miser* says: you forbid me to love money, to seek after the means of acquiring it: alas! does not every thing tell me that, in this world, money is the greatest blessing; that it is amply sufficient to render me happy? In the country I inhabit, do I not see all my fellow citizens covetous of riches? but do I not also witness that they are little scrupulous in the means of obtaining wealth? As soon as they are enriched by the means which you censure, are they not cherished, considered and respected? By what authority, then, do you defend me from amassing treasure? What right have you to prevent my using means, which, although you call them sordid and criminal, I see approved by the sovereign? Will you have me renounce my happiness?

The *voluptuary* argues: you pretend that I should resist my desires; but was I the maker of my own temperament, which unceasingly invites me to pleasure? You call my pleasures disgraceful; but in the country in which I live, do I not witness the most dissipated men enjoying the most distinguished rank? Do I not behold that no one is ashamed of adultery but the husband it has outraged? Do not I see men making trophies of their debaucheries, boasting of their libertinism, rewarded with applause?

The *choleric man* vociferates: you advise me to put a curb on my passions, and to resist the desire of avenging myself: but can I conquer my nature? Can I alter the received opinions of the world? Shall I not be forever disgraced, infallibly dishonoured in society, if I do not wash out in the blood of my fellow creatures the injuries I have received?

The *zealous enthusiast* exclaims: you recommend me mildness; you advise me to be tolerant; to be indulgent to the opinions of my fellow men; but is not my temperament violent? Do I not ardently love my God? Do they not assure me, that zeal is pleasing to him; that sanguinary inhuman persecutors have been his friends? As I wish to render myself acceptable in his sight, I therefore adopt the same means.

In short, the actions of man are never free; they are always the necessary consequence of his temperament, of the received ideas, and of the notions, either true or false, which he has formed to himself of happiness; of his opinions, strengthened by example, by education, and by daily experience.

If he understood the play of his organs, if he were able to recall to himself all the impulsions they have received, all the modifications they have undergone, all the effects they have produced, he would perceive that all his actions are submitted to that fatality, which regulates his own particular system, as it does the entire system of the universe: no one effect in him, any more than in nature, produces itself by chance; this, as has been before proved, is word void of sense. All that passes in him; all that is done by him; as well as all that happens in nature, or that is attributed to her, is derived from necessary causes, which act according to necessary laws, and which produce necessary effects from whence necessarily flow others.

Fatality, is the eternal, the immutable, the necessary order, established in nature; or the indispensable connexion of causes that act, with the effects they operate.

Historical Postscript to Holbach. Holbach's *System of Nature* was published in 1770. H. T. Buckle, "who," says Sir Isaiah Berlin, "believed in the science of history more passionately, perhaps than any man who ever lived," published his *History of Civilization in England* in the years 1857–1861. Buckle offered the *History* as an embodiment of what he understood by history as a science. The natural sciences had nature as their subject matter. Buckle wanted the historians to look upon human history as the subject matter of historical science. In the course of expounding this conception he said:

> The believer in the possibility of a science of history is not called upon to hold either the doctrine of predestined events, or that of freedom of the will; and the only positions which, in this stage of inquiry, I shall expect him to concede are the following: That when we perform an action, we perform it in consequence of some motive or motives; that those motives are the results of some antecedents; and that, therefore, if we were acquainted with the whole of the antecedents, and with all the laws of their movements, we could with unerring certainty predict the whole of their immediate results. This, unless I am greatly mistaken, is the view which must be held by every man whose mind is unbiased by system, and who forms his opinions according to the evidence actually before him. If, for example, I am intimately acquainted with the character of any person, I can frequently tell how he will act under some given circumstances. Should I fail in this prediction, I must ascribe my error not to the arbitrary and capricious freedom of his will, nor to any supernatural prearrangement, for of neither of these things have we the slightest proof; but I must be content to suppose either that I had been misinformed as to some of the circumstances in which he was placed, or else that I had not sufficiently studied the ordinary operations of his mind. If, however, I were capable of correct reasoning, and if, at the same time, I had a complete knowledge both of his disposition and of all the events by which he was surrounded, I should be able to foresee the line of conduct which, in consequence of those events, he would adopt.

READING QUESTIONS

1. What is pretended in spite of what shackles?
2. Why religion and society and vanity have accepted the notion of man's free will.
3. What is Holbach's point in reference to all these matters: objects, sensations, ideas, brains, impulses, desires, habits, temperaments, motives, character traits, and so on?
4. What is his one point in reference to these: the thirsty man, the ambitious man, the miserly man, the voluptuary man, the choleric man, the zealous man?
5. Would he admit any sort of "man" to be an exception to his point in question 4?

6. "He himself is purely passive." Who is? How so? Is there anyone in Holbach's world who is *not* "purely passive"?
7. "Man is not a free-agent in any instant of his life." This is a clear and forthright statement of Holbach's thesis. Jot down two more, equally clear and forthright.
8. The only difference between throwing yourself out of a window and being thrown out of a window.
9. What is his point about complexity, multiplicity, variety, diversity?
10. The notion of free agency rests upon what ignorance?
11. If a moral man understood *what*, he would perceive *what*?
12. Holbach has a penchant for metaphor. Write a brief elucidation of his metaphor of the *line*, of the *bowl*, of the *heavy body*, of *gun powder*, and of a *swimmer*.
13. Do you notice anything telltale about the metaphors referred to in question 12?
14. Use the word *determinism* for Holbach's main thesis. Would he accept anything as a counterinstance, a negative instance, a contrary instance? If, not then he considers his thesis to be not falsifiable. What does that do for the thesis?

INDEPENDENT STUDY

1. Read the chapter "French Eighteenth-Century Materialism" by E. A. Gellner in *A Critical History of Western Philosophy* edited by D. J. O'Connor. Read also the article "Holbach" by A. Vartanian in the *Encyclopedia of Philosophy*. Write a paper on French eighteenth-century materialism centering your account on Holbach.
2. Read the article on determinism by R. Taylor and on determinism in history by W. H. Dray in the *Encyclopedia of Philosophy*. Note the excellent bibliographies. Write on determinism, pro or con as you wish.
3. Two closely reasoned expositions of determinism, more technical than Holbach's and in contemporary idiom, are those by (a) C. D. Broad, *Ethics and the History of Philosophy*, the chapter entitled "Determinism, Indeterminism and Libertarianism"; (b) W. D. Ross, *The Foundations of Ethics*, the chapter on determinism. An excellent bibliography for the entire freewill–determinism controversy is contained in Edwards and Pap, *A Modern Introduction to Philosophy*.

SECTION 3. WILLIAM JAMES: THE DILEMMA OF DETERMINISM

From Holbach to James. Holbach's *System of Nature* was published in 1770. Its eleventh chapter contained an emphatic rejection of the claim that any human behavior expresses free will in man. Free will is an illusion. Almost one century later, in 1878, William James contracted to produce a book on the conscious life of rational animals. The book, *The Principles of Psychology*, was published twelve years later, in 1890. During those intervening years James worked at certain questions, answers to which were needed if he proposed to have the conscious life of rational animals sit for a full-length portrait. These questions included the following: Does man have a free will? Is it expressed in any of his behavior? If so, how does such behavior differ from behavior in which free will is not expressed? Whether you subscribe to a doctrine of free will or to one of determinism, in respect to any human behavior, is going to make a difference to what will be put into the relevant chapters of a book on the principles of psychology. James published what has become a classic position paper on this question in 1884: "The Dilemma of Determinism." His findings in this paper contributed to the chapter on will in his *Principles*, six years later. (See p. 58.)

James's Dilemma paper contains a stimulating and valuable defense of free will against determinism. Holbach in his chapter and James in his paper between them offer a good introduction to this freewill–determinism question. They do not say everything that has been or might be said. Moreover they work with a broadax, not with a fret saw. But each considers the question important and does not propose to hedge on it. These are virtues.

James's essay contains some opening paragraphs in which he assures his reader that the question, "Does any human behavior express free will?" is by no means dead. No proponent of either side is entitled to any complacency on this matter. He also indicates that he proposes to appeal to what he had called, in an earlier paper, the "sentiment of rationality." If man is rational in Sense Two ("Can reason and be reasoned with") this is not an irrelevant court of appeal. If one position produces a greater sentiment of rationality than another, this is a mark in its favor. If it seems clearly more reasonable to claim X than Y; if, considered as a claim, X produces a greater "sentiment of rationality" than Y, James proposes to let this count heavily in favor of X. And, finally, he insists that rationality, considered as a feature of the world, and of our conceptions of the world, is a many-splendored thing. Neither mathematics nor natural science, nor both together, exhaust the possibility of rational claims and rational arguments. When you "appeal to reason," when you say, "it stands to reason that," you cast a wider net than do mathematics and natural science combined. These opening paragraphs are assigned numbers, which they do not have in the original paper, for ease in referring to them in discussion:

1. A common opinion prevails that the juice has ages ago been pressed out of the free-will controversy, and that no new champion can do more than warm up stale arguments which everyone has heard. This is a radical mistake. I know of no subject less worn out, or in which inventive genius has a better chance of breaking open new ground—not, perhaps, of forcing a conclusion or of coercing assent, but of deepening our sense of what the issue between the two parties really is, and of what the ideas of fate and of free will imply.

2. If I can make two of the necessarily implied corollaries of determinism clearer to you than they have been made before, I shall have made it possible for you to decide for or against that doctrine with a better understanding of what you are about. And if you prefer not to decide at all, but to remain doubters, you will at least see more plainly what the subject of your hesitation is. I thus disclaim openly on the threshold all pretension to prove to you that the freedom of the will is true. The most I hope is to induce some of you to follow my own example in assuming it true, and acting as if it were true.

3. The arguments I am about to urge all proceed on two suppositions: first, when we make theories about the world and discuss them with one another, we do so in order to attain a conception of things which shall give us subjective satisfaction; and, second, if there be two conceptions, and the one seems to us, on the whole, more rational than the other, we are entitled to suppose that the more rational one is truer of the two. I hope that you are all willing to make these suppositions with me.

4. I cannot stop to argue the point; but I myself believe that all the magnificent achievements of mathematical and physical science—our doctrines of evolution, of uniformity of law, and the rest—proceed from our indomitable desire to cast the world into a more rational shape in our minds than the shape into which it is thrown there by the crude order of our experience. The world has shown itself, to a great extent, plastic to this demand of ours for rationality. How much farther it will show itself plastic no one can say. Our only means of finding out is to try; and I, for one, feel as free to try conceptions of moral as of mechanical or of logical rationality. If a certain formula for expressing the nature of the world violates my moral demand, I shall feel free to throw it overboard, or at least to doubt it, as if it disappointed my demand for uniformity of sequence, for example; the one demand being, so far as I can see, quite as subjective and emotional as the other is.

5. All our scientific and philosophic ideals are altars to unknown gods. Uniformity is as much so as is free will. If this be admitted, we can debate

on even terms. But if any one pretends that while freedom and variety are, in the first instance, subjective demands, necessity and uniformity are something altogether different, I do not see how we can debate at all.

The question at issue can be worded retrospectively: "You being who you were, the circumstances being what they were, could you ever have done other than you did do?" Faced with this question, the determinist says, "No; you never could have done otherwise"; and the indeterminist, or freewillist, says equally emphatically, "Yes, under some circumstances you could have. It may be that *some* human behavior is determined, necessitated; but not *all* human behavior at all times." When the question is stated like this, in wholly general terms, James's first point is that neither answer can be proved by any single-fact evidence. It is not comparable to "yes" and "no" answers to the question "Is Jane older than John?" Or, "Is Chicago further west from New York than Cleveland is?" The most you are going to be able to do, on behalf of either answer, is "test" it for the amount of "sentiment of rationality" it produces. Doing this, as he began by noting, may lead to an impasse. In that case you pay your money and you take your choice. If some rational animals find "no" a reasonable answer and some find "yes" a reasonable answer, that is as far as you may get. James has already denied that you are entitled to write off those who vote "yes" for indeterminism and free will on the ground that their vote proves that they are not rational animals, and that therefore their vote does not count *for* their answer but counts against them as competent answerers.

To begin, then, I must suppose you acquainted with all the usual arguments on the subject. I cannot stop to take up the old proofs from causation, from statistics, from the certainty with which we can foretell one another's conduct, from the fixity of character, and all the rest.

Now, evidence of an external kind to decide between determinism and indeterminism is, as I intimated a while back, strictly impossible to find. Let us look at the difference between them and see for ourselves. What does determinism profess?

It professes that those parts of the universe already laid down absolutely appoint and decree what the other parts shall be. The future has no ambiguous possibilities hidden in its womb: the part we call the present is compatible with only one totality. Any other future complement than the one fixed from eternity is impossible. The whole is in each and every part, and welds it with the rest into an absolute unity, an iron block, in which there can be no equivocation or shadow of turning.

> With earth's first clay they did the last man knead,
> And there of the last harvest sowed the seed.
> And the first morning of creation wrote
> What the last dawn of reckoning shall read.

Indeterminism, on the contrary, says that the parts have a certain amount of loose play on one another, so that the laying down of one of them does not necessarily determine what the others shall be. It admits that possibilities may be in excess of actualities, and that things not yet revealed to our knowledge may really in themselves be ambiguous. Of two alternative futures which we conceive, both may now be really possible; and the one become impossible only at the very moment when the other excludes it by becoming real itself. Indeterminism thus denies the world to be one unbending unit of fact. It says there is a certain ultimate pluralism in it; and, so saying, it corroborates our ordinary unsophisticated view of things. To that view, actualities seem to float in a wider sea of possibilities from out of which they are chosen; and, somewhere, indeterminism says, such possibilities exist, and form a part of truth.

Determinism, on the contrary, says they exist *nowhere*, and that necessity on the one hand and impossibility on the other are the sole categories of the real. Possibilities that fail to get realized are, for determinism, pure illusions: they never were possibilities at all. There is nothing inchoate, it says, about this universe of ours, all that was or is or shall be actual in it having been from eternity virtually there. The cloud of alternatives our minds escort this mass of actuality withal is a cloud of sheer deceptions, to which "impossibilities" is the only name which rightfully belongs.

The issue, it will be seen, is a perfectly sharp one, which no eulogistic terminology can smear over or wipe out. The truth *must* lie with one side or the other, and its lying with one side makes the other false.

The question relates solely to the existence of possibilities, in the strict sense of the term, as things that may, but need not, be. Both sides admit that a volition, for instance, has occurred. The indeterminists say another volition might have occurred in its place: the determinists swear that nothing could possibly have occurred in its place. Now, can science be called in to tell us which of these two point-blank contradicters of each other is right? Science professes to draw no conclusions but such as are based on matters of fact, things that have actually happened; but how can any amount of assurance that something actually happened give us the least grain of information as to whether another thing might or might not have happened in its place?

And the truth is that facts practically have hardly anything to do with making us either determinists or indeterminists. Sure enough, we make a flourish of quoting facts this way or that; and if we are determinists, we talk about the infallibility with which we can predict one another's conduct; while if we are indeterminists, we lay great stress on the fact that it is just because we cannot fortell one another's conduct, either in war or statecraft or in any of the great and small intrigues and businesses of men, that life is so intensely anxious and hazardous a game. But who does not see the wretched insufficiency of this so-called objective testimony on both sides? What fills up the gaps in our minds is something not objective, not external. What divides us into *possibility* men and *anti-possibility* men is different faiths or postulates—postulates of rationality. To this man the world seems more rational with possibilities in it—to that man more rational with possibilities excluded; and talk as we will about having to yield to evidence, what makes us monists or pluralists, determinists or indeterminists, is at bottom always some sentiment like this.

There is a sense in which James might well stop right there. The question is not a scientific one. Neither answer can claim to be a, or the, scientific answer. A few years later he would say that the question was "metaphysical" and that the case for either answer was therefore "pragmatic," therefore an appeal to us to put forth our "will to believe" on behalf of whichever answer produced the greatest amount of the "sentiment of rationality" in us. However, he has a few more points he wishes a hearing for. One of these is that the friends of determinism vote against indeterminism and free will because it says that some events (some human behavior) happen "by chance," and they are turned off by the notion that *any* events happen by "chance." If the world is the place that they think it is, it does not contain *any* "chance" events. A chance event would be one that did not happen according to any law. In the scientific, but not in the legislative, sense of *law*, a "chance" event would be a "lawless" event. And they are totally opposed to any such notion. Given what might *appear* to be a chance or lawless event, they would *revise the law* until it included the event as an instance. So far as James is concerned, they need say no more. This shows what outrages their sentiment of rationality. This shows which "metaphysical" party they belong to. If they will recognize that others have an equal right to belong to some incompatible metaphysical party, James has nothing further to say. At this point he is nothing if not tolerant. He may be himself committed to the claim that they have got the world wrong, but he is willing, as between incompatible answers to metaphysical questions, to practice a policy of live and let live.

The stronghold of the deterministic sentiment is the antipathy to the idea of chance. As soon as we begin to talk indeterminism to our friends, we find a number of them shaking their heads. This notion of alternative possibility, they say, this admission that any one of several things may come to pass, is, after all, only a round-about name for chance; and chance is something the notion of which no sane mind can for an instant tolerate in the world. What is it, they ask, but barefaced crazy unreason, the negation of intelligibility and law? And if the slightest particle of it exists anywhere, what is to prevent the whole fabric from falling together, the stars from going out, and chaos from recommencing her topsy-turvy reign?

The sting of the word "chance" seems to lie in the assumption that it means something positive, and that if anything happens by chance, it must needs be something of an intrinsically irrational and preposterous sort. Now, chance means nothing of the kind. It is a purely negative and relative term, giving us no information about that of which it is predicated, except that it happens to be disconnected with something else—not controlled, secured, or necessitated by other things in advance of its own actual presence. As this point is the most subtle one of the whole lecture, and at the same time the point on which all the rest hinges, I beg you to pay particular attention to it. What I say is that it tells us nothing about what a thing may be in itself to call it "chance." All that its chance-character asserts about it is that there is something in it really of its own, something that is not the unconditional property of the whole. If the whole wants this property, the whole must wait till it can get it, if it be a matter of chance. That the universe may actually be a sort of joint-stock society of this sort, in which the sharers have both limited liabilities and limited powers, is of course a simple and conceivable notion.

Nevertheless, many persons talk as if the minutest dose of disconnectedness of one part with another, the smallest modicum of independence, the faintest tremor of ambiguity about the future, for example, would ruin everything, and turn this goodly universe into a sort of insane sand-heap or nulliverse—no universe at all. Since future human volitions are, as a matter of fact, the only ambiguous things we are tempted to believe in, let us stop for a moment to make ourselves sure whether their independent and accidental character need be fraught with such direful consequences to the universe as these.

What is meant by saying that my choice of which way to walk home after the lecture is ambiguous and matter of chance as far as the present moment is concerned? It means that both Divinity Avenue and Oxford Street are called; but that only one, and that one *either* one, shall be chosen. Now, I ask you seriously to suppose that this ambiguity of my choice is real; and then to make the impossible hypothesis that the choice is made twice over, and each time falls on a different street. In other words, imagine that I first walk through Divinity Avenue, and then imagine that the powers governing the universe annihilate ten minutes of time with all that it contained, and set me back at the door of this hall just as I was before the choice was made. Imagine then that, everything else being the same, I now make a different choice and traverse Oxford Street. You, as passive spectators, look on and see the two alternative universes—one of them with me walking through Divinity Avenue in it, the other with the same me walking through Oxford Street. Now, if you are determinists you believe one of these universes to have been from eternity impossible: you believe it to have been impossible because of the intrinsic irrationality or accidentality somewhere involved in it. But looking outwardly at these universes, can you say which is the impossible and accidental one, and which the rational and necessary one? I doubt if the most iron-clad determinist among you could have the slightest glimmer of light at this point. In other words, either universe *after the fact* and once there, would, to our means of observation and understanding, appear just as rational as the other. There would be absolutely no criterion by which we might judge one necessary and the other matter of chance. Suppose now we relieve the gods of their hypothetical task and assume my choice, once made, to be made forever. I go through Divinity Avenue for good and all. If, as good determinists, you now begin to affirm, what all good determinists punctually do affirm, that in the nature of things I couldn't have gone through Oxford Street—had I done so it would have been chance, irrationality, insanity, a horrid gap in nature—I simply call your attention to this, that your affirmation is what the Germans call a *Machtspruch*, a mere conception fulminated as a dogma and based on no insight into details. Before my choice, either street seemed as natural to you as to me.

The quarrel which determinism has with chance fortunately has nothing to do with this or that psychological detail. It is a quarrel altogether metaphysical. Determinism denies the ambiguity of future volitions, because it affirms that nothing future can be ambiguous. But we have said enough to meet the issue. Indeterminate future volitions *do* mean chance. Let us not fear to shout it from the house-tops if need be; for we now know that the idea of chance is, at bottom, exactly the same thing as the idea of gift—the one simply being a disparaging, and the other a eulogistic, name for anything on which we have no effective *claim*.

But what a hollow outcry, then, is this against a chance which, if it were present to us, we could by no character whatever distinguish from a rational necessity! I have taken the most trivial of examples, but no possible example could lead to any different result. For what are the alternatives which, in point of fact, offer themselves to human volition? What are those futures that now seem matters of chance? Are they not one and all like the Divinity Avenue and Oxford Street of our example? Are they not all of them *kinds* of things already here and based in the existing frame of nature? Is any one ever tempted to produce an *absolute* accident, something utterly irrelevant to the rest of the world? Do not all the motives that assail us, all the futures that offer themselves to our choice, spring equally from the soil of the past; and would not either one of them, whether realized through chance or through necessity, the moment it was realized, seem to us to fit that past, and in the completest and most continuous manner to interdigitate with the phenomena already there?

The more one thinks of the matter, the more one wonders that so empty and gratuitous a hubbub as this outcry against chance should have found so great an echo in the hearts of men. It is a word which tells us absolutely nothing about what chances, or about the *modus operandi* of the chancing; and the use of it as a war-cry shows only a temper of intellectual absolutism, a demand that the world shall be a solid block, subject to one control—which temper, which demand, the world may not be bound to gratify at all. But although, in discussing the word "chance," I may at moments have seemed to be arguing for its real existence, I have not meant to do so yet. We have not yet ascertained whether this be a world of chance or no; at most, we have agreed that it seems so. And I now repeat what I said at the outset, that, from any strict theoretical point of view, the question is insoluble. To deepen our theoretic sense of the *difference* between a world with chances in it and a deterministic world is the most I can hope to do.

Up to this point James has been formulating the question, "Does any human behavior express free will?" To this question determinists and indeterminists propose incompatible answers. James has been fending off one objection that determinists bring against free will—that it implies that some human behavior is a matter of chance.

From this point on, he begins to develop the claims and counterclaims implied in the title of his essay "The Dilemma of Determinism." His aim is to formulate a dilemma that you face if you
subscribe to determinism. His first move is to draw attention to the
fact that all of us make regret judgments:

> I wish first of all to show you just what the notion that this is a deter-
> ministic world implies. The implications I call your attention to are all
> bound up with the fact that it is a world in which we constantly have to make
> what I shall, with your permission, call judgments of regret. Hardly an hour
> passes in which we do not wish that something might be otherwise.
> Hardly any one can remain *entirely* optimistic after reading the confes-
> sion of the murderer at Brockton the other day: how, to get rid of the wife
> whose continued existence bored him, he inveigled her into a deserted spot,
> shot her four times, and then, as she lay on the ground and said to him, "You
> didn't do it on purpose, did you, dear?" replied, "No, I didn't do it on pur-
> pose," as he raised a rock and smashed her skull. Such an occurrence, with
> the mild sentence and self-satisfaction of the prisoner, is a field for a crop of
> regrets, which one need not take up in detail. We feel that, although a per-
> fect mechanical fit to the rest of the universe, it is a bad moral fit, and that
> something else would really have been better in its place.

His next move is to point out that if you are a determinist and if
you authorize regret judgments, then you are committed to a pessimism with regard to anything in the world that you do or would
find regrettable. The claim that nothing ever could be or could have
been other than the way it is includes everything that is a matter for
regret, everything that would have been better otherwise. "No way,"
your determinism says to you. Thus:

> But for the deterministic philosophy the murder, the sentence, and the
> prisoner's optimism were all necessary from eternity; and nothing else for a
> moment had a ghost of a chance of being put in their place. To admit such a
> chance, the determinists tell us, would be to make a suicide of reason; so we
> must steel our hearts against the thought. And here our plot thickens, for we
> see the first of those difficult implications of determinism and monism which
> it is my purpose to make you feel. If this Brockton murder was called for by
> the rest of the universe, if it had come at its preappointed hour, and if
> nothing else would have been consistent with the sense of the whole, what
> are we to think of the universe? Are we stubbornly to stick to our judgment
> of regret, and say, though it *couldn't* be, yet it *would* have been a better uni-
> verse with something different from this Brockton murder in it? That, of
> course, seems the natural and spontaneous thing for us to do; and yet is is
> nothing short of deliberately espousing a kind of pessimism. The judgment
> of regret calls the murder bad. Calling a thing bad means, if it means any-
> thing at all, that the thing ought not be, that something else ought to be in its
> stead. Determinism, in denying that anything else can be in its stead, vir-
> tually defines the universe as a place in which what ought to be is impos-

sible—in other words, as an organism whose constitution is afflicted with an incurable taint, and irremediable flaw. The pessimism of a Schopenhauer says no more than this—that the murder is a symptom; and that it is a vicious symptom because it belongs to a vicious whole, which can express its nature no otherwise than by bringing forth just such a symptom as that at this particular spot. Regret for the murder must transform itself, if we are determinists and wise, into a larger regret. It is absurd to regret the murder alone. Other things being what they are, *it* could not be different. What we should regret is that whole frame of things of which the murder is one member. I see no escape whatever from this pessimistic conclusion if, being determinists, our judgment of regret is to be allowed to stand at all.

If you make regret judgments, then determinism will commit you to pessimism in regard to all things regrettable: none of them could have been otherwise. Suppose you do not relish this commitment, is there any way out of it or around it? James notes a move you might make:

The only deterministic escape from pessimism is everywhere to abandon the judgment of regret. That this can be done, history shows to be not impossible. The devil, *quoad existentiam,* may be good. That is, although he be a *principle* of evil, yet the universe, with such a principle in it, may practically be a better universe than it could have been without. On every hand, in a small way, we find that a certain amount of evil is a condition by which a higher form of good is brought. There is nothing to prevent anybody from generalizing this view, and trusting that if we could but see things in the largest of all ways, even such matters as this Brockton murder would appear to be paid for by the uses which follow in their train. An optimism *quand même,* a systematic and infatuated optimism like that ridiculed by Voltaire in his *Candide,* is one of the possible ideal ways in which a man may train himself to look upon life.

James has two dilemmas that he wants to put to the person who subscribes to determinism. The first is this: If you are a determinist and you judge anything to be regrettable, then your determinism will commit you to pessimism about all things regrettable. If, to avoid being committed to pessimism, you abandon all regret judgments ("They are wrong-headed," your determinism assures you), then what about these wrong-headed regret judgments? If they are wrong, at least in the sense of being wrong-headed, aren't *they* matter for regret? Would it not have been better if your regret judgments, being wrong-headed, had never been made? So you decide to make a clean sweep: first, no regret judgments about any actions or events; then, no regret judgments because they are *all* wrong-headed.

Thus, our deterministic pessimism may become a deterministic optimism at the price of extinguishing our judgments of regret.

But does not this immediately bring us into a curious logical predicament? Our determinism leads us to call our judgments of regret wrong, because they are pessimistic in implying that what is impossible yet ought to be. But how then about the judgments of regret themselves? If they are wrong, other judgments, judgments of approval presumably, ought to be in their place. But as they are necessitated, nothing else *can* be in their place; and the universe is just what it was before—namely, a place in which what ought to be appears impossible. We have got one foot out of the pessimistic bog, but the other one sinks all the deeper. We have rescued our actions from the bonds of evil, but our judgments are now held fast. When murders and treacheries cease to be sins, regrets are theoretic absurdities and errors. The theoretic and the active life thus play a kind of see-saw with each other on the ground of evil. The rise of either sends the other down. Murder and treachery cannot be good without regret being bad: regret cannot be good without treachery and murder being bad. Both, however, are supposed to have been foredoomed; so something must be fatally unreasonable, absurd, and wrong in the world. It must be a place of which either sin or error forms a necessary part. From this dilemma there seems at first sight no escape. Are we then so soon to fall back into the pessimism from which we thought we had emerged? And is there no possible way by which we may, with good intellectual consciences, call the cruelties and the treacheries, the reluctances and the regrets, *all* good together?

James is not ready to construct his second dilemma. It is this second dilemma that is referred to in the title of the essay. He begins:

The refuge from the quandary lies, as I said, not far off. The necessary acts we erroneously regret may be good, and yet our error in so regretting them may be also good, on one simple condition; and that condition is this: The world must not be regarded as a machine whose final purpose is the making real of any outward good, but rather as a contrivance for deepening the theoretic consciousness of what goodness and evil in their intrinsic natures are. Not the doing either of good or of evil is what nature cares for, but the knowing of them. Life is one long eating of the fruit of the tree of *knowledge.*

We have thus clearly revealed to our view what may be called the dilemma of determinism, so far as determinism pretends to think things out at all. A merely mechanical determinism, it is true, rather rejoices in not thinking them out. It is very sure that the universe must satisfy its postulate of a physical continuity and coherence, but it smiles at any one who comes forward with a postulate of moral coherence as well. I may suppose, however, that the number of purely mechanical or hard determinists among you this evening is small. The determinism to whose seductions you are most exposed is what I have called soft determinism,—the determinism which allows considerations of good and bad to mingle with those of cause and effect in deciding what sort of a universe this may rationally be held to be. The dilemma of this determinism is one whose left horn is pessimism and whose right horn is subjectivism. In other words, if determinism is to escape pessimism, it must leave off looking at the goods and ills of life in a simple objective way, and regard them as materials, indifferent in themselves, for the production of consciousness, scientific and ethical, in us.

This second dilemma is between pessimism and subjectivism. The first had been between pessimism and optimism. The first said, "If you are a determinist, you must choose between pessimism and optimism." The second says, "If you are a determinist, you must choose between pessimism and subjectivism." James now increases the pressures exerted by this second dilemma.

To escape pessimism is, as we all know, no easy task. Your own studies have sufficiently shown you the almost desperate difficulty of making the notion that there is a single principle of things, and that principle absolute perfection, rhyme together with our daily vision of the facts of life. If perfection be the principle, how comes there any imperfection here? If God be good, how came he to create—or, if he did not create, how comes he to permit— the devil? The evil facts must be explained as seeming: the devil must be whitewashed, the universe must be disinfected, if neither God's goodness nor his unity and power are to remain impugned. And of all the various ways of operating the disinfection, and making bad seem less bad, the way of subjectivism appears by far the best.[1]

For, after all, is there not something rather absurd in our ordinary notion of external things being good or bad in themselves? Can murders and treacheries, considered as mere outward happenings, or motions of matter, be bad without any one to feel their badness? And could paradise properly be good in the absence of a sentient principle by which the goodness was perceived? Outward goods and evils seem practically indistinguishable except in so far as they result in getting moral judgments made about them. But then the moral judgments seem the main thing, and the outward facts mere perishing instruments for their production. This is subjectivism. Every one must at some time have wondered at that strange paradox of our moral nature, that, though the pursuit of outward good is the breath of its nostrils, the attainment of outward good would seem to be in suffocation and death. Why does the painting of any paradise or utopia, in heaven or on earth, awaken such yawnings for nirvana and escape? The white-robed harp-playing heaven of our sabbath-schools and the ladylike tea-table elysium represented in Mr. Spencer's Data of Ethics, as the final consummation of progress, are exactly on a par in this respect—lubberlands, pure and simple, one and all. We look upon them from this delicious mess of insanities and realities, strivings and deadnesses, hopes and fears, agonies and exultations, which forms out present state, and *tedium vitæ* is the only sentiment

[1] To a reader who says he is satisfied with a pessimism, and has no objection to thinking the whole bad, I have no more to say: he makes fewer demands on the world than I, who, making them, wish to look a little further before I give up all hope of having them satisfied. If, however, all he means is that the badness of some parts does not prevent his acceptance of a universe whose *other* parts give him satisfaction, I welcome him as an ally. He has abandoned the notion of the *Whole*, which is the essence of deterministic monism, and views things as a pluralism, just as I do in this paper.

they awaken in our breasts. To our crepuscular natures, born for the conflict, the Rembrandtesque moral chiaroscuro, the shifting struggle of the sunbeam in the gloom, such pictures of light upon light are vacuous and expressionless, and neither to be enjoyed nor understood. If *this* be the whole fruit of the victory, we say; if the generations of mankind suffered and laid down their lives; if prophets confessed and martyrs sang in the fire, and all the sacred tears were shed for no other end than that a race of creatures of such unexampled insipidity should succeed, and protract *in saecula saeculorum* their contented and inoffensive lives—why, at such a rate, better lose than win the battle, or at all events better ring down the curtain before the last act of the play, so that a business that began so importantly may be saved from so singularly flat a winding-up.

All this is what I should instantly say, were I called on to plead for gnosticism; and its real friends, of whom you will presently perceive I am not one, would say without difficulty a great deal more. Regarded as a stable finality, every outward good becomes a mere weariness to the flesh. It must be menaced, be occasionally lost, for its goodness to be fully felt as such. Nay, more than occasionally lost. No one knows the worth of innocence till he knows it is gone forever, and that money cannot buy it back. Not the saint, but the sinner that repenteth, is he to whom the full length and breadth, and height and depth, of life's meaning is revealed. Not the absence of vice, but vice there, and virtue holding her by the throat, seems the ideal human state. And there seems no reason to suppose it not a permanent human state. There is a deep truth in what the school of Schopenhauer insists on,—the illusoriness of the notion of moral progress. The more brutal forms of evil that go are replaced by others more subtle and more poisonous. Our moral horizon moves with us as we move, and never do we draw nearer to the far-off line where the black waves and the azure meet. The final purpose of our creation seems most plausibly to be the greatest possible enrichment of our ethical consciousness, through the intensest play of contrasts and the widest diversity of characters. This of course obliges some of us to be vessels of wrath, while it calls others to be vessels of honor. But the subjectivist point of view reduces all these outward distinctions to a common denominator. The wretch languishing in the felon's cell may be drinking draughts of the wine of truth that will never pass the lips of the so-called favorite of fortune. And the peculiar consciousness of each of them is an indispensable note in the great ethical concert which the centuries as they roll are grinding out of the living heart of man.

James's proposition to the determinist is that he opt for a combination of determinism and subjectivism. Then, to reassure the determinist, he does what he can to polish up a case for subjectivism when it is to be chosen as an alternative to pessimism. As he says, with something of a flourish:

So much for subjectivism! If the dilemma of determinism be to choose between it and pessimism, I see little room for hesitation from the strictly theoretical point of view. Subjectivism seems the more rational scheme. And the world may, possibly, for aught I know, be nothing else. When the healthy love of life is on one, and all its forms and its appetites seem so unutterably real; when the most brutal and the most spiritual things are lit by the same sun, and each is an integral part of the total richness—why, then it seems a grudging and sickly way of meeting so robust a universe to shrink from any of its facts and wish them not to be. Rather take the strictly dramatic point of view, and treat the whole thing as a great unending romance which the spirit of the universe, striving to realize its own content, is eternally thinking out and representing to itself.

At this point James starts to back away from subjectivism as a payable price on determinism. If he puts too high a gloss on subjectivism, someone might ask why he did not subscribe to subjectivism and *then* subscribe to determinism. But James neither desires nor intends to subscribe to determinism. He must therefore make clear why he, at least, will not subscribe to subjectivism. Thus:

No one, I hope, will accuse me, after I have said all this, of underrating the reasons in favor of subjectivism. And now that I proceed to say why those reasons, strong as they are, fail to convince my own mind, I trust the presumption may be that my objections are stronger still.

I frankly confess that they are of a practical order. If we practically take up subjectivism in a sincere and radical manner and follow its consequences, we meet with some that make us pause. Let a subjectivism begin in never so severe and intellectual a way, it is forced by the law of its nature to develop another side of itself and end with the corruptest curiosity. Once dismiss the notion that certain duties are good in themselves, and that we are here to do them, no matter how we feel about them; once consecrate the opposite notion that our performances and our violations of duty are for a common purpose, the attainment of subjective knowledge and feeling, and that the deepening of these is the chief end of our lives—and at what point on the downward slope are we to stop? In theology, subjectivism develops as its "left wing" antinomianism. In literature, its left wing is romanticism. And in practical life it is either a nerveless sentimentality or a sensualism without bounds.

Everywhere it fosters the fatalistic mood of mind. It makes those who are already too inert more passive still; it renders wholly reckless those whose energy is already in excess. All through history we find how subjectivism, as soon as it has a free career, exhausts itself in every sort of spiritual, moral, and practical license. Its optimism turns to an ethical indifference, which infallibly brings dissolution in its train. It is perfectly safe to say now that if the Hegelian gnosticism, which has begun to show itself here and in Great Britain, were to become a popular philosophy, as it once was in Germany, it would certainly develop its left wing here as there, and produce a reaction of disgust. Already I have heard a graduate of this very school express in the pulpit his willingness to sin like David, if only he might repent like David. You may tell me he was only sowing his wild, or rather his tame, oats; and perhaps he was. But the point is that in the subjectivistic or gnostical philosophy oat sowing, wild or tame, becomes a systematic necessity and the chief function of life. After the pure and classic truths, the exciting and rancid ones must be experienced; and if the stupid virtues of the philistine herd do not then come in and save society from the influence of the children of light, a sort of inward putrefaction becomes its inevitable doom.

The heart of the romantic utterances, whether poetical, critical, or historical, is this inward remedilessness, what Carlyle calls this far-off whimpering of wail and woe. And from this romantic state of mind there is absolutely no possible *theoretic* escape. Whether, like Renan, we look upon life in a more refined way, as a romance of the spirit; or whether, like the friends of M. Zola, we pique ourselves on our "scientific" and "analytic" character, and prefer to be cynical, and call the world a "roman expérimental" on an infinite scale—in either case the world appears to us potentially as what the same Carlyle once called it, a vast, gloomy, solitary Golgotha and mill of death.

The only escape is by the practical way. And since I have mentioned the nowadays much-reviled name of Carlyle, let me mention it once more, and say it is the way of his teaching. No matter for Carlyle's life, no matter for a great deal of his writing. What was the most important thing he said to us? He said: "Hang your sensibilities! Stop your snivelling complaints, and your equally snivelling raptures! Leave off your general emotional tomfoolery, and get to WORK like men!" But this means a complete rupture with the subjectivist philosophy of things. It says conduct, and not sensibility, is the ultimate fact for our recognition. With the vision of certain works to be done, of certain outward changes to be wrought or resisted, it says our intellectual horizon terminates. No matter how we succeed in doing these outward duties, whether gladly and spontaneously, or heavily and unwillingly, do them we somehow must; for the leaving of them undone is perdition. No matter how we feel; if we are only faithful in the outward act and refuse to do wrong, the world will in so far be safe, and we quit of our debt toward it. Take, then, the yoke upon our shoulders; bend our neck beneath the heavy legality of its weight; regard something else than our feeling as our limit, our master, and our law; be willing to live and die in its service—and, at a stroke, we have passed from the subjective into the objective philosophy of things, much as one awakens from some feverish dream, full of bad lights and noises, to find one's self bathed in the sacred coolness and quiet of the air of the night.

But what is the essence of this philosophy of objective conduct, so old-fashioned and finite, but so chaste and sane and strong, when compared with its romantic rival? It is the recognition of limits, foreign and opaque to our understanding. It is the willingness, after bringing about some external good, to feel at peace; for our responsibility ends with the performance of that duty, and the burden of the rest we may lay on higher powers.

> Look to thyself, O Universe,
> Thou art better and not worse,

we may say in that philosophy, the moment we have done our stroke of conduct, however small. For in the view of that philosophy the universe belongs

to a plurality of semi-independent forces, each one of which may help or
hinder, and be helped or hindered by, the operations of the rest.

As James makes clear, his grounds for rejecting subjectivism are
"practical," not "theoretical." His point is not that if you commit
yourself to subjectivism you may find yourself committed to an impossible conception of the world. His point is rather that if you commit yourself to subjectivism you may find yourself committed to a
life-style that he, for one, rejects. He therefore refuses to subscribe to
subjectivism as a way of going on to subscribe to determinism. So he
stands committed against determinism and in favor of freewillism,
indeterminism. This conjures up, all over again, the objections and
protests that center on such notions as "chance," "alternative possibilities," "lawless events," and so on. He resumes:

But this brings us right back, after such a long détour, to the question of
indeterminism and to the conclusion of all I came here to say to-night. For
the only consistent way of representing a pluralism and a world whose parts
may affect one another through their conduct being either good or bad is the
indeterministic way. What interest, zest, or excitement can there be in
achieving the right way, unless we are enabled to feel that the wrong way is
also a possible and a natural way—nay, more, a menacing and an imminent
way? And what sense can there be in condemning ourselves for taking the
wrong way, unless we need have done nothing of the sort, unless the right
way was open to us as well? I cannot understand the willingness to act, no
matter how we feel, without the belief that acts are really good and bad. I
cannot understand the belief that an act is bad, without regret at its happening. I cannot understand regret without the admission of real, genuine possibilities in the world. Only *then* is it other than a mockery to feel, after we
have failed to do our best, that an irreparable opportunity is gone from the
universe, the loss of which it must forever after mourn.

If you insist that this is all superstition, that possibility is in the eye of
science and reason impossibility, and that if I act badly it is that the universe
was foredoomed to suffer this defect, you fall right back into the dilemma,
the labyrinth, of pessimism and subjectivism, from out of whose toils we
have just wound our way.

Now, we are of course free to fall back, if we please. For my own part,
though, whatever difficulties may beset the philosophy of objective right and
wrong, and the indeterminism it seems to imply, determinism, with its alternative of pessimism or romanticism, contains difficulties that are greater still.
But you will remember that I expressly repudiated awhile ago the pretension to offer any arguments which could be coercive in a so-called scientific
fashion in this matter. And I consequently find myself, at the end of this long
talk, obliged to state my conclusions in an altogether personal way. This personal method of appeal seems to be among the very conditions of the problem; and the most any one can do is to confess as candidly as he can the
grounds for the faith that is in him, and leave his example to work on others
as it may.

What then has he to say for himself? To fend off a commitment to determinism and subjectivism, is he willing to subscribe to a potentially loose and chaotic universe, to stab the entire scientific enterprise in the back, to give aid and comfort to all manner of tenderminded true believers? It may not be quite all that; but the chips are down and James does not hesitate to make clear where he proposes to place his wager:

Let me, then, without circumlocution say just this. The world is enigmatical enough in all conscience, whatever theory we may take up toward it. The indeterminism I defend, the free-will theory of popular sense based on the judgment of regret, represents that world as vulnerable, and liable to be injured by certain of its parts if they act wrong. And it represents their acting wrong as a matter of possibility or accident, neither inevitable nor yet to be infallibly warded off. In all this, it is a theory devoid either of transparency or of stability. It gives us a pluralistic, restless universe, in which no single point of view can ever take in the whole scene; and to a mind possessed of the love of unity at any cost, it will, no doubt, remain forever inacceptable. A friend with such a mind once told me that the thought of my universe made him sick, like the sight of the horrible motion of a mass of maggots in their carrion bed.

But while I freely admit that the pluralism and the restlessness are repugnant and irrational in a certain way, I find that every alternative to them is irrational in a deeper way. The indeterminism with its maggots, if you please to speak so about it, offends only the native absolutism of my intellect—an absolutism which, after all, perhaps, deserves to be snubbed and kept in check. But the determinism with its necessary carrion, to continue the figure of speech, and with no possible maggots to eat the latter up, violates my sense of moral reality through and through. When, for example, I imagine such carrion as the Brockton murder, I cannot conceive it as an act by which the universe, as a whole, logically and necessarily expresses its nature without shrinking from complicity with such a whole. And I deliberately refuse to keep on terms of loyalty with the universe by saying blankly that the murder, since it does flow from the nature of the whole, is not carrion. There are *some* instinctive reactions which I, for one, will not tamper with. The only remaining alternative, the attitude of gnostical romanticism, wrenches my personal instincts in quite as violent a way. It falsifies the simple objectivity of their deliverance. It makes the goose-flesh the murder excites in me a sufficient reason for the perpetration of the crime. It transforms life from a tragic reality into an insincere melodramatic exhibition, as foul or as tawdry as any one's diseased curiosity pleases to carry it out. And with its consecration of the "roman naturaliste" state of mind, and its enthronement of the baser crew of Parisian *littérateurs* among the eternally indispensable organs by which the infinite spirit of things attains to that subjective illumination which is the task of its life, it leaves me in presence of a sort of subjective carrion considerably more noisome than the objective carrion I called it in to take away.

No! better a thousand times, than such systematic corruption of our moral sanity, the plainest pessimism, so that it be straightforward; but better far than that the world of chance. Make as great an uproar about chance as you please, I know that chance means pluralism and nothing more. If some of the members of the pluralism are bad, the philosophy of pluralism, whatever broad views it may deny me, permits me, at least, to turn to the other members with a clean breast of affection and an unsophisticated moral sense. And if I still wish to think of the world as a totality, it lets me feel that a world with a *chance* in it of being altogether good, even if the chance never come to pass, is better than a world with no such chance at all. That 'chance' whose very notion I am exhorted and conjured to banish from my view of the future as the suicide of reason concerning it, that 'chance' is—what? Just this—the chance that in moral respects the future may be other and better than the past has been. This is the only chance we have any motive for supposing to exist. Shame, rather, on its repudiation and its denial! For its presence is the vital air which lets the world live, the salt which keeps it sweet.

There is one remaining consideration. Up to this point James has been fending off determinism against the urgings of those who insist that determinism is a presupposition of science: if the choice is between human free will, human autonomy, and human achievement in natural sciences, then let him be sensible and remember that he is by profession a scientist, and that this means no fiddle-faddle about free will in man. James has made his position clear in relation to these science-oriented friends of determinism. However, determinism has other friends, among whom are those who insist that determinism is a presupposition of the sovereignty, the omnipotence, and omniscience of God. Before quitting this freewill–determinism argument, James addresses himself to these theology-oriented friends of determinism. He begins with one last word about "chance," because it is objected to by both scientists and theologians:

And here I might legitimately stop, having expressed all I care to see admitted by others to-night. But I know that if I do stop here, misapprehensions will remain in the minds of some of you, and keep all I have said from having its effect; so I judge it best to add a few more words.

In the first place, in spite of all my explanations, the word "chance" will still be giving trouble. Though you may yourselves be adverse to the deterministic doctrine, you wish a pleasanter word than "chance" to name the opposite doctrine by; and you very likely consider my preference for such a word a perverse sort of a partiality on my part. It certainly *is* a bad word to make converts with; and you wish I had not thrust it so butt-foremost at you—you wish to use a milder term.

Well, I admit there may be just a dash of perversity in its choice. The spectacle of the mere word-grabbing game played by the soft determinists has perhaps driven me too violently the other way; and, rather than be found wrangling with them for the good words, I am willing to take the first bad one which comes along, provided it be unequivocal. The question is of things, not of eulogistic names for them; and the best word is the one that enables men to know the quickest whether they disagree or not about the things. But the word "chance," with its singular negativity, is just the word for this purpose. Whoever uses it instead of "freedom," squarely and resolutely gives up all pretence to control the things he says are free. For *him*, he confesses that they are no better than mere chance would be. It is a word of *impotence*, and is therefore the only sincere word we can use, if, in granting freedom to certain things, we grant it honestly, and really risk the game. "Who chooses me must give and forfeit all he hath." Any other word permits of quibbling, and lets us, after the fashion of the soft determinists, make a pretence of restoring the caged bird to liberty with one hand, while with the other we anxiously tie a string to its leg to make sure it does not get beyond our sight.

So much for science-oriented friends of determinism, and repudiators of "chance." James moves to conclude by considering "a final doubt."

But now you will bring up your final doubt. Does not the admission of such an unguaranteed chance or freedom preclude utterly the notion of a Providence governing the world? Does it not leave the fate of the universe at the mercy of the chance-possibilities, and so far insecure? Does it not, in short, deny the craving of our nature for an ultimate peace behind all tempests, for a blue zenith above all clouds?

To this my answer must be very brief. The belief in free-will is not in the least incompatible with the belief in Providence, provided you do not restrict the Providence to fulminating nothing but *fatal* decrees. If you allow him to provide possibilities as well as actualities to the universe, and to carry on his own thinking in those two categories just as we do ours, chances may be there, uncontrolled even by him, and the course of the universe be really ambiguous; and yet the end of all things may be just what he intended it to be from all eternity.

An analogy will make the meaning of this clear. Suppose two men before a chessboard,—the one a novice, the other an expert player of the game. The expert intends to beat. But he cannot foresee exactly what any one actual move of his adversary may be. He knows, however, all the *possible* moves of the latter; and he knows in advance how to meet each of them by a move of his own which leads in the direction of victory. And the victory infallibly arrives, after no matter how devious a course, in the one predestined form of check-mate to the novice's king.

Let now the novice stand for us finite free agents, and the expert for the infinite mind in which the universe lies. Suppose the latter to be thinking out his universe before he actually creates it. Suppose him to say, I will lead things to a certain end, but I will not *now* decide on all the steps thereto. At various points, ambiguous possibilities shall be left open, *either* of which, at a given instant, may become actual. But whichever branch of these bifurcations become real, I know what I shall do at the *next* bifurcation to keep things from drifting away from the final result I intend.

The creator's plan of the universe would thus be left blank as to many of its actual details, but all possibilities would be marked down. The realization of some of these would be left absolutely to chance; that is, would only be determined when the moment of realization came. Other possibilities would be *contingently* determined; that is, their decision would have to wait till it was seen how the matters of absolute chance fell out. But the rest of the plan, including its final upshot, would be rigorously determined once for all. So the creator himself would not need to know *all* the details of actuality until they came; and at any time his own view of the world would be a view partly of facts and partly of possibilities, exactly as ours is now. Of one thing, however, he might be certain; and that is that his world was safe, and that no matter how much it might zigzag he could surely bring it home at last.

Now, it is entirely immaterial, in this scheme, whether the creator leave the absolute chance-possibilities to be decided by himself, each when its proper moment arrives, or whether, on the contrary, he alienate this power from himself, and leave the decision out and out to finite creatures such as we men are. The great point is that the possibilities are really *here*. Whether it be we who solve them, or he working through us, at those soul-trying moments when fate's scales seem to quiver, and good snatches the victory from evil or shrinks nerveless from the fight, is of small account, so long as we admit that the issue is decided nowhere else than *here* and *now*. *That* is what gives the palpitating reality to our moral life and makes it tingle, as Mr. Mallock says, with so strange and elaborate an excitement. This reality, this excitement, are what the determinisms, hard and soft alike, suppress by their denial that *anything* is decided here and now, and their dogma that all things were foredoomed and settled long ago. If it be so, may you and I then have been foredoomed to the error of continuing to believe in liberty. It is fortunate for the winding up of controversy that in every discussion with determinism this *argumentum ad hominem* can be its adversary's last word.

READING QUESTIONS

1. James says, "The arguments I am about to urge all proceed on two assumptions." (a) State these assumptions. (b) Any questions or comments on them? (c) Can you suggest any other issue (i.e., not free will vs. determinism) in reference to which these assumptions might be introduced? (d) What is the status of these assumptions themselves? How would *they* be defended or proved?

2. He differentiates three kinds of rationality: mechanical, logical, and moral. (a) Can you give an illustration of each? (b) Can you suggest still another kind? (c) Given two or more kinds of rationality, does he think that any pecking order can be either detected or instituted?

3. Just for the record: What does determinism profess? And what does indeterminism, libertarianism, profess?

4. He says, "Facts . . . have hardly anything to do with making us either determinists or indeterminists." (a) What does, then? (b) Can you suggest any other ism option to which facts would be similarly irrelevant? (c) Do you agree with James's claim here? If not, why not?

5. Use the Brockton murder case to explain what James means by a regret judgment. Why does he introduce the notion of a regret judgment anyway? Is it as crucial (for his purposes) as he thinks it is?

6. He says, "Thus, our deterministic pessimism may become a deterministic optimism." How so? Why the reference to Voltaire's *Candide?*

7. Formulate the dilemma of determinism as James sees it. If you are a satisfied pessimist, you will not feel it as a dilemma. Why not? What would James say to you?

8. What does he mean by *subjectivism?* As between it and pessimism, which would he choose? Why? Why, however, he has reservations about subjectivism.

9. He says, "But now you will bring up your final doubt." (a) What doubt? (b) Do you regard this as a serious doubt? (c) How does he propose to deal with it?

10. As between Holbach and James, where do you stand? Formulate one or more questions you would put to James.

INDEPENDENT STUDY

1. Read the essay (article) on James by W. J. Earle in the *Encyclopedia of Philosophy;* and the articles by D. Mackenzie on "Freewill" and on "Libertarianism vs Necessitarianism" in the *Encyclopedia of Religion and Ethics.*

2. Read the first two papers in *In Defence of Freewill* by C. A. Campbell, and the chapter on free will in the same author's *Selfhood and Godhood.* The papers overlap. Ignore that. State the author's position.

3. Consult the relevant chapters in *Freedom and Responsibility,* edited by H. Morris. This is an excellent collection of readings.

SECTION 4. JEAN PAUL SARTRE: EXISTENTIALISM
IS A HUMANISM

From James to Sartre. If you read relevantly in William James
you will discover what the founder of American pragmatism thought
about the nature of man considered as a rational animal. His paper
"The Dilemma of Determinism" is an excellent starting point, but
other essays and chapters would be needed to fill out the picture,
especially chapters of his *Principles of Psychology*. If you read relevantly in Jean-Paul Sartre you will discover what the founder of
French existentialism thought about the nature of man considered as
a rational animal. His published lecture "Existentialism Is a Humanism" is an excellent starting point, but other essays and chapters
would be needed to fill out the picture, especially chapters of his
large volume *Being and Nothingness*.

There is much in Sartre that is reminiscent of Descartes; e.g., Sartre's distinction between a *pour soi* and an *en soi* is some sort of de-
scendant of Descartes' distinction between a *res cogitans* and a *res
extensa*. Descartes' efforts to track down a not-doubtable as a starting
point is detectable in the following passage paraphrased from Sartre's lecture:

Our point of departure is the subjectivity of the individual [the individual
regarded as a *subject* who thinks, not as an *object* thought about]. It is
because we seek to base our teaching upon the truth. Any doctrine of probabilities which is not attached to a truth, will crumble. To define the probable
one must possess the true. And there is such a truth, At the point of departure there cannot be any other truth than this: "I think, therefore I am." This
theory does not begin by taking man as an object but as a subject. All kinds
of materialism treat man as an object, a set of predetermined reactions, no
different in this respect from a table or a chair or a stone. [See
pp. 154–155.]

Sartre's insistence on starting with man as subject, as one who
knows and wills and judges, not as some external object that is
known and willed and judged, is fundamental to his existentialism. A
subject, in contrast to an object, is come at through the activities that
it performs, and in performing which it is conscious, aware, of itself
as free. Unlike Holbach, Sartre sees no reason to write off this consciousness, this awareness, this experience as illusory. If freedom is
an ineluctable fact about man apprehended as *subject*—as knower,
willer, and judger—and if, as Sartre says, man is "condemned to be
free," then he (man) makes himself to be whatever he essentially
becomes. He does this as he goes along, in the exercise of his free-

dom. He is the author of his own essential nature. In his case, then, his existence *precedes* his "essence." Whatever he now essentially is, he has made himself to be, and he *existed* before and while he was doing so. This is a step beyond Descartes.

Sartre refers to his position as atheistic existentialism or existentialist atheism. Can you see why? To make sure, sort out the possibilities. Is Sartre telling us (1) "I call myself an atheist and also an existentialist, but there is no necessary connection between these two facts about me. It is not that I am an atheist because I am an existentialist, nor that I am an existentialist because I am an atheist. I am simply both"? (He says this in the way that he might say, "I am both a Frenchman and a writer of plays.") Or is he telling us (2) "I am an existentialist; therefore, to be consistent, I must be an atheist. If I freely make myself to be what I now essentially am, if my existence thus precedes my essence, then it is not possible that there exists any traditionally omnipotent God who has made me to be what I essentially am. My freedom and self-creativity are incompatible with His existence. Hence, my atheism is a corollary of my existentialism"? Or is he telling us (3) "I am an atheist, therefore to be consistent I must be an existentialist. God does not make me to be what I essentially am. *Dieu n'existe pas* so how could He? I make myself to be what I essentially am. In doing this I am not determined by the omnipotence of God. *Dieu n'existe pas,* so how could I be? With Him out of the way, I am free, as *subject,* to act on my own, to make myself what I decide and choose to become. Hence my existentialism is a corollary of my atheism"?

Biographical Note on Sartre.   Jean-Paul Sartre was born in Paris in 1905. His academic training in philosophy was received in colleges and universities in France and Germany. He taught philosophy in French colleges before and for a few years after World War II. His war experiences included service in the French army, prisoner of war in Germany, and work with the French Resistance movement. He wrote many philosophical monographs, novels, plays, and literary essays. He was a founder and editor of the journal *Modern Times.* He refused the Nobel Prize for literature in 1964. Of his many publications, between the early 1930's and the early 1960's, three are specifically noted here: in 1938, *Nausea,* an existentialist novel; in 1943, *Being and Nothingness,* his major philosophical statement of his existentialism; and in 1946, *Existentialism Is a Humanism,* a philosophical conference paper, reproduced in this chapter.

Sartre's treatise *L'Être et le Néant (Being and Nothingness)* was published in 1943. It contained the major exposition of his existentialism. His lecture "Existentialism Is a Humanism," reproduced in this section, was published three years later, in 1946. It contains a brief formulation of his existentialism and a defense of it against typical reproaches that had meanwhile been brought against it. Some readers question the value of this 1946 lecture as an introductory statement of Sartre's existentialism. They claim that it is too condensed, that it does not contain an adequate formulation of the author's position, that it glosses over important technical points worked out in the 1943 treatise, that it presupposes a familiarity with that treatise that only the treatise itself could supply, and so on. All this is as it may be. The fact remains that, short of reading at considerable length in the 1943 treatise, there is no other document of manageable length and simplicity by Sartre himself on his existentialism. The design of his lecture is clear and straightforward: he announces his intention to defend his position against some typical reproaches; formulates the position that is under reproach, explaining how it causes certain terms to become diagnostic; and proceeds to fend off specific examples of two major reproaches.

The first five paragraphs are numbered in this section to facilitate reference. They are not numbered in the text of the original lecture. He states his over-all purpose: to defend his doctrine against some typical reproaches. He indicates some typical reproaches. He comments briefly on the term *humanism* in the title of his lecture: "Existentialism Is a Humanism." What does it mean to say that? The suggestion is that there are humanistic doctrines, and that existentialism is one of these. What does it mean to say that? One possibility is that *his* existentialism is neither a naturalism nor a supernaturalism, neither a version of theism nor a version of materialism, neither a theology nor a doctrine about the order of nature; it is instead about man or human nature. Thus:

1. My purpose here is to offer a defence of existentialism against several reproaches that have been laid against it.

2. First, it has been reproached as an invitation to people to dwell in quietism of despair. For if every way to a solution is barred, one would have to regard any action in this world as entirely ineffective, and one would arrive finally at a contemplative philosophy. Moreoever, since contemplation is a luxury, this would be only another bourgeois philosophy. This is, especially, the reproach made by the Communists.

3. From another quarter we are reproached for having underlined all that is ignominious in the human situation, for depicting what is mean, sordid or base to the neglect of certain things that possess charm and beauty and belong to the brighter side of human nature: for example, according to the Catholic critic, Mlle. Mercier, we forget how an infant smiles. Both from this side and from the other we are also reproached for leaving out of account the solidarity of mankind and considering man in isolation. And this, say the Communists, is because we base our doctrine upon pure subjec-

tivity—upon the Cartesian "I think": which is the moment in which solitary man attains to himself; a position from which it is impossible to regain solidarity with other men who exist outside of the self. The *ego* cannot reach them through the *cogito*.

4. From the Christian side, we are reproached as people who deny the reality and seriousness of human affairs. For since we ignore the commandments of God and all values prescribed as eternal, nothing remains but what is strictly voluntary. Everyone can do what he likes, and will be incapable, from such a point of view, of condemning either the point of view or the action of anyone else.

5. It is to these various reproaches that I shall endeavor to reply today; that is why I have entitled this brief exposition "Existentialism is a Humanism." Many may be surprised at the mention of humanism in this connection, but we shall try to see in what sense we understand it. In any case, we can begin by saying that existentialism, in our sense of the word, is a doctrine that does render human life possible; a doctrine, also, which affirms that every truth and every action imply both an environment and a human subjectivity. The essential charge laid against us is, of course, that of overemphasis upon the evil side of human life. I have lately been told of a lady who, whenever she lets slip a vulgar expression in a moment of nervousness, excuses herself by exclaiming. "I believe I am becoming an existentialist." So it appears that ugliness is being identified with existentialism. That is why some people say we are "naturalistic," and if we are, it is strange to see how much we scandalize and horrify them, for no one seems to be much frightened or humiliated nowadays by what is properly called naturalism. Those who can quite well keep down a novel by Zola such as *La Terre* are sickened as soon as they read an existentialist novel. Those who appeal to the wisdom of the people—which is a sad wisdom—find ours sadder still. And yet, what could be more disillusioned than such sayings as "Charity begins at home" or "Promote a rogue and he'll sue you for damage, knock him down and he'll do you homage"? We all know how many common sayings can be quoted to this effect, and they all mean much the same—that you must not oppose the powers-that-be; that you must not fight against superior force; must not meddle in matters that are above your station. Or that any action not in accordance with some tradition is mere romanticism; or that any undertaking which has not the support of proven experience is foredoomed to frustration; and that since experience has shown men to be invariably inclined to evil, there must be firm rules to restrain them, otherwise we shall have anarchy. It is, however, the people who are forever mouthing these dismal proverbs and, whenever they are told of some more or less repulsive action, say "How like human nature!"—it is these very people, always harping upon realism, who complain that existentialism is too gloomy a view of things. Indeed their excessive protests make me suspect that what is annoying them is not so much our pessimism, but, much more likely, our optimism. For at bottom, what is alarming in the doctrine that I am about to try to explain to you is—is it not?—that it confronts man with a possibility of choice. To verify this, let us review the whole question upon the strictly philosophic level. What, then, is this that we call existentialism?

2. Well, what does an existentialist typically and centrally claim? Sartre acknowledges that this question is complicated at the outset by a division within the ranks of existentialists: some existentialists believe in God and some do not. Furthermore, the latter, the atheist existentialists, insist that existentialism's typical and central claim is incompatible with all or most traditional forms of theism. However, allowing for this source of ambiguity, Sartre answers along three lines. First, in the case of human being, existence precedes essence. Second, every human being is a subject who knows, values, wills, and acts freely and responsibly. Third, any activity by any individual human being is performed as holding for all other individual human beings: no subject says, "When I act, He acts *in* me," but, "When I act, I act *for* every other subject." Every human being, qua subject, is a *pour soi*. Every being that is not a subject but only an object is an *en soi*. Existentialism is a doctrine, a set of claims, purporting to answer the question: "What is it to be a *pour soi?*"

Most of those who are making use of this word would be highly confused if required to explain its meaning. For since it has become fashionable, people cheerfully declare that this musician or that painter is "existentialist." A columnist in *Clartés* signs himself "The Existentialist," and, indeed, the word is now so loosely applied to so many things that it no longer means anything at all. It would appear that, for the lack of any novel doctrine such as that of surrealism, all those who are eager to join in the latest scandal or movement now seize upon this philosophy in which, however, they can find nothing to their purpose. For in truth this is of all teachings the least scandalous and the most austere: it is intended strictly for technicians and philosophers. All the same, it can easily be defined.

The question is only complicated because there are two kinds of existentialists. There are, on the one hand, the Christians, amongst whom I shall name Jaspers and Gabriel Marcel, both professed Catholics; and on the other the existential atheists, amongst whom we must place Heidegger as well as the French existentialists and myself. What they have in common is simply the fact that they believe that *existence* comes before *essence*—or, if you will, that we must begin from the subjective. What exactly do we mean by that?

If one considers an article of manufacture—as, for example, a book or a paper-knife—one sees that it has been made by an artisan who had a conception of it; and he has paid attention, equally, to the conception of a paper-knife and to the pre-existent technique of production which is a part of that conception and is, at bottom, a formula. Thus the paper-knife is at the same time an article producible in a certain manner and one which, on the other hand, serves a definite purpose, for one cannot suppose that a man would produce a paper-knife without knowing what it was for. Let us say, then, of the paper-knife that its essence—that is to say the sum of the formulae and the qualities which made its production and its definition possible—precedes its existence. The presence of such-and-such a paper-knife or book is thus determined before my eyes. Here, then, we are viewing the world from a technical standpoint, and we can say that production precedes existence.

When we think of God as the creator, we are thinking of him, most of the time, as a supernal artisan. Whatever doctrine we may be considering, whether it be a doctrine like that of Descartes, or of Leibnitz himself, we always imply that the will follows, more or less, from the understanding or at least accompanies it, so that when God creates he knows precisely what he is creating. Thus, the conception of man in the mind of God is comparable to that of the paper-knife in the mind of the artisan: God makes man according to a procedure and a conception, exactly as the artisan manufactures a paper-knife, following a definition and a formula. Thus each individual man is the realization of a certain conception which dwells in the divine understanding. In the philosophic atheism of the eighteenth century, the notion of God is suppressed, but not, for all that, the idea that essence is prior to existence; something of that idea we still find everywhere, in Diderot, in Voltaire and even in Kant. Man possesses a human nature; that "human nature," which is the conception of human being, is found in every man; which means that each man is a particular example of a universal conception, the conception of Man. In Kant, this universality goes so far that the wild man of the woods, man in the state of nature and the bourgeois are all contained in the same definition and have the same fundamental qualities. Here again, the essence of man precedes that historic existence which we confront in experience.

Atheistic existentialism, of which I am a representative, declares with greater consistency that if God does not exist there is at least one being whose existence comes before its essence, a being which exists before it can be defined by any conception of it. That being is man or, as Heidegger has it, the human reality. What do we mean by saying that existence precedes essence? We mean that man first of all exists, encounters himself, surges up in the world—and defines himself afterwards. If man as the existentialist sees him is not definable, it is because to begin with he is nothing. He will not be anything until later, and then he will be what he makes of himself. Thus, there is no human nature, because there is no God to have a conception of it. Man simply is. Not that he is simply what he conceives himself to be, but he is what he wills, and as he conceives himself after already existing—as he wills to be after that leap towards existence. Man is nothing else but that which he makes of himself. That is the first principle of existentialism. And this is what people call its "subjectivity," using the word as a reproach against us. But what do we mean to say by this, but that man is of a greater dignity than a stone or a table? For we mean to say that man primarily exists—that man is, before all else, something which propels itself towards a future and is aware that it is doing so. Man is, indeed, a project which possesses a subjective life, instead of being a kind of moss, or a fungus or a cauliflower. Before that projection of the self nothing exists; not even in the heaven of intelligence: man will only attain existence when he is what he purposes to be. Not, however, what he may wish to be. For what we usually understand by wishing or willing is a conscious decision taken—much more often than not—after we have made ourselves what we are. I may wish to join a party, to write a book or to marry—but in such a case what is usually called my will is probably a manifestation of a prior and more spontaneous decision. If, however, it is true that existence is prior to essence, man is responsible for what he is. Thus, the first effect of existentialism is that it puts every man in possession of himself as he is, and places the entire responsibility for his existence squarely upon his own shoulders. And, when we say that man is responsible for himself, we do not mean that he is responsible only for his own individuality, but that he is responsible for all men. The word "subjectivism" is to be understood in two senses, and our adversaries play upon only one of them. Subjectivism means, on the one hand, the freedom of the individual subject and, on the other, that man cannot pass beyond human subjectivity. It is the latter which is the deeper meaning of existentialism. When we say that man chooses himself, we do mean that every one of us must choose himself; but by that we also mean that in choosing for himself he chooses for all men. For in effect, of all the actions a man may take in order to create himself as he wills to be, there is not one which is not creative, at the same time, of an image of man such as he believes he ought to be. To choose between this or that is at the same time to affirm the value of that which is chosen; for we are unable ever to choose the worse. What we choose is always the better; and nothing can be better for us unless it is better for all. If, moreover, existence precedes essence and we will to exist at the same time as we fashion our image, that image is valid for all and for the entire epoch in which we find ourselves. Our responsibility is thus much greater than we had supposed, for it concerns mankind as a whole. If I am a worker, for instance, I may choose to join a Christian rather than a Communist trade union. And if, by that membership, I choose to signify that resignation is, after all, the attitude that best becomes a man, that man's kingdom is not upon this earth, I do not commit myself alone to that view. Resignation is my will for everyone, and my action is, in consequence, a commitment on behalf of all mankind. Or if, to take a more personal case, I decide to marry and to have children, even though this decision proceeds simply from my situation, from my passion or my desire, I am thereby committing not only myself, but humanity as a whole, to the practice of monogamy. I am thus responsible for myself and for all men, and I am creating a certain image of man as I would have him to be. In fashioning myself I fashion man.

3. Suppose you have given a concise exposition of the typical and central claims of some doctrine. You might then go on to single out three or four particular notions consequent upon, diagnostic of, the doctrine you had expounded. Sartre is now at that point. He has provided a concise account of his existentialism. He now selects three notions familiar and important to any Sartrean existentialist, namely, anguish, abandonment, and despair. There are others he might have chosen—bad faith, nausea, absurdity, for example. Given the doctrine that there are two modes of being in the world, *être en soi* and *être pour soi,* being which is not conscious or aware of itself and being which is conscious or aware of itself; call the mode of being that is conscious or aware of itself *existence pour soi.* Sartre's

doctrine, existentialism, is about beings whose mode of existence is *pour soi*. You and I are such beings. We are conscious or aware that we exist. Our mode of existence is *pour soi*. A rock or a tree is not such a being. They are not conscious or aware that they exist. Their mode of existence is merely *en soi*. The present question is this: If you are a *pour soi*, why will anguish, abandonment, and despair be important, diagnostic, terms for you?

This may enable us to understand what is meant by such terms—perhaps a little grandiloquent—as anguish, abandonment and despair. As you will soon see, it is very simple. *First*, what do we mean by *anguish?* The existentialist frankly states that man is in anguish. His meaning is as follows—When a man commits himself to anything, fully realizing that he is not only choosing what he will be, but is thereby at the same time a legislator deciding for the whole of mankind—in such a moment a man cannot escape from the sense of complete and profound responsibility. There are many, indeed, who show no such anxiety. But we affirm that they are merely disguising their anguish or are in flight from it. Certainly, many people think that in what they are doing they commit no one but themselves to anything: and if you ask them, "What would happen if everyone did so?" they shrug their shoulders and reply, "Everyone does not do so." But in truth, one ought always to ask oneself what would happen if everyone did as one is doing; nor can one escape from that disturbing thought except by a kind of self-deception. The man who lies in self-excuse, by saying "Everyone will not do it" must be ill at ease in his conscience, for the act of lying implies the universal value which it denies. By its very disguise his anguish reveals itself. This is the anguish that Kierkegaard called "the anguish of Abraham." You know the story: An angel commanded Abraham to sacrifice his son: and obedience was obligatory, if it really was an angel who had appeared and said, "Thou, Abraham, shalt sacrifice thy son." But anyone in such a case would wonder, first, whether it was indeed an angel and secondly, whether I am really Abraham. Where are the proofs? A certain mad woman who suffered from hallucinations said that people were telephoning to her, and giving her orders. The doctor asked, "But who is it that speaks to you?" She replied: "He says it is God." And what, indeed, could prove to her that it was God? If an angel appears to me, what is the proof that it is an angel; or, if I hear voices, who can prove that they proceed from heaven and not from hell, or from my own subconsciousness or some pathological condition? Who can prove that they are really addressed to me?

Who, then, can prove that I am the proper person to impose, by my own choice, my conception of man upon mankind? I shall never find any proof whatever; there will be no sign to convince me of it. If a voice speaks to me, it is still I myself who must decide whether the voice is or is not that of an angel. If I regard a certain course of action as good, it is only I who choose to say that is is good and not bad. There is nothing to show that I am Abraham: nevertheless I also am obliged at every instant to perform actions which are examples. Everything happens to every man as though the whole human race had its eyes fixed upon what he is doing and regulated its conduct accordingly. So every man ought to say, "Am I really a man who has the right to act in such a manner that humanity regulates itself by what I do." If a man does not say that, he is dissembling his anguish. Clearly, the anguish with which we are concerned here is not one that could lead to quietism or inaction. It is anguish pure and simple, of the kind well known to all those who have borne responsibilities. When, for instance, a military leader takes upon himself the responsibility for an attack and sends a number of men to their death, he chooses to do it and at bottom he alone chooses. No doubt he acts under a higher command, but its orders, which are more general, require interpretation by him and upon that interpretation depends the life of ten, fourteen or twenty men. In making the decision, he cannot but feel a certain anguish. All leaders know that anguish. It does not prevent their acting, on the contrary it is the very condition of their action, for the action presupposes that there is a plurality of possibilities, and in choosing one of these, they realize that it has value only because it is chosen. Now it is anguish of that kind which existentialism describes, and moreover, as we shall see, makes explicit through direct responsibility towards other men who are concerned. Far from being a screen which could separate us from action, it is a condition of action itself.

4. So much for existentialist anguish. Sartre's point has been this: if you are a *pour soi,* conscious or aware of existence, especially of your own existence, in a world containing only others who are also *pour soi,* and objects that are merely *en soi,* and that is all, you will know anguish. Why so? Why is anguish one of the facts of life for a *pour soi?* He moves on now to consider his second notion, *abandonment.* Thus:

And when we speak of *"abandonment"*—a favorite word of Heidegger— we only mean to say that God does not exist, and that it is necessary to draw the consequences of his absence right to the end. The existentialist is strongly opposed to a certain type of secular moralism which seeks to suppress God at the least possible expense. Towards 1880, when the French professors endeavored to formulate a secular morality, they said something like this:—God is a useless and costly hypothesis, so we will do without it. However, if we are to have morality, a society and a law-abiding world, it is essential that certain values should be taken seriously; they must have an *à priori* existence ascribed to them. It must be considered obligatory *à priori* to be honest, not to lie, not to beat one's wife, to bring up children and so forth; so we are going to do a little work on this subject, which will enable us to show that these values exist all the same, inscribed in an intelligible heaven although, of course, there is no God. In other words—and this is, I believe, the purport of all that we in France call radicalism—nothing will be changed if God does not exist; we shall rediscover the same norms of honesty, progress and humanity, and we shall have disposed of God as an out-of-date hypothesis which will die away quietly of itself. The existentialist, on the contrary, finds it extremely embarrassing that God does not exist, for there disappears with Him all possibility of finding values in an intelligible heaven. There can no longer be any good *à priori,* since there is no infinite and perfect consciousness to think it. It is nowhere written that "the good" exists, that one must be honest or must not lie, since we are now upon the plane where there are only men. Dostoevsky once wrote "If God did not exist, everything would be permitted"; and that, for existentialism, is the starting point. Everything is indeed permitted if God does not exist, and man is in consequence forlorn, for he cannot find anything to depend upon either within or outside himself. He discovers forthwith, that he is without excuse. For if indeed existence precedes essence, one will never be able to explain one's action by reference to a given and specific human nature; in other words, there is no determinism—man is free, man *is* freedom. Nor, on the other hand, if God does not exist, are we provided with any values or commands that could legitimize our behavior. Thus we have neither behind us, nor before us in a luminous realm of values, any means of justification or excuse. We are left alone, without excuse. That is what I mean when I say that man is condemned to be free. Condemned, because he did not create himself, yet is nevertheless at liberty, and from the moment that he is thrown into this world he is responsible for everything he does. The existentialist does not believe in the power of passion. He will never regard a grand passion as a destructive torrent upon which a man is swept into certain actions as by fate, and which, therefore, is an excuse for them. He thinks that man is responsible for his passion. Neither will an existentialist think that a man can find help through some sign being vouchsafed upon earth for his orientation: for he thinks that the man himself interprets the sign as he chooses. He thinks that every man, without any support or help whatever, is condemned at every instant to invent man. As Ponge has written in a very fine article, "Man is the future of man." That is exactly true. Only, if one took this to mean that the future is laid up in Heaven, that God knows what it is, it would be false, for then it would no longer even be a future. If, however, it means that, whatever man may now appear to be, there is a future to be fashioned, a virgin future that awaits him—then it is a true saying. But in the present one is forsaken.

As an example by which you may the better understand this state of abandonment, I will refer to the case of a pupil of mine, who sought me out in the following circumstances. His father was quarrelling with his mother and was also inclined to be a "collaborator"; his elder brother had been killed in the German offensive of 1940 and this young man, with a sentiment somewhat primitive but generous, burned to avenge him. His mother was living alone with him, deeply afflicted by the semi-treason of his father and by the death of her eldest son, and her one consolation was in this young man. But he, at this moment, had the choice between going to England to join the Free French Forces or of staying near his mother and helping her to live. He fully realized that this woman lived only for him and that his disappearance—or perhaps his death—would plunge her into despair. He also realized that, concretely and in fact, every action he performed on his mother's behalf would be sure of effect in the sense of aiding her to live, whereas anything he did in order to go and fight would be an ambiguous action which might vanish like water into sand and serve no purpose. For instance, to set out for England he would have to wait indefinitely in a Spanish camp on the way through Spain; or, on arriving in England or in Algiers he might be put into an office to fill up forms. Consequently, he found himself confronted by two very different modes of action; the one concrete, immediate, but directed towards only one individual; and the other an action addressed to an end infinitely greater, a national collectivity, but for that very reason ambiguous—and it might be frustrated on the way. At the same time, he was hesitating between two kinds of morality; on the one side the morality of sympathy, of personal devotion and, on the other side, a morality of wider scope but of more debatable validity. He had to choose between those two. What could help him to choose? Could the Christian doctrine? No. Christian doctrine says: Act with charity, love your neighbour, deny yourself for others, choose the way which is hardest, and so forth. But which is the harder road? To whom does one owe the more brotherly love, the patriot or the mother? Which is the more useful aim, the general one of fighting in and for the whole community, or the precise aim of helping one particular person to live? Who can give an answer to that *à priori?* No one. Nor is it given in any ethical scripture. The Kantian ethic says, Never regard another as a means, but always as an end. Very well; if I remain with my mother, I shall be regarding her as the end and not as a means: but by the same token I am in danger of treating as means those who are fighting on my behalf; and the converse is also true, that if I go to the aid of the combatants I shall be treating them as the end at the risk of treating my mother as a means.

If values are uncertain, if they are still too abstract to determine the particular, concrete case under consideration, nothing remains but to trust in our instincts. That is what this young man tried to do; and when I saw him he said, "In the end, it is feeling that counts; the direction in which it is really pushing me is the one I ought to choose. If I feel that I love my mother enough to sacrifice everything else for her—my will to be avenged, all my longings for action and adventure—then I stay with her. If, on the contrary, I feel that my love for her is not enough, I go." But how does one estimate the strength of a feeling? The value of his feeling for his mother was determined precisely by the fact that he was standing by her. I may say that I love a certain friend enough to sacrifice such or such a sum of money for him, but I cannot prove that unless I have done it. I may say, "I love my mother enough to remain with her," if actually I have remained with her. I can only estimate the strength of this affection if I have performed an action by which it is defined and ratified. But if I then appeal to this affection to justify my action, I find myself drawn into a vicious circle.

Moreover, as Gide has very well said, a sentiment which is play-acting and one which is vital are two things that are hardly distinguishable one from another. To decide that I love my mother by staying beside her, and to play a comedy the upshot of which is that I do so—these are nearly the same thing. In other words, feeling is formed by the deeds that one does; therefore I cannot consult it as a guide to action. And that is to say that I can neither seek within myself for an authentic impulse to action, nor can I expect, from some ethic, formulae that will enable me to act. You may say that the youth did, at least, go to a professor to ask for advice. But if you seek counsel—from a priest, for example—you have selected that priest; and at bottom you already knew, more or less, what he would advise. In other words, to choose an adviser is nevertheless to commit oneself by that choice.

If you are a Christian, you will say, Consult a priest; but there are collabo-
rationists, priests who are resisters and priests who wait for the tide to turn:
which will you choose? Had this young man chosen a priest of the resistance, or one of the collaboration, he would have decided beforehand the
kind of advice he was to receive. Similarly, in coming to me, he knew what
advice I should give him, and I had but one reply to make. You are free,
therefore choose—that is to say, invent. No rule of general morality can show
you what you ought to do: no signs are vouchsafed in this world. The Catholics will reply, "Oh, but they are!" Very well; still, it is I myself, in every
case, who have to interpret the signs. While I was imprisoned, I made the
acquaintance of a somewhat remarkable man, a Jesuit, who had become a
member of that order in the following manner. In his life he had suffered a
succession of rather severe setbacks. His father had died when he was a
child, leaving him in poverty, and he had been awarded a free scholarship in
a religious institution, where he had been made continually to feel that he
was accepted for charity's sake, and, in consequence, he had been denied
several of those distinctions and honours which gratify children. Later, about
the age of eighteen, he came to grief in a sentimental affair; and finally, at
twenty-two—this was a trifle in itself, but it was the last drop that overflowed
his cup—he failed in his military examination. This young man, then, could
regard himself as a total failure: it was a sign—but a sign of what? He might
have taken refuge in bitterness or despair. But he took it—very cleverly for
him—as a sign that he was not intended for secular successes, and that only
the attainments of religion, those of sanctity and of faith, were accessible to
him. He interpreted his record as a message from God, and became a
member of the Order. Who can doubt but that this decision as to the meaning of the sign was his, and his alone? One could have drawn quite different
conclusions from such a series of reverses—as, for example, that he had better become a carpenter or a revolutionary. For the decipherment of the sign,
however, he bears the entire responsibility. That is what "abandonment"
implies, that we ourselves decide our being. And with this abandonment
goes anguish.

5. Thus far Sartre has claimed that if you are an existentialist you
will hold that there are in the world only two modes of existence: existence that is conscious or aware of itself, *être pour soi*, and existence that is not conscious or aware of itself, *être en soi*. He went on
to claim that if you are a *pour soi* among others who are *pour soi*,
anguish will be one of the facts of life for you. There will be no
avoiding that encounter. He has now added the further claim that if
you are an atheist *pour soi*, then abandonment, lostness, cosmic alone-
ness, forlornness will be one of the ineluctable facts of life for you
and your kind. There will be no avoiding encounter with the vast
"emptiness" of the world. You will realize that you, and all others
who are *pour soi*, are abandoned, lost, forlorn, alone. You are not an
object of concern to any *en soi;* that would be impossible. And because for Sartre you are also an atheist *pour soi*, an atheist aware that

he exists but committed to claiming that there is no super *pour soi*—no God, no Deity, no Creator and Sustainer—you are not an object of concern to any superhuman *pour soi*. There is, for the atheist existentialist, no God, but only other finite *pour soi* and *en soi*. Neither humanity nor nature is any substitute for God at this point. The knowledge that there are others, like yourself, who are *pour soi* will not rid you of this sense of being abandoned in and cast upon the world; *thrown*. The knowledge that every other being who is not a *pour soi* is merely an *en soi*, similar to a rock or a tree, will not rid you of this sense of abandonment, thrownness. He now turns to the existentialist concept of despair:

As for *"despair,"* the meaning of this expression is extremely simple. It merely means that we limit ourselves to a reliance upon that which is within our wills, or within the sum of the probabilities which render our action feasible. Whenever one wills anything, there are always these elements of probability. If I am counting upon a visit from a friend, who may be coming by train or by tram, I presuppose that the train will arrive at the appointed time, or that the tram will not be derailed. I remain in the realm of possibilities; but one does not rely upon any possibilities beyond those that are strictly concerned in one's action. Beyond the point at which the possibilities under consideration cease to affect my action, I ought to disinterest myself. For there is no God and no prevenient design, which can adapt the world and all its possibilities to my will. When Descartes said, "Conquer yourself rather than the world," what he meant was, at bottom, the same— that we should act without hope.

Marxists, to whom I have said this, have answered: "Your action is limited, obviously, by your death; but you can rely upon the help of others. That is, you can count both upon what the others are doing to help you elsewhere, as in China and in Russia, and upon what they will do later, after your death, to take up your action and carry it forward to its final accomplishment which will be the revolution. Moreover you must rely upon this; not to do so is immoral." To this I rejoin, first, that I shall always count upon my comrades-in-arms in the struggle, in so far as they are committed, as I am, to a definite, common cause; and in the unity of a party or a group which I can more or less control—that is, in which I am enrolled as a militant and whose movements at every moment are known to me. In that respect, to rely upon the unity and the will of the party is exactly like my reckoning that the train will run to time or that the tram will not be derailed. But I cannot count upon men whom I do not know, I cannot base my confidence upon human goodness or upon man's interest in the good of society, seeing that man is free and that there is no human nature which I can take as foundational. I do not know where the Russian revolution will lead. I can admire it and take it as an example in so far as it is evident, today, that the proletariat plays a part in Russia which it has attained in no other nation. But I cannot affirm that this will necessarily lead to the triumph of the proletariat: I must confine myself to what I can see. Nor can I be sure that comrades-in-arms will take up my work after my death and carry it to the maximum perfection, seeing that those men are free agents and will freely decide, tomorrow, what man is then to be. Tomorrow, after my death, some men may decide to establish Fascism, and the others may be so cowardly or so slack as to let them do so. If so, Fascism will then be the truth of man, and so much the worse for us. In reality, things will be such as men have decided they shall be. Does that mean that I should abandon myself to quietism? No. First I ought to commit myself and then act my commitment, according to the time-honored formula that "one need not hope in order to undertake one's work." Nor does this mean that I should not belong to a party, but only that I should be without illusion and that I should do what I can. For instance, if I ask myself "Will the social ideal as such, ever become a reality?" I cannot tell, I only know that whatever may be in my power to make it so, I shall do; beyond that, I can count upon nothing.

6. Sartre is about midpoint in his lecture. He has told us that he will defend his atheist existentialism against certain charges, certain reproaches. He has given us an account of his doctrine and some of its corollaries. He has explained that his doctrine is a form of human-ism. In the second half of his lecture he will deal with some of the charges brought against this atheist or humanist existentialism. The first charge ("reproach") is that an existentialism such as his will lead to quietism and pessimism. Thus:

Quietism is the attitude of people who say, "let others do what I cannot do." The doctrine I am presenting before you is precisely the opposite of this, since it declares that there is no reality except in action. It goes further, indeed, and adds, "Man is nothing else but what he purposes, he exists only in so far as he realizes himself, he is therefore nothing else but the sum of his actions, nothing else but what his life is." Hence we can well understand why some people are horrified by our teaching. For many have but one resource to sustain them in their misery, and that is to think, "Circumstances have been against me, I was worthy to be something much better than I have been. I admit I have never had a great love or a great friendship; but that is because I never met a man or a woman who were worthy of it; if I have not written any very good books, it is because I had not the leisure to do so; or, if I have had no children to whom I could devote myself it is because I did not find the man I could have lived with. So there remains within me a wide range of abilities, inclinations and potentialities, unused but perfectly via-ble, which endow me with a worthiness that could never be inferred from the mere history of my actions." But in reality and for the existentialist, there is no love apart from the deeds of love; no potentiality of love other than that which is manifested in loving; there is no genius other than that which is expressed in works of art. The genius of Proust is the totality of the works of Proust; the genius of Racine is the series of his tragedies, outside of which there is nothing. Why should we attribute to Racine the capacity to write yet another tragedy when that is precisely what he did not write? In life, a man commits himself, draws his own portrait and there is nothing but that por-trait. No doubt this thought may seem comfortless to one who has not made a success of his life. On the other hand, it puts everyone in a position to understand that reality alone is reliable; that dreams, expectations and hopes serve to define a man only as deceptive dreams, abortive hopes, expectations unfulfilled; that is to say, they define him negatively, not positively. Nevertheless, when one says, "You are nothing else but what you live," it does not imply that an artist is to be judged solely by his works of art, for a thousand other things contribute no less to his definition as a man. What we mean to say is that a man is no other than a series of undertakings, that he is the sum, the organization, the set of relations that constitute these undertakings.

In the light of all this, what people reproach us with is not, after all, our pessimism, but the sternness of our optimism. If people condemn our works of fiction, in which we describe characters that are base, weak, cowardly and sometimes even frankly evil, it is not only because those characters are base, weak, cowardly or evil. For suppose that, like Zola, we showed that the behavior of these characters was caused by their heredity, or by the action of their environment upon them, or by determining factors, psychic or organic. People would be reassured, they would say, "You see, that is what we are like, no one can do anything about it." But the existentialist, when he portrays a coward, shows him as responsible for his cowardice. He is not like that on account of a cowardly heart or lungs or cerebrum, he has not become like that through his physiological organism; he is like that because he has made himself into a coward by his actions. There is no such thing as a cowardly temperament. There are nervous temperaments; there is what is called impoverished blood, and there are also rich temperaments. But the man whose blood is poor is not a coward for all that, for what produces cowardice is the act of giving up or giving way; and a temperament is not an action. A coward is defined by the deed that he has done. What people feel obscurely, and with horror, is that the coward as we present him is guilty of being a coward. What people would prefer would be to be born either a coward or a hero. One of the charges most often laid against the *Chemins de la Liberté* is something like this—"But, after all, these people being so base, how can you make them into heroes?" That objection is really rather comic, for it implies that people are born heroes: and that is, at bottom, what such people would like to think. If you are born cowards, you can be quite content. You can do nothing about it and you will be cowards all your lives whatever you do; and if you are born heroes you can again be quite content; you will be heroes all your lives, eating and drinking heroically. Whereas the existentialist says that the coward makes himself cowardly, the hero makes himself heroic; and that there is always a possibility for the coward to give up cowardice and for the hero to stop being a hero. What counts is the total commitment, and it is not by a particular case or particular action that you are committed altogether.

7. What has Sartre said in reference to this reproach that his doctrine leads to quietism and pessimism, to the conclusion that people are essentially helpless and that their world is essentially evil? Something like this, perhaps: If, as existentialist, you tell a person that he is a *pour soi*, one who exists and is conscious of, aware of, ex-

isting, he may begin by agreeing with you. Why not? Your doctrine rates him above the world of the *en soi*. That is a gratifying, indeed a flattering, perception. However, if you go on to explain to him that his status as a *pour soi* endows him with free will, with perception of alternatives, with power to choose, hence with responsibility, with power to make of himself what he, not external events and forces, decides—if you go on to make this application of your existentialism to his handling of his life and affairs, he will take a dim view of your doctrine. He does not want to think of himself as essentially the architect of his own wrongdoings and of his character as a person. And he does not want your doctrine to constrain him into thinking that way about himself. He prefers to cop out, and your existentialism forbids him to do so. It tells him that he is the author of whatever he is. He has not "become" what he is. That is the way of the *en soi*. He has made of himself what he is, by his own wrong-headed and bad-willed thinking and acting. Hence, your doctrine denies or distorts the image he wants of himself. So what does he do? He contrives to misunderstand, to misinterpret, your doctrine. He will claim that your doctrine ends by inducing those who accept it to become quietists and pessimists. But as Sartre hastens to point out, such a person is only rationalizing his rejection of existentialism by refusing to understand that doctrine correctly. This refusal is an example of what Sartre means by *mauvaise foi*, bad faith. If the person will only snap out of his protective obtuseness, he will see that he is not "refuting" existentialism, not even proposing a relevant criticism, but merely setting up a straw man, and then clobbering it, only spitefully misunderstanding it.

Sartre is now left with the major reproach, namely, that his existentialism is a form of subjectivism. He distinguishes, under this safety-pin label, two reproaches: first, that his doctrine leads to a denial of human solidarity, and second, that it trivializes human affairs. As to the first of these:

We have now, I think, dealt with a certain number of the reproaches against existentialism. You have seen that it cannot be regarded as a philosophy of quietism since it defines man by his action; nor as a pessimistic description of man, for no doctrine is more optimistic, the destiny of man is placed within himself. Nor is it an attempt to discourage man from action since it tells him that there is no hope except in his action, and that the one thing which permits him to have life is the deed. Upon this level therefore, what we are considering is an ethic of action and self-commitment. However, we are still reproached, upon these few data, for confining man within his individual subjectivity. There again people badly misunderstand us.

Our point of departure is, indeed, the subjectivity of the individual, and that for strictly philosophic reasons. It is not because we are bourgeois, but because we seek to base our teaching upon the truth, and not upon a collection of fine theories, full of hope but lacking real foundations. And at the point of departure there cannot be any other truth than this, *I think, therefore I am,* which is the absolute truth of consciousness as it attains to itself. Every theory which begins with man, outside of this moment of self-attainment, is a theory which thereby suppresses the truth, for outside of the Cartesian *cogito,* all objects are no more than probable, and any doctrine of probabilities which is not attached to a truth will crumble into nothing. In order to define the probable one must possess the true. Before there can be any truth whatever, then, there must be an absolute truth, and there is such a truth which is simple, easily attained and within the reach of everybody; it consists in one's immediate sense of one's self.

In the second place, this theory alone is compatible with the dignity of man, it is the only one which does not make man into an object. All kinds of materialism lead one to treat every man including oneself as an object—that is, as a set of pre-determined reactions, in no way different from the patterns of qualities and phenomena which constitute a table, or a chair or a stone. Our aim is precisely to establish the human kingdom as a pattern of values in distinction from the material world. But the subjectivity which we thus postulate as the standard of truth is no narrowly individual subjectivism, for as we have demonstrated, it is not only one's own self that one discovers in the *cogito,* but those of others too. Contrary to the philosophy of Descartes, contrary to that of Kant, when we say "I think" we are attaining to ourselves in the presence of the other, and we are just as certain of the other as we are of ourselves. Thus the man who discovers himself directly in the *cogito* also discovers all the others, and discovers them as the condition of his own existence. He recognizes that he cannot be anything (in the sense in which one says one is spiritual, or that one is wicked or jealous) unless others recognize him as such. I cannot obtain any truth whatsoever about myself, except through the mediation of another. The other is indispensable to my existence, and equally so to any knowledge I can have of myself. Under these conditions, the intimate discovery of myself is at the same time the revelation of the other as a freedom which confronts mine, and which cannot think or will without doing so either for or against me. Thus, at once, we find ourselves in a world which is, let us say, that of "inter-subjectivity." It is in this world that man has to decide what he is and what others are.

Furthermore, although it is impossible to find in each and every man a universal essence that can be called human nature, there is nevertheless a human universality of *condition.* It is not by chance that the thinkers of today are so much more ready to speak of the condition than of the nature of man. By his condition they understand, with more or less clarity, all the *limitations* which *à priori* define man's fundamental situation in the universe. His historical situations are variable: man may be born a slave in a pagan society, or may be a feudal baron, or a proletarian. But what never vary are the necessities of being in the world, of having to labor and to die there. These limitations are neither subjective nor objective, or rather there is both a subjective and an objective aspect of them. Objective, because we meet with them everywhere and they are everywhere recognizable: and subjective because they are *lived* and are nothing if man does not live them—if, that is to say, he does not freely determine himself and his existence in relation to them. And, diverse though man's purposes may be, at least none of them is wholly foreign to me, since every human purpose presents itself as an attempt either to surpass these limitations, or to widen them, or else to deny or to accommodate oneself to them. Consequently every purpose, however individual it may be, is of universal value. Every purpose, even that of a Chinese, an Indian or a Negro, can be understood by a European. To say it can be understood, means that the European of 1945 may be striving out of a certain situation towards the same limitations in the same way, and that he may reconceive in himself the purpose of the Chinese, of the Indian or the African. In every purpose there is universality, in this sense that every purpose is comprehensible to every man. Not that this or that purpose defines man for ever, but that it may be entertained again and again. There is always some way of understanding an idiot, a child, a primitive man or a foreigner if one has sufficient information. In this sense we must say that there is a human universality, but it is not something given; it is being perpetually made. I make this universality in choosing myself; I also make it by understanding the purpose of any other man, of whatever epoch. This absoluteness of the act of choice does not alter the relativity of each epoch.

What is at the very heart and center of existentialism, is the absolute character of the free commitment, by which every man realizes himself in realizing a type of humanity—a commitment always understandable, to no matter whom in no matter what epoch—and its bearing upon the relativity of the cultural pattern which may result from such absolute commitment. One must observe equally the relativity of Cartesianism and the absolute character of the Cartesian commitment. In this sense you may say, if you like, that every one of us makes the absolute by breathing, by eating, by sleeping or by behaving in any fashion whatsoever. There is no difference between free being—being as self-committal, as existence choosing its essence—and absolute being. And there is no difference whatever between being as an absolute, temporarily localized—that is, localized in history—and universally intelligible being.

8. The charge dealt with in the preceding five paragraphs is that a Sartrean *pour soi* is, or could be, a radically individualized entity, not essentially related or relatable to or dependent on the existence of any other *pour soi*. It is not necessary for any "you" to exist in order that an "I" may exist. If every *pour soi* but one were to perish, it would make no essential, no "existential," difference, no difference in the mode of being, the mode of existence, enjoyed by the sole remaining *pour soi*. To be a Sartrean *pour soi*, an individualized center of awareness, to exist and to be conscious that you exist, performing activities freely and creatively and responsibly, it is not necessary that there be any other *pour soi*. To be a *pour soi* is to be an isolated, or isolatable, subject (i.e., not an object), for whom no mode of solidarity with another or others is a necessary condition for the mode of existence ascribed by Sartre's existentialism to an "I" or a "he" or a "you." No *pour soi* need say of himself and any other, "We

are members one of another." If you are a *pour soi* you have a mode
of existence that makes you radically sufficient unto yourself so far as
concerns your mode of being. To be a *pour soi* is to exist and to be
aware of yourself as existing, and that is all. The existence or nonexistence of another or others is not the ground for your having the
mode of being that you have, is not the ground for your existence as a
pour soi. For me to exist and to be aware of it, it is not necessary that
you or any other *pour soi* exist and be aware of existing. As he says,
the reproach is that existentialism, in its fundamental claim, confines
man within his individual subjectivity. That is the reproach. Let us
ask: Is it a *corollary* of his existentialism? He had claimed that his
existentialism, considered as a doctrine about man, could afford to
dispense with God, could afford to be an atheist existentialism. Is the
reproach that if he will look closer at his existentialist doctrine of
man he will see that so long as there exists only one *pour soi*, the
doctrine can afford to dispense with all others? That men are not
necessary to the existence of a man? Is it a *reproach* to his existentialism? Is he able to salvage his doctrine from this charge? Do both
Christians and communists have a stake in the validity of this reproach? In reflecting upon these questions the reader will do well to
pay careful attention to the second of the five paragraphs (pp. 154–155)
that Sartre gives to fending off this reproach.

The charge that his atheist existentialism is, or might well be, a
radical subjectivism in the manner explained above seems to have
been the most serious in Sartre's own judgment. However, other
forms of subjectivism remain. He notes three, and says, "these three
are not very serious objections." The charges are three different
ways of claiming that by subjectivizing his existentialism, making a
free-wheeling radically autonomous subject the center of his doctrine of man, he trivializes human life and human affairs: (a) If no
pour soi is answerable to anyone but himself in what he does, and
what he makes of himself, then "it does not matter what anyone
does; it does not matter what anyone chooses." (b) If every *pour soi*
is his own ultimate court of appeal, is answerable neither to God
(who does not exist) nor to any other *pour soi* because nothing final
depends on the admitted existence of other finite selves, then no one
can judge anyone else, "you are unable to judge others." This is not
the outcome of a doctrine of judgmental humility: "Judge not, that ye
be not judged." It is an outcome of "subjectivizing," placing only the
individual *pour soi* back of, human judgments. As people say, when
they catch sight of this theoretical possibility, "All judgments are
purely subjective. No judgment possesses any objectivity. No one is
in a position to judge anyone else." (c) If each of us is a Sartrean
pour soi, a center of existence conscious of existing, this promises
great ranges of individual autonomy, freedom, responsibility, crea-

tivity, and so on. That's what existentialism gives with one hand, or promises out of one side of its mouth. But the outcome is bleak. First, the existence of God is denied. That produces a drastically empty world. Second, the existence of other persons turns out to be finally unnecessary and impotent. That does not empty the world of others, but it trivializes their existence, and in so doing trivializes one's own existence. Finally, the power to authorize judgment evaporates because it is found to be not applicable in one's judgments of others. This is existentialism taking away with the other hand, talking now out of the other side of its mouth.

Sartre begins work on the first of these three objections, which "are not very serious":

This does not completely refute the charge of subjectivism. Indeed that objection appears in several other forms, of which the first is as follows. People say to us, "Then it does not matter what you do," and they say this in various ways. First they tax us with anarchy; then they say, "You cannot judge others, for there is no reason for preferring one purpose to another"; finally, they may say, "Everything being merely voluntary in this choice of yours, you give away with one hand what you pretend to gain with the other." These three are not very serious objections. As to the *first*, to say that it does not matter what you choose is not correct. In one sense choice is possible, but what is not possible is not to choose. I can always choose, but I must know that if I do not choose, that is still a choice. This, although it may appear merely formal, is of great importance as a limit to fantasy and caprice. For, when I confront a real situation—for example, that I am a sexual being, able to have relations with a being of the other sex and able to have children—I am obliged to choose my attitude to it, and in every respect I bear the responsibility of the choice which, in committing myself, also commits the whole of humanity. Even if my choice is determined by no *à priori* value whatever, it can have nothing to do with caprice: and if anyone thinks that this is only Gide's theory of the *acte gratuit* over again, he has failed to see the enormous difference between this theory and that of Gide. Gide does not know what a situation is, his "act" is one of pure caprice. In our view, on the contrary, man finds himself in an organized situation in which he is himself involved: his choice involves mankind in its entirety, and he cannot avoid choosing. Either he must remain single, or he must marry without having children, or he must marry and have children. In any case, and whichever he may choose, it is impossible for him, in respect of this situation, not to take complete responsibility. Doubtless he chooses without reference to any pre-established values, but it is unjust to tax him with caprice. Rather let us say that the moral choice is comparable to the construction of a work of art.

But here I must at once digress to make it quite clear that we are not propounding an aesthetic morality, for our adversaries are disingenuous enough to reproach us even with that. I mention the work of art only by way of comparison. That being understood, does anyone reproach an artist, when he paints a picture, for not following rules established *à priori?* Does one ever ask what is the picture that he ought to paint? As everyone knows, there is no pre-defined picture for him to make; the artist applies himself to the composition of a picture, and the picture that ought to be made is precisely that which he will have made. As everyone knows, there are no aesthetic values *à priori*, but there are values which will appear in due course in the coherence of the picture, in the relation between the will to create and the finished work. No one can tell what the painting of tomorrow will be like; one cannot judge a painting until it is done. What has that to do with morality? We are in the same creative situation. We never speak of a work of art as irresponsible; when we are discussing a canvas by Picasso, we understand very well that the composition became what it is at the time when he was painting it, and that his works are part and parcel of his entire life.

It is the same upon the plane of morality. There is this in common between art and morality, that in both we have to do with creation and invention. We cannot decide *à priori* what it is that should be done. I think it was made sufficiently clear to you in the case of that student who came to see me, that to whatever ethical system he might appeal, the Kantian or any other, he could find no sort of guidance whatever; he was obliged to invent the law for himself. Certainly we cannot say that this man, in choosing to remain with his mother—that is, in taking sentiment, personal devotion and concrete charity as his moral foundations—would be making an irresponsible choice, nor could we do so if he preferred the sacrifice of going away to England. Man makes himself; he is not found ready-made; he makes himself by the choice of his morality, and he cannot but choose a morality, such is the pressure of circumstances upon him. We define man only in relation to his commitments; it is therefore absurd to reproach us for irresponsibility in our choice.

So the first of these less serious reproaches is essentially a misunderstanding of his existentialism. Far from telling a person that it does not matter what he does, that there is no obligation, no ought, no duty, to be committed to, Sartre's existentialism tells a man that he makes himself, forms his own character, and that he does this by the choice of a morality, and that he cannot but choose a morality, such is the pressure of circumstances upon him. He is free; therefore he *is* responsible. He *must* exercise his freedom; therefore he *cannot* be irresponsible.

The second of these less serious reproaches, to which Sartre now turns, is that a Sartrean existentialist cannot pass judgment on any other *pour soi*. He may judge himself, but never anyone else. Thus:

In the *second* place, people say to us, "You are unable to judge others." This is true in one sense and false in another. It is true in this sense, that whenever a man chooses his purpose and his commitment in all clearness and in all sincerity, whatever that purpose may be, it is impossible for him to prefer another. It is true in the sense that we do not believe in progress. Progress implies amelioration; but man is always the same, facing a situation which is always changing, and choice remains always a choice in the situation. The moral problem has not changed since the time when it was a choice between slavery and anti-slavery—from the time of the war of Secession, for example, until the present moment when one chooses between the M.R.P. [*Mouvement Rèpublicain Populaire*] and the Communists.

We can judge, nevertheless, for, as I have said, one chooses in view of others, and in view of others one chooses himself. One can judge, first—and perhaps this is not a judgment of value, but it is a logical judgment—that in certain cases choice is founded upon an error, and in others upon the truth. One can judge a man by saying that he deceives himself. Since we have defined the situation of man as one of free choice, without excuse and without help, any man who takes refuge behind the excuse of his passions, or by inventing some deterministic doctrine, is a self-deceiver. One may object: "But why should he not choose to deceive himself?" I reply that it is not for me to judge him morally, but I define his self-deception as an error. Here one cannot avoid pronouncing a judgment of truth. The self-deception is evidently a falsehood, because it is a dissimulation of man's complete liberty of commitment. Upon this same level, I say that it is also a self-deception if I choose to declare that certain values are incumbent upon me; I am in contradiction with myself if I will these values and at the same time say that they impose themselves upon me. If anyone says to me, "And what if I wish to deceive myself?" I answer, "There is no reason why you should not, but I declare that you are doing so, and that the attitude of strict consistency alone is that of good faith." Furthermore, I can pronounce a moral judgment. For I declare that freedom, in respect of concrete circumstances, can have no other end and aim but itself; and when once a man has seen that values depend upon himself, in that state of forsakenness he can will only one thing, and that is freedom as the foundation of all values. That does not mean that he wills it in the abstract: it simply means that the actions of men of good faith have, as their ultimate significance, the quest of freedom itself as such. A man who belongs to some communist or revolutionary society wills certain concrete ends, which imply the will to freedom, but that freedom is willed in community. We will freedom for freedom's sake, in and through particular circumstances. And in thus willing freedom, we discover that it depends entirely upon the freedom of others and that the freedom of others depends upon our own. Obviously, freedom as the definition of a man does not depend upon others, but as soon as there is a commitment, I am obliged to will the liberty of others at the same time as my own. I cannot make liberty my aim unless I make that of others equally my aim. Consequently, when I recognize, as entirely authentic, that man is a being whose existence precedes his essence, and that he is a free being who cannot, in any circumstances, but will his freedom, at the same time I realize that I cannot not will the freedom of others. Thus, in the name of that will to freedom which is implied in freedom itself, I can form judgments upon those who seek to hide from themselves the wholly voluntary nature of their existence and its complete freedom. Those who hide from this total freedom, in a guise of solemnity or with deterministic excuses, I shall call cowards. Others, who try to show that their existence is necessary, when it is merely an accident of the appearance of the human race on earth—I shall call scum. But neither cowards nor scum can be identified except upon the plane of strict authenticity. Thus, although the content of morality is variable, a certain form of this morality is universal. Kant declared that freedom is a will both to itself and to the freedom of others. Agreed: but he thinks that the formal and the universal suffice for the constitution of a morality. We think, on the contrary, that principles that are too abstract break down when we come to defining action. To take once again the case of that student; by what authority, in the name of what golden rule of morality, do you think he could have decided, in perfect peace of mind, either to abandon his mother or to remain with her? There are no means of judging. The content is always concrete, and therefore unpredictable; it has always to be invented. The one thing that counts, is to know whether the invention is made in the name of freedom.

Let us, for example, examine the two following cases, and you will see how far they are similar in spite of their difference. Let us take *The Mill on the Floss*. We find here a certain young woman, Maggie Tulliver, who is an incarnation of the value of passion and is aware of it. She is in love with a young man, Stephen, who is engaged to another, an insignificant young woman. This Maggie Tulliver, instead of heedlessly seeking her own happiness, chooses in the name of human solidarity to sacrifice herself and to give up the man she loves. On the other hand, La Sanseverina in Stendhal's *Chartreuse de Parme*, believing that it is passion which endows man with his real value, would have declared that a grand passion justifies its sacrifices, and must be preferred to the banality of such conjugal love as would unite Stephen to the little goose he was engaged to marry. It is the latter that she would have chosen to sacrifice in realizing her own happiness, and, as Stendhal shows, she would also sacrifice herself upon the plane of passion if life made that demand upon her. Here we are facing two clearly opposed moralities; but I claim that they are equivalent, seeing that in both cases the overruling aim is freedom. You can imagine two attitudes exactly similar in effect, in that one girl might prefer, in resignation, to give up her lover while the other preferred, in fulfillment of sexual desire, to ignore the prior engagement of the man she loved; and, externally, these two cases might appear the same as the two we have just cited, while being in fact entirely different. The attitude of La Sanseverina is much nearer to that of Maggie Tulliver than to one of careless greed. Thus, you see, the second objection is at once true and false. One can choose anything, but only if it is upon the plane of free commitment.

The third of these less serious reproaches is that when a Sartrean *pour soi* "chooses his values," or "invents new values," it is essentially a trivial because merely idiosyncratic affair. There is no independently existing value that he *ought* to choose. His *oughts* are consequent upon his value choices. There are no "a priori values" that he cannot but choose. He is footloose and fancyfree in this matter, free to "shop around" as pleases him in value choices. There is no God ("*Dieu n'existe pas*") whose values a human *pour soi* is obligated to choose. It is all up to him as a self-sufficient *pour soi*.

And this, the reproach says, trivializes the *pour soi* "choosing his values." Sartre's comments on this third less serious reproach bring his lecture to a close.

The *third* objection, stated by saying, "You take with one hand what you give with the other," means, at bottom, "your values are not serious, since you choose them yourselves." To that I can only say that I am very sorry that it should be so; but if I have excluded God the Father, there must be somebody to invent values. We have to take things as they are. And moreover, to say that we invent values means neither more nor less than this; that there is no sense in life *à priori*. Life is nothing until it is lived; but it is yours to make sense of, and the value of it is nothing else but the sense that you choose. Therefore, you can see that there is a possibility of creating a human community. I have been reproached for suggesting that existentialism is a form of humanism: people have said to me, "But you have written in your *Nausée* that the humanists are wrong, you have even ridiculed a certain type of humanism, why do you now go back upon that?" In reality, the word humanism has two very different meanings. One may understand by humanism a theory which upholds man as the end-in-itself and as the supreme value. Humanism in this sense appears, for instance, in Cocteau's story *Round the World in 80 Hours*, in which one of the characters declares, because he is flying over mountains in an airplane, "Man is magnificent!" This signifies that although I, personally, have not built airplanes I have the benefit of those particular inventions and that I personally, being a man, can consider myself responsible for, and honored by, achievements that are peculiar to some men. It is to assume that we can ascribe value to man according to the most distinguished deeds of certain men. That kind of humanism is absurd, for only the dog or the horse would be in a position to pronounce a general judgment upon man and declare that he is magnificent, which they have never been such fools as to do—at least, not as far as I know. But neither is it admissible that a man should pronounce judgment upon Man. Existentialism dispenses with any judgment of this sort: an existentialist will never take man as the end, since man is still to be determined. And we have no right to believe that humanity is something to which we could set up a cult, after the manner of Auguste Comte. The cult of humanity ends in Comtian humanism, shut-in upon itself, and—this must be said—in Fascism. We do not want a humanism like that.

But there is another sense of the word, of which the fundamental meaning is this: Man is all the time outside of himself: it is in projecting and losing himself beyond himself that he makes man to exist; and, on the other hand, it is by pursuing transcendent aims that he himself is able to exist. Since man is thus self-surpassing, and can grasp objects only in relation to his self-surpassing, he is himself the heart and center of his transcendence. There is no other universe except the human universe, the universe of human subjectivity. This relation of transcendence as constitutive of man (not in the sense that God is transcendent, but in the sense of self-surpassing) with subjectivity (in such a sense that man is not shut up in himself but forever present in a human universe)—it is this that we call existential humanism. This is humanism, because we remind man that there is no legislator but himself; that he himself, thus abandoned, must decide for himself; also because we show that it is not by turning back upon himself, but always by seeking, beyond himself, an aim which is one of liberation or of some particular realization, that man can realize himself as truly human.

You can see from these few reflections that nothing could be more unjust than the objections people raise against us. Existentialism is nothing else but an attempt to draw the full conclusions from a consistently atheistic position. Its intention is not in the least that of plunging men into despair. And if by despair one means—as the Christians do—any attitude of unbelief, the despair of the existentialists is something different. Existentialism is not atheist in the sense that it would exhaust itself in demonstrations of the non-existence of God. It declares, rather, that even if God existed that would make no difference from its point of view. Not that we believe God does exist, but we think that the real problem is not that of His existence; what man needs is to find himself again and to understand that nothing can save him from himself, not even a valid proof of the existence of God. In this sense existentialism is optimistic. It is a doctrine of action, and it is only by self-deception, by confusing their own despair with ours that Christians can describe us as without hope.

READING QUESTIONS

1. He proposes to defend his existentialism against certain reproaches. Jot down any three of these reproaches.
2. For *your* money, which is the most serious objection? Make clear why you think so.
3. For any one objection, show how he meets it.
4. Which objection is he least successful in fending off? Indicate why you think so.
5. "There are two kinds of existentialists." Namely?
6. What do we mean by saying that "existence precedes essence"?
7. A Sartrean existentialist needs such terms as *anguish, abandonment, despair.* Choose one, and explain why.
8. Formulate briefly an *existentialist* reading of the predicament of the wartime student who consulted him.
9. He says, "Any doctrine of probabilities which is not attached to a truth will crumble . . . to define the probable, one must possess the true." Produce an illustration of his point; or, if that is too difficult, an explanation of his point.
10. He says that when people talk about *la condition humaine* (the human condition, the human predicament) they understand, have in mind, the limitations that define man's fundamental situation in the universe. Give an example of this.

11. He says that nowadays people talk more about the "human con-
    dition" than about "human nature." Why do they do this? Give
    an example illustrating the distinction.
12. He says that he is reproached for "confining man within his indi-
    vidual subjectivity." What does it mean to do that? Is it valid
    grounds for reproach?
13. How does he deal with the reproach in question 12?
14. He says, after meeting the charge in question 12, that even yet
    he has not completely refuted the charge of subjectivism. What
    further points in this charge does he refer to?
15. Select one of the "further reproaches" referred to in question 14
    and show how he deals with it.
16. The lecture reproduced in this section was delivered to the Club
    Maintenant. How would you translate that into colloquial En-
    glish? The title of the lecture was *L'Existentialisme est un hu-
    manisme*. How do you interpret that?

INDEPENDENT STUDY

Before tackling any of the following items for independent study,
read F. A. Olafson's article "Sartre" and A. MacIntyre's article "Existentialism," both in the *Encyclopedia of Philosophy*. Also, whatever
you can find on existentialism in the *Critical History of Western Philosophy* edited by D. J. O'Connor.

1. Read one of Sartre's existentialist novels (e.g., *Nausea*), plays
   (e.g., *No Exit*), or short stories (e.g., *The Wall*) and make clear its
   existentialist character.
2. Acquaint yourself sufficiently with the thinking of Sartre's contemporary, Albert Camus, to write an essay on any important doctrinal differences between Sartre and Camus.
3. Contrast any Christian existentialist (e.g., Gabriel Marcel) with
   any atheist existentialist (e.g., Sartre or Heidegger) on points relevant to that difference.
4. Sartre spent time clearing his mind on theories of Marx and
   Freud. Make clear why his existentialism constrained him to do
   this. Indicate briefly the outcome in each case.
5. Consult the portion of *Being and Nothingness* needed for an understanding of Sartre's notion of bad faith (*mauvaise foi*). What
   does he mean by bad faith? Why is that notion an essential component in his existentialism? If a person took no stock in the notion of bad faith, would that show he was not a genuine existentialist?

SECTION 5. CURT JOHN DUCASSE: IS LIFE
AFTER DEATH POSSIBLE?

From Sartre to Ducasse. Each author thus far in this topic ("the nature of man") can be read as addressing himself to the question "What am I? If it is said that I am human, then what is it to be human?" Descartes' answer was "You are a *res cogitans,* a thinking being." Holbach's thesis was negative: "You do not have free will," and this, it seemed, was for him a corollary of the prior claim: "You are part of nature, and there is no free will in nature." James's essay contains a counterattack, working up a dilemma you face if you deny free will to men. Sartre uses Descartes as a point of departure: "You are a being whose existence precedes his essence. You create your essence, your 'nature,' as you live along. In this activity you are radically free. You are a *pour soi.*" So: You are a *res cogitans.* You do not have free will. You do have free will. You are a *pour soi.*

Our author in this section is Curt John Ducasse, a Frenchman who spent most of his life in the United States. Unlike Descartes and Sartre, Ducasse does not address himself directly to the question, "What am I? What is it to be human?" Instead he asks the question, "Do I survive the death of my body?" Like James's, his is an attribute question: "Is free will an attribute of man? Is immortality, survival, an attribute of man?" Also, like James, Ducasse does not propose a categorical "yes," but raises difficulties for the person who proposes a categorical "no." Hence the somewhat modest wording of the title of his lecture: "Is a life after death possible?" indicating that he is addressing himself not so much to the person who says, "I do not survive the death of my body," as to the person who says, "I would go further than that. I would insist that it is not *possible* for a person to survive the death of his body." This is to enter a stronger claim. If something is not possible, then a fortiori it is not actual. If it is not possible for a person to survive the death of his body, then there is no point to asking whether there are any reasons for believing that he in fact does. On the other hand, as the title of Ducasse's lecture indicates, if it is at least possible for a person to survive the death of his body, then it is not silly to ask whether there are any reasons for believing that he may in fact do so. One may then even go on to ask whether these reasons are good and what form such survival might take.

It will be remembered that in the opening sentence of James's lecture on free will versus determinism he remarks that for many persons ("a common opinion prevails") the juice has been pressed out of the free will-determinism controversy. Everyone has heard all the arguments pro and con. This is not to say that determinists are in victorious possession of the field, having sent the friends of free will down to inglorious defeat. It is rather to say that the opposing positions are clear, the arguments on both sides are familiar, and it remains to choose up sides.

That is not the situation in regard to the question of personal immortality as Ducasse sees it. It is rather that for most persons the answer is in, and the question closed: No person survives the death of his body; such a thing is not possible. We must therefore ask ourselves why persons rule out personal immortality as "not possible." What do such persons know, or believe that they know, that is simply and flatly incompatible with the very possibility of personal immortality? From reading and conversation I would propose that their answer would run along these lines:

Natural science has taken away the delusion of a personal God and the delusion of personal free will and the delusion of personal immorality. Science meets the notion of immortality with a direct negative. God, free will, and immortality would mean an end to a science of nature. Physiology declares categorically against immortality. What we know about the human brain and nervous system rules out any notion of survival. A person *is* so many processes studied by physiology, and ultimately by chemistry and physics; or he is by-product of such processes. In either case, when they go, he goes. A person could no more survive the death of his body than two and two could make five.

So much for the "not possible" people. There are also those who insist that, possible or not, many or most people simply do not believe in immortality. I think they would tell you this sort of thing:

Not one person in ten really believes he is going to survive the death of his body. The other nine will tell you that when they are finished, they are finished altogether. For them belief in immortality died on the vine long ago. What issues, great and grave, are decided with reference to belief in personal immortality? Does it enter into the decisions of statesmen, educators, scientists, economists, psychologists, businessmen, labor organizers, military and industrial leaders, and so on? If people believe in a "life after death" why are they so reluctant to "pass on"? Why is not the planet depopulating? There is little evidence that people do, in fact, take serious stock in personal immortality. As one college president said: "Personal immortality may or may not be a truth. It is an idea which has never interested me in the slightest." As Swinburne wrote:

> From too much love of living,
> From hope and fear set free,
> We thank with brief thanksgiving
> Whatever gods may be,

> That no life lives forever,
> That dead men rise up never,
> That even the weariest river
> Winds somewhere safe to sea.

As an English philosopher said: "I have had my share of life. I desire no more, here or hereafter. It is mere restricted imagination to conceive of it." As an American psychologist observed: "A considerable number of people abhor the idea of personal immortality." And let us not forget Bernard Shaw: "Personal immortality is repugnant to me. There is no such thing as personal immortality."

These are the listeners, and subsequent readers, whom Ducasse had in mind when he delivered his California lecture on the question, "Is life after death possible?" His intention is to reopen discussion, to at least get a hearing for the question, to account for intransigent dismissal. He says he will do five things:

1. Ask why people desire and believe in some sort of life after death.
2. State the arguments commonly advanced to prove that such a life after death is impossible.
3. Show that these arguments fail to prove their point.
4. Point out the tacit assumptions that cause them to appear convincing, even though they are not.
5. Consider what forms a life after death might take.

Immanuel Kant used to say that metaphysics, to the extent that it was colorful and humanly important, shook down to a reflective concern with three questions: God, freedom (meaning free will), and immortality. Can the existence of God be demonstrated and His nature defined? Does any human behavior express genuine free will, self-originating, spontaneous autonomy? Does a human being survive the death of his body? Our present author, the late C. J. Ducasse, thought and wrote on all three of Kant's questions. In the present section we are to examine his widely read lecture "Is Life After Death Possible?" The text of this lecture begins with three introductory paragraphs, which are here given numbers that they do not have in the original:

1. The question whether human personality survives death is sometimes asserted to be one upon which reflection is futile. Only empirical evidence, it is said, can be relevant, since the question is purely one of fact.
2. But no question is purely one of fact until it is clearly understood; and this one is, on the contrary, ambiguous and replete with tacit assumptions. Until the ambiguities have been removed and the assumptions critically ex-

amined, we do not really know just what it is we want to know when we ask whether a life after death is possible. Nor, therefore, can we tell until then what bearing on this question various facts empirically known to us may have.

3. To clarify its meaning is chiefly what I now propose to attempt. I shall ask first why a future life is so generally desired and believed in. Then I shall state, as convincingly as I can in the time available, the arguments commonly advanced to prove that such a life is impossible. After that, I shall consider the logic of these arguments, and show that they quite fail to establish the impossibility. Next, the tacit but arbitrary assumption, which makes them nevertheless appear convincing, will be pointed out.

These assumptions, it may be, cause these arguments to appear sound and convincing. If, however, these assumptions themselves are arbitrary, then they do not provide a rational foundation for those arguments.

Why, then, do people desire and believe in a life after death?

To begin with, let us note that each of us here has been alive and conscious at all times in the past which he can remember. It is true that sometimes our bodies are in deep sleep, or made inert by anesthetics or injuries. But even at such times we do not experience unconsciousness in ourselves, for to experience it would mean being conscious of being unconscious, and this is a contradiction. The only experience of unconsciousness in ourselves we ever have is, not experience of total unconsciousness, but of unconsciousness *of this or that;* as when we report: "I am not conscious of any pain," or "of any bell-sound," or "of any difference between those two colors," etc. Nor do we ever experience unconsciousness in another person, but only the fact that, sometimes, some or all of the ordinary activities of his body cease to occur. That consciousness itself is extinguished at such times is thus only a hypothesis which we construct to account for certain changes in the behavior of another person's body or to explain in him or in ourselves the eventual lack of memories relating to the given period.

Being alive and conscious is thus, with all men, a lifelong experience and habit; and conscious life is therefore something they naturally—even if tacitly—expect to continue. As J. B. Pratt has pointed out, the child takes the continuity of life for granted. It is the fact of death that has to be taught him. But when he has learned it, and the idea of a future life is then put explicitly before his mind, it seems to him the most natural thing in the world.

The witnessing of death, however, is a rare experience for most of us, and, because it breaks so sharply into our habits, it forces on us the question whether the mind, which until then was manifested by the body now dead, continues somehow to live on, or, on the contrary, has become totally extinct. This question is commonly phrased as concerning "the immortality of the soul," and immortality, strictly speaking, means survival forever. But assurance of survival for some considerable period—say a thousand, or even a hundred, years—would probably have almost as much present psychological value as would assurance of survival strictly forever. Most men would be troubled very little by the idea of extinction at so distant a time—even less troubled than is now a healthy and happy youth by the idea that he will die in fifty or sixty years. Therefore, it is survival for some time, rather than survival specifically forever, that I shall alone consider.

The craving for continued existence is very widespread. Even persons who believe that death means complete extinction of the individual's consciousness often find comfort in various substitute conceptions of survival. They may, for instance, dwell on the continuity of the individual's germ plasm in his descendants. Or they find solace in the thought that, the past being indestructible, their individual life remains eternally an intrinsic part of the history of the world. Also—and more satisfying to one's craving for personal importance—there is the fact that since the acts of one's life have effects, and these in turn further effects, and so on, therefore what one has done goes on forever influencing remotely, and sometimes greatly, the course of future events.

Gratifying to one's vanity, too, is the prospect that, if the achievements of one's life have been great or even only conspicuous, or one's benefactions or evil deeds have been notable, one's name may not only be remembered by acquaintances and relatives for a little while, but may live on in recorded history. But evidently survival in any of these senses is but a consolation prize—but a thin substitute for the continuation of conscious individual life, which may not be a fact, but which most men crave nonetheless.

The roots of this craving are certain desires which death appears to frustrate. For some, the chief of these is for reunion with persons dearly loved. For others, whose lives have been wretched, it is the desire for another chance at the happiness they have missed. For others yet, it is desire for further opportunity to grow in ability, knowledge or character. Often, there is also the desire, already mentioned, to go on counting for something in the affairs of men. And again, a future life for oneself and others is often desired in order that the redressing of the many injustices of this life shall be possible. But it goes without saying that, although desires such as these are often sufficient to cause belief in a future life, they constitute no evidence at all that it is a fact.

In this connection, it may be well to point out that, although both the belief in survival and the belief in the existence of a god or gods are found in most religions, nevertheless there is no necessary connection between the two beliefs. No contradiction would be involved in supposing either that there is a God but no life after death or that there is a life after death but no God. The belief that there is a life after death may be tied to a religion, but it is no more intrinsically religious than would be a belief that there is life on the planet Mars. The after-death world, if it exists, is just another region or dimension of the universe.

But although belief in survival of death is natural and easy and has always been held in one form or another by a large majority of mankind, critical reflection quickly bring forth a number of apparently strong reasons to regard that belief as quite illusory.

A belief in some kind of life after death comes easily and naturally to most people. That has been Ducasse's first point thus far.

However, it is equally true that critical reflection has come up with apparently strong reasons for regarding such belief as groundless, as exercises in wishful thinking. So these deflationary reasons will be reviewed. The first is that consciousness *depends* on the nervous system. Thus:

> There are, *first* of all, a number of facts which definitely suggest that both the existence and the nature of consciousness wholly depend on the presence of a functioning nervous system. It is pointed out, for example, that wherever consciousness is observed, it is found associated with a living and functioning body. Further, when the body dies, or the head is struck a heavy blow, or some anesthetic is administered, the familiar outward evidences of consciousness terminate, permanently or temporarily. Again, we know well that drugs of various kinds—alcohol, caffein, opium, heroin, and many others—cause specific changes at the time in the nature of a person's mental states. Also, by stimulating in appropriate ways the body's sense organs, corresponding states of consciousness—namely, the various kinds of sensations—can be caused at will. On the other hand, cutting a sensory nerve immediately eliminates a whole range of sensations.
>
> Again, the contents of consciousness, the mental powers, or even the personality, are modified in characteristic ways when certain regions of the brain are destroyed by disease or injury or are disconnected from the rest by such an operation as prefrontal lobotomy. And that the nervous system is the indispensable basis of mind is further suggested by the fact that, in the evolutionary scale, the degree of intelligence of various species of animals keeps pace closely with the degree of development of their brain.

The first reason against a belief in personal survival came down to this: Consciousness *depends* on the proper functioning of a living nervous system. When, therefore, the nervous system dies, consciousness loses its hold on existence. When your nervous system dies, you go out like a light. The *second* reason is the claim not that consciousness depends on the nervous system, but that it *is identical with* minute physical or chemical events that take place in the brain. Identity is a much closer relation than dependence:

> That continued existence of mind after death is impossible has been argued also on the basis of theoretical considerations. It has been contended, for instance, that what we call states of consciousness—or more particularly, ideas, sensations, volitions, feelings, and the like—are really nothing but the minute physical or chemical events which take place in the tissues of the brain. For, it is urged, it would be absurd to suppose that an idea or a volition, if it is not itself a material thing or process, could cause material effects such as contractions of muscles.

The argument from dependence and the argument from identity are perhaps the most compelling reasons, for most people, against a belief that a person lives on after his body dies. However, Ducasse draws attention to several more; for example:

Moreover, it is maintained that the possibility of causation of a material event by an immaterial, mental cause is ruled out *a priori* by the principle of the conservation of energy; for such causation would mean that an additional quantity of energy suddenly pops into the nervous system out of nowhere.

Another conception of consciousness, which is more often met with today than the one just mentioned, but which also implies that consciousness cannot survive death, is that "consciousness" is only the name we give to certain types of behavior, which differentiate the higher animals from all other things in nature. According to this view, to say, for example, that an animal is conscious of a difference between two stimuli means nothing more than that it responds to each by different behavior. That is, the difference of *behavior* is what consciousness of difference between the stimuli *consists in;* and is not, as is commonly assumed, only the behavioral *sign* of something mental and not public, called "consciousness that the stimuli are different."

Or *again,* consciousness, of the typically human sort called thought, is identified with the typically human sort of behavior called speech; and this, again not in the sense that speech *expresses* or *manifests* something different from itself, called "thought," but in the sense that speech—whether uttered or only whispered—*is* thought itself. And obviously, if thought, or any mental activity, is thus but some mode of behavior of the living body, the mind cannot possibly survive death.

Still *another* difficulty confronting the hypothesis of survival becomes evident when one imagines in some detail what survival would have to include in order to satisfy the desires which cause man to crave it. It would, of course, have to include persistence not alone of consciousness, but also of personality; that is, of the individual's character, acquired knowledge, cultural skills and interests, memories, and awareness of personal identity. But even this would not be enough, for what man desires is not bare survival, but to go on living in some objective way. And this means to go on meeting new situations and, by exerting himself to deal with them, to broaden and deepen his experience and develop his latent capacities.

But it is hard to imagine this possible without a body and an environment for it, upon which to act and from which to receive impressions. And, if a body and an environment were supposed, but not material and corruptible ones, then it is paradoxical to think that, under such radically different conditions, a given personality could persist.

To take a crude but telling analogy, it is past belief that, if the body of any one of us were suddenly changed into that of a shark or an octopus, and placed in the ocean, his personality could, for more than a very short time, if at all, survive intact so radical a change of environment and of bodily form.

Thus far Professor Ducasse has asked why so many people find some form of personal survival to be both desirable and credible, and why, nevertheless, other people, more tough-minded perhaps, consider such belief to be lacking sufficient objective evidence. He now asks why these skeptics find their reasons for rejecting a belief in life after death to be strong enough to justify such rejection. Thus:

Such, in brief, are the chief reasons commonly advanced for holding that survival is impossible. Scrutiny of them, however, will, I think, reveal that they are not as strong as they first seem and far from strong enough to show that there can be no life after death.

Let us consider *first* the assertion that "thought," or "consciousness," is but another name for subvocal speech, or for some other form of behavior, or for molecular processes in the tissues of the brain. As Paulsen and others have pointed out, no evidence ever is or can be offered to support that assertion, because it is in fact but a disguised proposal to make the words "thought," "feeling," "sensation," "desire," and so on, denote facts quite different from those which these words are commonly employed to denote. To say that those words are but other names for certain chemical or behavioral events is as grossly arbitrary as it would be to say that "wood" is but another name for glass, or "potato" but another name for cabbage. What thought, desire, sensation, and other mental states are like, each of us can observe directly by introspection; and what introspection reveals is that they do not in the least resemble muscular contraction, or glandular secretion, or any other known bodily events. No tampering with language can alter the observable fact that thinking is one thing and muttering quite another; that the feeling called anger has no resemblance to the bodily behavior which usually goes with it; or that an act of will is not in the least like anything we find when we open the skull and examine the brain. Certain mental events are doubtless connected in some way with certain bodily events, but they are not those bodily events themselves. The connection is not identity.

This being clear, let us *next* consider the arguments offered to show that mental processes, although not identical with bodily processes, nevertheless depend on them. We are told, for instance, that some head injuries, or anesthetics, totally extinguish consciousness for the time being. As already pointed out, however, the strict fact is only that the usual bodily signs of consciousness are then absent. But they are also absent when a person is asleep; and yet, at the same time, dreams, which are states of consciousness, may be occurring.

It is true that when the person concerned awakens, he often remembers his dreams, whereas the person that has been anesthetized or injured has usually no memories relating to the period of apparent blankness. But this could mean that his consciousness was, for the first time, dissociated from its ordinary channels of manifestation, as was reported of the co-conscious personalities of some of the patients of Dr. Morton Prince. Moreover, it sometimes occurs that a person who has been in an accident reports lack of memories not only for the period during which his body was unresponsive but also for a period of several hours *before* the accident, during which he had given to his associates all the ordinary external signs of being conscious as usual.

But, more generally, if absence of memories relating to a given period proved unconsciousness for that period, this would force us to conclude that we were unconscious during the first few years of our lives, and indeed have been so most of the time since; for the fact is that we have no memories whatever of most of our days. That we were alive and conscious on any long past specific date is, with only a few exceptions, not something we actually remember, but only something which we infer must be true.

At this point Professor Ducasse launches into a protracted exposition and defense of psychical research. He finds this necessary because some persons argue that we have no evidence that a person (or his mind) survives the death of his body, and because this rejects as mistaken all the research and findings and theorizings of the members of the Society for Psychical Research, and because he (Professor Ducasse) is a committed member of many years' standing of the society in question. So:

Another argument advanced against survival was, it will be remembered, that death must extinguish the mind, since all manifestations of it then cease. But to assert that they invariably then cease is to ignore altogether the considerable amount of evidence to the contrary, gathered over many years and carefully checked by the Society for Psychical Research. This evidence, which is of a variety of kinds, has been reviewed by Professor Gardner Murphy in an article published in the Journal of the Society. He mentions first the numerous well-authenticated cases of apparition of a dead person to others as yet unaware that he had died or even been ill or in danger. The more strongly evidential cases of apparition are those in which the apparition conveys to the person who sees it specific facts until then secret. An example would be that of the apparition of a girl to her brother nine years after her death, with a conspicuous scratch on her cheek. Their mother then revealed to him that she herself had made that scratch accidentally while preparing her daughter's body for burial, but that she had then at once covered it with powder and never mentioned it to anyone.

Another famous case is that of a father whose apparition some time after death revealed to one of his sons the existence and location of an unsuspected second will, benefiting him, which was then found as indicated. Still another case would be the report by General Barter, then a subaltern in the British Army in India, of the apparition to him of a lieutenant he had not seen for two or three years. The lieutenant's apparition was riding a brown pony with black mane and tail. He was much stouter than at their last meeting, and, whereas formerly clean-shaven, he now wore a peculiar beard in the form of a fringe encircling his face. On inquiry the next day from a person who had known the lieutenant at the time he died, it turned out that he had indeed become very bloated before his death; that he had grown just such a beard while on the sick list; and that he had some time before bought and eventually ridden to death a pony of that very description.

Other striking instances are those of an apparition seen simultaneously by several persons. It is on record that an apparition of a child was perceived first by a dog, that the animal's rushing at it, loudly barking, interrupted the conversation of the seven persons present in the room, thus drawing their attention to the apparition, and that the latter then moved through the room for some fifteen seconds, followed by the barking dog.

Another type of empirical evidence of survival consists of communications, purporting to come from the dead, made through the persons commonly called sensitives, mediums, or automatists. Some of the most remarkable of these communications were given by the celebrated American medium, Mrs. Piper, who for many years was studied by the Society for Psychical Research, London, with the most elaborate precautions against all possibility of fraud. Twice, particularly, the evidences of identity supplied by the dead persons who purportedly were thus communicating with the living were of the very kinds, and of the same precision and detail which would ordinarily satisfy a living person of the identity of another living person with whom he was not able to communicate directly, but only through an intermediary, or by letter or telephone.

Again, sometimes the same mark of identity of a dead person, or the same message from him, or complementary parts of one message, are obtained independently from two mediums in different parts of the world.

Of course, when facts of these kinds are recounted, as I have just done, only in abstract summary, they make little if any impression upon us. And the very word "medium" at once brings to our minds the innumerable instances of demonstrated fraud perpetrated by charlatans to extract money from the credulous bereaved. But the modes of trickery and sources of error, which immediately suggest themselves to us as easy, natural explanations of the seemingly extraordinary facts, suggest themselves just as quickly to the members of the research committees of the Society for Psychical Research. Usually, these men have had a good deal more experience than the rest of us with the tricks of conjurers and fraudulent mediums, and take against them precautions far more strict and ingenious than would occur to the average sceptic.

But when, instead of stopping at summaries, one takes the trouble to study the detailed, original reports, it then becomes evident that they cannot all be just laughed off; for to accept the hypothesis of fraud or mal-observation would often require more credulity than to accept the facts reported.

To *explain* those facts, however, is quite another thing. Only two hypotheses at all adequate to do so have yet been advanced. One is that the communications really come, as they purport to do, from persons who have died and have survived death. The other is the hypothesis of telepathy—that is, the supposition, itself startling enough, that the medium is able to gather information directly from the minds of others, and that this is the true source of the information communicated. To account for all the facts, however, this hypothesis has to be stretched very far, for some of them require us to suppose that the medium can tap the minds even of persons far away and quite unknown to him, and can tap even the subconscious part of their minds.

Diverse highly ingenious attempts have been made to devise conditions that would rule out telepathy as a possible explanation of the communications received; but some of the most critical and best-documented investigators still hold that it has not yet been absolutely excluded. Hence, although some of the facts recorded by psychical research constitute, prima facie, strong empirical evidence of survival, they cannot be said to establish it beyond question. But they do show that we need to revise rather radically in some respects our ordinary ideas of what is and is not possible in nature.

Having spoken up on behalf of psychical research as a not impossible, not intellectually disreputable source of evidence that persons, at least some persons, do apparently live on after the deaths of their bodies, Professor Ducasse returns to his critical review of stock arguments against belief in such survival. Thus:

Let us now turn to *another* of the arguments against survival. That states of consciousness entirely depend on bodily processes, and therefore cannot continue when the latter have ceased, is proved, it is argued, by the fact that various states of consciousness—in particular, the several kinds of sensations—can be caused at will by appropriately stimulating the body.

Now, it is very true that sensations and some other mental states can be so caused; but we have just as good and abundant evidence that mental states can cause various bodily events. John Laird mentions, among others, the fact that merely willing to raise one's arm normally suffices to cause it to rise; that a hungry person's mouth is caused to water by the idea of food; that feelings of rage, fear or excitement cause digestion to stop; that anxiety causes changes in the quantity and quality of the milk of a nursing mother; that certain thoughts cause tears, pallor, blushing or fainting; and so on. The evidence we have that the relation is one of cause and effect is exactly the same here as where bodily processes cause mental states.

It is said, of course, that to suppose something non-physical, such as thought, to be capable of causing motion of a physical object, such as the body, is absurd. But I submit that if the heterogeneity of mind and matter makes this absurd, then it makes equally absurd the causation of mental states by stimulation of the body. Yet no absurdity is commonly found in the assertion that cutting the skin causes a feeling of pain, or that alcohol, caffein, bromides, and other drugs, cause characteristic states of consciousness. As David Hume made clear long ago, no kind of causal connection is intrinsically absurd. Anything might cause anything; and only observation can tell us what in fact can cause what.

Somewhat similar remarks would apply to the allegation that the principle of the conservation of energy precludes the possibility of causation of a physical event by a mental event. For if it does, then it equally precludes causation in the converse direction, and this, of course, would leave us totally at a loss to explain the occurrence of sensations. But, as Keeton and others have pointed out, that energy is conserved is not something observation has revealed or could reveal, but only a postulate—a defining postulate for the notion of an "isolated physical system."

That is, conservation of energy is something one has to have if, but only if, one insists on conceiving the physical world as wholly self-contained, independent, isolated. And just because the metaphysics which the natural sciences tacitly assume does insist on so conceiving the physical world, this metaphysics compels them to save conservation by postulations *ad hoc* whenever dissipation of energy is what observation reveals. It postulates, for instance, that something else, which appears at such times but was not until then regarded as energy, is energy too, but it is then said, "in a different form."

Furthermore, as Broad has emphasized, all that the principle of conservation requires is that when a quantity Q of energy disappears at one place in the physical world an equal quantity of it should appear at some other place there. And the supposition that, in some cases, what causes it to disappear here and appear there is some mental event, such perhaps as a volition, does not violate at all the supposition that energy is conserved.

A word, next, on the parallelism between the degree of development of the nervous systems of various animals and the degree of their intelligence. This is alleged to prove that the latter is the product of the former. But the facts lend themselves equally well to the supposition that, on the contrary, an obscurely felt need for greater intelligence in the circumstances the animal faced was what brought about the variations which eventually resulted in a more adequate nervous organization.

In the development of the individual, at all events, it seems clear that the specific, highly complex nerve connections which become established in the brain and cerebellum of, for instance, a skilled pianist are the results of his will over many years to acquire the skill.

We must not forget in this context that there is a converse, equally consistent with the facts, for the theory, called epiphenomenalism, that mental states are related to the brain much as the halo is to the saint, that is, as effects but never as causes. The converse theory which might be called hypophenomenalism, and which is pretty well that of Schopenhauer, is that the instruments which the various mechanisms of the body constitute are the objective products of obscure cravings for the corresponding powers; and, in particular, that the organization of the nervous system is the effect and material isomorph of the variety of mental functions exercised at a given level of animal or human existence.

Professor Ducasse has now scrutinized most of the stock reasons that skeptics produce in defense of their doubts and rejections. He has found these "skeptical doubts" less than convincing. If stronger, better reasons for their doubts and denials are not forthcoming, he, for one, will feel free to consider survival as *not* a proven impossibility." By way of concluding this part of his lecture, Professor Ducasse asks why so many persons find these arguments against survival to be convincing. This is usually a good question to ask. If you have examined a man's arguments on a certain matter, and found them uniformly weak and unconvincing, it is a good thing to ask why, nevertheless, he finds them convincing. Why does he?

It is, I believe, because these persons approach the question of survival with a certain unconscious metaphysical bias. It derives from a particular initial assumption which they tacitly make. It is that *to be real is to be material.* And to be material, of course, is to be some process or part of the perceptually public world, that is, of the world we all perceive by means of our so-called five senses.

Now the assumption that to be real is to be material is a useful and appropriate one for the purpose of investigating the material world and of operating upon it; and this purpose is a legitimate and frequent one. But those persons, and most of us, do not realize that the validity of that assumption is strictly relative to that specific purpose. Hence they, and most of us, continue making the assumption, and it continues to rule judgment, even when, as now, the purpose in view is a different one, for which the assumption is no longer useful or even congruous.

The point is all-important here and therefore worth stressing. Its essence is that the conception of the nature of reality that proposes to define the real as the material is not the expression of an observable fact to which everyone would have to bow, but is the expression only of a certain direction of interest on the part of the persons who so define reality—of interest, namely, which they have chosen to center wholly in the material, perceptually public world. This specialized interest is of course as legitimate as any other, but it automatically ignores all the facts, commonly called facts of mind, which only introspection reveals. And that specialized interest is what alone compels persons in its grip to employ the word "mind" to denote, instead of what it commonly does denote, something else altogether, namely, the public behavior of bodies that have minds.

Only so long as one's judgment is swayed unawares by that special interest do the logically weak arguments against the possibility of survival which we have examined, seem strong.

It is possible, however, and just as legitimate, as well as more conducive to a fair view of our question, to center one's interest at the start on the facts of mind as introspectively observable, ranking them as most real in the sense that they are the facts the intrinsic nature of which we most directly experience, the facts which we most certainly know to exist; and moreover, that they are the facts without the experiencing of which we should not know any other facts whatever—such, for instance, as those of the material world.

The sort of perspective one gets from this point of view is what I propose now to sketch briefly. For one thing, the material world is then seen to be but one among other objects of our consciousness. Moreover, one becomes aware of the crucially important fact that it is an object postulated rather than strictly given. What this means may be made clearer by an example. Suppose that, perhaps in a restaurant we visit for the first time, an entire wall is occupied by a large mirror and we look into it without realizing that it is a mirror. We then perceive, in the part of space beyond it, various material objects, notwithstanding that in fact they have no existence there at all. A certain set of the vivid color images which we call visual sensations was all that was strictly given to us, and these we construed, automatically and instantaneously, but nonetheless erroneously, as signs or appearances of the existence of certain material objects at a certain place.

Again, and similarly, we perceive in our dreams various objects which at the time we take as physical but which eventually we come to believe were not so. And this eventual conclusion, let it be noted, is forced upon us not because we then detect that something, called "physical substance," was lacking in those objects, but only because we notice, as we did not at the time, that their behavior was erratic—incoherent with their ordinary one.

That is, their appearance was a *mere* appearance, deceptive in the sense that it did not then predict truly, as ordinarily it does, their later appearances. This, it is important to notice, is the *only* way in which we ever discover that an object we perceive was not really physical, or was not the particular sort of physical object we judged it to be.

These two examples illustrate the fact that our perception of physical objects is sometimes erroneous. But the essential point is that, even when it is veridical instead of erroneous, *all* that is literally and directly given to our minds is still only *some set of sensations*. These, on a given occasion, may be only color sensations; but they often include also tactual sensations, sounds, odors, and so on. It is especially interesting, however, to remark here in passing that, with respect to almost all the many thousands of persons and other "physical" objects we have perceived in a life time, *vivid color images* were the only data our perceiving strictly had to go by; so that, if the truth should happen to have been that those objects, like ghosts or images in a mirror, were actually intangible—that is, were *only* color images—we should never have discovered that this was the fact. For all we *directly* know, it *may* have been the fact!

To perceive a physical object, then, instead of merely experiencing passively certain sensations (something which perhaps hardly ever occurs), is always to *interpret*, that is to *construe*, given sensations as signs of, and appearances to us of, a postulated something other than themselves, which we believe is causing them in us and is capable of causing in us others of specific kinds. We believe this because we believe that our sensations too must have some cause, and we find none of them among our other mental states.

Such a postulated extramental something we call "a physical object." We say that we observe physical objects, and this is true. But it is important for the present purpose to be clear that we "observe" them never in any more direct or literal manner than is constituted by the process of interpretive postulation just described—never, for example, in the wholly direct and literal manner in which we are able to observe our sensations themselves and our other mental states.

That perception of a physical object is thus always the product of two factors—one, a set of sensations simply given to us, and the other an act of interpretation of these, performed by us—is something which easily escapes notice and has even been denied. This, however, is only because the interpretive act is almost always automatic, instantaneous, and correct—like, for instance, that of thinking of the meaning of any familiar word we hear. But that an interpretive act does occur is forced on our attention when, in a particular case, we discover that we misconstrued the meaning of the sensations. Or, again, the interpretive act is noticeable when, because the sensations are too scant and therefore ambiguous, we catch ourselves hesitating between two or more possible interpretations of them and say that we are not sure what object it is we see.

The reader should recall Ducasse's intentions as expressed in the title that he chose for his lecture. The title was, "Is Life After Death Possible?" The author's stated intentions do not go beyond that. He is not trying to prove that a person does indeed survive the death of his body. How would he go about doing that? His lecture is a defensive skirmish directed against those persons who insist that survival is not possible, and that therefore any belief in it is an "impossible belief." Ducasse's defensive strategy is to insist that their arguments are not coercive and that their obliviousness to this may well stem from an unsuspected or unacknowledged metaphysical bias.

READING QUESTIONS

1. Ducasse proposes to do five things in his lecture. Jot them down in the right order.
2. "Survival in any of these senses is but a consolation prize, a thin substitute." Three examples of what Ducasse means here.
3. "Desires such as these often cause belief in a future life but they constitute no evidence for such a belief." Two examples. Could you add a possibly more urgent desire than those Ducasse mentions? If, as he says, desires cause belief in a future life, can it also be said that desires cause disbelief in a future life?
4. Ducasse says there is no necessary connection between belief in God and belief in personal survival. Why have people thought there was?
5. Ducasse reviews five reasons that people give for doubting or denying "life after death." State each briefly. Which of those reasons you find (a) most, (b) least convincing. Why?
6. Ducasse reviews those five reasons and criticizes them. State each criticism briefly.
7. "Only two hypotheses explain adequately the evidence gathered by SPR." Namely. Which does Ducasse prefer? Why?
8. Perception of a physical object is the product of two factors, neither of which is the physical object. (a) Namely? (b) Therefore what?

INDEPENDENT STUDY

1. Read the article "Ducasse" by V. Tomas and the article "Immortality" by A. Flew in the *Encyclopedia of Philosophy*. If you need more, read the article "Immortality" by S. H. Mellone in Hastings's *Encyclopedia of Religion and Ethics*. With Ducasse, Flew, and Mellone to draw on, write a paper making clear *what* you

think on the question of personal immortality and *why* you think it.

2. Read Plato's dialogue "Phaedo" and some helpful commentary on it. This dialogue is one of the ancient world's classic handlings of the question of personal immortality, as great in its way as Plato's "Symposium" on love. Give an account of the argument between Socrates and his friends. Are they persuaded? Are you? If not, why not?

3. You may prefer to ignore Ducasse, Flew, Mellone, and Plato and to concentrate on yourself. Purely as a pump primer, just to get your own mind turning over, you could read William James's lecture "Human Immortality." Then study the following questions. Use them as aids, as goads to finding out what *you* think and why *you* think it. There are eight of these questions. Arrange them in any order you see fit. Write out your answers. Do not be surprised if each answer takes a page of writing.

   a. Would you get a bigger jolt from discovering (1) that you do or (2) that you do not survive the death of your body? Why?

   b. What, in your judgment, is the greatest obstacle to believing in such survival?

   c. Which: (1) we have no evidence for such survival, or (2) we have evidence that there is no such survival.

   d. Is an atheist being inconsistent if he believes in a personal life after death?

   e. Why does discussion of the survival question frequently lead to discussion of (1) materialism and (2) empiricism? Are those two beliefs compatible? Is either of them true? Can we speak of evidence for or against either?

   f. State the verifiability theory of meaning. Does it have any bearing on the claim that a person survives the death of his body?

   g. Can you use the belief in personal survival to illustrate what is meant by (1) inductive, (2) deductive, (3) pragmatic support for belief?

   h. Is belief in such survival similar to the belief that

   (1) The radii of a circle are equal.

   (2) There is another side to the moon.

   (3) The sun will rise tomorrow.

   (4) Other people have minds.

   (5) Every event has a cause.

   (6) No surface is both red all over and green all over.

   (7) Sense data do not have a reverse side.

   (8) If the act was wrong, you should not have done it.

   (9) If a proposition is true, then it is consistent with every other true proposition.

SECTION 6. GILBERT RYLE: DESCARTES' MYTH

In the tradition that Descartes inherited, a human mind was said to be a *created* (not procreated) *spiritual* (not material) *substance* (not attribute), obscurely related to body, rational, active, free, and immortal. For him the question was how many of these claims he could show were not-doubtables, or were dependent upon claims that were not-doubtables. In respect to one or another of these claims, Descartes, James, Sartre, and Ducasse were supportive of this tradition. Holbach in the middle span of the eighteenth century (1730–1770) and Ryle in the middle span of the twentieth century (1930–1970) rejected the tradition. Holbach spoke of the illusion of free will, and Ryle speaks of Descartes' myth. In point of style, however, where Holbach works with a broadax, Ryle works with a fret saw or a scalpel.

Biographical Note on Ryle.   Gilbert Ryle was born in 1900. His academic education was received at Oxford. He taught there until his recent retirement. He succeeded R. G. Collingwood as Waynfleet professor of metaphysical philosophy at the University of Oxford at the end of World War II. He succeeded G. E. Moore as editor of the distinguished philosophical journal *Mind* in 1947. He published his most important and influential book, *The Concept of Mind,* in 1949. For the years 1945–1960 he was one of the most widely read and influential philosophers in the Anglo-American academic world. The reasons for this are to be found in the volumes of *Mind*, in his *Concept of Mind* (1949), his *Dilemmas* (1954), his *Plato's Progress* (1966), and his two volumes of *Collected Papers* (1971).

The Argument of the Selection.   The following selection, *Descartes' Myth,* is Chapter One of Gilbert Ryle's *Concept of Mind,* published in 1949. In this chapter Ryle sets the problem for his book: How should we conceive of the nature of a mind and its relation to a body? This chapter is a famous document. It describes what its author calls the "official doctrine" held by most persons in the Western world, especially since Descartes' lifetime, concerning the nature of a mind and its relation to a body. As formulated by the author, the theory is seen to bristle with "theoretical" difficulties.

The chapter is divided into three sections and a brief terminal historical note. The first section states the so-called official theory, underscoring some of its major "difficult" consequences. The second section formulates these difficulties as so many "absurdities"; and traces these absurdity-producing difficulties to one all-inclusive, all-encompassing, theoretical mistake, called by the author the "category-mistake." This mistake is then described, illustrated, and claimed to be the major source of the absurdities that mark the traditional "official" view of the nature of a person's mind and its relation to his body. The third section tries to account for this major "category-mistake" in modern thinking about person's minds in relation to their bodies. That is, what aspects of intellectual history lent plausibility to the "official" view and led those who hold it to overlook the theoretical absurdities in that view?

Section One, "The Official Doctrine," is a vivid and deflationary account of how, in point of historical fact, many, indeed most, people conceive of a person in terms of a body–mind dualism. It repays careful reading and reflection. Try it on for size. Is this how you think about your mind in relation to your body? Every person, the view runs, has a mind and a body, or *is* a combination, a union, of his mind and his body. Bodies are located in space and are subject to mechanical laws. Not so minds. They are not located in space, have no spatial dimensions, no spatial size or shape; and are not subject to mechanical laws. Frequently the terms *external* and *internal, outer* and *inner,* used in a metaphorical sense, are applied to bodies and minds, respectively. Bodies have surfaces, can meet and collide and jolt; minds have no surfaces, cannot meet "head on." The relation between spatial bodies and nonspatial minds is obscure indeed. How they can influence each other, "interact," is a difficult theoretical question; and the question will threaten the theory as long as the theory is held. Events in one body can directly cause events in another body. Events in one mind, it would seem, do not because they could not directly cause events in a body. If so, can it be claimed that events in one mind can cause events in another mind? If not, minds are shut out from their bodies and shut off from each other. The difficulties do not stop there. Bodily processes can be observed by second-party observers: I can observe that your body is blanching and sweating and trembling. But I cannot thus observe workings in your mind. They are not witnessable by me. They are "private" to you. I can observe your body wince. I cannot feel your pain. Each of us has direct and unchallengeable knowledge of at least some events in our own minds, but none of events in each other's minds. I can observe what happens to or goes on in your body. I may infer from that to what happens to or goes on in your mind; but I have no way of confirming that inference by any observation. To sharpen the question: Does any person have any good reason for believing in the existence of other minds? Other bodies, yes; other minds, how so? Each person has two "histories": the history of his bodily events and the history of his mental events. But what is the relation between these two "histories"?

(1) *The Official Doctrine*

There is a doctrine about the nature and place of minds which is so prevalent among theorists and even among laymen that it deserves to be described as the official theory. Most philosophers, psychologists and religious teachers subscribe, with minor reservations, to its main articles and, although they admit certain theoretical difficulties in it, they tend to assume that these can be overcome without serious modifications being made to the architecture of the theory. It will be argued here that the central principles of the doctrine are unsound and conflict with the whole body of what we know about minds when we are not speculating about them.

The official doctrine, which hails chiefly from Descartes, is something like this. With the doubtful exceptions of idiots and infants in arms every human being has both a body and a mind. Some would prefer to say that every human being is both a body and a mind. His body and his mind are ordinarily harnessed together, but after the death of the body his mind may continue to exist and function.

Human bodies are in space and are subject to the mechanical laws which govern all other bodies in space. Bodily processes and states can be inspected by external observers. So a man's bodily life is as much a public affair as are the lives of animals and reptiles and even as the careers of trees, crystals and planets.

But minds are not in space, nor are their operations subject to mechanical laws. The workings of one mind are not witnessable by other observers; its career is private. Only I can take direct cognisance of the states and processes of my own mind. A person therefore lives through two collateral histories, one consisting of what happens in and to his body, the other consisting of what happens in and to his mind. The first is public, the second private. The events in the first history are events in the physical world, those in the second are events in the mental world.

It has been disputed whether a person does or can directly monitor all or only some of the episodes of his own private history; but, according to the official doctrine, of at least some of these episodes he has direct and unchallengeable cognisance. In consciousness, self-consciousness and introspection he is directly and authentically apprised of the present states and operations of his mind. He may have great or small uncertainties about concurrent and adjacent episodes in the physical world, but he can have none about at least part of what is momentarily occupying his mind.

It is customary to express this bifurcation of his two lives and of his two worlds by saying that the things and events which belong to the physical world, including his own body, are external, while the workings of his own mind are internal. This antithesis of outer and inner is of course meant to be construed as a metaphor, since minds, not being in space, could not be described as being spatially inside anything else, or as having things going on spatially inside themselves. But relapses from this good intention are common and theorists are found speculating how stimuli, the physical sources of which are yards or miles outside a person's skin, can generate mental responses inside his skull, or how decisions framed inside his cranium can set going movements of his extremities.

Even when "inner" and "outer" are construed as metaphors, the problem how a person's mind and body influence one another is notoriously charged with theoretical difficulties. What the mind wills, the legs, arms and the tongue execute; what effects the ear and the eye has something to do with what the mind perceives; grimaces and smiles betray the mind's moods and bodily castigations lead, it is hoped, to moral improvement. But the actual transactions between the episodes of the private history and those of the public history remain mysterious, since by definition they can belong to neither series. They could not be reported among the happenings described in a person's autobiography of his inner life, but nor could they be reported among those described in some one else's biography of that person's overt career. They can be inspected neither by introspection nor by laboratory experiment. They are theoretical shuttlecocks which are forever being bandied from the physiologist back to the psychologist and from the psychologist back to the physiologist.

Underlying this partly metaphorical representation of the bifurcation of a person's two lives there is a seemingly more profound and philosophical assumption. It is assumed that there are two different kinds of existence or status. What exists or happens may have the status of physical existence, or it may have the status of mental existence. Somewhat as the faces of coins are either heads or tails, or somewhat as living creatures are either male or female, so, it is supposed, some existing is physical existing, other existing is mental existing. It is a necessary feature of what has physical existence that it is in space and time; it is a necessary feature of what has mental existence that it is in time but not in space. What has physical existence is composed of matter, or else is a function of matter; what has mental existence consists of consciousness, or else is a function of consciousness.

There is thus a polar opposition between mind and matter, an opposition which is often brought out as follows. Material objects are situated in a common field, known as "space," and what happens to one body in one part of space is mechanically connected with what happens to other bodies in other parts of space. But mental happenings occur in insulated fields, known as "minds," and there is, apart maybe from telepathy, no direct causal connection between what happens in one mind and what happens in another. Only through the medium of the public physical world can the mind of one person make a difference to the mind of another. The mind is its own place and in his inner life each of us lives the life of a ghostly Robinson Crusoe. People can see, hear and jolt one another's bodies, but they are irremediably blind and deaf to the workings of one another's minds and inoperative upon them.

What sort of knowledge can be secured of the workings of a mind? On the one side, according to the official theory, a person has direct knowledge of the best imaginable kind of the workings of his own mind. Mental states and processes are (or are normally) conscious states and processes, and the consciousness which irradiates them can engender no illusions and leaves the door open for no doubts. A person's present thinkings, feelings and willings, his perceivings, rememberings and imaginings are intrinsically "phosphorescent"; their existence and their nature are inevitably betrayed to their owner. The inner life is a stream of consciousness of such a sort that it would be absurd to suggest that the mind whose life is that stream might be unaware of what is passing down it.

True, the evidence adduced recently by Freud seems to show that there exist channels tributary to this stream, which run hidden from their owner. People are actuated by impulses the existence of which they vigorously disavow; some of their thoughts differ from the thoughts which they acknowledge; and some of the actions which they think they will to perform they do not really will. They are thoroughly gulled by some of their own hypocrisies and they successfully ignore facts about their mental lives which on the official theory ought to be patent to them. Holders of the official theory tend, however, to maintain that anyhow in normal circumstances a person must be directly and authentically seized of the present state and workings of his own mind.

Besides being currently supplied with these alleged immediate data of consciousness, a person is also generally supposed to be able to exercise from time to time a special kind of perception, namely inner perception, or introspection. He can take a (non-optical) "look" at what is passing in his mind. Not only can he view and scrutinize a flower through his sense of sight and listen to and discriminate the notes of a bell through his sense of hearing; he can also reflectively or introspectively watch, without any bodily organ of sense, the current episodes of his inner life. This self-observation is also commonly supposed to be immune from illusion, confusion or doubt. A mind's reports of its own affairs have a certainty superior to the best that is possessed by its reports of matters in the physical world. Sense-perceptions can, but consciousness and introspection cannot, be mistaken or confused.

On the other side, one person has no direct access of any sort to the events of the inner life of another. He cannot do better than make problematic inferences from the observed behavior of the other person's body to the states of mind which, by analogy from his own conduct, he supposes to be signalized by that behavior. Direct access to the workings of a mind is the privilege of that mind itself; in default of such privileged access, the workings of one mind are inevitably occult to everyone else. For the supposed arguments from bodily movements similar to their own to mental workings similar to their own would lack any possibility of observational corroboration. Not unnaturally, therefore, an adherent of the official theory finds it difficult to resist this consequence of his premises, that he has no good reason to believe that there do exist minds other than his own. Even if he prefers to believe that to other human bodies there are harnessed minds not unlike his own, he cannot claim to be able to discover their individual characteristics, or the particular things that they undergo and do. Absolute solitude is on this showing the ineluctable destiny of the soul. Only our bodies can meet.

As a necessary corollary of this general scheme there is implicitly prescribed a special way of construing our ordinary concepts of mental powers and operations. The verbs, nouns, and adjectives, with which in ordinary life we describe the wits, characters, and higher-grade performances of the people with whom we have to do, are required to be construed as signifying special episodes in their secret histories, or else as signifying tendencies for such episodes to occur. When someone is described as knowing, believing, or guessing something, as hoping, dreading, intending, or shirking something, as designing this or being amused at that, these verbs are supposed to denote the occurrence or specific modifications in his (to us) occult stream of consciousness. Only his own privileged access to this stream in direct awareness and introspection could provide authentic testimony that these mental-conduct verbs are correctly or incorrectly applied. The onlooker, be he teacher, critic, biographer, or friend, can never assure himself that his comments have any vestige of truth. Yet it was just because we do in fact all know how to make such comments, make them with general correctness and correct them when they turn out to be confused or mistaken, that philosophers found it necessary to construct their theories of the nature and place of minds. Finding mental-conduct concepts being regularly and effectively used, they properly sought to fix their logical geography. But the logical geography officially recommended would entail that there could be no regular or effective use of these mental-conduct concepts in our descriptions of, and prescriptions for, other people's minds.

Ryle's claim, then, is that the "official" doctrine is that a person's body is a "machine" intimately but obscurely related to his mind, which "inhabits" or "animates" his body machine. He refers to this traditional body–mind dualism as the doctrine of the "ghost in the machine," and claims that those who hold it are thereby involved in a number of theoretical absurdities, all of which express in one way or another a gross and flagrant "category-mistake." He gives examples of category-mistakes, none of which is the particular category-mistake present in the untenable notion of a person as a "ghost in a machine." A person who, having seen the colleges that make up Oxford University, asked, "Where, now, is the university?" would be guilty of a category-mistake, imagining that the university itself existed in the same way that the colleges did. Similarly, with a person who, having witnessed the marching of the battalions that make up a division, should then ask to see the division, ignoring the fact that a division does not exist in the way that its battalions do. His other examples are to the same effect. A more blatantly nonsensical example of a category-mistake would be made by a person who should say, "She came in a taxi and left in a rage," and then go on to ask questions about the rage that presupposed that it had the same order of existence as the taxi; for example, "How fast did it travel?" "What fuel did it use?" and so on. To such a person we would say, "Your questions do not arise; a rage belongs in a radically different category from a taxi." In this second section of Chapter One, Ryle is more concerned to illustrate the notion of a category-mistake, and how it could give rise to completely pointless and misleading questions, than to spell out the particular category-mistake that gives rise to the "impossible" "ghost-in-the-machine" notion of a person as a body united with a mind. It takes the rest of the book to spell out *that* category-mistake and to suggest some other way of conceiving of the body–mind relation.

(2) The Absurdity of the Official Doctrine

Such in outline is the official theory. I shall often speak of it, with deliberate abusiveness, as "the dogma of the Ghost in the Machine." I hope to prove that it is entirely false, and false not in detail but in principle. It is not merely an assemblage of particular mistakes. It is one big mistake and a mistake of a special kind. It is namely, a category-mistake. It represents the facts of mental life as if they belonged to one logical type or category (or range of types or categories), when they actually belong to another. The dogma is, therefore, a philosopher's myth. In attempting to explode the myth I shall probably be taken to be denying well-known facts about the mental life of human beings, and my plea that I aim at doing nothing more than rectify the logic of mental-conduct concepts will probably be disallowed as mere subterfuge.

I must first indicate what is meant by the phrase "category-mistake." This I do in a series of illustrations.

A foreigner visiting Oxford or Cambridge for the first time is shown a number of colleges, libraries, playing fields, museums, scientific departments, and administrative offices. He then asks, "But where is the University? I have seen where the members of the Colleges live, where the Registrar works, where the scientists experiment and the rest. But I have not yet seen the University in which reside and work the members of your University." It has then to be explained to him that the University is not another collateral institution, some ulterior counterpart to the colleges, laboratories and offices which he has seen. The University is just the way in which all that he has already seen is organized. When they are seen and when their co-ordination is understood, the University has been seen. His mistake lay in his innocent assumption that it was correct to speak of Christ Church, the Bodleian Library, the Ashmolean Museum, *and* the University, to speak, that is, as if "the University" stood for an extra member of the class of which these other units are members. He was mistakenly allocating the University to the same category as that to which the other institutions belong.

The same mistake would be made by a child witnessing the march-past of a division, who, having had pointed out to him such and such battalions, batteries, squadrons, etc., asked when the division was going to appear. He would be supposing that a division was a counterpart to the units already seen, partly similar to them and partly unlike them. He would be shown his mistake by being told that in watching the battalions, batteries, and squadrons marching past he had been watching the division marching past. The march-past was not a parade of battalions, batteries, squadrons, *and* a division; it was a parade of battalions, batteries, and squadrons *of* a division.

One more illustration. A foreigner watching his first game of cricket learns what are the functions of the bowlers, the batsmen, the fielders, the umpires, and the scorers. He then says, "But there is no one left on the field to contribute the famous element of team-spirit. I see who does the bowling, the batting, and the wicketkeeping; but I do not see whose role it is to exercise *esprit de corps*." Once more, it would have to be explained that he was looking for the wrong type of thing. Team-spirit is not another cricketing-operation supplementary to all of the other special tasks. It is, roughly, the keeness with which each of the special tasks is performed, and performing a task keenly is not performing two tasks. Certainly exhibiting team-spirit is not the same thing as bowling or catching, but nor is it a third thing such that we can say that the bowler first bowls *and* then exhibits team-spirit or that a fielder is at a given moment *either* catching *or* displaying *esprit de corps*.

These illustrations of category-mistakes have a common feature which must be noticed. The mistakes were made by people who did not know how to wield the concepts *University, division* and *team-spirit*. Their puzzles arose from inability to use certain items in the English vocabulary.

The theoretically interesting category-mistakes are those made by people who are perfectly competent to apply concepts, at least in the situations with which they are familiar, but are still liable in their abstract thinking to allocate those concepts to logical types to which they do not belong. An instance of a mistake of this sort would be the following story. A student of politics has learned the main differences between the British, the French and the American Constitutions, and has learned also the differences and connections between the Cabinet, Parliament, the various Ministries, the Judicature and the Church of England. But he still becomes embarrassed when asked questions about the connections between the Church of England, the Home Office and the British Constitution. For while the Church and the Home Office are institutions, the British Constitution is not another institution in the same sense of that noun. So inter-institutional relations which can be asserted or denied to hold between the Church and the Home Office cannot be asserted or denied to hold between either of them and the British Constitution. "The British Constitution" is not a term of the same logical type as "the Home Office" and "the Church of England." In a partially similar way, John Doe may be a relative, a friend, an enemy or a stranger to Richard Roe; but he cannot be any of these things to the Average Taxpayer. He knows how to talk sense in certain sorts of discussions about the Average Taxpayer, but he is baffled to say why he could not come across him in the street as he can come across Richard Roe.

It is pertinent to our main subject to notice that, so long as the student of politics continues to think of the British Constitution as a counterpart to the other institutions, he will tend to describe it as a mysteriously occult institution; and so long as John Doe continues to think of the Average Taxpayer as a fellow-citizen, he will tend to think of him as an elusive insubstantial man, a ghost who is everywhere yet nowhere.

My destructive purpose is to show that a family of radical category-mistakes is the source of the double-life theory. The representation of a person as a ghost mysteriously ensconced in a machine derives from this argument. Because, as is true, a person's thinking, feeling and purposive doing cannot be described solely in the idioms of physics, chemistry and physiology, therefore they must be described in counterpart idioms. As the human body is a complex organised unit, so the human mind must be another complex organised unit, though one made of a different sort of stuff and with a different sort of structure. Or, again, as the human body, like any other parcel of matter, is a field of causes and effects, so the mind must be another field of causes and effects, though not (Heaven be praised) mechanical causes and effects.

In the upcoming third section Ryle asks how this body–mind category-mistake ever came to be made anyway. To use his own words to frame this question we could ask, "What was the intellectual origin of what I have yet to prove to be the Cartesian category-mistake?" His answer is along this line: finding that such sciences as physics, chemistry, and physiology made good sense of processes that go on in the body, it occurred to some persons that another science, say, psychology, would investigate the processes that go on in the mind. This of course presupposed bodies *and* minds, bodily substances and processes, *and* mental substances and processes. The more the scheme "worked," the more it "confirmed" this body–mind dualism. Once the dualism was thoroughly installed, there arose all the tangle of cross-category questions and puzzles that have made a theoretical shambles of our notion of a person and of our notion of the relation of physics to psychology.

(3) *The Origin of the Category-Mistake*

One of the chief intellectual origins of what I have yet to prove to be the Cartesian category-mistake seems to be this. When Galileo showed that his methods of scientific discovery were competent to provide a mechanical theory which should cover every occupant of space, Descartes found in himself two conflicting motives. As a man of scientific genius he could not but endorse the claims of mechanics, yet as a religious and moral man he could not accept, as Hobbs accepted, the discouraging rider to those claims, namely that human nature differs only in degree of complexity from clockwork. The mental could not be just a variety of the mechanical.

He and subsequent philosophers naturally but erroneously availed themselves of the following escape-route. Since mental-conduct words are not to be construed as signifying the occurrence of mechanical processes, they must be construed as signifying the occurrence of nonmechanical processes; since mechanical laws explain movements in space as the effects of other movements in space, other laws must explain some of the non-spatial workings of minds as the effects of other non-spatial workings of minds. The difference between the human behaviours which we describe as intelligent and those which we describe as unintelligent must be a difference in their causation; so, while some movements of human tongues and limbs are the effects of mechanical causes, others must be the effects of non-mechanical causes, i.e. some issue from movements of particles of matter, others from workings of the mind.

The differences between the physical and the mental were thus repre-sented as differences inside the common framework of the categories of "thing," "stuff," "attribute," "state," "process," "change," "cause" and "ef-fect." Minds are things, but different sorts of things from bodies; mental processes are causes and effects, but different sorts of causes and effects from bodily movements. And so on. Somewhat as the foreigner expected the University to be an extra edifice, rather like a college but also considerably different, so the repudiators of mechanism represented minds as extra centres of causal processes, rather like machines but also considerably dif-ferent from them. Their theory was a para-mechanical hypothesis.

That this assumption was at the heart of the doctrine is shown by the fact that there was from the beginning felt to be a major theoretical difficulty in explaining how minds can influence and be influenced by bodies. How can a mental process, such as willing, cause spatial movements like the move-ments of the tongue? How can a physical change in the optic nerve have among its effects a mind's perception of a flash of light? This notorious crux by itself shows the logical mould into which Descartes pressed his theory of the mind. It was the self-same mould into which he and Galileo set their mechanics. Still unwittingly adhering to the grammar of mechanics, he tried to avert disaster by describing minds in what was merely an obverse vocabu-lary. The workings of minds had to be described by the mere negatives of the specific descriptions given to bodies; they are not in space, they are not motions, they are not modifications of matter, they are not accessible to public observation. Minds are not bits of clockwork, they are just bits of not-clockwork.

As thus represented, minds are not merely ghosts harnessed to machines, they are themselves just spectral machines. Though the human body is an engine, it is not quite an ordinary engine, since some of its workings are gov-erned by another engine inside it—this interior governor-engine being one of a very special sort. It is invisible, inaudible and it has no size or weight. It cannot be taken to bits and the laws it obeys are not those known to ordinary engineers. Nothing is known of how it governs the bodily engine.

A second major crux points the same moral. Since, according to the doc-trine, minds belong to the same category as bodies and since bodies are rigidly governed by mechanical laws, it seemed to many theorists to follow that minds must be similarly governed by rigid non-mechanical laws. The physical world is a deterministic system, so the mental world must be a de-terministic system. Bodies cannot help the modifications that they undergo, so minds cannot help pursuing the careers fixed for them. *Responsibility, choice, merit* and *demerit* are therefor inapplicable concepts—unless the compromise solution is adopted of saying that the laws governing mental processes, unlike those governing physical processes, have the congenial at-tribute of being only rather rigid. The problem of the Freedom of the Will was the problem how to reconcile the hypothesis that minds are to be de-scribed in terms drawn from the categories of mechanics with the knowledge that higher-grade human conduct is not of a piece with the behaviour of machines.

It is an historical curiosity that it was not noticed that the entire argument was broken-backed. Theorists correctly assumed that any sane man could already recognise the differences between, say, rational and non-rational utterances or between purposive and automatic behaviour. Else there would have been nothing requiring to be salved from mechanism. Yet the explanation given presupposed that one person could in principle never recognise the difference between the rational and the irrational utterances issuing from other human bodies, since he could never get access to the postulated immaterial causes of some of their utterances. Save for the doubtful exception of himself, he could never tell the difference between a man and a Robot. It would have to be conceded, for example, that, for all that we can tell, the inner lives of persons who are classed as idiots or lunatics are as rational as those of anyone else. Perhaps only their overt behaviour is disappointing; that is to say, perhaps "idiots" are not really idiotic, or "lunatics" lunatic. Perhaps, too, some of those who are classed as sane are really idiots. According to the theory, external observers could never know how the overt behaviour of others is correlated with their mental powers and processes and so they could never know or even plausibly conjecture whether their applications of mental-conduct concepts to these other people were correct or incorrect. It would then be hazardous or impossible for a man to claim sanity or logical consistency even for himself, since he would be debarred from comparing his own performances with those of others. In short, our characterisations of persons and their performances as intelligent, prudent and virtuous or as stupid, hypocritical and cowardly could never have been made, so the problem of providing a special causal hypothesis to serve as the basis of such diagnoses would never have arisen. The question, "How do persons differ from machines?" arose just because everyone already knew how to apply mental-conduct concepts before the new causal hypothesis was introduced. This hypothesis could not therefore be the source of the criteria used in those applications. Nor, of course, has the causal hypothesis in any degree improved our handling of those criteria. We still distinguish good from bad arithmetic, politic from impolitic conduct and fertile from infertile imaginations in the ways in which Descartes himself distinguished them before and after he speculated how the applicability of these criteria was compatible with the principle of mechanical causation.

He had mistaken the logic of his problem. Instead of asking by what criteria intelligent behaviour is actually distinguished from non-intelligent behaviour, he asked "Given that the principle of mechanical causation does not tell us the difference, what other causal principle will tell it us?" He realised that the problem was not one of mechanics and assumed that it must therefore be one of some counterpart to mechanics. Not unnaturally psychology is often cast for just this role.

When two terms belong to the same category, it is proper to construct conjunctive propositions embodying them. Thus a purchaser may say that he bought a left-hand glove and a right-hand glove, but not that he bought a left-hand glove, a right-hand glove and a pair of gloves. "She came home in a flood of tears and a sedan-chair" is a well-known joke based on the absurdity of conjoining terms of different types. It would have been equally ridiculous to construct the disjunction "She came home either in a flood of tears or else in a sedan-chair." Now the dogma of the Ghost in the Machine does just this. It maintains that there exist both bodies and minds; that there occur physical processes and mental processes; that there are mechanical causes of corporeal movements and mental causes of corporeal movements. I shall argue that these and other analogous conjunctions are absurd; but, it must be noticed, the argument will not show that either of the illegitimately conjoined propositions is absurd in itself. I am not, for example, denying that there occur mental processes. Doing long division is a mental process and so is making a joke. But I am saying that the phrase "there occur mental processes" does not mean the same sort of thing as "there occur physical processes," and, therefore, that it makes no sense to conjoin or disjoin the two.

If my argument is successful, there will follow some interesting consequences. First, the hallowed contrast between Mind and Matter will be dissipated, but dissipated not by either of the equally hallowed absorptions of Mind by Matter or of Matter by Mind, but in quite a different way. For the seeming contrast of the two will be shown to be as illegitimate as would be the contrast of "she came home in a flood of tears" and "she came home in a sedan-chair." The belief that there is a polar opposition between Mind and Matter is the belief that they are terms of the same logical type.

It will also follow that both Idealism and Materialism are answers to an improper question. The "reduction" of the material world to mental states and processes, as well as the "reduction" of mental states and processes to physical states and processes, presuppose the legitimacy of the disjunction "Either there exist minds or there exist bodies (but not both)." It would be like saying, "Either she bought a left-hand and a right-hand glove or she bought a pair of gloves (but not both)."

It is perfectly proper to say, in one logical tone of voice, that there exist minds and to say, in another logical tone of voice, that there exist bodies. But these expressions do not indicate two different species of existence, for "existence" is not a generic word like "coloured" or "sexed." They indicate two different senses of "exist," somewhat as "rising" has different senses in "the tide is rising," "hopes are rising," and "the average age of death is rising." A man would be thought to be making a poor joke who said that three things are now rising, namely the tide, hopes and the average age of death. It would be just as good or bad a joke to say that there exist prime numbers and Wednesdays and public opinions and navies; or that there exist both minds and bodies. In the succeeding chapters I try to prove that the official theory does rest on a batch of category-mistakes by showing that logically absurd corollaries follow from it. The exhibition of these absurdities will have the constructive effect of bringing out part of the correct logic of mental-conduct concepts.

Historical Note

It would not be true to say that the official theory derives solely from Descartes' theories, or even from a more widespread anxiety about the implications of seventeenth century mechanics. Scholastic and Reformation theology had schooled the intellects of the scientists as well as of the laymen, philosophers and clerics of that age. Stoic-Augustinian theories of the will were embedded in the Calvinist doctrines of sin and grace; Platonic and Aristotelian theories of the intellect shaped the orthodox doctrines of the immortality of the soul in the new syntax of Galileo. The theologian's privacy of conscience became the philosopher's privacy of consciousness, and what had been the bogy of Predestination reappeared as the bogy of Determinism.

It would also not be true to say that the two-worlds myth did no theoretical good. Myths often do a lot of theoretical good, while they are still new. One benefit bestowed by the para-political myth was that it partly superannuated the then prevalent para-political myth. Minds and their Faculties had previously been described by analogies with political superiors and political subordinates. The idioms used were those of ruling, obeying, collaborating and rebelling. They survived and still survive in many ethical and some epistemological discussions. As, in physics, the new myth of occult Forces was a scientific improvement on the old myth of Final Causes, so, in anthropological and psychological theory, the new myth of hidden operations, impulses and agencies was an improvement on the old myth of dictations, deferences and disobediences.

READING QUESTIONS

1. What is the "official" theory about the nature of human minds? Where will you encounter it in use?
2. Ryle refers to the "official" theory as "Descartes' myth." Why Descartes? Why myth? Was geocentric astronomy a *myth*? What causes a myth to be a myth?
3. In what sense are the terms *inner* and *outer* metaphors when applied by the official theory to the mind and the body? Is a metaphor a myth?
4. Is Ryle speaking literally or in metaphor when he refers to a mind as a "ghost in a machine"? Is it a good metaphor?
5. He claims that one who subscribes to the official theory has, on his own premises, no good reason to believe in the existence of minds other than his own. How so? Therefore what?
6. What does he refer to by "privileged access"? Who is privileged? In his access to what?
7. What does he mean by a category-mistake? If you asked what color the square root of 9 is, would you be making one? Or what Santa Claus feeds his reindeer? Or what the geometrical shape of justice is? Spell out your point.
8. How he uses (a) the university, (b) the division, (c) espirit de corps, team-spirit, to illustrate his notion of a category-mistake. What causes any mistake to be a category-mistake?

9. Ryle claims that if you subscribe to the official theory, you can never tell the difference between another person and a robot. How so? Therefore what? Can you tell the difference? How? What is the difference?

10. In this chapter it is said that the official theory claims *a* and *b* and *c* about the mind. And that its reasons for so doing are (or were) *d* and *e* and *f*. And that it has absurd consequences *g* and *h* and *i*. And that these absurd consequences have their source in a category-mistake, which is *j* and *k* and *l*. The official theory should therefore be dropped and replaced by another theory. And there any flash-points of question or counterclaims for you?

INDEPENDENT STUDY

1. There are ten chapters in *The Concept of Mind*. You have read Chapter One. Secure a copy of the book. Study the titles and subheadings of the remaining chapters. Select Chapter Two and any two others. In regard to each chapter make clear what Ryle is talking about; why, in view of Chapter One, he is talking about it; what he says about it; and whether you agree with what he says.

2. Read Chapter Nine carefully. Then read Chapter Thirteen in C. A. Campbell's book *In Defence of Freewill and Other Essays*. Make clear what Ryle says, and what Campbell says in criticism.

3. If you know your way around in American academic psychology read Chapter Ten and any two other chapters relevant to Chapter Ten. As an overseas spokesman for you, or for American academic psychology, does Ryle make good sense? If so, why? If not why not?

topic **three**
right and wrong

THE PROBLEM STATED

Ethics may be defined as an inquiry into the principles and the presuppositions which are operative in your moral judgments. Not to know your principles and presuppositions is to be naïve. To get to know them is to achieve sophistication.

Upon what principle do we discriminate between right and wrong? Compile a list of acts or ways of acting that you would judge to be wrong. What fact, about all of these acts, is your reason for calling them cases of wrongdoing? The fact that they are contrary to the will of God? The fact that they are contrary to custom or convention? The fact that they are contrary to nature, "unnatural"? The fact that they militate against human happiness? Whatever the fact is, call it X. You can then say, "An act is wrong if and only if it is X or an X." When you spell out that X, you have formulated the principle that is operative in your moral judgments. You use such a principle when you authorize moral judgments on conduct, on character, on institutions, on laws, on customs. We say, of a given act, that it is right or wrong; of a type of character, that it is the right type or the wrong type; of an institution, for example, private property, that it is right or wrong; of a law, say, capital punishment, that it is right or wrong; of a custom, that it is right or wrong. Our present problem is not which particular act, or character, or institution, or law, or custom is right or wrong. Our problem is the more general one: On what principle do we judge these things right or wrong?

The sets of passages that follow present six different approaches to this question. The first set, drawn from the writings of an eighteenth-century moralist, William Paley, argues that *right* means "according to the will of God." This way of grounding morality in theology is something with which we are all familiar. Paley's statement is therefore valuable as a starting point.

The second set, drawn from the writings of Immanuel Kant, argues that *right* means "according to reason," or "what reason prescribes." Kant wrote in the Age of Reason, which produced such characteristic figures as Voltaire, Rousseau, Thomas Paine, and others. His attempt to ground morality on an appeal to reason, with no reference to theological doctrine, represents one perennial possibility. In any age that understands by *reason* what Kant intended by that term, his appeal would be instant and profound.

The third set, drawn from the writings of John Stuart Mill, argues that *right* means "producing human happiness," "producing the greatest amount of happiness possible under the circumstances." Mill was a spokesman for an age of social reform. His position in moral philosophy was inspired by his experience of great and far-reaching changes in the social order, widespread wealth and poverty, the rise of nineteenth-century democratic governments, the emergence of new economic classes, and the rapid decay of old customs and institutions. It is in this context that we must understand his somewhat abrupt and impatient dismissal of the moral philosophies typified by Paley and Kant, and his forthright appeal to happiness as the foundation principle of human morality.

In the fourth set, Friedrich Nietzsche argues that *right* means "productive of or giving expression to the superman." The notion that man has evolved from lower animals suggested that something higher may evolve from man. This, when it comes, will be the superman, and anything is right that either hastens his arrival or expresses his nature when arrived.

In the fifth set, A. J. Ayer presents a repudiation of the entire problem as common to Paley, Kant, and Mill. In this regard Professor Ayer has affinities with Nietzsche. His thesis is that moral judgments are expressions of emotion, and hence call for a psychological theory to account for them, not an ethical theory to elucidate them.

In the sixth set, Brand Blanshard presents a general criticism of subjective theories in ethics. Subjectivism is the theory that judgments tell you about the person, the subject, who makes them but not about the object to which, as judgments, they seem to refer. A subjectivist would say that Paul's opinion of Peter tells you about Paul but not about Peter. If subjectivism is correct, then moral judgments are subjectively true, or valid; that is, they are true, or bold for and of the judger, the person who authorizes the judgments.

SECTION 1. WILLIAM PALEY: THE APPEAL TO THE WILL OF GOD

One important question we can direct at any human act is this: "Was it right or wrong? Did the agent do as he ought to have done, or as he ought not to have done?" Implicit in any answer to this question is a moral principle; that is, a criterion in terms of which we distinguish between right and wrong. As long as men entertain a lively belief in the existence of God, and ascribe to Him an interest in human affairs, many are likely to base their moral judgments upon what they consider to be His will. They are going to say that *right* means "according to the will of God," and *wrong* means "contrary to the will of God." William Paley, a popular moralist in the eighteenth century, was a man of precisely this turn of mind. One can do worse than examine the essentials of the appeal to theology in ethics as these are to be found in his writings. Any virtues that reside in this view will be obvious in the simplicity and sincerity of his language. Any shortcomings can be the more readily pointed out, since his stand is clear and straightforward. The following passage by Sir Leslie Stephen in his *History of English Thought in the Eighteenth Century* is worth reading before proceeding to Paley.

The different religions of the world tell us, each in its own fashion, what is the plan and meaning of this universe. Thence believers may infer what is the best method of employing our brief existence within it. We ought to be good, say all moralists, and the question remains: What is meant by *ought* and by *goodness?* Theology, so long as it was a vital belief in the world, affords a complete and satisfactory answer to these questions. Morality was, of necessity, its handmaid. Believe in an active ruler of the universe, who reveals his will to men, who distributes rewards and punishments to the good and the evil, and we have a plain answer to most of the problems of morality. God's will, so far as known to us, determines what is good. We are obliged to be good, whether from love or from fear.

Biographical Note. William Paley was born in England in 1743 and died in 1805 at the age of sixty-two. His father was headmaster of the school of Giggleswick in Yorkshire. His early education was obtained under the paternal eye. At the age of fifteen, young Paley went to Cambridge University. That his father had great expectations may be gathered from a remark he made to a friend: "My son is now gone to college. He'll turn out a great man. Very great, indeed. I am certain of it. He has by far the clearest head I ever met in my life."

Paley spent four years at Cambridge, obtaining his B.A. in 1762. The following anecdote suggests that he was a normal young man during these years:

I spent the first two years of my undergraduate life happily, but unprofitably. I was constantly in society, where we were not immoral, but idle and rather expensive. At the commencement of my third year, however, after having left the usual party at a rather late hour in the evening, I was awakened at five in the morning by one of my companions, who stood at my bedside. He said: "Paley, I have been thinking what a fool you are. I could achieve nothing worth while, even were I to try, and anyway I can afford the idle life I lead. You could achieve anything, if you were to try, and you cannot afford to waste your time. I have had no sleep during the whole night on account of these reflections, and am now come solemnly to inform you that if you persist in your indolence, I must renounce your society." I was so struck with the visit and the visitor that I laid in bed a great part of the day, and formed my plan. I ordered my bedmaker to prepare my fire every evening, in order that it might be lighted by myself the next morning. I rose at five o'clock, read during the whole of the day, except such hours as chapel and lectures required, allotting to each portion of time its peculiar branch of study; and, just before the closing of the gates (9:00 P.M.) I went to a neighboring coffeehouse, where I constantly regaled upon a mutton chop and a dose of milk punch.

After graduating, Paley rose slowly but steadily in the ecclesiastical world. In 1785 he published his *Principles of Moral and Political Philosophy*. It passed through fifteen editions during his own lifetime. One of his contemporaries remarked of this book: "It may be said to be the only work on moral philosophy fitted to be understood by every class of readers."

The Argument of the Passages.   Paley's formulation of the fundamental principle of morality is simple and clear: Right is that which agrees with the will of God; wrong is that which does not. Having stated this controlling idea, he sets himself to elaborate it. He provides first a definition of *virtue,* consistent with his basic propositions; he moves on, then, to examine the meaning of moral obligation and the distinction between prudence and duty. These matters settled, he turns to the question: if *right* means "according to the will of God," how are we to tell what is and is not the will of God? His answer here is twofold: scriptural revelation and the "light of nature." The sense in which God's will may be gathered from Scripture is then explained. But what of the light of nature; what, that is, about the morality of acts where we do not have God's express declaration? Here Paley meets a real problem, and knowing, as he did, that many occasions arise with respect to which Scripture is silent, he could not treat this matter lightly. To solve his problem he assumed that human happiness is God's primary concern. Realizing, as he says, that "this assumption is the foundation of the whole system," he sets himself to "explain the reasons upon which it rests." The explanation in question occupies the remainder of the passages. The following quotation from a seventeenth-century moralist expresses the idea that Paley proposes to develop:

> That God has given a rule whereby men should govern themselves, I think there is no one so brutish as to deny. He has a right to do it. We are His creatures. He has goodness and wisdom to direct our actions to what is best, and He has power to enforce it by rewards and punishments of infinite weight and duration in another life; for nobody can take us out of His hands. This is the only touchstone of moral rectitude, and by comparing them to this law, it is that men judge of the most considerable moral good or evil of their actions; that is, whether as duty or as sins, they are like to procure them happiness or misery from the hands of the Almighty.

Now Paley. First, as to ethics in general:

> Ethics is that science which teaches men their duty and the reasons of it. The use of such a study depends upon this, that, without it, the rules of life by which men are ordinarily governed, oftentimes mislead them, through a defect in either the rule or in the application.

Then, as to the meaning of *right:*

> *Right* signifies being consistent with the will of God.
> Right is a quality of persons or of actions. Of persons, as when we say, "He has a right to his property"; of actions, as when we say, "His action was right on that occasion." Whether of persons or of actions, *right* means "consistent with, or according to, the will of God." In the one case, substituting the definition for the term, you may say, "It is consistent with or according to the will of God that he have his property"; in the other case, "His action, on that occasion, was consistent with or according to the will of God."

From this it follows that:

> Virtue is doing good to mankind, in obedience to the will of God, and for the sake of everlasting happiness.
> The division of virtues to which we are nowadays most accustomed is into duties: duties toward God; duties toward other men; duties toward ourselves. There are more of these distinctions, but it is not worth while to set them down.

And we are now in a position to explain what is meant by *duty* or *moral obligation.*

What are we to understand by *moral obligation?* Truthfulness, we say, is a moral obligation. What do we intend by this expression? Why am I obliged to keep my word?

When I first turned my thoughts to moral speculations, an air of mystery seemed to hang over the whole subject. This arose, I believe, from hence—that I supposed that to be obliged to do a thing was very different from being induced or urged to do it; that the obligation to practice virtue, for example, was quite another thing, and of another kind, than the obligation which a soldier is under to obey his officer, or a servant his master. Now in what does the difference consist?

I shall argue to the following effect: A man is said to be *obliged* when he is urged by a violent motive resulting from the command of another. First, the motive must be violent, strong, powerful. A person has done me some little service. Suppose, then, he asks me for my vote. From a motive of gratitude, or expectation, I may give it to him. But I should hardly say I was obliged to give it to him; because the motive, or incentive, or inducement, does not rise high enough. Second, it must result from the command of another. Offer a man a gratuity for doing anything. He is not obliged by your offer to do it. But if a magistrate were to command it, he would then consider himself obligated to do it.

Wherever, then, the motive is violent enough and is coupled with the idea of a command, an authority, a law, a will, there, I take it, we always reckon ourselves to be obliged. Let it be remembered that to be obliged is to be urged by a violent motive resulting from the command of another.

And then let it be asked: Why am I "obliged" to keep my word? The answer will be: Because I am urged by the expectation of being rewarded after this life if I do, and punished if I do not, follow, in this respect, the command of God. This solution goes to the bottom of the subject, as no further question can reasonably be asked.

There is always understood to be a difference between an act of prudence and an act of duty. Thus, if I distrusted a man who owed me money, I should reckon it an act of prudence to get another bound with him; but I should hardly call it an act of duty. On the other hand, it would be a loose kind of language to say that, as my friend had placed a box of jewels in my hands when he went abroad, it would be prudent of me to preserve it for him until he returned.

Now, wherein does the difference consist? The difference, and the only difference, is this, that, in the one case, we consider what we shall gain or lose in the present world; in the other case, we consider also what we shall gain or lose in the world to come. Prudence has regard to the former; duty, to the latter. Those who would establish a system of morality, independent of a future state, must look out for some different idea of moral obligation.

To us, therefore, there are two great questions. Will there be, after this life, any distribution of rewards and punishments at all? If so, what actions will be rewarded and what actions will be punished? The first question comprises the credibility of the Christian religion. Proof of an affirmative answer to it, although we confess that it is the foundation upon which the whole fabric rests, must in this treatise be taken for granted. The second question comprises morality itself, and to this we shall now address ourselves.

By now the fundamental role of the will of God in Paley's moral philosophy should be clear. From it proceed all the principal terms in such a moralists's vocabulary. The question hence begins to press: How do we determine what is and is not the will of God?

As the will of God is our rule, to inquire, in any instance, what is our duty or what we are obliged to do, is, in effect, to inquire what is the will of God in that instance. This consequently becomes the whole business of morality.

Now, there are two methods of coming at the will of God on any point: by his express declarations, when they are to be had, and which must be sought for in Scripture; by what we can discover of his designs and disposition from his works, or, as we usually call it, the light of nature. The object of both is the same—to discover the will of God; and, provided we do but discover it, it matters nothing by what means.

An ambassador may guide himself in many cases with safety by judging only from what he knows of his sovereign's disposition, by arguing from what he has observed of his conduct or what he knows of his designs. But if he have his commission and instructions in his pocket, it would be strange never to look into them. He will, naturally, conduct himself by both rules. When his instructions are clear and positive, there is an end of all further deliberation, unless, indeed, he suspects their authenticity. Where his instructions are silent or dubious, he will endeavor to supply or explain them by what he has been able to collect from other quarters of his master's general inclination or intentions.

Whoever expects to find in the Scriptures particular directions for every moral doubt that arises looks for more than he will meet with. Such a detail of particular precepts would have so enlarged the sacred volume that it would have been too bulky either to be read or circulated; or rather, as St. John says, "even the world itself could not contain the books that should be written."

Morality is taught in the Scriptures in this wise: General rules are laid down, of piety, justice, benevolence, and purity. Several of these rules are occasionally illustrated, either in fictitious examples, as in the parable of the good Samaritan; or in instances which actually presented themselves, as in Christ's reproof of his disciples or his praise of the poor widow; or, in the resolution of questions proposed to Christ, as in his answer to the young man who asked him, "What lack I yet?"

This is the way in which all practical sciences are taught, as arithmetic, grammar, navigation, and the like. Rules are laid down, and examples are subjoined, by way of explaining the principle of the rule, and as so many specimens of the method of applying it.

So far, so good. By reference to the will of God we determine what is right and wrong. By reference to Scripture we determine, in part, what is the will of God. But what of that part which is not provided for by Scripture?

The method of coming at the will of God concerning any action, where we do not have this express declaration, is to inquire into the tendency of the action to promote or diminish the general happiness. This rule proceeds on the assumption that God Almighty wills and wishes the happiness of His creatures, and, consequently, that those actions which promote that will and wish must be agreeable to Him; and the contrary.

As this assumption is the foundation of the whole system, it becomes necessary to explain the reasons upon which it rests.

When God created the human species, either He wished their happiness or He wished their misery or He was indifferent to both.

If He wished their misery, He might have made sure of His purpose, e.g., by forming our senses to be as many sores and pains to us as they are now instruments of gratification and enjoyment. He might, e.g., have made everything we tasted, bitter; everything we saw, loathsome; everything we touched, a sting; every smell, a stench; every sound, a discord.

If He had been indifferent to our happiness or misery, we must impute to our good fortune both the capacity of our senses to receive pleasure and the supply of external objects fitted to excite it. But either of these—and still more both of them—is too much to be attributed to accident, i.e., mere "good fortune." Nothing remains, therefore, other than the first supposition; namely, that when God created the human species, He intended their happiness.

The same argument may be proposed in different terms, thus: The world abounds in contrivances, and all the contrivances with which we are acquainted are directed to beneficial purposes. Evil, no doubt, exists. But it is never, that we can perceive, the object of contrivance. Teeth are contrived to eat, not to ache. Their aching now and then is incidental to the contrivance, perhaps inseparable from it, perhaps even a defect in it; but it is not the object of it.

This is a distinction which well deserves to be attended to. In describing implements of husbandry, you would hardly say of a sickle that it is made to cut the reaper's fingers, though from the construction of the instrument, and the manner of using it, this mischief often happens.

On the other hand, if you had occasion to describe instruments of torture, the case would be different. This, you would say, is to stretch the sinews; this, to dislocate the joints; this, to break the bones; this, to scorch the soles of the feet; and so forth. Here pain and misery are the very objects of the contrivance.

Now, nothing of this sort is to be found in nature. We never discover a contrivance whose object is to bring about pain and misery. No anatomist ever discovered anything in the organism calculated to produce pain and disease. No anatomist, in explaining the parts of the human body, ever said, "This is to irritate, this is to inflame, this is to conduct stones to the kidneys, this is to secrete the humor which forms gout." The most he will say is that he does not understand some part or other, or that it is useless. He never suspects that it is put there to incommode, to annoy, to torment.

Since, then, God hath called forth His consummate wisdom to contrive and provide for our happiness, and the world appears to have been constituted with this design at first, then, so long as this constitution is upheld by Him, we must suppose the same design to continue.

We conclude, therefore, that God wills and wishes the happiness of His creatures. This conclusion being once established, we are at liberty to go on with the rule built upon it, namely, that the method of coming at the will of God concerning any action, where we do not have his express declaration, is to inquire into the tendency of that action to promote or diminish the general happiness.

By virtue of the two principles, that God wills the happiness of His creatures, and that God's will is the measure of right and wrong, we arrive at certain conclusions. These conclusions become rules. And soon we learn to pronounce actions right or wrong according as they agree or disagree with our rules, without looking any further.

Paley is of interest for the difficulties that his position suggests. Stated briefly, what he says comes to this: "*Right* means according to God's will. An act is right if and only if it is according to the will of God. This is the principle of morality. The phrase 'if and only if' indicates that you are trying to define rightness in principle. God's will is to be found in the Scriptures, or discovered by the light of nature. The light of nature tells us that God intends above all to produce and promote human happiness. Where, therefore, the Scriptures are silent, we determine the rightness of an act by the fact that it produces more happiness than any other act possible at the time." This is both clear and confused. It raises more questions than it settles. For example, does Paley mean that an act is right because it agrees with God's will, or that it agrees with God's will because it is right? These two are not the same. Also, what is the relation between a man's will and God's will? Does Paley believe that God's will causes and governs all things. If so, could a human act ever be contrary to God's will? If it could not, then it would follow that no act is ever wrong. Does Paley want *that?*

Then, of course, there is the problem connected with detecting God's will in the Scriptures. Why the Scriptures? Why not in Plato's dialogues? Or in the Mohammedan *Koran?* In which parts of the Scriptures? In these parts which enjoin an eye for an eye? Or in those parts which enjoin the golden rule? If in both, what about clashes? If in one, how choose which? Passing to the second half of his argument, has he proved, at all conclusively, that God's will is directed to creating and promoting human happiness? This hypothesis may account for some of the facts. But it does not account for all of them. See Hume and Schopenhauer on the misery of man's estate. Going a step further, and admitting his argument, are we justified in arguing that an act is right if and only if it produces more happiness

204 an introduction to modern philosophy

than any other act possible under the circumstances? Is this not to formulate a moral principle that swings clear of the first part of Paley's argument, and could stand on its own feet, without any aid from Scripture? If so, what about cases where the "appeal to Scripture" and "the appeal to happiness" appear to clash? Finally is it or is it not the case that we are more sure of what is right and wrong than we are of God's very existence? If so, would it not be wiser to begin with what we are more sure of, than to begin with what we are less sure of? These, and other problems that suggest themselves, were engaging the attention of Immanuel Kant during the years in which Paley was writing his *Principles of Moral and Political Philosophy.* Paley published in 1785. Kant had published his *Critique of Pure Reason* in 1781, and was meanwhile engaged on a second *Critique,* directed this time not at the problem of knowledge but at the problem of morality. From this prosperous and rather worldly Anglican divine one turns with something like eagerness to the austere and searching professorial moralist at Königsberg.

Note on Sources. The Paley materials in this section are quoted, abridged, or paraphrased from his volume *The Principles of Moral and Political Philosophy.* That work is divided into six Books. The materials in this section are from Books I and II. Each Book is divided into brief chapters. The titles of the chapters in Books I and II will indicate the points at which material has been used for this section.

READING QUESTIONS

1. Use the "If and only if" formula to state Paley's principle.
2. Two ways of getting to know the will of God.
3. Is Paley's principle the same as the Golden Rule?
4. Suppose you affirm Paley's principle. Mention at least three things you thereby presuppose. Can you mention more than three?
5. Relation between Paley's principle and (a) the Scriptures, (b) the light of nature. Does he cite either (a) or (b) as authority for his principle?
6. Why he wants to prove that God wills the happiness of men. Why it would not do for him to use the Scriptures to prove that. What logical fallacy would have been involved?
7. How in the course of his argument Paley uses the contrast between a sickle and an instrument of torture.

8. What fact common to all cases of wrongdoing would, according to Paley, be the reason for calling them cases of wrongdoing?
9. What fact common to all cases of wrongdoing would, according to the light of nature, be the reason for calling them cases of wrongdoing?
10. Why Paley should hesitate to judge any act wrong unless he is willing to presuppose free will in man.
11. Which of Paley's presuppositions would be placed in jeopardy by a strict theological determinism?
12. Use Paley's position to illustrate (a) the distinction, (b) the relation between a principle and a presupposition.
13. If you were inclined to reject Paley's principle, which presupposition(s) would incline you to do so?
14. Which of these statements Paley would endorse: (a) God wills a line of action because it is right; (b) a line of action is right because God wills it.
15. What you would do with this question if you were Paley: "Why does agreeing with the will of God make an act right?"
16. Wherein you find Paley (a) most, (b) least worth your while.

INDEPENDENT STUDY

1. Read the article on William Paley by E. Sprague in the *Encyclopedia of Philosophy* and that by Leslie Stephen in the *Dictionary of National Biography*. These will acquaint you with your author. Then read two brief articles in the *Encyclopedia of Philosophy:* (1) "Teleological Ethics" by W. P. Alston, and (2) "Deontological Ethics" by R. G. Olson. These will introduce you to two widely divergent views of ethics. Then read the article "Utilitarianism" by A. W. Hastings from the beginning through William Paley, in Hastings's *Encyclopedia of Religion and Ethics*. Write a philosophical letter to Paley, or a philosophical dialogue between Paley and yourself, bringing before him points gathered from the above articles that you would like to have him comment upon.
2. Read the articles "Ethics and Morality: Greek" by A. C. Pearson and "Ethics and Morality: Christian" by D. MacKenzie—both in Hastings's *Encyclopedia of Religion and Ethics*. Write a paper comparing Greek and Christian ideas and practices on ethics and morality.
3. Read the article "Ultimate Moral Principles: Their Justification," by A. P. Griffiths in the *Encyclopedia of Philosophy*. The article is brief, and, given the abstractness of its subject matter, not unclear.

Suppose Paley says that an act is right if and only if it agrees with the will of God, and adds that that is his ultimate moral principle. Suppose someone were to ask Paley, "Why does agreeing with the will of God make an act right?" If you were Paley, how would you handle that question? As you tried, you would be engaged in argument about Mr. Griffith's topic: the justification of ultimate moral principles. Write a paper clearing your mind on this issue.

SECTION 2. IMMANUEL KANT: THE CATEGORICAL IMPERATIVE

From Paley to Kant. While Paley was engaged in arguing that morality has its roots in theology, Immanuel Kant was engaged in showing that such is not the case. Paley, it will be remembered, published in 1785.

Kant lived in the Age of Reason, the age of Hume and Rousseau and Voltaire and the revolutions in America and France. He was a firm believer in the rationality of man. He sought to develop the notion of a rational morality: what, in the way of action, does reason require of man? He worked with the conception of man as a rational animal. By *rational* as applied to man he meant having (1) the power to discover what is the case, and to guide conduct by such knowledge, i.e., to develop pure and applied sciences; (2) the power to discover what ought to be the case, and to guide conduct by such knowledge, i.e., to make moral judgments and act them out. Just as he could speak of rational science, so he would speak of rational morality. Just as, by *rational science* he would mean knowledge valid and binding for all rational minds, so by *rational morality* he would mean morality valid and binding for all rational minds. To the first kind of rationality he devoted his *Critique of Pure Reason;* to the second, his *Critique of Practical Reason.* (See pp. 586–587.)

The Argument of the Passages. Kant's handling of the problem of moral principle follows from his conception of what morality is. Without a firm grip on this, one is likely to miss the point of his analysis. For that reason, it is necessary to emphasize his starting point. He begins by assuming that morality, whatever it may be in detail, is something which is universally binding on all rational minds, comparable, in this respect, to science. Thus, if it is true that two and two make four, then it is binding on all rational creatures to accept this proposition. If this is a truth, it is true for everyone, not merely true for those who care to believe it. If it is true, it is true necessarily and always. It is true, in and of itself, without any reference to why it is true, without any reference to who does or does not believe it, without any reference to consequences that follow from its being true or from its being believed. It is, to use a favorite phrase of Kant's, true categorically, without any strings or qualifications. To repeat, it is not true because God commands it, nor because it is according to nature, nor because it pays in the long run to believe it, nor because all or most people agree to it, nor for any other reason. It is simply true because it is true. Moreover, it is true of all cases of two's and two's. There are no possible exceptions. It is not something that holds for one period of time and not for another, for one pair of two's and not for another, for one stage of civilization and not for another. In this universality, necessity, objectivity, Kant finds the differential mark of rational knowledge. He has his own word for it. It is, he says, true *a priori.* It will be recalled that he began his *Critique of Pure Reason* by accepting and exploring the implications of *a priori* knowledge.

This notion of *a priori* he carries over into the field of morality. If there is such a thing as rational science, it is *a priori.* If there is such a thing as rational morality, it is *a priori.* Moreover, just as in the case of *a priori* knowledge he did not undertake to prove that there is such a thing, but assumed its existence as a fact, so in the case of morality he does not undertake to show that there is such a thing, but assumes its existence as a fact. His argument is after this manner: If you admit that there is any rational knowledge, then you must admit that it is *a priori* in character, and if you admit that there is any rational morality, you must admit that it is *a priori* in character. If you admit that there is any rational knowledge, you must recognize that it is binding on all rational beings; so, by analogy, if you admit that there is any rational morality, you must recognize that it is binding on all rational beings. He is content to accept both rational knowledge and rational morality as facts to be recognized, not as hypotheses to be proved.

Once the notion of a rational morality is admitted, Kant is in a position to formulate his problem. It is this: What must be its principle? It will be noticed that he is not seeking to justify morality, any more than one would seek to justify arithmetic; not seeking to explain why right is right and wrong is wrong, any more than one would seek to explain why true is true, or false is false. He is merely saying: The facts of morality are categorical facts, not dependent for their moral quality upon anything beyond themselves. Such being the case, we ask again, what principle must run through all the cases of morality, and be absent from all the cases of immorality?

His answer is simple: an act is moral if and only if the principle that it embodies is capable of universalization without self-contradiction. This notion once stated, Kant proceeds to illustrate his meaning by some examples. His next step is to approach this same notion of categorical rightness from two other angles, namely, duty and good will. When these matters have been settled, he turns to consider a question that had been hanging fire since his studies in the problem of knowledge. I mean the problem of man's free will. Here the findings of the first *Critique* are called in to help solve the difficulty. As a moralist, his fundamental problem is, "What ought I to do?" But if, as would appear from the "scientific" view of the world, everything happens "of necessity," what sense if there to claiming that some things "ought" or "ought not" to be done? Here Kant is at once clarifying and baffling. Clarifying because he has the insight and tenacity to hold on to the "ought" as being every bit as much as reality as the "is," baffling because he concludes by admitting his inability to solve the paradox involved in their joint acceptance. His treatment of this question would require too much space to be summarized here. From freedom he passes on to God and immortality. As in the case of Kant's handling of the problem of knowledge, it will be necessary to state a few of his claims in the form of a condensed summary. His own language is too involved to permit direct quotation. Wherever possible, however, his own words will be introduced.

Morality, the rightness and wrongness of actions, is categorical (not dependent upon anything) and *a priori* (valid for all persons and all times and all cases). In this it resembles rational knowledge. To quote: "The morality of an action is quite a peculiar thing. When we are considering the goodness of an action, we are concerned with what constitutes the goodness in and of itself."

If morality is of this categorical and *a priori* nature, then we can rule out several misleading attempts to formulate its principle. For example, the morality of an act is said, by some, to reside in the "feeling" that one has about the act. But this could not be for two reasons: (1) If morality is a matter of someone's feelings, then it is not categorical; that is, an act would depend, for its morality, upon the fact (external to the act itself) that it was or was not felt about in some way or other by some person or other. (2) If morality is a matter of feeling, then it is not anything universally binding and valid for all men, because feelings vary notoriously from time to time and from person to person; that is, one and the same act could be both right and wrong provided merely that two persons had opposite feelings about it. But this is to rob morality of its categorical nature, to give as the defining characteristic of morality a quality in virtue of which it would fail to be categorical and *a priori*.

Much the same line of reasoning is adduced by Kant against those who seek to locate the rightness of an act in its agreement with God's will. He says:

There are those who argue that we must first have God and then morality—a very convenient principle. But ethics and theology are neither of them a principle of the other. We are not discussing, here, the fact that theology is a motive for ethics—which it is—but we are asking whether the principle of ethical discrimination is theological—and it cannot be that.

Were it so, then before a nation could have any conception of duties it would first have to know God. Nations which had no right conception of God would have no duties, and this is not the case. Nations had a right idea of their duties, e.g., were aware that lies were detestable, without having the proper notion of God. Duties must therefore be derived from some other source.

If we do as God commanded, because He has commanded, and because He is so mighty that He can force us to, or punish us if we do not, we act under orders from fear and fright, not appreciating the propriety of our actions and knowing why we should do as God has commanded. Might cannot constitute a *vis obligandi*. Threats do not impose a (moral) obligation; they extort. Such conduct does not make the heart better.

Moral laws can be right without any commander, promulgator, obligator. How do we know the divine will? None of us feels it in his heart. We cannot know the moral law from any revelation, for if we did so, then those who had no revelation would be wholly ignorant of it.

We imagine God as possessing the most holy and most perfect will. But what then is the most perfect will? The moral law shows us what it is. We say the divine will accords with the moral law and is, therefore, holiest and most perfect. Thus we recognize the perfection of the divine will from the moral law. God wills all that is morally good and proper, and His will is, therefore, holy and perfect. But what is it that is morally good? Ethics supplies the answer to this question.

These strictures may be summarized. To locate the rightness of an act in its agreement with God's will is to deny its categorical nature, i.e., to make it depend, for its rightness, upon something other than or outside of itself. It is, too, to render morality an impossibility for all who do not know what God's will is, or who have a wrong notion of that will, or (it may be) deny His existence. There is, Kant would say, such a thing as morality apart from God's existence or our knowledge of the same. Finally, the view fails to take into account that when we say, "God is good," we are making goodness prior to and independent of God. He is good because His will or His action corresponds to the good; not vice versa.

There remains for consideration what Kant calls the *pragmatic* view of morality. The pragmatic view of morality is that an act is right because of the nature of its consequences; not right in itself, but because of the results that do or do not follow from it. Kant does not need to concern himself with the question of the nature of the results. He has two objections to doing so: (1) To locate the rightness of an act in the nature of its consequences is to deny the categorical nature of morality. It is to make its morality depend upon something other than the act. (2) To find the morality of an act in its consequences is to deprive morality of its *a priori* nature, because we can never know the consequences of an act until after the act is done, and even then never know them completely. This would reduce morality to a matter of probability; make it, as Kant says, *a posteriori,* instead of *a priori*. At this point, we can get closer to Kant's own words.

Having examined what the principle of morality is not, we must now examine what it is.

What is the one principle of morality, the criterion by which to judge everything and in which lies the distinction between moral goodness and all other goodness? What is the principle upon which we establish morality, and through which we are able to discriminate between what is moral and what immoral?

In this connection we must first notice that there are two points to be considered: the principle upon which we discriminate, and the mainspring or motive of performance. We must distinguish between the measuring rod and the mainspring. The measuring rod is the principle of discriminating; the mainspring is the motive of the performance of our obligation. If we ask, "What is morally good and what is not?" it is the principle of discrimination that is in question; but if we ask, "What is it that leads me to be moral?" it is the motive that is in question. We must guard against confusing the principle of morality with the motive to morality. The first is the norm. The second is the incentive.

The essence of morality is that our actions are motivated by a general rule. If we make it the foundation of our conduct that our actions shall be consistent with a universal rule, valid at all times and for everyone, then our actions exemplify the principle of morality.

In all moral judgments the idea which we frame is this: What is the character of the action taken by itself? If the principle of the action can, without self-contradiction, be universalized, it is moral; if it cannot be so universalized without contradicting itself, it is immoral. That action is immoral whose principle cancels and destroys itself when it is made a universal rule.

From this general statement of the nature of rightness Kant turns to some concrete illustrations. He considers the case of lying and suicide. These, being instances of wrongness, illustrate his notion of rightness only indirectly.

May I, when in distress, make a promise with the intention not to keep it? Considerations of prudence aside, would such an act be moral? The shortest way to answer this question is to ask, "Would I be content that the principle (getting out of difficulties by making false promises) should hold good as a universal law, for myself and all others?"

If I ask, "Can the principle of making deceitful promises to get out of difficulties be universalized?" I realize that it cannot. For with such a law there would be no promises at all. With such a principle made universal, it would be in vain to allege my intentions in regard to future actions. As soon as it were made a universal law, the principle would necessarily destroy itself, necessarily defeat its own end.

A man finds himself forced to borrow money. He knows that he will not be able to repay it, but he sees also that nothing will be lent to him unless he promises to repay it. Would it be right to promise? The principle of his action would be: When in need, to borrow and promise to repay, knowing that I cannot do so. Could this principle become a universal law? I see at once that it could not. As a universal law, it would contradict itself. For if this principle were a universal law, such promises would become impossible. For no one would consider such promises as binding, and all would ridicule them as vain pretenses.

A man reduced to despair by a series of misfortunes feels wearied of life. Would it be right to take his own life? Could the principle of his action become a universal law of nature? The principle would be: To shorten life when its longer duration is likely to bring more evil than satisfaction. Could this principle become a universal law of nature? Clearly not. A system of nature in which it was a law to destroy life by means of the very feeling whose special office it is to impel to the improvement of life, would contradict itself, and therefore could not exist as a system of nature. Hence that principle could not possibly exist as a universal law of nature. Hence it would be wholly inconsistent with the supreme principle of all duty.

If we attend to ourselves, on occasion of any transgression of duty, we shall find that we do not will that the principle of our action should become a universal law. On the contrary, we will that the opposite should remain a universal law, only we assume the liberty of making an exception in our own favor—just for this time only, it may be. This cannot be justified to our own impartial judgment, and it proves that we do recognize the validity of the moral principle I have formulated, even while we allow ourselves a few exceptions which we think important and forced upon us.

Thus far Kant has been developing the notion of a rational morality as something categorical and *a priori*. He has used this conception of morality to eliminate certain other theories that are incompatible with it, e.g., the theory that morality is a matter of feeling or emotion. He has disentangled what he takes to be the underlying principle of morality so conceived and advanced a few illustrations of his thesis. He returns again and again throughout his ethical writings to these basic claims. One example of such a reworking is contained in his distinction between hypothetical and categorical imperatives. The statement of this is given below. But a word first on Kant's use of these terms. The term *imperative*, used as a noun, means "a command." Kant inclines to use it in this sense. We shall, I think, come closer to his real meaning if we construe it by the word *ought*. We do, as a matter of everyday usage, employ the term *ought* in precisely the sense Kant would appear to have in mind. We say, for example, "If you wish to be there on time, you *ought* to leave early." Here the force of the *ought* is hypothetical; that is, it depends on whether you do or do not wish to get there on time. But there are occasions, Kant would claim, when we do not so use the term; when, for instance, we are pointing out what we take to be a duty. Thus, "you *ought* to be honest," "you *ought* to respect the rights of others." Here, we might feel, the *ought* is not dependent upon any *if*. It is not a hypothetical *ought*. It is, Kant would say, a categorical *ought*. The same idea could also be expressed in the distinction between a hypothetical obligation and a categorical obligation. Kant says:

All imperatives command either hypothetically or categorically. The former represent the practical necessity of a possible action as means to something else that is willed or might be willed. The latter would be that which represented an action as obligatory of itself without reference to some other end.

If an action is good only as a means to something else, then the imperative which commands it is hypothetical only; but if it is conceived to be good in itself, that is, without reference to any further end, the imperative which commands it is categorical.

The hypothetical imperative only says that the action is good for some purpose, actual or possible. The categorical imperative declares an action to be binding in itself, without reference to any purpose or end beyond itself.

All sciences have a practical part, consisting of problems connected with ends or purposes possible for us, and of imperatives directing how these may be attained. Here there is no question whether the end is good or rational, but only what one must do in order to attain it. The precepts for the physician to make his patient healthy and for a prisoner to insure his victim's death, are of equal value in this respect, namely that each serves to effect its purpose.

There is one imperative which commands certain conduct immediately, without having as its condition any other purpose to be attained by it. This imperative is categorical. It concerns not the matter of the action, nor its intended result, but its form and principle. This imperative may be called the imperative of morality.

There is but one categorical imperative, namely, "Act only on that principle which thou canst will should become a universal law."

This imperative of duty may be expressed, by analogy with natural laws, as follows: "Act as if the principle of thy action were to become by thy will a universal law of nature."

If there is a supreme practical principle or categorical imperative it must be one which constitutes an objective principle, and can therefore serve as a universal practical law. From this, as a supreme practical law, all laws of the will must be capable of being deduced. Accordingly the categorical imperative may be stated in a third way: "So act as to treat humanity, whether in thine own person or in the person of another, as an end withal, never as a means only."

If all the imperatives of duty can be deduced from this one imperative, from it as their principle, then, although it should remain undecided whether what is called *duty* is not merely a vain notion, yet at least we shall be able to show what we understand by it; be able, that is, to show what the notion means.

To act out of respect for this principle constitutes duty. To this every other motive must give place, because it is the condition of a will being good in itself, good absolutely, good without qualification; and the worth of such a will is above everything.

The direct opposite of acting on the principle of morality is acting on the principle of private happiness. This would ruin morality altogether, were not the voice of reason so clear, so irrepressible, so distinctly audible even to the commonest men. That action should be based on the principle of private happiness can only be maintained by such as are bold enough to shut their ears against that heavenly voice in order to support a theory that costs no trouble.

Two things fill the mind with ever new and increasing admiration and awe, the oftener and more steadily we reflect on them: the starry heavens above and the moral law within. I have not to search for them and conjecture them as though they were veiled in darkness or in a region transcending my horizon. I see them before me and connect them directly with the consciousness of my existence.

Duty! Thou sublime and mighty name! Thou seekest not to move the will by threatening nor by charming. Thou merely holdest forth a law which finds entrance into the mind, a law before which all inclinations and desires are dumb. What origin is worthy of thee? Where is to be found the root of thy noble descent?

I do not, therefore, need any far-reaching penetration to discern what I have to do in order that my will may be morally good. Inexperienced in the course of the world, incapable of being prepared for all its contingencies, I need only ask, "Can I will that the principle of my action should become a universal law?" If not, then it must be rejected.

A second reworking of his fundamental insight is contained in his remarks on the intrinsic goodness of a good will. This thought requires a few words of explanation. Kant has spoken thus far of the morality of acts and wherein it resides. He has, also, restated the same notion in terms of *ought* and *ought not*. But, he is quite aware, there is no such thing us an act apart from someone who does the act. We may analyze and define the morality of an act, but we must end by addressing our remarks, not to acts, but to persons who act. There can be right acts only insofar as persons act rightly; hence the need to restate the matter in terms of will or intention. Every moralist, no matter what his principle of morality, is brought around at last to this point; hence Kant's genuine concern over a good will, i.e., a will inspired and controlled by the principle he has defined.

Nothing can be called *good*, without qualifications, except a good will. We now proceed to examine what exactly constitutes that will, simply good in itself, on which moral goodness depends.

Intelligence, wit, judgment, courage, resolution, perseverance, and so on, are no doubt good and desirable in many respects. But these gifts of nature may also be bad and mischievous if the will which is to make use of them is not good.

It is the same with gifts of fortune. Power, riches, honor, even health and happiness, inspire pride and often presumption if there is not a good will to check their influence.

A good will is good, not because of what it performs or accomplishes, not because of its usefulness or fruitfulness, but is simply good in itself. Even if it should happen that, owing to a special disfavor of fortune or the niggardly provision of a stepmotherly nature, a good will should wholly lack power to achieve its purpose, should by its greatest efforts achieve nothing, yet, like a jewel it would shine by its own light as a thing which has its whole value in itself.

We have, then, to develop the notion of a will good in itself and without reference to anything further. This notion already exists in the sound natural understanding, and requires rather to be clarified than taught or proved. In order to define more closely the notion of a good will, we will consider the wider notion of duty which includes the notion of a good will.

To have moral worth an act must be done from a sense of duty alone. We must distinguish between acts which accord with what duty requires, and acts done because duty requires. The latter alone have moral worth. We must distinguish between doing what duty requires, and doing because duty requires. Only the latter possesses moral worth.

If I do a thing because it is commanded, or because it brings advantage, my action is not moral. But if I do a thing because it is absolutely right in itself, my disposition is a moral one. We ought to do a thing, not because God wills it, but because it is righteous and good in itself.

Thus, it is a matter of duty that a dealer should not overcharge an inexperienced customer. Refraining from so doing for any other motive than that duty requires it, has no moral worth. It is one's duty to maintain life and happiness. Doing so for any other reason than that duty requires it, has no moral worth. It is one's duty to be generous, kind, honest, and so on. Being so for any reason except that duty requires it, has no moral worth. An action done from a sense of duty must wholly exclude the influence of inclination. An action, to be wholly moral, must exclude wholly the influence of inclination.

Take for instance a man who pays his debts. He may be swayed by the fear of being punished if he defaults, or he may pay because it is right that he should. In the first case his conduct is legally right, but it is only in the latter case that it is morally right.

It is a very beautiful thing to do good to men out of love for them or to be just from love of order. But this is not the true moral principle, suitable to our position among rational beings as men. To pretend it were, would be to set ourselves, with fanciful pride, above the thought of duty, like volunteers independent of command; to want to do, of our own pleasure, what we think we need no command to do.

An action done from a sense of duty derives its moral worth, not from the purpose which is to be attained by it, but from the principle upon which it is done. . . . The moral worth of an action does not lie in the results expected from it, but from the principle which it embodies.

What sort of principle, or moral law, can that be, the conception of which must determine the will, without regard to expected consequences, in order that the will may be called *good* absolutely and without qualifications?

It is this: "So act that the principle of your action might become a universal law." Canst thou will that the principle of thy action should become a universal law? If not, then it must be rejected.

Kant has now declared himself on one fundamental problem in moral philosophy. Another problem remains. It grows out of his remarks on the nature and importance of a good will. A *good* will may be defined, after Kant, as a will to do what ought to be done. Here the crucial term is *ought*. And it is crucial because it implies that the will in question is a free will. There would be no point to the remark that a man ought to do so-and-so if, as a matter of fact, he cannot; i.e., has no free will. Furthermore, we hold a man responsible for his action, but only if his action expresses his free will in the matter. The moralist in all of us is brought up short by any denial of man's free will. Such a denial would deprive much of our everyday ethical language of meaning. If you doubt this, try some time to be a moralist about your own or other people's conduct, and refrain from using such words as, *ought, ought not, obligation, responsible, accountable, answerable, deserved, undeserved,* and so on.

Without freedom of the will, no moral law and no moral responsibility are possible.

A man commits a theft. By the physical law of causality this deed is a necessary result of the causes preceding it in time; it was impossible that it could not have happened. How then can the moral judgment make any difference, and suppose it could have been omitted? The moral judgment says it ought to have been omitted. How can this be? How can a man be called free, at the same moment and with respect to the same act in which he is subject to an inevitable physical necessity?

Actions which are not free, and do not involve one's personality, do not give rise to obligations. Thus no man can be placed under an obligation to give up swallowing for the very reason that it would not be within his powers. Obligation, therefore, presupposes the use of freedom.

That is the difficulty. No free will, no morality. Deny freedom of will, and you annihilate morality. This is not to say that by denying freedom of will you "discourage" people, so that they will "give up trying to do what is right"; but rather that you make the term *morality* a meaningless term. Kant spent years thinking out a theory of knowledge which would legitimate the notion of free will. In this sense his *Critique of Pure Reason* was thought out with an eye to the

Critique of Practical Reason that followed it. In the next sentence, we are back in the ideas of the first *Critique:*

If we take things in time as things-in-themselves, as is commonly done, then it is impossible to reconcile the necessity of the causal relation with freedom. They are contradictory. From the former, it follows that every event, every action, is a necessary result of what existed in time preceding. So, since time past is no longer in my power, it would follow that every action I perform is the necessary result of causes which are not in my power. That is, it would follow that at the moment in which I act, I am never free.

Obligation expresses a sort of necessity which occurs nowhere else in nature except in man. It is impossible that anything in nature *ought to be* other than in fact it is. In truth, obligation, if one has before one's eyes only the succession in nature, has simply and solely no meaning. We can as little ask what ought to happen in nature as what attributes a circle ought to have.

If existence in time, that is, existence as phenomena, were the only kind we could ascribe to things-in-themselves, freedom would have to be rejected as a vain and impossible suggestion.

Consequently, if we would save freedom, no other way remains but to consider that the existence of a thing in time and therefore according to the law of physical necessity, is appearance only. Freedom we must attribute to the thing as a reality, as a thing-in-itself. This is inevitable, if we would retain both these contradictory conceptions of necessity and freedom. However, when we try to explain their combination in one and the same action, great difficulties present themselves.

Now, in order to remove the apparent contradiction between freedom and mechanism in one and the same action, we must recall what was said in the *Critique of Pure Reason,* or what follows from what was said there. It was said there that the necessity of nature—which cannot coexist with the freedom of the will—pertains only to things as phenomena. The category of causation, it was argued, extends to phenomena or appearances only. The possibility of freedom was thus left open, although its reality was not thereby proved.

Kant's words are important. He says, "The possibility of freedom was thus left open." That is all the help he claims from his theory of knowledge. It is sufficient, however. As his discourse shows, he proposes to use the undeniable *ought.* That we ought to do some things and ought not to do others is a point upon which all moralists would agree. They might differ as to what we ought or ought not to do. The essential point is that they would all use the notions of "oughtness" and "ought-notness." Returning to the argument, the only point is to change this "may be free," which Kant's theory of knowledge permits, into an "is free," which his moral insight demands.

The only point is to change this "may be free" into "is free." That is, to show, in an actual case, that certain actions do imply freedom. Now, it is a duty to realize the moral law in our acts. Therefore it must be possible. ("I

ought" implies "I can.") Therefore every rational being must assume whatever is implied by this possibility. Freedom of the will, independence of
causal necessity, is implied by this possibility. The assumption is as necessary as the moral law, in connection with which alone it is valid.

Freedom and duty reciprocally imply each other. It is the moral law, of
which we become directly conscious, that leads directly to the conception of
freedom. It is morality that first discovers to us the notion of freedom. The
moral law—"I ought"—which itself does not require any proof, proves the
actuality of freedom in those who recognize it as binding on themselves. A
man judges he can do, or refrain from doing, a certain act because he is conscious that he ought to. No one would ever have been so rash as to introduce
freedom into science had not the moral law forced it upon us.

Morality requires us only to be able to think freedom without self-contradiction, not to understand it. It is enough that our notion of the act as free
puts no obstacle in the way of the notion of it as mechanically necessary. Our
notion is that the act stands in quite a different relation to freedom from that
in which it stands to the mechanism of nature. From the point of view of my
Critique of Pure Reason this is possible; the doctrine of nature and necessity
and the doctrine of morality and freedom may each be true in its own
sphere.

How freedom of the will is possible, how we are to conceive it theoretically and positively, how man is a member of two worlds, how man's moral
actions must always appear necessitated while they are nonetheless free—all
this is not discoverable. Only that there is such a freedom, is postulated by
the moral law. How freedom is possible no human intelligence will ever
fully fathom. That freedom is possible, on the other hand, no sophistry will
ever wrest from the conviction of even the commonest man.

It will be said that the solution here proposed to the problem of freedom
involves great difficulty. But is any other solution easier and more intelligible?

Thus far Kant gives a clarifying and convincing presentation of
what is implied in moral judgment. A transition from moral philosophy to theology comes about in connection with his account of two
other "postulates" of morality. One of these postulates we have already seen, namely, free will. But there are two more to come,
namely, immortality and God. It is perhaps as well to let Kant tell his
own story. First, immortality:

The immortality of the soul is also a postulate of the moral law. By a
postulate I mean a theoretical proposition, not demonstrable as such, but
which is an inseparable result of an unconditional, *a priori*, practical (i.e.,
moral) law.

The connection is this. The moral law commands the perfect accordance
of the will with it. This must be possible, since it is commanded. But perfect
accordance of the will with the moral law is a perfection of which no rational
being of the sensible world is capable at any moment of his existence. Since,
nevertheless, it is commanded, it can only be realized in an infinite progres-

sion toward that perfect accordance. Now, this endless progress is only possible on the supposition of an endless duration of the existence and personality of the same rational being. This is called the *immortality of the soul*. The highest good for man, the perfect accord of his will with the moral law, is only possible on the supposition of the immortality of the soul. Consequently, this immortality, being inseparably connected with the moral law, is a postulate of pure practical reason.

For a rational but finite being, the only thing possible is an endless progress from the lower to higher degrees of perfection. . . . And thus he may hope, not indeed here nor at any imaginable point of his future existence, but only in the endlessness of his duration, to be perfectly adequate in his will.

This principle of the moral destination of our nature, namely, that it is only in an endless progress that we can attain perfect accordance with the moral law, is of the greatest use, not merely for supplementing the impotence of speculative reason, but also with respect to religion.

It is interesting to note that Kant has here reversed the usual order of things, according to which morality is deduced from theology. The argument continues:

The existence of God is also a postulate of the moral law. We proceed to exhibit this connection in a convincing manner.

Happiness is the condition of a rational being in the world with whom everything goes according to his wish and will. It rests, thus, on the harmony of physical nature with his ends and purposes. But the rational being in the world is not the cause of the world and of physical nature. There is, therefore, not the least ground in the moral law for any necessary connection between morality (i.e., virtue) and proportionate happiness.

To repeat: In a being that belongs to the world as part of it, is therefore dependent on it, and for that reason cannot by his will be a cause of nature nor by his own power make it completely harmonize, as far as his happiness is concerned, with his practical (i.e., moral) principles, in such a being there is not the least ground for any connection between morality and proportionate happiness.

Therefore, *the summum bonum,* the union of virtue and happiness, is possible in the world only on the supposition of a Supreme Being having a causality corresponding to moral character.

Accordingly, the existence of a cause of nature, distinct from nature itself, and containing the principle of this connection, this exact harmony of happiness with morality, is postulated.

Now, a being that is capable of acting on the conception of laws is an intelligence, and the causality of such a being according to this conception of laws, is his will. Therefore, the supreme cause of nature, which must be presupposed as a condition of the *summum bonum* (the union of virtue and happiness) is a being who is the cause of nature by intelligence and will, that is, its author; that is, God.

Now, in as much as it is a duty for us to promote the *summum bonum,* it is not merely allowable but a duty to presuppose the possibility of this *summum bonum*. And so, as this is possible only on condition of the existence of God, it is morally necessary, it is a matter of duty, to assume the existence of God.

These postulates of immortality, freedom, and the existence of God, all proceed from the principle of morality which is itself not a postulate but a law, an imperative. . . . These postulates are not theoretical dogmas, but suppositions practically necessary, i.e., required in the interests of practice. While they do not extend our speculative knowledge, they do give objective reality to the ideas of speculative reason in general, do give it a right to conceptions the possibility of which it could not otherwise venture to affirm. . . . Thus respect for the moral law leads, through these postulates, to conceptions which speculation might indeed present as problems but could never solve.

By way of conclusion it might be well to repeat the main turns of Kant's argument. He begins by assuming that a rational morality is the only morality. He shows that this means categorical and *a priori*. This enables him to eliminate three misleading conceptions—that it is a matter of feelings, that it is a matter of consequences, that it is a matter of agreeing with God's will, since on these counts it would be neither categorical nor *a priori*. He returns again to the conception of rational morality as categorical and *a priori*, and formulates its principle. This central thesis he then works over in terms of the notion of *ought* or *duty*, and in terms of the *good will*. These considerations raise the problem of free will. He sharpens the point of this problem. He then reaches back to his theory of knowledge for justification of the claim that free will "may be so." He returns, finally, to the conception of morality as necessitating free will as a postulate. There his moral philosophy proper stops, and his theology begins. Kant's moral philosophy, I think, contains some of the soundest and most clarifying analyses to be found anywhere in the history of human thought.

Note on Sources. The Kant materials in this section are quoted, abridged, or paraphrased from three books: *Lectures on Ethics*, translated by Louis Infield and published (1930) by Methuen and Co., Ltd.; *Fundamental Principles of the Metaphysics of Morals;* and *Critique of Practical Reason*. The Kant material, pages 208–209 this section, is from Kant's essay "The Supreme Principle of Morality" in the volume of Kant's essays translated by Louis Infield, pages 36–46. The material expounding and illustrating the categorical imperative is from the first two sections of Kant's *Fundamental Principles*. The material setting forth the postulates of morality is from the third section of the same work, and from Part I, Book II, Chapter II, of Kant's *Critique of Practical Reason*.

READING QUESTIONS

1. Kant begins by considering three theories about what makes an act right. Use the "If and only if" formula to state each.
2. Show that according to each of those theories an act is right because of its relation to something external to the act.
3. Kant's claim is that an act is right if and only if it is done out of respect for the moral law. Does this "internalize" the criterion?
4. Suppose defenders of the three positions mentioned above were to say that an act is right if and only if it is done (a) out of respect for how I feel about the act, (b) out of respect for the will of God, (c) out of respect for the consequences of the act. Would they thereby "internalize" their criteria, and so meet Kant's objections?
5. "Out of respect for the moral law." Which is (a) mainspring, (b) measuring rod.
6. Does acting "out of respect for" mean (a) doing what the moral law says, or (b) doing it because the moral law says to.
7. How Kant formulates the moral law.
8. Given his formulation of the moral law, he says, "I do not need any far-reaching penetration to discern what I have to do in order that my will may be morally good." Why not?
9. Is Kant's moral law the same as the Golden Rule?
10. He says that acting on the principle of private happiness is the direct opposite of acting on the principle of morality. His point here.
11. He says that the moral law confronts us as a "categorical" imperative. What that means. If a categorical imperative, then not what other kind of imperative?
12. He says that obeying the moral law is not a "hypothetical" imperative. What that means. If not a hypothetical imperative, then what other kind?
13. Use Kant's notion of acting out of respect for the moral law to show what he would mean by (a) right act, (b) good will, (c) categorical imperative, (d) duty.
14. Use courage (a gift of nature) and wealth (a gift of fortune) to explain Kant's claim that only a good will is good unconditionally, good without qualification.
15. How Kant's moral law differs from a scientific law. Which is descriptive? Which is prescriptive?
16. Why Kant is concerned with the free will problem. What makes it a problem?
17. How he uses his distinction between phenomenon and thing-in-

itself to show *that* freedom is possible. What about *"how* freedom is possible"?

18. What it means to say that free will is a "postulate" of morality. Kant mentions two other postulates. Namely.

19. Wherein you find Kant (a) most, (b) least convincing.

INDEPENDENT STUDY

1. A great deal of Kant's philosophizing outside of ethics has a supportive, defensive, and explanatory bearing on his position in ethics. The job is to see this without getting lost in the woods. In this book you have Kant in three topics (see table of contents). Begin with those. Supplement them with W. H. Walsh's article "Kant" in the *Encyclopedia of Philosophy.* If the Walsh overview is not enough to enable you to relate Kant's views in ethics to other parts of his philosophy, try E. Troeltsch's article "Kant" in Hastings' *Encyclopedia of Religion and Ethics,* or G. J. Warnock's article on Kant in *Critical History of Western Philosophy,* edited by D. J. O'Connor.

2. Read Chapters 6 and 7 in S. Körner's small paperback, *Kant,* in the Pelican series. Guided by Körner, write a paper on Kant's account of moral experience and its relation to science and religion.

SECTION 3. JOHN STUART MILL: THE APPEAL TO HAPPINESS

From Kant to Mill.   Our subject is still the principle of morality. We began with Paley's attempt to ground morality in theology, to distinguish between right and wrong by reference to God's will: that is right which agrees, and wrong which disagrees with God's will. Difficulties latent in Paley's position were noted and need not be repeated here. In Kant's attempt to argue that morality is categorical, that it is not grounded in anything, but "stands on its own feet," we met a complete antithesis to the position represented by Paley. Kant's effort to disengage morality from theology, as well as from happiness, stands alone. The trend of moral philosophizing has been for the most part away from Kant. In J. S. Mill one meets a moralist who is prepared to argue that an act is right if, and only if, it produces more happiness than any other act possible under the circumstances.

Biographical Note.   John Stuart Mill grew up in the group that included Jeremy Bentham, James Mill (father of J. S.), T. R. Malthus, David Ricardo, George Grote, and others. These men were interested primarily in political, economic, and social reform. They were the driving force behind the first Reform Bill, the early Factory Acts, and so on. They were known, in their own day, as the Utilitarians and as the Philosophical Radicals: Utilitarians because they enquired of any law, custom, or institution, "What is its utility? Of what use is it?" If no answer were forthcoming, beyond some vague statement about its prestige or its long standing, they proposed to scrap it. Philosophical radicals because they aimed to go to the roots of things, the word *root* being English for the Latin word *radix*. The root to which these men proposed to go was human happiness. That, for them, was the "root question" to be addressed to any law, custom, or institution. For the most part they did not spend time seeking to justify this principle. This task J. S. Mill undertook to do. They applied the principle that *right* means "producing human happiness," or "being maximally productive of human happiness." He undertook to clarify and defend the principle in his book *Utilitarianism*. Most of his other writings are related to his *Utilitarianism*. Thus, in his essay "On Liberty," written a few years before his *Utilitarianism*, but based on the principles subsequently given in the later book, he argued that the greatest happiness of the greatest number is more likely to be achieved by allowing as much freedom of thought and action as possible. In his treatise "Considerations on Representative Government," he argued that government by elected representatives would offer a better guarantee of human happiness than government by monarchs or aristocrats. In his monograph *The Subjection of Women* he argued that the purpose of representative government was, in part, frustrated by refusing votes to women. The range and sincerity of his writings have given him great influence in the past hundred years. For other biographical notes, see pp. 32 and 312.

The Argument of the Passages.   Mill's exposition and defense of the appeal to happiness as the basis of morality moves through five turns. He first states the problem: What is the basis or principle of morality? He then explores two "false leads," and shows grounds for rejecting them. He then states his own position at some length. He then asks the question: Is this belief open to any kind of proof or disproof? and answers as best he can. He turns then to a review of objections and misunderstandings which, he knows, will be brought against his claim. These he seeks to answer. With this accomplished, he is in a position to say, "I have posed an age-long problem. I have criticized two widely held theories. I have advanced my own answer. I have shown what sort of proof it is amenable to. I have stated and removed as many objections as I can think of. The defense rests."

The *Utilitarianism* begins as follows:

There are few circumstances more significant of the backward state of speculation than the little progress which has been made in the controversy respecting the criterion of right and wrong.

From the dawn of philosophy the question concerning the foundation of morality has been accounted the main problem in speculative thought, has occupied the most gifted intellects, and divided them into sects and schools carrying on a vigorous warfare against one another.

After more than two thousand years the same discussions continue. Philosophers are still ranged under the same contending banners. Neither thinkers nor mankind at large seem nearer to agreement than when the youthful Socrates listened to the old Protagoras.

The problem is now before us: What is the foundation of morality? He proposes to examine two familiar answers. The first of these is the observation that this is a matter of personal opinion. Thus one reads the remarks, "There's nothing right or wrong, but thinking makes it so." "Right you are, if you think you are." That is, an act is right if you, or the community, or all mankind, think it is; right and wrong are mere matters of opinion, are merely subjective. There are many different ways of stating this notion. Of all moralists who hold this view Mill says:

They all, in one phrase or another, place the test of right and wrong in a feeling of approval or disapproval . . . they find certain feelings of approval and disapproval in themselves . . . a great part of all the ethical reasoning in books and in the world is of this sort.

His criticism of this appeal to moral feeling to settle the matter is short and pointed:

All experience shows that "moral feelings" are eminently artificial, and the product of culture; that the most senseless and pernicious "feelings" can be raised to the utmost intensity by inculcation, as hemlock and thistles could be reared to luxuriant growth by sowing them instead of wheat.

Things which have been really believed by all mankind have been proved to be false, as that the sun rises and sets. Can immunity from similar error be claimed for the "moral feelings"?

I do not found the morality of actions upon anybody's opinion or feeling of them. I found it upon facts.

"What facts?" we ask. Let us first glance at another doctrine: the appeal to nature. A thing is right, it will be said, if it is according to nature, if it is natural; wrong, if it is contrary to nature, if it is unnatural.

We will inquire into the truth of the doctrines which make nature a test of right and wrong, good and evil, or which in any mode or degree attach merit or approval to following, imitating, or obeying nature. A reference to that supposed standard is the predominant ingredient in the vein of thought and feeling which was opened by Rousseau, and which has infiltrated itself most widely into the modern mind.

That any mode of thinking, feeling, or acting is "according to nature" is usually accepted as a strong argument for its goodness. If it can be said, with any plausibility, that "nature enjoins" anything, the propriety of obeying the injunction is considered to be made out. And, conversely, the imputation of being "contrary to nature" is thought to bar the thing so designated from being tolerated or excused. It is thought that nature affords some criterion of what we ought to do.

Mill's handling of the appeal to nature is a good example of condensed refutation. He first points out that the term *nature,* or the phrase *according to nature,* is ambiguous. He states the two senses in which it might be used. He then shows that, given the first sense, the appeal to nature is meaningless; and, given the second sense, it is irrational and immoral.

The word *nature* has two principal meanings: it either denotes the entire system of things, with the aggregate of all their properties, or it denotes things as they would be, apart from human intervention.

Such being the two principal senses of the word *nature,* in which of these is it taken when the word and its derivatives are used to convey ideas of commendation, approval, and even moral obligation?

In the first of these senses, the doctrine that man ought to follow nature is unmeaning, since man has no power to do anything else than follow nature; all his actions are done through, and in obedience to, some one or many of nature's physical or mental laws.

In the other sense of the term, the doctrine that man ought to follow nature, or in other words, ought to make the spontaneous course of things the model of his voluntary actions, is equally irrational and immoral.

Irrational, because all human action whatever, consists in altering, and all useful action in improving the spontaneous course of nature. Immoral, because the course of natural phenomena being replete with everything which when committed by human beings is most worthy of abhorrence, any one who endeavored in his actions to imitate the natural course of things would be universally seen and acknowledged to be the wickedest of men.

The doctrine that the existing order of things is the natural order, and that, being natural, all innovation upon it is criminal, is vicious. Conformity to nature has no connection whatever with right and wrong. The idea can never be fitly introduced into ethical discussions at all. That a thing is unnatural is no argument for it being blamable.

At this point we may give Mill's own position. We have now two alternatives with which to compare it. He says:

All action is for the sake of some end, and rules of action must take their whole character and color from the end to which they are subservient.

The creed which accepts the greatest happiness principle as the foundation of morals holds that actions are right in proportion as they tend to promote happiness, wrong as they tend to produce the reverse of happiness. By happiness is intended pleasure, and the absence of pain; by unhappiness, pain, and the privation of pleasure. This theory I propose to expound and defend.

The standard is not the agent's own greatest happiness, but the greatest amount of happiness altogether. As between his own happiness and that of others, utilitarianism requires him to be as strictly impartial as a disinterested and benevolent spectator.

The test of morality is not the greatest happiness of the agent himself. Utilitarianism does not dream of defining morality to be the self-interest of the agent. The greatest happiness principle is the greatest happiness of mankind and of all sentient creatures.

He who does anything for any other purpose than to increase the amount of happiness in the world is no more deserving of admiration than the ascetic mounted on his pillar. He may be an inspiring proof of what men can do, but assuredly not an example of what they should do.

Pleasure and freedom from pain are the only things desirable as ends, and all desirable things are desirable either for the pleasure inherent in them or as means to the promotion of pleasure and the prevention of pain.

Mill has stated that morality is a matter of consequences. An act is right or wrong, according to its consequences, not because it agrees with someone's opinion, or with universal opinion, or with nature, or (by implication) with God's will. He pauses a moment to elaborate this point:

By "calculating the consequences" is meant, generally, calculating the consequences of classes of actions. There are, as we shall note, exceptions to this, but over all we must look at actions as though multiplied, and in large masses. Take murder for example. There are many persons, to kill whom would be to remove men who are a cause of no good to any human being, who are a cause of cruel physical and moral suffering to several, and whose whole influence tends to increase the mass of unhappiness and vice. Were such a man to be murdered, the balance of traceable consequences would be greatly in favor of the act. But, the counter consideration, still on the principle of utility, is that unless persons were punished for killing, and taught not to kill, nobody's life would be safe.

We say, "generally," not "universally." For the admission of exceptions to rules is a necessity equally felt in all systems of morality. To take an obvious instance: The rule against homicide, the rule against deceiving, the rule against taking advantage of superior strength, are suspended against enemies in the field and partially against malefactors in private life. In each case, the rule is suspended as far as is required by the peculiar nature of the case. That the moralities arising from special circumstances of the action may be so important as to over-rule those arising from the class of acts to which it belongs, is a liability common to all ethical systems.

The existence of exceptions to moral rules is no stumbling block peculiar to the principle of utility. The essential is that the exception should itself be a general rule; so that, being definite, and not left to the partial judgment of the individual, it might not shake the stability of the wider rule in the cases to which the reason of the exception does not extend. This is an ample foundation for "the construction of a scheme of morality."

With respect to the means of inducing people to conform in their actions to the scheme so formed, the utilitarian system depends, like all other schemes of morality, on the external motives supplied by law and opinion and the internal motives produced by education or reason.

The greatest happiness principle is now before us. Is the principle open to any kind of proof? Mill's answer amounts to a denial. The rationale of this denial is as follows:

Of what sort of proof is this principle of the greatest happiness susceptible?

It is evident that it cannot be proof in the ordinary and popular meaning of the term. Questions of ultimate ends are not amenable to direct proof. Whatever can be proved to be good must be shown to be a means to something admitted to be good without proof.

The medical art is proved to be good by its conducing to health. But how is it possible to prove that health is good? The art of music is good, for the reason among others, that it produces pleasure. But what proof is it possible to give that pleasure is good?

No comprehensive formula, including all things good in themselves and not as means to things good in themselves, is a subject of what is commonly meant by *proof*. It may be accepted or rejected, but not proved in the usual sense of that term.

There is a larger meaning of the word *proof* in which this question of ultimate principles is as amendable to proof as any other of the disputed questions of philosophy. The subject is within the cognizance of the rational faculty. Its acceptance or rejection does not depend on blind impulse or arbitrary choice.

The problem has been stated. False solutions have been exposed. His own solution has been given. The meaning of *proof* in these matters has been made clear. He turns to objections that may be raised. A study of these objections and replies will clarify and fix the doctrine in one's mind.

It may not be superfluous to notice a few of the common misapprehensions of utilitarian ethics, even those which are so obvious and gross that it might appear impossible for any person of candor and intelligence to fall into them.

The first objection is that such a moral philosophy is a godless doctrine:

Utilitarianism is a godless doctrine: The appeal to happiness, instead of the appeal to the will of God, is a godless, i.e., irreligious, principle of morality.

Mill's answer is to carry the war into the enemy's camp:

The question [whether the appeal to happiness is a godless doctrine] depends upon what idea we have formed of the moral character of the Deity. If it be a true belief that God desires above all things the happiness of His creatures, and that this was His purpose in their creation, then utilitarianism is not only not a godless doctrine, but more profoundly religious than any other.

Although the existence of God as a wise and just lawgiver is not a necessary part of the feelings of morality, it may still be maintained that those feelings make His existence eminently desirable. No doubt they do, and that is the great reason why we find that good men and women cling to the belief and are pained by its being questioned.

If the objection [that utilitarianism is a godless doctrine] means that utilitarianism does not recognize the revealed will of God as the supreme law of morals, I answer: An utilitarian who believes in the perfect goodness and wisdom of God, necessarily believes that whatever God has thought fit to reveal on the subject of morals must fulfill the requirements of utilitarianism in a supreme degree.

A second objection:

To suppose that life has no higher end than pleasure, no better and nobler object of desire and pursuit, is utterly mean and groveling; a doctrine worthy only of swine.

Mill's answer:

This supposes that human beings are capable of no pleasure except those of which swine are capable. If this supposition were true, the charge could not be denied; but it would then be no charge, for if the sources of pleasure were precisely the same for human beings and for swine, then the rule of life which is good enough for the one would be good enough for the other.

The comparison is felt to be degrading precisely because a beast's pleasures do not satisfy a human being's conception of happiness. Human beings have faculties more elevated than the animal appetites, and do not regard anything as happiness which does not include their gratification.

A third objection:

That utilitarianism [the appeal to the pleasure-pain consequences of action] renders men cold and unsympathizing; that it chills their moral feelings toward individuals; that is makes them regard only the consequences of actions, not taking into account the personal qualities from which those actions emanate.

Mill's answer:

If this means that utilitarians do not allow their judgment concerning the rightness or wrongness of an act to be influenced by their opinion of the quality of the person who does it, then it is a complaint not against utilitarianism but against having any standard of morality at all. For certainly no known ethical standard decides an action to be good or bad because it is done by a good or bad man; still less because it is done by an amiable, brave, or benevolent man, or the contrary. These considerations are relevant, not to the estimation of actions, but of persons; and there is nothing in utilitarianism inconsistent with the fact that there are other things which interest us in persons besides the rightness or wrongness of their actions.

The stoic moralists, indeed, were fond of saying that he who has virtue has everything. But no claim of this description is made for the virtuous man by the utilitarian moralist. There are other desirable possessions and qualities besides virtue. A right action does not necessarily indicate a virtuous character. Actions that are blamable often proceed from qualities entitled to praise. When this is so in any particular case, it modifies one's moral estimation of the agent, but not of the act.

A fourth objection is that the morality of an action depends upon the motive, not upon the consequences. Mill answers:

As to motive, the utilitarian position is this: Motive has nothing to do with the morality of the action, though much with the worth of the agent. He who saves a fellow creature from drowning does what is morally right, whether his motive be duty or the hope of being paid for his trouble.

A fifth objection:

A stock argument against utilitarianism consists in saying that an utilitarian will be apt to make his own particular case an exception to moral rules, and when under temptation, will see an utility in the breach of a rule, greater than he will see in its observance.

Mill's answer:

But is utilitarianism the only creed which is able to furnish us with excuses for evil doing and means of cheating our own conscience? They are afforded in abundance by all doctrines which recognize as a fact in morals the existence of conflicting considerations; which all doctrines do that have been believed by sane persons.

It is not the fault of any creed, but of the complicated nature of human affairs, that rules of conduct cannot be so framed as to require no exceptions, and that hardly any kind of action can safely be laid down as either always obligatory or always condemnable.

There is no ethical creed which does not temper its laws by giving a certain latitude, under the moral responsibility of the agent, for accommodation to peculiarities of circumstances. At the opening thus made, self-deception and dishonest casuistry get in.

There exists no moral system under which cases of conflicting obligation do not arise. These are the real difficulties, the knotty points, both in a theory of ethics and in the conscientious guidance of personal conduct. But is any one less qualified to deal with cases of conflicting obligations by reason of the fact that he possesses an ultimate standard to which such cases can be referred?

A sixth objection:

Utilitarianism is only an appeal to expedience, and an appeal to expedience is not as high morally as an appeal to principle.

Mill's answer:

This objection rests on a loose use of the term *expedience*. Generally, the *expedient* means that which is expedient for the particular interests of the agent himself; as when a minister of state sacrifices the interests of his country to keep himself in place. The expedient in this sense is a branch of the hurtful; and to claim that utilitarianism is an appeal to the expedient, in this sense, is simply to misunderstand or misrepresent its meaning.

Utilitarianism does recognize in human beings the power of sacrificing their own greatest good for the good of others. I must repeat again, what critics seldom have the justice to acknowledge, that the happiness which forms the standard of what is right in conduct, is not the agent's own happiness but the happiness of all concerned.

Utilitarianism does, however, refuse to admit that sacrifice of one's own good is itself a good. A sacrifice which does not increase the sum of happiness is wasted. The only sacrifice which utilitarianism applauds is that which is made in the interests of the happiness either of mankind or of individuals within the limits imposed by the interests of mankind.

A seventh objection:

Happiness cannot be the rational purpose of life, because it is unattainable.

Mill's answer:

This objection, were it well founded, would go to the root of the matter; for if no happiness is to be had at all by human beings, the attainment of it cannot be the end of morality. However, the assertion that it is impossible that human life be happy is an exaggeration.

If by *happiness* be meant a continuity of highly pleasurable excitement, it is evident that this is impossible. A state of exalted pleasure lasts only for a few moments, or in some cases for somewhat longer periods. If this kind of intense rapture be meant by *happiness*, then happiness is unattainable.

But this is not what philosophers have meant by *happiness* when they taught that happiness was the end of life. The happiness which they meant was not a life of rapture, but moments of such in an existence made up of few and transitory pains, many and various pleasures, with a decided predominance of the active over the passive, and having as the foundation not to expect more from life than it is capable of bestowing. A life thus composed, to those who have been fortunate enough to obtain it, has always appeared worthy of the name of happiness. And such an existence is even now the lot of many.

An eighth objection:

We cannot calculate all the consequences of any action and thus cannot estimate the degree in which it promotes human happiness.

Mill's answer:

Is there any department of human affairs in which we can do all that is desirable? Because we cannot foresee everything, is there no such thing as foresight? Can no estimate be formed of consequences, which would be any guide for our conduct, unless we can calculate all consequences? Because we cannot predict every effect which may follow from a person's death, are we to say that we cannot know that murder would be destructive to human happiness? Whether morality is or is not a question of consequences, it cannot be denied that prudence is a question of consequences, and if there is such a thing as prudence, it is because the consequences of actions can be calculated.

A ninth objection:

There is not time, previous to action, for calculating and weighing the effects of any line of conduct on the general happiness.

Mill's answer:

This is exactly as if any one were to say that it is impossible to guide our conduct by Christianity, because there is not time, on every occasion on which everything has to be done, to read through the Old and New Testaments.

The answer to the objection is that there has been ample time, namely, the whole past duration of the human species. During all that time mankind have been learning by experience the tendencies of action; on which experience all the prudence, as well as all the morality, of life is dependent.

Nobody argues that the art of navigation is not founded on astronomy, because sailors cannot wait to calculate the nautical almanac. Being rational creatures, they go to sea with it ready calculated, and all rational creatures go out upon the sea of life with their minds made up on the common questions of right and wrong.

There is no difficulty in proving any ethical standard whatever to work ill, if we suppose universal idiocy to be conjoined with it, but on any hypothesis short of that, mankind must by this time have acquired positive beliefs as to the effects of some actions on their happiness. To inform a traveler respecting the place of his ultimate destination is not to forbid the use of landmarks and direction posts on the way.

A tenth objection:

If happiness is made the ultimate standard by which other things are judged to be good or bad, then we are not in a position to distinguish among kinds of happiness with respect to their goodness or badness.

Mill's answer:

It is quite compatible with the principle of utility to recognize the fact that some kinds of pleasure are more desirable and more valuable than others. It would be absurd that while, in estimating all other things, quality is considered as well as quantity, the estimation of pleasures should be supposed to depend on quantity alone.

Of two pleasures, if there be one to which all or almost all who have experience of both give a decided preference, irrespective of any feeling of moral obligation to prefer it, that is the more desirable pleasure.

Now it is an unquestionable fact that those who are equally acquainted with, and equally capable of appreciating and enjoying, both, do give a most marked preference to the manner of existence which employs their higher faculties. It is better to be a human being dissatisfied than a pig satisfied; better to be Socrates dissatisfied than a fool satisfied. And if the fool, or the pig, is of a different opinion, it is because they know only their side of the question. The other party to the comparison knows both sides.

Few human creatures would consent to be changed into any of the lower animals for a promise of the fullest allowance of an animal's pleasures. No intelligent human being would consent to be a fool, no instructed person would consent to be an ignoramus, no person of feeling and conscience would consent to be selfish and base, even though they should be persuaded that the fool, the dunce or the rascal is better satisfied with his lot than they are with theirs.

From this verdict of the only competent judges, I apprehend there can be no appeal. On the question which of two pleasures is the best worth having, which of two modes of existence is the most grateful to the feelings, the judgment of those who are qualified by knowledge of both must be admitted as final. . . . There is no other tribunal to be referred to.

Note on Sources. The Mill material in this section is quoted, abridged, or paraphrased from his essay "Nature" and from Chapters I, II, and IV of his *Utilitarianism.*

Reading References. It is not easy to find a sympathetic account of Mill as a moralist. In a little book by George Santayana, *Some Turns of Thought in Modern Philosophy,* there is a passage, beginning on page 55, "With this dissolution always in prospect . . . ," which is an exception to this rule. The trouble arose, even in Mill's own day, over his somewhat unsatisfactory handling of the tenth objection: The appeal *to* happiness does not permit criticism *of* happiness. Nor does it. F. H. Bradley's *Ethical Studies,* Chapter 3, "Pleasure for Pleasure's Sake," contains a criticism of Mill's argument. Mill's *Autobiography* is worth reading. It gives a picture of the man who made a firm stand for happiness in moral philosophy. Courtney's *Life of Mill* and the third volume of Stephen's *English Utilitarians* are good books on Mill. The subsequent elaboration and defense and modification of Mill's position is to be traced in Henry Sidgwick's *Method of Ethics* and G. E. Moore's *Principia Ethica.*

READING QUESTIONS

1. Mill begins by considering two theories about what makes a right act right. Use the "If and only if" formula to state each.
2. His criticism of the first theory is that "moral feelings" can be mistaken, are not infallible. But, to speak strictly, can a feeling, simply as a feeling, ever be either true or false? How, for example, is the feeling of hunger, simply as a feeling, ever either true or false?
3. Suppose the first theory is revised: "An act is right if and only if I judge or state that it is right." (A judgment or statement, unlike a feeling, can be either true or false.) Mill's criticism, revised to meet this reformulation, would be that judgments or statements can be mistaken, are not infallible. Would that dispose of the theory? If not, what criticism of the theory would you propose?
4. His criticism of the second theory is (a) its key phrase ("according to nature") is ambiguous. How so? (b) If you develop this ambiguity you get a dilemma. Namely?
5. Use the "If and only if" formula to state Mill's own theory. Why this theory is called utilitarianism.
6. What points about his own theory is he making in his reference

to (a) a disinterested and benevolent spectator, (b) an ascetic mounted on his pillar.

7. Mill seems willing to admit exceptions to particular moral rules. For example. One general moral rule, however, to which he would admit no exceptions.

8. The principle of utility admits of (a) no exceptions, (b) no proof. Show why, in each case.

9. The principle of utility, he says, admits of no proof. However, its acceptance or rejection, he goes on to say, does not depend on blind impulse or arbitrary choice. On what does it depend, then?

10. If you were Mill, what would you do with this question: "Why does producing the greatest amount of happiness make an act right?"

11. Mill is seeking to formulate the first or ultimate principle of morality. It is a mark of such a principle, when found, that it admits of no exceptions and no proof. Would this hold of first or ultimate principles in other fields besides morality?

12. Mill meets the first objection to utilitarianism ("It is a godless doctrine") by arguing that it is no objection if God is Himself a utilitarian. But suppose God is Himself not a utilitarian. Then what?

13. Put this question to Mill: "If you believe that God is good, then you should believe that He cares more about our goodness than about our happiness." Can you suggest Mill's reply?

14. Suppose a person has a swinish conception of happiness. What would Mill be entitled to say to him? On what grounds would he be entitled to say it?

15. "A right action does not necessarily indicate a virtuous character." Why not?

16. "The motive has nothing to do with the morality of the action." (a) Why not? (b) Would Kant agree to this?

17. What Mill would say to the statements (a) The road to hell is paved with good intentions. (b) The end justifies the means.

18. What, precisely is an act, considered apart from the agent's purpose or intention? How would you tell what act it was? Would it differ from an event in nature, e.g., a stone rolling down a hill? If not, should we speak of a stone's behavior as moral or immoral, depending on the consequences?

19. How he meets the objections (a) Happiness is unattainable. (b) We cannot calculate all the consequences of any action.

20. He says it is quite compatible with the principle of utility to recognize that some kinds of pleasure are more desirable, more valuable, than others. Is it? If not, why not? If so, on what grounds?

21. Wherein you find Mill (a) most, (b) least convincing.

INDEPENDENT STUDY

1. Read the articles on (a) Bentham by D. H. Munro, (b) James Mill by D. H. Munro, (c) J. S. Mill by J. B. Schneewind, all in the *Encyclopedia of Philosophy*. [If you desire another round, read the articles on (a) Bentham by J. Mew, (b) James Mill, and (c) J. S. Mill by Leslie Stephen, all in the *Dictionary of National Biography*.] These articles on Bentham and James Mill and J. S. Mill will acquaint you with three important founders of English utilitarianism. Read the article "Utilitarianism" by J. J. C. Smart in the *Encyclopedia of Philosophy;* and "Utilitarianism" by A. W. Hastings in the *Encyclopedia of Religion and Ethics*. Write an essay on English utilitarianism with reference to Bentham and the two Mills.
2. You have by now read brief statements of their position by Paley, Kant, and Mill. At this point, reassemble three articles mentioned earlier in reference to Paley: "Teleological Ethics" by W. P. Alston, "Deontological Ethics" by R. G. Olson, and "Ultimate Moral Principles" by A. P. Griffiths—all in the *Encyclopedia of Philosophy*. You now have more to go on. Use what you have learned about Paley and Kant and Mill to set forth your opinions on the essential points being made by Alston and Olson and Griffiths.
3. Read the brief but compact article "The Ethical Movement" by G. Spiller in Hastings's *Encyclopedia of Religion and Ethics*. Then write a paper that you would read to your town's Ethical Society, on John Stuart Mill, explaining to your fellow members why they would, or would not, benefit from reading Mill's writings on ethics.

SECTION 4. FRIEDRICH NIETZSCHE: TWO MORALITIES: MASTER AND SLAVE

From Mill to Nietzsche. We have examined three attempts to formulate the principle of morality, to state what makes a right act right. Paley found the rightness of an act to depend upon its agreement with the will of God. Kant denied that the rightness of an act depended upon anything, asserting that an act, if right, is so categorically, without reference to anything outside of itself. Mill found the rightness of an act to depend upon its consequences, these consequences being the amount of happiness that it brought about. We have now to examine the claim of a fourth moralist whose findings differ radically from any of the other three. The difference is so great that it is rather difficult to institute a comparison. The point may be approached in terms of an example. Consider honesty, the habit of telling the truth and being square in one's dealings. Let us suppose each of our moralists to be asked, "Why is it right to be honest and wrong to be dishonest?" "Because it agrees with God's will," Paley would say. "There is no reason why honesty is right," Kant would say, "It is right simply because it is right." "Because it makes for the great amount of happiness in the long run and for the most people," Mill would say. Now our fourth moralist would be inclined to answer the question by asking another: "Who said that honesty is right, and dishonesty wrong?" That is, he would ask whether the very wording of the question doesn't beg the question. You first accept certain things as right and wrong, he would argue, then you ask what principle is involved in thus distinguishing them. That is to beg the question. In other words, you can only ask this question by first assuming, without inquiry, that some things are right and others wrong, but if you query *that* fact, then where are you?

Biographical Note.   Friedrich Nietzsche was born in Germany in 1844 and died in 1900 at the age of fifty-six. His biography may be epitomized in terms of three periods: years of preparation, years of production, and years of insanity. (1) He was born into a puritanical, religious family and was intended by his parents to enter the church. To this end he was educated privately and at a denominational school. In the university at Bonn he broke completely with his family in doctrinal matters. He moved on to the university at Leipzig. There he met Wagner, the German composer, and became a fervent Wagnerite. He discovered Schopenhauer's writings in a second-hand bookshop and became a convinced Schopenhauerian. He met Erwin Rhode, the historian of Greek culture, and became engrossed in the problems and perspectives of the cultural history of mankind. He did military service for a year in a war with Austria, returning to the University of Leipzig to complete his studies. The following year he was appointed to the chair of classical philology in the university at Bâle, received his Ph.D., and began work on his important book *The Birth of Tragedy.* The next year he was called once more into military service in the Franco-Prussian War which had just begun, 1870. He was head of an ambulance corps, but did only three weeks' service. Diphtheria ended his military career. He returned to the university at Bâle and resumed lectures. For eight years he remained at this work. During this period he was arriving at conclusions which formed the basis of his future writings. He published *The Birth of Tragedy.* It met with a chilly reception. His prestige began to decline. His next book, *Thoughts Out of Season,* contained four essays in which he criticized Strauss, Schopenhauer, German historians, and others. Two years later for reasons of poor health he retired on a small pension from the university.

(2) It should never be forgotten that Nietzsche was, first and last, a cultural historian; that is, he was interested in, and drew his inspiration from, the study of the cultures achieved by various peoples, ancient and modern. He wrote a series of books that develop really one theme. His investigations into mankind's cultural history, understanding by the term *culture* such things as art, religion, science, morality, government, and so on, impressed him with the enormous diversity that has obtained in these things at different times and places. But that was not all. He was equally impressed with the fact that cultural values are local and transitory affairs. He expressed this in the notion of the relativity of cultural values. By this he meant that cultural values are relative to time and place, relative to the needs peculiar to the peoples among whom they flourish. In other words, there is nothing eternal or absolute or immutable about them, and this, he felt, holds for values of all descriptions: religious, artistic, social, moral, scientific, and so on. On the rebound from his earlier orthodox training, he dismissed them with a flourish of his pen in his book *Human, All Too Human*. That was his "great discovery." Values, one and all, are "human-all-too-human." The rest of his work may be described as a series of studies in the natural history of human values. *Human, All Too Human*, was followed by *Dawn of Day*, and it in turn by *Joyful Wisdom*. Clearly, a new note was being struck.

What idea was Nietzsche working out in these books? It was something like this: The cultural history of mankind shows that aristocratic qualities flourish in the early stages of a culture and disappear gradually as that culture becomes old. In Homer's time, the Greeks were "heroes"; by the time of Pericles and the Spartan war, they had become mere "sophists" and "philosophers" and "scientists." In early Roman history there were great kings who founded a race that conquered the ancient world, but centuries later, in the days of imperial decline, this nation of "strong, silent men" had become helpless victims of their own weakening civilization and the new races of barbarians as yet "untouched" by such things. These newcomers swept over Europe, and another page in cultural history was begun, but with the same result. By the nineteenth century these "Germanic" peoples who had made over the civilization of ancient Rome had become democratic, even socialistic; they cultivated "science," "art," "morality" or (in some instances) decadent forms of "immorality," wealth, ease, the "emancipation of women," optimism, pessimism, philosophy, and so on.

There is no quarreling with Nietzsche's likes and dislikes in these matters. The sight of Achilles sulking in his tent was simply something he admired more than the sight of Karl Marx sulking in the library of the British Museum. A Greek athlete or a Roman warrior was simply not in the same degenerate class with J. S. Mill pleading for representative government and the political enfranchisement of women, or Schopenhauer brooding over the misery and folly of human affairs. Hence, the titles of his books. To "see through" modern degeneration was "the dawn of day"; to realize that "real virtues" belong in the context of fresh and vigorous young cultures was the first step in "joyful wisdom." Nietzsche was carried away on the wings of this sort of thing. Lonely, poor, sickly, unpopular, a bachelor *malgré lui*, he nevertheless lived on in the private world of "transvalued values," heaping scorn on "art" and "science" and "morality" and "religion" and "emancipation" and "democracy" and "socialism" and "humanitarianism." He poured his soul into the mold of one beautiful book, *Thus Spake Zarathustra*. This was the fine flower of his genius. Through the mouth of Zarathustra, the prophet of his doctrine, he preached and exhorted and satirized in pages of marvelous beauty and suggestiveness. But the nineteenth century passed Zarathustra by on the other side. Only a handful took the trouble to read him, and even these few were puzzled and disturbed. For their enlightenment, Nietzsche wrote two more books, *Beyond Good and Evil* and *The Genealogy of Morals*. They were intended as commentaries on the *Zarathustra*. The substance of their argument is given in the passages that follow. The balance of Nietzsche's writings carry further the ideas presented already. The Zarathustra group was followed by *The Twilight of the Idols, Antichrist, The Will to Power* (unfinished), and his own autobiography bearing the significant title *Ecce Homo*.

In 1889, now forty-five, Nietzsche began to lose the use of his mind. For the next eleven years he was caught in the toils of a steadily increasing insanity. The picture brings to mind Schopenhauer's gloomy hypothesis and leaves one impatient with the century that had allowed the man's genius to flicker out alone and unheeded.

The Argument of the Passages. The following passages, chosen principally from Nietzsche's *Beyond Good and Evil* and *The Genealogy of Morals,* exhibit six turns of thought. He begins by repudiating the whole notion of trying to formulate any principle of morality, in the sense that moralists have traditionally sought to do this. He insists that there is no such thing as morality having one fundamental principle running through it; that, on the contrary, there have been and are many moralities; and that any attempt to think philosophically about morality must begin by recognizing its diversity and the fact of its having had a history like any other phase of human culture. He propounds then a tentative natural history or genealogy of morals. From this he undertakes to draw some far-reaching conclusions. These he calls collectively his *immoralism*, or *transvaluation of values*. One fundamental distinction, arising out of his account of the natural history of morals and forming the foundation of his immoralism, is that between master morality and slave morality. The characteristics of each he then describes at some length. The doctrine is now substantially complete. However, to illustrate it more concretely, he applies it in a critical way to two phenomena of modern morality, namely, the emancipation of woman, and the close connection between modern morality and Christianity. He closes with a few reflections on his own significance.

The opening passages are fundamental. In these Nietzsche draws the searching distinction between accepting morality and trying to formulate its principle, and making moralities the subject of descriptive investigation. It is the historian of humanity's manifold cultures and cultural values who speaks:

Hitherto all moralists, with a pedantic and ridiculous seriousness, have wanted to give a "basis" to morality, and each has believed that he has given this "basis" to morality. Morality itself, however, has been regarded as something "given."

That which moralists have called "giving a basis to morality," has proved merely a learned form of good faith in prevailing morality, a new means of expressing prevailing morality, consequently just a phenomenon within one definite morality, a sort of denial that it is lawful for this particular morality to be called in question. In no case has the attempt to "provide a basis for morality" ever involved a testing, analyzing, doubting, and vivisecting of the prevailing moral faith.

The philosophical workers, after the pattern of Kant and Hegel, have to fix and systematize some existing body of valuations, that is to say, creations of value which have become prevalent and are for a time called "the truth." It is for these thinkers to make conspicuous, conceivable, intelligible, manageable what has happened and been esteemed hitherto.

Apart from the value of such assertions as "there is a categorical imperative in us," we can always ask: "What does such an assertion indicate about him who makes it?"

Because moralists have known the moral facts imperfectly, in an arbitrary epitome, perhaps the morality of their environment, their position, their church, their *Zeitgeist*, their climate; because they have been badly instructed with regard to nations, eras, and past ages, and were by no means eager to know about these matters; precisely because of this fact, they did not even come in sight of the real problems of morality, problems which disclose themselves only to a comparison of many kinds of morality.

There are systems of morals which are meant to justify their author in the eyes of other people; systems which are meant to tranquilize him and make him self-satisfied; systems which are meant to enable him to crucify and humble himself. By means of one system of morals, he wishes to take revenge; by means of another, to conceal himself; by means of another, to glorify himself and gain superiority and distinction. In short, systems of morals are only sign languages of the emotions.

What is still necessary is the collection of material, the comprehensive survey and classification of sentiments of worth, distinctions of worth, which live, grow, propagate, and perish; and the attempt, perhaps, to give a clear idea of the recurring and more common forms of these living crystallizations. This is necessary as preparation for a theory of types of morality.

So much as a start. The primary problem is not to formulate the principle of morality, but to recognize the existence and study the natural history of many moralities. An acquaintance with these matters, Nietzsche feels, will reveal the fact that genuine moralities arise from the presence in any group of an aristocratic or ruling-class element. He offers a hypothetical reconstruction of the natural history or genealogy of morals.

Every elevation of the type "man" has hitherto been the work of an aristocratic society, and so it will always be: a society believing in a long gradation of rank and differences of worth among human beings, and requiring slavery in some form or other.

Without the pathos of distance, such as grows out of the difference of classes, out of the constant outlooking and downlooking of the ruling class on subordinates and instruments, out of the constant practice of obeying and commanding, out of the keeping down and keeping at a distance, without these, that other more mysterious pathos could never have arisen: the longing for the continued self-surmounting of man.

To be sure, one must cherish no humanitarian illusions about the origin of aristocratic societies. The truth is hard. Every higher civilization has originated in barbarism. Men, barbarians in every respect, men of prey, still in possession of unbroken strength of will and desire for power, threw themselves upon weaker, more moral, more peaceful races, upon old mellow civilizations in which the final vital force was flickering out in brilliant fireworks of wit and depravity. In the beginnings, the noble caste was always the barbarian caste.

The essential thing in a good and healthy aristocracy is that it should regard itself not as a function of the king or the people but as the significance and highest justification thereof; that it should accept with a clear conscience the sacrifice of a legion of individuals, who, for its sake, must be suppressed and reduced to imperfect men, to slaves and instruments. Its fundamental belief must be that society is not allowed to exist for its own sake, but only as a foundation and scaffolding by which a select class may be able to elevate themselves to their higher duties: like those climbing, sun-seeking plants in Java which encircle a tree till, high above it but supported by it, they can unfold their tops in the open light and exhibit their happiness.

Consider an aristocratic commonwealth, e.g., an ancient Greek city state, as a voluntary or involuntary contrivance for rearing human beings. There men are beside one another, thrown on their own resources, who want to make their species prevail, chiefly because they must prevail or be in danger of extermination. The favor, the abundance, the protection, are lacking under which variations are fostered. The species needs itself as species; as something which by its hardness, its uniformity, its simplicity of structure, can prevail in the struggle against neighbors or rebellious vassals. Experience teaches it what are the qualities to which it owes its continued existence in spite of gods and men. These qualities it calls *virtues*, and these virtues alone it develops to maturity.

These virtues it develops with severity. Every aristocratic morality is intolerant in the education of its youth, in the control of its women, in the customs which control marriage, in the relations between old and young, in the penal laws (which have an eye only for the degenerating). It counts intolerance itself among the virtues.

Thus is established a type, with few but very marked features. The constant struggle with unfavorable conditions is the cause of the type becoming stable and hard.

Finally, however, a happy state of security results, and the enormous tension is relaxed. Perhaps there are no more enemies among neighboring peoples; perhaps the means of life and enjoyment are present in abundance. With one stroke the bond and constraint of the old discipline snaps. It is no longer regarded as a necessary condition of existence and survival. If it would continue, it can do so only as an archaizing "taste." Variations appear suddenly in the greatest exuberance and splendor. The individual dares to be individual and detach himself.

At this turning point of history there manifest themselves a magnificent manifold growth and an extraordinary decay, owing to the savagely opposed and seemingly exploded egoisms which strive for "light and sun" and can no longer assign any limit or restraint to themselves by the hitherto existing morality. It was this morality itself which piled up the enormous strength, which bent the bow in so threatening a manner, but it is now out of date, or getting out of date.

The dangerous and disquieting point has now been reached. The greater, more manifold, more comprehensive life now coming into existence is lived beyond the old morality. The "individual" stands out and is obliged to have recourse to his own law giving, his own arts and artifices for self-preservation, self-elevation, self-deliverance. Nothing but new "whys"; nothing but new "hows." No longer any common formulae; misunderstanding and disregard in league together; decay, deterioration, lofty desire, frightfully entangled; the genius of the race overflowing from all the cornucopias of good and bad; new charms and mysteries peculiar to the still inexhausted, still unwearied, corruption.

Danger, the mother of morality, is present once more. This time the danger point has shifted, into the individual, the neighbor, the friend; into the street, into their own child, into all the most personal and secret recesses of their desires and volitions.

After the fabric of a society seems established and secure against external dangers, it is the fear of our neighbor which creates new perspectives of moral evaluation.

It is by the loftiest and strongest instincts, when they break out and carry the individual above and beyond the average, above and beyond the low level of the herd conscience, that the self-reliance of the community is destroyed. Its belief in itself breaks. Consequently these instincts will be most branded and most defamed.

Strong and dangerous instincts, e.g., the love of enterprise, foolhardiness, revengefulness, astuteness, rapacity, love of power, which, up till then had to be honored and fostered and cultivated because required in the common dangers against common enemies, are now felt to be themselves dangerous, are gradually branded as immoral and given over to calumny. The opposite instincts and inclinations now attain to moral honor. The herd instinct gradually draws its conclusions.

How much danger to the community or its equality is contained in an opinion, a condition, an emotion, a character, a disposition? That is now the moral perspective. Here again fear is the mother of morals.

The lofty, independent spirit, the will to stand alone, are felt to be dangers. Everything that elevates the individual above the herd, and is a source of fear to the neighbor, is henceforth called evil. The tolerant, unassuming, self-adapting, self-equalizing disposition, the middle-of-the road desires, attain to moral distinction and honor.

Under peaceful circumstances there is always less opportunity and less need for training the feelings to severity and rigor. Now every form of severity, even severity in justice, begins to disturb the conscience. A lofty and rigorous nobleness and self-responsibility becomes now almost an offense.

The man of an age of dissolution, of an age which mixes the races with one another; who has the inheritance of a diversified descent in his body, contrary instincts and standards of value which struggle among themselves and are seldom at peace; such a man, of late culture and broken lights, will, as a rule, be a weak man.

His fundamental desire is that the war which is in him should come to an end. Happiness appears to him in the character of a soothing medicine and mode of thought; it is above all things the happiness of repose, of undisturbedness, of repetition, of final unity.

All systems of morals which address themselves to "happiness" are only suggestions for behavior adapted to the degree of danger from themselves in which the individuals live. They are thus recipes for their passions, their good and bad propensities, insofar as the individuals would like to play the master. They are all so many small and great expediences, permeated with the musty odor of old family medicines and old wives' wisdom; all grotesque and absurd because they are generalizations where generalization is not justified.

The rank-and-file man assumes an air of being the only kind of man that is allowable. He glorifies, as the peculiarly human virtues, his qualities, such as public spirit, kindness, deference, industry, temperance, modesty, indulgence, sympathy (by virtue of which he is gentle, endurable, and useful to the herd).

In cases where it is believed that a leader cannot be dispensed with, attempt after attempt is made to replace rulers by summing together clever herdminded men. All representative constitutions, for example, are of this origin.

There arises what I call the moral hypocrisy of the ruling class. They know no other way to protect themselves from bad conscience than to play the role of executors of older and higher orders. (Those "older and higher orders" may be predecessors, the constitution, justice, the law, or God himself.) Or they even justify themselves by maxims drawn from the current opinions of the herd, as, for example, "the first servants of their people," or "instruments of public weal."

The end is quickly approaching; everything decays and produces decay; nothing will endure until the day after tomorrow; nothing, that is, except one species of man, the incurably mediocre. The mediocre alone have a prospect of continuing, of propagating themselves. They will be the men of the future, the sole survivors. "Be like them! Be mediocre!" is now the only morality which has still a significance or obtains a hearing. But it is difficult to preach this morality of mediocrity. It can never avow what it is and what it desires. It has to talk of "moderation," and "dignity," and "duty," and "brotherly love." It will have difficulty in concealing its irony!

But this herding-animal morality is only one kind of morality, beside which, before which, and after which, many other moralities, above all, higher moralities, are or should be possible. Against such a possibility, this herd morality defends itself with all its strength. It says obstinately and inexorably: "I am morality and nothing else is morality."

The first corollary that follows from Nietzsche's conception of the genealogy of morals is what he calls his *immoralism,* or his proposed *transvaluation of values.* Thus:

What will the moralists who appear at this time have to preach? What shall be the message of these sharp on-lookers, these unhurried ones?

What is essential and invaluable in every system of morals, is that it is a long constraint.

A species originates, a type becomes established and strong in the long struggle with essentially unfavorable conditions. On the other hand, species which receive abundant nourishment, a surplus of protection and care, tend to develop variations, become fertile in prodigies and monstrosities.

The essential thing, to repeat, is that there should be a long obedience in the same direction. Thereby results something which makes life worth living; for instance, virtue, art, music, dancing, reason, spirituality; whatever, in short, is transfiguring, refined, or divine.

One may look at every system of morals in this light. It teaches us to hate the lax, the too great freedom. It implants the need for limited horizons, for immediate duties, for narrow perspectives. "Thou must obey some one, and for a long time; otherwise thou wilt come to grief, and lose all respect for thyself."

The tension of the soul in misfortune, its shuddering in view of rack and ruin, its inventiveness and heroism in enduring and exploiting misfortune, its depth, mystery, greatness; have these not been bestowed through the discipline of great suffering?

Up to now man has been in the worst hands, has been ruled by the misfits, the physiologically botched, the cunning and revengeful, the so-called *saints*—slanderers of the world, traducers of humanity. The morality of decadence, the will to nothingness, passes as morality *par excellence*. Proof of this: Altruism is considered an absolute value, while egoism meets with hostility everywhere. He who disagrees with me on this point I regard as infected.

For a physiologist, such an opposition of altruism and egoism would leave no room for doubt. If the smallest organ in the body neglects its self-preservation, its recuperative powers, its "egoism," the whole organism will degenerate. The physiologist insists that such decayed parts be cut out. He pities them not at all. But the priest wants precisely the degeneration of mankind; hence he strives to preserve the decayed elements in humanity. This is the price of his rule. This is the "harm that good men do."

When one is no longer serious about self-preservation and the increase of bodily energy, when anemia is made an ideal and contempt of the body is construed as "salvation of the soul," what can all this be, if not a recipe for decadence? Loss of ballast, resistance to natural instincts, "selflessness," these have hitherto been called *morality*.

You want, if possible, to do away with suffering. There is not a more foolish "if possible." We would rather have it increased and made worse. Wellbeing, as you understand it, is certainly not a goal. The discipline of great suffering is the only dicipline that has produced all the elevations of humanity hitherto.

To consider distress as something to be destroyed is sheer idiocy. Generally, it is actually harmful in its consequences, a fatal stupidity, almost as mad as the desire to abolish bad weather out of pity for the poor. In the great economy of the universe the terrors of reality, e.g., the passions, the desires, the will to power, are incalculably more essential than that petty happiness, so-called *goodness*.

It is only among decadents that pity is called a virtue. They are too ready to forget modesty, reverence, and that delicacy of feeling which knows how to keep at a distance. They forget that this sentimental emotion stinks of the mob; that pity is only one step removed from bad manners; that pitying hands may be thrust with destructive results into a great destiny, into a wounded isolation. . . . The overcoming of pity I reckon among the noble virtues.

There is nowadays a sickly irritability and sensitiveness to pain, a repulsive complaining, an effeminizing, which, with the aid of religious and philosophical nonsense, seeks to deck itself out as something superior. There is a regular cult of suffering. The unmanliness of what such groups of visionaries call *sympathy* is, I believe, the first thing that strikes the eye. One must resolutely taboo this latest form of bad taste.

There is a point of diseased mellowness and effeminacy in the history of society, at which society itself takes the part of him who injures it, the part of the criminal. To punish now appears to be somehow "unfair." Is it not sufficient, it is asked, if the criminal be rendered harmless? Why should we still punish? Punishment is barbarous! And so on. With these questions, the herd morality, the morality of fear, draws its ultimate conclusion.

On no point is the ordinary mind of Europe more unwilling to be corrected, than on this matter. People rave nowadays, even under the guise of "science," about coming social conditions in which the "exploiting character" of human relations is to be absent. Particularly is this true of socialistic shallowpates and howling anarchistic dogs. Their words sound to me as if they were promising a mode of life which should refrain from all organic functions. "Exploitation" is not the mark of a depraved or primitive society; it belongs to the nature of the living, as a primary organic function; it is a consequence of the will to power which is precisely the will to life.

You may note that I do not care to see rudeness undervalued. It is by far the most humane form of contradiction, and amid modern effeminacy, it is one of our first virtues.

To be able to be an enemy, to be an enemy, presupposes a strong nature. Strong natures need resistance, accordingly they seek it. The pathos of aggression belongs to strength as much as feelings of revenge and rancor belong to weakness. The strength of the aggressor is determined by the opposition he needs; every increase of strength betrays itself by a search for a more formidable opponent.

To refrain from mutual injury, from violence, from exploitation, to put one's will on a par with others' may result in a kind of good conduct among individuals; but only when the necessary conditions are given, namely, an equality of the individuals in force and worth, and their correlation within one organization.

To take this principle more generally, however, to use it as the fundamental principle of society, would immediately reveal what it actually amounts to, namely, a principle of dissolution and decay. Here one must think profoundly and resist all sentimentality; life itself is essentially appropriation, injury, exploitation, conquest, suppression, severity, obtrusion, incorporation.

Even the organization within which the members treat each other as equal, must, itself, do that toward other organizations which its members refrain from doing to each other; if, that is, it be a living, growing, and not a dying organization. It will endeavor to grow, to gain ground, to attract to itself, to acquire ascendency; not owing to any morality or immorality, but simply because it lives, and because life is precisely will to power.

Fortunately, the world is not built merely on those instincts in which the good-natured herd-animal would find his paltry happiness. To demand that everyone become a "good man," a gregarious animal, a blue-eyed benevolent "beautiful soul," or (as Herbert Spencer wished) an altruist, would mean robbing existence of its greatest character, emasculating mankind. And this has been attempted. It is just this that men call *morality*.

The "good" man is the most harmful kind of man. He secures his existence at the cost of truth. He cannot create. He crucifies the man who writeth new values on new tables. He crucifies the whole future of humanity. Whatever harm the slanderers of the world may do, the harm which good men do is the most calamitous of all harm.

Let me say again what I have already said a hundred times. In all our principal moral judgments, that which is sure of itself, that which glorifies itself with praise and blame, that which calls itself good, is the instinct of the herding human animal: the instinct which is coming more and more to the front, coming more and more to dominate other instincts. Morality at present is herding-animal morality.

All questions of politics, of the social order, of education, have been falsified from top to bottom, because the most harmful men have been taken for great men, and because people were taught to despise the fundamentals of life.

Nietzsche's characteristic doctrines have their basis in these conceptions of the genealogy of morals and the transvaluation of values. His distinction between man and superman, between master morality and slave morality, his reiterated criticisms of the softer, more humanitarian virtues and customs, follow reasonably enough. Perhaps the most famous of all Nietzsche's teachings is in his distinction between master morality and slave morality. Its point is this:

Moral systems must be compelled to bow before the gradations of rank. Their presumption must be driven home, until they thoroughly understand that it is immoral to say that "what is right and proper for one is right and proper for another."

In a tour through the many finer and coarser moralities which have hitherto prevailed, or still prevail, on the earth, I have found certain traits recurring regularly together, until finally two primary types revealed themselves to me: there are master morality and slave morality.

Moral valuations have originated, either in a ruling class pleasantly conscious of being different from the ruled, or in a ruled class, among slaves and dependents of all sorts.

In the master morality, when it is the rulers who determine the notion of "goodness," it is the exalted, proud type of character which is regarded as the distinguishing feature, as that which determines the order of rank. The noble man separates from himself the persons in whom these characteristics are absent; them he despises.

They say: "Thus shall it be." They determine the whither and the why of mankind. They grasp at the future with a creative hand. Whatever is and was becomes for them a means, an instrument, a hammer. Their knowing is creating. Their creating is law-giving. Their will to truth is will to power.

In master morality the antithesis is between "noble" and "despicable." The cowardly, the timid, the no-accounts, the narrowly utilitarian, the distrustful, the self-abasing, the doglike who submit to abuse, the mendicant flatterers, and above all the liars, are despised.

A man who says, "I like that, I take it for my own, I mean to guard it and protect it"; a man who can carry out a resolution, keep hold of a woman, punish and overthrow insolence; a man who has his indignation and his sword; a man whom the weak, the suffering, even the animals, willingly submit to and naturally belong to; such a man is a master by nature.

The noble type of man regards himself as the determiner of values; he does not require to be approved of; he passes the judgment: "What is injurious to me is injurious in itself"; he knows that it is he himself only who confers honor on things; he is a creator of values. He honors whatever he recognizes in himself: such morality is self-glorification. In the foreground there is the feeling of plenitude, of power which seeks to overflow, the consciousness of a wealth which would fain give and bestow.

The noble man honors in himself the powerful one, him who has power over himself, who knows how to speak and how to keep silent, who takes pleasure in subjecting himself to severity and hardness and has reverence for all that is severe and hard. "Wotan placed a hard heart in my breast," says an old Scandinavian saga: it is thus rightly expressed from the soul of a proud Viking.

The noble man is furthest removed from the morality which sees the essence of the moral in sympathy, or in "acting for the good of others." Faith in oneself, pride in oneself, a radical irony and enmity toward "selflessness," belong as definitely to master morality as do scorn and precaution in the presence of sympathy and the "warm heart."

A man of this sort is carved from a single block, which is hard, sweet, fragrant. He enjoys only what is good for him. His desire ceases when the limits of what is good for him are overstepped. . . . Whatever does not kill him makes him stronger. He gathers his material from all he sees, hears, and experiences. He is a selective principle: he rejects much. . . . He reacts slowly to all kinds of stimuli, with that slowness which long caution and pride have bred in him. . . . He is always in his own company, whether mingling with men or books or nature. . . . He honors the thing he chooses.

There is an instinct for rank, which, more than anything else, is the sign of a high rank. The refinement, the goodness, the loftiness of a soul are put to a real test when something of the highest rank passes by but is not yet protected with the awe of authority; something that goes its way like a living touchstone, undistinguished, undiscovered, tentative, perhaps veiled and disguised.

The noble and powerful know how to honor; it is their art, their domain for invention. The profound reverence for age and tradition, the belief and prejudice in favor of ancestors and against newcomers, is typical of master morality. If, contrariwise, men of "modern ideas" believe in "progress" and the "future," and are increasingly lacking in respect for the past, the ignoble origin of these "ideas" is thereby betrayed.

He whose task is to investigate souls will avail himself of many varieties of this very art to determine the ultimate value of a soul, the innate order of rank to which it belongs. He will test it by its instinct for reverence. The vulgarity of many a soul spurts up like dirty water when any holy vessel, any jewel from closed shrines, any book bearing the marks of great destiny, is brought before it. Contrariwise, there is an involuntary silence, a hesitation, a cessation, by which is indicated that a soul feels the nearness of what is worthy of respect.

In the so-called *cultured* classes today, the dealers in "modern ideas," nothing is perhaps so repulsive as their lack of shame, their lack of reverence, the easy insolence of hand and eye with which they touch, finger, and examine everything. It is possible that more tact for reverence exists among the lower classes and peasants than among the newspaper-reading demi-monde of "intellect" and "culture."

Much has been achieved when the sentiment of reverence has been finally instilled into the masses, when they realize that they are not allowed to touch everything, that there are some experiences before which they must take off their shoes and restrain their hand.

The master morality is especially foreign and irritating to present-day taste. It is disliked and distrusted for the sternness of its principle that one has duties only to one's equals; that one may act toward persons of a lower rank, toward all that is foreign, just as one pleases; that its values are "beyond good and evil."

It is typical of the master morality to be able and obliged to exercise prolonged gratitude and prolonged revenge, but both only within the circle of one's equals; artfulness in retaliation; a need for enemies as outlets for emotions of envy, quarrelsomeness, arrogance. This, of course, is not "modern morality," and is therefore difficult to realize, to discover.

In contrast to the master morality stands the slave morality:

It is otherwise with the second type of morality; what I have named slave morality. If the abused, the oppressed, the suffering, the unemancipated, the weary, the uncertain-of-themselves, should moralize, what will be the common element in their moral evaluations?

The slave has an unfavorable eye for the virtues of the powerful. He has a skepticism and distrust of everything which they honor. He would fain persuade himself that their happiness is not genuine.

On the other hand, those qualities which serve to alleviate the existence of sufferers are brought into prominence and flooded with light. It is here that sympathy, the kind helping hand, the warm heart, patience, diligence, humility, friendliness, attain to honor. For here these are the most useful equalities, almost the only means of supporting the burden of existence.

Slave morality is essentially the morality of utility. It is oriented around the idea of the "useful." Here is the seat of the origin of the famous antithesis of "good" and "evil," which I have distinguished from the antithesis of "good" and "bad." According to slave morality, the "evil" man rouses fear. According to master morality, the "good" man rouses fear, and seeks to rouse it, while the "bad" man is regarded as the despicable being.

According to slave morality, the good man must be the "safe" man: he must be good-natured, easily hoodwinked, perhaps a little stupid. Wherever slave morality gains the ascendency, language shows a tendency to approximate the significations of the words *good* and *stupid*.

A last fundamental difference: the desire for freedom, the enthusiasm for "liberty" the instinct of being "happy" belong as inherently to slave morality as artifice in reverence and enthusiasm in devotion belong to master morality. Hence, we can understand, love as a passion, romantic love, with its ardors and endurances and binding ties, is a phenomenon of master morality.

Nietzsche never wearied of criticizing those phases of modern morality that smacked of "degeneration" and "slaves." Among the topics singled out for castigation was the nineteenth-century enthusiasm for the emancipation of women. Says Nietzsche:

To be mistaken in the fundamental problem of "man and woman" is the typical sign of a shallow mind. To deny here the profoundest antagonism, the need for hostile tension; to dream here of "equal rights," equal training, equal claims and obligations; to prove oneself shallow at this dangerous spot, may be regarded as suspicious, nay more, as betrayed. Such an one may probably prove "too short" for all the fundamental issues of life, unable to descend into any of the depths.

In no previous age have women been treated with so much respect by men as at present. This belongs to the tendency and fundamental taste of democracy. Is it any wonder that abuse should be made of this respect? Women want more; they learn to make claims; they become rivals for rights. In a word, they lose their modesty. And, let me add, they also lose their taste.

They unlearn their fear of men. But the woman who "unlearns" her fear of men, sacrifices her most womanly instincts. That woman should venture forward when man has ceased to inspire fear, is reasonable enough, and intelligible enough. But what is more difficult to grasp is that precisely thereby woman deteriorates. That is happening these days: let us not deceive ourselves about it.

Wherever the industrial spirit has triumphed over the military and aristocratic spirit, woman strives for the economic and legal independence of a clerk. "Woman as clerk" is inscribed on the portal of that modern society which is in course of formation.

While she thus appropriates new rights, aspires to be master, and inscribes the "progress" of woman on her flags and banners, the very opposite realizes itself with terrible obviousness—woman retrogrades.

There is stupidity in this movement, an almost masculine stupidity, of which a well-bred sensible woman might be heartily ashamed. To lose the ground on which she can most surely achieve victory; to neglect her proper weapons; to let herself go before man where formerly she kept herself in control in artful humility; to neutralize man's faith in a fundamentally different ideal in woman, something eternally feminine; to emphatically and loquaciously dissuade man from the idea that woman must be preserved, protected, and indulged like some delicate, strangely wild, and often pleasant domestic animal; what does all this betoken, if not a disintegration of womanly instincts?

There are, to be sure, enough of idiotic friends and corrupters of woman amongst the learned asses of the male sex, who advise woman to defeminize herself in this manner, and to imitate all the stupidities from which man suffers, who would like to lower woman to "general culture," indeed, even to newspaper reading and meddling with politics.

In their efforts to rise to the ideal woman, to the higher woman, they have really wished to lower the general level of women, and there are no more certain means to this end than university education, trousers, and the rights of voting like cattle. Fundamentally, the "emancipated" and the "emancipators" (for example, that typical old maid, Henrik Ibsen) are anarchists, misbegotten souls whose most deep-rooted instinct is revenge.

Almost everywhere her nerves are being ruined, and she is daily being made more hysterical and more incapable of fulfilling her first and last function, namely, the rearing of robust children. These "friends of woman" wish to "cultivate" her, to make the weaker sex strong by "culture," as if history did not teach that the "cultivating" of mankind and the weakening of mankind have always kept pace with one another.

That which inspires respect in woman, and often also fear, is her real nature, her genuine, carnivora-like cunning and flexibility, her tiger claws beneath the glove, her naïveté in egoism, her untrainableness, her innate wildness, her incomprehensibleness, the extent and deviation of her virtues.

That which, in spite of fear, excites one's sympathy for the dangerous and beautiful in woman, is that she seems more afflicted, more vulnerable, more needful of love and more condemned to disillusion, than any other creature. Fear and sympathy—it is with these feelings that man hitherto stood in the presence of woman, always with one foot in tragedy which rends while it delights. And all that is now to be at an end? The disenchantment of women is in progress? The tediousness of woman is slowly evolving?

Another object of Nietzsche's criticism was what he describes as "Christian morality." He never tires of railing at it. From among pages and pages, the following passages may be taken as representative:

All the things men have valued heretofore are not even realities. They are mere fantasies; more strictly speaking, they are lies. All the concepts, "God," "soul," "virtue," "sin," "Beyond," "truth," "eternal life," are lies arising from the evil instincts of diseased and harmful natures.

I am the first immoralist. Basically, there are two denials included in this term. First, I deny the type of man who formerly passed as the highest, the "good" man, the "benevolent" man, the "charitable" man. Second, I deny that kind of morality which has become recognized and dominant, namely Christian morality. . . . The second of these denials is the more decisive.

No one before me has felt Christian morality beneath him. To do that one must have height, far vision, depth. Up to now, Christian morality has been the Circe of all thinkers; they stood at her service. What man before me has descended into the caves from which the poisonous fumes of this ideal burst forth? Who before me ever dared to suspect they were caves? What philosopher before me was a real moralist and not a superior swindler, an idealist?

Have you understood me? What defines me is the fact that I unmasked Christian morality. For this reason I needed a word which would contain the idea of a universal challenge: immoralist. Blindness in the face of Christian morality is the essential crime. It is the great uncleanliness.

Christian morality is the most pernicious form of the will to falsehood, the denial of life. It is not error as error which infuriates me here. It is not the age-long lack of "good will," of discipline, of decency, of spiritual courage, which betrays itself in the triumph of Christian morality. It is the ghastly fact that what was unnatural received the highest honors as morality, and remained suspended over man as the law of the categorical imperative. This is the great blundering. To teach contempt of the primal life instincts; to set up a "soul," a spirit, in order to overthrow the body; to teach man to find impurity in sex; to look for the principle of evil in the need for expansion; to see a "higher moral value" in "selflessness," in "objectivity," in "neighbor love"; these things are the will to nothingness, the denial of life, the great nay-saying.

The Jews performed the miracle of the inversion of valuations, by means of which life on earth obtained a new and dangerous charm for a couple of thousand years. Their prophets fused the expressions *rich, godless, wicked, violent, sensual,* into one expression, and for the first time coined the word *world* as a term of reproach. In this inversion of values (which included the use of *poor* as synonymous with *saint* and *friend*) the significance of the Jewish people is to be found. It is with them that slave morality begins.

From the beginning, Christian morality was essentially the surfeit of life which disguised itself under the belief in "another" and "better" life. The hatred of the world, the condemnation of emotion, the fear of beauty, the distrust of sensuality, all these have always appeared to me as the most dangerous forms of the "will to perish," symptoms of the deepest weariness, exhaustion, anaemia.

The teachers and preachers and leaders of mankind, including the theologians, have been decadents. Hence their inversion of values into a hostility to life; hence "morality." Here is a definition of *morality:* the idiosyncrasy of decadents actuated by a desire to avenge themselves successfully upon life. I attach great value to this definition.

Have you understood me? The unmasking of Christian morality is a unique event. It breaks the history of mankind in two. Man lives either before or after that. Everything which was until then called the *truth,* is now recognized as the most harmful, spiteful, and concealed falsehood. The sacred pretext, the "improvement of man," is recognized as a ruse to drain life of its blood. This morality is vampirism.

He who unmasks Christian morality unmasks the worthlessness of the values in which men believe. He sees in them only the most fatal kind of abortions; fatal, because they fascinate. The notion of "God" was invented as the counternotion to life. The notion of a "Beyond" was invented to depreciate the only world that exists. The notion of an "immortal soul" was invented to despise the body. The notion of "sin" was invented to mislead our instincts. Finally, the notion of a "good man" has come to mean everything that is weak, ill, misshapen, everything which should be obliterated. The law of selection is thwarted. And all this was believed in as morality! *Ecrasez l'infâme!*

We who hold a different view, we who regard Christian morality and democratic politics to be a degenerating form of organization, where have we to fix our hopes?

In new moralists and a new morality. There is no other alternative. In minds strong enough and original enough to initiate a transvaluation of values, to invert "eternal valuations," lies our only hope. In forerunners, in men of the future, who shall fix the constraints and fasten the knots which will compel millenniums to take new paths; make preparations for vast hazardous enterprises and collective attempts in rearing and educating; put an end to the frightful rule of folly and chance which has hitherto gone by the name of *history;* in such do we fix our hopes.

For these purposes a new type of moralist and ruler will some time be needed, at the very idea of which everything that has existed might look pale and dwarfed. The image of such leaders hovers before our eyes.

But their image fills our hearts with anxiety and gloom. How are they to be born? How are they to be bred? How nurtured to that elevation and power which will feel the present needs as their tasks? Of them is demanded a transvaluation of values. In them is needed a new conscience of steel, a new heart of brass, to bear the weight of such responsibility. There is always the danger that they may be lacking, or miscarry and degenerate. These are our real anxieties and glooms. These are the heavy thoughts and storms which sweep across our skies.

There are few pains so grievous as to have seen an exceptional man miss his way and deteriorate. But he who has the rare eye to see the danger of mankind itself missing its way and deteriorating; he who has recognized the element of wild chance in human affairs; he who has detected the fate that is hidden under the idiotic unwariness and blind confidence of "modern ideas," and still more of Christian morality and democratic politics; suffers from an anguish beyond comparison.

The universal degeneracy of mankind to the level of the ideals of socialistic fools and humanitarian shallowpates, the dwarfing of man to an absolutely gregarious animal, the brutalizing of man into pigmy with equal "rights" and "claims"—this is undoubtedly possible. He who has foreseen this possibility knows another loathing unknown to the rest of mankind.

From these themes, Nietzsche turns to the question of his own significance for the modern mind. Nietzsche on the genealogy of morals is interesting. Nietzsche on the distinction between master morality and slave morality is suggestive. Nietzsche on woman and Christianity is challenging. But Nietzsche on himself is unique:

Idealism is alien to me. Where you see ideal things I see human things, alas all-too-human.

He who would be a creator in good and evil must first be a destroyer, and break values into pieces. I am the most terrible man that has ever existed. But I shall be the most beneficent. I know the joy of annihilation. I am the first immoralist. I am thus the essential destroyer.

I know my destiny. I am not a man. I am a fatality. I am dynamite. Some day my name will be bound up with the recollection of something terrific, a crisis, a profound clash of consciences, a decisive condemnation of all that before me had been believed, required, hallowed.

I am the voice of truth. But my truth is terrible, for hitherto lies have been called truth. "The transvaluation of all values" is my formula for mankind's act of highest self-recognition. I contradict as no one has contradicted before. For when truth engages in a struggle with the falsehoods of ages, we must expect shocks, earthquakes, rearrangements of hills and valleys, such as never yet have been dreamt of. All the mighty forms of the old social structure I blow into space, for they rest on falsehoods. Politics on a grand scale will date from me.

My life task is to prepare humanity for a moment of supreme self-consciousness, a great noontide, a transvaluation of all values, an emancipation from all moral values, a yea-saying, a confidence in all that has formerly been forbidden, despised, and damned; when it will gaze both backwards and forwards, emerge from the tyranny of accident and priesthood, and, for the first time, pose the question of the why and wherefore of humanity as a whole.

But with all this there is nothing in me to suggest the founder of a "religion." Religions are the business of the mob. After coming in contact with a religious man, I have always to wash my hands. I want no "believers." I never address myself to the masses. I do not wish to be a saint: I would rather be a clown. Perhaps I am a clown.

Note on Sources. The Nietzsche materials in this section are quoted, abridged, or paraphrased from many different books, essays, and chapters. The basic "argument" of the section is derived principally from his book *Beyond Good and Evil*, particularly Chapters 1, 5, and 9; and somewhat also from his book *The Genealogy of Morals*, particularly essays I and II. The materials taken from those two sources were used to construct the "framework." But a number of passages from his other writings were then fitted into that framework. These passages were taken from his *Zarathustra*, his *Dawn of Day*, his *Joyful Wisdom*, his *Will to Power*, and his *Ecce Homo*.

Reading References. The best thing to do with Nietzsche, having read carefully the selections given here, is to try his *Thus Spake Zarathustra*. This is at first a somewhat difficult book, but it has a strange, exotic charm.

It may be supplemented by chapters from *Beyond Good and Evil* and *The Genealogy of Morals*. Among items that may be consulted with profit, for a beginning, is Will Durant's chapter in his *Story of Philosophy*. A good book on Nietzsche is George A. Morgan's *What Nietzsche Means*. The author of the Philo Vance detective novels was a student of Nietzsche's works. His name was W. H. Wright, and his book *What Nietzsche Taught* is a good introduction. The same goes for H. L. Mencken's *The Philosophy of Friedrich Nietzsche*. Among books of a more academic character may be mentioned W. K. Salter's *Nietzsche the Thinker*.

READING QUESTIONS

1. Nietzsche begins by repudiating traditional moral philosophy, as represented e.g., in Paley or Kant or Mill. What such moralists have sought to do. Why Nietzsche will have none of it.
2. A traditional moralist might say that he was trying to formulate a theory of morality. Nietzsche wants a theory of moralities or of types of morality. What is the difference here?
3. If you study a morality with an eye to its genealogy, its natural history, rather than its defining principle, you will (says Nietzsche) find that it originates during the early aristocratic period of the people whose morality it is. His point here: (a) the pathos of distance, (b) the long constraint, (c) that other more mysterious pathos, (d) the sun-seeking plants in Java, (e) intolerance.
4. Under the protection and control of its early aristocracy a people achieves security. The need for the early morality disappears. A morality emerges expressive of the needs and desires of a more democratic age. His point here: (a) the dangerous and disquieting point; (b) new whys; new hows; (c) fear of the neighbor, i.e., not of an external enemy; (d) the herd instinct; (e) happiness-moralities; (f) the moral hypocrisy of the ruling class; (g) "I am morality and nothing else is morality."
5. Nietzsche believed that, within most of Western civilization, moralities had reached the "democratic," the herding-animal, stage. He took a dim view of such latter-day moralities. His point here: (a) altruism, (b) the discipline of great suffering, (c) pity, (d) sympathy, (e) the criminal, (f) exploitation, (g) rudeness, (h) the "good" man, (i) socialistic shallow-pates and howling anarchistic dogs.
6. When a morality is in its aristocratic phase you have "master-morality." When it is in its democratic, herding-animal phase, you have "slave-morality," i.e., the morality of those who once were slaves. Nietzsche favored the former over the latter. His point here: (a) noble versus despicable; (b) a determiner, a creator of values; (c) an instinct for rank, a sentiment of reverence; (d) "beyond good and evil"; (e) "good and bad" versus "good and evil"; (f) liberty and happiness; (g) the morality of utility.
7. How wrong-headed is Nietzsche on the subject of women? What would he have thought about Women's Liberation?
8. What is Nietzsche's indictment of Christian morality? If you grant that the indictment ("unmasking") is essentially correct, would you attach as much importance to it as he does?
9. "These are our real anxieties and glooms." Elaborate.

10. Point here: (a) an anguish beyond comparison, (b) loathing unknown to the rest of mankind.
11. Wherein you find Nietzsche (a) most, (b) least worth your while. Why?

INDEPENDENT STUDY

1. Read the article on Nietzsche by W. Kaufmann in the *Encyclopedia of Philosophy* and that by H. Ellis in Hastings's *Encyclopedia of Religion and Ethics*. These are excellent brief essays on Nietzsche's life and thought. They should combine effectively with the Nietzsche material in this section. Work out a general paper on Nietzsche: his times, his life, his teachings.
2. Read as much as you need to in *Nietzsche in England 1890–1914*, by David Thatcher. You will encounter chapters on Havelock Ellis, William Butler Yeats, George Bernard Shaw, and others. If you know your way around among these English authors, a good paper could be done by selecting any two, and comparing Nietzsche's influence on them.
3. Read H. L. Mencken's translation of and introduction to Nietzsche's small volume *The Antichrist*. Write an essay on Nietzsche's position in that book.
4. Read around among the books on existentialism until you find what you need for a paper on Nietzsche and existentialism.
5. Read the prologue and Parts One and Two of Nietzsche's book *Thus Spake Zarathustra*. The book is written as a series of "sermons" preached by Zarathustra. Select any ten of these preachments. Write out your interpretation of them. You can get a good start with *The Portable Nietzsche*, edited by Walter Kaufmann.
6. Taking off from what Schopenhauer and Nietzsche claim about women, in this book, work out a fuller statement, basing your account on a reading in their own books. Then add J. S. Mill, *The Subjection of Women*. Now you have materials for an interesting and colorful essay: What Three Nineteenth-Century Philosophers Wrote About Woman.

SECTION 5. A. J. AYER: EMOTIVISM IN ETHICS [1]

From Nietzsche to Ayer. You begin by being able and willing to authorize moral judgments; e.g., stealing is wrong, truth-telling is

[1] For biographical note see pp. 600–601.

right, and so on. You then face a question: What fact, common to all your cases of wrongdoing is the reason for calling them cases of wrongdoing? Or, what fact, common to all your cases of right-doing is the reason for calling them cases of right-doing?

Much traditional ethical theory centers in those questions. If you get an answer, you are in a position to say, "An act is wrong if and only if. . . ." or "right if and only if. . . ." and supply what is needed to finish the statement. The completed sentence formulates the *principle* that is operative in your moral judgments. Much traditional ethical theory centers in the attempt to formulate the principle of moral judgment.

It will be recalled that Paley, Kant, and Mill each tried to formulate the principle of morality. Paley did so with reference to the will of God; and Mill, with reference to happiness. Other end-of-the-rope alternatives would be possible. Let all of them be set down side by side. Then let the question be asked, "What *logical* type do these statements belong to?" This is Professor. Ayer's question. In his hands this question presupposes that there are two possible answers: a statement is either empirical or tautological. He is clear that when you formulate the principle of morality, the resulting proposition is neither empirical nor tautological. His conclusion is that it is not a proposition at all, but a pseudoproposition; that is to say, it looks like a proposition because it is formulated in words and "reads" like a sentence expressing a proposition, but it is nevertheless not a proposition because to be a proposition it would have to be either empirical or tautological, and it is neither.

If it is not a proposition, then what is it? To say that it is a pseudoproposition is merely to say that it is not a proposition but looks as though it were. The question remains, "What is it?" Professor Ayer's point could be expressed by saying that it is a symbol, something used to express what is in the mind; and by distinguishing between two kinds of symbols—cognitive and emotive. A cognitive symbol is one that is used to express what you know or could know; an emotive symbol is one that is used to express what you feel or could feel. His claim would then be that when the principle of morality is expressed in words it is an emotive, not a cognitive symbol. In using it you express what you feel or could feel, not what you know or could know. This is the emotive theory about moral concepts and the judgments in which they occur.

Our business is to give an account of "judgements of value" which is both satisfactory in itself and consistent with our general empiricist principles. We shall set ourselves to show that in so far as statements of value are significant, they are ordinary "scientific" statements; and that in so far as they are not scientific, they are not in the literal sense significant, but are simply expressions of emotion which can be neither true nor false. In maintaining this view, we may confine ourselves for the present to the case of ethical statements. What is said about them will be found to apply, *mutatis mutandis*, to the case of aesthetic statements also.

The ordinary system of ethics, as elaborated in the works of ethical philosophers, contains, first of all, propositions which express definitions of ethical terms, or judgements about the legitimacy or possibility of certain definitions. Secondly, there are propositions describing the phenomena of moral virtue. And, lastly, there are actual ethical judgements.

Only the first of our four classes, namely that which comprises the propositions relating to the definitions of ethical terms, can be said to constitute ethical philosophy. The propositions which describe the phenomena of moral experience, and their causes, must be assigned to the science of psychology, or sociology. The exhortations to moral virtue are not propositions at all, but ejaculations or commands which are designed to provoke the reader to action of a certain sort. Accordingly, they do not belong to any branch of philosophy or science. As for ethical judgements, inasmuch as they are neither definitions nor comments upon definitions, nor quotations, we may say that they do not belong to ethical philosophy. A strictly philosophical treatise on ethics should therefore make no ethical pronouncements. But it should, by giving an analysis of ethical terms, show what is the category to which all such pronouncements belong. And this is what we are now about to do.

A question which is often discussed by ethical philosophers is whether it is possible to find definitions which would reduce all ethical terms to one or two fundamental terms. But this question, though it undeniably belongs to ethical philosophy, is not relevant to our present enquiry. We are not now concerned to discover which term, within the sphere of ethical terms, is to be taken as fundamental; whether, for example, "good" can be defined in terms of "right" or "right" in terms of "good," or both in terms of "value." What we are interested in is the possibility of reducing the whole sphere of ethical terms to non-ethical terms. We are enquiring whether statements of ethical value can be translated into statements of empirical fact.

That they can be so translated is the contention of those ethical philosophers who are commonly called subjectivists, and of those who are known as utilitarians. For the utilitarian defines the rightness of actions, and the goodness of ends, in terms of the pleasure, or happiness, or satisfaction, to which they give rise; the subjectivist, in terms of the feelings of approval which a certain person, or group of people, has towards them. Each of these types of definition makes moral judgements into a sub-class of psychological or sociological judgements; and for this reason they are very attractive to us. For, if either was correct, it would follow that ethical assertions were not generically different from the factual assertions which are ordinarily contrasted with them.

Nevertheless we shall not adopt either a subjectivist or a utilitarian analysis of ethical terms. We reject the subjectivist view that to call an action right, or a thing good, is to say that it is generally approved of, because it is not self-contradictory to assert that some actions which are generally approved of are not right, or that some things which are generally approved of are not good. And we reject the alternative subjectivist view that a man who asserts that a certain action is right, or that a certain thing is good, is saying that he himself approves of it, on the ground that a man who confessed that he sometimes approved of what was bad or wrong would not be contradicting himself. And a similar argument is fatal to utilitarianism. We cannot agree that to call an action right is to say that of all the actions possible in the circumstances it would cause, or be likely to cause, the greatest happiness, or the greatest balance of pleasure over pain, or the greatest balance of satisfied over unsatisfied desire, because we find that it is not self-contradictory to say that it is sometimes wrong to perform the action which would actually or probably cause the greatest happiness, or the greatest balance of pleasure over pain, or of satisfied over unsatisfied desire. And since it it not self-contradictory to say that some pleasant things are not good, or that some bad things are desired, it cannot be the case that the sentence "x is good" is equivalent to "x is pleasant," or to "x is desired." And to every other variant of utilitarianism with which I am acquainted the same objection can be made. Therefore the validity of ethical judgements is not determined by the felicific tendencies of actions, any more than by the nature of people's feelings; it must be regarded as "absolute" or "intrinsic," and not empirically calculable.

We are not denying that it is possible to invent a language in which all ethical symbols are definable in non-ethical terms; what we are denying is that the suggested reduction of ethical to non-ethical statements is consistent with the conventions of our actual language. That is, we reject utilitarianism and subjectivism, not as proposals to replace our existing ethical notions by new ones, but as analyses of our existing ethical notions. Our contention is simply that, in our language, sentences which contain normative ethical symbols are not equivalent to sentences which express psychological propositions, or indeed empirical propositions of any kind.

It is only normative ethical symbols, and not descriptive ethical symbols, that are indefinable in factual terms. There is a danger of confusing these two, because they are commonly constituted by signs of the same sensible form. Thus "x is wrong" may express a moral judgement concerning a certain type of conduct, or it may state that a certain type of conduct is repugnant to the moral sense of a particular society. In the latter case, the symbol "wrong" is a descriptive ethical symbol, and the sentence in which it occurs expresses an ordinary sociological proposition; in the former case, the symbol "wrong" is a normative ethical symbol, and the sentence in which it occurs does not, we maintain, express an empirical proposition at all. It is only with normative ethics that we are at present concerned; so that whenever ethical symbols are used in the course of this argument without qualification, they are to be interpreted as symbols of the normative type.

In admitting that normative ethical concepts are not reducible to empirical concepts, we seem to be leaving the way clear for the view that statements of value are not controlled by observation, as ordinary empirical propositions are, but only by a mysterious "intellectual intuition." This would make statements of value unverifiable. For it is notorious that what seems intuitively certain to one person may seem doubtful, or even false, to another. So that unless it is possible to provide some criterion by which one may decide between conflicting intuitions, a mere appeal to intuition is worthless as a test of a proposition's validity. But in the case of moral judgements, no such criterion can be given. Some moralists claim to settle the matter by saying that they "know" that their own moral judgements are correct. But such an assertion is of purely psychological interest, and has not the slightest tendency to prove the validity of any moral judgement. For dissentient moralists may equally well "know" that their ethical views are correct. And, as far as subjective certainty goes, there will be nothing to choose between them. When such differences of opinion arise in connection with an ordinary empirical proposition, one may attempt to resolve them by referring to, or actually carrying out, some relevant empirical test. But with regard to ethical statements, there is, on the "intuitionist" theory, no relevant empirical test. Therefore on this theory ethical statements are held to be unverifiable. They are, of course, also held to be genuine synthetic propositions.

Considering the use which we have made of the principle that a synthetic proposition is significant only if it is empirically verifiable, it is clear that the acceptance of an "absolutist" theory of ethics would undermine the whole of our main argument. And as we have already rejected the "naturalistic" theories which are commonly supposed to provide the only alternative to "absolutism" in ethics, we seem to have reached a difficult position. We shall meet the difficulty by showing that the correct treatment of ethical statements is afforded by a third theory, which is wholly compatible with our radical empiricism.

We begin by admitting that the fundamental ethical concepts are unanalysable, inasmuch as there is no criterion by which one can test the validity of the judgements in which they occur. So far we are in agreement with the absolutists. But, unlike the absolutists, we are able to give an explanation of this fact about ethical concepts. We say that the reason why they are unanalysable is that they are mere pseudo-concepts. The presence of an ethical symbol in a proposition adds nothing to its factual content. Thus if I say to someone, "You acted wrongly in stealing that money," I am not stating anything more than if I had simply said, "You stole that money." In adding that this action is wrong I am not making any further statement about it. I am simply evincing my moral disapproval of it. It is as if I had said, "You stole that money," in a peculiar tone of horror, or written it with the addition of some special exclamation mark. The tone, or the exclamation mark, adds nothing to the literal meaning of the sentence. It merely serves to show that the expression of it is attended by certain feelings in the speaker.

If now I generalise my previous statement and say, "Stealing money is wrong," I produce a sentence which has no factual meaning—that is, expresses no proposition which can be either true or false. It is as if I had written "Stealing money!!"—where the shape and thickness of the exclamation marks shows, by a suitable convention, that a special sort of moral disapproval is the feeling which is being expressed. It is clear that there is nothing said here which can be true or false. Another man may disagree with me about the wrongness of stealing, in the sense that he may not have the same feelings about stealing as I have, and he may quarrel with me on account of my moral sentiments. But he cannot, strictly speaking, contradict me. For in saying that a certain type of action is right or wrong, I am not making any factual statement, not even a statement about my own state of mind. I am merely expressing certain moral sentiments. And the man who is ostensibly contradicting me is merely expressing his moral sentiments. So that there is plainly no sense in asking which of us is in the right. For neither of us is asserting a genuine proposition.

What we have just been saying about the symbol "wrong" applies to all normative ethical symbols. Sometimes they occur in sentences which record ordinary empirical facts besides expressing ethical feeling about those facts: sometimes they occur in sentences which simply express ethical feeling about a certain type of action, or situation, without making any statement of fact. But in every case in which one would commonly be said to be making an ethical judgement, the function of the relevant ethical word is purely "emotive." It is used to express feeling about certain objects, but not to make any assertion about them.

It is worth mentioning that ethical terms do not serve only to express feeling. They are calculated also to arouse feeling, and so to stimulate action. Indeed some of them are used in such a way as to give the sentences in which they occur the effect of commands. Thus the sentence "It is your duty to tell the truth" may be regarded both as the expression of a certain sort of ethical feeling about truthfulness and as the expression of the command "Tell the truth." The sentence "You ought to tell the truth" also involves the command "Tell the truth," but here the tone of the command is less emphatic. In the sentence "It is good to tell the truth" the command has become little more than a suggestion. And thus the "meaning" of the word "good," in its ethical usage, is differentiated from that of the word "duty" or the word "ought." In fact we may define the meaning of the various ethical words in terms both of the different feelings they are ordinarily taken to express, and also the different responses which they are calculated to provoke.

We can now see why it is impossible to find a criterion for determining the validity of ethical judgements. It is not because they have an "absolute" validity which is mysteriously independent of ordinary sense-experience, but because they have no objective validity whatsoever. If a sentence makes no statement at all, there is obviously no sense in asking whether what it says is true or false. And we have seen that sentences which simply express moral judgements do not say anything. They are pure expressions of feeling and as such do not come under the category of truth and falsehood. They are unverifiable for the same reason as a cry of pain or a word of command is unverifiable—because they do not express genuine propositions.

Thus, although our theory of ethics might fairly be said to be radically subjectivist, it differs in a very important respect from the orthodox subjectivist theory. For the orthodox subjectivist does not deny, as we do, that the sentences of a moralizer express genuine propositions. All he denies is that they express propositions of a unique non-empirical character. His own view is that they express propositions about the speaker's feelings. If this were so, ethical judgements clearly would be capable of being true or false. They would be true if the speaker had the relevant feelings, and false if he had not. And this is a matter which is, in principle, empirically verifiable. Furthermore they could be significantly contradicted. For if I say, "Tolerance is a virtue," and someone answers, "You don't approve of it," he would, on the ordinary subjectivist theory, be contradicting me. On our theory, he would not be contradicting me, because, in saying that tolerance was a virtue, I should not be making any statement about my own feelings or about anything else. I should simply be evincing my feelings, which is not at all the same thing as saying that I have them.

The distinction between the expression of feeling and the assertion of feeling is complicated by the fact that the assertion that one has a certain feeling often accompanies the expression of that feeling, and is then, indeed, a factor in the expression of that feeling. Thus I may simultaneously express boredom and say that I am bored, and in that case my utterance of the words, "I am bored," is one of the circumstances which make it true to say that I am expressing or evincing boredom. But I can express boredom without actually saying that I am bored. I can express it by my tone and gestures, while making a statement about something wholly unconnected with it, or by an ejaculation, or without uttering any words at all. So that even if the assertion that one has a certain feeling always involves the expression of that feeling, the expression of a feeling assuredly does not always involve the assertion that one has it. And this is the important point to grasp in considering the distinction between our theory and the ordinary subjectivist theory. For whereas the subjectivist holds that ethical statements actually assert the existence of certain feelings, we hold that ethical statements are expressions and excitants of feeling which do not necessarily involve any assertions.

We have already remarked that the main objection to the ordinary subjectivist theory is that the validity of ethical judgements is not determined by the nature of their author's feelings. And this is an objection which our theory escapes. For it does not imply that the existence of any feelings is a necessary and sufficient condition of the validity of an ethical judgement. It implies, on the contrary, that ethical judgements have no validity.

There is, however, a celebrated argument against subjectivist theories which our theory does not escape. It has been pointed out by Moore that if ethical statements were simply statements about the speaker's feelings, it would be impossible to argue about questions of value. To take a typical example: if a man said that thrift was a virtue, and another replied that it was a vice, they would not, on this theory, be disputing with one another. One would be saying that he approved of thrift, and the other that *he* didn't; and there is no reason why both these statements should not be true. Now Moore held it to be obvious that we do dispute about questions of value, and accordingly concluded that the particular form of subjectivism which he was discussing was false.

It is plain that the conclusion that it is impossible to dispute about questions of value follows from our theory also. For as we hold that such sentences as "Thrift is a virtue" and "Thrift is a vice" do not express propositions at all, we clearly cannot hold that they express incompatible propositions. We must therefore admit that if Moore's argument refutes the ordinary subjectivist theory, it also refutes ours. But, in fact, we deny that it does refute even the ordinary subjectivist theory. For we hold that one really never does dispute about questions of value.

This may seem, at first sight, to be a very paradoxical assertion. For we certainly do engage in disputes which are ordinarily regarded as disputes about questions of value. But, in all such cases, we find, if we consider the matter closely, that the dispute is not really about a question of value, but about a question of fact. When someone disagrees with us about the moral value of a certain action or type of action, we do admittedly resort to argument in order to win him over to our way of thinking. But we do not attempt to show by our arguments that he has the "wrong" ethical feeling towards a situation whose nature he has correctly apprehended. What we attempt to show is that he is mistaken about the facts of the case. We argue that he has misconceived the agent's motive: or that he has misjudged the effects of the action, or its probable effects in view of the agent's knowledge; or that he has failed to take into account the special circumstances in which the agent was placed. Or else we employ more general arguments about the effects which actions of a certain type tend to produce, or the qualities which are usually manifested in their performance. We do this in the hope that we have only to get our opponent to agree with us about the nature of the empirical facts for him to adopt the same moral attitude towards them as we do. And as the people with whom we argue have generally received the same moral education as ourselves, and live in the same social order, our expectation is usually justified. But if our opponent happens to have undergone a different process of moral "conditioning" from ourselves, so that, even when he acknowledges all the facts, he still disagrees with us about the moral value of the actions under discussion, then we abandon the attempt to convince him by argument. We say that it is impossible to argue with him because he has a distorted or undeveloped moral sense; which signifies merely that he employs a different set of values from our own. We feel that our own system of values is superior, and therefore speak in such derogatory terms of his. But we cannot bring forward any arguments to show that our system is superior. For our judgement that it is so is itself a judgement of value, and accordingly outside the scope of argument. It is because argument fails us when we come to deal with pure questions of value, as distinct from questions of fact, that we finally resort to mere abuse.

In short, we find that argument is possible on moral questions only if some system of values is presupposed. If our opponent concurs with us in expressing moral disapproval of all actions of a given type *t*, then we may get him to condemn a particular action A, by bringing forward arguments to show that A is of type *t*. For the question whether A does or does not belong to that type is a plain question of fact. Given that a man has certain moral principles, we argue that he must, in order to be consistent, react morally to certain things in a certain way. What we do not and cannot argue about is the validity of these moral principles. We merely praise or condemn them in the light of our own feelings.

If anyone doubts the accuracy of this account of moral disputes, let him try to construct even an imaginary argument on a question of value which does not reduce itself to an argument about a question of logic or about an empirical matter of fact. I am confident that he will not succeed in producing a single example. And if that is the case, he must allow that its involving the impossibility of purely ethical arguments is not, as Moore thought, a ground of objection to our theory, but rather a point in favour of it.

Having upheld our theory against the only criticism which appeared to threaten it, we may now use it to define the nature of all ethical enquiries. We find that ethical philosophy consists simply in saying that ethical concepts are pseudo-concepts and therefore unanalysable. The further task of describing the different feelings that the different ethical terms are used to express, and the different reactions that they customarily provoke, is a task for the psychologist. There cannot be such a thing as ethical science, if by ethical science one means the elaboration of a "true" system of morals. For we have seen that, as ethical judgements are mere expressions of feeling, there can be no way of determining the validity of any ethical system, and, indeed, no sense in asking whether any such system is true. All that one may legitimately enquire in this connection is, What are the moral habits of a given person or group of people, and what causes them to have precisely those habits and feelings? And this enquiry falls wholly within the scope of the existing social sciences.

It appears, then, that ethics, as a branch of knowledge, is nothing more than a department of psychology and sociology. And in case anyone thinks that we are overlooking the existence of casuistry, we may remark that casuistry is not a science, but is a purely analytical investigation of the structure of a given moral system. In other words it is an exercise in formal logic.

When one comes to pursue the psychological enquiries which constitute ethical science, one is immediately enabled to account for the Kantian and hedonistic theories of morals. For one finds that one of the chief causes of moral behaviour is fear, both conscious and unconscious, of a god's displeasure, and fear of the enmity of society. And this, indeed, is the reason why moral precepts present themselves to some people as "categorical" commands. And one finds, also, that the moral code of a society is partly determined by the beliefs of that society concerning the conditions of its own happiness—or, in other words, that a society tends to encourage or discourage a given type of conduct by the use of moral sanctions according as it appears to promote or detract from the contentment of the society as a whole. And this is the reason why altruism is recommended in most moral codes and egotism condemned. It is from the observation of this connection between morality and happiness that hedonistic or eudæmonistic theories of morals ultimately spring, just as the moral theory of Kant is based on the fact, previously explained, that moral precepts have for some people the force of inexorable commands. As each of these theories ignores the fact which lies at the root of the other, both may be criticized as being one-sided; but this is not the main objection to either of them. Their essential defect is that they treat propositions which refer to the causes and attributes of our ethical feelings as if they were definitions of ethical concepts. And thus they fail to recognize that ethical concepts are pseudoconcepts and consequently indefinable.

As we have already said, our conclusions about the nature of ethics apply to æsthetics also. Æsthetic terms are used in exactly the same way as ethical terms. Such æsthetic words as "beautiful" and "hideous" are employed, as ethical words are employed, not to make statements of fact, but simply to express certain feelings and evoke a certain response. It follows, as in ethics, that there is no sense in attributing objective validity to æsthetic judgements, and no possibility of arguing about questions of value in æsthetics, but only about questions of fact. A scientific treatment of æsthetics would show us what in general were the causes of æsthetic feeling, why various societies produced and admired the works of art they did, why taste varies as it does within a given society, and so forth. And these are ordinary psychological or sociological questions. They have, of course, little or nothing to do with æsthetic criticism as we understand it. But that is because the purpose of æsthetic criticism is not so much to give knowledge as to communicate emotion. The critic, by calling attention to certain features of the work under review, and expressing his own feelings about them, endeavours to make us share his attitude towards the work as a whole. The only relevant propositions that he formulates are propositions describing the nature of the work. And these are plain records of fact. We conclude, therefore, that there is nothing in æsthetics, any more than there is in ethics, to justify the view that it embodies a unique type of knowledge.

It should now be clear that the only information which we can legitimately derive from the study of our æsthetic and moral experiences is information about our own mental and physical make-up. We take note of these experiences as providing data for our psychological and sociological generalisations. And this is the only way in which they serve to increase our knowledge. It follows that any attempt to make our use of ethical and æsthetic concepts the basis of a metaphysical theory concerning the existence of a world of values, as distinct from the world of facts, involves a false analysis of these concepts. Our own analysis has shown that the phenomena of moral experience cannot fairly be used to support any rationalist or metaphysical doctrine whatsoever. In particular, they cannot, as Kant hoped, be used to establish the existence of a transcendent god.

This mention of God brings us to the question of the possibility of religious knowledge. We shall see that this possibility has already been ruled out by our treatment of metaphysics. But, as this is a point of considerable interest, we may be permitted to discuss it at some length.

Note on Sources. The passages just quoted are from Chapter 6, "Critique of Ethics and Theology," in the book *Language, Truth, and Logic.*

Reading References. A second formulation of emotivism will be found in Professor Charles Stevenson's book *Ethics and Language.* A good criticism of emotivism will be found in Professor Brand Blanshard's *Reason and Goodness,* especially Chapter 8. Exposition and criticism of emotivism will be found in the author's book *An Elementary Ethics.*

READING QUESTIONS

1. How you would formulate the emotivist theory in ethics.
2. Contrast emotivism with (a) utilitarianism, (b) subjectivism.

3. At what point the emotive theory presupposes the verifiability theory of meaning.
4. Use the distinction between cognitive and emotive symbols to state the emotivist position.
5. Contrast emotivism in ethics with emotivism in aesthetics.
6. Suggest one criticism of emotivism in terms of the grounds on which it rests; and one in terms of the consequences that follow from it.
7. Wherein you find emotivism (a) most, (b) least convincing.

INDEPENDENT STUDY

1. Read the articles "Emotive Meaning" by W. P. Alston and "Emotive Theory of Ethics" by R. B. Brandt, both in the *Encyclopedia of Philosophy*. Each article is supplied with a usable bibliography. Work out a paper expounding or criticizing the emotive theory in ethics.
2. There is an emotive theory in aesthetics. You will find brief statements of it in this book, in the topic "The world of art," by Véron and Collingwood. Compare these two emotivisms. Do the criticisms directed at emotivism in ethics apply to emotivism in aesthetics? If not, why not?
3. Read as much as you need in C. L. Stevenson's *Ethics and Language* and in his *Facts and Values* to write a comparison–contrast paper on Stevenson and Ayer with reference to their emotivism.
4. Read *Ethical Theory*, Chapter 9, by Richard B. Brandt. Use that chapter and the bibliographical leads that it provides, to write a paper on criticisms of emotivism in ethics.

SECTION 6. BRAND BLANSHARD: THE NEW SUBJECTIVISM IN ETHICS

From Ayer to Blanshard.   In the preceding section we examined A. J. Ayer's exposition and defense of a theory about moral concepts and the moral judgments and moral principles in which they are used. The position is called emotivism. It is the claim that moral concepts (e.g., right, good, duty, together with their negatives, synonyms, and derivatives) do not refer to any facts about any acts or agents, are cognitively meaningless, and serve only to express or arouse emotions, feelings, in those who use them or those to whom they are used. Thus, when you say "Stealing is wrong" or, "You did wrong to steal," the term *wrong*, being a moral concept, does not tell you anything about either stealing or you. What it does is to express an emotion, a feeling, had by the person who made those "moral judgments," or intended to excite some emotion or feeling in the person addressed. An emotive term, or the emotive use of a term, is one that enables you to express an emotion or feeling (e.g., anger, disapproval, contempt, hatred, and so on.) The use of the term therefore tells you, or enables you to infer, something about the person who uses it; namely, that he has a certain emotion or feeling and that he is expressing it, or that he is endeavoring to excite some feeling in the person whom he is addressing. Since expressing or arousing a feeling is *all* that emotive language, or the emotive use of language, accomplishes, it follows that the "moral judgments" or "moral principles" in which they are used are, in the usual sense of the term, meaningless; have no objective reference; are neither true nor false; and so on. The emotive theory of moral "concepts," "judgments," and "principles" was drastically deflationary of all such "concepts," "judgments," and "principles." The deflationary intention was expressed by saying that, according to the emotive theory, these "concepts," "judgments," and "principles" were not concepts, judgments, and principles. They were pseudoconcepts, pseudojudgments, and pseudoprinciples.

Professor Blanshard has this deflationary theory in antiethics under attack. His paper, published in 1949, is an interesting example of an essay in counterattack. Emotivism was one road to antiethics. There may be others. The point of the antilabel is that such theories propose to abolish ethics. Professor Blanshard's argument, if successful, would put ethics back in business again, asking questions and making claims about moral concepts, and the judgments and principles in which they are used. The word *emotivism* draws attention to the fact that the theory claims that moral "concepts" do nothing but express or excite emotions or feelings. The word *subjectivism* draws attention to the fact that the theory claims that moral "concepts" tell you nothing about any "objects" (i.e., acts or agents) to which they "apply," but only about the subject, the person, the judger, who uses the pseudoconcept in question. What it tells you about him, the subject, is that he has a certain emotion or feeling, and that he is using the pseudoconcept to express said emotion or feeling, or to excite it in someone else.

Professor Blanshard uses his first four paragraphs to introduce the position that he proposes to attack, and to talk about it with reference to such lead-in questions as, "What does it claim?" "Who are its sponsors?" "What are their interests or specialties or positions or commitments in philosophy?" "What motivated them to develop this antiethical theory?" The opening paragraphs have been assigned numbers for ease in referring to them in discussion. The numbers do not occur in the original article.

1. By the new subjectivism in ethics I mean the view that when anyone says "this is right" or "this is good," he is only expressing his own feeling; he is not asserting anything true or false, because he is not asserting or judging at all; he is really making an exclamation that expresses a favorable feeling.

2. This view has recently come into much favor. With variations of detail, it is being advocated by Russell, Wittgenstein and Ayer in England, and by Carnap, Stevenson, Feigl, and others, in this country. Why is it that the theory has come into so rapid a popularity? Is it because moralists of insight have been making a fresh and searching examination of moral experience and its expression? No, I think not. A consideration of the names just mentioned suggests a truer reason. All these names belong, roughly speaking, to a single school of thought in the theory of knowledge. If the new view has become popular in ethics, it is because certain persons who were at work in the theory of knowledge arrived at a new view *there*, and found, on thinking it out, that it required the new view in ethics; the view comes less from ethical analysis than from logical positivism.

3. As positivists, these writers held that every judgment belongs to one or other of two types. On the one hand, it may be *a priori* or necessary. But then it is always analytic, i.e., it unpacks in its predicate part or all of its subject. Can we safely say that 7 + 5 make 12? Yes, because 12 is what we mean by "7 + 5." On the other hand, the judgment may be empirical, and then, if we are to verify it, we can no longer look to our meanings only; it refers to sense experience and there we must look for its warrant. Having arrived at this division of judgments, the positivists raised the question where value judgments fall. The judgment that knowledge is good, for example, did not seem to be analytic; the value that knowledge might have did not seem to be part of our concept of knowledge. But neither was the statement empirical, for goodness was not a quality like red or squeaky that could be seen or heard. What were they to do, then, with these awkward judgments of value? To find a place for them in their theory of knowledge would require them to revise the theory radically, and yet that theory was what they regarded as their most important discovery. It appeared that the theory could be saved in one way only. If it could be shown that judgments of good and bad were not judgments at all, that they asserted nothing true or false, but merely expressed emotions like "Hurrah" or "Fiddlesticks," then these wayward judgments would cease from troubling and weary heads could be at rest. This is the course the positivists took. They explained value judgments by explaining them away.

4. Now I do not think their view will do. But before discussing it, I should like to record one vote of thanks to them for the clarity with which they have stated their case. It has been said of John Stuart Mill that he wrote so clearly that he could be found out. This theory has been put so clearly and precisely that it deserves criticism of the same kind, and this I will do my best to supply. The theory claims to show by analysis that when we say,

"That is good," we do not mean to assert a character of the subject of which we are thinking. I shall argue that we do mean to do just that.

The position is now before us. It is an essay, an exercise, in antiethics, directed against any or all traditional ethics from Socrates to the present day. Is it open to any criticisms, or even to refutation? Professor Blanshard begins by describing a test case: a rabbit that has been caught in a trap, suffered great pain, and died. He then develops five criticisms of the emotivist or subjectivist position in antiethics. The example is this:

Let us work through an example, and the simpler and commoner the better. There is perhaps no value statement on which people would more universally agree than the statement that intense pain is bad. Let us take a set of circumstances in which I happen to be interested on the legislative side and in which I think every one of us might naturally make such a statement. We come upon a rabbit that has been caught in one of the brutal traps in common use. There are signs that it has struggled for days to escape and that in a frenzy of hunger, pain, and fear, it has all but eaten off its own leg. The attempt failed: the animal is now dead. As we think of the long and excruciating pain it must have suffered, we are very likely to say: "It was a bad thing that the little animal should suffer so." The positivist tells us that when we say this we are only expressing our present emotion. I hold, on the contrary, that we mean to assert something of the pain itself, namely, that it was bad—bad when and as it occurred.

Professor Blanshard's *first* criticism comes about this way: If you are *not* a committed emotivist or subjectivist, it would be open to you to say, "It was a bad thing that the little animal suffered so," and use the term *bad* to refer to the animal's pain and suffering, especially, I suppose, under those conditions. In your use, the term would have an objective referent, namely, the animal's pain and suffering; and it would have a judgmental force, namely, judging it to be a bad thing that the animal suffered this pain in this way. There would be nothing linguistically incorrect in your judgment. You knew what you were referring to, and you meant what you said. Suppose, however, that you have subscribed to emotivism, or subjectivism, in antiethics. Then what?

Consider what follows from the positivist view. On that view, nothing good or bad happened in the case until I came on the scene and made my remark. For what I express in my remark is something going on in me at the time, and that of course did not exist until I did come on the scene. The pain of the rabbit was not itself bad; nothing evil was happening when that pain was being endured; badness, in the only sense in which it is involved at all, waited for its appearance till I came and looked and felt. Now that this is at odds with our meaning may be shown as follows. Let us put to ourselves the hypothesis that we had not come on the scene and that the rabbit never was discovered. Are we prepared to say that in that case nothing bad occurred in the sense in which we said it did? Clearly not. Indeed we should say, on the contrary, that the accident of our later discovery made no difference whatever to the badness of the animal's pain, that it would have been every whit as bad whether a chance passer-by happened later to discover the body and feel repugnance or not. If so, then it is clear that in saying the suffering was bad we are not expressing our feelings only. We are saying that the pain was bad when and as it occurred and before anyone took an attitude toward it.

The first criticism, then, is that if you subscribe to the theory it will constrain you to say, or refrain from saying, things that, if it were not for the theory, you would not say, or would not refrain from saying. These coercions, constraints, are exercised by the theory, not by your knowledge of and judgment upon the animal's entrapment, suffering, and death. There is nothing to be said for these constraints except that they are required by this antiethical theory.

Professor Blanshard's *second* criticism asks us to suppose that we were mistaken about the facts: the animal was not caught in the trap, did not suffer great pain, and did not die. If you are *not* an emotivist or subjectivist, you will, upon discovering your mistake, retract your judgment on the grounds that the relevant facts were not what you (mistakenly) took them to be. Your judgment, being erroneous as to the facts, lost its point: "There is no point to saying that it was a bad thing for it to suffer if it did not suffer." An error about the objective referent of your judgment requires you to retract your judgment. Suppose, however, that you are an emotivist or subjectivist. In what otherwise odd ways will your theory constrain you?

Let us suppose that the animal did not in fact fall into the trap and did not suffer at all, but that we mistakenly believe it did, and say as before that its suffering was an evil thing. On the positivist theory, everything I sought to express by calling it evil in the first case is still present in the second. In the only sense in which badness is involved at all, whatever was bad in the first case is still present in its entirety, since all that is expressed in either case is a state of feeling, and that feeling is still there. And our question is, is such an implication consistent with what we meant? Clearly it is not. If anyone asked us, after we made the remark that the suffering was a bad thing, whether we should think it was relevant to what we said to learn that the incident had never occurred and no pain had been suffered at all, we should say that it made all the difference in the world, that what we were asserting to be bad was precisely the suffering we thought had occurred back there, that if this had not occurred, there was nothing left to be bad, and that our assertion was in that case mistaken. The suggestion that in saying something evil had occurred we were after all making no mistake, because we had never meant anyhow to say anything about the past suffering, seems to me merely frivolous. If we did not mean to say this, why should we be so relieved on finding that the suffering had not occurred? On the theory before us, such relief would be groundless, for in that suffering itself there was nothing bad at all, hence in its non-occurrence there would be nothing to be relieved about. The positivist theory would here distort our meaning beyond recognition.

So far as I can see, there is only one way out for the positivist. He holds that goodness and badness lie in feelings of approval or disapproval. And there is a way in which he might hold that badness did in this case precede our own feeling of disapproval without belonging to the pain itself. The pain in itself was neutral; but unfortunately the rabbit, on no grounds at all, took up toward this neutral object an attitude of disapproval, and that made it for the first time, and in the only intelligible sense, bad. This way of escape is theoretically possible, but since it has grave difficulties of its own and has not, so far as I know, been urged by positivists, it is perhaps best not to spend time over it.

Professor Blanshard's *third* criticism asks us to suppose that when we authorized the moral judgment ("It is bad for an animal to suffer such pain and such a death," "It is wrong for people to cause such pain and death," and so on), we did so with considerable feeling, and that this feeling was expressed in our moral judgment. The words we used expressed two things: our moral judgment and our feelings of, say, sympathy and outrage. He further asks us to suppose that sometime later, after our feelings had "died down," we repeated our moral judgment. We might recall our feelings, we might remember that when we originally pronounced the moral judgment we were wrought up, whereas it is now a matter of "emotion recollected in tranquillity." Nevertheless we do reiterate our original judgment: "It is bad for an animal to suffer such pain and such a death," "It is wrong for people to cause such pain and death," and so on. If you are *not* an emotivist, what account do you give of your two moral judgments? If you *are* an emotivist, what will your commitment constrain you to say, or to refrain from saying?

I come now to a third argument, which again is very simple. When we come upon the rabbit and make our remark about its suffering being a bad thing, we presumably make it with some feeling; the positivists are plainly right in saying that such remarks do usually express feeling. But suppose that a week later we revert to the incident in thought and make our statement again. And suppose that the circumstances have now so changed that the feeling with which we made the remark in the first place has faded. The pathetic evidence is no longer before us; and we are now so fatigued in body and mind that feeling is, as we say, quite dead. In these circumstances, since what was expressed by the remark when first made is, on the theory before us, simply absent, the remark now expresses nothing. It is as empty as the word "Hurrah" would be when there was no enthusiasm behind it. And this seems to me untrue. When we repeat the remark that such suffering was a bad thing, the feeling with which we made it last week may be at or near the vanishing point, but if we were asked whether we meant to say what we did before, we should certainly answer Yes. We should say that we made our point with feeling the first time and little or no feeling the second time, but that it was the same point we were making. And if we can see that what we meant to say remains the same, while the feeling varies from intensity to near zero, it is not the feeling that we primarily meant to express.

Professor Blanshard's *fourth* criticism of emotivism as a theory about moral concepts and the judgments and principles in which they are used turns on a question about the attitudes that we may take up toward agents or actions and then express in our moral judgments. Suppose someone is needlessly and flagrantly cruel to animals and little children. They are in no position to defend themselves, so he enjoys himself by causing them to squeal and squirm. Suppose our attitude toward him is one of disapproval. The question on which Professor Blanshard's fourth criticism turns is whether our attitude of disapproval is fitting, unfitting, or neither. Is it fitting that we should take up an attitude of disapproval, and proceed to express it in a moral judgment? If it is fitting, what does this fittingness depend on? If it is unfitting, why is it unfitting? If you are not an emotivist, you might say that the fittingness of your attitude of disapproval depends on, derives from, the character of the agent or action toward which you have this attitude. It is unlikely that you would say that the fittingness of your attitude depends on the fact that you have this attitude. You might say, "The action [needless and flagrant cruelty to animals and children who cannot protect themselves] is wrong. That is why I disapprove of it. That is the reason for my attitude. In view of the wrongness of the action, my attitude is quite fitting. Indeed, it would be quite *unfitting* for me, or anyone else, to have toward such action an attitude of approval." Here the order is (1) the agent, (2) his action, (3) its wrongness, (4) your attitude of disapproval, (5) the fittingness of your attitude, (6) the expression of the fitting attitude in your moral judgment. You could talk this way so long as you were not an emotivist. But how would emotivism require you to talk? What account would it constrain you to give of the fittingness of your attitude?

I come now to a fourth consideration. We all believe that toward acts or effects of a certain kind one attitude is fitting and another not; but on the theory before us such a belief would not make sense. Broad and Ross have lately contended that this fitness is one of the main facts of ethics, and I suspect they are right. But that is not exactly my point. My point is this: whether there is such fitness or not, we all assume that there is, and if we do, we express in moral judgments more than the subjectivists say we do. Let me illustrate.

In his novel *The House of the Dead*, Dostoevsky tells of his experiences in a Siberian prison camp. Whatever the unhappy inmates of such camps are like today, Dostoevsky's companions were about as grim a lot as can be imagined. "I have heard stories," he writes, "of the most terrible, the most unnatural actions, of the most monstrous murders, told with the most spontaneous, childishly merry laughter." Most of us would say that in this delight at the killing of others or the causing of suffering there is something very unfitting. If we were asked why we thought so, we should say that these things involve great evil and are wrong, and that to take delight in what is evil or wrong is plainly unfitting. Now on the subjectivist view, this answer is ruled out. For before someone takes up an attitude toward death, suffering, or their infliction, they have no moral quality at all. There is therefore nothing about them to which an attitude of approval or condemnation could be fitting. They are in themselves neutral, and, so far as they get a moral quality, they get it only through being invested with it by the attitude of the onlooker. But if that is true, why is any attitude more fitting than any other? Would applause, for example, be fitting if, apart from the applause, there were nothing good to applaud? Would condemnation be fitting if, independently of the condemnation, there were nothing bad to condemn? In such a case, any attitude would be as fitting or unfitting as any other, which means that the notion of fitness has lost all point.

Indeed we are forced to go much farther. If goodness and badness lie in attitudes only and hence are brought into being by them, those men who greeted death and misery with childishly merry laughter are taking the only sensible line. If there is nothing evil in these things, if they get their moral complexion only from our feeling about them, why shouldn't they be greeted with a cheer? To greet them with repulsion would turn what before was neutral into something bad; it would needlessly bring badness into the world; and even on subjectivist assumptions that does not seem very bright. On the other hand, to greet them with delight would convert what before was neutral into something good; it would bring goodness into the world. If I have murdered a man and wish to remove the stain, the way is clear. It is to cry, "Hurrah for murder."

What is the subjectivist to reply? I can only guess. He may point out that the inflicting of death is *not* really neutral before the onlooker takes his attitude, for the man who inflicted the death no doubt himself took an attitude, and thus the act had a moral quality derived from this. But that makes the case more incredible still, for the man who did the act presumably approved it, and if so it was good in the only sense in which anything is good, and then our conviction that the laughter is unfit is more unaccountable still. It may be replied that the victim, too, had his attitude and that since this was unfavorable, the act was not unqualifiedly good. But the answer is plain. Let the killer be expert at his job; let him despatch his victim instantly before he has time to take an attitude, and then gloat about his perfect crime without ever telling anyone. Then, so far as I can see, his act will be good without any qualification. It would become bad only if someone found out about it and disliked it. And that would be a curiously irrational procedure, since the man's approving of his own killing is in itself as neutral as the killing that it approves. Why then should anyone dislike it?

It may be replied that we can defend our dislike on this ground that, if the approval of killing were to go unchecked and spread, most men would have to live in insecurity and fear, and these things are undesirable. But surely this reply is not open; these things are not, on the theory, undesirable, for nothing is; in themselves they are neutral. Why then should I disapprove men's living in this state? The answer may come that if other men live in insecurity and fear, I shall in time be infected myself. But even in my own insecurity and fear there is, on the theory before us, nothing bad whatever, and therefore, if I disapprove them, it is without a shadow of ground and with no more fitness in my attitude than if I cordially cheered them. The theory thus conflicts with our judgments of fitness all along the line.

Professor Blanshard's *fifth* criticism of emotivism, or subjectivism, turns on the traditional and, as he says, merciful distinction between an act being subjectively right and objectively right. He first explains this distinction, and illustrates its plausibility. He then points out that emotivism, or subjectivism, would abolish this distinction, regardless of how plausible it may be. He then points out, further, that if you abolish the distinction between subjectively right and objectively right you find you have thereby abolished the notion of duty. Your losses pile up; and they are forced upon you by, they are the price you pay for, your commitment to emotivism or subjectivism. At what point does a philosophical commitment price itself out of the market of ideas?

I come now to a fifth and final difficulty with the theory. It makes mistakes about values impossible. There is a whole nest of inter-connected criticisms here, some of which have been made so often that I shall not develop them again, such as that I can never agree or disagree in opinion with anyone else about an ethical matter, and that in these matters I can never be inconsistent with others or with myself. I am not at all content with the sort of analysis which says that the only contradictions in such cases have regard to facts and that contradictions about value are only differences of feeling. I think that if anyone tells me that having a bicuspid out without an anaesthetic is not a bad experience and I say it is a very nasty exprience indeed, I am differing with him in opinion, and differing about the degrees of badness of the experience. But without pressing this further, let me apply the argument in what is perhaps a fresh direction.

There is an old and merciful distinction that moralists have made for many centuries about conduct—the distinction between what is subjectively and what is objectively right. They have said that in any given situation there is some act which, in view of all the circumstances, would be the best act to do; and this is what would be objectively right. The notion of an objectively right act is the ground of our notion of duty: our duty is always to find and do this act if we can. But of course we often don't find it. We often hit upon and do acts that we think are the right ones, but we are mistaken; and then our act is only subjectively right. Between these two acts the disparity may be continual; Professor Prichard suggested that probably few of us in the course of our lives ever succeed in doing *the* right act.

Now so far as I can see, the new subjectivism would abolish this difference at a stroke. Let us take a case. A boy abuses his small brother. We should commonly say, "That is wrong, but perhaps he doesn't know any better. By reason of bad teaching and a feeble imagination, he may see nothing wrong in what he is doing, and may even be proud of it. If so, his act may be subjectively right, though it is miles away from what is objectively right." What concerns me about the new subjectivism is that it prohibits this distinction. If the boy feels this way about his act, then it is right in the only sense in which anything is right. The notion of an objective right lying beyond what he has discovered, and which he ought to seek and do is meaningless. There might, to be sure, be an act that would more generally arouse favorable feelings in others, but that would not make it right for him unless he thought of it and approved it, which he doesn't. Even if he did think of it, it would not be obligatory for him to feel about it in any particular way, since there is nothing in any act, as we have seen, which would make any feeling more suitable than any other.

Now if there is no such thing as an objectively right act, what becomes of the idea of duty? I have suggested that the idea of duty rests on the idea of such an act, since it is always our duty to find that act and do it if we can. But if whatever we feel approval for at the time is right, what is the point of doubting and searching further? Like the little girl in Boston who was asked if she would like to travel, we can answer, "Why should I travel when I'm already there?" If I am reconciled in feeling to my present act, no act I could discover by reflection could be better, and therefore why reflect or seek at all? Such a view seems to me to break the mainspring of duty, to destroy the motive for self-improvement, and to remove the ground for self-criticism. It may be replied that by further reflection I can find an act that would satisfy my feelings more widely than the present one, and that this is the act I should seek. But this reply means either that such general satisfaction is objectively better, which would contradict the theory, or else that, if at the time I don't feel it better, it isn't better, in which case I have no motive for seeking it.

When certain self-righteous persons took an inflexible line with Oliver Cromwell, his very Cromwellian reply was, "Bethink ye, gentlemen, by the bowels of Christ, that ye may be mistaken." It was good advice. I hope nobody will take from me the privilege of finding myself mistaken. I should be sorry to think that the self of thirty years ago was as far along the path as the self of today, merely because he was a smug young jackanapes, or even that the paragon of today has as little room for improvement as would be allowed by his myopic complacency.

Professor Blanshard's criticisms have consisted in pointing out constraints that emotivism imposes upon those who subscribe to it. It requires them to say things they would not otherwise say, or to refrain from saying things they would otherwise say. The constraints are no evidence that emotivism is true considered as a theory of moral concepts and the judgments and principles in which they are used. They are concessions you make if you are an emotivist, ways in which you are theory-bound if you are an emotivist. As a parting shot, Professor Blanshard draws attention to a less theoretical, more practical, consequence: what emotivism would lead to if it were applied in international law, international politics, international relations.

One final remark. The great problems of the day are international problems. Has the new subjectivism any bearing upon these problems? I think it has, and a somewhat sinister bearing. I would not suggest, of course, that those who hold the theory are one whit less public-spirited than others; surely there are few who could call themselves citizens of the world with more right (if "rights" have meaning any longer) than Mr. Russell. But Mr. Russell has confessed himself discontented with his ethical theory, and in view of his breadth of concern, one cannot wonder. For its general acceptance would, so far as one can see, be an international disaster. The assumption behind the old League and the new United Nations was that there is such a thing as right and wrong in the conduct of a nation, a right and wrong that do not depend on how it happens to feel at the time. It is implied, for example, that when Japan invaded Manchuria in 1931 she might be wrong, and that by discussion and argument she might be shown to be wrong. It was implied that when the Nazis invaded Poland they might be wrong, even though German public sentiment overwhelmingly approved it. On the theory before us, it would be meaningless to call these nations mistaken; if they felt approval for what they did, then it was right with as complete a justification as could be supplied for the disapproval felt by the rest of the world. In the present dispute between Russia and our own country over southeast Europe, it is nonsense to speak of the right or rational course for either of us to take; if with all the facts before the two parties, each feels approval for its own course, both attitudes are equally justified or unjustified; neither is mistaken; there is no common reason to which they can take an appeal; there are no principles by which an international court could pronounce on the matter; nor would there be any obligation to obey the pronouncement if it were made. This cuts the ground from under any attempt to establish one's case as right or anyone else's case as wrong. So if our friends the subjectivists still hold their theory after I have applied my little ruler to their knuckles, which of course they will, I have but one request to make of them: Do keep it from Mr. Molotov and Mr. Vishinsky.

READING QUESTIONS

1. What Mr. Blanshard means by the new subjectivism in ethics.
2. How does he account for the popularity of the theory?

3. How the positivists arrived at emotivism.
4. How he used the case of the trapped rabbit to arrive at his first criticism of emotivism.
5. Ditto for his second criticism.
6. Ditto for his third criticism.
7. How he uses the example from Dostoievsky's *House of the Dead* to arrive at his fourth criticism of emotivism.
8. How he used the distinction between subjective rightness and objective rightness to arrive at his fifth criticism of emotivism.
9. And the idea of duty, to arrive at another criticism.
10. And the idea of international relations, to arrive at another criticism.
11. Why he requests the subjectivists to keep their theory from Mr. Molotov and Mr. Vishinsky.
12. Which of his criticism you find most incisive. Why?

INDEPENDENT STUDY

1. Read the relevant chapters in G. E. Moore's *Ethics* and W. T. Stace's *Concept of Morals.* Compare their arguments with Blanshard's.
2. Read Chapter 1, "Men Without Chests," in C. S. Lewis's little book, *The Abolition of Man.* Which, Blanshard or Lewis, does a better job of criticizing the antiethical isms?

topic four
state and law

THE PROBLEM STATED

The fact that men have religions, and that most religions include beliefs about God, and that members of religions have sometimes used what they know, or claim to know, about nature in support of what they believe about God, gave us our first topic. The fact that persons sometimes distinguish between nature and humanity, the order of nature and the order of the human, and have sometimes used what they know, or claim to know, about nature in support of what they believe about man, gave us our second topic. The fact that men distinguish between right and wrong, and sometimes try to formulate the principle upon which this distinction rests, gave us our third topic. The fact that some human behavior is regulated by man-made laws and that such a legislated way of life requires that humans be politically organized, organized as a state having a government, gives us our fourth topic.

Our present topic is the legislative way of life, the way of life that is productive of those contrived regularities to obtain which men devise, revise, administer, and enforce laws in the legislative, not the scientific, sense. We use the term *law* in two senses. In Sense One we use it to refer to those statements, produced by scientists, in which they formulate or describe regularities that they detect in the order of nature. In Sense Two we use it to refer to those demands, produced by legislators, in which they prescribe regularities that they desire to produce. "Do not park by a fire plug" would be a simple and familiar example of a law produced by a legislator, or a legislative body. To the degree that this law is obeyed, a regularity results: it becomes regularly the case that vehicles are not parked within a prescribed distance of fire hydrants. These and other humanly contrived regularities have considerable value. Increasingly, civilized communities are dependent upon laws produced by scientists and laws produced by legislators.

In communities committed to the legislative way of life, laws propose to remove options from the behavior of those who obey them; and to impose penalties upon those who disobey them. As a consequence, sometimes both parties are irked. The person who no longer has the option of parking by a fire hydrant is irked; and the person who is punished for having parked by the fire hydrant is also irked. Since a law's demands and threats are backed by very considerable power, the question eventually arises, "Where do those who possess and exercise this power obtain the authority, the right, to do so?" It will not do to say that they get it by law, because that law is itself here in question. So you have the question, "Is there anything, not produced by human legislation, that is 'above,' or 'higher than,' human legislation, which is the source from which legislative bodies derive their *authority* to exercise their *powers;* derive, as the Declaration of Independence says, their 'just powers'?"

Our authors direct attention to essential features of the legislative way of life, and to the questions that thereby arise. Rousseau, in the *Social Contract,* observes that, typically, men live under laws; also typically, laws make demands that are backed by threats. He therefore says that men live under "chains" and asks how this came to pass, and how it can be justified. Mill, in *On Liberty,* observes that as you democratize a state, a community committed to the legislative way of life, you enable an increasing majority to prescribe for deviant minorities. As majorities increasingly become the source of the powers exercised in their name by legislatures and executives, the chance for individuals and minorities to think and act for themselves is increasingly circumscribed. Marx, in the *Communist Manifesto,* observes that to the degree that the industrial revolution has been marked by laissez-faire capitalism, it has separated peoples into workers and employers, proletariate and capitalists, poor and rich, and that legislatures and executives have become the agents of the capitalist masters of the economy. As a consequence laws become demands, backed by threats, for regularities favorable to the class interests of the capitalists. Hart, in his *Concept of Law,* observes that if laws are nothing more than "orders backed by threats," then the legislative way of life is nothing but the institutionalization of tyranny. To amount to anything more than that, laws must incorporate obligations, and then propose that such obligations be enforced.

TRIGGER QUESTIONS

1. Civilized nations are, apparently, increasingly dependent upon (1) laws produced by scientists and (2) laws produced by legislators. Why is this so?

2. The word *polis* is Greek for "a Community committed to the legislative way of life," to the regulation of some human behavior by man-made laws. Mention any half-dozen words derived from the word *polis*.

3. Why, in a polis-community, you might expect to find (a) lawmakers, (b) courts, (c) higher and lower courts, (d) trials, (e) judges, (f) lawyers, (g) police, (h) jails, (i) law schools.

4. Contrast the *civil disobedient* with (a) the criminal, (b) the anarchist, (c) the rebel, (d) the invader. How the *civil disobedient* can be an important symbol of the legislative way of life.

5. As directed at laws produced by legislators, make clear what would be meant by (a) an economic criticism, (b) a constitutional criticism, and (c) a moral criticism. Can you think of a fourth kind of criticism?

6. Suppose you are authorized to legislate three revisions in the "shape" of any one major institution. (a) Which institution would you choose? (b) What three revisions would you propose?

7. How about this: "If there is to be widespread and enduring embodiment of moral principles, it will be in great part because human affairs are amenable to the legislative way of life, and because institutions are amenable to legislative definition and redefinition."

8. Jot down any four difficulties and drawbacks that typically beset the legislative way of life. What is there about human beings, and/or the legislative way of life, that accounts for these difficulties and drawbacks?

9. Experience of apparently built-in difficulties and drawbacks attaching to the legislative way of life has led some persons to ask whether there are any viable alternatives to the legislative way of life. Do you know of any viable alternative?

10. Is there anything not produced by human legislative activity that is "higher than" or "above" legislative activity, with reference to

which legislative activity is to be judged? If so, what? If not, what?

11. Does a lawmaker have a stake in the freewill–determinism hassle?

12. What do you understand by *moral skepticism?* Is it directed at moral judgments or moral principles? Suppose a civil disobedient took little or no stock in moral principles. Can you suggest any line he might take in defense of his position? If none, then what?

SECTION 1. JEAN JACQUES ROUSSEAU: THE SOCIAL CONTRACT AND THE COMMON GOOD

Masterpieces have been written about man considered as a political animal, a species committed to the legislative way of life, the way of life in which some human behavior is regulated by man-made laws. Examples from classical Greek times are Plato's *Republic* and Aristotle's *Politics.* If you take in view the time between Plato and Aristotle in the ancient world, and Marx and Lenin in the modern world, the period between is certainly notable for Machiavelli's *Prince* and Rousseau's *Social Contract.* When its argument is finally clarified and formulated, it possesses relevance and universality that place it among the great scriptures of the legislative way of life. When you say that, you do not say everything that makes it memorable, but what you say does make it memorable. The little book is among the primary clarifiers of *la condition humaine.*

Biographical Note. Jean Jacques Rousseau was born in Switzerland in 1712, and died in 1778 at the age of sixty-six. From 1712 to 1748 he was acquiring the elements of a formal education and something more than the elements of a worldly education. These matters are set down in his *Confessions.* As might be expected from the haphazard and undisciplined way in which he conducted himself during these years, Rousseau arrived at a state of some maladjustment. The times looked out of joint. The *mores* looked cramped and artificial. Civilization looked decadent. Rousseau, had he lived at a later time, might have claimed to be "alienated."

From 1749 to 1762 he formulated his criticisms of the then modern world in a series of tracts that have given him his place in the scheme of things. The first of these (1749) was addressed to the question, "Have the sciences and arts contributed to purify morals?" Rousseau's answer was, "No." The second (1755), *On the Origin of Inequality Among Men,* argued that the root of inequality is the institution of property, which permits the strong and wealthy to subject the mass of mankind to toil and poverty. The third (1760), *The New Heloise*, was a protest against the artificialities of marriage and the family. The fourth (1762), *Émile*, was an indictment of education conceived as discipline and restraint. It stated the case for education, conceived as expression and development. The fifth (1762), *The Social Contract*, was addressed to the problem: Man is born free, and is everywhere in chains. How can this be justified? In these writings, Rousseau touched on important phases of eighteenth-century civilization. His pronouncements were usually in terms of such words as *artificial, unnatural, narrow, selfish, ignoble, crass*. Art, science, society, education, religion, the family, the state—all gave evidence that mankind was paying too great a price for the fruits of "civilized" living.

From 1763 to 1778 he was again a wanderer. The authorities ordered him out of France. He moved to Switzerland. The authorities ordered him out of Switzerland. He moved, at the invitation of David Hume, to England. This proved no better. He returned to France. During the last years of his life his mind became unbalanced. He died suddenly in 1778, two years after the American Revolution had begun and eleven years before the French Revolution began, for both of which in *The Social Contract* he had formulated principles of justification.

The Argument of the Passages. The question that Rousseau set himself has been stated already: "Man is born free, and is everywhere in chains. How did this come about? I do not know. What can make it legitimate? That question I think I can answer." It is clear that Rousseau does not propose to account for the fact that man is everywhere in chains. He is not proposing historical research into origins. Nor is he proposing to remove the chains in question. He is not proposing an argument for anarchism. His question is the more searching one: Granted that men must live in chains (i.e., under laws) what considerations will justify the fact? He begins by rejecting the notion that the right of this condition is to be found in the might that enforces it. Might does not make right. What does, then? His answer is common need, common confrontation with conditions that no individual could handle if left to himself. This idea is contained in the notion of the social contract. The terms of the contract are noted. The attributes of the sovereignty created and sustained by the contract are noted. The role of lawmaker is noted. The nature of law is noted. The separation of powers within government is argued for. The alternative forms of government (monarchy, aristocracy, democracy) are noted, together with their defining virtues and vices. He notes, finally, "the unavoidable and inherent defect which tends ceaselessly to destroy" any form of political organization in any society. The argument begins as follows:

Man is born free, and is everywhere in chains. One thinks himself the master of others, and still remains a greater slave than they. How did this come about? I do not know. What can make it legitimate? That question I think I can answer.

The first thing to be clear about is that the restrictions that law imposes cannot be justified by any appeal to the fact of force that lies back of them. Might does not make right. Thus:

Suppose that "force" creates "right." The result is a mass of nonsense. For, if force creates right, then every force that is greater than the first succeeds to its right. As soon as it were possible to disobey with impunity, disobedience would become legitimate; and, the strongest being always in the right, the only thing that would matter (so far as concerns "justification") would be to act so as to become the strongest.

But what kind of "right" is it that perishes when force fails? If we "must" obey, there is no question that we "ought" to obey. And, on the principle that force makes right, if we are not forced to obey, we are under no obligation to do so. A brigand surprises me at the edge of a wood. The pistol he holds gives him power. Does it also give him right? Even if I could withhold my purse, am I in conscience bound to give it up? Does his "might" create a "right"?

Force is a physical power, and I fail to see what moral effect it can have. To yield to force is an act of necessity, not of will; at most, an act of prudence. In what sense can it be a duty?

"Obey the powers that be." If this means "yield to force," it is a good precept; but superfluous: I can answer for its never being violated. If it means "Yield, because all power comes from God," the case is no better. All power comes from God, I admit; but so does sickness. Does that mean that we are forbidden to call in a doctor?

Let us admit then that force does not create right, and that we are obligated to obey only legitimate powers. In that case my original question recurs: What is the basis of political obligations?

If might does not make right, if the "chains" are not justified by the fact that we are forced to wear them, what can we say? Rousseau shifts from the force that is admittedly necessary to the existence of law, to the conditions that justify law backed by force. Thus:

Suppose men to have reached the point at which the obstacles in the way of their preservation in the state of nature are greater than the resources at the disposal of each individual. That primitive condition can then subsist no longer, and the human race would perish unless it changed its manner of existence.

The problem is to find a form of association which will protect the person and goods of each individual with the whole common force of all; and in which each, uniting himself with all, may still obey himself alone and remain as free as before. This is the fundmental problem of which the "social compact" provides the solution.

If we disregard what is not of the essence of the social compact we shall find that it reduces itself to the following terms: "Each of us puts his person and his power in common under the supreme direction of the general will; and, in our corporate capacity, we receive each member as a part of the whole."

At one stroke, in place of the individual personality of each contracting party, this act of association creates a collective body, receiving from this act is unity, its common identity, its life, and its will. This public person, so formed by the union of all other persons, takes the name of *body politic*. It is called *state* when passive, *sovereign* when active, and *power* when compared with others like itself. Those who are associated in it take collectively the name of *people*, are severally called *citizens* as sharing in the sovereign power, and *subjects* as being under the laws of the state.

As soon as this multitude is united in one body politic, it becomes impossible to offend against one of the members without attacking the body politic, and still more to offend against the body politic. Duty and interest, therefore, equally obligate the two contracting parties to give each other help.

The social contract creates the state. It thereby creates the "chains" he had referred to. But it does more than that. The chains are seen to be, in principle, self-imposed restrictions; and they bring with them compensating advantages. Thus:

In the social compact there is no real "renunciation" on the part of the individuals. The position in which they find themselves, as a result of the compact, is really preferable to that in which they were before. Instead of a "renunciation," they have made an advantageous exchange; instead of an uncertain and precarious way of living, they have got one that is better and more secure; instead of natural independence, they have got liberty; instead of the power to harm others, they have got security for themselves; instead of their strength, which others might overcome, they have got a right which social union makes invincible.

What a man loses by the social compact is his natural liberty, and an unlimited right to everything he tries to get and succeeds in getting. What he gains is civil liberty and the proprietorship of all he possesses. If we are to avoid mistake in weighing one against the other, we must distinguish natural liberty, bounded only by the strength of the individual, from civil liberty, limited by the general will; and we must distinguish possession, the effect of force, from property, founded only on a positive title.

For such physical inequalities as nature may have set up between men, the social compact substitutes an equality that is moral and legitimate: by it, men who may be unequal in strength or intelligence, become every one equal by convention and legal right.

Under bad governments, this equality is only apparent and illusory: it serves only to keep the pauper in his poverty and the rich man in the position he has usurped. In fact, laws are always of use to those who possess, and harmful to those who have nothing: from which it follows that the social state is advantageous to men only when all have something and none have too much.

The general will alone can direct the state according to the object for which it was instituted, i.e., the common good: for, if the clashing of particular interests made the establishing of societies necessary, the agreement of these interests made it possible. The common element in these different interests is what forms the social tie; and, were there no point of agreement between them all, no society could exist. It is solely on the basis of this common interest that every society should be governed.

There is often a great difference between the "will of all" and the "general will." The latter considers only the common interest; the former takes private interest into account, and is no more than a sum of particular wills. But deduct from the sum of particular wills the plusses and minuses that cancel one another, and the general will remains.

Each individual may have a particular will contrary or dissimilar to the general will which he has as a citizen. His particular interest may speak to him quite different from the common interest; may make him look upon what he owes to the common cause as a gratuitous contribution, the loss of which will do less harm to others than the payment of it is burdensome to himself. He may come to regard the moral person which constitutes the state as a *persona ficta*, because not a man; and, as a result, may wish to enjoy the rights of citizenship without being ready to fulfill the duties of a subject. This, continued, would prove the undoing of the body politic.

The social contract creates sovereignty, i.e., a society organized to define and enforce its laws. The sovereignty inheres in the people. Rousseau proceeds to note several of its defining properties:

In order that the social compact may not be an empty formula, it includes the undertaking, that whoever refuses to obey the general will shall be compelled to do so. In this lies the key to the working of the body politic. This alone legitimizes civil undertakings which, without it, would be absurd, tyrannical and liable to the most frightful abuses. The social compact gives the body politic absolute power over all its members. It is this power, under the direction of the general will, which bears the name of *sovereignty.*

The sovereign, being formed wholly of the individuals who compose it, neither has nor can have any interest contrary to theirs. The sovereign, therefore, need give no guarantee to its subjects. Merely by virtue of what it is, the sovereign is always what it should be.

Sovereignty, being nothing less than the exercise of the general will, is inalienable, and the sovereign, who is no less than a collective being, cannot be represented except by himself. The power may be delegated, but not the general will from which it derives. To be "general," the will need not be unanimous, but every vote must count; any exclusion is a breach of generality. For the same reason that it is inalienable, sovereignty is indivisible.

The social compact sets up among the citizens an equality of such a kind that they all bind themselves to observe the same conditions and should therefore all enjoy the same rights. Thus, from the very nature of the compact, every act of sovereignty binds or favors all the citizens equally; so that the sovereign recognizes only the body of the nation and draws no distinctions between those of whom it is made up.

What, then, is an act of sovereignty? It is not a convention between a superior and an inferior, but a convention between the body politic and each of its members. It is legitimate, because based on the social contract; equitable, because common to all; useful because it can have no other object than the general good; and stable, because guaranteed by the public force and the supreme power.

The people are sovereign. Granted. But what can they do about it? They can delegate their sovereignty to a legislature and an administration. Of themselves the sovereign people cannot draw up good law nor can they administer it.

But how are the people to "regulate the conditions of society"? By a common agreement? By a sudden inspiration? Has the body politic an organ to declare its will? Who can give it the foresight to formulate and announce its acts in advance? How is it to announce them in the hour of need? How can a blind multitude, who often does not know what is good for it and hence what it wills, carry out for itself so great and difficult an enterprise as a system of legislation?

Of itself, the people always wills the good, but of itself it by no means always sees it. The general will is always in the right, but the judgment which guides it is not always enlightened. It must be got to see things as they are, and, sometimes, as they ought to appear to it. It must be shown the good road it is in search of, secured against the seductive influences of individual wills. It must be taught to see times and places, made to weigh the attractions of present and sensible advantages against the dangers of distant and hidden evils.

All stand equally in need of guidance. Individuals must be compelled to bring their wills into conformity with their reason. The public must be taught to know what is the good which it wills. If that is done, there is a union of understanding and will in the social body. The parts work together, and the whole is raised to its highest power. This makes a legislator necessary.

The function of lawmaker needs to be considered. The unique qualifications are noted. The "legislator" is a paradoxical ideal.

To discover the rules of society best suited to nations, a superior intelligence beholding all the passions of men without experiencing any of them, would be needed. This intelligence would have to be wholly unrelated to our nature, while knowing it through and through. Its happiness would have to be independent of our happiness and yet ready to occupy itself with it. It would have to look forward and, working in one century, to be able to enjoy the next. It would take gods to give men laws.

He who dares undertake the making of a people's institutions ought to feel himself capable of changing human nature, of transforming each individual into part of a greater whole, of altering men's constitution for the purpose of strengthening it, of substituting a shared and moral existence for the independent and natural existence which nature has conferred on us all. In a word, he must take away from man his own resources and give him in their stead new ones incapable of being used without the help of other men. The more completely these "natural" resources are annihilated, the greater and more lasting are those which supplant them, and the more stable and perfect are the new institutions.

The office of legislator, which gives form to the state, nowhere enters into its constitution. He who holds command over men (the government), ought not to hold command over the laws. He who holds command over the laws (the legislator) ought not to hold command over men. Else would his laws be the ministers of his passions serving to perpetuate his injustices, and his private aims mar the sanctity of his work.

Thus in the task of legislation we find two things which appear to be incompatible: an enterprise too difficult for human powers, and, for its execution, an authority that is no authority.

The great soul of the legislator is the only miracle that can prove his mission. Any man may engrave on tables, buy an oracle, feign secret connexion with the gods, train a bird to whisper into his ear, or find some other trumpery way to impose on the people. He whose knowledge goes no further may perhaps gather round him a band of fools, but he will never found an empire, and his extravagances will perish with him. Idle tricks form a passing tie; only wisdom can make it lasting.

Provided the miracle of a good law can be performed, what does society have at its disposal? An instrument, essentially, for dealing with general conditions. The particulars must be seen to fall under the law by the wisdom of the executive.

What is a law? When the whole people declares for the whole people, this is what I call a *law*.

The matter about which such decree is made is, like the decreeing will, general. When I say that the matter is "general," I mean that law considers subjects *en masse* and actions in the abstract, never a particular person or action. Thus law may declare that there shall be privileges; but it cannot confer them on any one by name. It may set up classes of citizens. It may specify qualifications for membership of these classes. But, as law, it cannot nominate such and such persons as belonging to these classes. Law may, e.g., establish a monarchical form of government and an hereditary succession. It cannot choose a king or nominate a royal family. In a word, no function which has a particular object in view can be a matter of law.

On this view, we see at once that it can no longer be asked whose business it is to make laws, since they are acts of the general will; nor whether "government is above the law," since governors are part of the state; nor whether laws can be unjust, since no one is unjust to himself; nor how we can be both "free" and at the same time subject to laws, since they are but registers of our wills.

The law unites universality of will with universality of object. What any man commands of his own motion cannot be law. Even what sovereignty commands with regard to some particular matter cannot be law; it is then merely a decree of the government.

Laws are, strictly speaking, the conditions of civil association. The people, being subject to the laws, ought to be their author: the conditions of the society ought to be regulated by those who unite to give it form.

Thus far we have had society, the contract, the sovereign people, the legislator, and laws. We come now to government, what we would call the executive arm of government. It is not to be confused with any of the other terms:

I have argued that the power to make laws belongs to the sovereign people, and can belong to it alone. On the other hand, the power to execute these laws cannot belong to the generality, because such power consists wholly of particular acts which fall outside the competency of lawmaking as such.

The body politic, therefore, needs an agent of its own to bind it together, to set it to work under the direction of the general will, to serve as a means of communication between the (people as) state and the (people as) sovereign. Here we have the basis of government, something which is often confused with the sovereign whose minister it is.

What then is government? It is an intermediate body, set up between the (people as) subjects and the (people as) sovereign, to secure their mutual correspondence, to execute the laws and to maintain liberty. The members of this body are called governors.

Government is hence simply and solely a commission, in which the governors, mere officials of the sovereign people, exercise in their own name the power which is invested in them by the people. This delegated power the sovereign people can limit, modify, or recover at pleasure.

The government gets from the (people as) sovereign the orders which it gives to the (people as) subjects. For the state to be properly balanced there must be an equality between the power of the government and the power of the citizens, for the latter are, on the one hand, sovereign, and, on the other hand, subject.

None of these three terms—*sovereign, subjects, government*—can be altered without the equality being instantly destroyed. If the sovereign tries to govern, if the government tries to give laws, or if the subjects refuse to obey, disorder replaces order, force and will no longer act together, and the state is dissolved into despotism or anarchy.

Government, then, is distinct from society, sovereignty, legislator, law, and so on. Its function is to administer the laws. What form should it have?

There has been at all times much dispute concerning the best form of government. Is it democratic? Aristocratic? Or monarchical? This question, "What, absolutely, is the best form of government?" is unanswerable and indeterminate. The fact is that each is in some cases the best, and in others the worst.

Let us see. Consider first the notion of democracy:

The sovereign people may commit the charge of the government to the whole people or to a majority of the people. The result would be that more citizens would be actual governors than mere private subjects. This form of government is called *democracy*.

If we take the term in the strict sense, there never has been a real democracy, and there never will be. It is unimaginable that the people should remain continually assembled to devote their time to public affairs.

Besides, how many conditions, difficult to unite, would such a form of government presuppose! First, a very small state, where the people can readily be got together and where each citizen can with ease know all the rest. Second, great simplicity of manners, to prevent business from multiplying and raising thorny problems. Third, a large measure of equality in rank and fortune, without which equality of rights and authority cannot long subsist. Fourth, little or no luxury, for luxury either comes of riches or makes them necessary.

Moreover, it is a certainty that promptitude in execution diminishes as more people are put in charge of it. Where prudence is made too much of, not enough is made of fortune; opportunity is let slip, and deliberation results in the loss of its object.

It may be added that no form of government is so subject to civil wars and intestinal agitations as democracy, because there is none which has so strong and persistent a tendency to change to another form, or which demands more vigilance and courage for its maintenance. Were there a people of gods, their government would be democratic. So perfect a government is not for men.

So, pure democracy is unsuited to the needs of the modern state. Another possibility is an elected aristocracy. It holds more promise:

The sovereign people may restrict the government to a small number, so that there are more private citizens than magistrates. This is named *aristocracy*.

There are three sorts of aristocracy: natural, elective, and hereditary. The first is only for simple peoples; the second is the best, and is aristocracy properly so-called; the third is the worst of all governments.

There is much to be said for an elective aristocracy. It has the advantage of keeping clear the distinction between the two powers, sovereignty and government. Besides this, its members are chosen to be governors, not born to this office, as in the case of a pure democracy or an hereditary aristocracy. By this means uprightness, understanding, experience, and all other claims to preeminence become so many guarantees of wise government.

It is more efficient. Assemblies are more easily held; affairs are better discussed and carried out with more order and diligence; the credit of the state is better sustained abroad.

It is more economical. There is no need to multiply instruments, or get twenty thousand men to do what a hundred picked men can do better.

However, if an elective aristocracy does not demand all the virtues needed by popular government, it demands others which are peculiar to itself; for instance, moderation on the side of the rich, and contentment on the side of the poor. If this form of government carries with it a certain inequality of fortune, this is justifiable on the grounds that the administration of public affairs may be entrusted to those who are most able to give them their whole time.

In Rousseau's day the commonest form of government was hereditary monarchy. It has its good points and its bad points. Thus:

The sovereign people may concentrate the whole government in the hands of a single person from whom all others hold their power. This form of government is the most usual, and is called *monarchy*.

No form of government is more vigorous than this. All answer to a single motive power. All the springs of the machine are in the same hands. The whole moves toward the same end. There are no conflicting movements to cancel one another. In no constitution does a smaller amount of effort produce a greater amount of action. Archimedes seated quietly on the bank of a river, easily drawing a great floating vessel, stands in my mind for a skillful monarch governing vast estates from his study, moving everything while he seems himself unmoved.

For a monarchical state to have a chance of being well governed, its population and extent must be proportionate to the abilities of its governor. It is easier to conquer than to rule. With a lever long enough, the world could be moved with a single finger; to sustain it requires the shoulders of Hercules.

These are some of the virtues to be expected in monarchy. However, Rousseau goes on to note possible defects:

Everything conspires to take away from a man who is set in authority the sense of justice and reason.

Kings desire to be absolute, and men are always crying out to them from afar that the best means is to get themselves loved by their people. This is all very well, and true enough in some respects. Unfortunately, it will always be derided at court. The power that comes of a people's love is no doubt the greatest; but it is precarious and conditional, and princes will never rest content with it. The best of kings desire to be in a position to be wicked, if they so please, without forfeiting thereby their mastery. Political sermonizers may tell them, to their hearts' content, that the people should be prosperous, numerous, and formidable. Kings know this to be untrue. Their personal interest is that the people should be weak, wretched, and unable to resist them.

There is an essential and inevitable defect which will always rank a monarchy below a republic. It is this. In a republic the people hardly ever raises men who are unenlightened and incapable to the highest positions; whereas, under a monarch, those who rise to power are most often petty blunderers, petty swindlers, petty intriguers, men whose petty talents cause them to get into stations of the greatest eminence at court. The people is far less often mistaken in its choice than the monarch. A man of real worth among the king's ministers is almost as rare as a fool at the head of a republic.

Another disadvantage in monarchical government is the lack of any continuous succession. When one king dies, another is needed. In the case of an elective monarchy, dangerous interregnums occur, and are full of storms; unless, that is, the citizens are upright and disinterested to a degree which seldom goes with this kind of government.

What has been done to prevent these evils? Succession has been made hereditary in certain families. That is to say, men have chosen rather to be ruled by children, monstrosities, or imbeciles than to endure disputes over the choice of good kings. Apparent tranquillity has been preferred to wise administration

These difficulties have not escaped our political writers. But they are not troubled by them. The remedy, they say, is to obey without a murmur: God sends bad kings in His wrath, and they are to be borne as the scourges of heaven. Such talk is doubtless edifying, but it would be more in place in a pulpit than in a political book. What are we to say of a doctor whose whole art is to exhort the sufferer to patience?

By way of conclusion we may note the fundamental fact from which political instability continually proceeds:

All forms of government contain within them the seeds of destruction and dissolution. As the particular will acts constantly in opposition to the general will, the government continually exerts itself against the sovereign. The greater this exertion becomes, the more the constitution changes. This is the unavoidable and inherent defect which, from the very birth of the body politic, tends ceaselessly to destroy it, as age and death end by destroying the human body.

Such is the natural and inevitable tendency of the best constituted governments. If Sparta and Rome perished, what state can hope to endure for ever? We desire a long-lived form of government? Let us not dream of making it eternal. If we are to succeed, we must not attempt the impossible; nor must we flatter ourselves that we are endowing the work of man with a stability which human conditions do not permit.

The body politic begins to die as soon as it is born, and carries in itself the causes of its own destruction. The state is a work of art, not of nature. It is for men to prolong its life as much as possible, by giving it the best possible constitution. But even the best will have an end.

The life principle of the body politic lies in the sovereign authority. The legislative power is the heart of the state; the executive power is its brain.

The brain may become paralyzed, and the body still live. But as soon as the heart ceases to perform its function, the organism is dead. Wherever the laws grow weak as they become old, there is no longer a legislative power, and the state is dead.

Note on Sources. The Rousseau material in this section is quoted, abridged, or paraphrased from his *Social Contract.*

Reading References. The number of books written on Rousseau is large. Each generation has found it necessary to take stock of his ideas. Lord Morley's *Rousseau* is good reading for those who continue to share Lord Morley's nineteenth-century rationalism and liberalism. A provocative chapter on *The Social Contract* is to be found in Bernard Bosanquet's *Philosophical Theory of the State.* The author stresses the fact that Rousseau's self-imposed problem was *not* how to justify revolution, but how to justify restraint of the individual by the state. A good biography is to be found in Matthew Josephson's *Jean Jacques Rousseau.* The best comprehensive accounts of Rousseau's ideas are to be found, as far as books written in English are concerned, in C. W. Hendel's two volumes, *Rousseau as Moralist,* and in Matthew Josephson's book.

READING QUESTIONS

1. It is well to distinguish these two matters at the beginning: (a) What it is he does not know. (b) Question he thinks he can answer.
2. Why he turns aside to deal with the "might makes right" doctrine. Any two of his criticisms.
3. Why men exchange the state of nature for a politically organized society.
4. This (No. 3) transition is effected, underwritten, marked, by the "social contract." The terms of this contract. The parties to it. Does it refer to the setting up of a state or the setting up of a government?
5. Losses and gains to be chalked up to passing from the state of nature to civil society.
6. Those who enter the social contract thereby create a "moral and collective body," a "public person." Is this metaphor?
7. What is the object of the general will? What, continued, would prove the undoing of the body politic?
8. Whoever refuses to obey the general will shall be compelled to do so. Why this is not tyranny, despotism, arbitrary coercion.

9. Rousseau's answer to the question, "Who are sovereign?"
10. Why a people needs a legislator or legislature.
11. Why it would take Gods to give men laws.
12. What a person sets himself to do, who undertakes to give institutions to a people.
13. Why there should be a separation between legislator and (a) the constitution, (b) the executive.
14. So long as laws express the general will, those who obey them obey their own wills. How so? (See question 8 on p. 290.)
15. Is a person's relation to the social contract the same as his relation to a law? If not, wherein not?
16. His distinction between state and government. Why this was a revolutionary distinction.
17. The sovereign people may commit the charge of government to the whole people or a majority, to a small number of the people, or to a single person. Rousseau's opinion of each resulting form of government.
18. The unavoidable and inherent defect which tends ceaselessly to destroy the body politic.
19. Why Rousseau would not speak of a democratic or aristocratic or monarchical state. How he would have revised Louis XIV's remark "I am the state."
20. Give a connected account of these notions according to Rousseau: (a) state of nature, (b) social contract, (c) civil state, (d) general will, (e) law, (f) legislator, (g) government, (h) dissolution.
21. Wherein you find Rousseau (a) most, (b) least convincing.

INDEPENDENT STUDY

1. There is a social contract doctrine in Hobbes's *Leviathan* (1651) and in Locke's second *Treatise on Civil Government* (1689). Compare either one of these with Rousseau's.
2. Rousseau's *Social Contract* was published in 1762, fourteen years before the American Revolution, in 1776, and twenty-seven years before the French Revolution, in 1789. Write an essay on the influence of Rousseau's thinking on the leaders of either revolution.

SECTION 2. KARL MARX: THE PROLETARIAN GOOD

From Rousseau to Marx. Rousseau's claim, in the 1762 *Social Contract*, had been that a government was justified in enforcing, indeed obligated to enforce, laws that expressed the General Will;

that is, defined and protected the Common Good or an aspect of the Common Good. Rousseau did not claim that all laws, nor perhaps even most laws, did in fact thus express the General Will for the Common Good. His argument therefore was not necessarily supportive of all, nor perhaps even most, governments. His *Social Contract* was, therefore, sometimes read by his contemporaries, or the next generation, as containing, if not actually propounding, a doctrine of justifiable revolution. Governments are not justified, let alone obligated, to enforce legislation that does not express the General Will for the Common Good. The inference was that governments would be justified in preventing, indeed obligated to prevent, the enforcement of laws that were incompatible with, destructive of, the General Will for the Common Good. When governments did not do this, a people was justified in revolution. Such revolution aimed to rid the state of a government that was failing in its duty, and to replace such government by one that would do its duty. So understood, Rousseau influenced revolutionary thinking in America and France.

Marx does not repudiate the essential claim of Rousseau's theory about laws and their justifiable enforcement. He purports to offer a closer and more accurate account of the conditions that called for revolutionary handling by the masses of the people, and for their organization and leadership by a new political party. His 1848 tract carries the title *The Manifesto of the Communist Party.* The Manifesto is addressed to the proletariat, recommending the leadership of the Communist Party; and to the members of the Party, urging them to assume leadership of the proletarian masses in revolutions against bourgeois or capitalist societies and their governments. If a society has a laissez-faire capitalist economy, as many societies had in Marx's day, then its laws and institutions will not express the General Will for the Common Good. They will express the will for the good of capitalists and their associated classes; and governments in such capitalist societies will use their powers to enforce such laws. The basis of this theory about government and law in the life of the state, a community committed to the legislative way of life, was what Marx, and his friend Engels, called the materialist or economic interpretation of history. It will be found in Topic Five of this book. Briefly, that interpretation of Western history was as follows: A state contains two great economic classes, one of which owns the materials and means of economic production, the other of which works for those who own. Referring to his own period in history, Marx spoke of the bourgeois or capitalist class, and the proletariat or wage-earning class. A capitalist society is organized as a state because in that way the bourgeoisie is able to use the government to rule over the proletariat. Between the property-owning class and the wage-earning class there is an irreconcilable antagonism. A government exercises a monopoly of legal violence to further and protect the class interests of the bourgeoisie. In earlier times the antagonism had been between the feudal land-owning class and the emerging bourgeois capital-owning class. The latter broke the feudal state as a way of achieving their political emancipation. Hence the feudal state was succeeded by the capitalist or bourgeois state. In time, the proletariat will break the bourgeois state as a way of achieving *their* political emancipation. Hence the bourgeois state will be succeeded by the proletariat state. The task of the Communist Party, he says, is to organize the proletariat so that this one-class state may be achieved.

Biographical Note. Marx was born in 1818 and died in 1883 at the age of sixty-five. He was educated in the universities at Bonn and Berlin, beginning with law, but subsequently devoting his entire attention to philosophy. Hegelianism was the fashionable doctrine at the time. It found no favor with young Marx. So, when he graduated and looked about for a job teaching philosophy, he found no openings. For the next few years, amid a life of newspaper work and radical agitation, he devoted his spare time to working out his economic interpretation of history. By 1848 he had joined the Communist League. For it he wrote the celebrated *Manifesto.* Exiled from Germany, from Belgium, from France, he settled in London. From here, in 1864, he organized the First International. In 1867 he published Volume One of *Capital.* The remainder was edited and published by Engels after Marx's death. In life, judged by ordinary standards, he was unhappy, unsuccessful, and largely unknown. In death he has become, like Darwin and Freud and Einstein, one of the makers of the modern mind.

The Argument of the Manifesto. The history of all hitherto existing society is the history of class struggles. In early modern times the bourgeosie triumphed over their feudal masters. They thus became masters of the modern world. An account of their multifarious doings. They have, among other things, brought into being a new class, the proletariat. The class struggle is now between bourgeosie and proletariat. When the latter win out, as they are destined to do, the world will see its first classless society. The bourgeois economy will be replaced by the communist economy. Injustices arising out of the fact that modern society has been, in respect to production and distribution, a capitalist economy, will cease to exist. The text:

A spectre is haunting Europe—the spectre of Communism. All the powers of old Europe have entered into a holy alliance to exorcise this spectre; Pope and Czar, Metternich and Guizot, French Radicals and German police-spies.

Where is the party in opposition that has not been decried as communistic by its opponents in power? Where the Opposition that has not hurled back the branding reproach of Communism, against the more advanced opposition parties, as well as against its reactionary adversaries?

Two things result from this fact.

I. Communism is already acknowledged by all European Powers to be itself a Power.

II. It is high time that Communists should openly, in the face of the whole world, publish their views, their aims, their tendencies, and meet this nursery tale of the Spectre of Communism with a Manifesto of the party itself.

To this end, Communists of various nationalities have assembled in London, and sketched the following manifesto, to be published in the English, French, German, Italian, Flemish and Danish languages.

Bourgeois and Proletarians

(1)

The history of all hitherto existing society is the history of class struggles.

Freeman and slave, patrician and plebeian, lord and serf, guild-master and journeyman, in a word, oppressor and oppressed, stood in constant opposition to one another, carried on an uninterrupted, now hidden, now open fight, a fight that each time ended, either in a revolutionary re-constitution of society at large, or in the common ruin of the contending classes.

In the earlier epochs of history, we find almost everywhere a complicated arrangement of society into various orders, a manifold gradation of social rank. In ancient Rome we have patricians, knights, plebeians, slaves; in the middle ages, feudal lords, vassals, guild-masters, journeymen, apprentices, serfs; in almost all of these classes, again, subordinate gradations.

The modern bourgeois society that has sprouted from the ruins of feudal society, has not done away with class antagonisms. It has but established new classes, new conditions of oppression, new forms of struggle in place of the old ones.

Our epoch, the epoch of the bourgeoisie, possesses, however, this distinctive feature; it has simplified the class antagonisms. Society as a whole is more and more splitting up into two great hostile camps, into two great classes directly facing each other: Bourgeoisie and Proletariat.

From the serfs of the middle ages sprang the chartered burghers of the earliest towns. From these burgesses the first elements of the bourgeoisie were developed.

The discovery of America, the rounding of the Cape, opened up fresh ground for the rising bourgeoisie. The East-Indian and Chinese markets, the colonization of America, trade with the colonies, the increase in the means of exchange and in commodities generally, gave to commerce, to navigation, to industry, an impulse never before known, and thereby, to the revolutionary element in the tottering feudal society, a rapid development.

The feudal system of industry, under which industrial production was monopolized by closed guilds, now no longer sufficed for the growing wants of the new markets. The manufacturing system took its place. The guild-masters were pushed on one side by the manufacturing middle-class; division of labor between the different corporate guilds vanished in the face of division of labor in each single workshop.

Meantime the markets kept ever growing, the demand, ever rising. Even manufacture no longer sufficed. Thereupon, steam and machinery revolutionized industrial production. The place of manufacture was taken by the giant, Modern Industry, the place of the industrial middle-class, by industrial millionaires, the leaders of whole industrial armies, the modern bourgeois.

Modern industry has established the world-market, for which the discovery of America paved the way. This market has given an immense development to commerce, to navigation, to communication by land. This development has, in its turn, reacted on the extension of industry; and in proportion as industry, commerce, navigation, railways extended, in the same proportion the bourgeoisie developed, increased its capital, and pushed into the background every class handed down from the Middle Ages.

We see, therefore, how the modern bourgeoisie is itself the product of a long course of development, of a series of revolutions in the modes of production and of exchange.

Each step in the development of the bourgeoisie was accompanied by a corresponding political advance of that class. An oppressed class under the sway of the feudal nobility, an armed and self-governing association in the mediaeval commune, here independent urban republic (as in Italy and Germany), there taxable "third estate" of the monarchy (as in France), afterwards, in the period of manufacture proper, serving either the semifeudal or the absolute monarchy as a counterpoise against the nobility, and, in fact, cornerstone of the great monarchies in general, the bourgeoisie has at last, since the establishment of Modern Industry and of the world-market, conquered for itself, in the modern representative State, exclusive political sway. *The executive of the modern State is but a committee for managing the common affairs of the whole bourgeoisie.*

(2)

The bourgeoisie, historically, has played a most revolutionary part.

The bourgeoisie, wherever it has got the upper hand, has put an end to all feudal, patriarchal, idyllic relations. It has pitilessly torn asunder the motley feudal ties that bound man to his "natural superiors," and has left remaining no other nexus between man and man than naked self-interest, callous "cash payment." It has drowned the most heavenly ecstasies of religious fervor, of chivalrous enthusiasm, of philistine sentimentalism, in the icy water of egotistical calculation. It has resolved personal worth into exchange value, and in place of the numberless indefeasible chartered freedoms, has set up that single, unconscionable freedom—Free Trade. In one word, for exploitation, veiled by religious and political illusions, it has substituted naked, shameless, direct, brutal exploitation.

The bourgeoisie has stripped of its halo every occupation hitherto honored and looked up to with reverent awe. It has converted the physician, the lawyer, the priest, the poet, the man of science, into its paid wage-laborers.

The bourgeoisie has torn away from the family its sentimental veil, and has reduced the family relation to a mere money relation.

The bourgeoisie has disclosed how it came to pass that the brutal display of vigor in the Middle Ages, which Reactionists so much admire, found its fitting complement in the most slothful indolence. It has been the first to show what man's activity can bring about. It has accomplished wonders far surpassing Egyptian pyramids, Roman aqueducts, and Gothic cathedrals; it has conducted expeditions that put in the shade all former Exoduses of nations and crusades.

The bourgeoisie cannot exist without constantly revolutionizing the instruments of production, and thereby the relations of production, and with them the whole relations of society. Conservation of the old modes of production in unaltered form, was, on the contrary, the first condition of existence for all earlier industrial classes. Constant revolutionizing of production, uninterrupted disturbance of all social conditions, everlasting uncertainty and agitation distinguish the bourgeois epoch from all earlier ones. All fixed, fast-frozen relations, with their train of ancient and venerable prejudices and opinions, are swept away, all new-formed ones become antiquated before they can ossify. All that is solid melts into air, all that is holy is profaned, and man is at last compelled to face, with sober senses, his real conditions of life, and his relations with his kind.

The need of a constantly expanding market for its products chases the bourgeoisie over the whole surface of the globe. It must nestle everywhere, settle everywhere, establish connections everywhere.

The bourgeoisie has through its exploitation of the world-market given a cosmopolitan character to production and consumption in every country. To the great chagrin of Reactionists, it has drawn from under the feet of industry the national ground on which it stood. All old-established national industries have been destroyed or are daily being destroyed. They are dislodged by new industries, whose introduction becomes a life and death question for all civilized nations, by industries that no longer work up indigenous raw material, but raw material drawn from the remotest zones; industries whose products are consumed, not only at home, but in every quarter of the globe. In place of the old wants, satisfied by the productions of the country, we find new wants, requiring for their satisfaction the products of distant lands and climes. In place of the old local and national seclusion and self-sufficiency, we have intercourse in every direction, universal inter-dependence of nations. And as in material, so also in intellectual production. The intellectual creations of individual nations become common property. National one-sidedness and narrow-mindedness become more and more impossible, and from the numerous national and local literatures there arises a world-literature.

The bourgeoisie, by the rapid improvement of all instruments of production, by the immensely facilitated means of communication, draws all, even the most barbarian, nations into civilization. The cheap prices of its commodities are the heavy artillery with which it batters down all Chinese walls, with which it forces the barbarians' intensely obstinate hatred of foreigners to capitulate. It compels all nations, on pain of extinction, to adopt the bourgeois mode of production; it compels them to introduce what it calls civilization into their midst, i.e., to become bourgeois themselves. In a word, it creates a world after its own image.

The bourgeoisie has subjected the country to the rule of the towns. It has created enormous cities, has greatly increased the urban population as compared with the rural, and has thus rescued a considerable part of the population from the idiocy of rural life. Just as it has made the country dependent on the towns, so it has made barbarian and semi-barbarian countries dependent on the civilized ones, nations of peasants on nations of bourgeois, the East on the West.

The bourgeoisie keeps more and more doing away with the scattered state of the population, of the means of production, and of property. It has agglomerated population, centralized means of production, and has concentrated property in a few hands. The necessary consequence of this was political centralization. Independent, or but loosely connected provinces, with separate interests, laws, governments and systems of taxation, became lumped together in one nation, with one government, one code of laws, one national class-interest, one frontier and one customs-tariff.

The bourgeoisie, during its rule of scarce one hundred years, has created more massive and more colossal productive forces than have all preceding generations together. Subjection of Nature's forces to man, machinery, application of chemistry to industry and agriculture, steam-navigation, railways, electric telegraphs, clearing of whole continents for cultivation, canalization of rivers, whole populations conjured out of the ground—what earlier century had even a presentiment that such productive forces slumbered in the lap of social labor?

We see then: the means of production and of exchange on whose foundation the bourgeoisie built itself up, were generated in feudal society. At a certain stage in the development of these means of production and of exchange, the conditions under which feudal society produced and exchanged, the feudal organization of agriculture and manufacturing industry, in one word, the feudal relations of property became no longer compatible with the already developed productive forces; they became so many fetters. They had to burst asunder; they were burst asunder.

Into their places stepped free competition, accompanied by a social and political constitution adapted to it, and by the economical and political sway of the bourgeois class.

A similar movement is going on before our own eyes. *Modern bourgeois* society with its relations of production, of exchange and of property, a society that has conjured up such gigantic means of production and of exchange, *is like the sorcerer, who is no longer able to control the powers of the nether world whom he has called up by his spells.* For many a decade past the history of industry and commerce is but the history of the revolt of modern productive forces against modern conditions of production, against the property relations that are the conditions for the existence of the bourgeoisie and of its rule. It is enough to mention the commercial crises that by their periodical return put on its trial, each time more threateningly, the existence of the entire bourgeois society. In these crises a great part not only of the existing products, but also of the previously created productive forces, are periodically destroyed. In these crises there breaks out an epidemic that, in all earlier epochs, would have seemed an absurdity—the epidemic of over-production. Society suddenly finds itself put back into a state of momentary barbarism; it appears as if a famine, a universal war of devastation had cut off the supply of every means of subsistence; industry and commerce seem to be destroyed; and why? Because there is too much civilization, too much means of subsistence, too much industry, too much commerce. The productive forces at the disposal of society no longer tend to further the development of the conditions of bourgeois property; on the contrary, they have become too powerful for these conditions, by which they are fettered, and so soon as they overcome these fetters, they bring disorder into the whole of bourgeois society, endanger the existence of bourgeois property. The conditions of bourgeois society are too narrow to comprise the wealth created by them. And how does the bourgeoisie get over these crises? On the one hand by enforced destruction of a mass of productive forces; on the other, by the conquest of new markets, and by the more thorough exploitation of the old ones. That is to say, by paving the way for more extensive and more destructive crises, and by diminishing the means whereby crises are prevented.

(3)

The weapons with which the bourgeoisie felled feudalism to the ground are now turned against the bourgeoisie itself.

But not only has the bourgeoisie forged the weapons that bring death to itself; it has also called into existence the men who are to wield those weapons—the modern working-class—the proletarians.

In proportion as the bourgeoisie, i.e., capital, is developed, in the same proportion is the proletariat, the modern working-class, developed, a class of laborers, who live only so long as they find work, and who find work only so long as their labor increases capital. These laborers, who must sell themselves piecemeal, are a commodity, like every other article of commerce, and are consequently exposed to all the vicissitudes of competition, to all the fluctuations of the market.

Owing to the extensive use of machinery and to division of labor, the work of the proletarians has lost all individual character, and, consequently, all charm for the workman. He becomes an appendage of the machine, and it is only the most simple, most monotonous, and most easily acquired knack that is required of him. Hence, the cost of production of a workman is restricted, almost entirely, to the means of subsistence that he requires for his maintenance, and for the propagation of his race. But the price of a commodity, and also of labor, is equal to its cost of production. In proportion, therefore, as the repulsiveness of the work increases, the wage decreases. Nay more, in proportion as the use of machinery and division of labor increases, in the same proportion the burden of toil also increases, whether by prolongation of the working hours, by increase of the work enacted in a given time, or by increased speed of the machinery, etc.

Modern industry has converted the little workshop of the patriarchal master into the great factory of the industrial capitalist. Masses of laborers, crowded into the factory, are organized like soldiers. As privates of the industrial army they are placed under the command of a perfect hierarchy of officers and sergeants. Not only are they the slaves of the bourgeois class, and of the bourgeois State, they are daily and hourly enslaved by the machine, by the over-looker, and, above all, by the individual bourgeois manufacturer himself. The more openly this despotism proclaims gain to be its end and aim, the more petty, the more hateful and the more embittering it is.

The less the skill and exertion or strength implied in manual labor, in other words, the more modern industry becomes developed, the more is the labor of men superseded by that of women. Differences of age and sex have no longer any distinctive social validity for the working class. All are instruments of labor, more or less expensive to use, according to their age and sex.

No sooner is the exploitation of the laborer by the manufacturer, so far at an end, that he receives his wages in cash, than he is set upon by the other portions of the bourgeoisie, the landlord, the shopkeeper, the pawnbroker, etc.

The lower strata of the middle class—the small tradespeople, shopkeepers, and retired tradesmen generally, the handicraftsmen and peasants—all these sink gradually into the proletariat, partly because their diminutive capital does not suffice for the scale on which Modern Industry is carried on, and is swamped in the competition with the large capitalists, partly because their specialized skill is rendered worthless by new methods of production. Thus the proletariat is recruited from all classes of the population.

The proletariat goes through various stages of development. With its birth begins its struggle with the bourgeoisie. At first the contest is carried on by individual laborers, then by the workpeople of a factory, then by the operatives of one trade, in one locality, against the individual bourgeois who directly exploits them. They direct their attacks not against the bourgeois conditions of production, but against the instruments of production themselves; they destroy imported wares that compete with their labor, they smash to pieces machinery, they set factories ablaze, they seek to restore by force the vanished status of the workman of the Middle Ages.

At this stage the laborers still form an incoherent mass scattered over the whole country, and broken up by their mutual competition. If anywhere they unite to form more compact bodies, this is not yet the consequence of their own active union, but of the union of the bourgeoisie, which class, in order to attain its own political ends, is compelled to set the whole proletariat in motion, and is moreover, yet, for a time, able to do so. At this stage, therefore, the proletarians do not fight their enemies, but the enemies of their enemies, the remnants of absolute monarchy, the landowners, the non-industrial bourgeois, the petty bourgeoisie. Thus the whole historical movement is concentrated in the hands of the bourgeoisie; every victory so obtained is a victory for the bourgeoisie.

But with the development of industry the proletariat not only increases in number, it becomes concentrated in greater masses, its strength grows, and it feels that strength more. The various interests and conditions of life within the ranks of the proletariat are more and more equalized, in proportion as machinery obliterates all distinctions of labor, and nearly everywhere reduces wages to the same low level. The growing competition among the bourgeois, and the resulting commercial crises, make the wages of the workers ever more fluctuating. The unceasing improvement of machinery, ever more rapidly developing, makes their livelihood more and more precarious; the collisions between individual workmen and individual bourgeois take more and more the character of collisions between two classes. Thereupon the workers begin to form combinations (Trades' Unions) against the bourgeois; they club together in order to keep up the rate of wages; they found permanent associations in order to make provision beforehand for these occasional revolts. Here and there the contest breaks out into riots.

Now and then the workers are victorious, but only for a time. The real fruit of their battle lies, not in the immediate result, but in the ever-expanding union of the workers. This union is helped on by the improved means of communication that are created by modern industry, and that place the workers of different localities in contact with one another. It was just this contact that was needed to centralize the numerous local struggles, all of the same character, into one national struggle between classes. But every class struggle is a political struggle. And that union, to attain which the burghers of the Middle Ages, with their miserable highways, required centuries, the modern proletarians, thanks to railways, achieve in a few years.

This organization of the proletarians into a class, and consequently into a political party, is continually being upset again by the competition between the workers themselves. But it ever rises up again, stronger, firmer, mightier. It compels legislative recognition of particular interest of the workers, by taking advantage of the divisions among the bourgeoisie itself. Thus the ten-hour bill in England was carried.

Altogether collisions between the classes of the old society further, in many ways, the course of development of the proletariat. The bourgeoisie finds itself involved in a constant battle. At first with the aristocracy; later on, with those portions of the bourgeoisie itself, whose interests have become antagonistic to the progress of industry; at all times, with the bourgeoisie of foreign countries. In all these battles it sees itself compelled to appeal to the proletariat, to ask for its help, and thus, to drag it into the political arena. The bourgeoisie itself, therefore, supplies the proletariat with its own elements of political and general education, in other words, it furnishes the proletariat with weapons for fighting the bourgeoisie.

Further, as we have already seen, entire sections of the ruling classes are, by the advance of industry, precipitated into the proletariat, or are at least threatened in their conditions of existence. These also supply the proletariat with fresh elements of enlightenment and progress.

Finally, in times when the class-struggle nears the decisive hour, the process of dissolution going on within the ruling class, in fact, within the whole range of old society, assumes such a violent, glaring character, that a small section of the ruling class cuts itself adrift, and joins the revolutionary class, the class that holds the future in its hands. Just as, therefore, at an earlier period, a section of the nobility went over to the bourgeoisie, so now a portion of the bourgeoisie goes over to the proletariat, and in particular, a portion of the bourgeois ideologists, who have raised themselves to the level of comprehending theoretically the historical movements as a whole.

(4)

Of all the classes that stand face to face with the bourgeoisie today, the proletariat alone is a really revolutionary class. The other classes decay and finally disappear in the face of modern industry; the proletariat is its special and essential product.

The lower middle-class, the small manufacturer, the shopkeeper, the artisan, the peasant, all these fight against the bourgeoisie, to save from extinction their existence as fractions of the middle class. They are, therefore, not revolutionary, but conservative. Nay more, they are reactionary, for they try to roll back the wheel of history. If by chance they are revolutionary, they are so, only in view of their impending transfer into the proletariat, they thus defend not their present, but their future interests, they desert their own standpoint to place themselves at that of the proletariat.

The "dangerous class," the social scum, that passively rotting mass thrown off by the lowest layers of old society, may, here and there, be swept into the movement by a proletarian revolution; its conditions of life, however, prepare it far more for the part of a bribed tool of reactionary intrigue.

In the conditions of the proletariat, those of old society at large are already virtually swamped. The proletarian is without property; his relation to his wife and children has no longer anything in common with the bourgeois family-relations; modern industrial labor, modern subjection to capital, the same in England as in France, in America as in Germany, has stripped him of every trace of national character. Law, morality, religion, are to him so many bourgeois prejudices, behind which lurk in ambush just as many bourgeois interests.

All the preceding classes that got the upper hand, sought to fortify their already acquired status by subjecting society at large to their conditions of appropriation. The proletarians cannot become masters of the productive forces of society, except by abolishing their own previous mode of appropriation, and thereby also every other previous mode of appropriation. They have nothing of their own to secure and to fortify; their mission is to destroy all previous securities for, and insurances of, individual property.

All previous historical movements were movements of minorities, or in the interest of minorities. The proletarian movement is the self-conscious, independent movement of the immense majority, in the interest of the immense majority. The proletariat, the lowest stratum of our present society, cannot stir, cannot raise itself up, without the whole superincumbent strata of official society being sprung into the air.

Though not in substance, yet in form, the struggle of the proletariat with the bourgeoisie is at first a national struggle. The proletariat of each country must, of course, first of all settle matters with its own bourgeoisie.

In depicting the most general phases of the development of the proletariat, we traced the more or less veiled civil war, raging within existing society, up to the point where that war breaks out into open revolution, and where the violent overthrow of the bourgeoisie lays the foundation for the sway of the proletariat.

Hitherto, every form of society has been based, as we have already seen, on the antagonism of oppressing and oppressed classes. But in order to oppress a class, certain conditions must be assured it under which it can, at least, continue its slavish existence. The serf, in the periof of serfdom, raised himself to membership in the commune, just as the petty bourgeois, under the yoke of feudal absolutism, managed to develop into a bourgeois. The modern laborer, on the contrary, instead of rising with the progress of industry, sinks deeper and deeper below the conditions of existence of his own class. He becomes a pauper, and pauperism develops more rapidly than population and wealth. And here it becomes evident, that the bourgeoisie is unfit any longer to be the ruling class in society, and to impose its conditions of existence upon society as an over-riding law. It is unfit to rule, because it is incompetent to assure an existence to its slave within his slavery, because it cannot help letting him sink into such a state that it has to feed him, instead of being fed by him. Society can no longer live under this bourgeoisie, in other words, its existence is no longer compatible with society.

The essential condition for the existence, and for the sway of the bourgeois class, is the formation and augmentation of capital; the condition for capital is wage labor. Wage labor rests exclusively on competition between the laborers. The advance of industry, whose involuntary promoter is the bourgeoisie, replaces the isolation of the laborers, due to competition, by their revolutionary combination, due to association. The development of Modern Industry, therefore, cuts from under its feet the very foundation in which the bourgeoisie produces and appropriates products. *What the bourgeoisie therefore produces, above all, are its own grave-diggers.* Its fall and the victory of the proletariat are equally inevitable.

Proletarians and Communists

(5)

[A] In what relation do the Communists stand to the proletarians as a whole?

The Communists do not form a separate party opposed to other working-class parties.

They have no interests separate and apart from those of the proletariat as a whole.

They do not set up any sectarian principles of their own, by which to shape and mould the proletarian movement.

The Communists are distinguished from the other working class parties by this only: 1. In the national struggles of the proletarians of the different countries, they point out and bring to the front the common interests of the entire proletariat independently of all nationality. 2. In the various stages of development which the struggle of the working class against the bourgeoisie has to pass through, they always and everywhere represent the interests of the movement as a whole.

The Communists, therefore, are on the one hand, practically, the most advanced and resolute section of the working class parties of every country, that section which pushes forward all others; on the other hand, theoretically, they have over the great mass of the proletariat the advantage of clearly understanding the line of march, the conditions, and the ultimate general results of the proletarian movement.

The immediate aim of the Communists is the same as that of all the other proletarian parties; formation of the proletariat into a class, overthrow of the bourgeois supremacy, conquest of political power by the proletariat.

The theoretical conclusions of the Communists are in no way based on ideas or principles that have been invented, or discovered, by this or that would-be universal reformer.

They merely express, in general terms, actual relations springing from an existing class struggle, from a historical movement going on under our very eyes. The abolition of existing property relations is not at all a distinctive feature of Communism.

All property relations in the past have continually been subject to historical change consequent upon the change in historical conditions.

The French Revolution, for example, abolished feudal property in favor of bourgeois property.

The distinguishing feature of Communism is not the abolition of property generally, but the abolition of bourgeois property. But modern bourgeois private property is the final and most complete expression of the system of producing and appropriating products, that is based on class antagonism, on the exploitation of the many by the few.

In this sense, the theory of the Communists may be summed up in the single sentence: Abolition of private property.

We Communists have been reproached with the desire of abolishing the right of personally acquiring property as the fruit of a man's own labor, which property is alleged to be the ground work of all personal freedom, activity and independence.

Hard-won, self-acquired, self-earned property! Do you mean the property of the petty artisan and of the small peasant, a form of property that preceded the bourgeois form? There is no need to abolish that; the development of industry has to a great extent already destroyed it, and is still destroying it daily.

Or do you mean modern bourgeois private property?

But does wage-labor create any property for the laborer? Not a bit. It creates capital, i.e., that kind of property which exploits wage-labor, and which cannot increase except upon condition of getting a new supply of wage-labor for fresh exploitation. Property, in its present form, is based on the antagonism of capital and wage-labor. Let us examine both sides of this antagonism.

To be a capitalist, is to have not only a purely personal, but a social status in production. Capital is a collective product, and only by the united action of many members, nay, in the last resort, only by the united action of all members of society, can it be set in motion.

Capital is therefore not a personal, it is a social power.

When, therefore, capital is converted into common property, into the property of all members of society, personal property is not thereby transformed into social property. It is only the social character of the property that is changed. It loses its class-character.

Let us now take wage-labor.

The average price of wage-labor is the minimum wage, i.e., that quantum of the means of subsistence, which is absolutely requisite to keep the laborer in bare existence as a laborer. What, therefore, the wage-laborer appropriates by means of his labor, merely suffices to prolong and reproduce a bare existence. We by no means intend to abolish this personal appropriation of the products of labor, an appropriation that is made for the maintenance and reproduction of human life, and that leaves no surplus wherewith to command the labor of others. All that we want to do away with is the miserable character of this appropriation, under which the laborer lives merely to increase capital, and is allowed to live only in so far as the interest of the ruling class requires it.

In bourgeois society, living labor is but a means to increase accumulated labor. In communist society, accumulated labor is but a means to widen, to enrich, to promote the existence of the laborer.

In bourgeois society, therefore, the past dominates the present; in communist society, the present dominates the past. In bourgeois society capital is independent and has individuality, while the living person is dependent and has no individuality.

And the abolition of this state of things is called by the bourgeois, abolition of individuality and freedom! And rightly so. The abolition of bourgeois individuality, bourgeois independence, and bourgeois freedom is undoubtedly aimed at.

By freedom is meant, under the present bourgeois conditions of production, free trade, free selling and buying.

But if selling and buying disappears, free selling and buying disappears also. This talk about free selling and buying, and all the other "brave words" of our bourgeoisie about freedom in general, have a meaning, if any, only in contrast with restricted selling and buying, with the fettered traders of the Middle Ages, but have no meaning when opposed to the Communistic abolition of buying and selling, of the bourgeois conditions of production, and of the bourgeoisie itself.

You are horrified at our intending to do away with private property. But in your existing society, private property is already done away with for nine-tenths of the population; its existence for the few is solely due to its non-existence in the hands of those nine-tenths. You reproach us, therefore, with intending to do away with a form of property, the necessary condition for whose existence is, the non-existence of any property for the immense majority of society.

In one word, you reproach us with intending to do away with your property. Precisely so; that is just what we intend.

From the moment when labor can no longer be converted into capital, money, or rent, into a social power capable of being monopolized, i.e., from the moment when individual property can no longer be transformed into bourgeois property, into capital, from that moment, you say, individuality vanishes.

You must, therefore, confess that by "individual" you mean no other person than the bourgeois, than the middle-class owner of property. This person must, indeed, be swept out of the way, and made impossible.

Communism deprives no man of the power to appropriate the products of society: all that it does is to deprive him of the power to subjugate the labor of others by means of such appropriation.

It has been objected, that upon the abolition of private property all work will cease, and universal laziness will overtake us.

According to this, bourgeois society ought long ago to have gone to the dogs through sheer idleness; for those of its members who work, acquire nothing, and those who acquire anything, do not work. The whole of this objection is but another expression of the tautology: that there can no longer be any wage-labor when there is no longer any capital.

All objections urged against the Communistic mode of producing and appropriating material products, have, in the same way, been urged against the Communistic modes of producing and appropriating intellectual products. Just as, to the bourgeois, the disappearance of class property is the disappearance of production itself, so the disappearance of class culture is to him identical with the disappearance of all culture.

That culture, the loss of which he laments, is, for the enormous majority, a mere training to act as a machine.

But don't wrangle with us so long as you apply, to our intended abolition of bourgeois property, the standard of your bourgeois notions of freedom, culture, law, etc. Your very ideas are but the outgrowth of the conditions of your bourgeois production and bourgeois property, just as your jurisprudence is but the will of your class made into a law for all, a will, whose essential character and direction are determined by the economic conditions of existence of your class.

The selfish misconception that induces you to transform into eternal laws of nature and of reason, the social forms springing from your present mode of production and form of property—historical relations that rise and disappear in the progress of production—this misconception you share with every ruling class that has preceded you. What you see clearly in the case of ancient property, what you admit in the case of feudal property, you are of course forbidden to admit in the case of your own bourgeois form of property.

Abolition of the family! Even the most radical flare up at this infamous proposal of the Communists.

On what foundation is the present family, the bourgeois family, based? On capital, on private gain. In its completely developed form this family exists only among the bourgeoisie. But this state of things finds its complement in the practical absence of the family among the proletarians, and in public prostitution.

The bourgeois family will vanish as a matter of course when its complement vanishes, and both will vanish with the vanishing of capital.

Do you charge us with wanting to stop the exploitation of children by their parents? To this crime we plead guilty.

But, you will say, we destroy the most hallowed of relations, when we replace home education by social.

And your education! Is not that also social, and determined by the social conditions under which you educate, by the intervention, direct or indirect, of society by means of schools, etc.? The Communists have not invented the intervention of society in education; they do but seek to alter the character of that intervention, and to rescue education from the influence of the ruling class.

The bourgeois clap-trap about the family and education, about the hallowed co-relation of parent and child, becomes all the more disgusting, the more, by the action of Modern Industry, all family ties among the proletarians are torn asunder, and their children transformed into simple articles of commerce and instruments of labor.

But you Communists would introduce community of women, screams the whole bourgeoisie in chorus.

The bourgeois sees in his wife a mere instrument of production. He hears that the instruments of production are to be exploited in common, and, naturally, can come to no other conclusion, than that the lot of being common to all will likewise fall to the women.

He has not even a suspicion that the real point aimed at is to do away with the status of women as mere instruments of production.

For the rest, nothing is more ridiculous than the virtuous indignation of our bourgeois at the community of women which, they pretend, is to be openly and offically established by the Communists. The Communists have no need to introduce community of women; it has existed almost from time immemorial.

Our bourgeois, not content with having the wives and daughters of their proletarians at their disposal, not to speak of common prostitutes, take the greatest pleasure in seducing each other's wives.

Bourgeois marriage is in reality a system of wives in common and thus, at the most, what the Communists might possibly be reproached with, is that they desire to introduce, in substitution for a hypocritically concealed, an openly legalized community of women. For the rest, it is self-evident, that the abolition of the present system of production must bring with it the abolition of the community of women springing from the system, i.e., of prostitution both public and private.

The Communists are further reproached with desiring to abolish countries and nationalities.

The working men have no country. We cannot take from them what they have not got. Since the proletariat must first of all acquire political supremacy, must rise to be the leading class of the nation, must constitute itself the nation, it is, so far, itself national, though not in the bourgeois sense of the word.

National differences, and antagonisms between peoples, are daily more and more vanishing, owing to the development of the bourgeoisie, to freedom of commerce, to the world-market, to uniformity in the mode of production and in the conditions of life corresponding thereto.

The supremacy of the proletariat will cause them to vanish still faster. United action, of the leading civilized countries at least, is one of the first conditions for the emancipation of the proletariat.

In proportion as the exploitation of one individual by another is put an end to, the exploitation of one nation by another will also be put an end to. In proportion as the antagonism between classes within the nation vanishes, the hostility of one nation to another will come to an end.

The charges against Communism made from a religious, a philosophical, and generally, from an ideological standpoint, are not deserving of serious examination.

[B] Does it require deep intuition to comprehend that man's ideas, views, and conceptions, in one word, man's consciousness, changes with every change in the conditions of his material existence, in his social relations and in his social life?

What else does the history of ideas prove, than that intellectual production changes in character in proportion as material production is changed? The ruling ideas of each age have ever been the ideas of its ruling class.

When people speak of ideas that revolutionize society, they do but express the fact, that within the old society, the elements of a new one have been created, and that the dissolution of the old ideas keeps even pace with the dissolution of the old conditions of existence.

When the ancient world was in its last throes, the ancient religions were overcome by Christianity. When Christian ideas succumbed in the 18th century to rationalist ideas, feudal society fought its death-battle with the then revolutionary bourgeoisie. The ideas of religious liberty and freedom of conscience, merely gave expression to the sway of free competition within the domain of knowledge.

"Undoubtedly," it will be said, "religious, moral, philosophical, and juridical ideas have been modified in the course of historical development. But religion, morality, philosophy, political science, and law, constantly survived this change.

"There are, besides, eternal truths, such as Freedom, Justice, etc., that are common to all states of Society. But Communism abolishes eternal truths, it abolishes all religion, and all morality, instead of constituting them on a new basis; it therefore acts in contradiction to all past historical experience."

What does this accusation reduce itself to? The history of all past society has consisted in the development of class antagonisms, antagonisms that assumed different forms at different epochs.

But whatever form they may have taken, one fact is common to all past ages, viz., the exploitation of one part of society by the other. No wonder, then, that the social consciousness of past ages, despite all the multiplicity and variety it displays, moves within certain common forms, or general ideas, which cannot completely vanish except with the total disappearance of class antagonisms.

The Communist revolution is the most radical rupture with traditional property-relations; no wonder that its development involves the most radical rupture with traditional ideas.

But let us have done with bourgeois objections to Communism.

[C] We have seen above that the first step in the revolution by the working class is to raise the proletariat to the position of ruling class, to win the battle of democracy.

The proletariat will use its political supremacy, to wrest, by degrees, all capital from the bourgeoisie, to centralize all instruments of production in the hands of the State, i.e., of the proletariat organized as the ruling class; and to increase the total of productive forces as rapidly as possible.

Of course, in the beginning, this cannot be effected except by means of despotic inroads on the rights of property, and on the conditions of bourgeois production; by means of measures, therefore, which appear economically insufficient and untenable, but which, in the course of the movement, outstrip themselves, necessitate further inroads upon the old social order, and are unavoidable as a means of entirely revolutionizing the mode of production.

These measures will of course be different in different countries.

Nevertheless in the most advanced countries the following will be pretty generally applicable:

1. Abolition of property in land and application of all rents of land to public purposes.
2. A heavy progressive or graduated income tax.
3. Abolition of all right of inheritance.
4. Confiscation of the property of all emigrants and rebels.
5. Centralization of credit in the hands of the State, by means of a national bank with State capital and an exclusively monopoly.
6. Centralization of the means of communication and transport in the hands of the State.
7. Extension of factories and instruments of production owned by the State; the bringing into cultivation of waste lands, and the improvement of the soil generally in accordance with a common plan.
8. Equal liability of all to labor. Establishment of industrial armies, especially for agriculture.
9. Combination of agriculture with manufacturing industries; gradual abolition of the distinction between town and country, by a more equable distribution of population over the country.
10. Free education for all children in public schools. Abolition of children's factory labor in its present form. Combination of education with industrial production, etc., etc.

When, in the course of development, class distinctions have disappeared, and all production has been concentrated in the hands of a vast association of the whole nation, the public power will lose its political character. Political power, properly so called, is merely the organized power of one class for oppressing another. If the proletariat during its contest with the bourgeoisie is compelled, by the force of circumstances, to organize itself as a class, if, by means of a revolution, it makes itself the ruling class, and, as such, sweeps away by force the old conditions of production, then it will, along with these conditions, have swept away the conditions for the existence of class antagonisms, and of classes generally, and will thereby have abolished its own supremacy as a class.

In place of the old bourgeois society, with its classes and class antagonisms, we shall have an association, in which the free development of each is the condition for the free development of all.

Position of the Communists in Relation to the Various Existing Opposition Parties

(6)

Section II [pp. 302–309] has made clear the relations of the Communists to the existing working class parties, such as the Chartists in England and the Agrarian Reformers in America.

The Communists fight for the attainment of the immediate aims, for the enforcement of the momentary interests of the working class; but in the movement of the present, they also represent and take care of the future of that movement. In France the Communists ally themselves with the Social-Democrats, against the conservative and radical bourgeoisie, reserving, however, the right to take up a critical position in regard to phrases and illusions traditionally handed down from the great Revolution.

In Switzerland they support the Radicals, without losing sight of the fact that this party consists of antagonistic elements, partly of Democratic Socialists, in the French sense, partly of radical bourgeois.

In Poland they support the party that insists on an agrarian revolution, as the prime condition of national emancipation, that party which fomented the insurrection of Cracow in 1846.

In Germany they fight with the bourgeoisie whenever it acts in a revolutionary way, against the absolute monarchy, the feudal squirearchy, and the petty bourgeoisie.

But they never cease, for a single instant, to instill into the working class the clearest possible recognition of the hostile antagonism between bourgeoisie and proletariat, in order that the German workers may straightway use, as so many weapons against the bourgeoisie, the social and political conditions that the bourgeoisie must necessarily introduce along with its supremacy, and in order that, after the fall of the reactionary classes in Germany, the fight against the bourgeoisie itself may immediately begin.

The Communists turn their attention chiefly to Germany, because that country is on the eve of a bourgeois revolution, that is bound to be carried out under more advanced conditions of European civilization, and with a more developed proletariat, than that of England was in the seventeenth, and of France in the eighteenth century, and because the bourgeois revolution in Germany will be but the prelude to an immediately following proletarian revolution.

In short, the Communists everywhere support every revolutionary movement against the existing social and political order of things.

In all these movements they bring to the front, as the leading question in each, the property question, no matter what its degree of development at the time.

Finally, they labor everywhere for the union and agreement of the democratic parties of all countries.

The Communists disdain to conceal their views and aims. They openly declare that their ends can be attained only by the forcible overthrow of all existing social conditions. Let the ruling classes tremble at a Communistic revolution. The proletarians have nothing to lose but their chains. They have a world to win.

Working men of all countries, unite!

Note on Sources. The above material comprises sections I, II, and IV of Karl Marx and Friedrich Engels, *The Manifesto of the Communist Party.* Section III is omitted.

Reading References. For Marx as philosopher, one can consult Sidney Hook's *Toward an Understanding of Karl Marx.* It may be supplemented by the same author's paper on "Marxism" in his volume *Reason, Social Myth, and Democracy.* Bertrand Russell's *Freedom versus Organization* is also excellent on Marx as theoretical philosopher. A. D. Lindsay's little book *Karl Marx's Capital* is well worth the effort required to read it.

For Marx as social critic, one can consult Edmund Wilson's book *To the Finland Station.* This is one of the finest pieces of historical writing so far published upon the revolutionary movement. Less deftly written, but valuable, is Max Nomad's *Apostles of Revolution.*

The standard biography of Marx is by Franz Mehring. Another, not so exhaustive, by Otto Ruhle, is good reading. A short work, *Karl Marx,* by I. Berlin, in the *Home University Library* series, is perhaps the best single item for busy students.

READING QUESTIONS

1. Marx's footnote definition of (a) *bourgeoisie* and (b) *proletariat.*
2. What about the history of all hitherto existing society? Who are the "antagonistic classes" in our epoch?
3. To what medieval economic groups does he trace the bourgeoisie? How did geographical discovery lead to the overthrow of feudalism?

4. Elucidate: "The bourgeoisie is the product of . . . a series of revolutions in the modes of production and exchange."
5. The development of the bourgeoisie as an economic class was accompanied by their political advance. Cite an example.
6. Elucidate: "The executive of the modern state is but a committee for managing the common affairs of the whole bourgeoisie."
7. The bourgeoisie, historically, has played a most revolutionizing part. Mention three examples.
8. They cannot exist without constantly revolutionizing the instruments of production. Why not? (See question 4 above.)
9. What about the bourgeoisie "during its rule of scarce one hundred years"?
10. Elucidate: "Modern bourgeois society . . . is like the sorcerer. . . ."
11. What "crises" and "epidemics" mark the career of the bourgeois economy? How are they dealt with?
12. What class has the bourgeoisie called into existence? How?
13. The proletariat is recruited from all classes of society. How so?
14. The proletariat goes through various stages of development. Mention two.
15. What "division among the bourgeoisie itself" produced the ten-hour bill in England?
16. The bourgeoisie supplies the proletariat with its own political and general education. Why? With what result?
17. A portion of the bourgeois ideologists goes over to the proletariat. When? Which portion?
18. Why the proletariat is today the only revolutionary class.
19. To the proletariat "law, morality, religion" are so many bourgeois prejudices: Why?
20. "The bourgeoisie is unfit any longer to be the ruling class in society." Why so?
21. Elucidate: "The bourgeoisie produces its own gravediggers."
22. What is the relation of the communist party to the proletarian class?
23. Marx mentions five or six bourgeois objections to communism. Namely. How does he handle any two of these?
24. The ten-point program is suggested as a step toward abolishing what? Show, for any two of these, how they would be that.
25. What is the position of the communists in relation to the various existing opposition parties?
26. This document deals with three groups (bourgeoisie, proletariat, communist). What, briefly, is the relation between bourgeoisie, and proletariat, proletariat and communist, and therefore between bourgeoisie and communist?

INDEPENDENT STUDY

1. Marx's vision of the economic class struggles of the modern world provided poets, novelists, and dramatists with a point of view from which to work. Read Emile Zola's proletarian novel *Germinal,* and make clear the ways in which it is a striking example of "Marxism in literature."
2. Much has been written in recent years on the idea of "alienation" as set forth in Marx's early writings, i.e., those that precede the *Manifesto.* Acquaint yourself with these early essays of Marx. Set forth his conception of alienation. Do you see any vitality, any relevance, in that idea, given circumstances in your own time?
3. Read a standard account of any major political revolution in the modern world; for example, the English revolution in the seventeenth century, the American revolution in the eighteenth century, the French revolutions of 1789, 1830, 1848, or 1870. When you have studied the "standard" account, read what Marx had to say by way of interpretation of the revolution in question.
4. Read essential chapters in C. A. Beard's *Economic Interpretation of the American Constitution.* Make clear wherein Beard writes as Marx might have done, and wherein he does not.

SECTION 3. JOHN STUART MILL: LIBERTY AND LAW

From Marx to Mill. Thus far we have examined Rousseau's position as set forth in his *Social Contract,* published in 1762 and Marx's position as set forth in the *Communist Manifesto,* published in 1848. Their positions are not the same, partly because they are not advancing answers to the same question. Each writes with an eye on the fact that in any community organized as a state, organized to make law possible, force will be brought to bear upon individuals and groups to conform to the law's demands. At this point Rousseau and Marx diverge. Rousseau asks, "How did this come about?" And answers, "I do not know." He goes on and asks, "How can it be justified?" And answers, "That I think I can tell." His question, then, is not historical. It is expressible this way: "When is a person *obligated* to conform to a law?" And this way: "When is a community, acting through its government, *justified* in enforcing a law?" His answer was, "The use of force, of coercion, to produce conformity to law, is justified when, and only when, it is introduced to protect a common good, a good common to all members of the politically organized group. When this is done, a law backed by force can say to each individual: "I am what you demand of others; I am therefore what you ought to demand of yourself. If we (the laws) force you to do what you *ought* to do, then you have no reasonable grounds for complaint. Agreeing to this is the social contract, the social cement that holds a community together as a state."

Marx begins with a historical question to which he proposes an answer: "How did it happen that communities have laws backed by force? Why is coercive restraint a mark of politically organized communities? Why do governments, acting in the name of states, claim and try to exercise a monopoly of legal violence?" His question is not what *justifies* this widespread political phenomenon. It is doubtful that he thought it justifiable. His question is what accounts for this phenomenon. His answer is a round-about one. It involves an *economic* interpretation of politics and law. On the face of it, a community is organized politically to make possible regulation of some human behavior by laws backed by force. This is the *prima facie* fact. But how is it to be interpreted? Why are communities thus organized? His answer is that "beneath the political face of things," a community is an economic order. That it is organized to make *production* possible is a more basic fact about it than that it is organized to make law possible. Its essential features—such as political community, political society—are to be explained, interpreted, understood, by reference to the more basic fact that it is an economy, an economic order. Unless this were so, it would not be organized as a political order, an order permitting control by laws backed by force. This is the fundamental claim of Marx's *economic* interpretation of politics and political history.

If you look *beneath* the surface of political orders you discover economic orders. If you look *at* economic orders you find that they consist of economic classes, and that between these classes there is a relation of class antagonism that can become class war. One of the economic classes, the "dominant" one, organizes the community into a political order so that it may suppress the other class, keep it in line, exploit it, by means of laws backed by force. Marx mentions the "feudal" class as having done this to the "bourgeois" class, and the bourgeois class as staging a "political" revolution enabling them to throw off the feudal class and impose their own modes of "law and order" upon the "proletarian" class. Marx's economic interpretation of politics and political history, law and legal history, thus consists in "class-angling" political organization, domination, revolution, and beginning anew. So long as this recurring cycle marks the political life of a community, there will be class legislation, and the use of force to produce conformity to the laws.

However, Marx foresees an end to these cycles. When the proletarians overthrow the bourgeoisie, they will not in turn be overthrown by a new economic class. Their triumph will mark the end of economic classes within the economic order, and the end of the need for laws backed by force. Thereafter, communities will be *administered,* not coercively governed. There will be no other economic class threatening the proletarian class. Rousseau's "common good" will become the proletarian good. The proletarians will not require to be coerced into acting with reference to *their* common good.

Mill's small book *On Liberty* was published in 1859, ninety-seven years after Rousseau's *Social Contract* and eleven years after Marx's *Manifesto.* It became, and has remained, a classic defense of the right of the individual to think and act for himself. So construed, it is not a defense of the individual's right to think what he pleases and do what he pleases. It is not a theoretical defense of the idiosyncratic or the anarchical as such. Its claim is along these lines: when a community is organized to make law enforcement possible, and has a government backed by police and an army as its agent, such a community has much more power at its disposal than any dissenting individual. In such a community, whether a democracy or a republic or a constitutional monarchy or an absolute monarchy, a dissenting individual or minority can find itself confronted with virtually irresistible force. Mill's little book is written on behalf of persons so circumstanced. It is addressed to communities and their governments where a monopoly of coercive restraint is exercised in the name of the common good. It is no less applicable to communities and their governments where such restraint is exercised in the name of the proletarian good. Victoria's Britain, Lincoln's America, Lenin's Russia, or Hitler's Germany are, or would be thought of as, answerable to Mill's argument. (See pp. 32 and 222.)

The Argument of the Passages. Suppose you are appointed to a law-making group charged with the responsibility of providing legislative definition or redefinition of one of society's major institutions; say, marriage. How would you handle such an assignment? Along what lines would you propose legislative definitions for this institution? What do's and don't's connected with this institution would you make mandatory upon all who would participate in the institution, placing the full weight of the law back of these demands?" A reader so circumstanced would be in a position to wield considerable power. As modern communities go, few persons have more power over others than those who devise or revise the laws. To an increasing degree, as legislators decide, the members of a community act or refrain from acting. Such power is not absolute, but it is great. To wield such power is to be responsible for much of what others do or refrain from doing.

A slight familiarity with the history of legislative social control shows that legislative power may be *misused* in either (or both) of two ways:

(1) It may be used to require people to do what is wrong. That is not frequent, but it is by no means impossible. If a certain way of acting is wrong, and a law is passed requiring people to act in that way, then, to the degree that people are law-abiding, they are being required to do what is wrong. No conscientious legislator would want to be responsible for that state of affairs.

(2) It may be used to require people to do what should be left up to them to do or leave undone. Here the rightness or wrongness of the way of acting is not in question; the point is that it is a way of acting which law should say nothing about. An instance might be found in what is called "breach of promise," in the sense of promise to marry. If a man engages to marry a woman, he should, as we say, "live up to his promise." But do we want the law to force him to do so? If a woman engages to marry a man, she should live up to her promise. But do we want the law to force her to do so? If we hesitate, or say "no" at this point, it is not that we regard such promises lightly, nor that we feel that it is right to break them; it is rather that we regard such matters as better left up to individuals to settle for themselves. A man does right, often, in sending his sons to college; but do we want a law requiring him to do so? A man does wrong if he deliberately destroys a masterpiece of painting which he has bought and paid for; but do we want a law forbidding him to do so? A man does wrong to be mean to his friends or miserly or wasteful with his money; but do we want a law forbidding him to be so? There are an indefinite number of ways in which a man of good will would act, but we would not want bad men forced by law to act in these ways. There are matters that we want people "left alone" about, left legally free to do them or not do them, regardless of what good men would do. In some matters we want people left legally free to do what is foolish; in some matters, to do what is wrong. In other words, we don't want the law to force men to do what is wrong; but we also don't want the law to prohibit them in all instances from doing what is wrong nor force them in all instances to do what is right.

These are reflections that might well occur to a person possessing the power to devise and revise a community's laws. In proportion as you possess the power to force people to act or refrain from acting in a certain way, you might well ask whether, in regard to a particular matter, you should use or refrain from using that power.

The balance of this section contains selections from John Stuart

Mill's *On Liberty*. The selections are Chapter I and passages from chapters II, III, IV, and V. In this book Mill was concerned to defend the right of the individual to think and act for himself. This right meant a great deal to the author. He believed that societies and governments frequently intrude where they have no right to do so. He wrote his book to point out this fact and to protest against it. His book is Western man's finest handling of the theme. It became the testament of liberalism.

Chapter I is reproduced in full. It formulates the issue to which Mill addresses himself in successive chapters. Chapter I is here divided into two parts. Part 1, beginning with the phrase "The *subject* of this essay," points out that the problem of liberty throughout most of its history has arisen between individuals and nondemocratic governments, but that, in recent years, since the increase of democratic governments answerable to all or most of the adult population of their states, it is now between individuals and minorities, and democratically elected governments claiming to rule in the name of a political majority. This "majoritarianism," Mill insists, has done little or nothing to solve or dissolve the problem. Part 2 begins with the phrase "The object of this essay."

(1)

The subject of this Essay is not the so-called Liberty of the Will, so unfortunately opposed to the misnamed doctrine of Philosophical Necessity; but Civil, or Social Liberty: the nature and limits of the power which can be legitimately exercised by society over the individual. A question seldom stated, and hardly ever discussed, in general terms, but which profoundly influences the practical controversies of the age by its latent presence, and is likely soon to make itself recognised as the vital question of the future. It is so far from being new, that, in a certain sense, it has divided mankind, almost from the remotest ages; but in the stage of progress into which the more civilised portions of the species have now entered, it presents itself under new conditions, and requires a different and more fundamental treatment.

The struggle between Liberty and Authority is the most conspicuous feature in the portions of history with which we are earliest familiar, particularly in that of Greece, Rome, and England. But in old times this contest was between subjects, or some classes of subjects, and the Government. By liberty, was meant protection against the tyranny of the political rulers. The rulers were conceived (except in some of the popular governments of Greece) as in a necessarily antagonistic position to the people whom they ruled. They consisted of a governing One, or a governing tribe or caste, who derived their authority from inheritance or conquest, who, at all events, did not hold it at the pleasure of the governed, and whose supremacy men did not venture, perhaps did not desire, to contest, whatever precautions might be taken against its oppressive exercise. Their power was regarded as necessary, but also as highly dangerous; as a weapon which they would attempt to use against their subjects, no less than against external enemies. To prevent the weaker members of the community from being preyed upon by innumerable vultures, it was needful that there should be an animal of prey stronger than the rest, commissioned to keep them down. But as the king of the vultures would be no less bent upon preying on the flock than any of the minor harpies, it was indispensable to be in a perpetual attitude of defence against his beak and claws. The aim, therefore, of patriots was to set limits to the power which the ruler should be suffered to exercise over the community; and this limitation was what they meant by liberty. It was attempted in two ways. First, by obtaining a recognition of certain immunities, called political liberties or rights, which was to be regarded as a breach of duty in the ruler to infringe, and which if he did infringe, specific resistance, or general rebellion, was held to be justifiable. A second, and generally a later expedient, was the establishment of constitutional checks, by which the consent of the community, or of a body of some sort, supposed to represent its interests, was made a necessary condition to some of the more important acts of the governing power. To the first of these modes of limitation, the ruling power, in most European countries, was compelled, more or less, to submit. It was not so with the second; and, to attain this, or when already in some degree possessed, to attain it more completely, became everywhere the principal object of the lovers of liberty. And so long as mankind were content to combat one enemy by another, and to be ruled by a master, on condition of being guaranteed more or less efficaciously against his tyranny, they did not carry their aspirations beyond this point.

A time, however, came, in the progress of human affairs, when men ceased to think it a necessity of nature that their governors should be an independent power, opposed in interest to themselves. It appeared to them much better that the various magistrates of the State should be their tenants or delegates, revocable at their pleasure. In that way alone, it seemed, could they have complete security that the powers of government would never be abused to their disadvantage. By degrees this new demand for elective and temporary rulers became the prominent object of the exertions of the popular party, wherever any such party existed; and superseded, to a considerable extent, the previous efforts to limit the power of rulers. As the struggle proceeded for making the ruling power emanate from the periodical choice of the ruled, some persons began to think that too much importance had been attached to the limitation of the power itself. *That* (it might seem) was a resource against rulers whose interests were habitually opposed to those of the people. What was now wanted was, that the rulers should be identified with the people; that their interest and will should be the interest and will of the nation. The nation did not need to be protected against its own will. There was no fear of its tyrannising over itself. Let the rulers be effectually responsible to it, promptly removable by it, and it could afford to trust them with power of which it could itself dictate the use to be made. Their power was but the nation's own power, concentrated, and in a form convenient for exercise. This mode of thought, or rather perhaps of feeling, was common among the last generation of European liberalism, in the Continental section of which it still apparently predominates. Those who admit any limit to what a government may do, except in the case of such governments as they think ought not to exist, stand out as brilliant exceptions among the political thinkers of the Continent. A similar tone of sentiment might by this time have been prevalent in our own country, if the circumstances which for a time encouraged it had continued unaltered.

But, in political and philosophical theories, as well as in persons, success discloses faults and infirmities which failure might hve concealed from ob- servation. The notion, that the people have no need to limit their power over themselves, might seem axiomatic, when popular government was a thing only dreamed about, or read of as having existed at some distant period of the past. Neither was that notion necessarily disturbed by such temporary aberrations as those of the French Revolution, the worst of which were the work of a usurping few, and which, in any case, belonged, not to the perma- nent working of popular institutions, but to a sudden and convulsive out- break against monarchical and aristocratic despotism. In time, however, a democratic republic came to occupy a large portion of the earth's surface, and made itself felt as one of the most powerful members of the community of nations; and elective and responsible government became subject to the observations and criticisms which wait upon a great existing fact. It was now perceived that such phrases as "self-government," and "the power of the people over themselves," do not express the true state of the case. The "peo- ple" who exercise the power are not always the same people with those over whom it is exercised; and the "self-government" spoken of is not the govern- ment of each by himself, but of each by all the rest. The will of the people, moreover, practically means the will of the most numerous or the most active *part* of the people; the majority, or those who succeed in making themselves accepted as the majority; the people, consequently *may* desire to oppress a part of their number; and precautions are as much needed against this as against any other abuse of power. The limitation, therefore, of the power of government over individuals loses none of its importance when the holders of power are regularly accountable to the community, that is, to the strongest party therein. This view of things, recommending itself equally to the in- telligence of thinkers and to the inclination of those important classes in Eu- ropean society to whose real or supposed interests democracy is adverse, has had no difficulty in establishing itself; and in political speculations "the tyr- anny of the majority" is now generally included among the evils against which society requires to be on its guard.

Like other tyrannies, the tyranny of the majority was at first, and is still vulgarly, held in dread, chiefly as operating through the acts of the public authorities. But reflecting persons perceived that when society is itself the tyrant—society collectively over the separate individuals who compose it—its means of tyrannising are not restricted to the acts which it may do by the hands of its political functionaries. Society can and does execute its own mandates: and if it issues wrong mandates instead of right, or any mandates at all in things with which it ought not to meddle, it practises a social tyr- anny more formidable than many kinds of political oppression, since, though not usually upheld by such extreme penalties, it leaves fewer means of es- cape, penetrating much more deeply into the details of life, and enslaving the soul itself. Protection, therefore, against the tyranny of the magistrate is not enough: there needs protection also against the tyranny of the prevailing opinion and feeling; against the tendency of society to impose, by other means than civil penalties, its own ideas and practices as rules of conduct on those who dissent from them; to fetter the development, and, if possible, prevent the formation, of any individuality not in harmony with its ways, and compels all characters to fashion themselves upon the model of its own. There is a limit to the legitimate interference of collective opinion with individual independence: and to find that limit, and maintain it against encroachment, is as indispensable to a good condition of human affairs, as protection against political despotism.

But though this proposition is not likely to be contested in general terms, the practical question, where to place the limit—how to make the fitting adjustment between individual independence and social control—is a subject on which nearly everything remains to be done. All that makes existence valuable to any one, depends on the enforcement of restraints upon the actions of other people. Some rules of conduct, therefore, must be imposed, by law in the first place, and by opinion on many things which are not fit subjects for the operation of law. What these rules should be is the principal question in human affairs; but if we except a few of the most obvious cases, it is one of those which least progress has been made in resolving. No two ages, and scarcely any two countries, have decided it alike; and the decision of one age or country is a wonder to another. Yet the people of any given age and country no more suspect any difficulty in it, than if it were a subject on which mankind had always been agreed. The rules which obtain among themselves appear to them self-evident and self-justifying.

This all but universal illusion is one of the examples of the magical influence of custom, which is not only, as the proverb says, a second nature, but is continually mistaken for the first. The effect of custom, in preventing any misgiving respecting the rules of conduct which mankind impose on one another, is all the more complete because the subject is one on which it is not generally considered necessary that reasons should be given, either by one person to others or by each to himself. People are accustomed to believe, and have been encouraged in the belief by some who aspire to the character of philosophers, that their feelings, on subjects of this nature, are better than reasons, and render reasons unnecessary. The practical principle which guides them to their opinions on the regulation of human conduct, is the feeling in each person's mind that everybody should be required to act as he, and those with whom he sympathises, would like them to act. No one, indeed, acknowledges to himself that his standard of judgment is his own liking; but an opinion on a point of conduct, not supported by reasons, can only count as one person's preference; and if the reasons, when given, are a mere appeal to a similar preference felt by other people, it is still only many people's liking instead of one. To an ordinary man, however, his own preference, thus supported, is not only a perfectly satisfactory reason, but the only one he generally has for any of his notions of morality, taste or propriety, which are not expressly written in his religious creed; and his chief guide in the interpretation even of that. Men's opinions, accordingly, on what is laudable or blamable, are affected by all the multifarious causes which influence their wishes in regard to the conduct of others, and which are as numerous as those which determine their wishes on any other subject. Sometimes their reason—at other times their prejudices or superstitions: often their social affections, not seldom their anti-social ones, their envy or jealousy, their arrogance or contemptuousness: but most commonly their desires or fears for themselves—their legitimate or illegitimate self-interest.

Wherever there is an ascendant class, a large portion of the morality of the country emanates from its class interests, and its feelings of class superiority. The morality between Spartans and Helots, between planters and negroes, between princes and subjects, between nobles and roturiers, between men and women, has been for the most part the creation of these class interests and feelings: and the sentiments thus generated react in turn upon the moral feelings of the members of the ascendant class, in their relations among themselves. Where, on the other hand, a class, formerly ascendant, has lost its ascendancy, or where its ascendancy is unpopular, the prevailing moral sentiments frequently bear the impress of an impatient dislike of superiority. Another grand determining principle of the rules of conduct, both in act and forbearance, which have been enforced by law or opinion, has been the servility of mankind towards the supposed preferences or aversions of their temporal masters or of their gods. This servility, though essentially selfish, is not hypocrisy; it gives rise to perfectly genuine sentiments of abhorrence; it made men burn magicians and heretics. Among so many baser influences, the general and obvious interests of society have of course had a share, and a large one, in the direction of the moral sentiments: less, however, as a matter of reason, and on their own account, than as a consequence of the sympathies and antipathies which grew out of them: and sympathies and antipathies which had little or nothing to do with the interests of society, have made themselves felt in the establishment of moralities with quite as great force.

The likings and dislikings of society, or of some powerful portion of it, are thus the main thing which has practically determined the rules laid down for general observance, under the penalties of law or opinion. And in general, those who have been in advance of society in thought and feeling, have left this condition of things unassailed in principle, however they may have come into conflict with it in some of its details. They have occupied themselves rather in inquiring what things society ought to like or dislike, than in questioning whether its likings or dislikings should be a law to individuals. They preferred endeavouring to alter the feelings of mankind on the particular points on which they were themselves heretical, rather than make common cause in defence of freedom, with heretics generally. The only case in which the higher ground has been taken on principle and maintained with consistency, by any but an individual here and there, is that of religious belief: a case instructive in many ways, and not least so as forming a most striking instance of the fallibility of what is called the moral sense: for the *odium theologicum*, in a sincere bigot, is one of the most unequivocal cases of moral feeling. Those who first broke the yoke of what called itself the Universal Church, were in general as little willing to permit difference of religious opinion as that church itself. But when the heat of the conflict was over, without giving a complete victory to any party, and each church or sect was reduced to limit its hopes to retaining possession of the ground it already occupied; minorities, seeing that they had no chance of becoming majorities, were under the necessity of pleading to those whom they could not convert, for permission to differ. It is accordingly on this battle field almost solely, that the rights of the individual against society have been asserted on broad grounds of principle, and the claim of society to exercise authority over dissentients openly controverted. The great writers to whom the world owes what religious liberty it possesses, have mostly asserted freedom of conscience as an indefeasible right, and denied absolutely that a human being is accountable to others for his religious belief. Yet so natural to mankind is intolerance in whatever they really care about, that religious freedom has hardly anywhere been practically realised, except where religious indifference, which dislikes to have its peace disturbed by theological quarrels, has added its weight to the scale. In the minds of almost all religious persons, even in the most tolerant countries, the duty of toleration is admitted with tacit reserves. One person will bear with dissent in matters of church government, but not of dogma; another can tolerate everybody, short of a Papist or a Unitarian; another every one who believes in revealed religion; a few extend their charity a little further, but stop at the belief in a God and in a future state. Wherever the sentiment of the majority is still genuine and intense, it is found to have abated little of its claim to be obeyed.

In England, from the peculiar circumstances of our political history, though the yoke of opinion is perhaps heavier, that of law is lighter, than in most other countries of Europe; and there is considerable jealousy of direct interference, by the legislative or the executive power, with private conduct; not so much from any just regard for the independence of the individual, as from the still subsisting habit of looking on the government as representing an opposite interest to the public. The majority have not yet learnt to feel the power of the government their power, or its opinions their opinions. When they do so, individual liberty will probably be as much exposed to invasion from the government, as it already is from public opinion. But, as yet, there is a considerable amount of feeling ready to be called forth against any attempt of the law to control individuals in things in which they have not hitherto been accustomed to be controlled by it; and this with very little discrimination as to whether the matter is, or is not, within the legitimate sphere of legal control; insomuch that the feeling, highly salutary on the whole, is perhaps quite as often misplaced as well grounded in the particular instances of its application. There is, fact, no recognised principle by which the propriety or impropriety of government interference is customarily tested. People decide according to their personal preferences. Some, whenever they see any good to be done, or evil to be remedied, would willingly instigate the government to undertake the business; while others prefer to bear almost any amount of social evil, rather than add one to the departments of human interests amenable to governmental control. And men range themselves on one or the other side in any particular case, according to this general direction of their sentiments; or according to the degree of interest which they feel in the particular thing which it is proposed that the government should do, or according to the belief they entertain that the government would, or would not, do it in the manner they prefer; but very rarely on account of any opinion to which they consistently adhere, as to what things are fit to be done by a government. And it seems to me that in consequence of this absence of rule or principle, one side is at present as often wrong as the other; the interference of government is, with about equal frequency, improperly invoked and improperly condemned.

In Part 2, beginning with the phrase "The *object* of this essay," Mill asks what principle should be used by societies and their governments in regulating the behaviors of individuals and minority groups. Most of Part 2 is given over to answering that question "in principle." Part 2 lays down some ground rules that are intended to govern what is said in each of the remaining four chapters. It should, therefore, be read carefully, and footnoted by examples from your own thinking as you go along.

(2)

The object of this Essay is to assert one very simple principle, as entitled to govern absolutely the dealings of society with the individual in the way of compulsion and control, whether the means used be physical force in the form of legal penalties, or the moral coercion of public opinion. That principle is, that the sole end for which mankind are warranted, individually or collectively, in interfering with the liberty of action of any of their number, is self-protection. That the only purpose for which power can be rightfully exercised over any member of a civilised community, against his will, is to prevent harm to others. His own good, either physical or moral, is not a sufficient warrant. He cannot rightfully be compelled to do or forbear because it will be better for him to do so, because it will make him happier, because, in the opinions of others, to do so would be wise, or even right. These are good reasons for remonstrating with him, or reasoning with him, or persuading him, or entreating him, but not for compelling him, or visiting him with any evil in case he do otherwise. To justify that, the conduct from which it is desired to deter him must be calculated to produce evil to some one else. The only part of the conduct of any one, for which he is amenable to society, is that which concerns others. In the part which merely concerns himself, his independence is, of right, absolute. Over himself, over his own body and mind, the individual is sovereign.

It is, perhaps, hardly necessary to say that this doctrine is meant to apply only to human beings in the maturity of their faculties. We are not speaking of children, or of young persons below the age which the law may fix as that of manhood or womanhood. Those who are still in a state to require being taken care of by others, must be protected against their own actions as well as against external injury. For the same reason, we may leave out of consideration those backward states of society in which the race itself may be considered as in its nonage. The early difficulties in the way of spontaneous progress are so great, that there is seldom any choice of means for overcoming them; and a ruler full of the spirit of improvement is warranted in the use of any expedients that will attain an end, perhaps otherwise unattainable. Despotism is a legitimate mode of government in dealing with barbarians, provided the end be their improvement, and the means justified by actually affecting that end. Liberty, as a principle, has no application to any state of things anterior to the time when mankind have become capable of being improved by free and equal discussion. Until then, there is nothing for them but implicit obedience to an Akbar or a Charlemagne, if they are so fortunate as to find one. But as soon as mankind have attained the capacity of being guided to their own improvement by conviction or persuasion (a period long since reached in all nations with whom we need here concern ourselves), compulsion, either in the direct form or in that of pains and penalties for non-compliance, is no longer admissible as a means to their own good, and justifiable only for the security of others.

It is proper to state that I forego any advantage which could be derived to my argument from the idea of abstract right, as a thing independent of utility. I regard utility as the ultimate appeal on all ethical questions; but it must be utility in the largest sense, grounded on the permanent interests of a man as a progressive being. Those interests, I contend, authorise the subjection of individual spontaneity to external control, only in respect to those actions of each, which concern the interest of other people. If any one does an act hurtful to others, there is a *prima facie* case for punishing him, by law, or, where legal penalties are not safely applicable, by general disapprobation. There are also many positive acts for the benefit of others, which he may rightfully be compelled to perform; such as to give evidence in a court of justice; to bear his fair share in the common defence, or in any other joint work necessary to the interest of the society of which he enjoys the protection; and to perform certain acts of individual beneficence, such as saving a fellow creature's life, or interposing to protect the defenceless against ill-usage, things which whenever it is obviously a man's duty to do, he may rightfully be made responsible to society for not doing. A person may cause evil to others not only by his actions but by his inaction, and in either case he is justly accountable to them for the injury. The latter case, it is true, requires a much more cautious exercise of compulsion than the former. To make any one answerable for doing evil to others is the rule; to make him answerable for not preventing evil is, comparatively speaking, the exception. Yet there are many cases clear enough and grave enough to justify that exception. In all things which regard the external relations of the individual, he is *de jure* amenable to those whose interests are concerned, and, if need be, to society as their protector. There are often good reasons for not holding him to the responsibility; but these reasons must arise from the special expediencies of the case: either because it is a kind of case in which he is on the whole likely to act better, when left to his own discretion, than when controlled in any way in which society have it in their power to control him; or because the attempt to exercise control would produce other evils, greater than those which it would prevent. When such reasons as these preclude the enforcement of responsibility, the conscience of the agent himself should step into the vacant judgment seat, and protect those interests of others which have no external protection; judging himself all the more rigidly, because the case does not admit of his being made accountable to the judgment of his fellow creatures.

But there is a sphere of action in which society, as distinguished from the individual, has, if any, only an indirect interest; comprehending all that portion of a person's life and conduct which affects only himself, or if it also affects others, only with their free, voluntary, and undeceived consent and participation. When I say only himself, I mean directly, and in the first instance; for whatever affects himself, may affect others through himself; and the objection which may be grounded on this contingency, will receive consideration in the sequel. This, then, is the appropriate region of human liberty. It comprises, first, the inward domain of consciousness; demanding liberty of conscience in the most comprehensive sense; liberty of thought and feeling; absolute freedom of opinion and sentiment on all subjects, practical or speculative, scientific, moral, or theological. The liberty of expressing and publishing opinions may seem to fall under a different principle, since it belongs to that part of the conduct of an individual which concerns other people; but, being almost of as much importance as the liberty of thought itself, and resting in great part on the same reasons, is practically inseparable from it. Secondly, the principle requires liberty of tastes and pursuits; of framing the plan of our life to suit our own character; of doing as we like, subject to such consequences as may follow: without impediment from our fellow creatures, so long as what we do does not harm them, even though they should think our conduct foolish, perverse, or wrong. Thirdly, from this liberty of each individual, follows the liberty, within the same limits, of combination among individuals; freedom to unite, for any purpose not involving harm to others: the persons combining being supposed to be of full age, and not forced or deceived.

No society in which these liberties are not, on the whole, respected, is free, whatever may be its form of government; and none is completely free in which they do not exist absolute and unqualified. The only freedom which deserves the name, is that of pursuing our own good in our own way, so long as we do not attempt to deprive others of theirs, or impede their efforts to obtain it. Each is the proper guardian of his own health, whether bodily, *or* mental and spiritual. Mankind are greater gainers by suffering each other to live as seems good to themselves, than by compelling each to live as seems good to the rest.

Though this doctrine is anything but new, and, to some persons, may have the air of a truism, there is no doctrine which stands more directly opposed to the general tendency of existing opinion and practice. Society has expended fully as much effort in the attempt (according to its lights) to compel people to conform to its notions of personal as of social excellence. The ancient commonwealths thought themselves entitled to practise, and the ancient philosophers countenanced, the regulation of every part of private conduct by public authority, on the ground that the State had a deep interest in the whole bodily and mental discipline of every one of its citizens; a mode of thinking which may have been admissible in small republics surrounded by powerful enemies, in constant peril of being subverted by foreign attack or internal commotion, and to which even a short interval of relaxed energy and self-command might so easily be fatal that they could not afford to wait for the salutary permanent effects of freedom. In the modern world, the greater size of political communities, and, above all, the separation between spiritual and temporal authority (which placed the direction of men's consciences in other hands than those which controlled their worldly affairs), prevented so great an interference by law in the details of private life; but the engines of moral repression have been wielded more strenuously against divergence from the reigning opinion in self-regarding, than even in social matters; religion, the most powerful of the elements which have entered into the formation of moral feeling, having almost always been governed either by the ambition of a hierarchy, seeking control over every department of human conduct, or by the spirit of Puritanism. And some of those modern reformers who have placed themselves in strongest opposition to the religions of the past, have been noway behind either churches or sects in their assertion of the right of spiritual domination: M. Comte, in particular, whose social system, as unfolded in his *Système de Politique Positive*, aims at establishing (though by moral more than by legal appliances) a despotism of society over the individual, surpassing anything contemplated in the political ideal of the most rigid disciplinarian among the ancient philosophers.

Apart from the peculiar tenets of individual thinkers, there is also in the world at large an increasing inclination to stretch unduly the powers of society over the individual, both by the force of opinion and even by that of legislation; and as the tendency of all the changes taking place in the world is to strengthen society, and diminish the power of the individual, this encroachment is not one of the evils which tend spontaneously to disappear, but, on the contrary, to grow more and more formidable. The disposition of mankind, whether as rulers or as fellow-citizens, to impose their own opinions and inclinations as a rule of conduct on others, is so energetically supported by some of the best and by some of the worst feelings incident to human nature, that it is hardly ever kept under restraint by anything but want of power; and as the power is not declining, but growing, unless a strong barrier of moral conviction can be raised against the mischief, we must expect, in the present circumstances of the world, to see it increase.

It will be convenient for the argument, if, instead of at once entering upon the general thesis, we confine ourselves in the first instance to a single branch of it, on which the principle here stated is, if not fully, yet to a certain point, recognised by the current opinions. This one branch is the Liberty of Thought: from which it is impossible to separate the cognate liberty of speaking and of writing. Although these liberties, to some considerable amount, form part of the political morality of all countries which profess religious toleration and free institutions, the grounds, both philosophical and practical, on which they rest, are perhaps not so familiar to the general mind, nor so thoroughly appreciated by many even of the leaders of opinion, as might have been expected. Those grounds, when rightly understood, are of much wider application than to only one division of the subject, and a thorough consideration of this part of the question will be found the best introduction to the remainder. Those to whom nothing which I am about to say will be new, may therefore, I hope, excuse me, if on a subject which for now three centuries has been so often discussed, I venture on one discussion more.

So much for Mill's introductory Chapter I. His over-all subject is to be the right of the individual to think and act for himself. For Mill this does not mean the right to think and act as you please. Mill's individualism was never pushed to anarchism. The appropriate word is *liberalism:* the right to give the best thought of which you are capable to any matter that challenges you to think about it, and then to act as wisely as you can on the conclusion you arrive at. In Chapter II he defends the right to think for oneself. His defense here is unqualified. This liberty he regards as an unconditional right. The chapter is one of humanity's great defenses of this right. After an opening paragraph and a footnote he tackles first those who would refuse to permit free discussion in the case of a false belief. Only his opening paragraph is quoted here. Many pages of closely argued test cases are omitted. Thus:

The time, it is to be hoped, is gone by, when any defence would be necessary of the "liberty of the press" as one of the securities against corrupt or tyrannical government. No argument, we may suppose, can now be needed, against permitting a legislature or an executive, not identified in interest with the people, to prescribe opinions to them, and determine what doctrines or what arguments they shall be allowed to hear. This aspect of the question, besides, has been so often and so triumphantly enforced by preceding writers, that it needs not be specially insisted on in this place. Though the law of England, on the subject of the press, is as servile to this day as it was in the time of the Tudors, there is little danger of its being actually put in force against political discussion, except during some temporary panic, when fear of insurrection drives ministers and judges from their propriety; [1] and, speaking generally, it is not, in constitutional countries, to be apprehended, that the government, whether completely responsible to the people or not, will often attempt to control the expression of opinion, except when in doing so it makes itself the organ of the general intolerance of the public. Let us suppose, therefore, that the government is entirely at one with the people, and never thinks of exerting any power of coercion unless in agreement with what it conceives to be their voice. But I deny the right of the people to exercise such coercion, either by themselves or by their government. The power itself is illegitimate. The best government has no more title to it than the worst. It is as noxious, or more noxious, when exerted in accordance with public opinion, than when in opposition to it. If all mankind minus one were of one opinion, and only one person were of the contrary

[1] These words had scarcely been written, when, as if to give them an emphatic contradiction, occurred the Government Press Prosecutions of 1858. That ill-judged interference with the liberty of public discussion has not, however, induced me to alter a single word in the text, nor has it at all weakened my conviction that, moments of panic excepted, the era of pains and penalties for political discussion has, in our own country, passed away. For, in the first place, the prosecutions were not persisted in; and, in the second, they were never, properly speaking, political prosecutions. The offence charged was not that of criticising institutions, or the acts or persons of rulers, but of circulating what was deemed an immoral doctrine, the lawfulness of Tyrannicide. If the arguments of the present chapter are of any validity, there ought to exist the fullest liberty of professing and discussing, as a matter of ethical conviction, any doc-

opinion, mankind would be no more justified in silencing that one person, than he, if he had the power, would be justified in silencing mankind. Were an opinion a personal possession of no value except to the owner; if to be obstructed in the enjoyment of it were simply a private injury, it would make some difference whether the injury was inflicted only on a few persons or on many. But the peculiar evil of silencing the expression of an opinion is, that it is robbing the human race; posterity as well as the existing generation; those who dissent from the opinion, still more than those who hold it. If the opinion is right, they are deprived of the opportunity of exchanging error for truth: if wrong, they lose, what is almost as great a benefit, the clearer perception and livelier impression of truth, produced by its collision with error.

It is necessary to consider separately these two hypotheses, each of which has a distinct branch of the argument corresponding to it. We can never be sure that the opinion we are endeavouring to stifle is a false opinion; and if we were sure, stifling it would be an evil still.

First: the opinion which it is attempted to suppress by authority may possibly be true. Those who desire to suppress it, of course deny its truth; but they are not infallible. They have no authority to decide the question for all mankind, and exclude every other person from the means of judging. To refuse a hearing to an opinion, because they are sure that it is false, is to assume that *their* certainty is the same thing as *absolute* certainty. All silencing of discussion is an assumption of infallibility. Its condemnation may be allowed to rest on this common argument, not the worse for being common. . . .

Mill now moves against those who would refuse to permit free discussion in the case of a false belief. Only two paragraphs are here quoted. Many pages of closely argued test cases are omitted. Thus:

Let us now pass to the *second* division of the argument, and dismissing the supposition that any of the received opinions may be false, let us assume them to be true and examine into the worth of the manner in which they are likely to be held when their truth is not freely and openly canvassed. However unwillingly a person who has a strong opinion may admit the possibil-

---

trine, however immoral it may be considered. It would, therefore, be irrelevant and out of place to examine here, whether the doctrine of Tyrannicide deserves that title. I shall content myself with saying that the subject has been at all times one of the open questions of morals; that the act of a private citizen in striking down a criminal, who, by raising himself above the law, has placed himself beyond the reach of legal punishment or control, has been accounted by whole nations, and by some of the best and wisest of men, not a crime, but an act of exalted virtue; and that, right or wrong, it is not of the nature of assassination, but of civil war. As such, I hold that the instigation to it, in a specific case, may be a proper subject of punishment, but only if an overt act has followed, and at least a probable connection can be established between the act and the instigation. Even then, it is not a foreign government, but the very government assailed, which alone, in the exercise of self-defence, can legitimately punish attacks directed against its own existence.

ity that his opinion may be false, he ought to be moved by the consideration that, however true it may be, if it is not fully, frequently, and fearlessly discussed, it will be held as a dead dogma, not a living truth.

There is a class of persons (happily not quite so numerous as formerly) who think it enough if a person assents undoubtingly to what they think true, though he has no knowledge whatever of the grounds of the opinion and could not make a tenable defense of it against the most superficial objections. Such persons, if they can once get their creed taught from authority, naturally think that no good, and some harm, comes of its being allowed to be questioned. Where their influence prevails, they make it nearly impossible for the received opinion to be rejected wisely and considerately, though it may still be rejected rashly and ignorantly; for to shut out discussion entirely is seldom possible, and when it once gets in, beliefs not grounded on conviction are apt to give way before the slightest semblance of an argument. Waiving, however, this possibility—assuming that the true opinion abides in the mind, but abides as a prejudice, a belief independent of, and proof against, argument—this is not the way in which truth ought to be held by a rational being. This is not knowing the truth. Truth, thus held, is but one superstition the more, accidentally clinging to the words which enunciate a truth. . . .

This brings him to the concluding portion of Chapter II. Here, after a brief resumé, he moves against those who would permit free discussion on condition that the manner be temperate and not pass the grounds of fair discussion. Mill rejects their proposed qualification. Thus:

We have now recognised the necessity to the mental well-being of mankind (on which all their other well-being depends) of freedom of opinion, and freedom of the expression of opinion, on four distinct grounds; which we will now briefly recapitulate.

First, if any opinion is compelled to silence, that opinion may, for aught we can certainly know, be true. To deny this is to assume our own infallibility.

Secondly, though the silenced opinion be an error, it may, and very commonly does, contain a portion of truth; and since the general or prevailing opinion on any subject is rarely or never the whole truth, it is only by the collision of adverse opinions that the remainder of the truth has any chance of being supplied.

Thirdly, even if the received opinion be not only true, but the whole truth; unless it is suffered to be, and actually is, vigorously and earnestly contested, it will, by most of those who receive it, be held in the manner of a prejudice, with little comprehension or feeling of its rational grounds. And not only this, but, fourthly, the meaning of the doctrine itself will be in danger of being lost, or enfeebled, and deprived of its vital effect on the character and conduct: the dogma becoming a mere formal profession, inefficacious for good, but cumbering the ground, and preventing the growth of any real and heartfelt conviction, from reason or personal experience.

Before quitting the subject of freedom of opinion, it is fit to take some notice of those who say that the free expression of all opinions should be permitted, on condition that the manner be temperate, and do not pass the
bounds of fair discussion. Much might be said on the impossibility of fixing
where these supposed bounds are to be placed; for if the test be offence to
those whose opinions are attacked, I think experience testifies that this offence is given whenever the attack is telling and powerful, and that every
opponent who pushes them hard, and whom they find it difficult to answer,
appears to them, if he shows any strong feeling on the subject, an intemperate opponent.

But this, though an important consideration in a practical point of view,
merges in a more fundamental objection. Undoubtedly the manner of asserting an opinion, even though it be a true one, may be very objectionable, and
may justly incur severe censure. But the principal offences of the kind are
such as it is mostly impossible, unless by accidental self-betrayal, to bring
home to conviction. The gravest of them is, to argue sophistically, to
suppress facts or arguments, to misstate the elements of the case, or misrepresent the opposite opinion. But all this, even to the most aggravated degree,
is so continually done in perfect good faith, by persons who are not considered, and in many other respects may not deserve to be considered, ignorant
or incompetent, that it is rarely possible, on adequate grounds, conscientiously to stamp the misrepresentation as morally culpable; and still less
could law presume to interfere with this kind of controversial misconduct.
With regard to what is commonly meant by intemperate discussion, namely
invective, sarcasm, personality, and the like, the denunciation of these
weapons would deserve more sympathy if it were ever proposed to interdict
them equally to both sides; but it is only desired to restrain the employment
of them against the prevailing opinion: against the unprevailing they may
not only be used without general disapproval, but will be likely to obtain for
him who uses them the praise of honest zeal and righteous indignation. Yet
whatever mischief arises from their use is greatest when they are employed
against the comparatively defenceless; and whatever unfair advantage can
be derived by any opinion from this mode of asserting it, accrues almost exclusively to receive opinions. The worst offence of this kind which can be
committed by a polemic is to stigmatise those who hold the contrary opinion
as bad and immoral men. To calumny of this sort, those who hold any unpopular opinion are peculiarly exposed, because they are in general few and
uninfluential, and nobody but themselves feels much interested in seeing
justice done them; but this weapon is, from the nature of the case, denied to
those who attack a prevailing opinion: they can neither use it with safety to
themselves, nor, if they could, would it do anything but recoil on their own
cause. In general, opinions contrary to those commonly received can only
obtain a hearing by studied moderation of language, and the most cautious
avoidance of unnecessary offence, from which they hardly ever deviate even
in a slight degree without losing ground: while unmeasured vituperation
employed on the side of the prevailing opinion really does deter people
from professing contrary opinions, and from listening to those who profess
them.

For the interest, therefore, of truth and justice, it is far more important to restrain this employment of vituperative language than the other; and, for example, if it were necessary to choose, there would be much more need to discourage offensive attacks on infidelity than on religion. It is, however, obvious that law and authority have no business with restraining either, while opinion ought, in every instance, to determine its verdict by the circumstances of the individual case; condemning every one, on whichever side of the argument he places himself, in whose mode of advocacy either want of candour, or malignity, bigotry, or intolerance of feeling manifest themselves; but not inferring these vices from the side which a person takes, though it be the contrary side of the question to our own; and giving merited honour to every one, whatever opinion he may hold, who has calmness to see and honesty to state what his opponents and their opinions really are, exaggerating nothing to their discredit, keeping nothing back which tells, or can be supposed to tell, in their favour. This is the real morality of public discussion: and if often violated, I am happy to think that there are many controversialists who to a great extent observe it, and a still greater number who conscientiously strive towards it.

The title of Chapter III is "Of Individuality as One of the Elements of Well-being." It is something of a breather between Mill's unqualified defense of the individual's right to think for himself and his qualified defense, in Chapters IV and V, of the individual's right to act for himself without restraints imposed by a society or its government. The argument here is that liberty is a condition for individuality ("being your own man"), and that individuality is a condition for well-being. The chapter is a closely argued exposition and defense of that claim. Only the first three paragraphs are quoted here:

Such being the reasons which make it imperative that human beings should be free to form opinions, and to express their opinions without reserve; and such the baneful consequences to the intellectual, and through that to the moral nature of man, unless this liberty is either conceded, or asserted in spite of prohibition; let us next examine whether the same reasons do not require that men should be free to act upon their opinions—to carry these out in their lives, without hindrance, either physical or moral, from their fellow-men, so long as it is at their own risk and peril.

This last proviso is of course indispensable. No one pretends that actions should be as free as opinions. On the contrary, even opinions lose their immunity when the circumstances in which they are expressed are such as to constitute their expression a positive instigation to some mischievous act. An opinion that corn-dealers are starvers of the poor, or that private property is robbery, ought to be unmolested when simply circulated through the press, but may justly incur punishment when delivered orally to an excited mob assembled before the house of a corn-dealer, or when handed about among the same mob in the form of a placard. Acts, of whatever kind, which, without justifiable cause, do harm to others, may be, and in the more important cases absolutely require to be, controlled by the unfavourable sentiments, and, when needful, by the active interference of mankind. The liberty of the individual must be thus far limited; he must not make himself a nuisance to other people. But if he refrains from molesting others in what concerns them, and merely acts according to his own inclination and judgment in things which concern himself, the same reasons which show that opinion should be free, prove also that he should be allowed, without molestation, to carry his opinions into practice at his own cost. That mankind are not infallible; that their truths, for the most part, are only half-truths; that unity of opinion, unless resulting from the fullest and freest comparison of opposite opinions, is not desirable, and diversity not an evil, but a good, until mankind are much more capable than at present of recognising all sides of the truth, are principles applicable to men's modes of action, not less than to their opinions. As it is useful that while mankind are imperfect there should be different opinions, so it is that there should be different experiments of living; that free scope should be given to varieties of character, short of injury to others; and that the worth of different modes of life should be proved practically, when any one thinks fit to try them. It is desirable, in short, that in things which do not primarily concern others, individuality should assert itself. Where, not the person's own character, but the traditions or customs of other people are the rule of conduct, there is wanting one of the principal ingredients of human happiness, and quite the chief ingredient of individual and social progress.

In maintaining this principle, the greatest difficulty to be encountered does not lie in the appreciation of means towards an acknowledged end, but in the indifference of persons in general to the end itself. If it were felt that the free development of individuality is one of the leading essentials of well-being; that it is not only a co-ordinate element with all that is designated by the terms civilization, instruction, education, culture, but is itself a necessary part and condition of all those things; there would be no danger that liberty should be under-valued, and the adjustment of the boundaries between it and social control would present no extraordinary difficulty. But the evil is, that individual spontaneity is hardly recognized by the common modes of thinking, as having any intrinsic worth, or deserving any regard on its own account. The majority, being satisfied with the ways of mankind as they now are (for it is they who make them what they are), cannot comprehend why those ways should not be good enough for everybody; and what is more, spontaneity forms no part of the ideal of the majority of moral and social reformers, but is rather looked on with jealousy, as a troublesome and perhaps rebellious obstruction to the general acceptance of what these reformers, in their own judgment, think would be best for mankind.

Granted that the thesis of Chapter III does not entitle an individual to an *unqualified* right to act for himself, without coercive intervention from society or its government; there is still the important question of what is the rightful limit of an individual to act for himself. How is this limit to be defined *in principle?* This turns out to be a large and thorny question. Before Mill was willing to stop pulling at it, he had written two substantial concluding chapters. In the first of these, Chapter IV, he develops his question and proposes his answer and reviews a number of illustrations of his claim. Most of the chapter ("Of the limits to the authority of society over the individual") is taken up with closely argued cases. Only the first three paragraphs are quoted here:

What, then, is the rightful limit to the sovereignty of the individual over himself? Where does the authority of society begin? How much of human life should be assigned to individuality, and how much to society?

Each will receive its proper share, if each has that which more particularly concerns it. To individuality should belong the part of life in which it is chiefly the individual that is interested; to society, the part which chiefly interests society.

Though society is not founded on a contract, and though no good purpose is answered by inventing a contract in order to deduce social obligations from it, every one who receives the protection of society owes a return for the benefit, and the fact of living in society renders it indispensable that each should be bound to observe a certain line of conduct towards the rest. This conduct consists, first, in not injuring the interests of one another; or rather certain interests, which, either by express legal provision or by tacit understanding, ought to be considered as rights; and secondly, in each person's bearing his share (to be fixed on some equitable principle) of the labours and sacrifices incurred for defending the society or its members from injury and molestation. These conditions society is justified in enforcing, at all costs to those who endeavour to withhold fulfilment. Nor is this all that society may do. The acts of an individual may be hurtful to others, or wanting in due consideration for their welfare, without going to the length of violating any of their constituted rights. The offender may then be justly punished by opinion, though not by law. As soon as any part of a person's conduct affects prejudicially the interests of others, society has jurisdiction over it, and the question whether the general welfare will or will not be promoted by interfering with it, becomes open to discussion. But there is no room for entertaining any such question when a person's conduct affects the interests of no persons besides himself, or needs not affect them unless they like (all the persons concerned being of full age, and the ordinary amount of understanding). In all such cases, there should be perfect freedom, legal and social, to do the action and stand the consequences.

In a sense, Chapter V, although of good length and careful thought, is little more than an extension of Chapter IV. Taken as a pair, they give you what Mill has to say on the right of the individual to *act* for himself. He had been able to deal with the individual's right to *think* for himself back in Chapter II. There a single chapter had sufficed. Now, in the matter of *acting* for himself, two chapters are needed. The reason is, perhaps, that Mill realized he was going to have to take up a qualified stand here and wanted the principles operative in arriving at this qualification to be argued out carefully and illustrated clearly. Two opening paragraphs are quoted here:

The principles asserted in these pages must be more generally admitted as the basis for discussion of details, before a consistent application of them to all the various departments of government and morals can be attempted with any prospect of advantage. The few observations I propose to make on questions of detail are designed to illustrate the principles, rather than to follow them out to their consequences. I offer, not so much applications, as specimens of application; which may serve to bring into greater clearness the meaning and limits of the two maxims which together form the entire doctrine of this Essay, and to assist the judgment in holding the balance between them, in the cases where it appears doubtful which of them is applicable to the case.

The maxims are, *first*, that the individual is not accountable to society for his actions, in so far as these concern the interests of no person but himself. Advice, instruction, persuasion, and avoidance by other people if thought necessary by them for their own good, are the only measures by which society can justifiably express its dislike or disapprobation of his conduct. *Secondly*, that for such actions as are prejudicial to the interests of others, the individual is accountable, and may be subjected either to social or to legal punishment, if society is of opinion that the one or the other is requisite for its protection. . . .

The remaining five paragraphs are quoted from near the end of Mill's fifth and final chapter. As he says, they introduce something of a new question, or a new qualification of his present question. What about government interference where the liberty principle is not involved?

I have reserved for the last place a large class of questions respecting the limits of government interference, which, though closely connected with the subject of this essay, do not, in strictness, belong to it. These are cases in which the reasons against interference do not turn upon the principle of liberty: the question is not about restraining the actions of individuals, but about helping them; it is asked whether the government should do, or cause to be done, something for their benefit instead of leaving it to be done by themselves, individually or in voluntary combination.

The objections to government interference, when it is not such as to involve infringement of liberty, may be of three kinds:

The first is when the thing to be done is likely to be better done by individuals than by the government. Speaking generally, there is no one so fit to conduct any business, or to determine how or by whom it shall be conducted, as those who are personally interested in it. This principle condemns the interferences, once so common, of the legislature, or the officers of government, with the ordinary process of industry. But this part of the subject has been sufficiently enlarged upon by political economists, and is not particularly related to the principles of this essay.

The second objection is more nearly allied to our subject. In many cases, though individuals may not do the particular thing so well, on the average, as the officers of government, it is nevertheless desirable that it should be done by them, rather than by the government, as a means to their own mental education—a mode of strengthening their active faculties, exercising their judgment, and giving them a familiar knowledge of the subjects with which they are thus left to deal. This is a principal, though not the sole, recommendation of jury trial (in cases not political); of free and popular local and municipal institutions; of the conduct of industrial and philanthropic enterprises by voluntary associations. These are not questions of liberty, and are connected with that subject only by remote tendencies, but they are questions of development. It belongs to a different occasion from the present to dwell on these things as parts of national education, as being, in truth, the peculiar training of a citizen, the practical part of the political education of a free people, taking them out of the narrow circle of personal and family selfishness, and accustoming them to the comprehension of joint interests, the management of joint concerns—habituating them to act from public or semipublic motives, and guide their conduct by aims which unite instead of isolating them from one another. Without these habits and powers, a free constitution can neither be worked nor preserved, as is exemplified by the too-often transitory nature of political freedom in countries where it does not rest upon a sufficient basis of local liberties. The management of purely local business by the localities, and of the great enterprises of industry by the union of those who voluntarily supply the pecuniary means, is further recommended by all the advantages which have been set forth in this essay as belonging to individuality of development and diversity of modes of action. Government operations tend to be everywhere alike. With individuals and voluntary associations, on the contrary, there are varied experiments and endless diversity of experience. What the State can usefully do is to make itself a central depository, and active circulator and diffuser, of the experience resulting from many trials. Its business is to enable each experimentalist to benefit by the experiments of others, instead of tolerating no experiments but its own.

The third and most cogent reason for restricting the interference of government is the great evil of adding unnecessarily to its power. Every function superadded to those already exercised by the government causes its influence over hopes and fears to be more widely diffused, and converts, more and more, the active and ambitious part of the public into hangers-on of the government, or of some party which aims at becoming the government. If the roads, the railways, the banks, the insurance offices, the great joint-stock companies, the universities, and the public charities were all of them branches of the government; if, in addition, the municipal corporations and local boards, with all that now devolves on them, became departments of the central administration; if the employees of all these different enterprises were appointed and paid by the government and looked to the government for every rise in life, not all the freedom of the press and popular constitution of the legislature would make this or any other country free otherwise than in name. And the evil would be greater, the more efficiently and scientifically the administrative machinery was constructed—the more skillful the arrangements for obtaining the best qualified hands and heads with which to work it. In England it has of late been proposed that all the members of the civil service of government should be selected by competitive examination, to obtain for these employments the most intelligent and instructed persons procurable; and much has been said and written for and against this proposal. One of the arguments most insisted on by its opponents is that the occupation of a permanent official servant of the State does not hold out sufficient prospects of emolument and importance to attract the highest talents, which will always be able to find a more inviting career in the professions or in the service of companies and other public bodies. One would not have been surprised if this argument had been used by the friends of the proposition as an answer to its principal difficulty. Coming from the opponents it is strange enough. What is urged as an objection is the safety valve of the proposed system. If, indeed, all the high talent of the country *could* be drawn into the service of the government, a proposal tending to bring about that result might well inspire uneasiness. If every part of the business of society which required organized concert, or large and comprehensive views, were in the hands of the government, and if government offices were universally filled by the ablest men, all the enlarged culture and practiced intelligence in the country, except the purely speculative, would be concentrated in a numerous bureaucracy, to whom alone the rest of the community would look for all things—the multitude for direction and dictation in all they had to do; the able and aspiring for personal advancement. To be admitted into the ranks of this bureaucracy, and when admitted, to rise therein, would be the sole objects of ambition. Under this *régime* not only is the outside public ill-qualified, for want of practical experience, to criticize or check the mode of operation of the bureaucracy, but even if the accidents of despotic or the natural working of popular institutions occasionally raise to the summit a ruler or rulers of reforming inclinations, no reform can be effected which is contrary to the interest of the bureaucracy. Such is the melancholy condition of the Russian empire, as shown in the accounts of those who have had sufficient opportunity of observation. The Czar himself is powerless against the bureaucratic body; he can send any one of them to Siberia, but he cannot govern without them, or against their will.

READING QUESTIONS

Following are some general statements that occur in the selection from Mill. Do they raise any questions for you? Do they move you to make any comment?

1. "The nature and limits of the power which can be legitimately exercised by society over the individual . . . is . . . the vital question of the future."
2. "The limitation of the power of government over individuals loses none of its importance when the holders of power are regularly accountable to the community."
3. "All that makes existence valuable to anyone depends on the enforcements of restraints upon the actions of other people."

4. "Some rules are necessary. What rules, is the principal question in human affairs. Little progress has been made here."

5. "Wherever there is an ascendent class, a large portion of the morality of the country emanates from its class interests."

6. ". . . religious freedom has hardly anywhere been practically realized, except where religious indifference . . . has added its weight. . . ."

7. "The only part of the conduct of anyone, for which he is answerable to society, is that which concerns others."

8. "Despotism is legitimate in dealing with barbarians provided the end be their improvement and the means effective to that end."

9. "I regard utility as the ultimate appeal on all ethical questions."

10. "To make anyone answerable for doing evil to others is the rule; to make him answerable for not preventing evil is . . . the exception."

11. "Mankind are greater gainers by allowing each other to live as seems good to themselves, than by compelling each to live as seems good to the rest."

12. "The only freedom which deserves the name, is that of pursuing our own good in our own way. . . ."

13. ". . . religion [is] the most powerful of the elements which have entered into the formation of moral feeling. . . ."

14. ". . . religion . . . [has] almost always been governed either by the ambition of a hierarchy, seeking control over every department of human conduct, or by the spirit of Puritanism."

15. ". . . the tendency of all the changes taking place in the world is to strengthen society, and diminish the power of the individual. . . ."

16. "The disposition of mankind, whether as rulers or as fellow-citizens, to impose their opinions and inclinations as a rule of conduct upon others, . . . is hardly ever kept under restraint by anything but want of power. . . ."

INDEPENDENT STUDY

1. Henry David Thoreau published his essay "On Civil Disobedience" in 1849, just ten years before Mill's *On Liberty*. George Bernard Shaw published his preface and play "Saint Joan" in 1924, just sixty-five years after Mill's *On Liberty*. Thoreau's essay deals with circumstances in America pressing on him at the time he wrote; Shaw's preface and play deal with circumstances pressing upon Joan of Arc in fifteenth-century France. Write a paper on Thoreau and on Saint Joan that would interest and satisfy Mill.

2. Read the chapter on John Stuart Mill in *Masters of Political Thought,* Volume 3, by L. W. Lancaster. Pay particular attention to the many substantial quotations from Mill's writings. The chapter provides a coverage of Mill going considerably beyond his *On Liberty.* Combine this overview of Mill with any one or two other chapters from the same volume—for example, Chapter 7, on Peter Kropotkin, the Russian anarchist; Chapter 8, on Georges Sorel, the French syndicalist; on Chapter 9, on Sidney and Beatrice Webb, the pioneer thinkers in English Fabian socialism. The point is not to make an overview comparison or contrast between Mill and any of these others, but to figure out what, given their positions, they would, or should, say on the right of the individual to think and act for himself. You can be sure they read Mill's little book. What do you suppose they thought about it?

3. Mill published *On Liberty* in 1859. Ten years later (1869) he published a small sequel, *The Subjection of Women,* in which he defended the right of women to think and act for themselves. Like his 1859 book, it is one of the best of its kind on the issue with which it deals. For a running start read the article "Liberalism" by D. C. Smith in the *International Encyclopedia of the Social Sciences.* Then read Mill on the subjection of woman, bearing in mind his earlier book on liberty.

SECTION 4. H. L. A. HART: OBLIGATION AND LAW

From Mill to Hart. John Stuart Mill published *On Liberty* in 1859. Mill had been a student and in some ways a disciple of John Austin, whose *Province of Jurisprudence Determined,* published in 1832, had greatly influenced Mill's thinking in the matter of the state and law. Austin's *Province* had claimed that a law is a command issued by a *Sovereign* to a *Subject.* The Sovereign has the power to enforce his command upon the Subject, or he is no longer "sovereign" over the "subjects." (The word *subject* is said to be derived from two Latin words *sub* and *jacere,* meaning "to throw under." A subject, in the legal sense, is "thrown under" a sovereign.) A sovereign's will, expressed in a law and enforced by his political power, sets limits to the subject's liberty or freedom. In this way Mill came by his problem: "What *principle* justifies a sovereign in setting limits to a subject's liberty? What *authorizes* (not *enables:* mere power will enable) a sovereign to use *power* upon a subject? When is a subject *obligated* (not *obliged:* mere power could oblige him) to obey a sovereign? Mill had given this question a careful going over in his 1859 book *On Liberty.* H. L. A. Hart's 1961 book returns to the question,

"Is there anything human, higher than power in a sovereign and higher than liberty in a subject, given which a sovereign is not merely able, but justified, entitled, indeed obligated, when imposing limits upon a subject's liberty?" And a subject is *obligated* (not merely obliged) to knuckle under? This is a way of asking whether there is anything, not itself the outcome or product of legislative activity, that justifies the use of force to produce conformity to law? If the answer is "no," then the legislative way of life necessarily involves an element of the arbitrary and tyrannical. If the answer is "yes," then the legislative way of life necessarily involves a principle that is not itself produced by legislative activity, which is "prior to," "higher than," "presupposed by," the legislative way of life. This question has not issued its last invitation, its last challenge, to the conduct of argument.

Mill died in 1873. Twenty-four years later, in 1897, Justice Oliver Wendell Holmes, at that time a member of the Massachusetts Supreme Court, and five years later (1902) a member of the United States Supreme Court, published a widely read and influential paper, "The Path of the Law." In this paper, originally delivered as a lecture at the dedication of a new hall at the Boston University School of Law, he formulated what has since been referred to as the "prediction" theory of law. This is the claim that laws produced by legislators are predictions of what the courts will do. A client consults a lawyer. The lawyer consults the relevant law. He is thereby in a position to predict what the courts will do in his client's case, provided, of course, that the judge follows what the law prescribes. This "prediction" theory of law caught on, as much perhaps as any theory in American jurisprudence in the twentieth century. Professor Hart, whose claim that law, or a legal system, is a union of primary and secondary rules we are to examine in this section, has the prediction theory much in mind, presupposing that his reader is familiar with it. For this reason, and for its own intrinsic interest, Holmes's claim is here quoted and paraphrased in an abridged version:

When we study law we are studying a well-known profession. We are studying what we shall want to know in order to appear before judges, or to advise people in such a way as to keep them out of court. The reason why it is a profession, why people will pay lawyers to argue for them or to advise them, is that in societies like ours the command of the public force is intrusted to the judges in certain cases, and the whole power of the state will be put forth, if necessary, to carry out their judgments and decrees. People want to know under what circumstances and how far they will run the risk of coming against what is so much stronger than themselves, and hence it becomes a business to find out when this danger is to be feared. The object of our study, then, is prediction, the prediction of the incidence of the public force through the instrumentality of the courts.

The means of the study are a body of reports, of treatises, and of statutes, in this country and in England, extending back for six hundred years, and now increasing annually by hundreds. In this are gathered the scattered prophecies of the past upon the cases in which the axe will fall. The most important and pretty nearly the whole meaning of every new effort of legal thought is to make these prophecies more precise, and to generalize them into a thoroughly connected system. The process is one, from a lawyer's statement of a case, eliminating all the dramatic elements with which his client's story has clothed it, and retaining only the facts of legal import. The reason a lawyer does not mention that his client wore a white hat when he made a contract, is that he foresees that the public force will act in the same way whatever his client had upon his head. It is to make the prophecies easier to be remembered and to be understood that the teachings of the decisions of the past are put into general propositions and gathered into textbooks, or that statutes are passed in a general form. The primary rights and duties with which jurisprudence busies itself again are nothing but prophecies. A legal duty so called is nothing but a prediction that if a man does or omits certain things he will be made to suffer in this or that way by judgment of the court—and so of a legal right.

The number of our predictions when generalized and reduced to a system is not unmanageably large. They may be mastered within a reasonable time. It is a great mistake to be frightened by the ever increasing number of reports.

I wish, if I can, to lay down some first principles for the study of this body of systematized prediction which we call the law, for men who want to use it as the instrument of their business to enable them to prophesy in their turn.

The first thing for a businesslike understanding of the matter is to understand its limits, and therefore I think it desirable at once to point out that a bad man has as much reason as a good one for wishing to avoid an encounter with the public force. A man who cares nothing for an ethical rule which is believed and practised by his neighbors is likely nevertheless to care a good deal to avoid being made to pay money, and will want to keep out of jail if he can.

I take it for granted that no hearer of mine will misinterpret what I have to say as the language of cynicism. The law is the witness and external deposit of our moral life. Its history is the history of the moral development of the race. The practice of it, in spite of popular jests, tends to make good citizens and good men. When I emphasize the difference between law and morals I do so with reference to a single end, that of learning and understanding the law. For that purpose you must definitely master its specific marks, and it is for that that I ask you for the moment to imagine yourselves indifferent to other and greater things.

If you want to know the law and nothing else, you must look at it as a bad man, who cares only for the material consequences which such knowledge enables him to predict, not as a good one, who finds his reasons for conduct, whether inside the law or outside of it, in the sanctions of conscience.

What constitutes the law? You will find some text writers telling you that it is something different from what is decided by the courts of Massachusetts or England, that it is a system of reason, that it is a deduction from principles of ethics or admitted axioms or what not, which may or may not coincide with the decisions. But if we take the view of our friend the bad man we shall find that he does not care two straws for the axioms or deductions, but that he does want to know what the Massachusetts or English courts are likely to do in fact. I am much of his mind. The prophecies of what the courts will do in fact, and nothing more pretentious, are what I mean by the law.

Take again a notion which as popularly understood is the widest conception which the law contains—the notion of legal duty. What does it mean to a bad man? Mainly, and in the first place, a prophecy that if he does certain things he will be subjected to disagreeable consequences by way of imprisonment or compulsory payment of money. What significance is there in calling one action right and another wrong from the point of view of the law? It does not matter, so far as the given consequence, the compulsory payment, is concerned, whether the act to which it is attached is described in terms of praise or in terms of blame, or whether the law purports to prohibit it or to allow it. If it matters at all, still speaking from the bad man's point of view, it must be because in one case and not in the other some further disadvantages, or at least some further consequences, are attached to the act by the law. You see how the vague circumference of the notion of duty shrinks and at the same time grows more precise when we wash it with cynical acid and expel everything except the object of our study, the operations of the law.

I trust that no one will understand me to be speaking with disrespect of the law. I venerate the law, and especially our system of law, as one of the vastest products of the human mind. No one knows better than I do the countless number of great intellects that have spent themselves in making some addition or improvement, the greatest of which is trifling when compared with the mighty whole. It has the final title to respect that it exists, that it is not a dream, but a part of the lives of men. But one may criticise even what one reveres. Law is the business to which my life is devoted, and I should show less than devotion if I did not do what in me lies to improve it, and, when I perceive what seems to me the ideal of its future, if I hesitated to point it out and to press toward it with all my heart.

The Argument of the Hart Selection. The following material is taken from the fifth and sixth chapters of H. L. A. Hart's 1961 volume *The Concept of Law.* At that time the author was professor of jurisprudence at Oxford University. His book is one of the most important and clarifying books in jurisprudence published in this country or in England since World War II. It has done much to restore, or to create, an interest in the philosophy of law. In addition to *The Concept of Law,* Professor Hart has also written *Law, Liberty and Morality* (1963) and *Punishment and Responsibility* (1968).

In the following selection the author begins by asking the reader to imagine a small, simple society having no legislature, no courts, no officials. They regulate some human behavior by a few simple rules, spelling out a few simple rights and duties. These Hart refers to as primary rules of obligation. They make up the legal life of the community. He then mentions three conditions that must be present if such a community is to live by such rules alone. He then mentions three defects that can be expected to mark the legal life of a community limited to primary rules of obligation alone. He then claims that these defects may be dealt with by the introduction of three kinds of secondary rules. These matters are covered in the first seven paragraphs. They are an important beginning. The paragraphs are here given numbers to enable them to be referred to in study and discussion. These numbers are not in the original text:

1. It is, of course, possible to imagine a society without a legislature, courts or officials of any kind. Indeed, there are many studies of primitive communities which not only claim that this possibility is realized but depict in detail the life of a society where the only means of social control is that general attitude of the group towards its own standard modes of behaviour in terms of which we have characterized rules of obligation. A social structure of this kind is often referred to as one of "custom"; but we shall not use this term, because it often implies that the customary rules are very old and supported with less social pressure than other rules. To avoid these implications we shall refer to such a social structure as one of primary rules of obligation.

2. If a society is to live by such primary rules alone, there are certain conditions which, granted a few of the most obvious truisms about human nature and the world we live in, must clearly be satisfied. The *first* of these conditions is that the rules must contain in some form restrictions on the free use of violence, theft, and deception to which human beings are tempted but which they must, in general, repress, if they are to coexist in close proximity to each other. Such rules are in fact always found in the primitive societies of which we have knowledge, together with a variety of others imposing on individuals various positive duties to perform services or make contributions to the common life. *Secondly,* though such a society may exhibit tension, between those who accept the rules and those who reject the rules except where fear of social pressure induces them to conform, it is plain that the latter cannot be more than a minority, if so loosely organized a society of persons, approximately equal in physical strength, is to endure: for otherwise those who reject the rules would have too little social pressure to fear. This too is confirmed by what we know of primitive communities where, though there are dissidents and malefactors, the majority live by the rules seen from the internal point of view.

3. More important for our present purpose is the following consideration. It is plain that only a small community closely knit by ties of kinship, common sentiment, and belief, and placed in a stable environment, could live successfully by such a régime of unofficial rules. In any other conditions such a simple form of social control must prove defective and will require supplementation in different ways.

4. In the *first* place, the rules by which the group lives will not form a system, but will simply be a set of separate standards, without any identifying or common mark, except of course that they are the rules which a particular

group of human beings accepts. They will in this respect resemble our own rules of etiquette. Hence if doubts arise as to what the rules are or as to the precise scope of some given rule, there will be no procedure for settling this doubt, either by reference to an authoritative text or to an official whose declarations on this point are authoritative. For, plainly, such a procedure and the acknowledgement of either authoritative text or persons involve the existence of rules of a type different from the rules of obligation or duty which *ex hypothesi* are all that the group has. This defect in the simple social structure of primary rules we may call its *uncertainty*.

5. A *second* defect is the *static* character of the rules. The only mode of change in the rules known to such a society will be the slow process of growth, whereby courses of conduct once thought optional become first habitual or usual, and then obligatory, and the converse process of decay, when deviations, once severely dealt with, are first tolerated and then pass unnoticed. There will be no means, in such a society, of deliberately adapting the rules to changing circumstances, either by eliminating old rules or introducing new ones: for, again, the possibility of doing this presupposes the existence of rules of a different type from the primary rules of obligation by which alone the society lives. In an extreme case the rules may be static in a more drastic sense. This, though never perhaps fully realized in any actual community, is worth considering because the remedy for it is something very characteristic of law. In this extreme case, not only would there be no way of deliberately changing the general rules, but the obligations which arise under the rules in particular cases could not be varied or modified by the deliberate choice of any individual. Each individual would simply have fixed obligations or duties to do or abstain from doing certain things. It might indeed very often be the case that others would benefit from the performance of these obligations; yet if there are only primary rules of obligation they would have no power to release those bound from performance or to transfer to others the benefits which would accrue from performance. For such operations of release or transfer create changes in the initial positions of individuals under the primary rules of obligation, and for these operations to be possible there must be rules of a sort different from the primary rules.

6. The *third* defect of this simple form of social life is the *inefficiency* of the diffuse social pressure by which the rules are maintained. Disputes as to whether an admitted rule has or has not been violated will always occur and will, in any but the smallest societies, continue interminably, if there is no agency specially empowered to ascertain finally, and authoritatively, the fact of violation. Lack of such final and authoritative determinations is to be distinguished from another weakness associated with it. This is the fact that punishments for violations of the rules, and other forms of social pressure involving physical effort or the use of force, are not administered by a special agency but are left to the individuals affected or to the group at large. It is obvious that the waste of time involved in the group's unorganized efforts to catch and punish offenders, and the smouldering vendettas which may result from self help in the absence of an official monopoly of "sanctions," may be serious. The history of law does, however, strongly suggest that the lack of official agencies to determine authoritatively the fact of violation of the rules

is a much more serious defect; for many societies have remedies for this defect long before the other.

7. The remedy for each of these three main defects in this simplest form of social structure consists in supplementing the *primary* rules of obligation with *secondary* rules which are rules of a different kind. The introduction of the remedy for each defect might, in itself, be considered a step from the pre-legal into the legal world; since each remedy brings with it many elements that permeate law: certainly all three remedies together are enough to convert the régime of primary rules into what is indisputably a legal system. We shall consider in turn each of these remedies and show why law may most illuminatingly be characterized as a union of primary rules of obligation with such secondary rules. Before we do this, however, the following general points should be noted. Though the remedies consist in the introduction of rules which are certainly different from each other, as well as from the primary rules of obligation which they supplement, they have important features in common and are connected in various ways. Thus they may all be said to be on a different level from the primary rules, for they are all *about* such rules; in the sense that while primary rules are concerned with the actions that individuals must or must not do, these secondary rules are all concerned with the primary rules themselves. They specify the ways in which the primary rules may be [1] conclusively ascertained, [2] introduced, eliminated, varied, and [3] the fact of their violation conclusively determined.

The three defects that mark a legal system having only primary rules of obligation are that it will be uncertain, static, and inefficient. The first of these defects, uncertainty, can be remedied by the introduction of what Hart calls a *rule of recognition*. This is the first of three classes of secondary rules. When all three classes of secondary rules have been introduced, the community's legal system will be a union of primary rules of obligation and secondary rules of recognition, change, and adjudication. As for the first defect:

The simplest form of remedy for the *uncertainty* of the régime of primary rules is the introduction of what we shall call a "rule of recognition." This will specify some feature or features possession of which by a suggested rule is taken as a conclusive affirmative indication that it is a rule of the group to be supported by the social pressure it exerts. The existence of such a rule of recognition may take any of a huge variety of forms, simple or complex. It may, as in the early law of many societies, be no more than that an authoritative list or text of the rules is to be found in a written document or carved on some public monument. No doubt as a matter of history this step from the pre-legal to the legal may be accomplished in distinguishable stages, of which the first is the mere reduction to writing of hitherto unwritten rules. This is not itself the crucial step, though it is a very important one: what is crucial is the acknowledgement of reference to the writing or inscription as *authoritative,* i.e. as the *proper* way of disposing of doubts as to the existence of the rule. Where there is such an acknowledgement there is a very simple form of secondary rule: a rule for conclusive identification of the primary rules of obligation.

In a developed legal system the rules of recognition are of course more complex; instead of identifying rules exclusively by reference to a text or list they do so by reference to some general characteristic possessed by the primary rules. This may be the fact of their having been enacted by a specific body, or their long customary practice, or their relation to judicial decisions. Moreover, where more than one of such general characteristics are treated as identifying criteria, provision may be made for their possible conflict by their arrangement in an order of superiority, as by the common subordination of custom or precedent to statute, the latter being a "superior source" of law. Such complexity may make the rules of recognition in a modern legal system seem very different from the simple acceptance of an authoritative text: yet even in this simplest form, such a rule brings with it many elements distinctive of law. By providing an authoritative mark it introduces, although in embryonic form, the idea of a legal system: for the rules are now not just a discrete unconnected set but are, in a simple way, unified. Further, in the simple operation of identifying a given rule as possessing the required feature of being an item on an authoritative list of rules we have the germ of the idea of legal validity.

The second defect, its static character, calls for the introduction of secondary rules of change. These rules of change will regularize the introduction of new primary rules of obligation, and the elimination of old rules:

The remedy for the *static* quality of the régime of primary rules consists in the introduction of what we shall call "rules of change." The simplest form of such a rule is that which empowers an individual or body of persons to introduce new primary rules for the conduct of the life of the group, or of some class within it, and to eliminate old rules. It is in terms of such a rule, and not in terms of orders backed by threats, that the ideas of legislative enactment and repeal are to be understood. Such rules of change may be very simple or very complex: the powers conferred may be unrestricted or limited in various ways: and the rules may, besides specifying the persons who are to legislate, define in more or less rigid terms the procedure to be followed in legislation. Plainly, there will be a very close connexion between the rules of change and the rules of recognition: for where the former exists the latter will necessarily incorporate a reference to legislation as an identifying feature of the rules, though it need not refer to all the details of procedure involved in legislation. Usually some official certificate or official copy will, under the rules of recognition, be taken as a sufficient proof of due enactment. Of course if there is a social structure so simple that the only "source of law" is legislation, the rule of recognition will simply specify enactment as the unique identifying mark or criterion of validity of the rules.

The third defect, inefficiency of operation, calls for the introduction of secondary *rules of adjudication*. A subclass of this third class, or an independent fourth class, might be called rules of punishment. By whatever name, they have to do with the appointment of judges and the fixing of guilt and penalties:

The third supplement to the simple régime of primary rules, intended to remedy the *inefficiency* of its diffused social pressure, consists of secondary rules empowering individuals to make authoritative determinations of the question whether, on a particular occasion, a primary rule has been broken. The minimal form of adjudication consists in such determinations, and we shall call the secondary rules which confer the power to make them "rules of adjudication." Besides identifying the individuals who are to adjudicate, such rules will also define the procedure to be followed. Like the other secondary rules these are on a different level from the primary rules: though they may be reinforced by further rules imposing duties on judges to adjudicate, they do not impose duties but confer judicial powers and a special status on judicial declarations about the breach of obligations. Again these rules, like the other secondary rules, define a group of important legal concepts: in this case the concepts of judge or court, jurisdiction and judgment. Besides these resemblances to the other secondary rules, rules of adjudication have intimate connexions with them. Indeed, a system which has rules of adjudication is necessarily also committed to a rule of recognition of an elementary and imperfect sort. This is so because, if courts are empowered to make authoritative determinations of the fact that a rule has been broken, these cannot avoid being taken as authoritative determinations of what the rules are. So the rule which confers jurisdiction will also be a rule of recognition, identifying the primary rules through the judgments of the courts and these judgments will become a "source" of law. It is true that this form of rule of recognition, inseparable from the minimum form of jurisdiction, will be very imperfect. Unlike an authoritative text or a statute book, judgments may not be couched in general terms and their use as authoritative guides to the rules depends on a somewhat shaky inference from particular decisions, and the reliability of this must fluctuate both with the skill of the interpreter and the consistency of the judges.

It need hardly be said that in few legal systems are judicial powers confined to authoritative determinations of the fact of violation of the primary rules. Most systems have, after some delay, seen the advantages of further centralization of social pressure; and have partially prohibited the use of physical punishments or violent self help by private individuals. Instead they have supplemented the primary rules of obligation by further secondary rules, specifying or at least limiting the penalties for violation, and have conferred upon judges, where they have ascertained the fact of violation, the exclusive power to direct the application of penalties by other officials. These secondary rules provide the centralized official "sanctions" of the system.

Professor Hart now has some conceptual "machinery" before his reader. There is more to come, but it derives from questions you can ask given his basic distinction between primary rules of obligation and secondary rules of recognition, change, and adjudication.

If we stand back and consider the structure which has resulted from the combination of primary rules of obligation with the secondary rules of recognition, change and adjudication, it is plain that we have here not only the heart of a legal system, but a most powerful tool for the analysis of much that has puzzled both the jurist and the political theorist.

Not only are the specifically legal concepts with which the lawyer is professionally concerned, such as those of obligation and rights, validity and source of law, legislation and jurisdiction, and sanction, best elucidated in terms of this combination of elements. The concepts (which bestride both law and political theory) of the state, of authority, and of an official require a similar analysis if the obscurity which still lingers about them is to be dissipated. The reason why an analysis in these terms of primary and secondary rules has this explanatory power is not far to seek. Most of the obscurities and distortions surrounding legal and political concepts arise from the fact that these essentially involve reference to what we have called the internal point of view: the view of those who do not merely record and predict behaviour conforming to rules, but *use* the rules as standards for the appraisal of their own and others' behaviour. This requires more detailed attention in the analysis of legal and political concepts than it has usually received. Under the simple régime of primary rules the internal point of view is manifested in its simplest form, in the use of those rules as the basis of criticism, and as the justification of demands for conformity, social pressure, and punishment. Reference to this most elementary manifestation of the internal point of view is required for the analysis of the basic concepts of obligation and duty. With the addition to the system of secondary rules, the range of what is said and done from the internal point of view is much extended and diversified. With this extension comes a whole set of new concepts and they demand a reference to the internal point of view for their analysis. These include the notions of legislation, jurisdiction, validity and, generally, of legal powers, private and public. There is a constant pull towards an analysis of these in the terms of ordinary or "scientific," fact-stating or predictive discourse. But this can only reproduce their external aspect: to do justice to their distinctive, internal aspect we need to see the different ways in which the law-making operations of the legislator, the adjudication of a court, the exercise of private or official powers, and other "acts-in-the-law" are related to secondary rules. We shall conclude this chapter with a warning: though the combination of primary and secondary rules merits, because it explains many aspects of law, the central place assigned to it, this cannot by itself illuminate every problem. The union of primary and secondary rules is at the centre of a legal system; but it is not the whole, and as we move away from the centre we shall have to accommodate, in ways indicated in later chapters, elements of a different character.

From here to the end of our selection Hart is raising questions and making claims that refer to his basic concept of law, or legal system, as a union or combination of primary rules of obligation and secondary rules of recognition, change, and adjudication. Indeed, this occupies him through the balance of his book. This section does not follow him beyond his fifth and sixth chapters. His seventh, eighth, ninth, and tenth chapters examine and elaborate his fundamental conception in ways, and to an extent, that is impressive indeed.

The first of these points that are consequent upon the basic conception is his distinction between an *internal* point of view and an *external* point of view that a person may take up toward the primary and secondary rules of a given legal system in a given community. He may accept them as applying to him, as binding on him, as relevant in the justification and criticism of his own behavior. Much of this is expressed in his acknowledging himself as a *member* of the community in question. A person who "relates" to "his" community in this way illustrates what Hart means by the *internal* point of view. Where there is commitment to the rule, or rules, of recognition, and acceptance of the rules of obligation thereby enacted, there Hart's "internal" point of view is present. By contrast, the view of a tourist, a visiting official, a visiting anthropologist, is external. They are "external" to a situation within which rights and duties confront a "member," a person whose view is "internal." This is one of Hart's basic distinctions. His claim would be that it is essential to spelling out the meaning of the legislative way of life. The external point of view marks the *alien*, the person who is *other* than a member. Given a group of persons all of whom took an external view of the primary and secondary rules, you would not have a legal community. It is a distinction that applies to persons in respect to community. It does not apply to the planets in relation to each other and to the sun. The solar system is, in one sense of the word *law*, a lawful system, but it is not a community living under a legal system. Neither the sun nor its planets takes either an internal or an external point of view toward the laws that "regulate" their planetary behavior.

In the day-to-day life of a legal system its rule of recognition is very seldom expressly formulated as a rule; though occasionally, courts in England may announce in general terms the relative place of one criterion of law in relation to another, as when they assert the supremacy of Acts of Parliament over other sources or suggested sources of law. For the most part the rule of recognition is not stated, but its existence is *shown* in the way in which particular rules are identified, either by courts or other officials or private persons or their advisers. There is, of course, a difference in the use made by courts of the criteria provided by the rule and the use of them by others: for when courts reach a particular conclusion on the footing that a particular rule has been correctly identified as law, what they say has a special authoritative status conferred on it by other rules. In this respect, as in many others, the rule of recognition of a legal system is like the scoring rule of a game. In the course of the game the general rule defining the activities which constitute scoring (runs, goals, &c.) is seldom formulated; instead it is *used* by officials and players in identifying the particular phases which count towards winning. Here too, the declarations of officials (umpire or scorer) have a special authoritative status attributed to them by other rules. Further, in both cases there is the possibility of a conflict between these authoritative applications of the rule and the general understanding of what the rule plainly requires according to its terms. This, as we shall see later, is a complication which must be catered for in any account of what it is for a system of rules of this sort to exist.

The use of unstated rules of recognition, by courts and others, in identifying particular rules of the system is characteristic of the internal point of view. Those who use them in this way thereby manifest their own acceptance of them as guiding rules and with this attitude there goes a characteristic vocabulary different from the natural expressions of the external point of view. Perhaps the simplest of these is the expression, "It is the law that . . . ," which we may find on the lips not only of judges, but of ordinary men living under a legal system, when they identify a given rule of the system. This, like the expression "Out" or "Goal," is the language of one assessing a situation by reference to rules which he in common with others acknowledges as appropriate for this purpose. This attitude of shared acceptance of rules is to be contrasted with that of an observer who records *ab extra* the fact that a social group accepts such rules but does not himself accept them. The natural expression of this external point of view is not "It is the law that . . ." but "In England they recognize as law . . . whatever the Queen in Parliament enacts. . . ." The first of these forms of expression we shall call an *internal statement* because it manifests the internal point of view and is naturally used by one who, accepting the rule of recognition and without stating the fact that it is accepted, applies the rule in recognizing some particular rule of the system as valid. The second form of expression we shall call an *external statement* because it is the natural language of an external observer of the system who, without himself accepting its rule of recognition, states the fact that others accept it.

A second point, consequent upon the distinction between internal and external view, is Hart's distinction between *validity* and *efficacy* as essential features of laws produced by legislators but not of laws produced by scientists. A law is *valid* if it passes all the tests provided by the rule of recognition, whereas it is efficacious if it is obeyed more often than not. Thus:

If this use of an accepted rule of recognition in making internal statements is understood and carefully distinguished from an external statement of fact that the rule is accepted, many obscurities concerning the notion of legal "validity" disappear. For the word "valid" is most frequently, though not always, used, in just such internal statements, applying to a particular rule of a legal system, an unstated but accepted rule of recognition. To say that a given rule is valid is to recognize it as passing all the tests provided by the rule of recognition and so as a rule of the system. We can indeed simply say that the statement that a particular rule is valid means that it satisfies all the criteria provided by the rule of recognition. This is incorrect only to the extent that it might obscure the internal character of such statements; for, like the cricketers' "Out," these statements of validity normally apply to a particular case a rule of recognition accepted by the speaker and others, rather than expressly state that the rule is satisfied.

Some of the puzzles connected with the idea of legal validity are said to concern the relation between the validity and the "efficacy" of law. If by "efficacy" is meant that the fact that a rule of law which requires certain behaviour is obeyed more often than not, it is plain that there is no necessary connexion between the validity of any particular rule and *its* efficacy, unless the rule of recognition of the system includes among its criteria, as some do, the provision (sometimes referred to as a rule of obsolescence) that no rule is to count as a rule of the system if it has long ceased to be efficacious.

Validity and efficacy are distinct though related notions. That a law is valid is no guarantee that it will be efficacious. That it is inefficacious is no proof that it is invalid. These and more here:

From the inefficacy of a particular rule, which may or may not count against its validity, we must distinguish a general disregard of the rules of the system. This may be so complete in character and so protracted that we should say, in the case of a new system, that it had never established itself as the legal system of a given group, or, in the case of a once-established system, that it had ceased to be the legal system of the group. In either case, the normal context or background for making any internal statement in terms of the rules of the system is absent. In such cases it would be generally *pointless* either to assess the rights and duties of particular persons by reference to the primary rules of a system or to assess the validity of any of its rules by reference to its rules of recognition. To insist on applying a system of rules which had either never actually been effective or had been discarded would, except in special circumstances mentioned below, be as futile as to assess the progress of a game by reference to a scoring rule which had never been accepted or had been discarded.

One who makes an internal statement concerning the validity of a particular rule of a system may be said to *presuppose* the truth of the external statement of fact that the system is generally efficacious. For the normal use of internal statements is in such a context of general efficacy. It would however be wrong to say that statements of validity "mean" that the system is generally efficacious. For though it is normally pointless or idle to talk of the validity of a rule of a system which has never established itself or has been discarded, none the less it is not meaningless nor is it always pointless. One vivid way of teaching Roman Law is to speak *as if* the system were efficacious still and to discuss the validity of particular rules and solve problems in their terms; and one way of nursing hopes for the restoration of an old social order destroyed by revolution, and rejecting the new, is to cling to the criteria of legal validity of the old régime. This is implicitly done by the White Russian who still claims property under some rule of descent which was a valid rule of Tsarist Russia.

A third point, consequent upon the distinction between validity and efficacy, is Hart's formulation and criticism of the prediction theory. His claim is that this celebrated theory derives whatever plausibility it possesses, largely because its proponents fudge the distinctions laid down thus far:

A grasp of the normal contextual connexion between the internal statement that a given rule of a system is valid and the external statement of fact that the system is generally efficacious, will help us see in its proper perspective the common theory that to assert the validity of a rule is to predict that it will be enforced by courts or some other official action taken. In many ways this theory is similar to the predictive analysis of obligation which we considered and rejected in the last chapter. In both cases alike the motive for advancing this predictive theory is the conviction that only thus can metaphysical interpretations be avoided: that either a statement that a rule is valid must ascribe some mysterious property which cannot be detected by empirical means or it must be a prediction of future behaviour of officials. In both cases also the plausibility of the theory is due to the same important fact: that the truth of the external statement of fact, which an observer might record, that the system is generally efficacious and likely to continue so, is normally presupposed by anyone who accepts the rules and makes an internal statement of obligation or validity. The two are certainly very closely associated. Finally, in both cases alike the mistake of the theory is the same: it consists in neglecting the special character of the internal statement and treating it as an external statement about official action.

This mistake becomes immediately apparent when we consider how the judge's own statement that a particular rule is valid functions in judicial decision; for, though here too, in making such a statement, the judge presupposes but does not state the general efficacy of the system, he plainly is not concerned to predict his own or others' official action. His statement that a rule is valid is an internal statement recognizing that the rule satisfies the tests for identifying what is to count as law in his court, and constitutes not a prophecy of but part of the *reason* for his decision. There is indeed a more plausible case for saying that a statement that a rule is valid in a prediction when such a statement is made by a private person; for in the case of conflict between unofficial statements of validity or invalidity and that of a court in deciding a case, there is often good sense in saying that the former must then be withdrawn.

A fourth point has to do with an essential feature of the rule of recognition deriving from its unique position among the class of secondary rules: it is an *ultimate* rule, and where it supplies two or more criteria ranked hierarchically, one of these criteria is *supreme*. So the question arises, "What is the distinction between, and the relation between, *supremacy* considered as a mark of criteria of recognition, and *ultimacy* considered as a mark of the rule of recognition?" Professor Hart deals with the question of *supremacy* first, disposing of it relatively briefly. Thus:

The rule of recognition providing the criteria by which the validity of other rules of the system is assessed is in an important sense, which we shall try to clarify, an *ultimate* rule: and where, as is usual, there are several criteria ranked in order of relative subordination and primacy one of them is *supreme*. These ideas of the ultimacy of the rule of recognition and the supremacy of one of its criteria merit some attention. It is important to disentangle them from the theory, which we have rejected, that somewhere in every legal system, even though it lurks behind legal forms, there must be a sovereign legislative power which is legally unlimited.

Of these two ideas, supreme criterion and ultimate rule, the first is the easiest to define. We may say that a criterion of legal validity or source of law is supreme if rules identified by reference to it are still recognized as rules of the system, even if they conflict with rules identified by reference to the other criteria, whereas rules identified by reference to the latter are not so recognized if they conflict with the rules identified by reference to the supreme criterion. A similar explanation in comparative terms can be given of the notions of "superior" and "subordinate" criteria which we have already used. It is plain that the notions of a superior and a supreme criterion merely refer to a *relative* place on a scale and do not import any notion of legally *unlimited* legislative power. Yet "supreme" and "unlimited" are easy to confuse—at least in legal theory. One reason for this is that in the simpler forms of legal system the ideas of ultimate rule of recognition, supreme criterion, and legally unlimited legislature seem to converge. For where there is a legislature subject to no constitutional limitations and competent by its enactment to deprive all other rules of law emanating from other sources of their status as law, it is part of the rule of recognition in such a system that enactment by that legislature is the supreme criterion of validity. This is, according to constitutional theory, the position in the United Kingdom. But even systems like that of the United States in which there is no such legally unlimited legislature may perfectly well contain an ultimate rule of recognition which provides a set of criteria of validity, one of which is supreme. This will be so, where the legislative competence of the ordinary legislature is limited by a constitution which contains no amending power, or places some clauses outside the scope of that power. Here there is no legally unlimited legislature, even in the widest interpretation of "legislature"; but the system of course contains an ultimate rule of recognition and, in the clauses of its constitution, a supreme criterion of validity.

In a given legal system the rule of recognition sets forth the criteria, possessing which a given rule of law is recognized as valid. It does this for primary rules of obligation and for the other secondary rules of change and adjudication. In a manner of speaking, it "goes bail" for them. Professor Hart's main point is that there is not *another* rule of recognition, which "goes bail" for *it*. It is end-of-the-rope, or, to use his word, *ultimate*. Thus:

The sense in which the rule of recognition is the *ultimate* rule of a system is best understood if we pursue a very familiar chain of legal reasoning.

If the question is raised whether some suggested rule is legally valid, we must, in order to answer the question, use a criterion of validity provided by some other rule. Is this purported by-law of the Oxfordshire County Council valid? Yes: because it was made in exercise of the powers conferred, and in accordance with the procedure specified, by a statutory order made by the Minister of Health. At this first stage the statutory order provides the criteria in terms of which the validity of the by-law is assessed. There may be no practical need to go farther; but there is a standing possibility of doing so. We may query the validity of the statutory order and assess its validity in terms of the statute empowering the minister to make such orders. Finally when the validity of the statute has been queried and assessed by reference to the rule that what the Queen in Parliament enacts is law, we are brought to a stop in inquiries concerning validity: for we have reached a rule which, like the intermediate statutory order and statute, provides criteria for the assessment of the validity of other rules; but it is also unlike them in that there is no rule providing criteria for the assessment of its own legal validity.

There are, indeed, many questions which we can raise about this ultimate rule. We can ask whether it is the practice of courts, legislatures, officials, or private citizens in England actually to use this rule as an ultimate rule of recognition. Or has our process of legal reasoning been an idle game with the criteria of validity of a system now discarded? We can ask whether it is a satisfactory form of legal system which has such a rule at its root. Does it produce more good than evil? Are there prudential reasons for supporting it? Is there a moral obligation to do so? These are plainly very important questions; but, equally plainly, when we ask about the rule of recognition, we are no longer attempting to answer the same kind of question about it as those which we answered about other rules with its aid. When we move from saying that a particular enactment is valid, because it satisfies the rule that what the Queen in Parliament enacts is law, to saying that in England this last rule is used by courts, officials, and private persons as the ultimate rule of recognition, we have moved from an internal statement of law asserting the validity of a rule of the system to an external statement of fact which an observer of the system might make even if he did not accept it. So too when we move from the statement that a particular enactment is valid, to the statement that the rule of recognition of the system is an excellent one and the system based on it is one worthy of support, we have moved from a statement of legal validity to a statement of value.

From here to the end of our selection Professor Hart works at clarifying the notion of *ultimate* as applied to his Rule of Recognition, and fending off any alternative interpretation of this notion. Throughout he wants to make two connected claims: first, the rule of recognition is the "source" from which all *other* rules get their validity; second, there is no *more ultimate* rule from which the rule of recognition gets *its* validity. You must therefore say of it—what you would not say of any *other* legal rule—that it is valid in itself, that it is the source of its own validity, that it is self-validating, or that, in the case of the rule of recognition, the question of validity versus invalidity does not arise. This is a unique and important sort of status. He wants it reserved for the rule of recognition and he wants no deflationary claims made about this mode of uniqueness and importance. His comparison of the status of the rule of recognition in a legal system to the status of the standard meter bar in a metric system helps to make his point: the validity of any measuring device is established by checking it against the *standard* meter bar; but there is no *further,* or *more* standard bar against which you check the *standard* bar. It *is* the standard. There is no future in calling the standard itself into question. If you could do *that,* then your original standard is no longer the standard. This is an excellent point on which to end the Hart section of this book.

Some writers, who have emphasized the legal ultimacy of the rule of recognition, have expressed this by saying that, whereas the legal validity of other rules of the system can be demonstrated by reference to it, its own validity can not be demonstrated but is "assumed" or "postulated" or is a "hypothesis." This may, however, be seriously misleading. Statements of legal validity made about particular rules in the day-to-day life of a legal system whether by judges, lawyers, or ordinary citizens do indeed carry with them certain presuppositions. They are internal statements of law expressing the point of view of those who accept the rule of recognition of the system and, as such, leave unstated much that could be stated in external statements of fact about the system. What is thus left unstated forms the normal background or context of statements of legal validity and is thus said to be "presupposed" by them. But it is important to see precisely what these presupposed matters are, and not to obscure their character. They consist of two things. First, a person who seriously asserts the validity of some given rule of law, say a particular statute, himself makes use of a rule of recognition which he accepts as appropriate for identifying the law. Secondly, it is the case that this rule of recognition, in terms of which he assesses the validity of a particular statute, is not only accepted by him but is the rule of recognition actually accepted and employed in the general operation of the system. If the truth of this presupposition were doubted, it could be established by reference to actual practice: to the way in which courts identify what is to count as law, and to the general acceptance of or acquiescence in these identifications.

Neither of these two presuppositions are well described as "assumptions" of a "validity" which cannot be demonstrated. We only need the word "validity," and commonly only use it, to answer questions which are *within* a system of rules where the status of a rule as a member of the system depends on its satisfying certain criteria provided by the rule of recognition. No such question can arise as to the validity of the very rule of recognition which provides the criteria; it can neither be valid nor invalid but is simply accepted as appropriate for use in this way. To express this simple fact by saying darkly that its validity is "assumed but cannot be demonstrated," is like saying that we assume, but can never demonstrate, that the standard metre bar in Paris which is the ultimate test of the correctness of all measurement in metres, is itself correct.

A more serious objection is that talk of the "assumption" that the ultimate rule of recognition is valid conceals the essentially factual character of the second presupposition which lies behind the lawyers' statements of validity. No doubt the practice of judges, officials, and others, in which the actual existence of a rule of recognition consists, is a complex matter. As we shall see later, there are certainly situations in which questions as to the precise content and scope of this kind of rule, and even as to its existence, may not admit of a clear or determinate answer. None the less it is important to distinguish "assuming the validity" from "presupposing the existence" of such a rule; if only because failure to do this obscures what is meant by the assertion that such a rule *exists*.

In the simple system of primary rules of obligation sketched in the last chapter, the assertion that a given rule existed could only be an external statement of fact such as an observer who did not accept the rules might make and verify by ascertaining whether or not, as a matter of fact, a given mode of behaviour was generally accepted as a standard and was accompanied by those features which, as we have seen, distinguish a social rule from mere convergent habits. It is in this way also that we should now interpret and verify the assertion that in England a rule—though not a legal one—exists that we must bare the head on entering a church. If such rules as these are found to exist in the actual practice of a social group, there is no separate question of their validity to be discussed, though of course their value or desirability is open to question. Once their existence has been established as a fact we should only confuse matters by affirming or denying that they were valid or by saying that "we assumed" but could not show their validity. Where, on the other hand, as in a mature legal system, we have a system of rules which includes a rule of recognition so that the status of a rule as a member of the system now depends on whether it satisfies certain criteria provided by the rule of recognition, this brings with it a new application of the word "exist." The statement that a rule exists may now no longer be what it was in the simple case of customary rules—an external statement of the *fact* that a certain mode of behaviour was generally accepted as a standard in practice. It may now be an internal statement applying an accepted but unstated rule of recognition and meaning (roughly) no more than "valid given the system's criteria of validity." In this respect, however, as in others a rule of recognition is unlike other rules of the system. The assertion that it exists can only be an external statement of fact. For whereas a subordinate rule of a system may be valid and in that sense "exist" even if it is generally disregarded, the rule of recognition exists only as a complex, but normally concordant, practice of the courts, officials, and private persons in identifying the law by reference to certain criteria. Its existence is a matter of fact.

READING QUESTIONS

The selection you have just read is almost the whole of Chapter 5 of
Hart's *The Concept of Law*. That chapter is center of gravity for the
book. After an introductory chapter, he used Chapters 2, 3, and 4 to
criticize the theory, set forth in John Austin's important and influential treatise *The Province of Jurisprudence Determined,* published in
1832, the year of the famous first reform act in British political and
constitutional history. As Hart reads Austin and the Austinians, their
essential claim had been that a law, in the sense of what a legislator
produces, is *an order backed by threats.* Since a gunman issues an
order backed by threats to his victim, Hart sometimes refers to the
essential claim of the Austin jurisprudence as "the gunman theory."
This theory he had subjected to criticism in Chapters 2, 3, and 4 of
his book. Now, in Chapter 5, he advances his own claim that a legal
system, or the laws that comprise it, is a union of primary and secondary rules, in which primary rules declare obligations and secondary
rules declare conditions under which primary rules can be identified, changed, and adjudicated. Hence the basic question, "What is
an obligation, or an obligation rule?"
1. What is the prediction theory of obligation rules? Why some persons find it attractive. Any one of Hart's criticisms of it. How it is
   related to Hart's distinction between internal and external points
   of view.
2. (a) Three conditions necessary if a society is to live by rules of
   obligation alone. (b) Three defects that would mark such a society. (c) The defects are remedied by the introduction of "secondary" rules. (d) Why "secondary"? His names for each secondary
   rule. (e) Which defect each secondary rule deals with. (f) Which is
   the most important secondary rule? Why? (g) Relate "secondary
   rules" to "power-conferring rules."
3. Where Austin claimed to have found "the key to the science of jurisprudence." Where, by contrast, Hart claims to have found it.
   Give your reason (or reasons) for siding with Austin or Hart. If
   with neither, then make clear where *you* find said "key."

INDEPENDENT STUDY

1. Read Chapters 2 and 3 in Hart's book *The Concept of Law*. Write
   a paper making clear the "monistic" position he is criticizing, e.g.,
   Austin's or Holmes's. Set out the essential criticisms contained in

these two chapters. Which criticism or criticisms do you consider most incisive? Why so?

2. Chapter 4 of Hart's book draws a bow on the claim that a law, in the sense of what a legislator or legislature produces, expresses a command issued by a Sovereign Power to a Subject People. Why must Hart discredit this position? How does he try to do so? Which of his objections do you find most incisive? Why so?

3. As you know, the central claim of Hart's jurisprudence is set forth in Chapter 5 of his book *The Concept of Law*. That claim is elaborated in Chapter 6. What is added? It is defended against criticisms and misunderstandings in Chapters 8 and 9. Write a paper making clear what these two chapters (8 and 9) deal with, why they must try to do so, and whether, in your judgment, they succeed.

4. Compare and contrast the positions in jurisprudence set forth in Hans Kelsen's *General Theory of Law and the State* and Hart's *Concept of Law*. A beginning can be made here by reading the selection from Kelsen's book contained in *The Nature of Law*, a volume of readings in legal philosophy edited by M. P. Golding.

5. Base a paper on selected essays in Hart's two paperbacks *Law, Liberty and Morality* and *Punishment and Responsibility*.

SECTION 5. MARTIN LUTHER KING: CIVIL DISOBEDIENCE

From Hart to King. Our last author is Martin Luther King, whose *Letter from Birmingham Jail* was written and published in 1963. Mr. King's *Letter* should be read with Hart and Mill and Marx and Rousseau in mind: Rousseau in 1762, Marx in 1848, Mill in 1859, and Hart in 1961. Mr. King's *Letter* was written in response to a public statement directed to him by eight Alabama clergymen, April 12, 1963. That statement reads as follows:

We clergymen are among those who, in January, issued "An Appeal for Law and Order and Common Sense," in dealing with racial problems in Alabama. We expressed understanding that honest convictions in racial matters could properly be pursued in the courts, but urged that decisions of those courts should in the meantime be peacefully obeyed.

Since that time there has been some evidence of increased forbearance and a willingness to face facts. Responsible citizens have undertaken to work on various problems which cause racial friction and unrest. In Birmingham, recent public events have given indication that we all have opportunity for a new constructive and realistic approach to racial problems.

However, we are now confronted by a series of demonstrations by some of our Negro citizens, directed and led in part by outsiders. We recognize the natural impatience of people who feel that their hopes are slow in being realized. But we are convinced that these demonstrations are unwise and untimely.

We agree rather with certain local Negro leadership which has called for honest and open negotiation of racial issues in our area. And we believe this kind of facing of issues can be best accomplished by citizens of our own metropolitan area, white and Negro, meeting with the knowledge and experience of the local situation. All of us need to face that responsibility and find proper channels for its accomplishment.

Just as we formerly pointed out that "hatred and violence have no sanction in our religious and political traditions," we also point out that such actions as incite to hatred and violence, however technically peaceful those actions may be, have not contributed to the resolution of our local problems. We do not believe that these days of new hope are days when extreme measures are justified in Birmingham.

We commend the community as a whole, and the local news media and law enforcement officials in particular, on the calm manner in which these demonstrations have been handled. We urge the public to continue to show restraint should the demonstrations continue, and the law enforcement officials to remain calm and continue to protect our city from violence.

We further strongly urge our own Negro community to withdraw support from these demonstrations, and to unite locally in working peacefully for a better Birmingham. When rights are consistently denied, a cause should be pressed in the courts and in negotiations among local leaders, and not in the streets. We appeal to both our white and Negro citizenry to observe the principles of law and order and common sense.

With the eight clergymen's statement in mind we could turn directly to the text of Mr. King's reply, but there is a figure waiting in the wings whom we would do well to remind ourselves of before giving our attention to Mr. King's *Letter from Birmingham Jail.* That figure is Henry David Thoreau, who had published an eloquent essay in 1849, "On the Duty of Civil Disobedience." Thoreau was not a Marxist. His 1849 plea for civil disobedience did not rest on premises set forth the year before in Marx's 1848 *Communist Manifesto.* He had refused to pay a state tax as a protest against slavery and against the war going on in Mexico. He had been jailed. There is a tradition that his friend Ralph Waldo Emerson had looked in through the jail window and demanded: "Henry, what are you doing in there?"; and that Thoreau had replied, "The question is, what are you doing out there?" That is the question to which he was led by reflecting on his own refusal to conform to the law. The citizens of Massachusetts, organized into a state under a government, demanded that he pay taxes. He refused on the grounds that his taxes would be used to help support measures and enforce laws that it would be wrong for him to countenance. This was civil disobedience, refusal to obey a law that violates a principle that is *higher* than any man-made law, a principle with reference to which laws themselves were to be judged, and either justified or condemned. His stand here is reminiscent of Antigone in Sophocles's play. The following eighteen paragraphs are quoted, abridged, or paraphrased from the full text of Thoreau's essay on civil disobedience:

I heartily accept the motto,—"That government is best which governs least"; and I should like to see it acted up to more readily and systematically. Carried out, it finally amounts to this, which also I believe,—"That government is best which governs not at all"; and when men are prepared for it, that will be the kind of government which they will have. Government is at best but an expedient; but most governments are usually, and all governments are sometimes, inexpedient. The objections which have been brought against a standing army, and they are many and weighty, and deserve to prevail, may also at last be brought against a standing government. The standing army is only an arm of the standing government. The government itself, which is only the mode which the people have chosen to execute their will, is equally liable to be abused and perverted before the people can act through it. Witness the present Mexican war, the work of comparatively a few individuals using the standing government as their tool; for, in the outset, the people would not have consented to this measure.

But, to speak practically and as a citizen, unlike those who call themselves no-government men, I ask for, not at once no government, but *at once* a better government. Let every man make known what kind of government would command his respect, and that will be one step toward obtaining it.

Must the citizen ever for a moment, or in the least degree, resign his conscience to the legislator? Why has every man a conscience, then? I think that we should be men first, and subjects afterward. It is not desirable to cultivate a respect for the law, so much as for the right. The only obligation which I have a right to assume, is to do at any time what I think right. It is truly enough said, that a corporation has no conscience; but a corporation of conscientious men is a corporation *with* a conscience. Law never made men a whit more just; and, by means of their respect for it, even the well-disposed are daily made the agents of injustice. A common and natural result of an undue respect for law is, that you may see a file of soldiers, colonel, captain, corporal, privates, powder-monkeys and all, marching in admirable order over hill and dale to the wars, against their wills, aye, against their common sense and consciences, which makes it very steep marching indeed, and produces a palpitation of the heart. They have no doubt that it is a damnable business in which they are concerned; they are all peaceably inclined. Now, what are they? Men at all? or small moveable forts and magazines, at the service of some unscrupulous man in power? Visit the Navy Yard, and behold a marine, such a man as an American government can make, or such as it can make a man with its black arts, a mere shadow and reminiscence of humanity, a man laid out alive and standing, and already, as one may say, buried under arms with funeral accompaniments.

The mass of men serve the State thus, not as men mainly, but as machines, with their bodies. They are the standing army, and the militia, jailers, constables, *posse comitatus*, etc. In most cases there is no free exercise whatever of the judgment or the moral sense; but they put themselves on a level with wood and earth and stones; and wooden men can perhaps be manufactured that will serve the purpose as well. Such command no more respect than men of straw, or a lump of dirt. They have the same sort of worth only as horses and dogs. Yet such as these even are commonly esteemed good citizens. Others, as most legislators, politicians, lawyers, ministers, and officeholders, serve the State chiefly with their heads; and, as they rarely make any moral distinctions, they are as likely to serve the devil, without intending it, as God. A very few, as heroes, patriots, martyrs, reformers in the great sense, and *men*, serve the State with their consciences also, and so necessarily resist it for the most part; and they are commonly treated by it as enemies.

How does it become a man to behave toward this American government to-day? I answer that he cannot without disgrace be associated with it. I cannot for an instant recognize that political organization as *my* government which is the *slave's* government also.

All men recognize the right of revolution; that is, the right to refuse allegiance to and to resist the government, when its tyranny or its inefficiency are great and unendurable. When a sixth of the population of a nation which has undertaken to be the refuge of liberty are slaves, and a whole country is unjustly overrun and conquered by a foreign army, and subjected to military law, I think that it is not too soon for honest men to rebel and revolutionize. What makes this duty the more urgent is the fact, that the country so overrun is not our own, but ours is the invading army.

If I have unjustly wrested a plank from a drowning man, I must restore it to him though I drown myself. This, according to Paley, would be inconvenient. But he that would save his life, in such a case, shall lose it. This people must cease to hold slaves, and to make war on Mexico, though it cost them their existence as a people.

Practically speaking, the opponents to a reform in Massachusetts are not a hundred thousand politicians at the South, but a hundred thousand merchants and farmers here, who are more interested in commerce and agriculture than they are in humanity, and are not prepared to do justice to the slave and to Mexico, *cost what it may*. I quarrel not with far-off foes, but with those who, near at home, cooperate with, and do the bidding of those far away, and without whom the latter would be harmless.

There are thousands who are *in opinion* opposed to slavery and to the war, who yet in effect do nothing to put an end to them; who esteeming themselves children of Washington and Franklin, sit down with their hands in their pockets, and say that they know not what to do, and do nothing; who even postpone the question of freedom to the question of free-trade, and quietly read the prices-current along with the latest advices from Mexico, after dinner, and, it may be, fall asleep over them both. What is the price-current of an honest man and patriot to-day? They hesitate, and they regret, and sometimes they petition; but they do nothing in earnest and with effect. They will wait, well disposed, for others to remedy the evil, that they may no longer have it to regret.

Unjust laws exist: shall we be content to obey them, or shall we endeavor to amend them, and obey them until we have succeeded or shall we transgress them at once? Men generally, under such a government as this, think that they ought to wait until they have persuaded the majority to alter them. They think that, if they should resist, the remedy would be worse than the evil. But it is the fault of the government itself that the remedy *is* worse than the evil. *It* makes it worse. Why is it not more apt to anticipate and provide for reform? Why does it not cherish its wise minority?

If the injustice is part of the necessary friction of the machine of government, let it go, let it go: perchance it will wear smooth,—certainly the machine will wear out. But if it is of such a nature that it requires you to be the agent of injustice to another, then, I say, break the law. Let your life be a counter friction to stop the machine. What I have to do is to see, at any rate, that I do not lend myself to the wrong which I condemn. As for adopting the ways which the State has provided for remedying the evil, I know not of such ways. They take too much time, and a man's life will be gone.

I do not hesitate to say, that those who call themselves abolitionists should at once effectually withdraw their support both in person and property from the government of Massachusetts.

I meet this American government, or its representative directly, and face to face, once a year, no more, in the person of its tax-gatherer; this is the only mode in which a man situated as I am necessarily meets it; and it then says distinctly, Recognize me; and the simplest, the most effectual, and in the present posture of affairs, the indispensablest mode of treating with it on this head, of expressing your little satisfaction with and love for it, is to deny it then.

Under a government which imprisons any unjustly, the true place for a just man is also a prison. The proper place to-day, the only place which Massachusetts has provided for her freer and less desponding spirits, is in her prisons, to be put out and locked out of the State by her own act, as they have already put themselves out by their principles. It is there that the fugitive slave, and the Mexican prisoner on parole, and the Indian come to plead the wrongs of his race, should find them; on that separate, but more free and honorable ground, where the State places those who are not *with* her but *against* her,—the only house in a slave-state in which a free man can abide with honor. A minority is powerless while it conforms to the majority; it is not even a minority then; but it is irresistible when it clogs by its whole weight. If the alternative is to keep all just men in prison, or give up war and slavery, the State will not hesitate which to choose. If a thousand men were not to pay their tax-bills this year, that would not be a violent and bloody measure, as it would be to pay them, and enable the State to commit violence and shed innocent blood. This is, in fact, the definition of a peaceable revolution if any such is possible. If the tax-gatherer, or any other public officer, asks me, as one has done, "But what shall I do?" my answer is, "If you really wish to do any thing, resign your office." When the subject has refused allegiance, and the officer has resigned his office, then the revolution is accomplished. But even suppose blood should flow. Is there not a sort of blood shed when the conscience is wounded? Through this wound a man's real manhood and immortality flow out, and he bleeds to an everlasting death, I see this blood flowing now.

I have never declined paying the highway tax, because I am as desirous of being a good neighbor as I am of being a bad subject; and, as for supporting schools, I am doing my part to educate my fellow-countrymen now. It is for no particular item in the taxbill that I refuse to pay it. I simply wish to refuse allegiance to the State, to withdraw and stand aloof from it effectually. I do not care to trace the course of my dollar, if I could, till it buys a man, or a musket to shoot one with—the dollar is innocent—but I am concerned to trace the effects of my allegiance. In fact, I quietly declare war with the State, after my fashion.

I do not wish to quarrel with any man or nation. I do not wish to split hairs, to make fine distinctions, or set myself up as better than my neighbors. I seek rather, I may say, even an excuse for conforming to the laws of the land. I am but too ready to conform to them. Indeed I have reason to suspect myself on this head; and each year, as the tax-gatherer comes round, I find myself disposed to review the acts and position of the general and state governments, and the spirit of the people, to discover a pretext for conformity. Seen from a lower point of view, the Constitution, with all its faults, is very good; the law and the courts are very respectable; even this State and this American government are, in many respects, very admirable and rare things, to be thankful for, such as a great many have described them; but seen from a point of view a little higher, they are what I have described them; seen from a higher still, and the highest who shall say what they are, or that they are worth looking at or thinking of at all?

The authority of government, even such as I am willing to submit to, for I will cheerfully obey those who know and can do better than I, and in many things even those who neither know or can do so well, is still an impure one: to be strictly just, it must have the sanction and consent of the governed. It can have no pure right over my person and property but what I concede to it. The progress from an absolute to a limited monarchy, from a limited monarchy to a democracy, is a progress toward a true respect for the individual. Is a democracy, such as we know it, the last improvement possible in government? Is it not possible to take a step further towards recognizing and organizing the rights of man? There will never be a really free and enlightened State, until the State comes to recognize the individual as a higher and independent power, from which all its own power and authority are derived, and treats him accordingly.

It would be interesting and enlightening to have King's letter of reply to the eight Birmingham clergymen read and commented on by Rousseau, Marx, Thoreau, Mill, and Hart. All five of them would be open to such an experiment. In their own writings they had taken positions that would entitle Mr. King to demand that they read his *Letter,* and stand up and be counted. Would they take their stand with the eight clergymen, or with the public authorities who had put Mr. King in jail? Or with Mr. King himself? Could he appeal to anything they had written, to justify himself in his act of civil disobedience?

The Argument of the Passages. Following are twenty-three paragraphs from Mr. King's letter. The complete letter is much longer than the part quoted here. These twenty-three paragraphs have been divided into five sequences. The numbers used to mark these divisions are not in the original text. In the first sequence Mr. King explains why he is in Birmingham. In the second sequence, which is the most important part of the letter, he sets forth his theory of civil disobedience and the conditions that justify it. In the third sequence he reminds his correspondents of some outstanding cases of civil disobedience. In the fourth sequence he expresses regret that the Christian church in the South has not identified itself with civil disobedience on behalf of Negro groups in this country. In the fifth sequence he refers to some exceptions to his criticism of churches. In the final paragraph he expresses a desire, and a hope, that he and his correspondents will be able to meet as fellow Christians.

My dear Fellow Clergymen,

(1)

. . . I think I should give the reason for my being in Birmingham, since you have been influenced by the argument of "outsiders coming in." I have the honor of serving as president of the Southern Christian Leadership Conference, an organization operating in every Southern state, with headquarters in Atlanta, Georgia. We have some eighty-five affiliate organizations all across the South—one being the Alabama Christian Movement of Human Rights. Whenever necessary and possible we share staff, educational and financial resources with our affiliates. Several months ago our local affiliate here in Birmingham invited us to be on call to engage in a nonviolent direct action program if such were deemed necessary. We readily consented and when the hour came we lived up to our promises. So I am here, along with several members of my staff, because we were invited here. I am here because I have basic organizational ties here.

Beyond this, I am in Birmingham because injustice is here. Just as the eighth century prophets left their little villages and carried their "thus saith the Lord" far beyond the boundaries of their home towns; and just as the Apostle Paul left his little village of Tarsus and carried the gospel of Jesus Christ to practically every hamlet and city of the Graeco-Roman world, I too am compelled to carry the gospel of freedom beyond my particular home town. Like Paul, I must constantly respond to the Macedonian call for aid.

Moreover, I am cognizant of the interrelatedness of all communities and states. I cannot sit idly by in Atlanta and not be concerned about what happens in Birmingham. Injustice anywhere is a threat to justice everywhere. We are caught in an inescapable network of mutuality, tied in a single garment of destiny. Whatever affects one directly affects all indirectly. Never again can we afford to live with the narrow, provincial "outside agitator" idea. Anyone who lives inside the United States can never be considered an outsider anywhere in this country.

You deplore the demonstrations that are presently taking place in Birmingham. But I am sorry that your statement did not express a similar concern for the conditions that brought the demonstrations into being. I am sure that each of you would want to go beyond the superficial social analyst who looks merely at effects, and does not grapple with underlying causes. I would not hesitate to say that it is unfortunate that so-called demonstrations are taking place in Birmingham at this time, but I would say in more emphatic terms that it is even more unfortunate that the white power structure of this city left the Negro community with no other alternative. . . .

(2)

We know through painful experience that freedom is never voluntarily given by the oppressor; it must be demanded by the oppressed. Frankly, I have never yet engaged in a direct action movement that was "well timed," according to the timetable of those who have not suffered unduly from the disease of segregation. For years now I have heard the words "Wait!" It rings in the ear of every Negro with a piercing familiarity. This "Wait" has almost always meant "Never." It has been a tranquilizing thalidomide, relieving the emotional stress for a moment, only to give birth to an ill-formed infant of frustration. We must come to see with the distinguished jurist of yesterday that "justice too long delayed is justice denied." We have waited for more than three hundred and forty years for our constitutional and God-given rights. The nations of Asia and Africa are moving with jet-like speed toward the goal of political independence, and we still creep at horse and buggy pace toward the gaining of a cup of coffee at a lunch counter. I guess it is easy for those who have never felt the stinging darts of segregation to say, "Wait." But when you have seen vicious mobs lynch your mothers and fathers at will and drown your sisters and brothers at whim; when you have seen hate-filled policemen curse, kick, brutalize and even kill your black brothers and sisters with impunity; when you see the vast majority of your twenty million Negro brothers smothering in an air-tight cage of poverty in the midst of an affluent society; when you suddenly find your tongue twisted and your speech stammering as you seek to explain to your six-year-old daughter why she can't go to the public amusement park that has just been advertised on television, and see tears welling up in her little eyes when she is told that Funtown is closed to colored children, and see the depressing clouds of inferiority begin to form in her little mental sky, and see her begin to distort her little personality by unconsciously developing a bitterness toward white people; when you have to concoct an answer for a five-year-old son asking in agonizing pathos: "Daddy, why do white people treat colored people so mean?"; when you take a cross country drive and find it necessary to sleep night after night in the uncomfortable corners of your automobile because no motel will accept you; when you are humiliated day in and day out by nagging signs reading "white" and "colored"; when your first name becomes "nigger" and your middle name becomes "boy" (however old you are) and your last name becomes "John," and when your wife and mother are never given the respected title "Mrs."; when you are harried by day and haunted at night by the fact that you are a Negro, living constantly at tip-toe stance never quite knowing what to expect next, and plagued with inner fears and outer resentments; when you are forever fighting a degenerating sense of "nobodiness"; then you will understand why we find it difficult to wait. There comes a time when the cup of endurance runs over, and men are no longer willing to be plunged into an abyss of injustice where they experience the blackness of corroding despair. I hope, sirs, you can understand our legitimate and unavoidable impatience.

You express a great deal of anxiety over our willingness to break laws. This is certainly a legitimate concern. Since we so diligently urge people to obey the Supreme Court's decision of 1954 outlawing segregation in the public schools, it is rather strange and paradoxical to find us consciously breaking laws. One may well ask, "How can you advocate breaking some laws and obeying others?" The answer is found in the fact that there are two types of laws: There are *just* and there are *unjust* laws. I would agree with Saint Augustine that "An unjust law is no law at all."

Now what is the difference between the two? How does one determine when a law is just or unjust? A just law is a man-made code that squares with the moral law or the law of God. An unjust law is a code that is out of harmony with the moral law. To put it in terms of Saint Thomas Aquinas, an unjust law is a human law that is not rooted in eternal and natural law. Any law that uplifts human personality is just. Any law that degrades human personality is unjust. All segregation statutes are unjust because segregation distorts the soul and damages the personality. It gives the segregator a false sense of superiority, and the segregated a false sense of inferiority. To use the words of Martin Buber, the great Jewish philosopher, segregation substitutes an "I-it" relationship for the "I-thou" relationship, and ends up relegating persons to the status of things. So segregation is not only politically, economically and sociologically unsound, but it is morally wrong and sinful. Paul Tillich has said that sin is separation. Isn't segregation an existential expression of man's tragic separation, an expression of his awful estrangement, his terrible sinfulness? So I can urge men to disobey segregation ordinances because they are morally wrong.

Let us turn to a more concrete example of just and unjust laws. An unjust law is a code that a majority inflicts on a minority that is not binding on itself. This is difference made legal. On the other hand a just law is a code that a majority compels a minority to follow that it is willing to follow itself. This is sameness made legal.

Let me give another explanation. An unjust law is a code inflicted upon a minority which that minority had no part in enacting or creating because they did not have the unhampered right to vote. Who can say that the legislature of Alabama which set up the segregation laws was democratically elected? Throughout the state of Alabama all types of conniving methods are used to prevent Negroes from becoming registered voters and there are some counties without a single Negro registered to vote despite the fact that the Negro constitutes a majority of the population. Can any law set up in such a state be considered democratically structured?

These are just a few examples of unjust and just laws. There are some instances when a law is just on its face and unjust in its application. For instance, I was arrested Friday on a charge of parading without a permit. Now there is nothing wrong with an ordinance which requires a permit for a parade, but when the ordinance is used to preserve segregation and to deny citizens the First Amendment privilege of peaceful assembly and peaceful protest, then it becomes unjust.

I hope you can see the distinction I am trying to point out. In no sense do I advocate evading or defying the law as the rabid segregationist would do. This would lead to anarchy. One who breaks an unjust law must do it *openly, lovingly* (not hatefully as the white mothers did in New Orleans when they were seen on television screaming "nigger, nigger, nigger"), and with a willingness to accept the penalty. I submit that an individual who breaks a law that conscience tells him is unjust, and willingly accepts the penalty by staying in jail to arouse the conscience of the community over its injustice, is in reality expressing the very highest respect for law.

Of course, there is nothing new about this kind of civil disobedience. It was seen sublimely in the refusal of Shadrach, Meschach and Abednego to obey the laws of Nebuchadnezzar because a higher moral law was involved. It was practiced superbly by the early Christians who were willing to face hungry lions and the excruciating pain of chopping blocks, before submitting to certain unjust laws of the Roman empire. To a degree academic freedom is a reality today because Socrates practised civil disobedience.

We can never forget that everything Hitler did in Germany was "legal" and everything the Hungarian freedom fighters did in Hungary was "illegal." It was "illegal" to aid and comfort a Jew in Hitler's Germany. But I am sure that if I had lived in Germany during that time I would have aided and comforted my Jewish brothers even though it was illegal. If I lived in a Communist country today where certain principles dear to the Christian faith are suppressed, I believe I would openly advocate disobeying these anti-religious laws. . . .

(3)

Oppressed people cannot remain oppressed forever. The urge for freedom will eventually come. This is what happened to the American Negro. Something within has reminded him of his birthright of freedom; something without has reminded him that he can gain it. Consciously and unconsciously, he has been swept in by what the Germans call the *Zeitgeist*, and with his black brothers of Africa, and his brown and yellow brothers of Asia, South America and the Caribbean, he is moving with a sense of cosmic urgency toward the promised land of racial justice. Recognizing this vital urge that has engulfed the Negro community, one should readily understand public demonstrations. The Negro has many pent-up resentments and latent frustrations. He has to get them out. So let him march sometime; let him have his prayer pilgrimages to the city hall; understand why he must have sit-ins and freedom rides. If his repressed emotions do not come out in these nonviolent ways, they will come out in ominous expressions of violence. This is not a threat; it is a fact of history. So I have not said to my people "get rid of your discontent." But I have tried to say that this normal and healthy discontent can be channelized through the creative outlet of nonviolent direct action. Now this approach is being dismissed as extremist. I must admit that I was initially disappointed in being so categorized.

But as I continued to think about the matter I gradually gained a bit of satisfaction from being considered an extremist. Was not Jesus an extremist in love—"Love your enemies, bless them that curse you, pray for them that despitefully use you." Was not Amos an extremist for justice—"Let justice roll down like waters and righteousness like a mighty stream." Was not Paul an extremist for the gospel of Jesus Christ—"I bear in my body the marks of the Lord Jesus." Was not Martin Luther an extremist—"Here I stand; I can do none other so help me God." Was not John Bunyan an extremist—"I will stay in jail to the end of my days before I make a butchery of my conscience." Was not Abraham Lincoln an extremist—"This nation cannot survive half slave and half free." Was not Thomas Jefferson an extremist—"We hold these truths to be self-evident, that all men are created equal." So the question is not whether we will be extremist but what kind of extremist will we be. Will we be extremists for hate or will we be extremists for love? Will we be extremists for the preservation of injustice—or will we be extremists for the cause of justice? In that dramatic scene on Calvary's hill, three men were crucified. We must not forget that all three were crucified for the same crime—the crime of extremism. Two were extremists for immorality, and thusly fell below their environment. The other, Jesus Christ, was an extremist for love, truth and goodness, and thereby rose above his environment. So, after all, maybe the south, the nation and the world are in dire need of creative extremists.

I had hoped that the white moderate would see this. Maybe I was too optimistic. Maybe I expected too much. I guess I should have realized that few members of a race that has oppressed another race can understand or appreciate the deep groans and passionate yearnings of those that have been oppressed and still fewer have the vision to see that injustice must be rooted out by strong, persistent and determined action. I am thankful, however, that some of our white brothers have grasped the meaning of this social revolution and committed themselves to it. They are still all too small in quantity, but they are big in quality. Some like Ralph McGill, Lillian Smith, Harry Golden and James Dabbs have written about our struggle in eloquent, prophetic and understanding terms. Others have marched with us down nameless streets of the South. They have languished in filthy roach-infested jails, suffering the abuse and brutality of angry policemen who see them as "dirty nigger lovers." They, unlike so many of their moderate brothers and sisters, have recognized the urgency of the moment and sensed the need for powerful "action" antidotes to combat the disease of segregation. . . .

(4)

In spite of my shattered dreams of the past, I came to Birmingham with the hope that the white religious leadership of this community would see the justice of our cause, and with deep moral concern, serve as the channel through which our just grievances would get to the power structure. I had hoped that each of you would understand. But again I have been disappointed. I have heard numerous religious leaders of the South call upon their worshippers to comply with a desegregation decision because it is the *law*, but I have longed to hear white ministers say, "Follow this decree because integration is morally *right* and the Negro is your brother." In the midst of blatant injustices inflicted upon the Negro, I have watched white churches stand on the sideline and merely mouth pious irrelevancies and sanctimonious trivialities. In the midst of a mighty struggle to rid our nation of racial and economic injustice, I have heard so many ministers say, "Those are social issues with which the gospel has no real concern," and I have watched so many churches commit themselves to a completely other-worldly religion which made a strange distinction between body and soul, the sacred and the secular.

So here we are moving toward the exit of the twentieth century with a religious community largely adjusted to the status quo, standing as a taillight behind other community agencies rather than a headlight leading men to higher levels of justice.

I have traveled the length and breadth of Alabama, Mississippi and all the other southern states. On sweltering summer days and crisp autumn mornings I have looked at her beautiful churches with their lofty spires pointing heavenward. I have beheld the impressive outlay of her massive religious education buildings. Over and over again I have found myself asking: "What kind of people worship here? Who is their God? Where were their voices when the lips of Governor Barnett dripped with words of interposition and nullification? Where were they when Governor Wallace gave the clarion call for defiance and hatred? Where were their voices of support when tired, bruised and weary Negro men and women decided to rise from the dark dungeons of complacency to the bright hills of creative protest?"

Yes, these questions are still in my mind. In deep disappointment. I have wept over the laxity of the church. But be assured that my tears have been tears of love. There can be no deep disappointment where there is not deep love. Yes, I love the church; I love her sacred walls. How could I do otherwise? I am in the rather unique position of being the son, the grandson and the great-grandson of preachers. Yes, I see the church as the body of Christ. But, oh! How we have blemished and scarred that body through social neglect and fear of being nonconformists.

There was a time when the church was very powerful. It was during that period when the early Christians rejoiced when they were deemed worthy to suffer for what they believed. In those days the church was not merely a thermometer that recorded the ideas and principles of popular opinion; it was a thermostat that transformed the *mores* of society. Wherever the early Christians entered a town the power structure got disturbed and immediately sought to convict them for being "disturbers of the peace" and "outside agitators." But they went on with the conviction that they were "a colony of heaven," and had to obey God rather than man. They were small in number but big in commitment. They were too God-intoxicated to be "astronomically intimidated." They brought an end to such ancient evils as infanticide and gladiatorial contest.

Things are different now. The contemporary church is often a weak, ineffectual voice with an uncertain sound. It is so often the arch supporter of the status quo. Far from being disturbed by the presence of the church, the power structure of the average community is consoled by the church's silent and often vocal sanction of things as they are.

But the judgment of God is upon the church as never before. If the church of today does not recapture the sacrificial spirit of the early church, it will lose its authentic ring, forfeit the loyalty of millions, and be dismissed as an irrelevant social club with no meaning for the twentieth century. I am meeting young people every day whose disappointment with the church has risen to outright disgust.

(5)

Maybe again, I have been too optimistic. Is organized religion too inextricably bound to the *status quo* to save our nation and the world? Maybe I must turn my faith to the inner spiritual church, the church within the church, as the true *ecclesia* and the hope of the world. But again I am thankful to God that some noble souls from the ranks of organized religion have broken loose from the paralyzing chains of conformity and joined us as active partners in the struggle for freedom. They have left their secure congregations and walked the streets of Albany, Georgia, with us. They have gone through the highways of the South on tortuous rides for freedom. Yes, they have gone to jail with us. Some have been kicked out of their churches, and lost support of their bishops and fellow ministers. But they have gone with the faith that right defeated is stronger than evil triumphant. These men have been the leaven in the lump of the race. Their witness has been the spiritual salt that has preserved the true meaning of the Gospel in these troubled times. They have carved a tunnel of hope through the dark mountain of disappointment.

I hope the church as a whole will meet the challenge of this decisive hour. But even if the church does not come to the aid of justice, I have no despair about the future. I have no fear about the outcome of our struggle in Birmingham, even if our motives are presently misunderstood. We will reach the goal of freedom in Birmingham and all over the nation, because the goal of America is freedom. Abused and scorned though we may be, our destiny is tied up with the destiny of America. Before the pilgrims landed at Plymouth we were here. Before the pen of Jefferson etched across the pages of history the majestic words of the Declaration of Independence, we were here. For more than two centuries our foreparents labored in this country without wages; they made cotton king; and they built the homes of their masters in the midst of brutal injustice and shameful humiliation—and yet out of a bottomless vitality they continued to thrive and develop. If the inexpressible cruelties of slavery could not stop us, the opposition we now face will surely fail. We will win our freedom because the sacred heritage of our nation and the eternal will of God are embodied in our echoing demands.

I must close now. But before closing I am impelled to mention one other point in your statement that troubled me profoundly. You warmly commended the Birmingham police force for keeping "order" and "preventing violence." I don't believe you would have so warmly commended the police force if you had seen its angry violent dogs literally biting six unarmed, non-violent Negroes. I don't believe you would so quickly commend the police-men if you would observe their ugly and inhuman treatment of Negroes here in the city jail; if you would watch them push and curse old Negro women and young Negro girls; if you would see them slap and kick old Negro men and young boys; if you will observe them, as they did on two occasions, re-fuse to give us food because we wanted to sing our grace together. I'm sorry that I can't join you in your praise for the police department.

It is true that they have been rather disciplined in their public handling of the demonstrators. In this sense they have been rather publicly "non-violent." But for what purpose? To preserve the evil system of segregation. Over the last few years I have consistently preached that nonviolence de-mands that the means we use must be as pure as the ends we seek. So I have tried to make it clear that it is wrong to use immoral means to attain moral ends. But now I must affirm that it is just as wrong, or even more so, to use moral means to preserve immoral ends. Maybe Mr. Connor and his police-men have been rather publicly nonviolent, as Chief Pritchett was in Albany, Georgia, but they have used the moral means of nonviolence to maintain the immoral end of flagrant racial injustice. T. S. Eliot has said that there is no greater treason than to do the right deed for the wrong reason.

I wish you had commended the Negro sit-inners and demonstrators of Birmingham for their sublime courage, their willingness to suffer and their amazing discipline in the midst of the most inhuman provocation. One day the South will recognize its real heroes. They will be the James Merediths, courageously and with a majestic sense of purpose facing jeering and hostile mobs and the agonizing loneliness that characterizes the life of the pioneer. They will be old, oppressed, battered Negro women, symbolized in a sev-enty-two year old woman of Montgomery, Alabama, who rose up with a sense of dignity and with her people decided not to ride the segregated buses, and responded to one who inquired about her tiredness with ungram-matical profundity: "My feet is tired, but my soul is rested." They will be the young high school and college students, young ministers of the Gospel and a host of their elders courageously and nonviolently sitting-in at lunch counters and willingly going to jail for conscience's sake. One day the South will know that when these disinherited children of God sat down at lunch counters they were in reality standing up for the best in the American dream and the most sacred values in our Judeo-Christian heritage, and thusly, car-rying our whole nation back to those great wells of democracy which were dug deep by the founding fathers in the formulation of the Constitution and the Declaration of Independence.

Never before have I written a letter this long (or should I say a book?). I'm afraid that it is much too long to take your precious time. I can assure you that it would have been much shorter if I had been writing from a com-fortable desk, but what else is there to do when you are alone for days in the dull monotony of a narrow jail cell other than write long letters, think strange thoughts, and pray long prayers?

If I have said anything in this letter that is an overstatement of the truth and is indicative of an unreasonable impatience, I beg you to forgive me. If I have said anything in this letter that is an understatement of the truth and is indicative of my having a patience that makes me patient with anything less than brotherhood, I beg God to forgive me.

I hope this letter finds you strong in the faith. I also hope that circumstances will soon make it possible for me to meet each of you, not as an integrationist or a civil-rights leader, but as a fellow clergyman and a Christian brother. Let us all hope that the dark clouds of racial prejudice will soon pass away and the deep fog of misunderstanding will be lifted from our fear-drenched communities and in some not too distant tomorrow the radiant stars of love and brotherhood will shine over our great nation with all of their scintillating beauty.

Yours for the cause of Peace and Brotherhood,
Martin Luther King, Jr.

READING QUESTIONS

1. Why Rousseau, Marx, Mill, and Hart should read Thoreau and King with genuine concern.
2. Thoreau and 1849: (a) Two reasons for Thoreau's dim view of the U.S. government in 1849. (b) Where slaves, Indians, and Mexicans should expect to find public-spirited citizens at that time. Why so? (c) Is the *Essay* as timely today as it was in 1849? Give your reason(s) for your answer. (d) Will lowering the franchise cause the *Essay* to become outdated? Why do you or do not think so.
3. Thoreau and the moral skeptic: (a) What do you understand by *moral skepticism?* (b) Why neither Antigone nor Thoreau could afford to be moral skeptics. (c) Could a moral skeptic defend civil disobedience? On what grounds? (d) Thoreau asks whether the citizen must resign his conscience to the legislator. What considerations would raise that question? How would a moral skeptic answer that question? Spell out Thoreau's answer to his own question. (e) Seen from the "highest" point of view, what Thoreau would say about government and its laws. Does that commit him to anarchism in jurisprudence?
4. Mr. King sets up a distinction between just and unjust laws. (a) Why does he do this, anyway? (b) What is the distinction in question? (c) Does he think that there is any *necessary* connection between law and justice? Do you? If so, what is the connection?
5. Is justice a *wider* notion than law?
6. When, according to Mr. King, the civil disobedient expresses "the very highest respect for law"?
7. Why civil disobedience, like crime, is a frequent feature of the legislative way of life. Why not so frequent a feature, however?

INDEPENDENT STUDY

1. Read the article "Civil Disobedience" by C. Bay in the *International Encyclopedia of the Social Sciences.* Study carefully the two-column bibliography at the end of the article. Carve out a topic.
2. Read Sophocles's drama "Antigone" and Shaw's drama "Saint Joan" and any one other dramatization of a civil disobedient. Work out a drama of your own around Martin Luther King.
3. Read the article "On Civil Disobedience" by H. Bedau in the *Journal of Philosophy,* Volume 58. Write a paper comparing and contrasting Martin Luther King with one or two of the following: Albert Camus, Mohandas Gandhi, Henry Thoreau, Leo Tolstoy.

topic five
history and historical thinking

THE PROBLEM STATED

We use the word *history* in at least two senses. In Sense One we use it to refer to the human past. The human past "contains" events that happened and acts that were performed. Thus the Lisbon earthquake happened in the human past in 1755, and the English defeated the French in the human past in 1815. Using the term history in Sense One we could say that the earthquake happened "back in history" and the defeat was inflicted "back in history." In Sense Two we use the term *history* to refer to the *study* of the human past, and to the *story* of the human past as worked out and written down by historians. In this second sense, history is something produced by historians, analogous, say, to science produced by scientists, to laws produced by legislators, or works of art produced by artists. Using *history* in the first sense we can say that Caesar and Napoleon, Washington and Lincoln made history. Using *history* in the second sense we can say that Herodotus and Thucydides, Beard and Macaulay produced history, produced an account of some portion of the human past intended to make it understandable. History, in this sense of what the historian produces, is sometimes referred to as historiography.

In this Topic we have two problems, one deriving from each sense of *history*. The first comes about in this way: using history in Sense One ("the human past"), we distinguish between event (or act) and history. We make this distinction readily enough. We distinguish between the death of Caesar and the history of Rome, between the fall of the Bastille and the French Revolution, between the production of "Hamlet" and the history of Elizabethan drama, between the invention of the steam engine and the history of the industrial revolution. We "stumble upon" events and acts, we "locate" events and acts in the context of a history. We "understand" events (and acts) in terms of a history. We "isolate" events within a history. We "abstract" events from a history. We sometimes even talk about "analyzing" a history into the events that "make it up." Where *history*, in Sense One, is used in contrast to *event* or *act*, can we say that a history is a pattern, a gestalt, a plot, a theme, a framework, a structure, a plan, a schema, an outline? Try the term *pattern*, as perhaps the most neutral of these metaphors. The idea that it is intended to convey is illustrated by the one-time familiar newspaper drawing containing scattered numbers that the reader is invited to connect up in arithmetical order by means of lines. The result was a "picture," perhaps of a fish or a horse or a man's head. The apparently scattered numbers occur in a pattern. When we first look at them we do not detect the pattern. Gradually, as we fill in the lines from number to number, we begin to "see" or "grasp" the pattern. It was "there" all the time.

Granted this metaphor, we can put our first question this way: "What is the pattern that holds the events of history together, that gradually emerges as we fill in the events, which was merely latent in the events taken in their "bare particularity"? Is there *one* such pattern that takes in all events? Or many limited patterns that do not fit together to form any "overall" pattern? If there is, "back there in the past," only one all-comprehensive pattern within which all events and acts are "located" and with reference to which they make whatever sense they make, let us speak of historical monism, meaning one pattern in the human past. If there are two or more patterns, each "independent" of the others, no one "reducible" to any other, let us speak of historical pluralism. Practicing and professional historians take a dim view of this question. They doubt that it is possible to show that either historical monism or some form of historical pluralism is true. Such claims they incline to dismiss as "mere speculation." So let us speak of the speculative problem in philosophy of history. Our first four authors—Kant, Hegel, Engels, Spengler—are speculative, in the sense that each believes that there is an overarching pattern, or rationale, to the human past; and each is trying to state what it is.

Our second question has to do with how the historian thinks, in contrast, say, to how the scientist or mathematician or even the "plain man" thinks. If there is such a thing as scientific method, a method productive of science, and you practice this method, you will produce some science. You will "think scientifically," producing some scientific knowledge. In this sense we may say that scientific thinking, and perhaps nothing else, produces scientific knowledge, or science. Is there an analogy here between the scientist, scientific method, and science, on the one hand, and the historian, historical method or thinking, and history in Sense Two? How must you think if you are to produce history in Sense Two, if you are to render the human past intelligible? If there is such a thing as historical method, a method productive of history in Sense Two, and you practice this method, you think methodically according to this method, you will produce some history in Sense Two. In this sense we may say that historical thinking, and perhaps nothing else, produces historical knowledge, or history in Sense Two. Our second question, then, is this: "What is the nature of historical thinking and the historical knowledge that it produces?" Our fifth author, Collingwood, addresses himself to this question. He is skeptical with regard to speculative philosophy of history. He wants to track down what goes on in historical thinking. If there are criteria of recognition and criteria of evaluation relevant to historical thinking, and he can track these down, then he will be in a position to produce, or read, history critically. We can therefore speak of his interest in critical, in contrast to speculative, philosophy of history.

Collingwood is curious about the rationale of history in the sense of what the historian produces. The historian's "field" is the past. His aim is to "recover" the past in terms that will make it intelligible. This is a difficult job, partly because the past is gone; we have no time machine to take us back into the past to "see for ourselves" what went on there. But despite its difficulty, the historian's job is important. We are historical animals. We need a knowledge of the past. I do not mean merely that it is useful. It is indispensable. Deprive yourself of *all* knowledge based on an understanding of the past, and you will not make sense to yourself. The great historians are men who have turned powerful and disciplined imaginations upon this task of making the past intelligible. It does not matter that their work is never wholly accurate and complete. What we know of the past does not differ in that respect from what we know of the present or the future; or of nature at large via the sciences. I am not concerned to defend the importance of what the historian tries to do. What would a person use for evidence if he denied the importance of activity directed toward making the past intelligible? How would he come by such evidence?

We began this introductory section by noting that we use the term *history* in two senses. This distinction is worth its keep in the economy of the enquiring mind. Suppose you want to get at the American and the French revolutions: 1776 and 1789. In working at this you will learn some history in the sense of what "went on" back there, what events happened and what acts were performed. You will also learn some history in the sense of what the historian produces. You will begin to distinguish between history in the sense that Washington and Robespierre produced it; and history in the sense that Bancroft and Michelet produced it. The question of the relation between these two is a sophisticating one. Eventually you will see that history in the sense that the historian makes it, authorizes what you claim to know about history in the sense that Washington and Robespierre make it. It is important to see that the historian as well as Washington and Robespierre is responsible for what you believe about Washington and Robespierre.

TRIGGER QUESTIONS

1. Theology and speculative metaphysics have been sitting ducks for skeptics, history only slightly less so. For similar reasons, do you suppose?
2. Is it (a) difficult or (b) impossible to verify or falsify a historical claim?
3. A historian, it seems, may address himself without misgivings to the question, "Did the Crucifixion and the Reformation happen?" However, what about the question, "Did the Incarnation and the Ascension happen?"
4. We know that interpretations of the past change. How do we know that the past itself does not change?
5. It is sometimes possible to detect among historians an ambivalence toward psychology and sociology. Why is there this ambivalence?
6. Is the distinction between *causing* and *causing intentionally*, important for the historian?
7. There is history in the sense that Cromwell or Napoleon produced it, and history in the sense that Carlyle or Michelet produced it. How do you relate these two senses of history? Which "goes bail" for the other?
8. Historians may generalize. Does that imply that there are "historical laws," "laws in history"?
9. Does the historian have any stake in the freewill–determinism hassle?

10. "Claims answer questions, and then give rise to questions." Illustrate, from historical thinking.
11. Is there any *essential* difference between a historical question and either a mathematical question or a scientific question?
12. Any questions or comments:
    a. "Between the historian and the past stands always the document."
    b. "A historian's claims are *relative*." Relative to *what?*
    c. "No historian, speaking as historian, is entitled to any value judgments about the past." Why not?
    d. "Historical knowledge is only scientific knowledge on the make."
    e. "The solar system has a past. Solar astronomy has a history."

SECTION 1. IMMANUEL KANT: NATURE'S PLAN IN HUMAN HISTORY [1]

The Argument of Kant's Essay. Until the twentieth century, and well into the twentieth century, writers on philosophy of history addressed themselves primarily to what might be called the "overall" question: "Is there any pattern or law, or any purpose and plan, in the over-all history of the human race?" The Biblical–Christian writers had proposed human history overall as setting forth the drama of salvation: man's creation, fall, redemption, and destiny in heaven. This had been done most influentially by Saint Augustine in his book *The City of God*, written in the fifth century A.D. This overall interpretation of human history died hard; indeed, it may be an exaggeration to say that it is dead yet. It is certainly less influential than it was for the thousand years between Saint Augustine and, say, Machiavelli. However, the overall *question* retained its power to give shape to reflection on the human past. Kant wrote toward the end of the eighteenth century, in the period following the rise of modern science, and itself crowded with the American Revolution, the French Revolution, the French Enlightenment, the Encyclopedists, Hume, Voltaire, Condorcet, Rousseau, Thomas Paine, Thomas Jefferson, Franklin, and many more. These movers and shakers did not, typically, subscribe to the Biblical–Christian or Augustinian interpretation of human history. What alternative interpretation would hold their attention or even command their belief? It is possible to read Kant's essay "Idea for a Universal History from a Cosmopolitan Standpoint," published in 1784, as having been written with that question in mind. The originating question is

[1] For biographical note on Kant, see pp. 586–587.

clearly before his mind: "Is there any clue to any purpose and plan in the overall history of the human race?" Kant is convinced that there is, but if you ask him *whose* purpose and plan it is, he carefully avoids claiming that it is God's, and insists emphatically that it is not humanity's, not man's. There *is* a purpose and a plan, being worked out in human history, but it is nature's plan. Nature has plans for man. These are being worked out in human history. His essay proposes to sketch out these matters.

Whatever difference there may be in our notions of the freedom of the will, it is evident that the manifestations of this will, viz., human actions, are as much under the control of universal laws of nature as any other physical phenomena. It is the province of history to narrate these manifestations; and let their causes be ever so secret, we know that history, simply by taking its station at a distance and contemplating the agency of the human will upon a large scale, aims at unfolding to our view a regular stream of tendency in the great succession of events; so that the very same course of incidents, which taken separately and individually would have seemed incoherent and lawless, yet viewed in their connection never fail to discover a steady and continuous though slow development of certain great predispositions in our nature. Thus for instance deaths, births, and marriages, considering how much they are separately dependent on the freedom of the human will, should seem to be subject to no law according to which any calculation could be made beforehand of their amount; and yet the yearly registers of these events in great countries prove that they go on with as much conformity to the laws of nature as the oscillations of the weather; the latter again are events which in detail are so far irregular that we cannot predict them individually, and yet taken as a whole series we find that they never fail to support the growth of plants, the currents of rivers, and other arrangements of nature in a uniform and uninterrupted course. Individual men, and even nations, are little aware that, while they are severally pursuing their own peculiar and often contradictory purposes, they are unconsciously following the guidance of a natural purpose which is wholly unnoticed by themselves, and are thus promoting and making efforts for a process which, even if they perceived it, they would little regard.

Considering that men, taken collectively as a body, do not proceed like animals under the law of an instinct, nor yet like wholly rational beings under the law of a preconcerted plan, one might imagine that no systematic history of their actions (such, for instance, as the history of bees or beavers) could be possible. At the sight of the actions of man displayed on the great stage of the world, it is impossible to escape a certain degree of disgust; with all the occasional indications of wisdom scattered here and there, we cannot but perceive the whole sum of these actions to be a web of folly, childish vanity, and often even of the idlest wickedness and spirit of destruction. Hence at last one is puzzled to know what judgment to form of our species so conceited of its high advantages. In this perplexity there is no resource for the philosopher but this: that, finding it impossible to presume in the human race any rational purpose of its own, he must endeavor to detect some natural purpose in such a senseless current of human actions, by means of which a history of creatures that pursue no plan of their own may yet admit a systematic form as the history of creatures that are blindly pursuing a plan of nature. Let us now see whether we can succeed in finding out a clue to such a history, leaving it to nature to produce a man capable of executing it.

After those introductory remarks, Kant develops his speculation about nature's purpose in human history by means of nine numbered propositions, each carrying the argument forward.

Proposition the First. All tendencies of any creature to which it is predisposed by nature, are destined in the end to develop themselves perfectly and agreeably to their final purpose.

External as well as internal (or anatomical) examination confirms this remark in all animals. An organ which is not to be used, a natural arrangement that misses its purpose, would be a contradiction in physics. Once departing from this fundamental proposition, we have a nature no longer tied to laws, but objectless and working at random; and a cheerless reign of chance steps into the place of reason.

In man, nature produced an animal rational in Sense Two, an animal that can reason and be reasoned with. Nature's purpose is to develop this power in man, and all other powers that are dependent on it. Most distinctively human powers depend on the power to reason and be reasoned with. Nature can accomplish this purpose only in the life of the species, i.e., not in the life of any one individual or generation.

Proposition the Second. In man, those tendencies which have the use of his reason for their object are destined to obtain their perfect development in the species only and not in the individual.

Reason in a creature is a faculty for extending the rules and purposes of the exercise of all its powers far beyond natural instinct, and it is illimitable in its plans. It works however not instinctively, but stands in need of trials, of practice, and of instruction in order to ascend gradually from one degree of illumination to another. On this account either it would be necessary for each man to live an inordinate length of time in order to learn how to make a perfect use of his natural tendencies; or else, supposing the actual case that nature has limited his term of life, she must then require an incalculable series of generations (each delivering its quota of knowledge to its immediate successor) in order to ripen the germs which she has laid in our species to that degree of development which corresponds with her final purpose. Otherwise man's own natural predispositions must of necessity be regarded as objectless; and this would at once take away all practical principles, and would expose nature—the wisdom of whose arrangements must in all other cases be assumed as a fundamental postulate—to the suspicion of capricious dealing in the case of man only.

Given her purpose (to develop those capacities that mark man as a rational animal), nature has adopted a plan: (a) man shall owe to himself alone everything beyond the physical, material processes that make up his animal body and material environment. (b) Man shall find satisfaction and perfection only or largely in what he produces by his own rational powers.

Proposition the Third. It is the will of nature that man should owe to himself alone everything which transcends the mere mechanical constitution of his animal existence, and that he should be susceptible of no other happiness or perfection than what he has created for himself, instinct apart, through his own reason.

Nature does nothing superfluously, and in the use of means to her ends does not play the prodigal. Having given to man reason, and freedom of the will grounded upon reason, she had hereby sufficiently made known the purpose which governed her in the choice of the furniture and appointments, intellectual and physical, with which she has accoutered him. Thus provided, he had no need for the guidance of instinct, or for knowledge and forethought created to his hand; for these he was to be indebted to himself. The means of providing for his own shelter from the elements—for his own security, and the whole superstructure of delights which add comfort and embellishment to life—were to be the work of his own hands. So far indeed has she pushed this principle, that she seems to have been frugal even to niggardliness in the dispensation of her animal endowments to man, and to have calculated her allowance to the nicest rigor of the demand in the very earliest stage of existence: as if it had been her intention hereby to proclaim that the highest degree of power—of intellectual perfection—and of happiness to which he should ever toil upwards from a condition utterly savage, must all be wrung and extorted from the difficulties and thwartings of his situation—and the merit therefore be exclusively his own, thus implying that she had at heart his own rational self-estimation rather than his convenience or comfort. She has indeed beset man with difficulties; and in no way could she have so clearly made known that her purpose with man was not that he might live in pleasure; but that by a strenuous wrestling with those difficulties he might make himself worthy of living in pleasure. Undoubtedly it seems surprising on this view of the case that the earlier generations appear to exist only for the sake of the latter—viz., for the sake of forwarding that edifice of man's grandeur in which only the latest generations are to dwell, though all have undesignedly taken part in raising it. Mysterious as this appears, it is however at the same time necessary, if we once assume a race of rational animals, as destined by means of this characteristic reason to a perfect development of their tendencies, and subject to mortality in the individual but immortal in the species.

By now Kant's overall conception of human history has been spelled out a bit: In man, nature has produced a rational animal possessing free will—he can reason and be reasoned with, and he can choose. Nature's purpose, in respect to man, is to develop these two powers, and all other powers that are dependent on these two powers; to develop, in humanity, the power to reason and be reasoned with, and the power to choose. Her plan, a means to goading humanity into realizing her purpose, is to see to it that man shall owe to her only the physical basis (his body) for thinking and choosing, and the physical environment upon which to exercise these powers. Beyond that, he must fend for himself. Nature has one more string to her bow, one more means to goad humanity into realizing her purpose:

Proposition the Fourth. The means, which nature employs to bring about the development of all the tendencies she has laid in man, is the antagonism of these tendencies in the social state—no farther however than to that point at which this antagonism becomes the cause of social arrangements founded in law.

By antagonism of this kind I mean the unsocial sociality of man; that is, a tendency to enter the social state combined with a perpetual resistance to that tendency which is continually threatening to dissolve it. Man has gregarious inclinations, feeling himself, in the social state, more than man by means of the development thus given to his natural tendencies. But he has also strong antigregarious inclinations prompting him to insulate himself, which arise out of the unsocial desire (existing concurrently with his social propensities) to force all things into compliance with his own humor; a propensity to which he naturally anticipates resistance from his consciousness of a similar spirit of resistance to others existing in himself. Now this resistance it is which awakens all the powers of man. It drives him to master his propensity to indolence, and, in the shape of ambition or avarice, impels him to procure distinction for himself amongst his fellows. In this way arise the first steps from the savage state to the state of culture, which consists peculiarly in the social worth of man: Talents of every kind are now unfolded, taste formed, and by gradual increase of light a preparation is made for such a mode of thinking as is capable of converting the rude natural tendency to moral distinctions into determinate practical principles, and finally of exalting a social concert that had been extorted from the mere necessities of the situation into a moral union founded on reasonable choice. But for these antisocial propensities, so unamiable in themselves, which give birth to that resistance which every man meets with in his own self-interested pretensions, an Arcadian life would arise of perfect harmony and mutual love such as must suffocate and stifle all talents in their very germs. Men, as gentle as the sheep they fed, would communicate to their existence no higher value than belongs to mere animal life, and would leave the vacuum which exists in reference to the final purpose of man's nature, as a rational being, unfilled. Thanks be, therefore, to nature for the enmity, for the jealous spirit of envious competition, for the insatiable thirst after wealth and power! These wanting, all the admirable tendencies in man's nature would remain for ever undeveloped. Man, for his own sake as an individual, wishes for concord; but nature knows better what is good for man as a species, and she ordains discord. He would live in ease and passive content; but nature wills that he shall precipitate himself out of his luxury of indolence into labors and hardships, in order that he may devise remedies against them and thus raise himself above them by an intellectual conquest—not sink below them by an unambitious evasion. The impulses, which she has laid in his moral constitution, the sources of that antisociality and universal antagonism from which so many evils arise, but which again stimulate a fresh reaction of the faculties and by consequence more and more aid the development of the primitive tendencies—all tend to betray the adjusting hand of a wise creator, not that of an evil spirit that has bungled the execution of his own designs, or has malevolently sought to perplex them with evil.

Nature has given man the power to reason and the power to choose; her purpose is to develop these powers in the race. To this end she leaves him to fend for himself by the exercise of these powers. He is on his own so far as nature is concerned; however, men are dependent on each other, and also antagonistic to each other: they are social, with antisocial tendencies. Hence we have dependence and conflict as built-in features of *la condition humaine.*

Proposition the Fifth. The highest problem for the human species, to the solution of which it is irresistibly urged by natural impulses, is the establishment of a universal civil society founded on political justice.

Since it is only in the social state that the development of all man's tendencies can be accomplished; since such a social state must combine with the utmost possible freedom, and consequent antagonism of its members, the most rigorous determination of the boundaries of this freedom in order that the freedom of such individual may coexist with the freedom of others; and since this as well as all other objects of man's destination should be the work of men's own efforts, on these accounts a society in which freedom under laws is united with the greatest possible degree of irresistible power is the highest problem nature sets for man; because it is only by the solution of this problem that nature can accomplish the rest of her purpose with our species. Into this state of restraint man, who is otherwise so much enamored of lawless freedom, is compelled to enter by necessity, his natural inclinations making it impossible for man to preserve a state of perfect liberty for any length of time in the neighborhood of his fellows. But, under the restraint of a civil community, these very inclinations lead to the best effects— just as trees in a forest, for the very reason that each endeavors to rob the other of air and sun, compel each other to shoot upwards in quest of both; and thus attain a fine erect growth; whereas those which stand aloof from each other under no mutual restraint, and throw out their boughs at pleasure, become crippled and distorted. All the gifts of art and cultivation which adorn the human race—in short, the most beautiful forms of social order—are the fruits of the antisocial principle—which is compelled to discipline itself, and by means won from the very resistance of man's situation in this world to give perfect development to all the germs of nature.

A rational animal, capable of action based on the power to choose, who is also dependent on his fellows but inveterately antisocial, will be driven finally to the legislative way of life, to the enforced regulation of some human behavior by man-made laws. This calls for political organization, and promises liberty under law. These are the human bases of civilization. As the history of this "civilizing" race proceeds, men become increasingly dependent on laws produced by scientists and laws produced by legislators, and human life becomes less regulated by personal habit and group customs. This massive transformation of the lives of political animals is the highest task that nature sets for humanity, the most demanding, and the latest to be accomplished. Thus Kant:

Proposition the Sixth. This problem is at the same time the most difficult of all, and the one which is latest solved by man.

The difficulty, which is involved in the bare idea of such a problem, is this: Man is an animal that, so long as he lives amongst others of his species, stands in need of a master. For he inevitably abuses his freedom in regard to his equals; and, although as a reasonable creature he wishes for a law that may set bounds to the liberty of all, yet do his self-interested animal propensities seduce him into making an exception in his own favor whensoever he dares. He requires a master therefore to curb his will, and to compel him into submission to a universal will which may secure the possibility of universal freedom. Now where is he to find this master? Of necessity amongst the human species. But, as a human being, this master will also be an animal that requires a master. Lodged in one or many, it is impossible that the supreme and irresponsible power can be certainly prevented from abusing its authority. Hence it is that this problem is the most difficult of any; nay, its perfect solution is impossible; out of wood so crooked and perverse as that which man is made of, nothing absolutely straight can ever be wrought. An approximation to this idea is therefore all which nature enjoins. That it is also the last of all problems, to which the human species addresses itself, is clear from this—that it presupposes just notions of the nature of a good constitution, great experience, and a will favorably disposed to the adoption of such a constitution; three elements that can hardly, and not until after many fruitless trials, be expected to concur.

The legislative way of life in separate political societies, based upon a rationally arrived at and rationally exploited knowledge of nature and her forces, threatens finally to wipe out human achievement, and so defeat nature's purposes with regard to humanity. This brings Kant to his seventh proposition, the longest in the essay, and perhaps the most famous. There is irony in all of this—Nature threatened with frustration and defeat by the success of her plans for goading mankind into carrying out her purpose and plans:

Proposition the Seventh. The problem of the establishment of a perfect constitution of society depends upon the problem of a system of international relations adjusted to law; and, apart from this latter problem, cannot be solved.

To what purpose is labor bestowed upon a civil constitution adjusted to law for individual men, i.e., upon the creation of a commonwealth? The same antisocial impulses, which first drove men to such a creation, is again the cause—that every commonwealth in its external relations, i.e., as a state in reference to other states, occupies the same ground of lawless and uncontrolled liberty. Consequently each must anticipate from the other the same evils which compelled individuals to enter the social state. Nature accordingly avails herself of the spirit of enmity in man, as existing even in the great national corporations of that animal, for the purpose of attaining through the inevitable antagonism of this spirit a state of rest and security. That is, by wars, by the exhaustion of incessant preparations for war, and by pressure of evil consequences which war at last entails even through the midst of peace, she drives nations to all sorts of experiments and expedients; and finally after devastations, ruin, and exhaustion of energy, to one which reason should have suggested without the cost of so sad an experience; viz., to quit the condition of lawless power, and to enter into a federal league of nations, in which even the weakest member looks for its rights and for protection not to its own power, or its own adjudication, but to this great confederation, to the united power, and the adjudication of the collective will. Visionary as this idea may seem, it is, notwithstanding, the inevitable resource and mode of escape under that pressure of evil which nations reciprocally inflict; and, hard as it may be to realize such an idea, states must of necessity be driven at last to the very same resolution to which the savage man of nature was driven with equal reluctance—viz., to sacrifice brutal liberty, and to seek peace and security in a civil constitution founded upon law. All wars therefore are so many tentative essays (not in the intention of man, but in the intention of nature) to bring about new relations of states, and by revolutions and dismemberments to form new political bodies. These again, either from internal defects or external attacks, cannot support themselves, but must undergo similar revolutions, until at last, partly by the best possible arrangement of civil government within and partly by common concert and legal compact without, a condition is attained which, like a well-ordered commonwealth, can maintain itself.

Now, whether (in the first place) it is to be anticipated that states, like atoms, by accidental shocking together, should go through all sorts of new combinations to be again dissolved by the fortuitous impulse of fresh shocks, until at length by pure accident some combination emerges capable of supporting itself; or whether (in the second place) we should assume that nature is pursuing her course of raising our species gradually from the lower steps of animal existence to the very highest of a human existence, and that not by any direct interposition in our favor but through man's own spontaneous and artificial efforts (spontaneous, but yet extorted from him by his situation), and in this apparently wild arrangement of things is developing with perfect regularity the original tendencies she has implanted; or whether (in the third place) it is more reasonable to believe that out of all this action and reaction of the human species upon itself nothing in the shape of a wise result will ever issue, that it will continue to be as it has been, and therefore that it cannot be known before hand but that the discord, which is so natural to our species, will finally prepare for us a hell of evils under the most moral condition of society such as may swallow up this very moral condition itself and all previous advance in culture by a reflex of the original barbaric spirit of desolation; to all this the answer turns upon the following question: Is it reasonable to assume a final purpose in all natural processes and arrangements in the parts, and yet a want of purpose in the whole?

What therefore the condition of savage life effected, viz., checked the development of the natural tendencies in the human species, but then, by the very evils thus caused, drove man into a state where those tendencies could unfold and mature themselves, that same service is performed for states by the barbaric freedom in which they are now existing—viz., by causing the dedication of all national energies and resources to war, it checks the full development of the natural tendencies in its progress; but on the other hand by these very evils and their consequences, it compels our species at last to discover some law of counterbalance to the principle of antagonism between nations, and in order to give effect to this law to introduce a federation of states and consequently an international police corresponding to national internal police.

This federation will itself not be exempt from danger, else the powers of the human race would go to sleep. It will be sufficient that it contain a principle for restoring the equilibrium between its own action and reaction, and thus checking the two functions from destroying each other. Before this last step is taken, human nature—then about half way advanced in its progress—is in the deepest abyss of evils under the deceitful semblance of external prosperity. We are at this time in a high degree of culture as to arts and sciences. We are civilized to superfluity in what regards the graces and decorums of life. But, to entitle us to consider ourselves moralized, much is still wanting. Nothing indeed of a true moral influence can be expected so long as states direct all their energies to idle plans of aggrandizement by force, and thus incessantly check the slow motions by which the intellect of the species is unfolding and forming itself, to say nothing of their shrinking from all positive aid to those motions. But all good, that is not engrafted upon moral good, is mere show and hollow speciousness—the dust and ashes of morality. And in this delusive condition will the human race linger, until it shall have toiled upwards in the way I have mentioned from its present chaotic abyss of political relations.

As individuals succeed in creating strong and well-ordered communities, they succeed only in reinstating at the political, community level the *bellum omnium contra omnes* ("war of all against all") that their political efforts were designed to moderate and control within communities. The survival of man as a political animal depends on his ability to create, to preserve, and to increase an international political order. This will result, finally, in a worldstate ruled by a world government; as Kant envisions it, an international republic of federated national republics. He has a great theme here:

Proposition the Eighth. The history of the human species as a whole may be regarded as the unraveling of a hidden plan of nature for accomplishing a perfect state of civil constitution for society in its internal relations (and, as the condition of that, in its external relations also) as the sole state of society in which the tendencies of human nature can be all and fully developed.

This proposition is an inference from the preceding. The question arises: Has experience yet observed any traces of such an unraveling in history? I answer: Some little. The entire period of this unraveling is probably too vast to admit of our detecting the relation of the parts to the whole from the small fraction of it which man has yet left behind him.

Meantime our human nature obliges us to take an interest even in the remotest epoch to which our species is destined, provided we can anticipate it with certainty. So much less can we be indifferent to it, inasmuch as it appears within our power by intellectual arrangements to contribute something toward the acceleration of the species in its advance to this great epoch. On this account the faintest traces of any approximation in such a direction becomes of importance to us. At present all states are so artificially interconnected, that no one can possibly become stationary without retrograding with respect to the rest; and thus if not the progress yet the nondeclension of this purpose of nature is sufficiently secured through the ambition of nations. Moreover, civil liberty cannot at this day any longer be arrested in its progress but that all the sources of livelihood, and more immediately trade, must betray a close sympathy with it, and sicken as that sickens; and hence a decay of the state in its external relations. Gradually too this liberty extends itself. If the citizen be hindered from pursuing his interest in any way most agreeable to himself, provided only it can coexist with the liberty of others, in that case the life of general business is palsied, and in connection with that again the powers of the whole. Hence it arises that all personal restriction is more and more withdrawn; religious liberty is established; and thus, with occasional interruptions, arises illumination; a blessing which the human race must win even from the self-interested purposes of its rulers, if they comprehend what is for their own advantage. Now this illumination, and with it a certain degree of cordial interest which the enlightened man cannot forbear taking in all the good which he perfectly comprehends must by degrees mount upwards even to the throne, and exert an influence on the principles of government.

Finally, war itself becomes gradually not only so artificial a process, so uncertain in its issue, but also in the afterpains of inextinguishable national debts so anxious and burthensome; and, at the same time, the influence which any convulsions of one state exert upon every other state is so remarkable in our quarter of the globe—linked as it is in all parts by the systematic intercourse of trade—that at length, those governments, which have no immediate participation in the war, under a sense of their own danger, offer themselves as mediators—though as yet without any authentic sanction of law, and thus prepare all things from afar for the formulation of a great primary state body, such as is wholly unprecedented in all preceding ages. Although this body at present exists only in rude outline, yet already a stirring is beginning to be perceptible in all its limbs—each of which is interested in the maintenance of the whole; even now there is enough to justify a hope that, after many revolutions and remodelings of states, the supreme purpose of nature will be accomplished in the establishment of an international state as the bosom in which all the original tendencies of the human species are to be developed.

Kant's ninth proposition is a glance back over the argument of the preceding eight. Nothing essentially new is added: (a) Only the powers (to reason and to choose) that nature has "planted" in man can achieve these outcomes: communities organized into the legislative way of life as nations, and these nations organized into a planetary republic of national republics. A stand of trees, or a herd of cattle, or a system of uninhabited planets could not do it. (b) Only the achievement of these national and international goals by men will make possible the indefinite realization of nature's purpose; namely, to produce conditions under which men can develop the powers that nature has "planted" in them, and the powers dependent on those powers. (c) Only a history of humanity, which made all this stand out clear, would cue man in on nature's purpose and plan, make him aware of what nature has been up to all these millions of years, and of humanity's destiny in relation to nature's intentions. So:

Proposition the Ninth. A philosophical attempt to compose a universal history tending to unfold the purpose of nature in a perfect civil union of the human species is to be regarded as possible, and as capable even of helping forward this very purpose of nature.

At first sight it is apparently an extravagant project—to propose a history of man founded on any idea of the course which human affairs would take if adjusted to certain reasonable ends. On such a plan, it may be thought, nothing better than a romance could result. Yet, if we assume that nature proceeds not without plan even in the motions of human free will, this idea may possibly turn out very useful; and, although we are too shortsighted to look through the secret mechanism of her arrangements, this idea may yet serve as a clue for connecting into something like unity the great abstract of human actions that else seem a chaotic and incoherent aggregate. For, if we take our beginning from Greek history; if we pursue down to our own times its influence upon the formation and malformation of the Roman people as a political body that swallowed up the Greek state, and the influence of Rome upon the barbarians by whom Rome itself was destroyed; and if to all this we add the political history of every other people so far as it has come to our knowledge through the records of the two enlightened nations above mentioned; we shall then discover a regular gradation of improvement in civil polity as it has grown up in our quarter of the globe, which quarter is in all probability destined to give laws to all the rest. If further we direct an exclusive attention to the civil constitution, with its laws, and the external relations of the state, insofar as both, by means of the good which they contained, served for a period to raise and to dignify other nations and with them the arts and sciences, yet again by their defects served also to precipitate them into ruin, but always so that some germ of illumination survived which, being more and more developed by every revolution, prepared continually a still higher step of improvement; in that case, I believe that a clue will be discovered not only for the unraveling of the intricate web of human affairs and for the guidance of future statesmen, but also such a clue as will open a consolatory prospect into futurity, in which at a remote distance we shall discover the human species seated upon an eminence won by infinite toil where all the germs are unfolded which nature has implanted—and its destination upon this earth accomplished. Such a justification of nature, or rather of providence, is no mean motive for choosing this station for the survey of history. For what does it avail to praise and to draw forth to view the magnificence and wisdom of the creation in the irrational kingdom of nature, if that part in the great stage of the supreme wisdom, which contains the object of all this mighty display—viz., the history of the human species—is to remain an eternal objection to it, the bare sight of which obliges us to turn away our eyes with displeasure, and (from the despair which it raises of ever discovering in it a perfect and rational purpose) finally leads us to look for such a purpose only in another world?

My object in this essay would be wholly misinterpreted, if it were supposed that under the idea of a universal history which to a certain degree has its course determined *a priori*, I had any wish to discourage the cultivation of empirical history in the ordinary sense. On the contrary, the philosopher must be well versed in history who could execute the plan I have sketched, which is indeed a most extensive survey of history, only taken from a new station. However, the extreme and, simply considered, praiseworthy circumstantiality, with which the history of every nation is written in our times, must naturally suggest a question of some embarrassment: In what way will our remote posterity be able to cope with the enormous accumulation of historical records which a few centuries will bequeath to them? There is no doubt that they will estimate the historical details of times far removed from their own, the original monuments of which will have long perished, simply by the value of that which will then concern themselves—viz., by the good or evil performed by nations and their governments in a universal view. To direct the eye upon this point as connected with the ambition of rulers and their servants, in order to guide them to the only means of bequeathing an honorable record of themselves to distant ages, may furnish some small motive (over and above the great one of justifying providence) for attempting a philosophic history on the plan I have here explained.

It is easy, but neither necessary nor desirable, for a reader in the last quarter of the twentieth century to sell Kant short in the matter of his 1784 essay. It invites comparison and contrast with Orwell's novel *1984*. Kant is more civilized and more civilizing than Orwell. It invites comparison and contrast with Skinner's *Walden Two*. Kant is more civilized and more civilizing than Skinner. A reader should not be put off by Kant's "Age of Reason" mythology about nature and her purposes and plans. Whether God or nature or accident is responsible for man's existence on this planet is one question, and not a trivial question. But, however he got here, the important question for an overall theory of human history is his nature now that he is here. Disregarding Kant's mythologizing about nature, his important claim is that human history will be what it is largely because man's nature is what it is. And what is it to be human? It is, he says, to have the power to reason and be reasoned with; and the power to choose based upon one's power to reason and be reasoned with; and to possess an indefinite number of other powers based upon those two. How wrong is that picture? Among readers of this page, who are prepared to say of themselves that they are not rational in Kant's sense, that they are incapable of choice in Kant's sense, and that they have no powers growing out of those features that Kant stipulates as essentially human? Having somehow produced such a creature, Kant tell us, nature found that she had only one overriding purpose: to so arrange matters that these powers would be indefinitely developed. What is so wrong about that, allowing for the mythological thinking? What alternative would we recommend to nature? Given her purpose, nature hatched out a plan. Given humanity, and given her purpose, what was so wrong about her plan?

READING QUESTIONS

1. What are Kant's views on history and man's free will?
2. Why must the philosopher endeavor to detect some natural purpose in human actions?
3. Be prepared to formulate each numbered proposition (e.g., Proposition the First) as briefly as you can.
4. "This would expose nature, the wisdom of whose arrangements must in all other cases be assumed, as a fundamental postulate, to the suspicion of capricious dealing with man only."
   a. What would expose nature thus?
   b. Why must the wisdom of her arrangements be assumed, in all other cases, as a fundamental postulate?
   c. What is the wisdom of her arrangements?
   d. Do you imagine that Kant would criticize the design argument in natural theology?
5. Where, do you suppose, Kant finds out that the arrangement noted in Proposition the Third is the will of nature? What does such an expression mean, if not the will of God? Can nature be said to have a will?
6. What *appears* mysterious, but *is* necessary, if we once assume what?

7. What is the means which nature employs to bring about the development of the tendencies she has laid in man?
8. "No farther, however, than to that point." What point?
9. "Man wishes for concord; but nature knows better, and she ordains discord." Why?
10. What is the highest problem for the human species?
11. "This problem is at the same time the most difficult of all." Elucidate.
12. "This problem depends upon a system of international relations adjusted to law." Elucidate.
13. "The human race will linger in this delusive condition until it shall have toiled upwards in the way I have mentioned." What delusive condition? What way?
14. "The history of the human species may be regarded as the unraveling of a hidden plan of nature." Namely?
15. Of what value is such a history?
16. "I have no wish to discourage, under the idea of a universal history, which is to a certain degree *a priori*, the cultivation of empirical history." Explain.

INDEPENDENT STUDY

1. Read the first 104 pages of R. G. Collingwood's book *The Idea of History*. Use your firsthand knowledge of Kant, gained from reading his 1784 essay, and Collingwood's account of men's ideas of history down to Kant, to write a paper showing Kant's position in relation to his forerunners.
2. When you have studied the next section in this book, containing Hegel's views on human history, write a paper relating Hegel to Kant. In what ways is Kant an important road to Hegel in speculative philosophy of history? What important changes do you find in Hegel?
3. Read the article "Philosophy of History" by W. H. Dray in the *Encyclopedia of Philosophy*. Write a paper contrasting critical and speculative philosophy of history. (Dray's bibliography omits his own important book, *Law and Explanation in History*.)

SECTION 2. G. W. F. HEGEL: THE POLITICAL
INTERPRETATION OF HISTORY

From Kant to Hegel. Kant's proposal for an interpretation of human history ("Nature has a plan, and humanity is working it out in history.") was published in 1784. It did not command much attention at that time. Hegel's views, while in some ways merely an extension of Kant's, have been more widely read and more influential. These were set forth in his *Philosophy of History,* delivered as lectures at the University of Berlin for some years prior to his death, and published posthumously in 1837.

Between Kant and Hegel there was much history in Sense One, including the French Revolution and the career of Napoleon. These made a difference, for persons who lived on into the period of reaction under Metternich, in the interpretation of history. The French Revolution, which began as a demand for liberty, seemed to culminate in a demand for licence; and its licence, in turn, seemed to have invoked the heavy-handed regime of Napoleon. The result, in the sphere of practical politics, was a period of illiberalism, of distrust of revolutionary politics, and of fear of the tyranny they seem to generate. From 1815 to 1830 this distrust was at its height. Hegel's philosophy of history is the attempt to restate the appeal to reason, such as one meets in Kant's pamphlet, by an appeal to reason somewhat disillusioned and chastened by the events that fell between him and Kant. Three things at least Hegel had to do: save the great concept of freedom, by means of the distinction between law and licence; provide recognition of the fact that history includes a place for the great man, or hero, e.g., Napoleon, whom Hegel referred to as the world-spirit on horseback; and justify the attempt of the reaction to save Europe from licence and tyranny in the name of "rational freedom" or freedom under law.

Biographical Note.   Georg Wilhelm Friedrich Hegel was born in 1770 and died in 1831 at the age of sixty-one. He wrote many volumes elucidating the general thesis that reality is spirit manifesting itself in nature, in man, and in their combination, which is history. These books are difficult reading, partly because the thought they contain is unfamiliar and elusive, partly because the words they contain are obscure and technical. Early in life, Hegel arrived at the conclusion that the totality of things is an objectification or manifestation of *Geist,* or spirit. This Spirit is manifested *as* nature and is present *in* man. With his reasons for this conclusion we are not here concerned. His writings are directed, for the most part, toward elaborating his central thesis, not proving it. In his *Phenomenology of Spirit* he offered an account of nature, of man, of society, of morality, of art, of religion, of philosophy, as so many "fields" in which the nature of *Geist* is disclosed. His *Philosophy of Right* was a treatise on the state and law in which these are analyzed and described to show wherein they disclose the nature of *Geist,* spirit. After his death, his disciples published his lectures in a series of volumes, *Philosophy of History, Philosophy of Art, Philosophy of Religion,* in which similarly motivated analyses and descriptions are carried out.

The external facts of Hegel's life are few and conventional. He was trained for the church. He early became an academic. Outwardly at least, he never ceased to be one. He taught at several universities before he was called to occupy the chair of philosophy in the University at Berlin. He died, at the height of his fame, from an attack of cholera, which had broken out in Berlin. His writings provided the great synthesis of European thought between the age of Newton and Kant before him, and Darwin and Marx after him.

The Argument of the Passages. After defending the notion of a philosophy of history against the charge of forcing facts to fit theories, Hegel proposes that history be construed as the realm of mind, in contrast to nature as the realm of matter. In history, mind, or spirit, is engaged in working out the form and substance of freedom. Freedom is the capacity to act. It presupposes rules. Rules that permit the exercise and growth of the capacity to act are rules that define freedom under law, which is true freedom, in contrast to false freedom or licence. The career of spirit has been marked by violence and conflict. This breeds pessimism and cynicism only in little men. Hegel's claim is that they (violence and conflict) are the necessary conditions under which freedom comes into being. The process is blind, in the sense that the successive steps are not marked out in advance. But it is also beneficent in the sense that each step forward, no matter what the cost in individual misery, marks an increase in the conditions that make freedom possible. The pain and sorrow that characterize the history of humanity, the conflicts within states and between states are blind stumblings toward that form of organized living in which spirit will achieve a maximum of realization in the freedom of individuals. This is a kind of long-range optimism, but in the short range it is harsh and grim.

The world-spirit makes use of certain individuals to initiate new and difficult turns in the history of civilization. These are the great men, or heroes, of history. They serve a power and an end that transcends them. The goal of history is the evolution of the state, that is, a union of rational wills making possible the continuous exercise and development of freedom. This is the march of God on earth. The state is the organization of the nation. Since there are many nations, war is a necessary ingredient in history. Such conflict purifies and strengthens the national state. There is no judge of the nations, beyond their survival in the strenuous march of God on earth. The world's history is the world's tribunal. Let us make a beginning:

The most general definition that can be given of the philosophical treatment of history is contained in the word *rational*. The *philosophy of history* means the "rationale of history." The only thought which philosophy brings to the contemplation of history is the simple conception of reason; that reason is the sovereign of the world; that the history of the world, therefore, presents us with a "rational" process. This conviction and intuition are an hypothesis in the domain of history as such.

Before elaborating this view of history, Hegel turns to consider a possible objection. May this not lead a man to set up a plan and then force the facts to fit it?

This presupposition that history has an essential and actual goal or end is called an *a priori* view of it. Philosophy is reproached with "*a priori* history-writing." On this point we must go into further detail. This seems to be the legitimate demand that the historian should proceed with impartiality; there should be no prepossession in favor of an idea or opinion, just as a judge should have no special sympathy for one of the contending parties.

Now, in the case of the judge it is admitted that he would administer his office ill and foolishly if he had no interest in justice; indeed, if he did not have an exclusive interest in justice. That is assumed to be his one sole aim. This requirement, which we make of a judge, may be called partiality for justice.

But, in speaking of the impartiality required from an historian, this self-satisfied, insipid, chatter lets the distinction between legitimate, responsible partiality and mere subjective partiality, disappear. It demands that the historian shall bring with him no definite aim, no definite conception by which he may sort out, describe, evaluate events. It demands that he shall narrate them exactly in the casual mode he finds them, in all their incoherent and unintelligent particularity. A history must have an object, e.g., Rome and its fortunes, or the greatness and decline of Rome. This lies at the basis of the events themselves, and therefore at the basis of the critical examination into their comparative importance. A history without some such criticism would be only an imbecile mental digression—not so good as a fairy tale, for even children expect a motif in their stories, at least dimly surmisable, with which events and actions are put in relation.

To presuppose such a theme is blameworthy only when the assumed conception is arbitrarily adopted, and when a determined attempt is made to force events and actions to conform to this conception. For this kind of *a priori* handling of history, however, those are chiefly to blame who profess to be "purely historical," who raise their voice against any attempt to deal philosophically with history. Philosophy is to them a troublesome neighbor; for she is the enemy of all arbitrariness and hasty suggestion.

So much, then, for an objection to his view. He asks of history what a scientist asks of nature, namely, that it be reasonable, that the use of reason on the details of history shall not *ipso facto* mislead a man. This granted, much may be expected. However, this rationality of history is not to be confused with a pious belief in a superintending providence:

The time must come for understanding that rich product of active Reason which world history offers to us. It was for a while the fashion to profess admiration for the wisdom of God as displayed in animals plants, and isolated occurrences. But, if it be allowed that Providence exhibits itself in such objects and forms of existence, why not also in world history? Is this too great a matter to be thus regarded? But divine wisdom, that is, reason, is one and the same in the great as well as in the little.

In those to whom such a conception is not familiar, I may at least presume the existence of a belief in reason, a desire, a thirst, for an understanding of it. Indeed, it is the wish for rational insight, not the ambition to amass a mere heap of facts, that should be presupposed in the mind of every learner. If the clear idea of reason, of pervading rationality, is not already in our minds, in beginning the study of history, we should at least have the firm faith that it does exist there, that the scene of intelligence and conscious volition—human history—is not abandoned to chance. . . . To him who looks upon the world rationally, the world in its turn presents a rational aspect. The relation is mutual.

This conviction involves much more than the mere belief in a "superintending Providence." Pious folk are encouraged to see in particular circumstances, something more than mere chance; to acknowledge the "guiding hand" of God when help has unexpectedly come to an individual in great perplexity and need. But these instances of "providential design" are of a limited kind. They concern the accomplishment of nothing more than the desires of the individual in question. But in world history the "individuals" we have to deal with are whole peoples, e.g., the Jews, the Greeks, the Romans. We cannot, therefore, be satisfied with what we may call this "trifling" view of Providence.

But *reason*, whose presence in the world and sovereignty over the world has been maintained, is as vague and indefinite a term as *Providence*. Unless we can characterize it distinctly, unless we can show wherein it consists, we cannot decide whether a thing is rational or irrational. An adequate definition of *reason* is therefore the first desideratum to an inquiry into "reason in history." Without such a definition we can get no further than mere words.

To begin with, it must be observed that world history belongs to the realm of spirit, not to the realm of matter. The term *world*, indeed, includes both physical and psychical. But our concern is not with nature at large. On the stage of world history spirit displays itself in its most concrete reality. The development of spirit is our central theme.

The nature of spirit may be understood by a glance at its direct opposite—matter. As the essence of matter is gravity, so the essence of spirit is freedom. It involves an appreciation of its own nature, a power to know itself as also an energy enabling it to realize itself, to make itself actually that which it is potentially. Accordingly it may be said of world history that it is the exhibition of spirit working out that which it is potentially.

The spirit which thinks in world history, stripping off the limitations of its several national manifestations and temporal restrictions, lays hold of its actual transcendence and universality, rises to apprehend itself for what it essentially is, while the necessity of nature and the necessity of history but minister to its revelation and are vessels of its honor.

It is the spirit which not merely broods over history as over the waters, but lives in it and is alone its principle of movement. And in the path of that spirit, liberty is the guiding principle and its development the final aim. Such a doctrine—reason in history—will be partly a plausible faith, partly a philosophical insight.

If the essence of spirit is freedom, then the history of the world, if it is the history of spirit, is none other than the progress of the consciousness of freedom.

The [ancient] Orientals had not attained the knowledge that spirit, man as such, is free. And because they did not know this, they lived in bondage. They knew only the freedom of one among the many. That one was therefore only a despot, a tyrant, not a free man. The freedom of that one was only caprice; ferocity, brutal recklessness of passion; or, equally an accident of nature, mildness and tameness of desire.

The consciousness of freedom first arose among the Greeks. And therefore they were free. But they, and the Romans likewise, knew only that some are free, not man as such. They therefore had slaves. Their whole life, and the maintenance of their splendid liberty, was implicated with the institution of slavery. Liberty, among them, was therefore only an accidental, a transient, a limited growth; and this very fact constituted it a rigorous thraldom of our common human nature.

The Germanic peoples, under the influence of Christianity, were the first to realize that man, as man, is free; that it is freedom which constitutes the essence of spirit. To introduce this realization into the various relations of the actual world was a large problem, whose solution required a severe and lengthened process of culture. Slavery did not cease immediately upon the reception of Christianity. Liberty did not all at once predominate in states. Governments and constitutions did not all at once adopt a rational organization, or recognize freedom as their basis. The application of the principle to political relations, the thorough molding and interpenetration of society by it, has been identical with history itself. But the history of the world has been none other than the progress of the consciousness of freedom.

In world history, the essential nature of freedom is displayed as coming to a consciousness of itself, as realizing itself. This is the result at which world history has been aiming. To this end have the sacrifices that have ever and anon been laid on the vast altar of the earth, through long lapse of ages, been offered. This is the only aim that sees itself realized and fulfilled; the only pole of repose amid the ceaseless change of events and conditions; the sole efficient principle that pervades the whole. Translating this into the language of religion, we may say that this realization by spirit of the nature and conditions of freedom is God's final aim and purpose with the world.

Freedom, the capacity to act, is the essence of spirit. Spirit is both manifested *as* nature and our bodies, and present *in* us. This "present-in-us" part is latent. We can potentially do many things that we cannot do actually; e.g., "I cannot, actually play bridge; but, potentially, I can; that is, I can develop that freedom." Now, Hegel asks, "By what means does the spirit present *in* humanity develop its freedoms?"

If, as we have argued, the history of the world is the history of the further and further realization of freedom, we are moved to pose a question: By what means does freedom develop? By what means is it brought to further and further realization?

A first glance at history convinces us that the actions of men proceed from their needs, their passions, their characters, their abilities. A first glance impresses us, too, with the belief that these needs, passions, private interests, are the sole springs of human action. Here and there may be found, perhaps, some aims of a liberal kind; benevolence, maybe; or noble patriotism. But such aims and virtues are insignificant on the broad canvas of history. They bear only a trifling proportion to the mass of the human race, and their influence is limited accordingly.

Passions, private aims, the satisfaction of selfish desires, are the most effective springs of human action. Let no illusions be cherished on this point. Their power lies in the fact that they respect none of the limitations which justice and morality would impose on them. These natural impulses have a more direct influence over men than the artificial and tedious discipline which tends to order and self-restraint, law and morality.

If I am to exert myself for any object, principle, aim, design, it must in some way or other be mine. In its realization I must find my satisfaction; although the purpose for which I exert myself includes a complication of results, many of which have no interest for me. This is the absolute right of personal existence—to find itself satisfied in its activity and labor. If men are to interest themselves in anything, they must find their individuality gratified by its attainment. Nothing therefore happens, nothing is accomplished, unless individuals seek their own satisfaction in the issue.

We assert, then, that nothing has been accomplished without interest on the part of those who brought it about. If *interest* be called *passion*, where the whole individuality is concentrating all its desires and powers to the neglect or exclusion of all other actual or possible interests or claims, we may affirm without qualification that nothing great has been accomplished in the world without passion.

Two elements, therefore, enter into our investigation: first, the aim, principle, destiny namely the realization of freedom; second, the complex of human passions. The one the warp, the other the woof, of the vast arras web of world history.

The spirit which is both manifested as and present in humanity must come out, must gain freedom, must achieve the capacity to act. It must learn and master the conditions of its freedom. Now, Hegel has it, the medium in which this spirit works is the totality of blind drives that compose an unenlightened and undisciplined humanity. The spirit must achieve its freedom through and in these drives, or not at all. In themselves these drives are neither good nor bad. They are, it happens, necessary to that freedom which spirit is seeking in the history of humanity.

Passion is by many regarded as a thing of sinister aspect, more or less immoral. Man is required to have no passions. We need only repeat, to silence such pallid moralizing, that nothing great has been accomplished without passion, without the concentration of energy and will upon some private interests—self-seeking, if you will—to the exclusion of all things else.

World history is controlled by a general aim—the realization of the essence of spirit, which is freedom. In the beginning this is only implicit—a profoundly hidden, unconscious instinct. The whole of history is directed to rendering this unconscious impulse a conscious one. At the very dawn of world history, physical craving, animal instinct, private interest, selfish passion, prejudiced opinion, spontaneously present themselves. This vast congeries of wills, interests, and activities constitute the instruments, the means, the media, of the world spirit for attaining its object.

At this point Hegel introduces a line of thought that is not easy to grasp. But it is central to his philosophy of history. We may approach it by way of what he has already said: The story of humanity is the story of the conquest by the spirit present in humanity of the conditions of its freedom, its power to act. The spirit that is present in man encounters no difficulty in acting, in exerting its will, in the realm of the natural order. And the reason is that "nature" is the realm of law and order. Nature is calculable. She "obeys" rules. When these are known they provide a basis for action. A law in nature is a possible basis for action by men. If there were no law, no order, no pattern, in nature, we could not act. We would be reduced to sheer guesswork; even lower, since if there were no law or order, we could not even guess. When we turn from nature to society, we turn from the realm of law to the realm of freedom. If the man is to act in the "medium" of private wills, there must be something corresponding to laws as they are in nature. To this end man needs the state. The *state* may be defined as "society organized to make law possible." Some laws are left without the pressure of the state immediately behind them. Such laws are moral. Law and morality then, between them, are self-imposed limitations for which the justification is that they make it possible to act. They extend the realm of freedom, from the natural into the social order.

The concrete union of the two elements which we find in history—that freedom which is the essence of spirit, and those individual needs and desires which supply the driving power—is liberty under the conditions of law and morality in the state.

A state is well constituted and internally powerful when the private interests of its citizens are one with the common interest of the state, when the one finds its gratification and realization in the other. The epoch during which a state attains this harmonious condition marks the period of its bloom, its vigor, its virtue and prosperity.

I will endeavor to make my point more vivid by means of an example. The building of a house is, on the one hand, a subjective aim and design. On the other hand we have, as means, the several substances required for the undertaking—iron, wood, stone, etc. The elements are used to work up this material—fire to melt the iron, wind to blow the fire, water to drive the wheels to cut the wood, and so on. The result is that the wind which has helped to build the house is shut out by the house. So also are the rains and floods which supplied the water to drive the wheels; and the destructive power of fire, so far as the house is fireproof. The stones and beams obey their law of gravity—press downwards—and so high walls are carried up.

Thus the elements are used according to their natures, and yet cooperate for a product by which their operation is limited. Thus, in the building of a state, where freedom is realized under conditions of law and order, the passions of men are gratified; they develop themselves and their aims in accordance with their natural tendencies, and build up the edifice of human society; thus fortifying a position for law and order against themselves.

Lest anyone should feel that Hegel is growing optimistic, viewing humanity and the state through rosy spectacles, he turns aside to note that the price of freedom is not merely eternal vigilance; it is eternal strife and violence.

When we contemplate this display of passions, and the consequences of their violence, the unreason which is associated with them; when we see the evil, the vice, the ruin that has befallen the most flourishing kingdom which the mind of man ever created, we can scarce avoid being filled with sorrow at this universal taint and corruption. Since, moreover, this perversion and decay are not the work of mere nature, but the work of human will, we are liable to a moral bitterness, a revolt of the good will, as a result of our reflections.

Without rhetorical exaggeration, a simple truthful account of the miseries that have overwhelmed the noblest of nations and the finest exemplars of private virtue, provides a picture of most fearful aspect, excites emotions of the profoundest and most hopeless sadness, counterbalanced by no consolatory results. History appears as the slaughter bench at which the happiness of peoples, the wisdom of states, and the virtue of individuals have been victimized.

In beholding it we endure a mental torture allowing no defense or escape save the consideration that what has happened could not have been otherwise; that it has been a fatality which no intervention could alter. We draw back at last in disgust. We turn from these intolerable sorrows, from these blackened pages of humanity's history, to the more agreeable environment of our own individual life.

The philosophy of history that Hegel has been marking out threatens to end in a kind of pessimism. Spirit is the capacity to act. It is therefore freedom. It is manifested as nature. It is present in humanity. It requires a social order comprising a moral and political order. These orders are the battleground of private wills controlled by private passions. The spirit must work out its destiny in terms of these factors, or not at all. They are the matter to which it will give the form, the form of freedom. This entails tension and conflict. We turn from it, as from a slaughter bench. But where to? To our own private selves. Only by withdrawing from humanity do we see any prospect of relief from the price that it continuously pays. This is "alienation," "estrangement." The German word is *Entfremdung.* But we withdraw from the human scene in the name of precisely those human values and ideals which the human scene alone makes possible, and toward which it is the endless struggle. Are we caught here in a vicious circle? The "great man" as hero is Hegel's partial answer. The "great man" is he who "breaks ground" for spirit's further advance.

But whither do we thus retreat? Into the present, formed by our own private aims and interests! In short, we retreat into the selfishness that stands on the quiet shore, enjoying thence in safety the distant spectacle of wreckage and confusion.

To what final aim have these enormous sacrifices been offered? To what paradox, moreover, have we come? We point to the gloomy facts presented by history—but we point to them as the very field which we regard as exhibiting the means for realizing what we have described as the essential destiny, the final aim, of world-history. In what terms can this paradox be resolved? We pick up our analysis again. The steps to which it will lead us will also evolve the conditions required for answering the question suggested by the panorama of sin and suffering that history unfolds.

Those manifestations of vitality on the part of individuals and nations, in which they seek and satisfy their own purposes, are at the same time the means and instruments of a higher and broader purpose of which they know nothing, which they realize unconsciously. This has been questioned, denied, condemned, as mere dreaming and "philosophy." So be it. On this point I announced my view at the very outset: Reason governs the world, and has consequently governed history. All else is subordinate to it, subservient to it, and the means for its development.

In the sphere of world history we see momentous collisions between established, acknowledged duties, laws, rights on the one hand and forces adverse to this fixed system on the other. These forces realize themselves in history. They involve principles different from those on which depend the permanence of a people or a state. They are an essential phase in the creative advance of the world spirit. Great historical men—world figures—are those in whose aims such principles are present.

Caesar belongs to this category. His enemies had the *status quo* and the power conferred by an appearance of justice on their side. Caesar was contending for his own position. But his victory secured for him the conquest of the empire. This realization of his own aim, however, was an independently necessary feature in the history of Rome and of the world. It was not merely his private gain. An unconscious impulse occasioned the accomplishment of that for which the time was ripe.

Such are all great historical men. Their own private aims involve those larger issues which are the will of the world spirit. They derive their purposes from a concealed fount, from that inner spirit still hidden beneath the surface which impinges on the outer world as on a shell and bursts it to pieces; not from the calm, regular course of things sanctioned by the existing order.

Such world figures have no consciousness of the general idea they are unfolding while prosecuting their own private aims. On the contrary, they are practical, political men, but possessed of an insight into the requirements of the time, an understanding of what was ripe for development. It is theirs to realize this nascent principle; the next step forward which their world is to take. It is theirs to make this their aim and spend their energies promoting it. They are the heroes of an epoch; must be recognized as its clear-sighted ones. Their deeds, their words, are the best of their time.

World-historical figures form purposes to satisfy themselves, not others. Whatever they might learn from others would limit their role. It is they who best understand. From them others learn; or with them, they acquiesce. For that spirit which, in their persons, takes a fresh step in history is the inmost soul of all individuals; but in them it is in a state of unconsciousness which great men arouse. Their fellows therefore follow them, for they feel the irresistible power of their own indwelling spirit embodied in them.

If we contemplate the fate of the world-historical person, whose destiny is to be the agent of the world spirit, we find it to be no happy one. He attains no calm enjoyment. His whole life is labor and trouble, driven by some master passion. And when his object is attained, he falls off like an empty shell from the kernel. He dies early, like Alexander; he is murdered, like Caesar; he is exiled, like Napoleon. This consolation those may draw from history who stand in need of it, vexed at what is great and transcendent, striving to belittle it because it is beyond them.

The special interests of private passion are thus inseparable from the development of general principles. But the principle is not implicated in the opposition and combat through which it comes into being. It remains in the hinterland, untouched. This may be called the cunning of reason; it sets the passions to work for it, while that which develops through the conflict of passions pays the penalty and suffers the loss.

A world-historical figure is not so unwise as to permit many wishes to divide his energies. He is devoted to one aim. He frequently overrides great and sacred interests. Such conduct is indeed morally reprehensible, but so mighty a form must trample down many an innocent flower, and crush to pieces many an object in its path.

What pedagogue has not demonstrated of Alexander the Great, or of Julius Caesar, that they were immoral men? Whence the conclusion follows that he—the pedagogue—is a better man than they, because he is not driven by their passion. For proof of this he can point to the fact that he does not conquer Asia, does not vanquish Darius, does not subdue an empire. He enjoys life and lets others enjoy it too.

No man is a hero to his valet. Not because he is no hero, but because his valet is only a valet. World-historical figures, waited upon in historical literature by psychological valets, come off poorly. They are brought down to the level—or usually a few degrees below the level—of their biographers, those exquisite discerners of true spirits!

Hegel returns, at this point, to his central thought about the state. It is society organized to make law possible. Under the shadow of political law, we can gradually get moral law. Under the discipline of "legal" law man may rise to "moral" law. Law is the possibility of action. It is therefore the basis of freedom, since freedom is the capacity to act. This Hegelian freedom, with its deification of the state, is sometimes confused with freedom in the sense of "permission" or absence of restraint. He wishes to obviate any such confusion.

In world-history, only those people can come under our notice which form a state. For it must be understood that the state is the realization of freedom.

The state exists for its own sake. All the worth which any human being possesses, he possesses only through the state. Thus only is he fully conscious. Thus only is he a partaker of morality—of a just and moral social and political life. The state is the march of God on earth. We have in it the object of history, that in which freedom obtains realization; for only that will which obeys law is free.

In our time various errors are current, respecting the state. We shall mention only one, but one which is the direct contradictory of our principle that the state is the realization of freedom. It is this misconception: that man is free by nature, but that in society, in the state, he must limit this natural freedom. In this sense a "state of nature" is assumed, in which mankind possess their "natural rights," with the unconstrained exercise and enjoyment of their freedom.

This assumption of "natural freedom" and "natural rights" is not, indeed, given the dignity of being an historical fact. It would be difficult to point to any such condition as existing or having existed. Examples of savage social organization can be pointed to; but not in support of this idea, for they are marked by brutal passion and violence, and, however primitive their conditions, they involve social organizations which actually function to restrain freedom.

Freedom does not exist as primitive and natural. On the contrary, freedom must be sought and won, and by an incalculable discipline of intellectual and moral powers. Then "state of nature" is a state of injustice and violence, of untamed natural impulse, of inhuman deeds and feelings. Limits are certainly imposed by social organization; but they are limits imposed on emotions and instincts. In more advanced stages, they are limits imposed on self-will, caprice, passion. Limitation of this kind is, in part, the means whereby rational freedom, contrasted with unbridled license, can be obtained.

To the conception of freedom, law and morality are indispensably necessary. They are discovered only by the activity of thought, separating itself from the merely sensuous and developing itself in opposition thereto. They must be introduced and incorporated into the originally desire-controlled will, contrarily to its "natural" inclination. The widespread misapprehension of the true nature of freedom consists in conceiving it to be a constraint imposed upon desire, something pertaining to the individual as such. Thus a limitation of caprice and selfwill is regarded as a limitation of freedom. Instead, we argue, such limitation is the indispensable proviso of freedom. Society and the state, with the law and morality upon which they rest, are the very conditions in which freedom is realized.

The state, its laws and morality, constitute the rights of its members. (Thus wide of the facts is the conception of "natural" rights.) Its natural features, its mountains, its rivers, its forests and fields, are their country, their homeland, their material property. Its history is their history. What their forefathers have produced, belongs to them and lives now in their memory. All is their possession, and they are possessed by it. It constitutes their being. This is the meaning of *patriotism*.

The state, then, is the hero of Hegel's philosophy of history. In it the spirit that is manifested as nature and present in man comes to self-realization. When these unions of wills clash, there is war. This conflict clarifies and strengthens the parties. War, like every other genuine expression of will, has its place in the growth of freedom.

In world history each nation is to be regarded as an individual. For world history is the story of the growth of spirit in its highest forms. The forms which this progress assumes are the characteristic "national spirits" of history; the peculiar tenor of their moral life, their government, their art, religion, science. To realize these successive forms is the boundless impulse of the world spirit, the goal of its irresistible longing. The state is the march of God through the world . . . the world which the spirit has made for itself . . . a great architectonic edifice, a hieroglyph of reason, manifesting itself in reality.

All the worth which any human being possesses, all his "spiritual reality," he possesses only through the state. For his "spiritual reality" consists in this, that his own essential nature—rationality—is objectively present to him. Thus only is he fully conscious. Thus only is he a partaker of morality, of a just and moral social and political life. For truth, in these matters, is the unity of the objective and subjective will; and the objective will is to be found in the state, in its laws and arrangements.

Just as the individual is not a real person unless related to other persons, so the state is not a real state unless it is related to other states.

The relation of one state to another presents, on the largest possible scale, the most shifting play of individual passions, interests, aims, talents, virtues, power, injustice, vice, and mere external chance. It is a play in which even the independence of the state is exposed to accident.

When the wills of the particular state can come to no agreement, the matter can only be settled by war. What shall be recognized as a violation of treaty, of respect, or honor, must remain indefinite since many and various injuries can accrue from the wide range of interests and complex relations among states. A state may identify its majesty and honor with any one of its aspects. And if a state, as a strong individuality, has experienced an unduly protracted internal rest, it will naturally be more inclined to irritability in order to find an occasion for intense activity.

There is a moral element in war. It must not be regarded as an absolute ill, or as merely an external calamity accidentally based upon the passions of despotic individuals or nations, upon acts of injustice and what ought not to be.

War has the deep meaning that by it the moral health of nations is preserved and their finite aims uprooted. And as the winds which sweep over the ocean prevent the decay that would result from its perpetual calm, so war protects a people from the corruption which an everlasting peace would bring on it.

In times of peace, civic life becomes more extended, every sphere is hedged in and grows immobile, and at last men stagnate, their particular nature becoming more and more hardened and ossified. Where the organs become still, there is death. Eternal peace is often demanded as an ideal toward which mankind should move. But nations issue forth invigorated from their wars. Nations torn by internal strife win internal peace as the result of war abroad. War indeed causes insecurity of property, but this is a necessary commotion.

From the pulpits one hears much concerning the insecurity, the vanity, the instability of temporal things. Everyone is touched by the words. Yet, let insecurity really come, in the form of Hussars with flashing sabers, and that edification which foresaw all this and acquiesced, now turns upon the enemy with curses. Wars break out whenever necessity demands them; but the seeds spring up anew, and speech is silenced before the grave repetitions of history.

The principles which control the many national spirits are limited. Each nation is guided by its particular principles. No judge exists to adjust differences, save the universal spirit of which these are but moments. Only as a particular individuality can each national spirit win objectivity and self-realization; but states, in their relation one to another, reveal the dialectic, the claims and counterclaims, which arise out of their finitude. Out of this dialectic of history rises the universal spirit, pronouncing its judgment upon the nations of the world. For the world's history is the world's tribunal.

Note on Sources. The preceding material is quoted, abridged, or paraphrased from Hegel's book *The Philosophy of History.* Except for a few passages, the material comes from his introduction to that book.

Reading References. Hegel has been much written about, but the result is not encouraging. In English, there is a small volume by

G. S. Morris, *Hegel's Philosophy of History*. It is more understandable, perhaps, than Hegel's own volumes, *Philosophy of History* and *Philosophy of Right*. The Hegelian conception of the state, and thus the central theme in his philosophy of history, is adopted with modifications by Bernard Bosanquet in his *Philosophical Theory of the State*. A sharply critical and not altogether satisfactory account of the Hegelian notion of the state as the significance of history may be found in L. T. Hobhouse's *The Metaphysical Theory of the State*. It should be offset by a few chapters from M. B. Foster's small volume *The Political Philosophies of Plato and Hegel*. The fact is that Hegel is difficult to read, and that no expositor has succeeded, as yet, in translating him into the language and idiom of ordinary discourse.

READING QUESTIONS

1. Hegel says that philosophy brings the notion of *Geist* to the study of history. (a) How this sets him going about a judge in a court; and about a Superintending Providence. (b) How *Geist* is related to Nature and to history. (c) *Geist* is a many-splendored notion. Use two senses of *rational* to spell out at least part of your answer to (b). (d) Why *Geist* in history needs *Geist* in nature.
2. *Geist*, manifested *as* nature, is everywhere lawful, everywhere rational in Sense One. (a) Why *Geist* present *in* man needs *Geist* manifested as nature. (b) Why, by analogy, *Geist* needs also the state.
3. Why he goes on about "private wills, interests, passions, desires," and so on. What is his main claim here? What is the point of his warp–woof–web metaphor?
4. How the development of the state in history can be likened to the building of a house.
5. What renders us liable to moral bitterness, cynicism, a revolt of the good will, and so on? What is ironic in the outcome of this?
6. Why the *Zeitgeist* (*Geist*-in-time) needs great men. Use an example to spell out any two points in his theory about great men in history.
7. Why the state ("a community organized to make law possible") is no accident in human history. One then current error about the state in history.
8. Why war is no accident in human history. What mankind owes to war. Contrast Kant and Hegel in respect to their claims about the state and war.

9. Hegel: "All the worth any human being possesses, he possesses only through the state." Over to you.
10. Hegel referred to his doctrine of *Geist* as "idealism": the doctrine that "Ultimate Reality" is spirit manifested *as* Nature and present *in* man. What do you understand by his "dialectical idealism," as applied to human history? What does this phrase become in Marxism?
11. Hegel was something of a phrase maker when he chose to be. How do you interpret these: (a) "The state is the march of God on earth"; (b) "Die Weltgeschicht ist das Weltgericht"; (c) "No man is a hero to his valet."

INDEPENDENT STUDY

1. Read the article "Hegel, Georg Wilhelm Friedrich" by H. B. Acton in the *Encyclopedia of Philosophy*. This will give you some sense for Hegel's general position in philosophy. Read *The Open Society and Its Enemies,* Volume II, Chapter 12, by K. Popper. Write on Popper's criticism of Hegel.
2. Read the article "Hegelianism" by S. D. Crites in the *Encyclopedia of Philosophy*. Read *From Hegel to Marx* by S. Hook. Write on Hegel with reference to any individual or movement that he influenced positively or negatively.

SECTION 3. FRIEDRICH ENGELS: THE ECONOMIC INTERPRETATION OF HISTORY

From Hegel to Marx and Engels. What came to be called the "idealistic" interpretation of history was the claim that in history, as opposed to nature, spirit was at work. There is spirit. It manifests itself as matter, the order of nature, which the natural sciences study. But it goes beyond that. In addition to being *manifested as* matter, spirit is also *present in* man, the order of human nature, and in all his activities. The German word for *spirit* is *Geist*. One therefore spoke of *Geisteswissenschaft*, the systematic and orderly study of what spirit does, considered apart from its manifestation as nature. This would give you "history and the social sciences." In all of this, the notion of spirit is ultimate. Given the notion of spirit, you knew how to try to think about "nature," the material order. In this way you arrived at the natural sciences. You knew also how to try to think about man. In this way you arrived at the historical sciences, those inquiries in which spirit sets forth the story of its own activities, the activities that it is itself present in.

Now, up to a point, this idealistic interpretation of history satisfied those who wished to extend their thinking beyond history into a philosophy of history. It was an attractive alternative for those who were skeptical of the biblical interpretation of history, but whose skepticism did not lead them to go further and reject also the conception of spirit working in nature and history. If you were able and willing to think of matter, the material order, as somehow produced by or derived from spirit, this speculative idealism held out hopes for you. But the friends of matter have never been willing to do this. They have always insisted that matter is fundamental and primary, and that spirit is produced by, a derivative from, matter. In the beginning was matter in motion. As a result, spirit gets produced. This speculative materialism is felt to underlie the natural sciences, and also the historical and social sciences. This gives you the materialist interpretation of history, the philosophy of history that makes matter primary and history the story of its motions and changes.

Karl Marx and his friend Friedrich Engels set themselves to work out what became a popular and influential version of the materialist interpretation of history. They called it historical materialism, and referred to it as the economic interpretation of history. They offered it as an alternative to all versions of the biblical or theological interpretation of history, and all versions of the Hegelian or idealist interpretation of history. Matter is primary. Man is made of matter. His activities are "material" activities. The most important of his activities are those that he performs upon matter, transforming it into food, clothing, shelter, and other material means to his material existence and well-being. To this end he everywhere finds it necessary to organize into associations and communities whereby his *working* on matter is made more productive of the means of subsistence. The result is an economy, a community of persons organized to make possible production by division of labor and, therefore, distribution by exchange. What men do as members of economies is therefore the fundamental answer to the question, "What goes on in history?" Hence the phrase "economic interpretation of history."

Note on Marx and Engels. Marx and Engels worked together at formulating the economic interpretation of history. Engels says that Marx was responsible for the fundamental idea, and for the intellectual drive required to work it out in detail, whereas he himself undertook to set it forth in simple, popular language. If you read their joint tract, *The Communist Manifesto*, published in 1848, you see the Marxist interpretation of history already at work. It tells you what has been happening to man, and what man has been doing about it, throughout human history. Marx himself wrote some historical accounts of events in his own time, basing his narrative on the assumption that his general interpretation of history would be granted; e.g., his *Class Struggles in France*, his *Eighteenth Brumaire of Louis Napoleon*, his *Civil War in France*. Late in the 1870's Engels wrote a statement of their historical materialism. He later published it in the form of a pamphlet, *Socialism: Utopian and Scientific*. This small document contains the clearest and most straightforward wording of the doctrine, particularly in its third section or chapter. That third section, slightly abridged but not otherwise changed, follows. In it Engels explains how, as members of economies, men have transformed economies from feudal, land-based economies into capitalist or bourgeois economies; and will transform these in turn into proletarian socialist economies. The joint *Manifesto*, and this similar tract by Engels alone, have done more to secure a hearing for the Marxist economic interpretation of history than any other writings by Marx or Engels or anyone else. (See also pp. 292–293.)

1. The materialist conception of history starts from the proposition that the production of the means to support human life and, next to production, the exchange of things produced, is the basis of all social structure; that the manner in which wealth is distributed and society divided into classes is dependent upon what is produced, how it is produced, and how the products are exchanged. From this point of view the final causes of all social changes and political revolutions are to be sought, not in men's brains, not in man's better insight into eternal truth and justice, but in changes in the modes of production and exchange. They are to be sought, not in the *philosophy*, but in the *economics* of each epoch. The perception that social institutions are unreasonable and unjust, only proves that in the modes of production and exchange changes have silently taken place, with which the social order, adapted to earlier economic conditions, is no longer in keeping. The means of getting rid of the incongruities must be present, in a more or less developed condition, within the changed modes of production themselves. These means are not to be invented by deduction from fundamental principles. They are to be discovered in the facts of the existing system of production.

2. What is, then, the position of modern socialism in this connection?

3. The present structure of society is the creation of the ruling class of today, of the bourgeoisie. The mode of production peculiar to the bourgeoisie, the capitalist mode, was incompatible with the feudal system. The bourgeoisie broke up the feudal system and built the capitalist order of society, the kingdom of free competition, of personal liberty, of equality before the law of all commodity owners, and all the rest of the capitalist blessings. Thenceforward the capitalist mode of production could develop in freedom. Since steam, machinery, and the making of machines by machinery, transformed the older manufacture into modern industry, the productive forces evolved under the bourgeoisie developed with a rapidity and in a degree unheard of before. But just as the older manufacture had come into collision

with the feudal system, so now modern industry, comes into collision with the bounds within which the capitalistic mode of production holds it confined. The new productive forces have already outgrown the capitalistic mode of using them. And this conflict between productive forces and modes of production exists independently of the will and actions even of the men that brought it on. Modern socialism is the reflex, in thought, of this conflict in fact.

4. In what does this conflict consist?

5. Before capitalistic production, the system of petty industry obtained generally, based upon the private property of the labourers in their means of production; in the country, the agriculture of the small peasant, freeman or serf; in the towns, the handicrafts organised in guilds. The instruments of labour were the instruments of single individuals, adapted for the use of one worker and therefore, small, dwarfish, circumscribed. They belonged, as a rule, to the producer himself. To concentrate these scattered, limited means of production, to enlarge them, to turn them into the powerful levers of production of the present day, was the rôle of capitalistic production and of its upholder, the bourgeoisie. Since the fifteenth century this has been worked out through the three phases of simple co-operation, manufacture and modern industry. But the bourgeoisie could not transform these puny means of production into mighty productive forces, without transforming them, at the same time, from means of production of the individual into *social* means of production only workable by a collectivity of men. The spinning-wheel, the hand-loom, the blacksmith's hammer were replaced by the spinning machine, the power-loom, the steam-hammer; the individual workshop, by the factory, implying the co-operation of hundreds and thousands of workmen. In like manner, production itself changed from a series of individual into a series of social acts, and the products from individual to social products. The yarn, the cloth, the metal articles that now came out of the factory were the joint product of many workers. No one person could say of them: "I made that; this is *my* product."

6. But where the form of production is that spontaneous division of labour which creeps in gradually and not upon any preconceived plan, there the products take on the form of *commodities*, whose mutual exchange, buying and selling, enable the individual producers to satisfy their wants. And this was the case in the Middle Ages. The peasant, e.g., sold to the artisan agricultural products and bought from him the products of handicraft. Into this society of individual producers, of commodity producers, the new mode of production thrust itself. In the midst of the old division of labour, grown up spontaneously and upon *no definite plan*, arose division of labour upon *a definite plan*, as organised in the factory; side by side with *individual* production appeared *social* production. The products of both were sold in the same market, and, therefore, at prices approximately equal. But organisation upon a definite plan was stronger than spontaneous division of labour. The factories working with the combined social forces of a collectivity of individuals produced their commodities more cheaply than the individual small producers. Individual production succumbed in one department after another. Socialised production revolutionised all the old methods of production. But its revolutionary character was so little recognized that it was in-

troduced as a means of increasing and developing the production of commodities. When it arose, it found ready-made, certain machinery for the production and exchange of commodities; merchants' capital, handicraft, wage labour. Socialised production thus introducing itself as a new form of the production of commodities, the old forms of appropriation remained in full swing, and were applied to its products as well.

7. In the mediaeval stage, the question as to the owner of the product of labour could not arise. The individual producer had, from raw material belonging to himself, and generally his own handiwork, produced it with his own tools, by the labour of his own hands or of his family. There was no need for him to appropriate the new product. It belonged to him, as a matter of course. His property in the product was based *upon his own labour.* Even where external help was used, this was, as a rule, of little importance, and was generally compensated by something other than wages.

8. Then came the concentration of production and producers in large workshops, their transformation into socialised means of production and socialised producers. But the socialised producers and means of production and their products were still treated, after this change, just as they had been before, i.e., as the means of production and the products of individuals. Hitherto, the owner of the instruments of labour had himself appropriated the product, because as a rule it was his own product and the assistance of others was the exception. Now the owner of the instruments of labour appropriated the product, although it was no longer *his* product but the product of the *labour of others.* Thus, the products now produced socially were not appropriated by those who had actually produced the commodities, but by the *capitalists.* The means of production, and production itself, had become in essence socialised. But they were subjected to a form of appropriation which presupposes the private production of individuals, under which every one owns his own product and brings it to market. The mode of production is subjected to this form of appropriation, although it abolishes the conditions upon which the latter rests.

9. This contradiction *contains the germ of the social antagonisms of today.* The greater the mastery obtained by the new mode of production, the more it reduced individual production to an insignificant residuum, *the more clearly was brought out the incompatibility of socialised production with capitalististic appropriation.*

10. The first capitalists found wage labour ready-made for them on the market. But it was exceptional, complementary, necessary, transitory wage labour. The agricultural labourer, though, upon occasion, he hired himself out by the day, had a few acres of his own on which he could live at a pinch. The guilds were so organised that the journeyman of today became the master of tomorrow. But all this changed, as the means of production became socialised and concentrated in the hands of capitalists. The means of production, as well as the product of the individual producer, became more and more worthless; there was nothing left for him but to turn wage worker under the capitalist. Wage labour, formerly the exception, now became the rule of production. The worker became a wage worker for life. The number of these wage workers was further increased by the breaking up of the feudal system, by the disbanding of the retainers of the feudal lords, the eviction of the

peasants from their homesteads, etc. The separation was made complete between the capitalists possessing the means of production, and the producers, possessing nothing but their labour power. *The contradiction between socialised production and capitalistic appropriation manifested itself as the antagonism of proletariat and bourgeoisie.*

11. The capitalistic mode of production thrust its way into a society of individual producers, whose social bond was the exchange of their products. But in every society based upon the production of commodities, the producers lose control over their social inter-relations. Each man produces for himself and for such exchange as he may require to satisfy his remaining wants. No one knows how much of his particular article is coming on the market, nor how much of it will be wanted. No one knows whether his individual product will meet an actual demand, whether he will be able to make good his cost of production or even to sell his commodity at all. Anarchy reigns in socialised production.

12. But the production of commodities has its peculiar laws; and these laws work in and through anarchy. They reveal themselves in exchange, and here they affect the individual producers as laws of competition. They are, at first, unknown and have to be discovered as the result of experience. They work themselves out, therefore, independently of the producers, and in antagonism to them, as laws of their particular form of production.

13. In mediaeval society, production was directed towards satisfying the wants of the individual. It satisfied the wants of the producer and his family. Where personal dependence existed, it also helped to satisfy the wants of the feudal lord. In all this there was no exchange; the products did not assume the character of commodities. The family of the peasant produced what they wanted: clothes and furniture, means of subsistence. Only when it began to produce more than was sufficient to its own wants and the payments in kind to the feudal lord, did it also produce commodities. This surplus became commodities.

14. The artisans of the towns also supplied the greatest part of their own individual wants. They had gardens and plots of land. They turned their cattle out into the communal forest, which, also, yielded them timber and firing. The women spun flax, wool, and so forth. Production for exchange, production of commodities, was only in its infancy. Hence, exchange was restricted, the market narrow, the methods of production stable.

15. But with the extension of the production of commodities, and especially with the introduction of the capitalist mode of production, the laws of commodity production came into action more openly and with greater force. Old bonds were loosened, old limits broken through, producers more and more turned into independent, isolated producers of commodities. It became apparent that the production of society at large was marked by absence of plan, by accident, by anarchy; and this anarchy grew greater and greater. But the chief means by which the capitalist mode of production intensified this anarchy of socialised production was the exact opposite of anarchy. It was the increasing organisation of production, upon a social basis, in every individual productive establishment. By this, the old, peaceful, stable condition of things was ended. Wherever this organisation of production was introduced, it brooked no other method of production. The field of labour

became a battle ground. The great geographical discoveries, and the colonisation following upon them, multiplied markets and quickened the transformation of handicraft into manufacture. War broke out between the individual producers of particular localities. The local struggles begat in their turn national conflicts, the commercial wars of the seventeenth and eighteenth centuries.

16. Finally, modern industry and the opening of the world market made the struggle universal and gave it an unheard-of virulence. Advantage in conditions of production now decide the existence or non-existence of individual capitalists, as well as of whole industries and countries. He that falls is cast aside. It is the Darwinian struggle of the individual for existence transferred from nature to society. The conditions of existence natural to the animal appear as the final term of human development. The contradiction between socialised production and capitalistic appropriation now presents itself as *an antagonism between the organisation of production in the individual workshop and the anarchy of production in society generally.*

17. The capitalistic mode of production moves in these two forms of antagonism. It is never able to get out of that "vicious circle." This circle is gradually narrowing. The movement becomes more and more a spiral, and must come to an end. It is anarchy in production in society at large that more and more turns the majority of men into proletarians; and it is the proletariat who will finally put an end to anarchy in production. It is the anarchy in social production that turns the perfectibility of machinery into a law by which every individual industrial capitalist must continually perfect his machinery under penalty of ruin.

18. But the perfecting of machinery makes human labour superfluous. The introduction and increases of machinery means the displacement of manual, by a few machine workers. Improvement in machinery means the displacement of the machine workers themselves. It means the production of wage workers in excess of the needs of capital, the formation of an industrial reserve army available when industry is working at high pressure, to be cast out when the crash comes, a constant weight upon the limbs of the working class in its struggle for existence with capital, keeping wages down to the level that suits the interests of capital. Thus machinery becomes the most powerful weapon in the war of capital against the working class; the instruments of labour tear the means of subsistence out of the hands of the labourer; the product of the worker is turned into an instrument for his subjugation. Thus economising the instrument of labour becomes the waste of labour power, and robbery based upon the normal conditions under which labour functions; machinery, the most powerful instrument for shortening labour time, becomes the means for placing the labourer's time at the disposal of the capitalist. Thus it comes about that overwork of some becomes the condition for the idleness of others, and that modern industry, which hunts after new consumers over the whole world, forces the consumption of the masses at home down to a starvation minimum, and so destroys its own home market. The law that equilibrates the surplus population, the industrial reserve army, to the extent and energy of accumulation, rivets the labourer to capital more firmly than ever. It establishes an accumulation of misery, corresponding with accumulation of capital. Accumulation of

wealth at one pole; accumulation of misery, agony of toil, slavery, ignorance, brutality, mental degradation, at the opposite pole.

19. The perfectibility of modern machinery is, by the anarchy of social production, turned into a law that forces the individual industrial capitalist to improve his machinery, to increase its productivity. The possibility of extending production is transformed for him into a compulsory law. The expansive force of modern industry, laughs at all resistance. Such resistance is offered by consumption, by sales, by the markets. The extension of the markets cannot keep pace with the extension of production. The collision becomes inevitable, and as this cannot produce any real solution so long as it does not break the capitalist mode of production, the collisions become periodic. Capitalist production has begotten another "vicious circle."

20. Since 1825, when the first general crisis broke out, the whole industrial and commercial world is thrown out of joint about once every ten years. Commerce is at a standstill, the markets are glutted, products accumulate, hard cash disappears, credit vanishes, factories are closed, workers are in want of the means of subsistence, because they have produced too much of the means of subsistence; bankruptcy follows bankruptcy. The stagnation lasts for years; productive forces and products are wasted and destroyed, until the accumulated commodities finally filter off depreciated in value, until production and exchange gradually begin to move again. Little by little the pace quickens. It becomes a trot. The trot breaks into a canter, the canter grows into the headlong gallop of a steeplechase of industry, commercial credit and speculation, which finally, after breakneck leaps, ends where it began—in the ditch of a crisis. And so over and over again. We have now, since 1825, gone through this five times, and at the present moment (1877) we are going through it for the sixth time.

21. In these crises, the contradiction between socialised production and capitalist appropriation ends in a violent explosion. The circulation of commodities is stopped. Money becomes a hindrance to circulation. The laws of production and circulation of commodities are turned upside down. The economic collision has reached its apogee. *The mode of production is in rebellion against the mode of exchange.*

22. The socialised organisation of production has become incompatible with the anarchy of production. This is brought home to the capitalists by the concentration of capital that occurs during crises, through the ruin of large and small capitalists. The mechanism of the capitalist mode of production breaks down under the pressure of the productive forces. It is no longer able to turn all this means of production into capital. They lie fallow, and hence the industrial reserve army must also lie fallow. Means of production, means of subsistence, available labourers, all the elements of production and of general wealth, are present in abundance. But abundance becomes the source of distress and want, because it prevents the transformation of the means of production and subsistence into capital. For in capitalistic society the means of production can only function when they have undergone transformation into capital, into the means of exploiting human labour power. The necessity of this transformation into capital of the means of production and subsistence stands like a ghost between these and the workers. It alone prevents the coming together of the material and personal levers of produc-

tion; it alone forbids the means of production to function, the workers to work and live. The capitalistic mode of production stands convicted of its own incapacity to direct these productive forces. These productive forces press forward to the removal of the existing contradiction, to the *recognition of their character as social productive forces.*

23. This rebellion of the productive forces, this command that their social character shall be recognized, forces the capitalist class to treat them more and more as social productive forces. The period of industrial high pressure, with its inflation of credit, not less than the crash itself, by the collapse of great capitalist establishments, tends to bring about the form of the socialisation of means of production which we meet in joint-stock companies. Many of these means of production and of distribution are, from the outset, so colossal, that, like the railroads, they exclude all other forms of capitalistic exploitation. At a further stage of evolution this form also becomes insufficient. The producers on a large scale in a particular branch of industry in a particular country unite in a "trust," for the purpose of regulating production. They determine the amount to be produced, parcel it out among themselves, and thus enforce the selling price fixed beforehand. But trusts of this kind, as soon as business becomes bad, are generally liable to break up, and, on this account, compel a yet greater concentration of association. The whole of the particular industry is turned into one gigantic joint-stock company; internal competition gives place to the internal monopoly of this one company.

24. In the trusts, competition changes into its opposite—monopoly; and the production without any definite plan of capitalistic society capitulates to the production upon a definite plan of the invading socialistic society. This is still to the advantage of the capitalists. But in this case the exploitation is so palpable that it must break down. No nation will put up with production conducted by trusts, with so barefaced an exploitation of the community by a small band of dividend mongers.

25. In any case, with trusts or without, the official representative of capitalist society—the state—will ultimately have to undertake the direction of production. This necessity of conversion into state property is felt first in the great institutions for intercourse and communication—the post-office, the telegraphs, the railways.

26. The crises demonstrate the incapacity of the bourgeoisie to manage modern productive forces. The transformation of the great establishments for production and distribution into joint-stock companies, trusts and state property, show how unnecessary the bourgeoisie are for that purpose. The social functions of the capitalist are now performed by salaried employees. The capitalist has no further social function than pocketing dividends, tearing off coupons, and gambling on the Stock Exchange, where the different capitalists despoil one another of their capital. At first the capitalistic mode of production forces out the workers. Now it forces out the capitalists, and reduces them, as it reduced the workers, to the ranks of the surplus population, although not immediately into those of the industrial reserve army.

27. But the transformation, into joint-stock companies and trusts, or into state ownership, does not do away with the capitalistic nature of the productive forces. In the joint-stock companies and trusts this is obvious. But the

modern state, is only the organisation that bourgeois society takes on to support the conditions of the capitalist mode of production against the encroachments of the workers and of individual capitalists. The modern state is essentially a capitalist machine, the state of the capitalists, the ideal personification of the total national capital. The more it takes over productive forces, the more it becomes the national capitalist, the more citizens it exploits. The workers remain wage workers—proletarians. The capitalist relation is not done away with. It is rather brought to a head. But, brought to a head, it topples over. State ownership of the productive forces is not the solution of the conflict, but concealed within it are the elements of that solution.

28. This solution consists in the recognition of the social nature of the modern forces of production, and therefore in the harmonising of the modes of production, appropriation and exchange with the socialised character of the means of production. And this can only come about by society taking possession of the productive forces which have outgrown all control except that of society as a whole. The social character of the means of production and of the products today reacts against the producers, periodically disrupts production and exchange. But with the taking over by society of the productive forces, the social character of the means of production and of the products will be utilised by the producers with an understanding of its nature, and instead of being a source of disturbance and periodical collapse, will become the most powerful lever of production itself.

29. Social forces work like natural forces; blindly, forcibly, destructively, so long as we do not understand and reckon with them. But when we understand them, when we grasp their action, their direction, their effects, it depends only upon ourselves to subject them to our own will, and by means of them to reach our own ends. And this holds especially of the mighty productive forces of today. As long as we refuse to understand the nature of these social means of action—and this understanding goes against the grain of the capitalist mode of production and its defenders—so long these forces work in opposition to us, so long they master us.

30. But when their nature is understood, they can, in the hands of the producers working together, be transformed from master demons into willing servants. With this recognition of the real nature of the productive forces of today, the social anarchy of production gives place to a social regulation of production upon a definite plan, according to the needs of the community and of each individual. Then the capitalist mode of appropriation, in which the product enslaves first the producer and then the appropriator, is replaced by the mode of appropriation of the products that is based upon the nature of the modern means of production; upon the one hand, direct social appropriation, as means to the maintenance and extension of production—on the other, direct individual appropriation, as means of subsistence and enjoyment.

31. Whilst the capitalist mode of production transforms the great majority of the population into proletarians, it creates the power which, under penalty of its own destruction, is forced to accomplish this revolution. Whilst it forces on the transformation of the means of production, already socialised, into state property, it shows the way to accomplishing this revolution. *The*

proletariat seizes political power and turns the means of production into state property.

32. In doing this, it abolishes itself as proletariat, abolishes class distinctions and antagonisms, abolishes also the state as state. Society thus far, based upon class antagonisms, had need of the state: that is, an organisation of the particular class which was *pro tempore* the exploiting class, an organisation to prevent interference with the existing conditions of production, and therefore, to keep the exploited classes in the condition of oppression corresponding with the given mode of production (slavery, serfdom, wage labour). The state was the official representative of society as a whole. But it was this only in so far as it was the state of that class which represented, for the time being, society as a whole; in ancient times, the state of slave-owning citizens; in the Middle Ages, the feudal lords; in our own time, the bourgeoisie. When it becomes the representative of the whole of society, it renders itself unnecessary. As soon as there is no longer any social class to be held in subjection; as soon as class rule and the individual struggle for existence based upon our present anarchy in production, with the collisions and excesses arising from these, are removed, nothing remains to be repressed, and a special repressive force, a state, is no longer necessary. The first act by which the state constitutes itself the representative of the whole of society— taking possession of the means of production in the name of society—is its last independent act as a state. State interferences in social relations becomes superfluous, and then dies out; the government of persons is replaced by the administration of things, and by the conduct of processes of production. The state is not "abolished." *It dies out.*

33. Since the appearance of the capitalist mode of production, the appropriation by society of the means of production has been dreamed of, by individuals and sects, as the ideal of the future. But it could become possible, could become a historical necessity, only when the actual conditions for its realisation were there. Like every other social advance, it becomes practicable, not by men understanding that the existence of classes is in contradiction to justice, equality, etc., not by the mere willingness to abolish these classes, but by virtue of certain new economic conditions. The separation of society into an exploiting and an exploited class, a ruling and an oppressed class, was the necessary consequence of the deficient and restricted development of production in former times. So long as the total social labour yields a product which but slightly exceeds that necessary for the existence of all; so long, therefore, as labour engages the great majority of the members of society—so long, of necessity, this society is divided into classes. Side by side with this great majority arises a class freed from directly productive labour, which looks after the general affairs of society, the direction of labour, state business, law, science, art, etc. It is, therefore, the law of division of labour that lies at the basis of the division into classes. But this does not prevent this division into classes from being carried out by violence and robbery, trickery and fraud. It does not prevent the ruling class from consolidating its power at the expense of the working class, turning their social leadership into an exploitation of the masses.

34. But if division into classes has a certain historical justification, it has

this only for a given period, under given social conditions. It was based upon the insufficiency of production. It will be swept away by the development of modern productive forces. And the abolition of classes presupposes a degree of historical evolution, at which the existence of any ruling class and, therefore, the existence of class distinction itself has become obsolete. It presupposes, therefore, the development of production to a point where appropriation of the means of production and of the products, of political domination, of the monopoly of culture, and of intellectual leadership by a particular class has become superfluous; economically, politically, intellectually a hindrance to development.

35. This point is now reached. Their political and intellectual bankruptcy is no longer a secret to the bourgeoisie. Their economic bankruptcy recurs every ten years. In every crisis, society is suffocated beneath its own productive forces and products, which it cannot use, and stands helpless before the absurd contradiction that the producers have nothing to consume, because consumers are wanting. The expansive force of the means of production bursts the bonds that the capitalist mode of production had imposed upon them. Their deliverance from these bonds is the one condition for an unbroken, constantly accelerated development of the productive forces, and therewith for a practically unlimited increase of production. Nor is this all. The socialised appropriation of the means of production does away not only with the artificial restrictions upon production, but also with the waste and devastation of productive forces and products that are at present the concomitants of production, and that reach their height in the crises. Further, it sets free for the community at large a mass of means of production and of products, by doing away with the senseless extravagance of the ruling classes and their political representatives. The possibility of securing for every member of society, by means of socialised production, an existence not only sufficient materially, but guaranteeing to all the free development and exercise of their physical and mental faculties is now for the first time here.

36. With the seizing of the means of production by society, production of commodities is done away with, and, simultaneously the mastery of the product over the producer. Anarchy in social production is replaced by definite organisation. The struggle for individual existence disappears. Then man is finally marked off from the rest of the animal kingdom, and emerges from mere animal conditions of existence into human ones. The conditions of life which environ man, and which have hitherto ruled man, now come under the control of man, who for the first time becomes the conscious lord of nature, because he has become master of his own social organisation. The laws of his own social action, hitherto standing face to face with man as laws of nature foreign to and dominating him, will then be used with understanding, and so mastered by him. Man's own social organisation, hitherto confronting him as a necessity imposed by nature and history, now becomes the result of his own free action. The forces that have hitherto governed history pass under the control of man himself. Only from that time will man, more and more consciously, make his own history—only from that time will the social causes set in movement by him have, in a constantly growing

measure, the results intended by him. It is the ascent of man from the kingdom of necessity to the kingdom of freedom.

37. Let us briefly sum up our sketch of historical evolution.

    I. *Medieval Society*—Individual production on a small scale. Means of production adapted for individual use; hence primitive, ungainly, petty, dwarfed. Production for immediate consumption, either of the producer himself or of his feudal lords. Only where an excess of production over this consumption occurs is such excess offered for sale, enters into exchange. Production of commodities, therefore, is only in its infancy. But already it contains within itself *anarchy in the production of society at large.*

   II. *Capitalist Revolution*—Transformation of industry, at first by means of simple co-operation and manufacture. Concentration of the means of production, hitherto scattered, into great workshops. As a consequence, their transformation from individual to social means of production—a transformation which does not, on the whole, affect the form of exchange. The old forms of appropriation remain in force. The capitalist appears. In his capacity as owner of the means of production, he appropriates the products and turns them into commodities. Production has become a *social* act. Exchange and appropriation continue to be *individual* acts, the acts of individuals. *The social product is appropriated by the individual capitalist.* Fundamental contradiction, whence arise all the contradictions in which our present day society moves, and which modern industry brings to light.

   A. Severance of the producer from the means of production. Condemnation of the worker to wage labour. *Antagonism between the proletariat and the bourgeoisie.*

   B. Growing predominance and increasing effectiveness of the laws governing the production of commodities. Unbridled competition. *Contradiction between socialised organisation in the individual factory and social anarchy in production as a whole.*

   C. On the one hand, perfecting of machinery, made by competition compulsory for each individual manufacturer, and complemented by a constantly growing displacement of labourers. *Industrial reserve army.* On the other hand, unlimited extension of production, also compulsory under competition, for every manufacturer. On both sides, unheard of development of productive forces, excess of supply over demand, overproduction, glutting of the markets, crises every ten years, the vicious circle: excess here, of means of production and products—excess there, of labourers, without employment and without means of existence. But these two levers of production and of social well-being are unable to work together because the capitalist form of production prevents the productive forces from working and the products from circulating, unless they are first turned into capital—which their very superabundance prevents. The contradiction has grown into an absurdity. *The mode of production rises in rebellion against the form of exchange.* The bourgeoisie are convicted of incapacity to manage their social productive forces.

D. Partial recognition of the social character of the productive forces forced upon the capitalists themselves. Taking over of the great institutions for production and communication, first by joint-stock companies, later on by trusts, then by the state. The bourgeoisie demonstrated to be a superfluous class. All its social functions performed by salaried employees.

III. *Proletarian Revolution*—Solution of the contradictions. The proletariat seizes the public power, and by means of this transforms the socialised means of production, slipping from the hands of the bourgeoisie, into public property. By this act, the proletariat frees the means of production from the character of capital they have thus far borne, and gives their socialised character freedom to work itself out. Socialised production upon a predetermined plan henceforth possible. The development of production makes the existence of different classes of society thenceforth an anachronism. In proportion as anarchy in social production vanishes, the political authority of the state dies out. Man, at last the master of his own form of social organisation, becomes at the same time the lord over nature, his own master—free.

To accomplish this act of universal emancipation is the historical mission of the modern proletariat. To thoroughly comprehend the historical conditions and thus the nature of this act, to impart to the now oppressed proletarian class a full knowledge of the conditions and of the meaning of the momentous act it is called upon to accomplish, this is the task of the theoretical expression of the proletarian movement, scientific socialism.

Reading References. Professor H. J. Laski's book *The Rise of European Liberalism* is a good piece of further reading. It will hand the interested reader on to other books by him and to other books by twentieth-century Marxists. Two alternatives to Marxism as a philosophy of history will be found in Toynbee's *Study of History* and in R. G. Collingwood's "The Idea of History." The reader who has come this far can find his own way in Toynbee: the terms of the assignment ("a pattern detectable in the details") carry over from our earlier authors. Professor Collingwood, however, proposes a new, or at least different, assignment; namely, an exploration and description of the *modes of thinking* that mark the historian's effort to make the past intelligible. When a historian addresses himself to that task, what principles and what presuppositions are operative in his thinking? This is to redefine philosophy's problem in respect to history. Collingwood's thoughts on these matters will be found in Section 5 of the present topic.

READING QUESTIONS

1. The "materialist" conception of history.
2. Why "economic interpretation of history" or "economic determism" are usable alternatives to "historical materialism."
3. Use his distinction between "individual" and "social" or "collective" to set forth the transition from a "medieval" economy to a "bourgeois" economy.
4. And his distinction between division of labor upon "no definite plan" vs. "a definite plan."
5. Individual production succumbed to what? Why?
6. In the medieval stage the question of the owner of the product could not arise. (a) Why not? (b) Whereas . . . ?
7. Anarchy reigns in socialized production when the products are *commodities*. (a) What is a commodity? (b) Why the anarchy?
8. What is the Industrial Reserve Army? Where does it come from?
9. "Capitalist production has begotten *another* vicious circle" (a) What was the first one? (b) What is this second one?
10. How the "anarchy" generates trusts, monopolies, state ownership.
11. At first the capitalistic mode of production forces out the workers. Then it forces out the capitalists. How so?
12. Why "state ownership" will not satisfy him.
13. What he wants instead.
14. In doing this, the proletariat abolishes itself as proletariat.
15. The state is not "abolished." It dies out. It withers away. How so?
16. If there is a country in which the proletarian revolution has taken place, and the state has emphatically *not* "withered away," then what?

INDEPENDENT STUDY

1. Read the article "Engels, Friedrich" by T. Ramm in the *International Encyclopedia of the Social Sciences* and the articles "Marx," "Marxism," "Marxist Sociology" in the same encyclopedia. Use these articles, and their bibliographies where relevant, to write on Engels's interpretation of history.
2. Take any major episode in American history (e.g., the founding of the colonies, the Revolutionary War, the Civil War) and work out an "economic" interpretation of it along lines laid down by Engels.

SECTION 4. OSWALD SPENGLER: THE CULTURAL INTERPRETATION OF HISTORY

From Marx and Engels to Spengler. Thus far we have examined three examples of speculative philosophy of history: Kant, Hegel, and Engels. Kant sees in history the story of nature's efforts, having produced in man an animal capable of living by the use of his rational powers, to force him to develop those powers by posing a problem for him. If he handles the problem it will be because he uses and develops his rational powers. If he does not, those powers may atrophy, but the species will not survive to tell about it. The exercise and development of his rational powers is a mandate of survival from nature to man. Hegel pushes this argument beyond the somewhat "fable" way in which Kant had left it. In Hegel there is no nature having designs on man whereby he will be goaded into developing his rational powers. There is reason in the world. History is the story of how reason develops, and in developing, produces, indeed *is*, the historical world of human beings and human society. The basic thought here is obscure. That spirit manifests itself *as* nature, and is present *in* man and society as developing reason, is not an easily apprehended claim. It may not be a "fable," as Kant's way of conceiving the matter was; but it is obscure, in a way that Kant was not. Marx, in setting forth his views on history, took Hegel, not Kant, as his point of departure. This was to accept the more obscure formulation. Marx seems to have clear intentions about this aspect of his relation to Hegel. He says he wanted to turn Hegel right way up; having found him standing on his head, to turn him right way up and stand him on his feet. His materialist conception of history, his historical materialism in contrast to Hegel's historical idealism, was the outcome. For reasons that Marx and Engels both make clear, their historical materialism became finally their "economic interpretation of history."

The Communist Manifesto was published by Marx and Engels in 1848. It broached the theory that history discloses a pattern of class struggles moving toward a social revolution that will end the class struggle by ushering in a classless social order based upon a socialist economy. Exactly seventy years later, in 1918, Oswald Spengler published his massive work *The Decline of the West.* The years between were crowded with events and activities. These should be recalled to mind in passing from Marx and Engels to Spengler.

1. In the first place, from 1848 to 1918 there was much lively history. Merely the list of wars and revolutions is imposing. In the year 1848 itself, revolutionary uprisings occurred throughout Europe on an unprecedented scale. The Crimean War and the Indian Mutiny

came in the 1850's; the American Civil War, in the 1860's; the Franco-Prussian War, the third French Revolution, and the rise of the Paris Commune in the 1870's; a number of colonial and "imperialistic" wars, in the 1880's and 1890's, culminating in the Boer War at the opening of the new century; the Russian–Japanese War and the first Russian revolution, in 1904–1905; an intricate tangle of Balkan wars, in the years preceding 1914; the important Chinese revolution, in 1912; the World War, in 1914; the two Russian revolutions under Kerensky and Lenin, in 1917; and the German revolution in 1918. This list is representative, not exhaustive. These wars and revolutions formed an accompaniment to enormous population growth, tremendous economic expansion, vast and complex political and social reform movements, the rise of organized labor, the formation of overseas empires by European great powers, and much more besides. Consult the table of contents of any good history of the world since 1848. The cultural history of the period is no less intense. The scientific theories of Darwin, Pavlov, Freud, and Einstein fall between Marx and Spengler. The challenging problem literatures of modern England, Russia, France, Germany, and the Scandinavias fall between Marx and Spengler. The heated controversies associated with the names of Colenso, Bradlaugh, Huxley, Pasteur, Dreyfus, Pankhurst, Nietzsche, to name only a few, fall between Marx and Spengler. The movements in the arts associated with such persons as Wagner, William Morris, Rodin, Cézanne, Matisse, and others, fall between Marx and Spengler. The tendencies in modern philosophy covered by such terms as *neo-Hegelianism, neo-positivism, pragmatism, creative evolutionism, instrumentalism, realism, anti-intellectualism*, and so on, fall between Marx and Spengler.

2. In the second place, the period from 1848 to 1918 was rich in historical writing. More and, with a few notable exceptions, greater histories were written during these years than during any comparable period in the past. In Germany the latter half of the historical writings of Leopold von Ranke, the historical writings of Theodor Mommsen, of Heinrich von Treitschke, of Eduard Zeller, of Kuno Fischer, of Adolph Harnack, of Theodor Gomperz, to name only a few, fall between Marx and Spengler. So, also, in France, do the historical writings of Jean Victor Duruy, Ernest Renan, Hippolyte Taine, and others. In England the historical writings of Macaulay, Froude, Stubbs, Green, Maine, Gardiner, Lecky, Seeley, Creighton, Acton, Maitland, the Trevelyans, fall within the same period; as, also, in the United States, do the works of John Lothrop Motley, of Francis Parkman, of John Fiske, of James Ford Rhodes, Alfred Mahan, Henry Adams, and others. The point of listing these names is to indicate that a philosophy of history formulated during or at the close of this period had to take account of a vastly increased amount

of sheer data. The inviting simplicity presented by the picture of world history between Augustine and Hegel is gone. The man who proposes discourse on these matters now, must be prepared to take account of a greater number and a larger range of facts than confronted his predecessors in other centuries.

3. In the third place, the period from 1848 to 1918 was prolific in theories or philosophies of history. In England, Carlyle's "great man" theory carried over from a previous generation. It was followed by the hypothesis of geographic determinism and the central role of intellectual progress, in the writings of H. T. Buckle. Buckle was followed by Walter Bagehot, whose *Physics and Politics* proposed an application to human history of categories applied to natural history by Darwin. On the Continent philosophies of history were set forth by Hippolyte Taine, by Friedrich Nietzsche, by Anatole France, by Benedetto Croce, by Vilfredo Pareto, and many others. And mention should be made, in the United States, of the interesting and suggestive theory advanced by Henry Adams in his two papers "The Tendency of History" and "The Rule of Phase Applied to History," and illustrated in his two books *Mont-Saint-Michel and Chartres* and *The Education of Henry Adams.*

No matter who is read, following Kant, Hegel, Marx and Engels, the history of the world since 1848 would have to be kept in mind. The problem of a speculative philosophy of history remains what it had been: a hypothesis in the light of which to interpret the events and actions. But, as already noted, the number and range of events and actions known is greater, and the tempo of reflection upon them has been stepped up. In selecting Spengler it is not suggested that valuable alternatives are lacking. Spengler, in our own day, is worth reading, in the wake of Kant and Hegel and Engels. But so, too, are several others, particularly Benedetto Croce, Flinders Petrie, Henry Adams, Vilfredo Pareto, Pitirim Sorokin, Arnold Toynbee, and R. G. Collingwood. If science has been the greatest fertilizer of modern philosophy, history runs it a close second.

Biographical Note. Oswald Spengler was born in Germany in 1880 and died in 1936, at the age of fifty-six. He was educated in the universities at Halle, Munich, and Berlin. He studied mathematics and philosophy particularly, we are told, but, like Francis Bacon, seems to have taken all knowledge for his field. After teaching for seven years in the secondary schools of Germany, he retired to do private tutoring and to write his books. His one great work, *The Decline of the West,* was published, Volume One in 1918 and Volume Two in 1922. Over a hundred thousand copies were sold in Germany in a few years. The *Decline* was followed by two small volumes, *Man and Technics* and *The Hour of Decision,* in which the author formulates a philosophy of life and a call to action, based upon the premise that the argument of the large treatise is substantially correct.

The Argument of the Passages. Spengler begins with the usual questions: "Is there a logic of history?" "Is there, beyond all the casual and incalculable elements of the separate events, something that we may call a structure of historic humanity?" "Does world history present certain grand traits?" The first step toward finding answers is the critique of what he calls the "ancient–medieval–modern" scheme of history. He gives his reasons for rejecting this "Ptolemaic" view of history. In place of it, he proposes his "Copernican" view, reminding us of Kant's earlier "Copernican revolution" in philosophy. Granted the Copernican hypothesis in history, he pauses to emphasize the fact that analogy thereby becomes fundamental in historical thinking. The essence of Spengler's Copernican revolution is the distinction between a culture and a civilization, and the claim that history reveals many cultures maturing and declining into civilizations. The culture of the West, declining into the civilization of the West, is a case in point. The book is to tell the story of this decline, once the general theory has been established. One feature of a culture degenerating into a civilization is the emergence of "world cities" and their contributory "provinces." Our own period is then given some attention. Finally, the futility and fate of philosophizing, in our own period, are pointed out.

Is there a logic of history? Is there, beyond all the casual and incalculable elements of the separate events, something that we may call a structure of historic humanity? Does world history present certain grand traits? And if so, what are the limits to which reasoning from such premises may be pushed?

The preceding quotation shows that Spengler is proposing the same question as Kant, Hegel, Marx, and Engels. Before presenting his own views to the reader, the author pauses to repudiate the usual textbook division of history into ancient, medieval, and modern. He calls this the Ptolemaic view of history, likening it to Ptolemaic astronomy, according to which our earth was the center of the universe.

What is world history? An ordered presentation of the past, no doubt. Everyone, if asked, would say that he knew "the form" of history, quite clearly and definitely. He would be under an illusion. The illusion is there because no one has seriously reflected upon the question of the form of world history, still less conceived any doubts as to his knowledge of it. In fact, the common notion of world history is an unproved and subjective affair handed down from generation to generation, and badly in need of a little of that skepticism which, from Galileo onward, has regulated and deepened our ideas of nature.

Thanks to the subdivision of history into "ancient," "medieval," and "modern"—an incredibly jejune and meaningless scheme, which has, however, entirely dominated our historical thinking—we have failed to perceive the true position in the general history of mankind of the little part-world that has developed in Western Europe from the time of the Roman Empire, to judge of its relative importance, and to estimate its direction.

The ages that are to come will find it difficult to believe that such a scheme, with its simple rectilinear progression and its meaningless proportions, becoming more preposterous with each century, incapable of bringing into itself the new fields of history as they come into the light of our knowledge, was never whole heartedly attacked.

The criticisms that it has long been the fashion for historical students to level at this scheme mean nothing. They have only obliterated the scheme without substituting any other for it. To toy with such phrases as "the Greek middle ages" or "Germanic antiquity" does not help us to form a clear picture in which China and Mexico, the empire of Axum and that of the Sassanids have their proper places. And the expedient of shifting the initial point of "modern history" from the Crusades to the Renaissance, or from the Renaissance to the French Revolution, only goes to show that the scheme is still regarded as unshakably sound.

It is not only that the ancient-medieval-modern scheme circumscribes the area of history. What is worse, it rigs the stage. Western Europe is treated as a steady pole, and great histories of millennial duration and mighty faraway cultures are made to revolve around this pole in all modesty. We select a single patch of ground, for no better reason, it seems, than because we live on it, and make it the center of the historical system. From it all the events of history receive their light; from it their importance is judged. But this phantom "world history," which a breath of skepticism would dissipate, is acted out only in our own West European conceit.

We have to thank this conceit of ours for the immense optical illusion whereby distant histories, such as those of China and Egypt, are made to shrink to mere episodes while in the neighborhoods of our own position the decades since Luther or Napoleon loom large as Brocken specters.

For the cultures of the West, it is evident that Athens, Florence, or Paris, is more important than Lo-Yang or Pataliputra. But is it permissible to found a scheme of world history on such estimates? The Chinese historian is equally entitled to frame a world history in which Caesar, the Crusades, the Renaissance, Frederick the Great are passed over in silence as insignificant. From the morphological point of view, why should our eighteenth century be more important than any of the sixty centuries that preceded it? Is it not ridiculous to oppose a "modern" history of a few centuries to an "ancient" history which covers as many millennia? This is no exaggeration. Do we not, for the sake of keeping the hoary scheme of ancient-medieval-modern, dispose of Egypt and Babylon as a prelude to classical history? Do we not relegate the vast cultures of India and China to footnotes? Do we not entirely ignore the great American cultures?

As mentioned above, this ancient–medieval–modern scheme is to be repudiated as Ptolemaic and replaced by a Copernican view of history.

The most appropriate designation for this ancient-medieval-modern scheme of history, in which great cultures are made to follow orbits around us, is the Ptolemaic system of history. The system that is put forward in this book, in place of it, I regard as the Copernican system in the historical sphere. It admits no privileged position to the classical culture, or the Western culture, as against the cultures of India, Babylon, China, Egypt, the Arabs, Mexico. Each of these non-Western cultures, being separate worlds, count, in point of mass for just as much in the general picture of history as the classical culture, while they frequently surpass it in point of spiritual greatness and soaring power.

I see, in place of that empty figment of ancient-medieval-modern, the drama of a number of mighty cultures, each springing from the soil of a mother region; each stamping its material in its own image; each having its own idea, its own passions, its own life, its own will and feeling, its own death. Here indeed are colors, lights, movements, that no eye has yet discovered.

Here cultures, peoples, languages, truths, gods, bloom and age as the oaks and the stone pines. Each culture has its own new possibilities of self-expression, which arise, ripen, decay, and never return. There is not just one sculpture, one painting, one mathematics, one physics, one religion, one morality, one philosophy, but many, each different from the others, each limited in duration, each having its special type of growth and decline. Each grows with the same superb aimlessness as the flowers of the field. I see world history as a picture of endless formations and transformations. The professional historian sees it as a sort of tapeworm industriously adding onto itself one epoch after another.

The substitution of the Copernican for the Ptolemaic view of history effects an unmeasurable widening of horizon. This idea once attained, the rest is easy. To this single idea one can refer all those separate problems of religion, art, philosophy, morals, politics, economics with which the modern mind has busied itself so passionately and so vainly. This idea is one of those truths that have only to be expressed with clarity to become indisputable. It is capable of transforming the world outlook of one who fully understands it. It immensely deepens the world historical picture. By its aid we are enabled to follow the broad lines into the future, a privilege till now permitted only to the physicist.

The Copernican view, then, resolves history into a number of different epochs. Each epoch, it is to be argued, begins as a "culture" and ends as a "civilization." The first step will be to clarify these terms *culture* and *civilization*. Do the epochs have any common characteristics? Does each have a "life" of its own?

Is it possible to find in life a series of stages which must be traversed? For everything organic, the notions of birth, youth, age, lifetime, death, are fundamentals. May not these notions possess, in the realm of history, a meaning which no one has yet extracted? In short, is all history founded upon general biographic archetypes?

At this point Spengler develops the thought that a history of many different epochs will develop analogies between one epoch and another. Something in one epoch will be "analogous" to something in another epoch. How reliable is the analogy?

The means whereby to identify dead forms is mathematical law. The means whereby to understand living forms is analogy.

From any technique of analogies we are far distant. It is neither a principle nor a sense of historic necessity, but simple inclination, that governs the choice of the analogies we draw. They throng up without scheme or unities. If they do hit upon something that is apt, it is thanks to luck, more rarely to instinct, never to a principle. No one has hitherto set himself to work out a technique or method for striking upon apt and revealing analogies in the region of world history. Nor has anyone had the slightest inkling that there is here a root, in fact the only root, from which can come a broad solution of the problems of history.

Insofar as they lay bare the structure of history, analogies might be a blessing to historical thought. Their technique, developing under the influence of a comprehensive idea, might eventuate in inevitable conclusions and logical mastery. But, as hitherto understood and practiced, they have been a curse, for they have enabled historians to follow their own tastes, instead of realizing that their first task was the symbolism of history and its analogies. Superficial in many cases, these analogies are worse than superficial in others, while occasionally they are bizarre to the point of perversity.

Napoleon has hardly ever been discussed without a side glance at Caesar and Alexander. Napoleon himself conceived of his situation as akin to Charlemagne's. The French Revolutionary Convention spoke of Carthage when it meant England, and the Jacobins styled themselves Romans. Cecil Rhodes, the organizer of British South Africa, felt himself akin to the Emperor Hadrian. And so on, through an indefinitely long list.

I have not hitherto found anyone who has carefully considered the morphological relationship that binds together the expression forms of all branches of a single culture; who has, e.g., gone beyond politics to grasp the ultimate and fundamental ideas in mathematics, ornamentation, architecture, philosophy, literature, craftsmanship, etc., within a single culture.

Who among historians realizes that there are deep uniformities between the differential calculus and the dynastic principle of politics in the age of Louis XIV; between the classical city state and Euclidean geometry; between the space perspective of Western oil painting and the conquest of space by railroad; between telephone and long-range weapon; between contrapuntal music and credit economics? Yet, viewed from this morphological standpoint, such things as the Egyptian administrative system, the classical coinage, analytical geometry, the cheque, the Suez Canal, the book printing of the Chinese, the Prussian army, the Roman road engineering, can be made uniformly understandable as symbols.

The historian, then, despite risks, must be prepared to make large use of analogies. He will be interested in noting what things in epoch A are "contemporary" with things in epoch B. The word *contemporary* in Spengler's use means happening in one epoch at relatively the same point as in another epoch. Two events can be contemporary, in this sense, even if the epochs in question are several centuries apart. However, the whole point of working up these analogies is to throw light on the common characteristics of an epoch. Now, an epoch, it was said, begins as a culture and ends as a civilization. Accordingly, we turn to these two key terms.

If we are to discover the form in which the destiny of Western culture will be accomplished, we must first be clear as to what a culture is. What are its relations to visible history? How far may we point to peoples, tongues and epochs, battles and ideas, states and goods, arts and crats, sciences, laws, economic types, great men, great events, world ideas, as symbols of a culture?

Every culture has its own civilization. In this book, these two words are used in a periodic sense, to express an organic succession. The civilization is the destiny of the culture. In this principle we obtain the viewpoint from which the problems of historical morphology become capable of solution. Civilizations are the most external and artificial states of which a species of developed humanity is capable. Civilizations are a conclusion, death following upon life, rigidity following expansion. They are an end, irrevocable, yet, by an inward necessity reached again and again. They consist in a progressive taking-down of forms that have become dead.

To the culture belongs gymnastics, the joust, the tournament. To the civilization belongs sport. Art itself becomes a sport, to be played before a highly intelligent audience of connoisseurs or buyers; and this, whether the feat consist in mastering absurd instrumental tone masses and taking harmonic fences, or in some *tour de force* of coloring. Then a new fact-philosophy appears, which can spare only a smile for metaphysical speculations; and a new literature that is a necessity for the megalopolitan palate and nerves but is both unintelligible and ugly to the provincial.

What is the hallmark of a politic of civilization, in contrast to a politic of culture? It is, for the classical and the West European, money. The money spirit penetrates the historical forms of the people's existence. Though the forms persist, the great political parties cease to be more than reputed centers of decision. The decisions in fact lie elsewhere. A small number of superior heads, whose names are often little known, settle everything, while below them are the great mass of second-rate politicians selected through a franchise to keep alive the illusion of popular self-determination.

Imperialism is to be taken as the typical symbol of passing away. Imperialism is civilization unadulterated. The energy of culture-man is directed inwards; of civilization-man, outwards. In this form the destiny of the West is now set. Thus I see in Cecil Rhodes a man of the age. He stands for the political style of a far-ranging future. His phrase "expansion is everything" is the Napoleonic reassertion of the tendency of every civilization that has fully ripened. It is not a matter of choice. The expansive tendency is a doom which grips man of the world-city stage.

Rhodes is to be regarded as the precursor of a Western type of Caesar whose day is to come, though yet distant. He stands midway between Napoleon and the force-men of the next centuries. It was only before his maps that he could fall into a sort of poetic trance, this son of a parson who, sent out to South Africa without means, made a gigantic fortune and employed it as the engine of political aims.

His idea of a trans-African railway from Cape to Cairo, his project of a South African empire, his hold on the hard metal souls of the mining magnates, his capital planned as the future residence of an all-powerful statesman who yet stood in no definite relation to the state, his wars, his diplomatic deals, his road systems, his syndicates, his armies, all this is the prelude of a future which is still in store for us and with which the history of Western man will be definitely closed.

The civilization of an epoch crystallizes always into the "world city" and the "province": megalopolis and its surrounding territory. What about these two units of social organization?

World city and province, the two basic ideas of every civilization, bring up a wholly new form-problem of history, the very problem that we are living through today with hardly any notion of its immensity. In place of a people true to a type, born of the soil and grown on the soil, there is a new sort of nomad, cohering unstably in fluid masses, the parasitical city dweller traditionless, utterly matter-of-fact, without religion, clever, unfruitful, contemptuous of the countryman. This is a great stride toward the end. What does it signify? France and England have already taken the step. Germany is beginning to do so. After Syracuse, Athens, Alexandria, comes Rome. After Madrid, Paris, London, comes Berlin and New York. It is the destiny of whole regions that lie outside the circle of one of these great cities to become "provinces."

The world city means cosmopolitanism in place of home, matter-of-fact coldness in place of reverence for tradition, scientific irreligion in place of the older religion of the heart, society in place of the state, "natural" in place of hard-earned rights. It was in the conception of money, entirely disconnected from the notion of the fruitful earth, that the Romans had the advantage over the Greeks. Thereafter any high ideal of life becomes largely a question of money. Unlike Greek stoicism, Roman stoicism presupposes a private income. Unlike the social and moral ideals of the eighteenth century, the ideals of the twentieth century are matters for millionaires. To the world city belongs not a folk, but a mass.

The uncomprehending hostility of the mass of the world city to all the traditions of the culture—nobility, church, privilege, dynasties, conventions in art, limits of knowledge—the keen and cold intelligence that confounds the wisdom of the peasant, the new-fashioned naturalism in sex and society, the reappearance of *panem et circenses* in the form of wage disputes and large-scale organized spectator sports, all these things betoken the definite closing down of the culture and the setting in of the civilization, antiprovincial, late, futureless, but inevitable.

At this level civilizations enter upon a stage of depopulation. The whole pyramid of culture vanishes. It crumbles from the summit, first the world cities, then the provinces, and finally the land itself whose best blood has incontinently poured into the towns. At last only the primitive blood remains alive, but robbed of its strongest and most promising elements. The residue is the Fellah type.

Thus far: Has history a logic? Repudiation of the Ptolemaic theory of history. Proposal of the Copernican theory. History deals with great epochs. Hence analogy as the historical method. Epochs begin as cultures and end as civilizations. The world city and its province characterize the end of an epoch. With these general ideas in mind Spengler turns to the particular subject of his book: the history of our own times or, as he calls it, *The Decline of the West*. We live at the end of an epoch. We live in a civilization, not in a culture. And his massive book is an inductive survey of the evidence for this claim. He says:

Our narrow task, then, is to determine, from such a survey of world history, the state of Western Europe and America for the epoch, 1800–2000; to establish the chronological position of this period in the cultural history of the West; to indicate its significance as a chapter that it found in the story of every culture; and to make clear the meaning of its political, artistic, intellectual, and social expression forms.

Every culture is a four-act drama with an ascending movement of religion, aristocracy, and art, and a descending movement of irreligion, democracy, socialism, and the great city. The culture of the West, whose "decline" is referred to in the title of this book, originated in that feudal system of lord and serf which Roman conquest left like a network over Europe. Its basis is a stolid peasantry, bearing on its back the economic life of the world.

Considered in the spirit of analogy the period appears as chronologically parallel to the epoch we call *Hellenism;* and its present culmination, marked by the World War, corresponds to the transition from the Hellenistic to the Roman age. Rome, with its rigorous realism, uninspired, barbaric, disciplined, practical, will always give us, working as we must by analogies, the key to our own future.

Long ago we should have seen in the classical culture a development which is the counterpart of our own, differing indeed in surface detail, but similar as regards the power driving the great organism toward its end. We might have established the correspondence, item by item, from the Trojan War and the Crusades, Homer and the *Nibelungenlied*, through Doric and Gothic, Dionysian and Renaissance, Polycletus and Bach, Athens and Paris, Aristotle and Kant, Alexander and Napoleon, to the world city and imperialism.

The transition from culture to civilization was accomplished for the classical world in the fourth century A.D.; for the Western world in the nineteenth century. From these periods onwards, the great decisions take place. And they take place in three or four world cities that have absorbed into themselves the whole content of history.

Let it be realized, then, that the nineteenth and twentieth centuries, hitherto looked upon as an ascending straight line of world history, are in reality a stage of life which may be observed in every culture that has ripened to its limit. Let it be realized, then, that the future of the West is not a limitless tending upwards and onwards toward our present ideals, but a single phenomenon of history, strictly limited and defined as to form and duration, covering a few centuries and, in essentials, calculated from available precedents.

He who does not understand that this outcome is obligatory, that our choice is between willing this and willing nothing, between cleaving to this destiny or despairing of the future; he who cannot feel that there is grandeur in the achievements of powerful intelligence, in the energy and discipline of metal-hard natures, in battles fought with the coldest and abstractest means; he who is obsessed with the ideals of past ages, must forego all desire to comprehend history, to live through history, or to make history.

So much, then, for a few of the analogies by means of which Spengler locates the West and the period of its decline. He turns to some of the characteristic phenomena of the period. Here we can only quote a few scattered items from an enormous mass comprising two stout volumes. For example, the press:

A more appalling caricature of freedom cannot be imagined. There is today no need to impose military service on people. Whip their souls with articles, telegrams, pictures, till they clamor for weapons and force their leaders into a conflict. In preparation for the World War the press of whole countries was brought financially under the control of a few world cities, and the peoples belonging to them reduced to an unqualified intellectual slavery.

As for the modern press, the sentimentalist may beam with contentment when it is constitutionally "free." But the realist merely asks at whose disposal it is. For the multitude, that is true which it continually reads and hears. Its "truth" is a product of the press. What the press wills is true. Three weeks of press work, and the truth is acknowledged by everybody. The press and the news service keep whole peoples and continents under a deafening drumfire of theses, catchwords, standpoints, scenes, feelings.

Or the modern omnipresent machine:

These machines become less and less human; more ascetic, mystic, esoteric. They weave over the earth an infinite web of subtle forces, currents, tensions. Their bodies become ever more immaterial, ever less noisy. The wheels, rollers, levers, are vocal no more. All that matters draws itself into the interior. The center of this artificial and complicated realm is the engineer, the priest of the machine.

Or the modern masses:

. . . the fluid megalopolitan populace; the newspaper readers of our time; the "educated" who makes a cult of intellectual mediocrity and a church of advertisement; the man of the theaters and places of amusement, of sport and "best sellers," of expressionism, the movies, theosophy, dances, poker, and racing. The Roman *panem et circenses* we have in our wage disputes and football games.

Such "men" constitute the "masses." The masses reject the matured culture of our epoch. The mass is formless. It persecutes with hatred all distinctions of rank, the orderliness of tradition, of property, of knowledge. They are the new nomads of cosmopolis. They recognize no past and possess no future. They are the end.

Or modern art:

It is all irretrievably over with the arts of the West. What is practiced as art today is impotence and falsehood: a faked music, filled with artificial noisiness of massed instruments; a faked painting, full of idiotic, exotic, and show-card effects; a lying plastic that steals from Assyria, Egypt, Mexico, indifferently. For Western people there can no longer be any question of great painting or great music. We are today playing out a tedious game with dead forms to keep up the illusion of a living art.

Coming, at last, to philosophy, the story makes unpalatable reading. To begin with, Herr Spengler dislikes and distrusts the "thinker" type:

There are born destiny-men and causality-men. A whole world separates the man born to prosper, to rule, to fight, to dare, to organize, from the man who is destined by the power of his mind or the defect of his blood to be an intellectual—the saint, the priest, the scholar, the idealist. The eye for men and situations, the belief in his star, things which every born man of action possesses, are something wholly different from the belief in the "correctness of a standpoint," and are denied to the critical, meditative man. Even the footfall of the fact man sounds different from that of the thinker.

With that as a beginning, one can expect what follows: Modern philosophers are nobodies and busybodies:

It still remains to consider the relation of a morphology of world history to philosophy. For me the test to be applied to a thinker is his eye for the great facts of his own time. Only this can settle whether he is merely a clever architect of systems and principles, versed in definitions and analyses, or one in whom the soul of his time speaks in his works and intuitions.

A philosopher who cannot grasp and command actuality will never be of the first rank. The early Greek philosophers were merchants and politicians *en grande*. The desire to put his political ideas into practice nearly cost Plato his life. Confucius was several times a minister of state. Pythagoras organized an important political movement. Goethe, besides being an executive minister, was interested in the Suez and Panama Canals and their effects upon the economy of the world. Hobbes was one of the originators of a plan for winning South America for England. Leibnitz, without doubt the greatest intellect in Western philosophy, founder of the differential calculus and the analysis situs, conceived or cooperated in a number of major political schemes.

Turning from men of this world to the "philosophers" of today, one is dismayed and ashamed. What they do not possess is real standing in actual life. Their personalities are poor. Their political and practical outlook is commonplace. Not one of them has intervened effectively in politics, in the development of modern techniques, in matters of communication, in economics, or in any other big actuality, with a single act or a single compelling idea. Not one of them counts in mathematics, in physics, in politics. Why is it that the mere idea of calling upon one of them to prove his intellectual eminence in government, diplomacy, large-scale organization, the direction of any big colonial or commercial or transport concern, is enough to evoke our pity? This insufficiency indicates, not that they possess profundity but that they lack weight. I look around in vain for an instance in which a modern "philosopher" has made a name by even one deep or far-seeing pronouncement on an important question of the day. I see nothing but provincial opinions of the same kind as any one else's. Whenever I take up a work by a modern philosopher I find myself asking: Has he any idea of the actualities of world politics, world-city problems, capitalism, the future of the state, the relation of techniques to the course of civilization, Russia, science? Goethe would have understood all this and reveled in it. There is not one living philosopher capable of taking it in. This sense for actualities is, of course, not the same thing as the content of a philosophy; but, I repeat, it is an infallible symptom of its necessity, fruitfulness and importance.

We must allow ourselves no illusions as to the gravity of this negative result. We have lost sight of the final significance of effective philosophizing. We have descended from the perspective of the bird to that of the frog. We confuse philosophy with preaching, with agitation, with novel-writing, with lecture-room jargon. It were better to become a colonist or an engineer, to do something that is real and true, than to chew over once more the old dried-up themes under cover of some "new wave of philosophic thought"; better to construct an aero-engine than a new theory of apperception that is not wanted. It is indeed a poor life's work to restate once more the views of a hundred predecessors on the will or on psychophysical parallelism. This may be a profession. It is emphatically not a philosophy. A doctrine that does not attack and affect the life of one's period is no doctrine, and had better not be taught.

To me, the depths and refinement of mathematical and physical theories are a joy. By comparison, the aesthete and the physiologist are fumblers. I would sooner have the fine mind-begotten forms of a fast steamer, a steel structure, a precision lathe, the subtlety and elegance of many chemical and optical processes, than all the pickings and stealings of present-day "arts and crafts."

This is a situation that regularly repeats itself at a certain historical level. I maintain that today many an inventor, many a diplomat, many a financier, is a sounder philosopher than all those who practice the dull craft of experimental psychology. It would have been absurd in a Roman of intellectual eminence, who might, as consul or praetor, have led armies, organized provinces, built cities and roads, to want to hatch out some new variant of post-Platonic philosophy at Athens. Consequently no one did so. It was not in harmony with the tendency of the age. Therefore it attracted only third-class men of the kind that always advances as far as the Zeitgeist of the day before yesterday.

I prefer one Roman aqueduct to all the Roman temples and statues. I love the Colosseum and the giant vault of the Palatine, for they display the real Rome and the grand practical sense of her engineers. It was not for nothing, that the genuine Roman despised the "artist" and the "philosopher." The time for art and philosophy had passed; they were exhausted, used up, superfluous, and his instinct for the realities of life told him so. One Roman law weighed more than all the lyrics and school metaphysics of the time put together.

Modern philosophy, like modern art, is played out. With Kant and Schopenhauer, the curtain went down for the last time. What remains is merely the possibility of becoming competent and understanding historians of philosophy.

Systematic philosophy closed with the end of the eighteenth century. Kant put its utmost possibilities in forms that are grand and, for the Western soul, final. He is followed, as Plato and Aristotle were followed, by a specifically megalopolitan philosophy that is not speculative, but practical, irreligious, social-moral. This philosophy begins in the West with Schopenhauer. He was the first to make the will-to-live a central thought. It is the same will-to-live that was Schopenhauer-wise denied in *Tristan* and Darwin-wise asserted in *Siegfried;* that led Marx to an economic and Darwin to a biological hypothesis which have together subtly transformed the world-outlook of the Western megalopolis; and that produced a series of tragedies from Hebbel to Ibsen and Hardy. It has embraced, therefore, all the possibilities of a philosophy, and has exhausted them.

We have not chosen our time. We cannot help it if we are born in the early winter of a civilization, instead of in the golden summer of a culture. Everything depends upon seeing our own position clearly; on realizing that we may lie to ourselves about it but cannot evade it. He who does not acknowledge this ceases to be counted among the men of his generation.

One must begin, therefore, by asking what today is possible and what is not. In the case of a genuine adept this question is answered in advance by a kind of instinct.

Systematic philosophy, then, lies far behind us, and ethical philosophy has been wound up. But a third possibility, corresponding to the classical skepticism, still remains. And it can be brought to light by the hitherto unknown methods of historical morphology. Classical skepticism was ahistoric.

Our skepticism, a symbol of the autumn of spirituality, is historical. Its solutions are got by treating everything as relative, as historical. Classical skepticism is the negation of philosophy, declaring it to be useless. Our skepticism, on the contrary, regards the history of philosophy as, in the last resort, philosophy's gravest theme. This is *skepsis* in the true sense; for, where classical skepticism is led to renounce absolute standpoints by contempt for the past, we are led to do so by comprehension of the past.

It is our task to sketch out this unphilosophical philosophy—the last that the West will know. Skepticism is the expression of a pure civilization, and it dissipates the world picture of the culture that has gone before. For us, its success will lie in resolving all the older problems into one, the historical. With that, the claim of higher thought to possess general and eternal truths falls to the ground. Truths are truths only in relation to a particular mankind. Thus, my own philosophy is able to express and reflect only the Western mind, and that mind only in its present civilized phase by which its conception of the world, its practical range, and its sphere of effect, are specified.

Note on Sources. The above material is quoted, abridged, or paraphrased from Spengler's *The Decline of the West;* for the most part, from his introduction to that book.

Reading References. An introductory account of Spengler and his *Decline* is to be found in Will Durant's book *Adventures in Genius.* This book was reissued under the title *Great Men of Literature.* A book on Spengler's interpretation of history, *Civilization or Civilizations,* has been written by E. H. Goddard and P. A. Gibbons. A volume of selections from the *Decline,* with introduction and notes by Edwin F. Dakin, has been published under the title *Today and Destiny.* The *Decline* itself is not easy reading. The author's style and his esoteric references slow things up. The two short books *Man and Technics* and *The Hour of Decision* are much less encumbered.

READING QUESTIONS

1. What is the Ptolemaic view of history?
2. Why is it so named?
3. Give three of Spengler's criticisms of this view.
4. What is the Copernican view of history?
5. Why is it so named?
6. Why is Spengler led to a consideration of analogy in history?
7. Name one or two he suggests.
8. In what sense does he propose to use the word *contemporary?*
9. What distinguishes a culture from its civilization?
10. What is a world city?

11. Name two or three from history.
12. How does Spengler characterize world cities?
13. What, roughly, is the period of the decline in our case?
14. What about the press in our day?
15. Or the machine?
16. Or the masses?
17. Or the fine arts?
18. What is a causality man?
19. Some items in Spengler's appraisal of modern philosophers.
20. "A third possibility . . . still remains." Namely?

INDEPENDENT STUDY

1. Read the essay on Spengler in Durant's book *Adventures in Genius*. Read one topic (any one you find interesting and congenial) in the full text of Spengler's book. Write a paper expounding what you find.
2. If you have the time and the ambition, write an essay comparing *or* contrasting Spengler and Toynbee. Allow plenty of time.
3. Read Spengler's long "Introduction" to his *Decline of the West*. Read the essays on history by Henry Adams. Compare or contrast Adams and Spengler.

SECTION 5. R. G. COLLINGWOOD: THE NATURE OF HISTORICAL THINKING [2]

From Spengler to Collingwood. Spengler's *Decline of the West*, Volume One, 1918, and Toynbee's *Study of History*, Volume One, 1934, were two widely read examples of speculative philosophy of history. In this respect they were written in the tradition of Kant, Hegel, Marx and Engels, and others. They were not the first to attempt the formulation of a speculative philosophy of history, and there is no conclusive reason for claiming that they will have been the last. However, beginning in the 1930's, another tradition in philosophy of history began to be increasingly cultivated. Here the center of interest is not the overall character of the human past as we have seen it to be in Kant, Hegel, Engels, Spengler, and Toynbee), but the character of the thinking performed by the historian, in contrast, say, to the thinking performed by the natural scientist. Here the

[2] For a biographical note on Collingwood, see p. 613.

question is, "What sort of thinking, if correctly performed, will be productive of history in Sense Two?"

Hegel's lectures on the philosophy of history were delivered in the 1820's and published in the 1830's. Just a century later, R. G. Collingwood, sometimes referred to as an English Hegelian, began lecturing on the philosophy of history, in the 1920's, and publishing essays and pamphlets on these matters, in the 1930's. One of these essays, "Historical Evidence," contains several paragraphs under a subheading "Pigeon-holing," in which the author breaks with the tradition of speculative philosophy of history. These paragraphs repay a careful reading. They show the author making a backward gesture pointing to the historically speculative labors of St. Augustine, Kant, Hegel, Marx and Engels, Spengler, Toynbee, and any others who have shared with them the desire to work out some large-scale time scheme into which the particulars of the human past can be fitted to form a coherent "pattern." Collingwood refers to this as "pigeon-holing," and will have none of it. Such historians, he says, invent these retrospective systems and use them as all-inclusive receptacles in which to arrange their learning. (The numbers assigned to these paragraphs do not occur in the original.) Thus:

1. This is the origin of all those schemes and patterns into which history has again and again, with surprising docility, allowed itself to be forced by such men as Vico, with his pattern of historical cycles based on Greco-Roman speculations; Kant, with his proposal for a "universal history from a cosmopolitan point of view"; Hegel, who followed Kant in conceiving universal history as the progressive realization of human freedom; Comte and Marx, two very great men who followed Hegel's lead each in his own way; and so on down to Flinders Petrie, Oswald Spengler, and Arnold Toynbee in our own time, whose affinities are less with Hegel than with Vico.

2. Although we find it as late as the twentieth century and as early as the eighteenth, not to mention isolated occurrences even earlier, this impulse towards arranging the whole of history in a single scheme (not a chronological scheme merely, but a qualitative scheme, in which "periods" each with its own pervasive character follow one another in time, according to a pattern which may be necessary *a priori* on logical grounds, or may be forced upon our minds by the fact of its frequent repetition, or may be a bit of both) is in the main a nineteenth-century phenomenon. It belongs to the period when scissors-and-paste history was on its last legs; when people were becoming dissatisfied with it but had not yet broken away from it. This is why the people who have indulged it have been, in general, men with a high degree of intelligence and a real talent for history, but a talent which has been to some extent thwarted and baffled by the limitations of scissors and paste.

3. It is typical of this condition that some of them described their pigeon-holing enterprise as "raising history to the rank of a science." History as they found it meant scissors-and-paste history; that, obviously, was no

science, because there was nothing autonomous, nothing creative, about it; it was merely the transhipment of ready-made information from one mind into another. They were conscious that history might be something more than this. It might have, and it ought to have, the characteristics of a science. But how was this to be brought about? At this point the analogy of the natural sciences came, they thought, to their aid. It had been a commonplace ever since Bacon that a natural science began by collecting facts, and then went on to construct theories, that is, to extrapolate the patterns discernible in the facts already collected. Very well: let us put together all the facts that are known to historians, look for patterns in them, and then extrapolate these patterns into a theory of universal history.

4. It proved to be not at all a difficult task for anybody with an active mind and a taste for hard work. For there was no need to collect all the facts known to historians. Any large collection of facts, it was found, revealed patterns in plenty; and extrapolating such patterns into the remote past, about which there was very little information, and into the future, about which there was none, gave the "scientific" historian just that sense of power which scissors-and-paste history denied him. After being taught to believe that he, as an historian, could never know anything except what his authorities told him, he found himself discovering, as he fancied, that this lesson had been a fraud; that by converting history into a science he could ascertain, entirely for himself, things that his authorities had concealed from him or did not know.

5. This was a delusion. The value of each and all of these pigeon-holing schemes, if that means their value as means for discovering historical truths not ascertainable by the interpretation of evidence, was exactly nil. And in fact none of them ever had any scientific value at all; for it is not enough that science should be autonomous or creative, it must also be cogent or objective; it must impress itself as inevitable on anyone who is able and willing to consider the grounds upon which it is based, and to think for himself what the conclusions are to which they point. That is what none of these schemes can do. They are the offspring of caprice. If any of them has ever been accepted by any considerable body of persons beside the one who invented it, that is not because it has struck them as scientifically cogent, but because it has become the orthodoxy of what is in fact, though not necessarily in name, a religious community. This was to some extent achieved by Comtism, and to a much greater extent by Marxism. In these cases, or at any rate in the case of Marxism, historical schemes of the kind in question proved to have an important magical value, as providing a focus for emotions and in consequence an incentive to action.

The Argument of the Selections. There are two sets of materials used in this Collingwood section. The first is from "Human Nature and Human History," Collingwood's inaugural lecture as Waynflete professor at Oxford University. In that lecture he gave an account of essential differences between the thinking productive of natural science and the thinking productive of history in the sense of what the historian produces. The second is from "The Historical Imagina-

history and historical thinking *437*

tion," his 1936 lecture to the British Academy. In that lecture he gave an extended criticism of what he calls the "common-sense theory of history." Having rejected this common-sense notion, he proposes to replace it by an account of historical thinking that has striking similarities to the account that Kant gave of thinking productive of natural science. The point of the resemblance is too complicated to be stated here. Let us put it this way: Kant claimed that thinking that produces natural science contains an *a priori* component contributed by the human imagination, and Collingwood makes the same claim about historical thinking.

These lectures, together with essays like them, were published posthumously in 1946 in his book *The Idea of History*. They have been widely read and commented upon, and almost as widely rejected. That is par for the course in writings that are both breaking with a tradition in one field and criticizing a way of thinking that is modish in another field. This fact about their reception during the last forty years does not destroy their value today. They are still much worth their reading time. They are clear, colorful, and thought-provoking. There are few better ways to make a beginning in critical philosophy of history than by reading what Collingwood has to say, finding out why you disagree with him if you do, and going on from there. He is a good starting point, a good point of departure, leaving you free to depart as far as you like in any direction you choose.

I Human Nature and Human History. The selection from *Human Nature and Human History* begins at the point where Collingwood is describing the views of what he calls the "ordinary historian":

According to him, all history properly so called is the history of human affairs. His special technique, depending as it does on the interpretation of documents in which human beings of the past have expressed or betrayed their thoughts, cannot be applied just as it stands to the study of natural processes; and the more this technique is elaborated in its details, the farther it is from being so applicable. There is a certain analogy between the archaeologist's interpretation of a stratified site and the geologist's interpretation of rock-horizons with their associated fossils; but the difference is no less clear than the similarity. The archaeologist's use of his stratified relics depends on his conceiving them as artifacts serving human purposes and thus expressing a particular way in which men have thought about their own life; and from his point of view the palaeontologist, arranging his fossils in a time-series, is not working as an historian, but only as a scientist thinking in a way which can at most be described as quasi-historical.

The question must therefore be raised, why do historians habitually identify history with the history of human affairs? In order to answer this question, it is not enough to consider the characteristics of historical method as it actually exists, for the question at issue is whether, as it actually exists, it covers the whole field which properly belongs to it. We must ask what is the general nature of the problems which this method is designed to solve. When we have done so, it will appear that the special problem of the historian is one which does not arise in the case of natural science.

The historian, investigating any event in the past, makes a distinction between what may be called the outside and the inside of an event. By the outside of the event I mean everything belonging to it which can be described in terms of bodies and their movements: the passage of Caesar, accompanied by certain men, across a river called the Rubicon at one date, or the spilling of his blood on the floor of the senate-house at another. By the inside of the event I mean that in it which can only be described in terms of thought: Caesar's defiance of Republican law, or the clash of constitutional policy between himself and his assassins. The historian is never concerned with either of these to the exclusion of the other. He is investigating not mere events (where by a mere event I mean one which has only an outside and no inside) but actions, and an action is the unity of the outside and inside of an event. He is interested in the crossing of the Rubicon only in its relation to Republican law, and in the spilling of Caesar's blood only in its relation to a constitutional conflict. His work may begin by discovering the outside of an event, but it can never end there; he must always remember that the event was an action, and that his main task is to think himself into this action, to discern the thought of its agent.

In the case of nature, this distinction between the outside and the inside of an event does not arise. The events of nature are mere events, not the acts of agents whose thought the scientist endeavours to trace. It is true that the scientist, like the historian, has to go beyond the mere discovery of events; but the direction in which he moves is very different. Instead of conceiving the event as an action and attempting to rediscover the thought of its agent, penetrating from the outside of the event to its inside, the scientist goes beyond the event, observes its relation to others, and thus brings it under a general formula or law of nature. To the scientist, nature is always and merely a "phenomenon," not in the sense of being defective in reality, but in the sense of being a spectacle presented to his intelligent observation; whereas the events of history are never mere phenomena, never mere spectacles for contemplation, but things which the historian looks, not at, but through, to discern the thought within them.

In thus penetrating to the inside of events and detecting the thought which they express, the historian is doing something which the scientist need not and cannot do. In this way the task of the historian is more complex than that of the scientist. In another way it is simpler: the historian need not and cannot (without ceasing to be an historian) emulate the scientist in searching for the causes or laws of events. For science, the event is discovered by perceiving it, and the further search for its cause is conducted by assigning it to its class and determining the relation between that class and others. For history, the object to be discovered is not the mere event, but the thought expressed in it. To discover that thought is already to understand it. After the historian has ascertained the facts, there is no further process of inquiring into their causes. When he knows what happened, he already knows why it happened.

This does not mean that words like "cause" are necessarily out of place in reference to history; it only means that they are used there in a special sense. When a scientist asks "Why did that piece of litmus paper turn pink?" he means "On what kinds of occasions do pieces of litmus paper turn pink?" When an historian asks "Why did Brutus stab Caesar?" he means "What did Brutus think, which made him decide to stab Caesar?" The cause of the event, for him, means the thought in the mind of the person by whose agency the event came about: and this is not something other than the event, it is the inside of the event itself.

The processes of nature can therefore be properly described as sequences of mere events, but those of history cannot. They are not processes of mere events but processes of actions, which have an inner side, consisting of processes of thought; and what the historian is looking for is these processes of thought. All history is the history of thought.

But how does the historian discern the thoughts which he is trying to discover? There is only one way in which it can be done: by re-thinking them in his own mind. The historian of philosophy, reading Plato, is trying to know what Plato thought when he expressed himself in certain words. The only way in which he can do this is by thinking it for himself. This, in fact, is what we mean when we speak of "understanding" the words. So the historian of politics or warfare, presented with an account of certain actions done by Julius Caeser, tries to understand these actions, that is, to discover what thoughts in Caesar's mind determined him to do them. This implies envisaging for himself the situation in which Caesar stood, and thinking for himself what Caesar thought about the situation and the possible ways of dealing with it. The history of thought, and therefore all history, is the re-enactment of past thought in the historian's own mind.

This re-enactment is only accomplished, in the case of Plato and Caesar respectively, so far as the historian brings to bear on the problem all the powers of his own mind and all his knowledge of philosophy and politics. It is not a passive surrender to the spell of another's mind; it is a labour of active and therefore critical thinking. The historian not only re-enacts past thought, he re-enacts it in the context of his own knowledge and therefore, in re-enacting it, criticizes it, forms his own judgement of its value, corrects whatever errors he can discern in it. This criticism of the thought whose history he traces is not something secondary to tracing the history of it. It is an indispensable condition of the historical knowledge itself. Nothing could be a completer error concerning the history of thought than to suppose that the historian as such merely ascertains "what so-and-so thought," leaving it to some one else to decide "whether it was true." All thinking is critical thinking; the thought which re-enacts past thoughts, therefore, criticizes them in re-enacting them.

It is now clear why historians habitually restrict the field of historical knowledge to human affairs. A natural process is a process of events, an historical process is a process of thoughts. Man is regarded as the only subject of historical process, because man is regarded as the only animal that thinks, or thinks enough, and clearly enough, to render his actions the expressions of his thoughts. The belief that man is the only animal that thinks at all is no doubt a superstition; but the belief that man thinks more, and more continuously and effectively, than any other animal, and is the only animal whose conduct is to any great extent determined by thought instead of by mere impulse and appetite, is probably well enough founded to justify the historian's rule of thumb.

There is only one hypothesis on which natural processes could be regarded as ultimately historical in character: namely, that these processes are in reality processes of action determined by a thought which is their own inner side. This would imply that natural events are expressions of thoughts, whether the thoughts of God, or of angelic or demonic finite intelligences, or of minds somewhat like our own inhabiting the organic and inorganic bodies of nature as our minds inhabit our bodies. Setting aside mere flights of metaphysical fancy, such an hypothesis could claim our serious attention only if it led to a better understanding of the natural world. In fact, however, the scientist can reasonably say of it "je n'ai pas eu besoin de cette hypothèse," and the theologian will recoil from any suggestion that God's action in the natural world resembles the action of a finite human mind under the conditions of historical life. This at least is certain: that, so far as our scientific and historical knowledge goes, the processes of events which constitute the world of nature are altogether different in kind from the processes of thought which constitute the world of history.

History, then, is not, as it has so often been mis-described, a story of successive events or an account of change. Unlike the natural scientist, the historian is not concerned with events as such at all. He is only concerned with those events which are the outward expression of thoughts, and is only concerned with these in so far as they express thoughts. At bottom, he is concerned with thoughts alone; with their outward expression in events he is concerned only by the way, in so far as these reveal to him the thoughts of which he is in search.

Historical knowledge is the knowledge of what mind has done in the past, and at the same time it is the redoing of this, the perpetuation of past acts in the present. Its object is therefore not a mere object, something outside the mind which knows it; it is an activity of thought, which can be known only in so far as the knowing mind re-enacts it and knows itself as so doing. To the historian, the activities whose history he is studying are not spectacles to be watched, but experiences to be lived through in his own mind; they are objective, or known to him, only because they are also subjective, or activities of his own.

It may thus be said that historical inquiry reveals to the historian the powers of his own mind. Since all he can know historically is thoughts that he can re-think for himself, the fact of his coming to know them shows him that his mind is able (or by the very effort of studying them has become able) to think in these ways. And conversely, whenever he finds certain historical matters unintelligible, he has discovered a limitation of his own mind; he has discovered that there are certain ways in which he is not, or no longer, or not yet, able to think. Certain historians, sometimes whole generations of historians, find in certain periods of history nothing intelligible, and call

them dark ages; but such phrases tell us nothing about those ages themselves, though they tell us a great deal about the persons who use them,
namely that they are unable to re-think the thoughts which were fundamental to their life. It has been said that *die Weltgeschichte ist das Weltgericht;*
and it is true, but in a sense not always recognized. It is the historian himself
who stands at the bar of judgement, and there reveals his own mind in its
strength and weakness, its virtues and its vices.

But historical knowledge is not concerned only with a remote past. If it is
by historical thinking that we re-think and so rediscover the thought of Ham-
murabi or Solon, it is in the same way that we discover the thought of a
friend who writes us a letter, or a stranger who crosses the street. Nor is it
necessary that the historian should be one person and the subject of his inquiry another. It is only by historical thinking that I can discover what I
thought ten years ago, by reading what I then wrote, or what I thought five
minutes ago, by reflecting on an action that I then did, which surprised me
when I realized what I had done. In this sense, all knowledge of mind is historical. The only way in which I can know my own mind is by performing
some mental act or other and then considering what the act is that I have
performed. If I want to know what I think about a certain subject, I try to put
my ideas about it in order, on paper or otherwise; and then, having thus arranged and formulated them, I can study the result as an historical document
and see what my ideas were when I did that piece of thinking: if I am dissatisfied with them, I can do it over again. If I want to know what powers my
mind possesses as yet unexplored, for example, whether I can write poetry, I
must try to write some, and see whether it strikes me and others as being the
real thing. If I want to know whether I am as good a man as I hope, or as bad
as I fear, I must examine acts that I have done, and understand what they really were: or else go and do some fresh acts and then examine those. All
these inquiries are historical. They proceed by studying accomplished facts,
ideas that I have thought out and expressed, acts that I have done. On what I
have only begun and am still doing, no judgement can as yet be passed.

Thus far we have seen Collingwood distinguish between
"pigeon-holing," constructing a schema of the past into which particular events and actions and sequences of events and actions are then
"fitted," and what he calls "historical thinking proper." He rejects
"pigeon-holing," and is thus left with "historical thinking proper."
In what does this consist? In the first place, historical thinking presupposes a distinction between the "outside" and the "inside." The
inside of an act is the thought on which the agent acted. In the case
of the scientific study of nature this distinction does not arise. Hence,
in penetrating to the "inside" of an act, the thought that was in the
mind of the agent, the historian does something that the natural scientist does not and cannot do. If this notion of the "inside" of past
acts is granted, then it can be said that all history, in the sense of
human history, is the history of thought. If events in nature do not
have an "inside," they cannot enter directly into the thinking of a

historian. If he is writing the history of a person blown out to sea in a small open boat, the wind events and sea events enter into his thinking only indirectly as providing the occasion for the thinking of the person blown out to sea. The wind events and sea-events do not have, or are not presupposed to have, any "inside." The historian discerns, "gets at," the "inside," the "thought side," of an act by re-thinking it for himself. In doing this he also evaluates it. If an agent in the past acted upon a false thought, the historian will discover this for himself. Events "in nature," in contrast to acts in human history, could be regarded "historically" only if they could be interpreted as acts performed by an agent, perhaps an Agent. Historical knowledge, then, is knowledge of what minds have done in the past. It hence reveals to the historian the powers of his own mind: if he lacks the power to think, in the sense of *rethink*, what Socrates thought or Euclid thought or Caesar thought, he will be unable to produce a historical account of their doings. Their lives will be for him a "closed book," or a book whose pages he cannot read. Historical thinking, thinking productive of historical knowledge, is not re-stricted to the remote past. It can deal with events of last week or yesterday or this morning.

Collingwood draws three conclusions at the end of his lecture. The *first* has to do with the difference between the thinking that is productive of historical knowledge and the thinking that is produc-tive of scientific knowledge. The second, which has to do with past attempts to construct a science of human nature and human behavior, is omitted here. The third has to do with psychology. Is it a historical science? Or a natural science? Or some third sort of science? If the latter, what is its proper subject matter? Thus:

It remains to draw a few conclusions from the thesis I have tried to main-tain.

First, as regards history itself. The methods of modern historical inquiry have grown up under the shadow of their elder sister, the method of natural science; in some ways helped by its example, in other ways hindered. Throughout this essay it has been necessary to engage in a running fight with what may be called a positivistic conception, or rather misconception, of history, as the study of successive events lying in a dead past, events to be understood as the scientist understands natural events, by classifying them and establishing relations between the classes thus defined. This misconcep-tion is not only an endemic error in modern philosophical thought about his-tory, it is also a constant peril to historical thought itself. So far as historians yield to it, they neglect their proper task of penetrating to the thought of the agents whose acts they are studying, and content themselves with determin-ing the externals of these acts, the kind of things about them which can be studied statistically. Statistical research is for the historian a good servant but a bad master. It profits him nothing to make statistical generalizations, unless

he can thereby detect the thought behind the facts about which he is generalizing. At the present day, historical thought is almost everywhere disentangling itself from the toils of the positivistic fallacy, and recognizing that in itself history is nothing but the re-enactment of past thought in the historian's
mind; but much still needs to be done if the full fruits of this recognition are
to be reaped. All kinds of historical fallacies are still current, due to confusion between historical process and natural process: not only the cruder
fallacies of mistaking historical facts of culture and tradition for functions of
biological facts like race and pedigree, but subtler fallacies affecting
methods of research and the organization of historical inquiry, which it
would take too long to enumerate here. It is not until these have been eradi-
cated that we can see how far historical thought, attaining at last its proper
shape and stature, is able to make good the claims long ago put forward on
behalf of the science of human nature.

Finally, there is the question what function can be assigned to the
science of psychology. At first sight its position appears equivocal. On the
one hand, it claims to be a science of mind; but if so, its apparatus of scientific method is merely the fruit of a false analogy, and it must pass over into
history and, as such, disappear. And this is certainly what ought to happen so
far as psychology claims to deal with the functions of reason itself. To speak
of the psychology of reasoning, or the psychology of the moral self (to quote
the titles of two well-known books), is to misuse words and confuse issues,
ascribing to a quasi-naturalistic science a subject-matter whose being and
development are not natural but historical. But if psychology avoids this
danger and renounces interference with what is properly the subject-matter
of history, it is likely to fall back into a pure science of nature and to become
a mere branch of physiology, dealing with muscular and nervous movements.

But there is a third alternative. In realizing its own rationality, mind also
realizes the presence in itself of elements that are not rational. They are not
body; they are mind, but not rational mind or thought. To use an old distinction, they are psyche or soul as distinct from spirit. These irrational elements
are the subject-matter of psychology. They are the blind forces and activities
in us which are part of human life as it consciously experiences itself, but are
not parts of the historical process: sensation as distinct from thought, feelings
as distinct from conceptions, appetite as distinct from will. Their importance
to us consists in the fact that they form the proximate environment in which
our reason lives, as our physiological organism is the proximate environment
in which they live. They are the basis of our rational life, though no part of
it. Our reason discovers them, but in studying them it is not studying itself.
By learning to know them, it finds out how it can help them to live in health,
so that they can feed and support it while it pursues its own proper task, the
self-conscious creation of its own historical life.

II The Historical Imagination.   In the first half of this section we
used Collingwood's lecture "Human Nature and Human History." In
the second half, we shall be using his lecture "The Historical Imagination." Near the beginning of that lecture he states that his purpose

is to offer an account of historical thinking as productive of historical knowledge, and that he will begin by setting forth what he calls the "common-sense theory" of it. This is the theory that most people believe, or think they believe, when they first reflect on the nature of historical thinking. He will then subject this common-sense theory to several disabling criticisms. This will clear the decks for a more promising conception and for an account of the role of imagination in historical thinking so conceived. He begins:

According to this [common-sense] theory, the essential things in history are memory and authority. If an event or a state of things is to be historically known, first of all some one must be acquainted with it; then he must remember it; then he must state his recollection of it in terms intelligible to another; and finally that other must accept the statement as true. History is thus the believing some one else when he says that he remembers something. The believer is the historian; the person believed is called his authority.

This doctrine implies that historical truth, so far as it is at all accessible to the historian, is accessible to him only because it exists ready made in the ready-made statements of his authorities. These statements are to him a sacred text, whose value depends wholly on the unbrokenness of the tradition they represent. He must therefore on no account tamper with them. He must not mutilate them; he must not add to them; and, above all, he must not contradict them. For if he takes it upon himself to pick and choose, to decide that some of his authority's statements are important and others not, he is going behind his authority's back and appealing to some other criterion; and this, on the theory, is exactly what he cannot do. If he adds to them, interpolating in them constructions of his own devising, and accepting these constructions as additions to his knowledge, he is believing something for a reason other than the fact that his authority has said it; and this again he has no right to do. Worst of all, if he contradicts them, presuming to decide that his authority has misrepresented the facts, and rejecting his statements as incredible, he is believing the opposite of what he has been told, and committing the worst possible offence against the rules of his craft. The authority may be garrulous, discursive, a gossip and a scandal-monger; he may have overlooked or forgotten or omitted facts; he may have ignorantly or wilfully misstated them; but against these defects the historian has no remedy. For him, on the theory, what his authorities tell him is the truth, the whole accessible truth, and nothing but the truth.

The common-sense theory is now before us. Is it a sound, recognizable account of how historians think? Collingwood is convinced that it is not, as the following programmatic paragraph makes clear:

These consequences of the common-sense theory have only to be stated in order to be repudiated. Every historian is aware that on occasion he does tamper in all these three ways with what he finds in his authorities. He selects from them what he thinks important, and omits the rest; he interpolates in them things which they do not explicitly say; and he criticizes them by rejecting or amending what he regards as due to misinformation or mendacity. But I am not sure whether we historians always realize the consequences of what we are doing. In general, when we reflect on our own work, we seem to accept what I have called the common-sense theory, while claiming our own rights of selection, construction, and criticism. No doubt these rights are inconsistent with the theory; but we attempt to soften the contradiction by minimizing the extent to which they are exercised, thinking of them as emergency measures, a kind of revolt into which the historian may be driven at times by the exceptional incompetence of his authorities, but which does not fundamentally disturb the normal peaceful régime in which he placidly believes what he is told because he is told to believe it. Yet these things, however seldom they are done, are either historical crimes or facts fatal to the theory: for on the theory they ought to be done, not rarely, but never. And in fact they are neither criminal nor exceptional. Throughout the course of his work the historian is *selecting, constructing,* and *criticizing;* it is only by doing these things that he maintains his thought upon the *sichere Gang einer Wissenschaft.* By explicitly recognizing this fact it is possible to effect what, again borrowing a Kantian phrase, one might call a Copernican revolution in the theory of history: the discovery that, so far from relying on an authority other than himself, to whose statements his thought must conform, the historian is his own authority and his thought *autonomous,* self-authorizing, possessed of a criterion to which his so-called authorities must conform and by reference to which they are criticized.

In what ways, then, is historical thinking *autonomous,* not based on any authority that is not authorized by the historian himself? Collingwood reminds us of three essential activities that historians perform, in each of which they are autonomous, "on their own": selection, construction, and criticism. First, selection:

The autonomy of historical thought is seen at its simplest in the work of selection. The historian who tries to work on the common-sense theory, and accurately reproduce what he finds in his authorities, resembles a landscape-painter who tries to work on that theory of art which bids the artist copy nature. He may fancy that he is reproducing in his own medium the actual shapes and colours of natural things; but however hard he tries to do this he is always selecting, simplifying, schematizing, leaving out what he thinks unimportant and putting in what he regards as essential. It is the artist, and not nature, that is responsible for what goes into the picture. In the same way, no historian, not even the worst, merely copies out his authorities; even if he puts in nothing of his own (which is never really possible), he is always leaving out things which, for one reason or another, he decides that his own work does not need or cannot use. It is he, therefore, and not his authority, that is responsible for what goes in. On that question he is his own master: his thought is to that extent autonomous.

Second, in historical construction:

An even clearer exhibition of this autonomy is found in what I have called historical construction. The historian's authorities tell him of this or that phase in a process whose intermediate phases they leave undescribed; he then interpolates these phases for himself. His picture of his subject, though it may consist in part of statements directly drawn from his authorities, consists also, and increasingly with every increase in his competence as an historian, of statements reached inferentially from those according to his own criteria, his own rules of method, and his own canons of relevance. In this part of his work he is never depending on his authorities in the sense of repeating what they tell him; he is relying on his own powers and constituting himself his own authority; while his so-called authorities are now not authorities at all but only evidence.

Third, in historical criticism:

The clearest demonstration of the historian's autonomy, however, is provided by historical criticism. As natural science finds its proper method when the scientist, in Bacon's metaphor, puts Nature to the question, tortures her by experiment in order to wring from her answers to his own questions, so history finds its proper method when the historian puts his authorities in the witness-box, and by cross-questioning extorts from them information which in their original statements they have withheld, either because they did not wish to give it or because they did not possess it. Thus, a commander's dispatches may claim a victory; the historian, reading them in a critical spirit, will ask: 'If it was a victory, why was it not followed up in this or that way?' and may thus convict the writer of concealing the truth. Or, by using the same method, he may convict of ignorance a less critical predecessor who has accepted the version of the battle given him by the same dispatches.

The historian's autonomy is here manifested in its extremest form, because it is here evident that somehow, in virtue of his activity as an historian, he has it in his power to reject something explicitly told him by his authorities and to substitute something else. If that is possible, the criterion of historical truth cannot be the fact that a statement is made by an authority. It is the truthfulness and the information of the so-called authority that are in question; and this question the historian has to answer for himself, on his own authority. Even if he accepts what his authorities tell him, therefore, he accepts it not on their authority but on his own; not because they say it, but because it satisfies his criterion of historical truth.

So much for the common-sense theory that would base history on memory and authority. If it cannot make good sense of three such essential historical-knowledge-producing activities as selecting, constructing, and criticizing, then as a theory it is out of the running.

The common-sense theory which bases history upon memory and authority needs no further refutation. Its bankruptcy is evident. For the historian there can never be authorities, because the so-called authorities abide a verdict which only he can give. Yet the common-sense theory may claim a qualified and relative truth. The historian, generally speaking, works at a subject which others have studied before him. In proportion as he is more of a novice, either in this particular subject or in history as a whole, his forerunners are, relatively to his incompetence, authoritative; and in the limiting case where his incompetence and ignorance were absolute, they could be called authorities without qualification. As he becomes more and more master of his craft and his subject, they become less and less his authorities, more and more his fellow students, to be treated with respect or contempt according to their deserts.

And as history does not depend on authority, so it does not depend upon memory. The historian can rediscover what has been completely forgotten, in the sense that no statement of it has reached him by an unbroken tradition from eyewitnesses. He can even discover what, until he discovered it, no one ever knew to have happened at all. This he does partly by the critical treatment of statements contained in his sources, partly by the use of what are called unwritten sources, which are increasingly employed as history becomes increasingly sure of its own proper methods and its own proper criterion.

However, the more the historian's thinking is conceded to be autonomous, and the common-sense theory therefore inadequate, the more we are faced with an important and difficult question: "By what criterion of historical truth does the historian regulate his autonomous thinking? And who or what authorizes this criterion?

I have spoken of the criterion of historical truth. What is this criterion? According to the common-sense theory, it is the agreement of the statements made by the historian with those which he finds in his authorities. This answer we now know to be false, and we must seek another. We cannot renounce the search. Some answer to the question there must be, for without a criterion there can be no criticism. One answer to this question was offered by Francis Herbert Bradley, the greatest English philosopher of our time in his pamphlet on *The Presuppositions of Critical History.* . . . In it Bradley faces the question how it is possible for the historian, in defiance of the common-sense theory, to turn the tables on his so-called authorities and to say 'This is what our authorities record, but what really happened must have been not this but that.'

His answer to this question was that our experience of the world teaches us that some kinds of things happen and others do not; this experience, then, is the criterion which the historian brings to bear on the statements of his authorities. If they tell him that things happened of a kind which, according to his experience, does not happen, he is obliged to disbelieve them; if the things which they report are of a kind which according to his experience does happen, he is free to accept their statements.

There are many obvious objections to this idea, on which I shall not insist. . . . But . . . there are certain special points in which the argument appears to me defective.

First, the proposed criterion is a criterion not of what did happen but of what could happen. It is in fact nothing but Aristotle's criterion of what is admissible in poetry; and hence it does not serve to discriminate history from fiction. It would no doubt be satisfied by the statements of an historian, but it would be satisfied no less adequately by those of an historical novelist. It cannot therefore be the criterion of critical history.

Secondly, because it can never tell us what did happen, we are left to rely for that on the sheer authority of our informant. We undertake, when we apply it, to believe everything our informant tells us so long as it satisfies the merely negative criterion of being possible. This is not to turn the tables on our authorities; it is blindly to accept what they tell us. The critical attitude has not been achieved.

Thirdly, the historian's experience of the world in which he lives can only help him to check, even negatively, the statements of his authorities in so far as they are concerned not with history but with nature, which has no history. The laws of nature have always been the same, and what is against nature now was against nature two thousand years ago; but the historical as distinct from the natural conditions of man's life differ so much at different times that no argument from analogy will hold. That the Greeks and Romans exposed their new-born children in order to control the numbers of their population is no less true for being unlike anything that happens in the experience of contributors to the *Cambridge Ancient History.*

Bradley's essay, inconclusive though it is, remains memorable for the fact that in it the Copernican revolution in the theory of historical knowledge has been in principle accomplished. For the common-sense theory, historical truth consists in the historian's beliefs conforming to the statements of his authorities; Bradley has seen that the historian brings with him to the study of his authorities a criterion of his own by reference to which the authorities themselves are judged. What it is, Bradley failed to discover. It remains to be seen whether, sixty years later, his problem, which in the meantime I believe no English-speaking philosopher has discussed in print, can be advanced beyond the point at which he left it.

I have already remarked that, in addition to selecting from among his authorities' statements those which he regards as important, the historian must in two ways go beyond what his authorities tell him. One is the critical way, and this is what Bradley has attempted to analyse. The other is the constructive way. Of this he has said nothing, and to this I now propose to return. I described constructive history as interpolating, between the statements borrowed from our authorities, other statements implied by them. Thus our authorities tell us that on one day Caesar was in Rome and on a later day in Gaul; they tell us nothing about his journey from one place to the other, but we interpolate this with a perfectly good conscience.

This act of interpolation has two significant characteristics. *First,* it is in no way arbitrary or merely fanciful: it is necessary or, in Kantian language, *a priori.* If we filled up the narrative of Caesar's doings with fanciful details such as the names of the persons he met on the way, and what he said to them, the construction would be arbitrary: it would be in fact the kind of construction which is done by an historical novelist. But if our construction involves nothing that is not necessitated by the evidence, it is a legitimate historical construction of a kind without which there can be no history at all.

Secondly, what is in this way inferred is essentially something imagined. If we look out over the sea and perceive a ship, and five minutes later look again and perceive it in a different place, we find ourselves obliged to imagine it as having occupied intermediate positions when we were not looking. That is already an example of historical thinking; and it is not otherwise that we find ourselves obliged to imagine Caesar as having travelled from Rome to Gaul when we are told that he was in these different places at these successive times.

This activity, with this double character, I shall call *a priori* imagination; and, though I shall have more to say of it hereafter, for the present I shall be content to remark that, however unconscious we may be of its operation, it is this activity which, bridging the gaps between what our authorities tell us, gives the historical narrative or description its continuity. That the historian must use his imagination is a commonplace; to quote Macaulay's *Essay on History*, 'a perfect historian must possess an imagination sufficiently powerful to make his narrative affecting and picturesque'; but this is to underestimate the part played by the historical imagination, which is properly not ornamental but structural. Without it the historian would have no narrative to adorn. The imagination, that 'blind but indispensable faculty' without which, as Kant has shown, we could never perceive the world around us, is indispensable in the same way to history: it is this which, operating not capriciously as fancy but in its *a priori* form, does the entire work of historical construction.

Two misunderstandings may here be forestalled. *First*, it may be thought that by imagining we can present to ourselves only what is imaginary in the sense of being fictitious or unreal. This prejudice need only be mentioned in order to be dispelled. If I imagine the friend who lately left my house now entering his own, the fact that I imagine this event gives me no reason to believe it unreal. The imaginary, simply as such, is neither unreal nor real.

Secondly, to speak of *a priori* imagination may seem a paradox, for it may be thought that imagination is essentially capricious, arbitrary, merely fanciful. But in addition to its historical function there are two other functions of *a priori* imagination which are, or ought to be, familiar to all. One is the pure or free, but by no means arbitrary, imagination of the artist. A man writing a novel composes a story where parts are played by various characters. Characters and incidents are all alike imaginary; yet the whole aim of the novelist is to show the characters acting and the incidents developing in a manner determined by a necessity internal to themselves. The story, if it is a good story, cannot develop otherwise than as it does; the novelist in imagining it cannot imagine it developing except as it does develop. Here, and equally in all other kinds of art, the *a priori* imagination is at work. Its other familiar function is what may be called the perceptual imagination, supplementing and consolidating the data of perception in the way so well analysed by Kant, by presenting to us objects of possible perception which are not actually perceived: the under side of this table, the inside of an unopened egg, the back of the moon. Here again the imagination is *a priori:* we cannot but imagine what cannot but be there. The historical imagination differs from these not in being *a priori*, but in having as its special task to imagine the past: not an object of possible perception, since it does not now exist, but able through this activity to become an object of our thought.

The historian's picture of his subject, whether that subject be a sequence of events or a past state of things, thus appears as a web of imaginative construction stretched between certain fixed points provided by the statements of his authorities; and if these points are frequent enough and the threads spun from each to the next are constructed with due care, always by the *a priori* imagination and never by merely arbitrary fancy, the whole picture is constantly verified by appeal to these data, and runs little risk of losing touch with the reality which it represents.

Actually, this is very much how we do think of historical work, when the common-sense theory has ceased to satisfy us, and we have become aware of the part played in it by the constructive imagination. But such a conception is in one way seriously at fault: it overlooks the no less important part played by criticism. We think of our web of construction as pegged down, so to speak, to the facts by the statements of authorities, which we regard as data or fixed points for the work of construction. But in so thinking we have slipped back into the theory, which we now know to be false, that truth is given us ready made in these statements. We know that truth is to be had, not by swallowing what our authorities tell us, but by criticizing it; and thus the supposedly fixed points between which the historical imagination spins its web are not given to us ready made, they must be achieved by critical thinking.

There is nothing other than historical thought itself, by appeal to which its conclusions may be verified.

Thus far Professor Collingwood's claim has been to this effect: Thinking that is productive of historical knowledge involves the exercise of the historical imagination; and the historical imagination works, in part, according to *a priori* principles or rules. We still do not have a clear answer to the question, "By what criterion of truth does the historian regulate his autonomous thinking?" But whatever it is, it must be compatible with the *a priori* imagination as that works to produce historical knowledge. To continue, then:

I began by considering a theory according to which everything is given: according to which all truth, so far as any truth is accessible to the historian, is provided for him ready made in the ready-made statements of his authorities. I then saw that much of what he takes for true is not given in this way but constructed by his *a priori* imagination; but I still fancied that this imagination worked inferentially from fixed points given in the same sense. I am now driven to confess that there are for historical thought no fixed points thus given: in other words, that in history, just as there are properly speaking no authorities, so there are properly speaking no data.

Historians certainly think of themselves as working from data; where by data they mean historical facts possessed by them ready made at the beginning of a certain piece of historical research. Such a datum, if the research concerns the Peloponesian War, would be, for example, a certain statement of Thucydides, accepted as substantially true. But when we ask what gives historical thought this datum, the answer is obvious: historical thought gives it to itself, and therefore in relation to historical thought at large it is not a datum but a result or achievement. It is only our historical knowledge which tells us that these curious marks on paper are Greek letters; that the words which they form have certain meanings in the Attic dialect; that the passage is authentic Thucydides, not an interpolation or corruption; and that on this occasion Thucydides knew what he was talking about and was trying to tell the truth. Apart from all this, the passage is merely a pattern of black marks on white paper: not any historical fact at all, but something existing here and now, and perceived by the historian. All that the historian means, when he describes certain historical facts as his data, is that for the purposes of a particular piece of work there are certain historical problems relevant to that work which for the present he proposes to treat as settled; though, if they are settled, it is only because historical thinking has settled them in the past, and they remain settled only until he or some one else decides to reopen them.

His web of imaginative construction, therefore, cannot derive its validity from being pegged down, as at first I described it, to certain given facts. That description represented an attempt to relieve him of the responsibility for the nodal points of his fabric, while admitting his responsibility for what he constructs between them. In point of fact, he is just as responsible for the one as for the other. Whether he accepts or rejects or modifies or reinterprets what his so-called authorities tell him, it is he that is responsible for the statement which, after duly criticizing them, he makes. The criterion that justifies him in making it can never be the fact that it has been given him by an authority.

Telling us what the criterion of truth in historical thinking is not, still does not tell us what it is. However, Collingwood has added another important point: in thinking productive of historical knowledge there are, strictly speaking, no data; in the last analysis there are only *accepta*. This is to radicalize the autonomy exercised by the historian, but it leaves the question of the criterion with reference to which he does his radically autonomous thinking still unanswered. As Collingwood says:

This brings me back to the question what this criterion is. And at this point a partial and provisional answer can be given. The web of imaginative construction is something far more solid and powerful than we have hitherto realized. So far from relying for its validity upon the support of given facts, it actually serves as the touchstone by which we decide whether alleged facts are genuine. Suetonius tells me that Nero at one time intended to evacuate Britain. I reject his statement, not because any better authority flatly contradicts it, for of course none does; but because my reconstruction of Nero's policy based on Tacitus will not allow me to think that Suetonius is right. And if I am told that this is merely to say I prefer Tacitus to Suetonius, I confess that I do: but I do so just because I find myself able to incorporate what Tacitus tells me into a coherent and continuous picture of my own, and cannot do this for Suetonius.

It is thus the historian's picture of the past, the product of his own *a priori* imagination, that has to justify the sources used in its construction. These sources are sources, that is to say, credence is given to them, only because they are in this way justified. For any source may be tainted: this writer prejudiced, that misinformed; this inscription misread by a bad epigraphist, that blundered by a careless stonemason; this potsherd placed out of its context by an incompetent excavator, that by a blameless rabbit. The critical historian has to discover and correct all these and many other kinds of falsification. He does it, and can only do it, by considering whether the picture of the past to which the evidence leads him is a coherent and continuous picture, one which makes sense. The *a priori* imagination which does the work of historical construction supplies the means of historical criticism as well.

Freed from its dependence on fixed points supplied from without, the historian's picture of the past is thus in every detail an imaginary picture, and its necessity is at every point the necessity of the *a priori* imagination. Whatever goes into it, goes into it not because his imagination passively accepts it, but because it actively demands it.

At this point Collingwood introduces something of a "breather," in the form of a comparison and contrast between the thinking that is productive of historical knowledge and the thinking that is productive of historical fiction. After this aside, he will return to his continuing question:

The resemblance between the historian and the novelist, to which I have already referred, here reaches its culmination. Each of them makes it his business to construct a picture which is partly a narrative of events, partly a description of situations, exhibition of motives, analysis of characters. Each aims at making his picture a coherent whole, where every character and every situation is so bound up with the rest that this character in this situation cannot but act in this way, and we cannot imagine him as acting otherwise. The novel and the history must both of them make sense; nothing is admissible in either except what is necessary, and the judge of this necessity is in both cases the imagination. Both the novel and the history are self-explanatory, self-justifying, the product of an autonomous or self-authorizing activity; and in both cases this activity is the *a priori* imagination.

As works of imagination, the historian's work and the novelist's do not differ. Where they do differ is that the historian's picture is meant to be true. The novelist has a single task only: to construct a coherent picture, one that makes sense. The historian has a double task: he has both to do this, and to construct a picture of things as they really were and of events as they really happened. This further necessity imposes upon him obedience to three rules of method, from which the novelist or artist in general is free.

First, his picture must be localized in space and time. The artist's need not; essentially, the things that he imagines are imagined as happening at no place and at no date. Of *Wuthering Heights* it has been well said that the scene is laid in Hell, though the place-names are English; and it was a sure instinct that led another great novelist to replace Oxford by Christminster, Wantage by Alfredston, and Fawley by Marychurch, recoiling against the discord of topographical fact in what should be a purely imaginary world.

Secondly, all history must be consistent with itself. Purely imaginary worlds cannot clash and need not agree; each is a world to itself. But there is only one historical world, and everything in it must stand in some relation to everything else, even if that relation is only topographical and chronological.

Thirdly, and most important, the historian's picture stands in a peculiar relation to something called evidence. The only way in which the historian or any one else can judge, even tentatively, of its truth is by considering this relation; and, in practice, what we mean by asking whether an historical statement is true is whether it can be justified by an appeal to the evidence: for a truth unable to be so justified is to the historian a thing of no interest. What is this thing called evidence, and what is its relation to the finished historical work?

Historical claims rest on evidence. The evidence consists of *accepta*, not data. The responsibility for accepting remains with the accepter. You have therefore the question, "Why do you *accept* this and that which you will then proceed to use *as* evidence? In this accepting, what criterion are you guided by?" Once you have *accepted* these prior claims, and move to use them as evidence, you have the follow-up question, "What do they prove? Your claim rests on them. Does it rest validly? Given them, are you entitled to say that your historical claim is true? What criterion of truth is operating here?" These are Collingwood's questions in the paragraphs that remain:

We already know what evidence is not. It is not ready-made historical knowledge, to be swallowed and regurgitated by the historian's mind. Everything is evidence which the historian can use as evidence. But what can he so use? It must be something here and now perceptible to him: this written page, this spoken utterance, this building, this finger-print. And of all the things perceptible to him there is not one which he might not conceivably use as evidence on some question, if he came to it with the right question in mind. The enlargement of historical knowledge comes about mainly through finding how to use as evidence this or that kind of perceived fact which historians have hitherto thought useless to them.

The whole perceptible world, then, is potentially and in principle evidence to the historian. It becomes actual evidence in so far as he can use it. And he cannot use it unless he comes to it with the right kind of historical knowledge. The more historical knowledge we have, the more we can learn from any given piece of evidence; if we had none, we could learn nothing. Evidence is evidence only when some one contemplates it historically. Otherwise it is merely perceived fact, historically dumb. It follows that historical knowledge can only grow out of historical knowledge; in other words, that historical thinking is an original and fundamental activity of the human mind, or, as Descartes might have said, that the idea of the past is an "innate" idea.

Historical thinking is that activity of the imagination by which we endeavour to provide this innate idea with detailed content. And this we do by using the present as evidence for its own past. Every present has a past of its own, and any imaginative reconstruction of the past aims at reconstructing the past of this present, the present in which the act of imagination is going on, as here and now perceived. In principle the aim of any such act is to use the entire perceptible here-and-now as evidence for the entire past through whose process it has come into being. In practice, this aim can never be achieved. The perceptible here-and-now can never be perceived, still less interpreted, in its entirety; and the infinite process of past time can never be envisaged as a whole. But this separation between what is attempted in principle and what is achieved in practice is the lot of mankind, not a peculiarity of historical thinking. The fact that it is found there only shows that herein history is like art, science, philosophy, the pursuit of virtue, and the search for happiness.

It is for the same reason that in history, as in all serious matters, no achievement is final. The evidence available for solving any given problem changes with every change of historical method and with every variation in the competence of historians. The principles by which this evidence is interpreted change too; since the interpreting of evidence is a task to which a man must bring everything he knows: historical knowledge, knowledge of nature and man, mathematical knowledge, philosophical knowledge; and not knowledge only, but mental habits and possessions of every kind: and none of these is unchanging. Because of these changes, which never cease, however slow they may appear to observers who take a short view, every new generation must rewrite history in its own way; every new historian, not content with giving new answers to old questions, must revise the questions themselves; and—since historical thought is a river into which none can step twice—even a single historian, working at a single subject for a certain length of time, finds when he tries to reopen an old question that the question has changed.

This is not an argument for historical scepticism. It is only the discovery of a second dimension of historical thought, the history of history: the discovery that the historian himself, together with the here-and-now which forms the total body of evidence available to him, is a part of the process he is studying, has his own place in that process, and can see it only from the point of view which at this present moment he occupies within it.

But neither the raw material of historical knowledge, the detail of the here-and-now as given him in perception, nor the various endowments that serve him as aids to interpreting this evidence, can give the historian his criterion of historical truth. That criterion is the idea of history itself: the idea of an imaginary picture of the past. That idea is, in Cartesian language, innate; in Kantian language, *a priori*. It is not a chance product of psychological causes; it is an idea which every man possesses as part of the furniture of his mind, and discovers himself to possess in so far as he becomes conscious of what it is to have a mind. Like other ideas of the same sort, it is one to which no fact of experience exactly corresponds. The historian, however long and faithfully he works, can never say that his work, even in crudest outline or in this or that smallest detail, is done once for all. He can never say that his picture of the past is at any point adequate to his idea of what it ought to be. But, however fragmentary and faulty the results of his work may be, the idea which governed its course is clear, rational, and universal. It is the idea of the historical imagination as a self-dependent, self-determining, and self-justifying form of thought.

READING QUESTIONS

1. What is Collingwood's distinction between the "outside" and the "inside"? To what use does he put this distinction?
2. "All history is the history of thought." How so?
3. "All history is the re-enactment of past thought in the historian's own mind." (a) How so? (b) Is Collingwood referring to history in Sense One or Sense Two here?
4. "There is only one hypothesis on which natural processes could be regarded as historical in character." Namely?
5. Use any half-dozen points to formulate what he calls the common-sense theory of history.
6. How he uses the notions of (a) selection, (b) construction, (c) criticism to torpedo the common-sense theory of history.
7. In which of those three notions in question 6 is the historian's autonomy manifested "in its extremest form"? How so?
8. What does Collingwood mean by the *a priori* imagination in history? Why it is important. Is there an *a priori* imagination in science? For example?
9. Illustrate: "Historical thinking is that activity of the imagination by which we endeavor to provide this *a priori* idea with detailed content."

INDEPENDENT STUDY

1. Read Collingwood's essay "Historical Evidence," essay 3, part 5, of his book *The Idea of History*. Write a paper setting forth his essential claims in a systematic and orderly manner.

2. Read Chapter 6, "The Grammar of Action," in L. O. Mink's book *Mind, History and Dialectic.* Professor Mink reviews six criticisms of Collingwood's views of historical thinking. Write a paper making clear each objection, and whether Professor Mink's handling satisfies you.

3. Read the article on R. G. Collingwood by A. Donagan in the *Encyclopedia of Philosophy.* Then read Collingwood's *Autobiography.* Write a biographical essay on Collingwood's philosophy, centering your account on his philosophy of history.

4. Collingwood's interest in the character of historical thinking is continued by W. H. Dray in *Law and Explanation in History.* This book opens with a chapter on the covering-law theory of explanation and its application to history, as proposed by C. Hempel. The rest of Dray's book is a critique of the covering-law theory of explanation applied to history. Write a paper on Dray's monograph.

topic SIX
art and feeling

THE PROBLEM STATED

We sometimes refer to poems, pictures, musical compositions, and status as works of art; and the activity that produces them as art. Is it possible to define these terms, *art* and *work of art?* What fact about any activity would be our reason for calling it art? What fact about any object would be our reason for calling it a work of art? There would seem to be *some* reason. On some occasions we withhold these terms; on others, we are in doubt. Such behavior on our part would suggest that we at least "know what we are talking about" when we use, or refuse, or are in doubt about using, the terms *art* and *work of art.* If there is *no* detectable reason for using these terms, why do we do so? Why do we refuse to do so? Why do we hesitate to do so?

In an inquiry of this kind, we might begin with judgments that we would be able and willing to authorize. Take, for example, Matthew Arnold's poem "Dover Beach." Is it a work of art? If so, why? If not, why not? Let the reader settle these questions for himself. Let him mention a dozen items, *any* dozen—poems, pictures, musical compositions, statues—about which he would be prepared to say, "There are works of art. Whatever else they are, they are works of art. Whatever other items are works of art, at least *these* are. Whatever other items are *not* works of art, at least these *are*. And the activ-

457

ity that produced them is art. You might add, "The agent who performs this activity is an artist." How about these three terms: *work of art, art, artist?* Are they a connected set? Does it matter at which end you begin? If the reader cannot or will not authorize *any* such judgments, then for him the problem dealt with in this Topic does not arise. But there is no *prima facie* reason to believe that the reader is thus either unable or unwilling. Why should he be?

Suppose, then, that these aesthetic judgments are forthcoming. "This and this and this are works of art; and the activity that produced them is art." Such judgments are data. Given them, the question arises, "What fact, common and peculiar to these and similar objects, is the reason for calling them *works of art?* And for calling the activity that produced them *art?* And for calling the agent who performed these activities an *artist?*" An answer to this question would define, set limits to, the class "work of art" and "art." Whatever satisfied the definition would fall inside these classes; whatever did not, would fall outside these classes. As these definitions took shape, they would suggest further questions; and as these questions were answered, the answers could be added on to the original definitions. The outcome would constitute a theory of art. The English word *theory* is said to be derived from the Greek word *theoria,* meaning a looking at, a viewing, a beholding. A theory of art is a looking at the particulars that together make up "the world of art." You could start by answering, "What makes these particulars to be works of art?" Your answer would spell out for you the criteria of recognition that are present and operative when you identify a particular as a work of art. It should be noted that the question, "Is this a work of art?" is not the same as the question, "Is this a good work of art?" Your criteria of recognition may not be your criteria of evaluation. Asking what *kind* an identifiable particular is, is not the same as asking whether it is good of its kind.

In the authors brought together in this Topic you have persons attempting to think about aesthetic judgments, definitions, and theories. They are endeavoring to define and theorize about art; or to theorize about the attempt to define and theorize about art. The first author, Eugene Véron, claims that art is an activity in which the agent expresses his feelings or emotions, and does this subject to the limitations imposed by some medium, e.g., words, sounds, lines, colors, or stone. This theory of art as expression stands in contrast to an older theory of art as imitation. The second author, Leo Tolstoy, would include communication as well as expression. There must be communication as well as expression, if the activity is to be art, and the outcome a work of art. The third, R. G. Collingwood, reverts to the first position, art as expression of emotion, and offers a more intimate and detailed account of the character of this activity. Criticism sets in with the fourth author, Professor John Hospers. Professor Hospers gives reasons for doubting that "expression of emotion" will enable one to formulate a definition of *art* or *work of art*. The fifth author, Professor Morris Weitz, rejects the entire enterprise of defining the terms *art* or *work of art;* he claims that these terms are essentially and in principle impossible to define. His point, to speak in metaphor, is that these terms are "alive" and "growing"; and that therefore *any* attempt to "contain" them by a definition or a theory is bound to be unsatisfactory.

TRIGGER QUESTIONS

1. Mention any half-dozen items that you would unhesitatingly claim to be *works of art*.
2. Relative to art, or works of art, or artists, is the distinction between *criteria of recognition* and *criteria of evaluation* an important one? Which of these criteria presupposes the other?
3. Which of the two criteria in question 2 would be involved if you said that a woodcarving might be a work of art, but that a piece of driftwood could not be?
4. Why does talk about *art,* if persisted in, usually lead to talk about feeling? Is there any necessary connection between the two?
5. What do you understand by the term *feelings?* Mention three.
6. What can we do with feelings?
7. How are feelings related to (a) experiences we have, and (b) activities we perform?
8. Why does the expression of feeling, or the attempt to express feeling, so frequently involve one in the use of metaphor?
9. We use these three terms: (a) *artist,* (b) *art,* (c) *work of art.* Which is the basic term? Are the other two definable with reference to it?
10. You have read nine "trigger questions." Can you formulate a tenth?

SECTION 1. EUGENE VÉRON: ART AS EXPRESSION OF EMOTION

A good beginning can be made with Eugene Véron (1825–1889). His book *Aesthetics* was published in 1878. It was translated into English a year later, but is now out of print and difficult to come by. This is regrettable because it has the virtues of simplicity and clarity.

Whether you agree with Véron or not, at least you know where he stands. If you agree, he leaves you free to develop beyond him if you see the necessity for doing so. If you disagree, he leaves you "in the clear" with respect to what it is you disagree with. These are helps, when one is making a beginning.

The Argument of the Passages. His proposal is that a work of art is an emotive symbol, something whereby the artist expresses his emotions, his feelings. An emotive symbol can be contrasted with a cognitive symbol, something whereby one expresses what one knows or believes, in contrast to what one feels. It is one thing to have emotions and to express them: this calls for an emotive symbol. It is another to have knowledge or belief, and to express them: this calls for a cognitive symbol. We all need and use both kinds of symbols. But we are not all equally talented at creating either kind. So we put artists and cognizers to work for us. If emotions are to be expressed, a symbol or vehicle must be created enabling them to be expressed. Art is the activity of creating these emotionally expressive symbols. The symbol is the work of art.

Véron distinguishes sharply between this way of conceiving art and the older way, which thought of art as the activity of producing a copy or imitation of some original. According to this Imitation Theory an artist looks at a man or a mountain and paints "what he sees." The result would be an imitation or copy or "picture" of some "original." On this way of thinking, the work of art would be something of a cognitive symbol. It would tell you what you would know if you knew the original. You could gauge its excellence by comparing it with the original. On this way of thinking a good camera might produce a better work of art than any painter could do. Compared to an original, a photograph can be more accurate than a painting. Even greater accuracy could be obtained by holding a mirror up to an original. Véron's essential claim would rule out mirror-images, photographs, contrived echoes, tape-recordings, and so on, as not works of art, and the activity of producing them as not art. The artist must have a certain feeling or emotion. The work of art must express that feeling or emotion.

This primary claim enables Véron to distinguish between decorative and expressive art. The latter is art proper. It is not to be judged by its power to please, but by its power to express. The claim—art as creation of emotive symbol—enables him also to develop the notions of artistic integrity and artistic style. Integrity demands that one express the emotions one has; not, e.g., the feelings one "ought to" have, or would like to have. Style is the way in which the person one basically is determines the way in which one gives expression to the emotions one has. His theory also enables Véron to distinguish between lyric and dramatic. When art is lyric, the intention is to express feelings, sensations, emotions that the artist himself has experienced. They may be sharable, but the point is they are his own in the first instance. Had you asked him, Matthew Arnold might have said as much about his "Dover Beach." Is it to be denied that his testimony would count as evidence? When art is dramatic, the intention is to express feelings that belong primarily to someone else. This someone else may be a historical person, as in Plato's Socrates; or an imaginary person, as in Goethe's Faust. These are a few of the good things to be had from a reading of Véron's statement of the Emotive Theory of Art. No matter what awkward questions that theory may give rise to, there is no dismissing it out of hand on the grounds that it does not lead one to think at all fruitfully about art.

Art, far from being the blossom and fruit of civilization, is rather its germ. It began to give evidence of its existence so soon as man became self-conscious, and is to be found clearly defined in his very earliest works.

By its psychological origin it is bound up with the constituent principles of humanity. The salient and essential characteristic of man is his incessant cerebral activity, which is propagated and developed by countless acts and works of varied kind. The aim and rule of this activity is the search after *the best;* that is to say, the more and more complete satisfaction of physical and moral wants. This instinct, common to all animals, is seconded in man by an exceptionally well-developed faculty to adapt the means to the end.

The effort to satisfy physical wants has given birth to all the industries that defend, preserve, and smooth the path of life; the effort to satisfy the moral wants—of which one of the most important is the gratification of our cerebral activity itself—has created the arts, long before it could give them power sufficient for the conscious elaboration of ideas. The life of sentiment preceded the manifestations of intellectual life by many centuries.

The gratification, *in esse* or *in posse,* of either real or imaginary wants, is the cause of happiness, joy, pleasure, and of all the feelings connected with them; the contrary is marked by grief, sadness, fear, etc.: but in both cases there is emotion to give more or less lively evidence by means of exterior signs. When expressed by gesture and rhythmic movement, such emotion produces the dance; when by rhythmic notes, music; when by rhythmic words, poetry.

As man is essentially sympathetic and his joy or pain is often caused as much by the good or evil fortunes of others as by his own; as, besides, he possesses in a very high degree the faculty of combining series of fictitious facts, and of representing them in colors even more lively than those of reality: it results that the domain of art is of infinite extent for him. For the causes of emotion are multiplied for every man—not only by the number of similar beings who live around him and are attached to him by the more or less closely knit bonds of affection, alliance, similitude of situation or community of ideas and interests; but also, by the never-ending multitude of beings and events that are able to originate or direct the imaginings of poets.

To these elements of emotion and moral enjoyment must be added the combinations of lines, of forms and of colors, the dispositions and opposition of light and shade, etc. The instinctive search after this kind of emotion or pleasure, the special organ of which is the eye, has given birth to what are called the arts of design—sculpture, painting and architecture.

We may say then, by way of general definition, that art is the manifestation of emotion, obtaining external interpretation, now by expressive arrangements of line, form or color, now by a series of gestures, sounds, or words governed by particular rhythmical cadence.

We must conclude, from our definition, that the merit of a work of art can be measured by the power with which it manifests or interprets the emotion that was its determining cause, and that, for a like reason, must constitute its innermost and supreme unity.

Imitation is not the aim of art. The poet arranging his verses, the musician composing his airs and harmonies, are well aware that their real object is not imitation. This distinction is perhaps less clear in matters of painting and sculpture. Some artists, and these not the least capable, are convinced that when they have a model before them, their one duty is to imitate it, copy it. And indeed they do nothing else; and, by virtue of such imitation, they succeed in producing works of incontestable artistic value.

Here we have simply a misunderstanding. If an artist were really able to reduce himself to the condition of a copying machine; if he could so far efface and suppress himself as to confine his work to the servile reproduction of all the details of an object or event, the only value his work would possess would be that of a more or less exact *procès verbal*, and it would perforce remain inferior to reality. Where is the artist who would attempt to depict sunlight without taking refuge in some legerdemain, calling to his aid devices which the true sun would despise? But enough of this. Just because he is endowed with sensibility and imaginative power, the artist, in presence of the facts of nature or the events of history, finds himself, whether he will or not, in a peculiar situation. However thorough a realist he may think himself, he does not leave himself to chance. Now, choice of subject alone is enough to prove that some preference has existed, the result of a more or less predeterminate impression, and of a more or less unconscious agreement between the character of the object and that of the artist. This impression and agreement he sets to work to embody in outward form; it is the real aim of his work, and its possession gives him his claim to the name of artist. Without wishing or even knowing it, he molds the features of nature to his dominant impression and to the idea that caused him to take pencil in hand. His work has an accidental stamp, in addition to that of the permanent genius which constitutes his individuality. Poet, musician, sculptor and architect, all pay more or less strict obedience to the same law. To it, point all those rules of artistic composition which pedantic academicism has subtly multiplied until they contradict each other.

The more of this personal character that a work possesses; the more harmonious its details and their combined expression; the more clearly each part communicates the impression of the artist, whether of grandeur, of melancholy or of joy; in fine, the more that expression of human sensation and will predominates over mere imitation, the better will be its chance of obtaining sooner or later the admiration of the world—always supposing that the sentiment expressed be a generous one, and that the execution be not of such a kind as to repel or baffle connoisseurs. It is not of course impossible that an artist endowed with an ill-regulated or morbid imagination may place himself outside all normal conditions and condemn himself to the eternal misapprehension of the public. Impressions that are too particular, eccentric feelings, fantastic execution or processes, which do nothing to raise the intrinsic value or power of inspiration of a work, may give it so strange and ultra-individual a character that it may become impossible for us to arrive at its real merit. The best qualities, when exaggerated, become faults; and that very personality or individuality which, when added to imitative power, results in a work of art, produces when pushed to extravagance nothing but an enigma.

We see, then, that the beautiful in art springs mainly from the intervention of the genius of man when excited by special emotion.

A work is beautiful when it bears strong marks of the individuality of its author, of the permanent personality of the artist, and of the more or less accidental impression produced upon him by the sight of the object or event rendered.

In a word, it is from the worth of the artist that the worth of his work is derived. It is the manifestation of the faculties and qualities he possesses which attracts and fascinates us. The more sympathetic power and individuality these faculties and qualities display, the easier it is for them to obtain our love and admiration. On the other hand, we, for a similar reason, reject and contemn bold and vulgar works that by their shortcomings demonstrate the moral and intellectual mediocrity of their authors, and prove the latter to have mistaken their vocation.

Consequently, then, beauty in art is a purely human creation. Imitation may be its means, as in sculpture and painting; or, on the other hand, it may have nothing to do with it, as in poetry and music. This beauty is of so peculiar a nature that it may exist even in ugliness itself; inasmuch as the reproduction of an ugly model may be a beautiful work of art, by the ensemble of qualities which the composition of it may prove are possessed by its author.

The theory of imitation is but the incomplete and superficial statement of the ideas which we are here advocating. What is it that we admire in imitation? The resemblance? We have that much better in the object itself. But how is it that the similitude of an ugly object can be beautiful? It is obvious that between the object and its counterfeit some new element intervenes. This element is the personality, or, at least, the skill of the artist. This latter, indeed, is what they admire who will have it that beauty consists in imitation. What these applaud, in fact, is the talent of the artist. If we look below the surface and analyze their admiration we shall find that it is so; whether they mean it or not, what they praise in a work is the worker.

This was the opinion of Bürger, who says: "In works which interest us the authors in a way substitute themselves for nature. However common or vulgar the latter may be, they have some rare and peculiar way of looking at it. It is Chardin himself whom we admire in his representation of a glass of water. We admire the genius of Rembrandt in the profound and individual character which he imparted to every head that posed before him. Thus did they seem to him, and this explains everything simple or fantastic in his expression and execution."

After all this, we need not stop to refute the theory which would found artistic beauty upon the imitation of "beautiful nature."

The only beauty in a work of art is that placed there by the artist. It is both the result of his efforts and the foundation of his success. As often as he is struck by any vivid impression—whether moral, intellectual, or physical—and expresses that impression by some outward activity, by poetry, music, sculpture, painting or architecture—in such a way as to cause its communication with the soul of spectator or auditor; so often does he produce a work of art the beauty of which will be in exact proportion to the intelligence and depth of the sentiment displayed, and the power shown in giving it outward form.

The union of all these conditions constitutes artistic beauty in its most complete expression. We may define aesthetics as the science of beauty in art. It is the science whose object is the study and elucidation of the manifestations of artistic genius.

There are two distinct kinds of art: decorative and expressive. The main object of decorative art is the gratification of the eye and ear. Its chief means to perfection of form are harmony and grace of contour, diction or sound. Such art rests upon the desire for beauty, and has nothing in view beyond the peculiar delight caused by the sight of beautiful objects. It has produced admirable works in the past, and may produce them again on condition that its inspiration be sought in actual and existing life, and not in the imitation of works sanctified by time.

Modern art has no tendency in this latter decorative direction. Decorative beauty no longer suffices for us in art. Something more has been required. The chief characteristic of modern art is power of expression. Through form this, the second kind of art, traces the moral life, and endeavors to occupy man, body and soul, but with no thought of sacrificing the one to the other.

The moral life is but the general result of the conditions of the physical. The one is bound to the other by necessary connections which cannot be broken without destroying both. The first care of the artist should be to seek out and grasp the methods of manifestation so as to comprehend and master their unity.

Art, thus understood, demands intellectual faculties higher and more robust than if founded solely upon an ideal of beauty. Art founded upon the latter notion would be sufficiently served by one possessing an acute sense of the beautiful—the degree of his sensibility being indicated by the plastic perfection of his work. But expressive art demands a capability of being moved by many sentiments, demands the power to penetrate beneath outward appearances and to seize a hidden thought, the power to grasp either the permanent characteristic or the particular and momentary emotion; in a word, it demands that complete eloquence of representation which art might have dispensed with while it confined itself to the investigation or delineation of a single expression, but which became indispensable the moment the interpretation of the entire man became its object.

We may say, too, that modern art is doubly expressive; because, while the artist is indicating by form and sound the sentiments and ideas of the personages whom he introduces, he is also by the power and manner of such manifestation giving an unerring measure of his own sensibility, imagination, and intelligence.

Expressive art is in no way hostile to beauty; it makes use of it as one element in the subjects which require it, but its domain is not enclosed within the bounds of such a conception. It is not indifferent to the pleasures of sight and hearing, but it sees something beyond them. Its worth must not be measured only by perfection of form, but also and chiefly, by the double power of expression which we have pointed out, and, we must add, by the value of the sentiments and ideas expressed. This latter point is too often and wrongly ignored by artists.

Between two works which give evidence of equal facility to grasp the accents and characteristics of nature, and equal power to bring out both the inner meaning of things and the personality of the artist—we, for our part, would prefer that one of which the *Conception* showed the more vigorous intelligence and elevated feeling. The art critics seem to have made it one of their principles to take no account of choice of subject, but only to look at the technical result. Such a principle is plausible rather than true. The individuality of the author can never be excluded from a work, and choice of subject is frequently one of the points by which this individuality is most clearly indicated.

It is true, of course, that elevation of sentiment can never take the place of art talent. On this point we cannot too strongly condemn the practice of academic juries who, on the one hand, reward mere mechanical labor simply because it has been exercised upon what are called classic subjects; and, on the other, persecute more independent artists to punish their obstinacy in deserting the beaten track. Nothing, then, can be further from our thoughts than to require critics to substitute, in every case, consideration of the subject for that of the work itself; or to condemn *a priori* all artists who remain faithful to the traditions, ideas, and sentiments of the past. In these, indeed, some find their only inspiration. We only wish to affirm our conviction that choice of subject is not so indifferent a matter as some say it is, and that it must be taken into account as of considerable weight in determining an opinion of a work of art.

This is one consequence of the distinction between decorative and expressive art. The former, solely devoted to the gratification of eye and ear, affords no measure of its success beyond the pleasure which it gives. The latter, whose chief object is to express the feelings and ideas, and, through them, to manifest the power of conception and expansion possessed by the artist, must obviously be estimated, partly at least, by the moral or other value of the ideas and sentiments in question. And, as the value of a work depends directly upon the capability of its author, and as many artists have been about equal in their technical ability, we must be ready to acknowledge that moral and intellectual superiority is a real superiority, and is naturally marked by the possession of an instinctive and spontaneous power of sympathy.

Style is the man. Get some one who *can* read, to read a page of Demosthenes *and* of Cicero, of Bossuet and of Massillon, of Corneille and of Racine, of Lamartine and of Victor Hugo. You will notice that no two of them sound the same. Apart from the subjects or ideas, which may be identical, each one has an air, an accent, which can never be confounded or replaced. In some of them we find elegance, finesse, grace, the most seductive and soothing harmony; in others, a force and *élan* like the sound of a trumpet.

Style only exists by virtue of *the law of separation.* "A being only exists in consequence of his separation from other beings. . . . This law of successive detachment—which alone renders progress possible—may be proved to influence the course of religion, of politics, of literature and of art." It is by style, by the manner of comprehension, of feeling and interpretation, that epochs, races, schools and individuals are separated and distinguished one from the other. In all the arts, analogous differences are to be found; plainly marked, in proportion as a more or less extensive field is offered for the development of artistic personality. Michelangelo and Raphael, Leonardo and Veronese, Titian and Correggio, Rubens and Rembrandt, resembled each other no more and no less than Beethoven resembled Rossini; Weber, Mozart; or Wagner resembles Verdi. Each has his own style, his peculiar mode of thinking and feeling, and of expressing those feelings and thoughts.

Why have mediocre artists no style? For the same reasons that they are mediocrities. The particular characteristic of mediocrity is commonness or vulgarity of thought and feeling. At each moment in the evolution of a social system, there is a general level which marks, for that moment, the average value of the human psyche and intellect. Such works as rise above this general level imply an amount of talent or genius in proportion to the amount of superior elevation and spontaneity which they display. Mediocrity comes up to the general level, but does not pass it; thus the mediocre artist thinks and feels like the ordinary run of mankind, and has nothing to "separate" him from the crowd. He may have a manner, an ensemble of habits of working, peculiar to himself; but he can have no style in the accurate sense of the word. Facility is not style; for the latter is a product, a reverberation from the soul itself, and can no more be artificially acquired than can the sonorousness of bronze or silver be acquired by lead. . . .

Style, which is a simple reflection of the artist's personality, is naturally found in the work of every artist who possesses any personality. The indescribable quality, the *je ne sais quoi,* is precisely the assemblage of qualities, the condition of being and temperament which caused Rubens to see things differently from Rembrandt. The two extracted, from one and the same object or subject, emotions widely different though congenial to their respective natures; just as a tightened string in a concert room will vibrate in response to the note which it would itself produce if struck. The one thing needful is the power to vibrate, which is too often wanting.

The question of style is important. We might even say that it includes the whole of aesthetics, which is in fact the question of personality in art. . . .

Truth and *personality:* these are the alpha and omega of art formulas; *truth* as to facts, and the *personality* of the artist. But, if we look more closely, we shall see that these two terms are in reality but one. Truth as to fact, so far as art is concerned, is above all the truth of our own sensations, of our own sentiments. It is truth as we see it, as it appears modified by our own temperaments, preferences, and physical organs. It is, in fact, our personality itself. Reality, as given by the photographer, reality taken from a point of view without connection with us or our impressions, is the negation of art. When this kind of truth predominates in a work of art, we cry, "There is realism for you!" Now, realism partakes of the nature of art, only because the most downright of realists must, whether he will or not, put something of his own individuality into his work. When, on the other hand, the dominant quality is what we call human or personal truth, then we at once exclaim, "Here is an artist!"

And the latter is the right meaning of the word. Art consists essentially in the predominance of subjectivity over objectivity; it is the chief distinction between it and science. The man intended for science is one whose imagination has no modifying influence over the results of his direct observation. The artist, on the other hand, is one whose imagination, impressionability—in a word, personality—is so lively and excitable that it spontaneously transforms everything, dyeing them in its own colors, and unconsciously exaggerating them in accordance with its own preferences.

We think ourselves justified, then, in calling art the direct and spontaneous manifestation of human personality. But we must not omit also the fact that personality—individual and particular as it is from some points of view—is nevertheless exposed to many successive and temporary modifications caused by the various kinds of civilization through which it has had to pass.

Note on Sources.   The above material is from Véron's book *Aesthetics,* published in 1878, and translated in 1879. A few brief passages have been deleted.

READING QUESTIONS

1. Bear the following in mind: "We may say then, by way of general definition, that art is the manifestation of emotion, obtaining external interpretation, now by expressive arrangements of line, form or color, now by a series of gestures, sounds, or words. . . . If our definition is exact, we must conclude from it that the merit of a work of art can be finally measured by the power with which it manifests or interprets the emotion which was its determining cause. . . ." Use any particular work of art to illustrate Véron's two claims.
2. Use the emotive theory to distinguish between art and a work of art; and between both of those and an artist.
3. Why, if you hold the emotive theory, you would be constrained to criticize the imitation theory.
4. Any two criticisms, your own or Véron's, of the imitation theory of art.

5. He says that the imitation theory is only an incomplete and superficial statement of the emotive or expression theory. How so?
6. Véron's distinction between decorative and expressive art.
7. Véron: "We may say that modern art is doubly expressive." How so? Can you use the distinction between *lyric* and *dramatic* to convey his point?
8. Why the emotive theory is much concerned with style and personality.
9. Distinguish between an emotive symbol and a cognitive symbol. Which is this : $2 + 2 = 4$. Why? Under any circumstances could it be an emotive symbol?
10. If you were in doubt whether a given symbol were emotive or cognitive, how would you settle the matter?
11. Distinguish between the emotive theory in aesthetics and the emotive theory in ethics. Is it a sounder theory in aesthetics than in ethics? Why, or why not.
12. Wherein you find the emotive theory of art (a) most, (b) least, convincing.

INDEPENDENT STUDY

1. Before doing anything else, read the brief three-column entry "Aesthetics" in the *Concise Encyclopedia of Western Philosophy and Philosophers*, edited by J. O. Urmson. What did you learn from it? What further points, compatible with a brief entry, would you have added? What questions does the article enable you to raise for discussion? Write your own article on aesthetics, for inclusion in such a volume, keeping to the same wordage.
2. Read the article "Aesthetics, History of," by M. C. Beardsley, in the *Encyclopedia of Philosophy*. What are the major historical or chronological divisions? Who were the major writers in each period? What major questions and claims mark each period? Select any one major period and write an essay on aesthetics as it was in that period.
3. Read Plato's dialogue *Ion*. Write an expository account of the questions and answers set forth.
4. Read T. L. Peacock's "The Four Ages of Poetry" and P. B. Shelley's reply "A Defence of Poetry," as you find them in *Critical Theory Since Plato*, edited by H. Adams; or in any comparable volume of readings in aesthetics. Write on the Peacock–Shelley "debate."

SECTION 2. LEO TOLSTOY: ART AS COMMUNICATION OF EMOTION

From Véron to Tolstoy. Véron published his reflections on art and works of art in 1878. The book was read, almost at once, by the Russian novelist Leo Tolstoy. By 1878 Tolstoy was himself a well-known European novelist, the author of *War and Peace* and *Anna Karenina.* There was no question but that these were works of art and their author an artist. It is not irrelevant therefore that Véron's thesis made a considerable impression upon Tolstoy. That a man is an artist does not *guarantee* his answer to the question, "What is art?" But it at least makes it difficult to say that, in addressing himself to this question, he "does not know what he is talking about." Tolstoy had read and thought about this question: What, as artist, was he seeking to do when he produced his great novels? In 1896 he published his conclusions in a small but important book, *What Is Art?*

Biographical Note. Leo Tolstoy was born in 1828 and died in 1910, aged eighty-two. He was born into one of the great families of the Russian aristocracy. His three books, *Childhood, Boyhood,* and *Youth,* give a vivid account of the life of a privileged young aristocrat. After completing his university education, he spent time in military service, following it with a period of European travel. He was married in 1863, and for fifteen years led a happy, successful, productive life, earning wealth and world-wide fame as a novelist. To this period belong his *War and Peace* and his *Anna Karenina.* Beginning in 1878, and lasting until his death in 1910, he became increasingly alienated from modern civilization in most of its "important" phases. Stages in this rejection of modern civilization are set forth in a series of small books which combine vivid autobiography with social and cultural criticism—e.g., *My Confession, What I Believe, What Then Shall We Do? The Kingdom of God Is Within You,* and *What Is Art?* These essays in criticism and repudiation contain an impressive attempt to formulate a "philosophy of life."

The Argument of the Passages. In his book *What Is Art?* Tolstoy admits that Véron's emotive theory of art is correct as far as it goes; but he insists that it does not go far enough. What it says is necessary but not sufficient. If you stop short with Véron's claim that art is the *expression* of emotion, you have told only half the story. You must add that it is the *communication* of emotion; the intentional successful communication to reader or listener or spectator of emotion felt by the artist. He has some refinements on this, but communication of emotion is the essential point. Tolstoy, like Véron, defends this thesis against the older idea of art as imitation. He also defends it, at great length, against the older thesis that art is the creating of beauty. Indeed the book gives the impression that Tolstoy's principal *bête noire* is the notion that there is any necessary connection between art and beauty.

The claim that art is the communication of emotion enables Tolstoy to distinguish between art and nonart; e.g., between a picture of a sunset and a sunset. A picture of a sunset, provided it communicates the emotion that the artist felt about the sunset, is a work of art. But the sunset itself, unless we think of it as the work of a Divine Artist, is not and cannot be a work of art. Once we have a principle that enables us to distinguish between art and nonart, we can raise the further question of the distinction, within art, between good art and bad art; that is, once we have got a criterion of recognition we can ask about a criterion of evaluation. The latter presupposes the former. This question Tolstoy handles by referring to the quality, the character, the nature, of the emotion communicated. If it is one kind of emotion, you have good art; if another kind, bad art. Friends of the emotive theory of art have taken less kindly to Tolstoy's way of distinguishing, within art, between good and bad. Indeed, they have been amused or scandalized by the conclusions he arrived at when he applied this secondary principle to specific works of art; e.g., when he found that his own great novels were art but perhaps neither good nor great.

In order to define art correctly it is necessary first of all to cease to consider it as a means to pleasure, and to consider it as one of the conditions of human life. Viewing it in this way we see that art is a means of intercourse between man and man.

Every work of art causes the receiver to enter into a certain kind of relationship both with him who produced or is producing the art, and with all those who receive the same artistic impression.

Speech transmitting the thoughts and experiences of men serves as a means of union among them. Art serves a similar purpose. The peculiarity of the latter consists in this, that whereas by words a man transmits his thoughts by art he transmits his feelings.

The activity of art is based on the fact that a man receiving through his sense of hearing or sight another man's expression of feeling, is capable of experiencing the emotion which moved the man who expressed it. To take the simplest example: one man laughs, and another who hears becomes merry, or a man weeps, and another who hears feels sorrow. A man is excited or irritated, and another man seeing him is brought to a similar state of mind. By his movements or by the sounds of his voice a man expresses courage and determination or sadness and calmness, and this state of mind passes on to others. A man suffers, manifesting his sufferings by groans and spasms, and this suffering transmits itself to other people; a man expresses his feelings of admiration, devotion, fear, respect, or love, to certain objects, persons, or phenomena, and others are infected by the same feelings of admiration, devotion, fear, respect, or love, to the same objects, persons, or phenomena.

It is on this capacity of man to receive another man's expression of feeling and to experience those feelings himself, that the activity of art is based.

If a man infects another directly, immediately, by his appearance or by the sounds he gives vent to at the time he experiences the feeling; if he causes another man to yawn when he himself cannot help yawning, or to laugh or cry when he himself is obliged to laugh or cry, or to suffer when he himself is suffering—that does not amount to art.

Art begins when one person with the object of joining another or others to himself in one and the same feeling, expresses that feeling by certain external indications. To take an example: a boy, having experienced fear on encountering a wolf, relates that encounter, and in order to evoke in others the feeling he has experienced, describes himself, his condition before the encounter, the surroundings, the wood, his own lightheartedness, and then the wolf's appearance, its movements, the distance between himself and the wolf, and so forth. All this, if only the boy when telling the story again experiences the feelings he had lived through, and infects the hearers and compels them to feel what he had experienced—is art. Even if the boy had not seen a wolf but had frequently been afraid of one, and if wishing to evoke in others the fear he had felt, he invented an encounter with a wolf and recounted it so as to make his hearers share the feelings he experienced when he feared the wolf, that also would be art. And in the same way it is art if a man, having experienced either the fear of suffering or the attraction of enjoyment (whether in reality or in imagination), expresses these feelings on canvas or in marble so that others are infected by them. And it is also art if a man feels, or imagines to himself, feelings of delight, gladness, sorrow, despair, courage, or despondency, and the transition from one to another of these feelings, and expresses them by sounds so that the hearers are infected by them and experience them as they were experienced by him.

The feelings with which the artist infects others may be very strong or very weak, very important or very insignificant, very bad or very good: feelings of love of one's country, self-devotion and submission to fate or to God expressed in a drama, raptures of lovers described in a novel, feelings of voluptuousness expressed in a picture, courage expressed in a triumphal march, merriment evoked by a dance, humor evoked by a funny story, the feeling of quietness transmitted by an evening landscape or by a lullaby, or the feeling of admiration evoked by a beautiful arabesque—it is all art.

If only the spectators or auditors are infected by the feelings which the author has felt, it is art.

To evoke in oneself a feeling one has once experienced and having evoked it in oneself then by means of movements, lines, colors, sounds, or forms expressed in words, so to transmit that feeling that others experience the same feeling—this is the activity of art.

Art is a human activity consisting in this, that one man consciously by means of certain external signs, hands on to others feelings he has lived through, and that others are infected by these feelings and also experience them.

Art is not the manifestation of some mysterious Idea of beauty or God; it is not a game in which man lets off his excess of stored-up energy; it is not the expression of man's emotions by external signs; it is not the production of pleasing objects; and, above all, it is not pleasure; but it is a means of union among men joining them together in the same feelings, and indispensable for the life and progress towards well-being of individuals and humanity.

As every man, thanks to man's capacity to express thoughts by words, may know all that has been done for him in the realms of thought by all humanity before his day, and can in the present, thanks to this capacity to understand the thoughts of others, become a sharer in their activity and also himself hand on to his contemporaries and descendants the thoughts he has assimilated from others as well as those that have arisen in himself; so, thanks to man's capacity to be infected with the feelings of others by means of art, all that is being lived through by his contemporaries is accessible to him, as well as the feelings experienced by men thousands of years ago, and he has also the possibility of transmitting his own feelings to others.

If people lacked the capacity to receive the thoughts conceived by men who preceded them and to pass on to others their own thoughts, men would be like wild beasts or like Kasper Hauser.[1]

And if men lacked this other capacity to be infected by art, people might be almost more savage still, and above all more separated from, and more hostile to, one another.

And therefore the activity of art is most important, as important as the activity of speech itself and as generally diffused.

As speech does not act on us only in sermons, orations, or books, but in all those remarks by which we interchange thoughts and experiences with one another, so also art in the wide sense of the word permeates our whole life, but it is only to some of its manifestations that we apply the term in the limited sense of the word.

We are accustomed to understand art to be only what we hear and see in theaters, concerts, and exhibitions; together with buildings, statues, poems, and novels. But all this is only the smallest part of the art by which we communicate with one another in life. All human life is filled with works of art of every kind—from cradle-song, jest, mimicry, the ornamentation of houses, dress, and utensils, to church services, buildings, monuments, and triumphal processions. It is all artistic activity. So that by art, in the limited sense of the word, we do not mean all human activity transmitting feelings but only that part we for some reason select from it and to which we attach special importance.

---

[1] "The foundling of Nuremberg," found in the marketplace of that town on 23rd May 1828, apparently some sixteen years old. He spoke little and was almost totally ignorant even of common objects. He subsequently explained that he had been brought up in confinement underground and visited by only one man, whom he saw but seldom.

This special importance has always been given by men to that part of this activity which transmits feelings flowing from their religious perception, and this small part they have specifically called art, attaching to it the full meaning of the word.

That was how men of old—Socrates, Plato, and Aristotle—looked on art. Thus did the Hebrew prophets and the ancient Christians regard art. Thus it was, and still is, understood by the Mohammedans, and thus it still is understood by religious folk among our own peasantry.

Some teachers of mankind—e.g., Plato in his *Republic*, the primitive Christians, the strict Mohammedans, and the Buddhists—have gone so far as to repudiate all art.

People viewing art in this way (in contradiction to the prevalent view of to-day which regards any art as good if only it affords pleasure) held and hold that art (as contrasted with speech, which need not be listened to) is so highly dangerous in its power to infect people against their wills, that mankind will lose far less by banishing all art than by tolerating each and every art.

Evidently such people were wrong in repudiating all art, for they denied what cannot be denied—one of the indispensable means of communication without which mankind could not exist. But not less wrong are the people of civilized European society of our class and day in favoring any art if it but gives people pleasure.

Formerly people feared lest among works of art there might chance to be some causing corruption, and they prohibited art altogether. Now they only fear lest they should be deprived of any enjoyment art can afford, and they patronize any art. And I think the last error is much grosser than the first and its consequences far more harmful.

.   .   .

Art in our society has become so perverted that not only has bad art come to be considered good, but even the very perception of what art really is has been lost. In order to be able to speak about the art of our society it is therefore, first of all necessary to distinguish art from counterfeit art.

There is one indubitable sign distinguishing real art from its counterfeit—namely, the infectiousness of art. If a man without exercising effort and without altering his standpoint, on reading, hearing, or seeing another man's work experiences a mental condition which unites him with that man and with others who are also affected by that work, then the object evoking that condition is a work of art. And however poetic, realistic, striking, or interesting, a work may be, it is not a work of art if it does not evoke that feeling (quite distinct from all other feelings) of joy and of spiritual union with another (the author) and with others (those who are also infected by it).

It is true that this indication is an *internal* one and that there are people who, having forgotten what the action of real art is, expect something else from art (in our society the great majority are in this state), and that therefore such people may mistake for this aesthetic feeling the feeling of diversion and a certain excitement which they receive from counterfeits of art. But though it is impossible to undeceive these people, just as it may be impossible to convince a man suffering from colour-blindness that green is not red, yet for all that, this indication remains perfectly definite to those whose feeling for art is neither perverted nor atrophied, and it clearly distinguishes the feeling produced by art from all other feelings.

The chief peculiarity of this feeling is that the recipient of a truly artistic impression is so united to the artist that he feels as if the work were his own and not some one else's—as if what it expresses were just what he had long been wishing to express. A real work of art destroys in the consciousness of the recipient the separation between himself and the artist, and not that alone, but also between himself and all whose minds receive this work of art. In this freeing of our personality from its separation and isolation, in this uniting of it with others, lies the chief characteristic and the great attractive force of art.

If a man is infected by the author's condition of psyche, if he feels this emotion and this union with others, then the object which has effected this is art; but if there be no such infection, if there be not this union with the author and with others who are moved by the same work—then it is not art. And not only is infection a sure sign of art, but the degree of infectiousness is also the sole measure of excellence in art.

The stronger the infection the better is the art, as art, speaking of it now apart from its subject-matter—that is, not considering the value of the feelings it transmits.

And the degree of the infectiousness of art depends on three conditions: (1) On the degree of individuality of the feeling transmitted; (2) on the degree of clearness with which the feeling is transmitted; (3) on the sincerity of the artist, that is, on the degree of force with which the artist himself feels the emotion he transmits.

The more individual the feeling transmitted the more strongly does it act on the recipient; the more individual the state of psyche into which he is transferred the more pleasure does the recipient obtain and therefore the more readily and strongly does he join in it.

Clearness of expression assists infection because the recipient who mingles in consciousness with the author is the better satisfied the more clearly that feeling is transmitted which, as it seems to him, he has long known and felt and for which he has only now found expression.

But most of all is the degree of infectiousness of art increased by the degree of sincerity in the artist. As soon as the spectator, hearer, or reader, feels that the artist is infected by his own production and writes, sings, or plays, for himself, and not merely to act on others, this mental condition of the artist infects the recipient; and, on the contrary, as soon as the spectator, reader, or hearer, feels that the author is not writing, singing, or playing, for his own satisfaction—does not himself feel what he wishes to express, but is doing it for him, the recipient—resistance immediately springs up, and the most individual and the newest feelings and the cleverest technique not only fail to produce any infection but actually repel.

I have mentioned three conditions of contagion in art, but they may all be summed up into one, the last, sincerity; that is, that the artist should be impelled by an inner need to express his feeling. That condition includes the first; for if the artist is sincere he will express the feeling as he experienced it. And as each man is different, his feeling will be individual; and the more individual it is—the more the artist has drawn it from the depths of his nature—the more sympathetic and sincere will it be. And this same sincerity will impel the artist to find clear expression for the feeling which he wishes to transmit.

Therefore this third condition—sincerity—is the most important of the three. It is always complied with in peasant art, and this explains why such art always acts so powerfully; but it is a condition almost entirely absent from our upper-class art, which is produced by artists actuated by personal aims of covetousness or vanity.

Such are the three conditions which divide art from its counterfeits, and which also decide the quality of every work of art considered apart from its subject-matter.

The absence of any one of these conditions excludes a work from the category of art and relegates it to that of art's counterfeits. If the work does not transmit the artist's peculiarity of feeling and is therefore not individual, if it is unintelligibly expressed, or if it has not proceeded from the author's inner need for expression—it is not a work of art. If all these conditions are present even in the smallest degree, then the work even if a weak one is yet a work of art.

The presence in various degrees of these three conditions: individuality, clearness, and sincerity, decides the merit of a work of art as art, apart from subject-matter. All works of art take order of merit according to the degree in which they fulfil the first, the second, and the third, of these conditions. In one the individuality of the feeling transmitted may predominate; in another, clearness of expression; in a third, sincerity; while a fourth may have sincerity and individuality but be deficient in clearness; a fifth, individuality and clearness, but less sincerity; and so forth, in all possible degrees and combinations.

Thus is art divided from what is not art, and thus is the quality of art, as art, decided, independently of its subject-matter, that is to say, apart from whether the feelings it transmits are good or bad.

But how are we to define good and bad art with reference to its content or subject-matter?

·   ·   ·

A few days ago I was returning home from a walk feeling depressed. On nearing the house I heard the loud singing of a large choir of peasant women. They were welcoming my daughter, celebrating her return home after her marriage. In this singing, with its cries and clanging of scythes, such a definite feeling of joy, cheerfulness, and energy, was expressed, that without noticing how it infected me I continued my way towards the house in a better mood and reached home smiling and in good spirits. That same evening a visitor, an admirable musician, famed for his execution of classical music and particularly of Beethoven, played us Beethoven's sonata, Opus 101. For the benefit of those who might attribute my judgment of that sonata of Beethoven to non-comprehension of it, I should mention that for a long time I used to attune myself to delight in those shapeless improvizations which form the subject-matter of the works of Beethoven's later period. But I had only to consider the question of art seriously, and to compare the impression I received from Beethoven's later works, with those pleasant, clear, and strong, musical impressions which are transmitted, for instance, by the melodies of Bach (his arias), Haydn, Mozart, Chopin (when his melodies are not overloaded with complications and ornamentation), of Beethoven himself in his earlier period, and above all, with the impressions produced by folk-songs,—Italian, Norwegian, or Russian,—by the Hungarian *csárdás*, and other such simple, clear, and powerful music, for the obscure, almost unhealthy, excitement from Beethoven's later pieces, which I had artifically evoked in myself, to be immediately destroyed.

On the completion of the performance (though it was noticeable that every one had become dull) those present warmly praised Beethoven's profound production in the accepted manner, and did not forget to add that formerly they had not been able to understand that last period of his, but that they now saw he was really then at his very best. And when I ventured to compare the impression made on me by the singing of the peasant women—an impression which had been shared by all who heard it—with the effect of this sonata, the admirers of Beethoven only smiled contemptuously, not considering it necessary to reply to such strange remarks.

But for all that, the song of the peasant women was real art transmitting a definite and strong feeling, while the 101st sonata of Beethoven was only an unsuccessful attempt of art containing no definite feeling and therefore not infectious.

For my work on art I have this winter read diligently, though with great effort, the celebrated novels and stories praised by all Europe, written by Zolá, Bourget, Huysmans, and Kipling. At the same time I chanced on a story in a child's magazine, by a quite unknown writer, which told of the Easter preparations in a poor widow's family. The story tells how the mother managed with difficulty to obtain some wheat-flour, which she poured on the table ready to knead. She then went out to procure some yeast, telling the children not to leave the hut and to take care of the flour. When the mother had gone, some other children ran shouting near the window calling those in the hut to come to play. The children forgot their mother's warning, ran into the street, and were soon engrossed in the game. The mother on her return with the yeast finds a hen on the table throwing the last of the flour to her chickens, who were busily picking it out of the dust of the earthen floor. The mother, in despair, scolds the children, who cry bitterly. And the mother begins to feel pity for them—but the white flour has all gone. So to mend matters she decides to make the Easter cake with sifted rye-flour, brushing it over with white of egg and surrounding it with eggs. "Rye-bread we bake is as good as a cake," says the mother, using a rhyming proverb to console the children for not having an Easter cake of white flour, and the children, quickly passing from despair to rapture, repeat the proverb and await the Easter cake more merrily even than before.

Well! the reading of the novels and stories by Zolá, Bourget, Huysmans, Kipling, and others, handling the most harrowing subjects, did not touch me for one moment, and I was provoked with the authors all the while as one is provoked with a man who considers you so naïve that he does not even conceal the trick by which he intends to take you in. From the first lines one sees the intention with which the book is written, the details all become superfluous, and one feels dull. Above all, one knows that the author had no other feeling all the time than a desire to write a story or a novel, and so one receives no artistic impression. On the other hand I could not tear myself away from the unknown author's tale of the children and the chickens, because I was at once infected by the feeling the author had evidently experienced, re-evoked in himself, and transmitted.

.   .   .

Beethoven's *Ninth Symphony* is considered a great work of art. To verify its claim to be such I must first ask myself whether this work transmits the highest religious feeling. I reply in the negative, since music in itself cannot transmit those feelings; and therefore I ask myself next: Since this work does not belong to the highest kind of religious art, has it the other characteristic of the good art of our time—the quality of uniting all men in one common feeling—does it rank as Christian universal art? And again I have no option but to reply in the negative; for not only do I not see how the feelings transmitted by this work could unite people not specially trained to submit themselves to its complex hypnotism, but I am unable to imagine to myself a crowd of normal people who could understand anything of this long, confused, and artificial production, except short snatches which are lost in a sea of what is incomprehensible. And therefore, whether I like it or not, I am compelled to conclude that this work belongs to the rank of bad art. It is curious to note in this connection, that attached to the end of this very symphony is a poem of Schiller's which (though somewhat obscurely) expresses this very thought, namely, that feeling (Schiller speaks only of the feeling of gladness) unites people and evokes love in them. But though this poem is sung at the end of the symphony, the music does not accord with the thought expressed in the verses; for the music is exclusive and does not unite all men, but unites only a few, dividing them off from the rest of mankind.

Note on Sources. The above material is quoted, with a few minor deletions, from Chapters 5 and 15 and 16 of Aylmer Maude's translation (1898) of Tolstoy's *What Is Art?*

Reading References. Tolstoy's book is short enough and challenging enough to be read through. Discussions will be found in most manuals on Aesthetics. H. W. Garrod's book *Tolstoi's Theory of Art* is a standard work. Israel Knox's paper "Tolstoi's Esthetic Definition of Art," in the *Journal of Philosophy*, Volume 27 (1930) is worthwhile.

READING QUESTIONS

1. The use that Tolstoy makes of the distinction between transmitting thoughts and transmitting feelings.

2. It is on *this* capacity . . . that the activity of art is based. Namely.
3. How he distinguishes real art from counterfeit art.
4. "The degree of infectiousness of art depends on three conditions." Namely.
5. Why the third condition is the most important of the three.
6. Apart from reference to what he calls "the subject matter," how would he distinguish between good art and poor art?
7. What he means by subject matter. How he would use subject matter to distinguish between good art and bad art.
8. Tolstoy's addition to Véron's position. Does this addition represent a step forward or backward?
9. Why Tolstoy would be constrained to deal polemically with the notion that art is imitation, and the notion that art is the creation of beauty.
10. Wherein you find Tolstoy's position (a) most, (b) least satisfactory.

INDEPENDENT STUDY

1. Read "Shakespeare and the Drama," an essay by Tolstoy, in *Recollections and Essays,* a volume of essays by Tolstoy, translated by Aylmer Maude. The essay contains sharp criticism of Shakespeare, centering on "Lear." Write an essay relating it to Tolstoy's position in *What Is art?*
2. Read the article on Tolstoy by E. Kamenka in the *Encyclopedia of Philosophy.* Select from the bibliography one or a few item(s) that deal with Tolstoy's views on art. Write a paper summarizing opinions on Tolstoy's aesthetic; e.g., H. W. Garrod's *Tolstoy's Theory of Art.*
3. The Tolstoy section in this textbook is based on Chapters 5, 15, and 16 of Tolstoy's *What Is Art?* Read further in that book; e.g., the chapter containing Tolstoy's review of European art in the then modern world. Criticize or defend what you find.

SECTION 3. COLLINGWOOD: ART AS EXPRESSION OF EMOTION [2]

From Véron and Tolstoy to Collingwood. We began our examination of Emotivism with a statement by Eugene Véron: art is the

---

[2] For biographical note on Collingwood see p. 613.

creation of emotive symbols. Tolstoy revised Véron's position slightly by insisting that expression, although necessary, is not sufficient: there must be communication of emotion; the expression must be infectious; and the more infectious, the more art. With Professor Collingwood, the reader is invited to return to Véron, and pick up again the aesthetic principle that art is an activity in which an agent expresses, or works at expressing, the emotional charge which marked his experience. This retake of the original formulation was worked out in Professor Collingwood's interesting and important book *The Principles of Art*, published in 1937. This book contains one of the twentieth century's most astute and persuasive statements of the emotive theory in aesthetics.

The Argument of the Passages.   Much of our experience, perhaps all of it, is marked by a certain "feeling tone," what Professor Collingwood calls its "emotional charge." For example, one lives through a love affair, or an earthquake or a military battle. One is thereby open to the question, "How does it *feel* to be in love, to encounter an earthquake, to engage an enemy in battle? What emotional charge marked the experience?" One may try to answer this question by *describing* the feelings. That would not be art. But one might compose a poem, or a piece of music, or paint a picture, in which one endeavored not to describe the feelings but to express them. That would be tackling the problem by producing or trying to produce a work of art. The author's emphasis here is on *expressing;* an activity that he does not want confused with describing or communicating, or arousing, or betraying, the emotion. These other activities might occur, but their occurrence would not be necessary to making the expressing activity art. It is basic and essential. It is the art activity. Its product or creation is the art object, or work of art.

Our first question is this. Since the artist proper has something to do with emotion, and what he does with it is not to arouse it, what is it that he does? It will be remembered that the kind of answer we expect to this question is an answer derived from what we all know and all habitually say; nothing original or recondite, but something entirely commonplace.

Nothing could be more entirely commonplace than to say he expresses them. The idea is familiar to every artist, and to every one else who has any acquaintance with the arts. To state it is not to state a philosophical theory or definition of art; it is to state a fact or supposed fact about which, when we have sufficiently identified it, we shall have later to theorize philosophically. For the present it does not matter whether the fact that is alleged, when it is said that the artist expresses emotion, is really a fact or only supposed to be one. Whichever it is, we have to identify it, that is, to decide what it is that people are saying when they use the phrase. Later on, we shall have to see whether it will fit into a coherent theory.

They are referring to a situation, real or supposed, of a definite kind. When a man is said to express emotion, what is being said about him comes to this. At first, he is conscious of having an emotion, but not conscious of what this emotion is. All he is conscious of is a perturbation or excitement, which he feels going on within him, but of whose nature he is ignorant. While in this state, all he can say about his emotion is: "I feel. . . . I don't know what I feel." From this helpless and oppressed condition he extricates himself by doing something which we call expressing himself. This is an activity which has something to do with the thing we call language: he expresses himself by speaking. It has also something to do with consciousness: the emotion expressed is an emotion of whose nature the person who feels it is no longer unconscious. It has also something to do with the way in which he feels the emotion. As unexpressed, he feels it in what we have called a helpless and oppressed way; as expressed, he feels it in a way from which this sense of oppression has vanished. His mind is somehow lightened and eased.

This lightening of emotions which is somehow connected with the expression of them has a certain resemblance to the "catharsis" by which emotions are earthed through being discharged into a make-believe situation; but the two things are not the same. Suppose the emotion is one of anger. If it is effectively earthed, for example by fancying oneself kicking some one down stairs, it is thereafter no longer present in the mind as anger at all: we have worked it off and are rid of it. If it is expressed, for example by putting it into hot and bitter words, it does not disappear from the mind; we remain angry; but instead of the sense of oppression which accompanies an emotion of anger not yet recognized as such, we have that sense of alleviation which comes when we are conscious of our own emotion as anger, instead of being conscious of it only as an unidentified perturbation. This is what we refer to when we say that it "does us good" to express our emotions.

The expression of an emotion by speech may be addressed to some one; but if so it is not done with the intention of arousing a like emotion in him. If there is any effect which we wish to produce in the hearer, it is only the effect which we call making him understand how we feel. But, as we have already seen, this is just the effect which expressing our emotions has on ourselves. It makes us, as well as the people to whom we talk, understand how we feel. A person *arousing* emotion sets out to affect his audience in a way in which he himself is not necessarily affected. He and his audience stand in quite different relations to the act, very much as physician and patient stand in quite different relations towards a drug administered by the one and taken by the other. A person expressing emotion, on the contrary, is treating himself and his audience in the same kind of way: he is making his emotions clear to his audience, and that is what he is doing to himself.

It follows from this that the expression of emotion, simply as expression, is not addressed to any particular audience. It is addressed primarily to the speaker himself, and secondarily to any one who can understand. Here again, the speaker's attitude towards his audience is quite unlike that of a person desiring to arouse in his audience a certain emotion. If that is what he wishes to do, he must know the audience he is addressing. He must know what type of stimulus will produce the desired kind of reaction in people of that particular sort; and he must adapt his language to his audience in the sense of making sure that it contains stimuli appropriate to their peculiarities. If what he wishes to do is to express his emotions intelligibly, he has to express them in such a way as to be intelligible to himself; his audience is then in the position of persons who overhear him doing this. Thus the stimulus-and-reaction terminology has no applicability to the situation.

The means-and-end, or technique, terminology too is inapplicable. Until a man has expressed his emotion, he does not yet know what emotion it is. The act of expressing it is therefore an exploration of his own emotions. He is trying to find out what these emotions are. There is certainly here a directed process: an effort, that is, directed upon a certain end; but the end is not something foreseen and preconceived, to which appropriate means can be thought out in the light of our knowledge of its special character. Expression is an activity of which there can be no technique.

Expressing an emotion is not the same thing as describing it. To say "I am angry" is to describe one's emotion, not to express it. The words in which it is expressed need not contain any reference to anger as such at all. Indeed, so far as they simply and solely express it, they cannot contain any such reference. The curse of Ernulphus, as invoked by Dr. Slop on the unknown person who tied certain knots, is a classical and supreme expression of anger; but it does not contain a single word descriptive of the emotion it expresses.

This is why, as literary critics well know, the use of epithets in poetry, or even in prose where expressiveness is aimed at, is a danger. If you want to express the terror which something causes, you must not give it an epithet like "dreadful." For that describes the emotion instead of expressing it, and your language becomes frigid, that is inexpressive, at once. A genuine poet, in his moments of genuine poetry, never mentions by name the emotions he is expressing.

Some people have thought that a poet who wishes to express a great variety of subtly differentiated emotions might be hampered by the lack of a vocabulary rich in words referring to the distinctions between them; and that psychology, by working out such a vocabulary, might render a valuable service to poetry. This is the opposite of the truth. The poet needs no such words at all; the existence or nonexistence of a scientific terminology describing the emotions he wishes to express is to him a matter of perfect indifference. If such a terminology, where it exists, is allowed to affect his own use of language, it effects it for the worse.

The reason why description, so far from helping expression, actually damages it, is that description generalizes. To describe a thing is to call it a thing of such and such a kind: to bring it under a conception, to classify it. Expression, on the contrary, individualizes. The anger which I feel here and now, with a certain person, for a certain cause, is no doubt an instance of anger, and in describing it as anger one is telling truth about it; but it is much more than mere anger: it is a peculiar anger, not quite like any anger that I ever felt before, and probably not quite like any anger I shall ever feel again. To become fully conscious of it means becoming conscious of it not merely as an instance of anger, but as this quite peculiar anger. Expressing it, we saw, has something to do with becoming conscious of it; therefore, if being fully conscious of it means being conscious of all its peculiarities, fully expressing it means expressing all its peculiarities. The poet, therefore, in proportion as he understands his business, gets as far away as possible from merely labelling his emotions as instances of this or that general kind, and takes enormous pains to individualize them by expressing them in terms which reveal their difference from any other emotion of the same sort.

This is a point in which art proper, as the expression of emotion, differs sharply and obviously from any craft whose aim it is to arouse emotion. The end which a craft sets out to realize is always conceived in general terms, never individualized. However accurately defined it may be, it is always defined as the production of a thing having characteristics that could be shared by other things. A joiner, making a table out of these pieces of wood and no others, makes it to measurements and specifications which, even if actually shared by no other table, might in principle be shared by other tables. A physician treating a patient for a certain complaint is trying to produce in him a condition which might be, and probably has been, often produced in others, namely, the condition of recovering from that complaint. So an "artist" setting out to produce a certain emotion in his audience is setting out to produce not an individual emotion, but an emotion of a certain kind. It follows that the means appropriate to its production will be not individual means but means of a certain kind: that is to say, means which are always in principle replaceable by other similar means. As every good craftsman insists, there is always a "right way" of performing any operation. A "way" of acting is a general pattern to which various individual actions may conform. In order that the "work of art" should produce its intended psychological effect, therefore, what is necessary is that it should satisfy certain conditions, possess certain characteristics: in other words be, not this work and no other, but a work of this kind and of no other.

This explains the meaning of the generalization which Aristotle and others have ascribed to art. Aristotle's *Poetics* is concerned not with art proper but with representative art, and representative art of one definite kind. He is not analyzing the religious drama of a hundred years before, he is analyzing the amusement literature of the fourth century, and giving rules for its composition. The end being not individual but general (the production of an emotion of a certain kind) the means too are general (the portrayal, not of this individual act, but of an act of this sort; not, as he himself puts it, what Alcibiades did, but what anybody of a certain kind would do). Sir Joshua Reynolds' idea of generalization is in principle the same; he expounds it in connexion with what he calls "the grand style," which means a style intended to produce emotions of a certain type. He is quite right; if you want to produce a typical case of a certain emotion, the way to do it is to put before your audience a representation of the typical features belonging to the kind of thing that produces it: make your kings very royal, your soldiers very soldierly, your women very feminine, your cottages very cottagesque, your oak-trees very oakish, and so on.

Art proper, as expression of emotion, has nothing to do with all this. The artist proper is a person who, grappling with the problem of expressing a certain emotion, says, "I want to get this clear." It is no use to him to get something else clear, however like it this other thing may be. Nothing will serve as a substitute. He does not want a thing of a certain kind, he wants a certain thing. This is why the kind of person who takes his literature as psychology, saying "How admirably this writer depicts the feelings of women, or bus-drivers, or homosexuals . . . ," necessarily misunderstands every real work of art with which he comes into contact, and takes for good art, with infallible precision, what is not art at all.

Finally, the expression of emotion must not be confused with what may be called the betraying of it, that is, exhibiting symptoms of it. When it is said that the artist in the proper sense of that word is a person who expresses his emotions, this does not mean that if he is afraid he turns pale and stammers; if he is angry he turns red and bellows; and so forth. These things are no doubt called expressions; but just as we distinguish proper and improper senses of the word "art," so we must distinguish proper and improper senses of the word "expression," and in the context of a discussion about art this sense of expression is an improper sense. The characteristic mark of expression proper is lucidity or intelligibility; a person who expresses something thereby becomes conscious of what it is that he is expressing, and enables others to become conscious of it in himself and in them. Turning pale and stammering is a natural accompaniment of fear, but a person who in addition to being afraid also turns pale and stammers does not thereby become conscious of the precise quality of his emotion. About that he is as much in the dark as he would be if (were that possible) he could feel fear without also exhibiting these symptoms of it.

Confusion between these two senses of the word "expression" may easily lead to false critical estimates, and so to false aesthetic theory. It is sometimes thought a merit in an actress that when she is acting a pathetic scene she can work herself up to such an extent as to weep real tears. There may be some ground for that opinion if acting is not an art but a craft, and if the actress's object in that scene is to produce grief in her audience; and even then the conclusion would follow only if it were true that grief cannot be produced in the audience unless symptoms of grief are exhibited by the performer. And no doubt this is how most people think of the actor's work. But if his business is art, the object at which he is aiming is not to produce a preconceived emotional effect on his audience but by means of a system of expressions, or language, composed partly of gesture, to explore his own emotions: to discover emotions in himself of which he was unaware, and, by permitting the audience to witness the discovery, enable them to make a similar discovery about themselves. In that case it is not her ability to weep real tears that would mark her out a good actress; it is her ability to make it clear to herself and her audience what the tears are about.

This applies to every kind of art. The artist never rants. A person who writes or paints or the like in order to blow off steam, using the traditional materials of art as means for exhibiting the symptoms of emotion, may deserve praise as an exhibitionist, but loses for the moment all claim to the title of artist. The second category will contain, for example, those young men who, learning in the torment of their own bodies and minds what war is like, have stammered their indignation in verses, and published them in the hope of infecting others and causing them to abolish it. But these verses have nothing to do with poetry.

Thomas Hardy, at the end of a fine and tragic novel in which he has magnificently expressed his sorrow and indignation for the suffering inflicted by callous sentimentalism on trusting innocence, spoils everything by a last paragraph fastening his accusation upon "the president of the immortals." The note rings false, not because it is blasphemous (it offends against no piety worthy of the name) but because it is rant. The case against God, so far as it exists, is complete already. The concluding paragraph adds nothing to it. All it does is to spoil the effect of the indictment by betraying a symptom of the emotion which the whole book has already expressed; as if a prosecuting counsel, at the end of his speech, spat in the prisoner's face.

The same fault is especially common in Beethoven. He was confirmed in it, no doubt, by his deafness; but the cause of it was not his deafness but a temperamental inclination to rant. It shows itself in the way his music screams and mutters instead of speaking, as in the soprano part of the Mass in D, on the layout of the opening pages of the *Hammerklavier* Sonata. He must have known his failing and tried to overcome it, or he would never have spent so many of his ripest years among string quartets, where screaming and muttering are almost, one might say, physically impossible. Yet even there, the old Adam struts out in certain passages of the *Grosse Fuge*.

It does not, of course, follow that a dramatic writer may not rant in character. The tremendous rant at the end of *The Ascent of F6*, like the Shaksperian [3] ranting on which it is modelled, is done with tongue in cheek. It is not the author who is ranting, but the unbalanced character he depicts; the emotion the author is expressing is the emotion with which he contemplates that character; or rather, the emotion he has towards that secret and disowned part of himself for which the character stands.

Note on Sources. The materials used in this section are quoted from R. G. Collingwood's book *The Principles of Art,* Book I, chapter VI, "Art as Expression."

Reading References. By all means, extend your acquaintance with Collingwood's own statement in *The Principles of Art* by reading the whole of Book I, "Art and Not-Art." Books II and III are equally valuable, but more difficult to follow. Collingwood's *Principles* can be supplemented by relevant chapters in Professor C. J. Ducasse's *The Philosophy of Art* and Professor E. F. Carritt's *The Theory of Beauty.*

[3] Shakespeare's characters rant (1) when they are characters in which he takes no interest at all, but which he simply uses as pegs on which to hang what the public wants, like Henry V; (2) when they are meant to be despicable, like Pistol; or (3) when they have lost their heads, like Hamlet in the graveyard.

READING QUESTIONS

1. Contrast Tolstoy and Collingwood on the question, "What is art?"
2. Collingwood's distinction between *expressing* and *arousing*. Which is a craft?
3. Between *expressing* and *betraying*.
4. Between *expressing* and *describing*.
5. Indicate some of the advantages that attend the study of the emotive theory of art.
6. Indicate the sense in which emotivism in aesthetics may be compared *and* contrasted with empiricism or utilitarianism, in their respective philosophical disciplines.
7. Some persons object to the notion that a work of art is an emotive symbol, created to express emotion. Unless you *were* the artist, or yourself knew him rather well, how could you know (a) that he was expressing emotion, or (b) what emotion he was expressing? Would the same objection hold for a cognitive symbol, e.g., $2 + 2 = 4$, or "The earth is spherical"?
8. Having read Véron and Tolstoy and Collingwood: (a) What is your principal reservation with reference to the emotive theory in aesthetics? (b) If you reject it, do you have an alternative that you would propose in its place?
9. Wherein you find Collingwood (a) most (b) least convincing.

INDEPENDENT STUDY

1. Read Collingwood's *Principles of Art*, Part I. Work out papers on any or all of the following: (a) Introduction and Chapters 6 and 7, (b) Chapters 2 and 3, (c) Chapters 4 and 5.
2. Read Collingwood's *Principles of Art*, Part III: "The Theory of Art." What is the theory? Write an essay expounding Part III and relating it to Part I.

SECTION 4. JOHN HOSPERS: CRITIQUE OF EXPRESSIONISM

From Collingwood to Hospers.   Any friend of emotivism in aesthetics will find a paper, presented by Professor John Hospers to the Aristotelian Society in 1954, both challenging and valuable. The title of Professor Hospers's paper was "The Concept of Artistic Expression." His purpose was to show that the use of "expression" in the statement of the emotive theory gives rise to difficult questions. This was to be expected. The key notions in any fundamental philosophical theory may be relied on to give trouble. They turn out to be vague, obscure, ambiguous, and metaphorical. What made Professor Hospers's paper something of a "hatchet job" was his patience in tracking down bothersome questions that the notion of *expression* gives rise to.

To see how this comes about, let us retrace our steps to the point where we began, namely by identifying certain activities as art, and the embodiments of these activities as works of art and those who perform those activities as artists. These identifications are primary data. As initially arrived at, they are preanalytical. Once obtained, they may be subjected to conceptual analysis with a view to detecting what they have in common. Professor Hospers emphasizes this point when he says, e.g., "It is, I think, more certain that these men (Bach, Shakespeare, Cézanne, Poe, Eliot, etc.) were artists than that any single theory of art, such as the expression theory, is true"; and again: "If we accept as being artists those men who have created unquestionably great works of art. . . ." The point is worth emphasizing: if you cannot tell chalk from cheese there is no future in asking what marks them as essentially different. If you cannot tell art from nonart, or good art from bad art, you have no *data* about which to ask philosopical questions or propose philosophical theses. This was Hegel's point in speaking of philosophy as a "night owl" that takes flight *after* the heat and battle of the day is over, i.e., after the preanalytical data have been assembled. To put the matter simply: if you don't know *what* you are talking about (e.g., artist, art, work of art), don't propound theories about it.

But suppose you *can* identify examples of artist, art, work of art. Proponents of emotivism, e.g., Véron, Tolstoy, Collingwood, were willing to assume this initial responsibility. Having done so, they then proposed the emotive theory about these examples. An artist is one who expresses his emotions in the creation of a poem, a picture, a statue, a musical composition, and so on. Art is the activity of doing this. What is thereby created is a work of art. It is clear that the concepts of *express, expressing, expression* are here essential vehicles. Let me suggest an analogy. Suppose you identify certain actions as "moral" and propose the theory that an action is moral if and only if it is done because believed to be right; or, going a step further; that an act is right if and only if it produces more pleasure than pain. There are essential vehicles here; e.g., "done because believed," or "right," or "produces more pleasure than." If you raise difficult questions about these essential vehicles you will embarrass these theories. That is Professor Hospers's strategy. He pitches on the concept of *expression* and proceeds to raise "hard questions" about it. And there is no denying that some, perhaps all, of his questions *are* hard to deal with if you subscribe to emotivism as a theory about artists, art, and works of art. It should be clear that in this strategy Professor Hospers is raising what might be called "second-order" questions; that is, questions about the theory, not about preanalytical data that the theory purports to deal with; and that the questions bear down on the concept of *expression*.

Biographical Note. Professor John Hospers is a member of the department of philosophy in the University of Southern California. His writings include: *Meaning and Truth in the Arts* (1946), *An Introduction to Philosophical Analysis* (1953), and *Human Conduct: An Introduction to the Problems of Ethics* (1961). He has taught at the University of Minnesota, the University of California (Los Angeles), and elsewhere.

The Argument of the Passages. The paper, as reprinted, contained four sections. Sections I and III are given below. In Section I Professor Hospers concentrates on *express* as the name for the activity that the artist performs. In Section II he concentrates on *express* as the name for what the work of art does, and particularly on the notion that its power to evoke something in us is a criterion of expressiveness in it. In Section III he returns to the activity of the artist and concentrates on *express* as meaning *communicate;* e.g., to express a feeling is to communicate it. In Section IV he returns to the work of art, and concentrates on *express* as the name for what it does, regardless of its relation to the artist or to the beholder. At the end of this final section, after pummelling the concept of expression till one wonders how the poor word will ever get back on its feet, Professor Hospers remarks, "in the field of aesthetics, where there are probably more promises and fewer fulfillments than aywhere else in philosophy, I am impelled to be suspicious of the promissory note, especially when the date due is repeatedly postponed, and to be content only with the cold hard cash of fulfillment." One does not begrudge Professor Hospers the right to his flourish; but flourish it is, because "second-order" questions, or "third-order" questions, can be used to raise just as much hob in ethics or logic or metaphysics or any other field of philosophy; and because, if you want "cold hard cash" in *any* of these fields, when second-order pressure or third-order pressure is being applied, you are going to be disappointed. When that hour strikes, aesthetics is no more a Cinderella than her sister disciplines.

The expression theory of art, in one form or another, has dominated the esthetic scene for the past two centuries as much, perhaps, as the imitation theory had done previously. It is often assumed without question that the distinctive function of the artist is to express emotions; that if the artist does not express in his work, what he does is to that extent less entitled to be called art; and that all art must be expressive of something or other, so much so that a non-expressive work of art is a contradiction in terms. Nor has the predominance of expression been limited to art; it has been extended to all objects of beauty. It is said that all truly beautiful objects are expressive, and some have even asserted their identity: beauty *is* expression.

In all this the terms "express," "expressive," and "expression" are, of course, all-important. It is of the utmost consequence, then, that we know what these terms are being used to mean. What is artistic expression? What does an artist do when he expresses? What is it for a work of art to be expressive? In this paper I shall try to do no more than give a brief critical examination of the principal senses which can be given to the notion of expression as it occurs in the literature of esthetics.

What, then, is expression? One answer seems obvious, though we shall see that it is not the only possible one: expression is an activity of the artist in the process of artistic creation; expressing is something that the artist *does*. What precisely is it that the artist does when he expresses? On this point accounts differ from one another considerably, and I can do no more than mention a few main points to indicate briefly the area in which esthetic philosophers are working when they discuss expression.

Most accounts of the expressive process emphasize the confusion and chaos with which the process begins in the artist's mind; gradually replaced by clarity and order as it approaches completion. Collingwood [in *The Principles of Art*], for example, says:

> When a man is said to express emotion, what is being said about him comes to this. At first, he is conscious of having an emotion, but not conscious of what that emotion is. All he is conscious of is a perturbation or excitement, which he feels going on within him, but of whose nature he is ignorant. While in this state, all he can say about his emotion is: "I feel . . . I don't know what I feel." From this helpless and oppressed condition he extricates himself by doing something which we call expressing himself.

At this point, he writes, he paints, or he carves in stone, and from doing this his emotions become channeled in the exercise of a medium, and his oppressed state is relieved; his inner turbulence ceases, and what was inchoate becomes clear and articulate.

Although Collingwood does not make clear what sense of the phrase "what it is" he is employing when he says that the aritst does not know what his emotion is, let us assume that what he is describing is in general clear enough and turn to another aspect of the expressive process which is usually included, namely, its springs in the artist's unconscious life. William James says:

> A man's conscious wit and will are aiming at something only dimly and inaccurately imagined. Yet all the while the forces of organic ripening

within him are going on to their own prefigured result, and his conscious strainings are letting loose subconscious allies behind the scenes which in their way work toward rearrangement, and the rearrangement toward which all these deeper forces tend is pretty surely definite, and definitely different from what he consciously conceives and determines. It may consequently be actually interfered with (jammed as it were) by his voluntary efforts slanting toward the true direction. When the new center of energy has been subconsciously incubated so long as to be just ready to burst into flower, "hands off" is the only word for us; it must burst forth unaided.

In all this, the expression of feeling or emotion is to be distinguished sharply from the deliberate *arousing* of it; accounts are fairly unanimous on this point. A writer of fiction, for example, may deliberately attempt to arouse feelings in his readers, which he does not experience himself. In this case he is expressing nothing, but cold-bloodedly adopting what devices he can to arouse feelings in others, remaining himself unmoved. Because the artist, while expressing his feeling, is clarifying it to himself, he cannot before expressing it know or state what he is going to express; therefore he cannot *calculate* in advance what effects he wants to produce and then proceed to produce them. If he could, he would have no need to express, since the emotion would already be clear to him. "Until a man has expressed his emotion," says Collingwood, "he does not yet know what emotion it is. The act of expressing it is therefore an exploration of his own emotions. He is trying to find out what these emotions are." The novelist who tries deliberately and consciously to arouse a certain emotion in his audience cannot, on the expression theory, be an artist; expression is the activity of an artist, while arousal is the activity of a clever craftsman or a trained technician.

In the foregoing characterization of the expressive process, attention has been given primarily to what is going on in the artist; and this, indeed, is the center of emphasis in the Croce-Collingwood school of esthetics. Though they do talk about the artistic medium, and insist that what the artist expresses must be conceived in the medium the artist is going to use—be it words or paints or musical tones—they tend to view the artist's actual manipulation of a physical medium outside himself as an accident or an afterthought. That such a bias, though perhaps affecting most accounts of expression, is no essential part of the expression theory is brought out most clearly by John Dewey in his account of expression in *Art as Experience.* Dewey conceives expression, as (one is tempted to add) he conceives of everything else, as an interaction between the organism and its environment: more specifically, in the case of art, as the recalcitrance of the medium and the artist's attempt to bend the medium to his will. To talk about expression in terms of the artist alone is to omit half the story; no amount of talk about the artist's inner experiences is enough.

There is no expression without excitement, without turmoil. Yet an inner agitation that is discharged at once in a laugh or a cry, passes away with its utterance. To discharge is to get rid of, to dismiss; to express is to stay by, to carry forward in development, to work out to completion. A gush of tears may bring relief, a spasm of destruction may give outlet to inward rage. But where there is no administration of objective conditions, no shaping of materials in the interest of embodying the excitement, there is no expression. What is sometimes called an act of self-expression might better be termed one of self-exposure; it discloses character—or lack of character—to others. In itself, it is only a spewing forth.

We have already distinguished expressing from arousing; Dewey asks us now to make another distinction, from the opposite direction, between expressing and discharging, getting rid of, or as Dewey puts it, "spewing forth." Esthetic theory, says Dewey, has made the mistake of supposing that the mere giving way to an impulsion, native or habitual, constitutes expression. Such an act is expressive not in itself but only in reflective interpretation on the part of some observer—as the nurse may interpret a sneeze as the sign of an impending cold. As far as the act itself is concerned, it is, if purely impulsive, just a boiling over. While there is no expression, unless there is urge from within outwards, the welling up must be clarified and ordered by taking into itself the values of prior experiences before it can be an act of expression. And these values are not called into play save through objects of the environment that offer resistance to the direct discharge of emotion and impulse. Emotional discharge is a necessary but not a sufficient condition of expression.

There are many questions which one might ask of the above accounts as descriptions of what goes on when artists create. But as a psychological account I shall leave it largely unquestioned. It becomes of interest for the philosopher when it is presented, as it often is, as a theory of art. And as such there are a few questions which should be put to it:

1. Expression theories usually speak of *emotions* as what is being expressed, although sometimes the phrase "expression of *feelings*" is used; but the meaning of these two terms, and their relation to one another, is not usually made clear. But let that pass: cannot other things be expressed as well, such as ideas? One wants to know more about *what* it is that the artist *qua* artist is expressing, and, if some things are appropriate for artistic expression and not others, why.

2. But no matter what the artist is said to be expressing, why should one assume that the artist in his distinctively artistic activity is always expressing? Why not say that he is sometimes representing, for example, or just playing around with tones or colors? Many composers do not begin with emotions or feelings at all, but with fragments of melody which they then develop. For them feelings do not particularly enter the picture at all, except possibly feelings of frustration at delays and jubilation at having finished the job. Artists have been creating great works of art for many centuries, yet only in the last two centuries or less would it have been customary, or even seemed natural, to say that *the* distinctive activity of the artist was that of expression.

Indeed, if we accept as being artists those men who have created unquestionably great works of art—Bach, Shakespeare, Cézanne, and so on—it is by no means clear that the creative processes through which they passed can be adequately labeled under the heading of "expression." In the first place, in the case of most artists we have very little idea of what their creative processes were like, since we have no record of them. And in the second place, even when we have such records, whether by the artist himself or his biographers, they do not always point to the kind of thing set forth by the expression theory. For example, what was Shakespeare doing—was he, necessarily and always, expressing? There are doubtless creative experiences in the life of every artist which could be described by talking about an inner turbulence gradually becoming clarified and ordered, and emotions being released through the manipulation of an artistic medium; but I suspect that, as a general description of artistic activity, this is far too narrow, and is a bit too reminiscent of the mystical concept of genius fostered by the Romantic era. I doubt whether Shakespeare was always expressing feelings; sometimes he probably wrote, although he did not feel like it, to meet a deadline, or to have money coming in for the next month, or because the plot he had borrowed from somewhere else intrigued him and he wondered how he could incorporate it into a five-act drama. The motivation, the ends and aims, as well as the inner springs of artistic activity are, I am sure, a very mixed lot; and to assume that the artist *qua* artist is always expressing seems just as one-sided as the earlier assumption that he is always imitating nature or human action.

The written records left by artists, when we have them, sometimes seem flatly to contradict the expression theory—even though artists as a whole probably tend to glamorize themselves and like to leave the impression that they are solitary geniuses engaged in mysterious acts of self-expression. Thus, Poe gives us an account of cold-blooded calculation in the composition of his poem "The Raven," which is such a far cry from the description of the artistic process given us by the expression theory that it would be difficult to make it fit in at any point. And T. S. Eliot said in *The Sacred Wood* that "poetry is not a turning loose of emotion but an escape from emotion." One may, of course, say that if these men did not go through the process described by the theory, they were therefore not true artists; but this is surely to allow an *a priori* dogma to take precedence over cold facts. It is, I think, more certain that these men were artists than that any single theory of art, such as the expression theory, is true. And if the theory is presented, not as an *a priori* pronouncement but as an actual account of the creative process in artists, it will have to stand the empirical test, namely: in all cases of admitted works of art, was the process of its creation such as the expression theory describes? And I do not see any evidence that it holds true in all cases.

3. If it is true that not all great art was created in the way the theory describes, it is, I think, even more plainly true that not everything created in the way the theory describes is great art. Let us assume that Shakespeare, Virgil, Mozart, Rembrandt, and Hokusai all went through the throes of creation as described by the expression theory; the same can be said of any number of would-be poets, painters, and composers whom one has never heard of for the very good reason that they have never produced anything worth looking at twice. I do not mean, now, the deliberate hacks and quacks, the detective-story writers who spin out half a dozen books a year with an eye on next season's market—these could be accused of trying to arouse emotions in others instead of expressing emotions of their own; I mean the host of deeply earnest would-be artists with delusions of grandeur, so dedi-

cated to Art that they would starve if need be to give proper expression to their genius—but who have neither genius nor, sometimes, even talent. The same turmoil and excitement, the same unpredictability of outcome, the feelings of compulsion and dedication, the surcease from emotion from working in a medium, are experienced not alone by the great creators of art but by their hosts of adoring imitators and camp-followers as well as the supreme individualists who sigh and die alone, ignored and unrecognized but devoted still. This is indeed the most disconcerting fact about the expression theory as a criterion of art: that [according to Harold Osborne in *Aesthetics and Criticism*]

> . . . all the characteristic phenomena of inspiration are described in undistinguishable terms by good and bad artists alike. Nor has the most penetrating psychological investigation succeeded in detecting any general differences between the mental processes which accompany the creation of a masterpiece and the inspirations of a third-rate botcher.

4. In any case, can anything at all relating to the artistic process be validly used as a criterion for evaluating the artistic product? Even if all artists did in fact go through the process described by the expression theory, and even if nobody but artists did this, would it be true to say that the work of art was a good one *because* the artist, in creating it, went through this or that series of experiences in plying his medium? Once the issue is put thus baldly, I cannot believe that anyone could easily reply in the affirmative; it seems much too plain that the merits of a work of art must be judged by what we can find in the work of art, quite regardless of the conditions under which the work of art came into being. Its genesis is strictly irrelevant; what we must judge is the work before us, not the process of the artist who created it. And yet much critical writing seems to be beset by the delusion that the artist's creative processes are relevant to judging his product—that a bad work is excused or a great work enhanced by considerations of how hard he tried or whether the conditions of work were unfavorable or whether he was inspired or in a mystical trance, and so on. And, perhaps, such considerations do excuse the *artist*, but they do not change the value of the work of art. It is a moral condemnation of Fitzgerald that he was lazy and indolent, and could have composed many poems like the *Rubaiyat* but failed to do so; but this is no criticism of the *Rubaiyat* itself; and it may be praise of Mozart's genius that every note in a concerto of his popped into his head in one afternoon, but not praise of his work—the concerto would be just as great if it had taken him ten years to complete. Even Collingwood, when he is distinguishing false art from art proper, does so on the basis of the artistic process: the artist is one who, during creation, expresses emotions formerly unclear to himself, while the false artist is the one who tries to evoke in others emotions which he does not feel. And I cannot emphasize too strongly that, however much this may be a criterion for judging the artist as a man (and I am not saying that it is a good one), it is not a criterion for judging his work. To fudge the distinction between these two is to fall victim to the process-product ambiguity with a vengeance: the word "art" is normally used to name both a process and the product of that process, and because of this fact

formulas like "art is expression" can be made to sound true and reasonable; the misfortune here is that this ambiguity, so obvious once it is pointed out, may help to make people think that any considerations about the artistic process can be relevant to judging the merits of the artistic product.

Our conclusion is, then, that when we make a judgment of esthetic value upon a work of art, we are in no way judging the process, including any expressive process, which led to its completion, and therefore the act of expression does not enter into a critical judgment. If we do not know what the process was like, we need not on that account hold our judgment of the work in abeyance; and if we do happen to know what it was like, we should not let this sway our judgment of the work of art. But there *are* times when we *seem* to invoke the process as a criterion of judgment, and these we should now briefly examine. Here is an example from Dewey [in *Art as Experience*]:

> If one examines into the reason why certain works of art offend us, one is likely to find that the cause is that there is no personally felt emotion guiding the selecting and assembling of the materials presented. We derive the impression that the artist . . . is trying to regulate by conscious intent the nature of the emotion aroused.

One example of this occurs, I suppose, when we fell that a novel is "plot-ridden"—for example that the novelist has forced his characters into conformity with the demands of a plot which he had outlined in full before giving much thought to his characters. This feeling, I take it, is familiar enough. But is our criticism here really of the author's creative processes? Are we blaming the novel because he outlined the plot first and then manufactured the characters to fit the plot? I do not think so: we criticize the work because the actions that these characters are made to perform are not such as characters of this kind would do; in other words, they oversimplify and falsify human nature, and it is because of this that we are offended. If the characters strike us as real human beings, we do not care what process the artist went through in creating them: whether he thought of the plot first and the characters afterward, or whatever it may have been.

The same considerations apply in other cases where we seem to make use of the process in criticizing the product. For example, we say, "One must feel that the work of art came out of the artist's own experience, that he himself lived through the things he was describing," or we say, "I don't like this work because I don't feel that the artist was being *sincere* when he wrote it." Now, living through something and being sincere about something are things we say about people; are we not therefore using the process in evaluating the product? Again, I think not. Perhaps we do require that the characters in the drama behave as if the dramatist had personally experienced all their emotions and shared all their fates; but as long as we feel this, must we reverse our judgment if we should subsequently discover that the dramatist had felt none of these things at all, or only a small part of them? Shakespeare could hardly have gone through the experiences of Hamlet, Macbeth, Iago, Cleopatra, Lear, Goneril, Prospero and Coriolanus in one lifetime, but what difference does this make as long as he could present us with a series of vivid, powerful, convincing characterizations? Or suppose we praise a work, say *Uncle Tom's Cabin,* for its sincerity. Does it really change our critical judgment when we know that Mrs. Stowe was weeping tears during many of the hours in which she wrote it, and if we should discover that it was written by a wealthy Southern slaveowner on a wager to prove how well he could present the feelings of "the other side," would it alter our critical judgment of his work? It would alter our judgment about the author, surely; it would change our judgment about the author's sincerity, and it would probably make us attribute to the author much more ingenuity than we now attribute to Mrs. Stowe. But our judgment of the work would not be changed; or, at any rate, I submit, it *should* not—for the novel, after we have made this discovery, would be just the same as before; not a jot or a title of it would be changed by our discovery. And as long as it is the *work* which we are judging, surely our judgment should remain unchanged as long as the work is unchanged.

What difference does it make *what* emotions the artist felt, so long as the work of art is a good one? If the artist was clever enough to compose a work of art without expressing emotion in anything like the manner described by the expression theory, or even if he felt nothing at all, this is of no importance so long as we find the work an enduring source of esthetic satisfaction. It may be true as an empirical fact about artists, that *unless* they really feel something, unless they are or have been on fire with emotion, or unless they have deep perturbations which demand resolution, they are not able to create great works of art. This may sometimes be true, though I doubt whether it is true in all cases. But even if it were true in all cases, we need still have no interest in the artist's creative processes as such; knowing facts about the artist's processes would at best be a good indicator of his having created great works of art, which we might then go on to examine, and test the correlation between process and product. To know (supposing it to be true) that a work of art could be produced only when the artist went through this or that kind of creative process would be to know an interesting correlation, but it would not be a means of judging the work of art itself. Even if Bach's Preludes and Fugues had been produced by machinery, would they not be as great as before?—and this in spite of the fact that there were no artist's emotions to be expressed because there was no artist. For appreciating the work of art, the artist's biography is not essential: "by their works shall ye know them."

But we may long since have become impatient with the line of reasoning just pursued. What we have been talking about all through it (it will be said) is evocation—trying to analyze expression in terms of certain effects, of whatever kind, evoked in the listener or reader or observer. And whatever expression is, it is not evocation; no theory of expression is merely a theory about evocation. So we shall have to look elsewhere if we want a sensible meaning for the term "expression," when used to characterize not artistic processes but works of art.

Why is this evocation-talk inadequate, one might ask, to deal with expression? One could imagine the following reply: To say that a work of art expresses something is not to say that the artist underwent certain creative processes, nor to say that the listener had certain experiences. Rather, it is to say that the artist had communicated something *to* the listener by means of his work. Expression is not just something evoked in us, it is something which the artist *did* which he then *communicated* to us. Thus far we have dealt with the two aspects—artist and audience—in isolation from each other; but we should have considered them both together; this has been our error. Let us pursue this line of thought a little.

The typical kind of view here is one hallowed by tradition; we might describe it roughly as follows: The artist feels a powerful emotion which he expresses by creating a work of art, in such a way that we, the audience, on reading or seeing or hearing the work of art, feel the same emotion ourselves. Whether the artist did this by intent—i.e., whether in creating he wanted us to feel this emotion, which is what Collingwood denies that a true artist will do—or whether he was working something out within himself without thinking of an audience, does not matter at this point; the important thing is that, whether by intent or not, whether he created with an audience in mind or only to express what he felt, the artist put something into his work which we, the audience, can get out of it; and what we get out is the same thing that he put in. In this way whatever it is that he put in is communicated to us who get it out. Expression is thus a "two-way deal" involving both the artist and his audience.

The language used just now in characterizing the view is deliberately crude, for I do not know how else to describe it with any accuracy. Indeed, this is the very feature of it which makes it, on reflection, extremely difficult to defend. Nor is it easy to remedy it by employing a more sophisticated language in formulating it, for the sophisticated terms usually turn out to be metaphorical. Yet these metaphors seem to be basic to the theory.

For example, it is said that the artist, by means of his work, *transmits* his emotion to us. But what is meant by "transmit" here? When water is transmitted through a pipe, the same water that comes into the pipe at one end comes out at the other; this is perhaps a paradigm case of transmission. When we speak of electricity as being transmitted through a wire, there is not in the same sense something that comes in at one end and out at the other, but at any rate there is a continuous flow of electricity; or if the word "flow" is itself metaphorical, it is perhaps enough to remark that at any point between its two ends the wire will affect instruments and produce shocks. When we transfer this talk about transmission from these contexts to works of art, we may tend to imagine a kind of wire connecting the work of art with the artist at one end and with the audience at the other; or, if we do not actually have such an image, at any rate the term "transmit" takes its meaning from situations such as we have just described; and the question arises, what does it mean in the very different context of art? If it is not like these orthodox cases of transmission, what makes it transmission? What is one committing himself to when he says that in art emotion is transmitted?

A metaphor that may seem to do better justice to the theory is that of deposition. The artist has, as it were, *deposited* his emotion in the work of art, where we can withdraw it at any time we choose. It is somewhat like the dog burying a bone, which another dog may dig up at his own pleasure. But of course, the artist has not literally buried or deposited emotion in his work; he has, rather, with or without the divine agonies of inspiration, painted in

oils or written a complicated set of notes on paper. It is true that on seeing
the one or hearing the other performed we may have certain feelings; but in
no literal sense has the artist *put* them there in the way that we put money
into the bank to withdraw at a later time. Moreover, the bone that is dug up
is one and the same bone that was previously buried; whereas the emotion
which we feel (I shall not say "extract") when we hear or see the work of art
cannot be one and the same numerical emotion as the one which the artist
felt (I shall not say "put in").

Let us then substitute the metaphor of *conveying*. Whatever it is that the
artist is said to be conveying to his audience, of what does such conveyance
consist? One person conveys the ball to another by throwing it; the postman
conveys letters from the postoffice to one's door. Is a material continuum
necessary for conveyance—the postman between the postoffice and the
house, the moving conveyor-belt for trays and machinery? If something mysteriously disappeared at one place and reappeared at another, would it be
said to be conveyed? If the emotion ceases in the artist and turns up in the
audience when they examine his work, has the artist's emotion been conveyed? Again it is not clear exactly what is involved in the talk about conveying. And even if the emotion ceased in the artist and thereupon occurred
in the audience, would it be the same emotion that occurred in the two? In
all the cases of conveyance—the ball, the letter, the water through the
pipe—it is one and the same thing that is conveyed from the one person or
place to the other. This condition is not fulfilled in the case of emotion. One
and the same emotion could no more occur in both artist and observer than
the same pain can be passed along from one person to another by each person in a row successively pricking his finger with the same pin.

Though the language of the expression theory leaves the impression that
it is one and the same emotion which occurs in both artist and observer, on
the analogy with the other examples, this is surely not essential to the
theory; perhaps it is enough that they be two emotions of the same kind or
class. It may be enough that the artist in composing may feel an emotion of
kind X, and the observer on seeing it may feel another emotion of kind X.
This probably occurs often enough. But suppose it does; is *this* sufficient for
saying that X is conveyed from the one to the other? Is this watered-down
formulation really what the theory means when it says that art expresses
emotion?

Let us, then, speak simply of "communication." The word "communicate" is somewhat more elastic than the previous words—people can
communicate in person, by wireless, even telepathically—but it is also more
vague and difficult to pin down. We could spend many hours discussing criteria for communication. Since we cannot do this here, let us take an example in which we would probably agree that communication had occurred.
A student summarizes the contents of a difficult essay, and the author looks
at the summary and says, "That's it exactly!" Similarly, one might say that an
emotion had been communicated if the listener to a symphony described a
movement as "haunting, tinged with gentle melancholy, becoming by degrees hopeful, ending on a note of triumph" and the composer said, "Exactly
so! that's just what I meant to communicate."

I have some doubts about whether even this last example would satisfy us as being a "communication of emotion." At any rate, what the listener did here was intellectual, not emotional—he *recognized* the emotions rather than experiencing them himself; and perhaps this suffices for communication, but it is worth pointing out that in the traditional expression theory the listener does not merely recognize the feeling, he himself *has* the feeling. But, so as not to spend more time tinkering with the highly vulnerable terminology of the expression theory (in the form we are considering in this section), let me state some objections that could be raised to any formulation of it known to me.

1. There are many experiences which the artist undergoes in the process of creation—the divine agonies of inception, the slow working through of ideas to fruition, and the technical details of execution—which the audience need not and probably should not share. This part of the artist's creative activity need in no sense be communicated. For example, much of the creative process may be agonizing or even boring, but the audience on viewing or hearing the work of art should not feel either agonized or bored. At most, then, it is only a selection of the artist's experiences in creation that should be communicated. One should not speak as if somehow the artist's whole experience in creation were somehow transferred bodily to the observer or listener.

2. Even for the part that the artist wants to communicate to his audience, it is not necessary that he be feeling this at the time of creation, as the theory so often seems to imply. When the artist is under the sway or spell of an emotion, he is all too inclined to be victim and not master of it, and therefore not to be in a good position to create a work of art, which demands a certain detachment and distance as well as considerable lucidity and studied self-discipline. Wordsworth himself said that the emotion should be recollected in tranquillity; and others, such as Eliot, have gone further and expunged emotion from the account altogether. Perhaps, then, it might be held essential only that the artist *have had* the emotion at some time or other. But if all that is required is that the artist have some emotion or other of type X, then, since most people of any sensitivity have experienced a considerable part of the gamut of human emotions, including some from type X or any other one chooses to mention, this feature in no way distinguishes the artist from other people, and the theory loses all its punch; it becomes innocuous and, like all highly diluted solutions, uninteresting and undistinctive.

3. To say that the audience should feel the same kind of emotion as the artist seems often to be simply not true. Perhaps, in lyric poems and some works of music, the listener may feel an emotion of the same kind as the artist once felt; but in many cases this is not so at all. Even when we do feel emotions in response to works of art (and most of the time what we experience should not, I think, be called "emotions" at all, at least if our attitude is esthetic), they are often of a quite different sort: if the author has expressed anger, we feel not anger but (perhaps) horror or repulsion; if he has expressed anguish, we may feel not anguish but pity.

Often it seems quite clear that the audience emotion should be quite different from anything that was or sometimes even could have been in the mind of the artist. We may experience fascination, horror, or sympathy when seeing *Hamlet* because of what we feel is the oedipal conflict unconsciously motivating his inaction; but this response, a result of Freudian psychology, could hardly have been in the mind of Shakespeare. And why indeed should it have been? It is enough that his drama can be consistently interpreted in this way, perhaps even giving it an added coherence; it is enough that he wrote a drama capable of arousing such feelings; it is not necessary that he have experienced them himself.

4. Epistemologically the most ticklish point for the expression theory is simply this: how can we ever know for sure that the feeling in the mind of the artist was anything like the feeling aroused in a listener or observer? Our judgments on this point, in cases where we do have evidence, have notoriously often been mistaken. We might feel absolutely certain that Mozart felt joy when he composed the Haffner Symphony, and be amazed to discover that during this whole period of his life he was quite miserable, full of domestic dissension, poverty, and disease. A happy composition does not imply a happy composer. Strictly speaking the only way we can know how a composer felt is to ask him, and then only if he is not lying. If he is dead, we have to consult his autobiography, if any, or other written records, if any, and hope that they do not misrepresent the facts and that they do not tell us what the composer or biographer wanted us to think rather than what really was the case. And of course [as Harold Osborne said in *Aesthetics and Criticism*] they often do this: "Artists who are dead have rarely left satisfactory psychological records, and the difficulties of appealing to living artists, whose motives and intentions are often mixed and their powers of introspective analysis small, are overwhelming."

This consequence is fatal if the expression theory is made a criterion of good art. For it would follow that if we do not know whether the emotion experienced by a listener is of the same kind as that experienced by the artist, we do not know whether or not this is a good work of art. Therefore in those cases where we have no records or they are of dubious value, we must hold our judgment of the work of art in abeyance. And such a consequence, it would seem, makes the theory in this form pass the bounds of the ridiculous.

"But," it may be said, "we don't have to find out from the artist himself or from written records what emotion the artist felt—we can tell this from seeing or hearing the work of art." But this is precisely what we cannot do. Though in this area conviction is strong and subjective feelings of certainty run high, our inferences from works of art to artists are as likely as not to be mistaken. We cannot tell from just listening to the symphony how Mozart felt; the work simply provides no safe clue to this. The best we can do is guess, after hearing the composition, what he was feeling; and then, if the available evidence should point to the conclusion that he actually was feeling so at the time, our inference would have been correct for at least this instance. But once we do this, we are already checking our inference (made from hearing the work) against the empirical evidence, and it is the evidence that is decisive.

We might, in the light of these objections, wish to revise the theory so as not to require that the audience should feel what the artist felt, but only what the artist wanted or *intended* the audience to feel. But when this is done, difficulties again confront us: (1) The same difficulties that attend our knowing how the artist felt are also present, though sometimes in lesser degree, in knowing what he intended. (2) The artist's whole intention may have misfired; he may have intended us to feel one thing, but if even the most careful and sensitive listeners for generations fail to feel anything like this when they hear his composition, shall we still say that we should feel what the artist intended us to feel? (3) The moment we abandon the stipulation that the audience should feel, not as the artist felt but as the artist intended the audience to feel, we seem to abandon anything that could be called the expression theory. For it is characteristic of the expression theory that the artist must have felt something which he "conveys" through his work and which we on observing the work also feel; if he did not feel it, but only tried to make us feel it or intended us to feel it, this is no longer an expression of feeling on his part but a deliberate attempt to evoke it in others—in other words, not expressing but arousing.

It may seem that in the last few pages we have been flogging a dead horse; yet if one examines much critical writing he must be aware how far from dead this horse is. Critics and laymen alike are dominated, quite unconsciously, by the metaphors of transmission, conveyance, and the like, the emotion in the analogy being usually a kind of liquid that is transmitted bodily from artist to audience. Although when made explicit this kind of formulation would doubtless be rejected, it is precisely these metaphors which are at the very roots (to use another metaphor) of the expression theory in the form we have been considering in this section. And the very strong objections to the theory seem seldom to be realized.

But then, one might say, why should the expression theory be held in any such form as this? What we have been discussing in this section concerns communication between artist and audience; and a theory of communication, one might say, is no more a theory of expression than a theory of evocation is. For an artist to *express* something, however irrelevant this may be to a judgment of its value, is one thing; for him to *communicate* it to an audience is another. For a work to be expressive is one thing; for an audience to feel so-and-so is another. If this is so—if reference to an audience has no place in a theory of expression—it immediately rules out both the evocation forms of the theory which we discussed, and the communication forms which we have been discussing.

Note on Source.   The material in the preceding section is quoted from Sections I and III of John Hospers's paper "The Concept of Artistic Expression," *Proceedings of the Aristotelian Society 1954–55.*

Reading References.   The student would do well to browse in one or more of the following collections of readings in aesthetics: E. F. Carritt, *Philosophies of Beauty from Socrates to Robert Bridges,* 1931. S. K. Langer, *Reflections on Art,* 1958. M. Rader, *A Modern Book of Aesthetics,* 3rd edition, 1960. E. Vivas and M. Krieger, *The Problems of Aesthetics,* 1953. M. Weitz, *Problems in Aesthetics,* 1959.

READING QUESTIONS

1. What it means to say that *expression* is an "essential vehicle" in the statement of the emotive theory of art.
2. Elucidate: "These identifications are primary data . . . preanalytical."
3. Hegel's point in comparing philosophy to a night owl.
4. What it means to say that Professor Hospers raises "second-order" questions. What would be an example of a first-order question? A third-order question?
5. Any two difficulties that Professor Hospers raises for *express* when that word refers to the activity the artist performs.
6. Any two difficulties he raises for *express* when that word is used to mean "communicate."
7. Professor Hospers raises second-order questions about emotivism in aesthetics. Suggest, by analogy, how you might employ the same strategy against, say, utilitarianism in ethics, or empiricism in theory of knowledge.

INDEPENDENT STUDY

1. Read the article "Aesthetics, Problems of," by J. Hospers in the *Encyclopedia of Philosophy*. Make clear what the problems are. Be sure Mr. Hospers does not ask questions and make claims that are incompatible with his essay in this section of this textbook.
2. Mr. Hospers's sand-papering of the emotivist (expressionist) position in aesthetics is a thorough job. Does it call for an *alternative* aesthetics? If so, can you find anything in books or articles by Mr. Hospers suggesting what that alternative might be? Or does it add up to an antiaesthetics? Can you find that anywhere in his relevant writings?
3. Read as you see lead-in themes in chapters of *Mind and Art* by G. Sircello. (Not recommended as a first assignment.)

SECTION 5. MORRIS WEITZ: IS AESTHETICS FOUNDED ON A MISTAKE?

From Hospers to Weitz. Our first three authors—Véron, Tolstoy, Collingwood—propounded the emotive theory about the arts and works of art. Our fourth author, Professor Hospers, selected one of the essential vehicles of that theory—the concept of expression—and subjected it to considerable criticism. Our fifth author, Professor Weitz, is more drastic in his treatment of the question to which the other four addressed themselves. If he is correct, they are in a worse state of confusion than they would seem to be aware of. Three of them are stating a theory and the fourth is criticizing it. Three of them are addressing themselves to a common question—"What is art?" (to use the title of Tolstoy's book)—and proposing an answer. The fourth is criticizing their answer; even, if you will, rejecting their answer. But to criticize or reject an answer is to leave open the possibility that the question makes sense, that it is susceptible of being answered. Professor Weitz proposes a clean sweep. He is convinced that the question itself is wrong-headed, and should not be asked. If this is so, then *no* answer will satisfy. If you are asking the wrong question, or an essentially pointless or meaningless or "impossible" question, then your trouble is more deep-rooted. There is no use in seeking *any* answer; what you must do is abandon the question. Professor Weitz is of the opinion that the question rests on a false or at least indefensible presupposition. If a person asks whether you have stopped beating your wife, you may reject the question on the grounds that it presupposes that you had been doing so, whereas you hadn't; or that you have a wife, whereas you haven't. You would say, "That question does not, because it cannot, arise." Professor Hospers had not proposed any such drastic criticism of the emotive theory. He seemed to allow the question but disallow the answer. He bore down on one particular answer to the question, "What is art?" Professor Weitz would rule out *all* answers to that question because he would rule out the question. As a Spanish proverb has it, these are major words.

Biographical Note. Morris Weitz was born in 1916. He is at present (1963) a professor of philosophy at Brandeis University. He is the author of *Philosophy of the Arts* (1950) and the editor of an anthology of readings of aesthetics, *Problems in Aesthetics* (1959). The article repudiating traditional aesthetic theory, "The Role of Theory in Esthetics," was published in *The Journal of Aesthetics and Art Criticism* (1956).

The Argument of the Passages. The traditional question, "What is art?" presupposes that works of art have some property or set of properties in common by virtue of which they are works of art. This Professor Weitz denies; works of art do not have *any* such common property or set of properties by virtue of which they are works of art. They are simply works of art, and that is the end of the matter. If you presuppose that there are *any* conditions that are necessary and sufficient to being a work of art—other than *being* a work of art—you are mistaken. As long as you entertain this false presupposition you will continue to be misled into posing the question "What makes a work of art to be a work of art?" and, in consequence, misled into proposing answers to your question. If you are convinced by Professor Weitz here, and abandon the presupposition, your question will die on the vine.

Then what will you do? Professor Weitz would have you begin all over again with a radically different question. Don't ask, "What is art?" instead ask, "What kind of concept is your concept of art? How do you conceive of your concept of art?" Two alternatives confront you here: a concept can be either "closed" or "open." A concept, of art or anything else, is closed when you do not entertain the possibility of amending it, extending it, revising it. It is fixed. You "stipulate" that it is not to be altered in any way for any reason. If cases occur that seem as though they ought to be included but don't exactly fit, you close them out. If cases occur that seem as though they ought not be included yet they do exactly fit, you rule them in. In proceeding thus you are, or may be, deliberately arbitrary, not to say "high-handed." You operate on the Humpty-Dumpty principle: "*I* stipulate the concept: let the cases fall where they may." Suppose you are a teacher and you stipulate that an *A* student shall be one who has a photographic memory, writes legibly, and never fails to show appreciation of your lectures; and you *hold* to this concept. You keep it closed. Professor Weitz would have you ask whether *this* is the way you conceive of your concept of art. As you conceive of your concept of art, would you say that you hold it thus "closed"? If you do, he would, I think, ask you *why* you do; and warn you against the dangers of having a "closed" mind on the question.

In contrast, a concept may be "open." You put it together as you go along. It is "open" to revision, amendment, extension. You "stipulate" nothing in advance. Instead, you "study the field," modifying your concept where you have to, retaining it where you can. Here you don't "stipulate" the concept; you form it and reform it. On these terms you may have no criterion or set of criteria of what constitutes an *A* student held in defiance of what your experience may bring forth. This does not mean that any and every student is an *A*. It means that your concept of an *A* student is not deliberately and unalterably fixed: you are "open" to what the field may produce. Professor Weitz would have you ask whether *this* is the way you conceive of your concept of art. Would you say that you hold it thus "open"? If you do, he would, I think, commend you for having an "open" (*not* a "vacant") mind on the question.

If your concept is "open," and you define it, you will treat your definition as, say, a scientist or a detective treats a hypothesis. If, however, it is "closed," and you define it, you will treat your definition more in the way a geometer treats a concept in geometry.

This is tempting business. The notion of definitions as hypotheses has great charm. On reading Professor Weitz's paper, one might feel a reservation in reference to his sweeping condemnation of his predecessors. It is not clear that they conceived of their conceptions of art as "closed." That is not the conception one has of one's conception of them. When great writers with an interest in philosophy turn their minds to questions connected with art, their thought is often characterized by considerable passion; there is such a thing as intellectual passion. And it may be that their manner of expressing themselves expresses both intellect and passion. Where this is so, one does well in reading them to proceed not only cautiously but *con amore*, with a mind held open by a combination of affection and respect.

(1)

Theory has been central in aesthetics and is still the preoccupation of the philosophy of art. Its main concern remains the determination of the nature of art which can be formulated into a definition of it. It construes definition as the statement of the necessary and sufficient properties of what is being defined, where the statement purports to be a true or false claim about the essence of art, what characterizes and distinguishes it from everything else. Each of the great theories of art converges on the attempt to state the defining properties of art. Each claims that it is the true theory because it has formulated correctly into a real definition the nature of art; and that the others are false because they have left out some necessary or sufficient property. Many theorists contend that their enterprise is no mere intellectual exercise but a necessity for any understanding of art and our proper evaluation of it. Unless we know what art is, they say, what are its necessary and sufficient properties, we cannot begin to respond to it adequately or to say why one work is good or better than another. Aesthetic theory, thus, is important not only in itself but for the foundations of both appreciation and criticism. Philosophers, critics, and even artists who have written on art, agree that what is primary in aesthetics is a theory about the nature of art.

Is aesthetic theory, in the sense of a true definition or set of necessary and sufficient properties of art, possible? If nothing else does, the history of aesthetics itself should give one enormous pause here. For, in spite of the many theories, we seem no nearer our goal today than we were in Plato's time. Each age, each art-movement, each philosophy of art, tries over and over again to establish the stated ideal only to be succeeded by a new or revised theory, rooted, at least in part, in the repudiation of preceding ones. Even today, almost everyone interested in aesthetic matters is still deeply wedded to the hope that the correct theory of art is forthcoming. We need only examine the numerous new books on art in which new definitions are proffered; or, in our own country especially, the basic textbooks and anthologies to recognize how strong the priority of a theory of art is.

I want to plead for the rejection of this problem. I want to show that theory—in the requisite classical sense—is *never* forthcoming in aesthetics, and that we would do much better as philosophers to supplant the question, "What is the nature of art?," by other questions, the answers to which will provide us with all the understanding of the arts there can be. I want to show that the inadequacies of the theories are not primarily occasioned by any legitimate difficulty such e.g., as the vast complexity of art, which might be corrected by further probing and research. Their basic inadequacies reside instead in a fundamental misconception of art. Aesthetic theory—all of it—is wrong in principle in thinking that a correct theory is possible because it radically misconstrues the logic of the concept of art. Its main contention—that "art" is amenable to real or any kind of true definition—is false. Its attempt to discover the necessary and sufficient properties of art is logically misbegotten for the simple reason that such a set and, consequently, such a formula about it, is never forthcoming. Art, as the logic of the concept shows, has no set of necessary and sufficient properties, hence a theory of it is logically impossible and not merely factually difficult. Aesthetic theory tries to define what cannot be defined in its requisite sense. But in recommending the repudiation of aesthetic theory I shall not argue from this, as too many others have done, that its logical confusions render it meaningless or worthless. On the contrary, I wish to reassess its role and its contribution primarily in order to show that it is of the greatest importance to our understanding of the arts.

(2)

Let us now survey briefly some of the more famous extant aesthetic theories in order to see if they do incorporate correct and adequate statements about the nature of art. In each of these there is the assumption that it is the true enumeration of the defining properties of art, with the implication that previous theories have stressed wrong definitions. Thus, to begin with, consider a famous version of Formalist theory, that propounded by Bell and Fry. It is true that they speak mostly of painting in their writings but both assert that what they find in that art can be generalized for what is "art" in the others as well. The essence of painting, they maintain, is the plastic elements in relation. Its defining property is significant form, i.e., certain combinations of lines, colors, shapes, volumes—everything on the canvas except the representational elements—which evoke a unique response to such combinations. Painting is definable as plastic organization. The nature of art, what it *really* is, so their theory goes, is a unique combination of certain elements (the specifiable plastic ones) in their relations. Anything which is art is an instance of significant form; and anything which is not art has no such form.

To this the Emotionalist replies that the truly essential property of art has been left out. Tolstoy, Ducasse, or any of the advocates of this theory, find that the requisite defining property is not significant form but rather the expression of emotion in some sensuous public medium. Without projection of emotion into some piece of stone or words or sounds, etc., there can be no art. Art is really such embodiment. It is this that uniquely characterizes art, and any true, real definition of it, contained in some adequate theory of art, must so state it.

The Intuitionist disclaims both emotion and form as defining properties. In Croce's version, for example, art is identified not with some physical, public object but with a specific creative, cognitive and spiritual act. Art is really a first stage of knowledge in which certain human beings (artists) bring their images and intuitions into lyrical clarification or expression. As such, it is an awareness, non-conceptual in character, of the unique individuality of things; and since it exists below the level of conceptualization or action, it is without scientific or moral content. Croce singles out as the defining essence of art this first stage of spiritual life and advances its identification with art as a philosophically true theory or definition.

The Organicist says to all of this that art is really a class of organic wholes consisting of distinguishable, albeit inseparable, elements in their causally efficacious relations which are presented in some sensuous medium. What is claimed is that anything which is a work of art is in its nature a unique complex of interrelated parts—in painting, for example, lines, colors, volumes, subjects, etc., all interacting upon one another on a paint surface of some sort. At one time it seemed to me that this organic theory constituted the one true and real definition of art.

My final example is the most interesting of all. This is the theory of Parker. In his writings on art, Parker persistently calls into question the traditional simple-minded definitions of aesthetics. "The assumption underlying every philosophy of art is the existence of some common nature present in all the arts." "All the so popular brief definitions of art—'significant form,' 'expression,' 'intuition,' 'objectified pleasure'—are fallacious, either because, while true of art, they are also true of much that is not art, and hence fail to differentiate art from other things; or else because they neglect some essential aspect of art." But instead of inveighing against the attempt at definition of art itself, Parker insists that what is needed is a complex definition rather than a simple one. "The definition of art must therefore be in terms of a complex of characteristics. Failure to recognize this has been the fault of all the well-known definitions." His own version is the theory that art is essentially three things: embodiment of wishes and desires imaginatively satisfied, language, which characterizes the public medium of art, and harmony, which unifies the language with the layers of imaginative projections. Thus, for Parker, it is a true definition to say of art that it is ". . . the provision of satisfaction through the imagination, social significance, and harmony. I am claiming that nothing except works of art possesses all three of these marks."

Now, all of these sample theories are inadequate in many different ways. Each purports to be a complete statement about the defining features of all works of art and yet each of them leaves out something which the others take to be central. Some are circular, e.g., the Bell-Fry theory of art as significant form which is defined in part in terms of our response to significant form. Some of them, in their search for necessary and sufficient properties, emphasize too few properties, like (again) the Bell-Fry definition which leaves out subject-representation in painting, or the Croce theory which omits inclusion of the very important feature of the public, physical character, say, of architecture. Others are too general and cover objects that are not art as well as works of art. Organicism is surely such a view since it can be applied to *any* causal unity in the natural world as well as to art. Still others rest on dubious principles, e.g., Parker's claim that art embodies imaginative satisfactions, rather than real ones; or Croce's assertion that there is nonconceptual knowledge. Consequently, even if art has one set of necessary and sufficient properties, none of the theories we have noted or, for that matter, no aesthetic theory yet proposed, has enumerated that set to the satisfaction of all concerned.

Then there is a different sort of difficulty. As real definitions, these theories are supposed to be factual reports on art. If they are, may we not ask, Are they empirical and open to verification or falsification? For example, what would confirm or disconfirm the theory that art is significant form or embodiment of emotion or creative synthesis of images? There does not even seem to be a hint of the kind of evidence which might be forthcoming to test these theories; and indeed one wonders if they are perhaps honorific definitions of "art," that is, proposed redefinitions in terms of some *chosen* conditions for applying the concept of art, and not true or false reports on the essential properties of art at all.

(3)

But all these criticisms of traditional aesthetic theories—that they are circular, incomplete, untestable, pseudo-factual, disguised proposals to change the meaning of concepts—have been made before. My intention is to go beyond these to make a much more fundamental criticism, namely, that aesthetic theory is a logically vain attempt to define what cannot be defined, to state the necessary and sufficient properties of that which has no necessary and sufficient properties, to conceive the concept of art as closed when its very use reveals and demands its openness.

The problem with which we must begin is not "What is art?," but "What sort of concept is 'art'?" Indeed, the root problem of philosophy itself is to explain the relation between the employment of certain kinds of concepts and the conditions under which they can be correctly applied. If I may paraphrase Wittgenstein, we must not ask, What is the nature of any philosophical "X"?, or even, according to the semanticist, What does "X" mean?, a transformation that leads to the disastrous interpretation of "art" as a name for some specifiable class of objects; but rather, What is the use or employment of "X"? What does "X" do in the language? This, I take it, is the initial question, the begin-all if not the end-all of any philosophical problem and solution. Thus, in aesthetics, our first problem is the elucidation of the actual employment of the concept of art, to give a logical description of the actual functioning of the concept, including a description of the conditions under which we correctly use it or its correlates.

My model in this type of logical description or philosophy derives from Wittgenstein. It is also he who, in his refutation of philosophical theorizing in the sense of constructing definitions of philosophical entities, has furnished contemporary aesthetics with a starting point for any future progress. In his new work, *Philosophical Investigations*, Wittgenstein raises as an illustrative question, What is a game? The traditional philosophical, theoretical answer would be in terms of some exhaustive set of properties common to all games. To this Wittgenstein says, let us consider what we call "games": "I mean board-games, card-games, ball-games, Olympic games, and so on. What is common to them all?—Don't say: 'there *must* be something common, or they would not be called "games" ' but *look and see* whether there is anything common to all.—For if you look at them you will not see something that is common to *all*, but similarities, relationships, and a whole series of them at that. . . ."

Card games are like board games in some respects but not in others. Not all games are amusing, nor is there always winning or losing or competition. Some games resemble others in some respects—that is all. What we find are no necessary and sufficient properties, only "a complicated network of similarities overlapping and crisscrossing," such that we can say of games that they form a family with family resemblances and no common trait. If one asks what a game is, we pick out sample games, describe these, and add, "This and *similar things* are called 'games.' " This is all we need to say and indeed all any of us knows about games. Knowing what a game is is not knowing some real definition or theory but being able to recognize and explain games and to decide which among imaginary and new examples would or would not be called "games."

The problem of the nature of art is like that of the nature of games, at least in these respects: If we actually look and see what it is that we call "art," we will also find no common properties—only strands of similarities. Knowing what art is is not apprehending some manifest or latent essence but being able to recognize, describe, and explain those things we call "art" in virtue of these similarities.

But the basic resemblance between these concepts is their open texture. In elucidating them, certain (paradigm) cases can be given, about which there can be no question as to their being correctly described as "art" or "game," but no exhaustive set of cases can be given. I can list some cases and some conditions under which I can apply correctly the concept of art but I cannot list all of them, for the all-important reason that unforeseeable or novel conditions are always forthcoming or envisageable.

A concept is open if its conditions of application are emendable and corrigible; i.e., if a situation or case can be imagined or secured which would call for some sort of *decision* on our part to extend the use of the concept to cover this, or to close the concept and invent a new one to deal with the new case and its new property. If necessary and sufficient conditions for the application of a concept can be stated, the concept is a closed one. But this can happen only in logic or mathematics where concepts are constructed and completely defined. It cannot occur with empirically-descriptive and normative concepts unless we arbitrarily close them by stipulating the ranges of their uses.

I can illustrate this open character of "art" best by examples drawn from its sub-concepts. Consider questions like "Is Dos Passos' *U. S. A.* a novel?," "Is V. Woolf's *To the Lighthouse* a novel?," "Is Joyce's *Finnegan's Wake* a

novel?" On the traditional view these are construed as factual problems to
be answered yes or no in accordance with the presence or absence of defining properties. But certainly this is not how any of these questions is answered. Once it arises, as it has many times in the development of the novel
from Richardson to Joyce (e.g., "Is Gide's *The School for Wives* a novel or a
diary?"), what is at stake is no factual analysis concerning necessary and sufficient properties but a decision as to whether the work under examination is
similar in certain respects to other works, already called "novels," and consequently warrants the extension of the concept to cover the new case. The
new work is narrative, fictional, contains character delineation and dialogue
but (say) it has no regular time-sequence in the plot or is interspersed with
actual newspaper reports. It is like recognized novels, A, B, C . . . , in some
respects but not like them in others. But then neither were B and C like A in
some respects when it was decided to extend the concept applied to A to B
and C. Because work N + 1 (the brand new work) is like A, B, C . . . N in
certain respects—has strands of similarity to them—the concept is extended
and a new phase of the novel engendered. "Is N + 1 a novel?," then, is no
factual, but rather a decision problem, where the verdict turns on whether or
not we enlarge our set of conditions for applying the concept.

What is true of the novel is, I think, true of every sub-concept of art:
"tragedy," "comedy," "painting," "opera," etc., of "art" itself. No "Is X a
novel, painting, opera, work of art, etc.?" question allows of a definitive answer in the sense of a factual yes or no report. "Is this *collage* a painting or
not?" does not rest on any set of necessary and sufficient properties of painting but on whether we decide—as we did!—to extend "painting" to cover
this case.

"Art," itself, is an open concept. New conditions (cases) have constantly
arisen and will undoubtedly constantly arise; new art forms, new movements
will emerge, which will demand decisions on the part of those interested,
usually professional critics, as to whether the concept should be extended or
nor. Aestheticians may lay down similarity conditions but never necessary
and sufficient ones for the correct application of the concept. With "art" its
conditions of application can never be exhaustively enumerated since new
cases can always be envisaged or created by artists, or even nature, which
would call for a decision on someone's part to extend or to close the old or to
invent a new concept. (E.g., "It's not a sculpture, it's a mobile.")

What I am arguing, then, is that the very expansive, adventurous character of art, its ever-present changes and novel creations, makes it logically impossible to ensure any set of defining properties. We can, of course, choose
to close the concept. But to do this with "art" or "tragedy" or "portraiture,"
etc., is ludicrous since it forecloses on the very conditions of creativity in the
arts.

(4)

Of course there are legitimate and serviceable closed concepts in art. But
these are always those whose boundaries of conditions have been drawn for
a *special* purpose. Consider the difference, for example, between "tragedy"
and "(extant) Greek tragedy." The first is open and must remain so to allow

for the possibility of new conditions, e.g., a play in which the hero is not noble or fallen or in which there is no hero but other elements that are like those of plays we already call "tragedy." The second is closed. The plays it can be applied to, the conditions under which it can be correctly used are all in, once the boundary, "Greek," is drawn. Here the critic can work out a theory or real definition in which he lists the common properties at least of the extant Greek tragedies. Aristotle's definition, false as it is as a theory of all the plays of Aeschylus, Sophocles, and Euripides, since it does not cover some of them, properly called "tragedies," can be interpreted as a real (albeit incorrect) definition of this closed concept; although it can also be, as it unfortunately has been, conceived as a purported real definition of "tragedy," in which case it suffers from the logical mistake of trying to define what cannot be defined—of trying to squeeze what is an open concept into an honorific formula for a closed concept.

What is supremely important, if the critic is not to become muddled, is to get clear about the way in which he conceives his concepts; otherwise he goes from the problem of trying to define "tragedy," etc., to an arbitrary closing of the concept in terms of certain preferred conditions or characteristics which he sums up in some linguistic recommendation that he mistakenly thinks is a real definition of the open concept. Thus, many critics and aestheticians ask, "What is tragedy?," choose a class of samples for which they may give a true account of its common properties, and then go on to construe this account of the chosen closed class as a true definition or theory of the whole open class of tragedy. This, I think, is the logical mechanism of most of the so-called theories of the subconcepts of art: "tragedy," "comedy," "novel," etc. In effect, this whole procedure, subtly deceptive as it is, amounts to a transformation of correct criteria for *recognizing* members of certain legitimately closed classes, of works of art into recommended criteria for *evaluating* any putative member of the class.

The primary task of aesthetics is not to seek a theory but to elucidate the concept of art. Specifically, it is to describe the conditions under which we employ the concept correctly. Definition, reconstruction, patterns of analysis are out of place here since they distort and add nothing to our understanding of art. What, then, is the logic of "X is a work of art"?

As we actually use the concept, "Art" is both descriptive (like "chair") and evaluative (like "good"); i.e., we sometimes say, "This is a work of art," to describe something and we sometimes say it to evaluate something. Neither use surprises anyone.

What, first, is the logic of "X is a work of art," when it is a descriptive utterance? What are the conditions under which we would be making such an utterance correctly? There are no necessary and sufficient conditions but there are the strands of similarity conditions, i.e., bundles of properties, none of which need be present but most of which are, when we describe things as works of art. I shall call these the "criteria of recognition" of works of art. All of these have served as the defining criteria of the individual traditional theories of art; so we are already familiar with them. Thus, mostly, when we describe something as a work of art, we do so under the conditions of there being present some sort of artifact, made by human skill, ingenuity, and imagination, which embodies in its sensuous, public medium—stone, wood, sounds, words, etc.—certain distinguishable elements and relations. Special theorists would add conditions like satisfaction of wishes, objectification or expression of emotion, some act of empathy, and so on; but these latter conditions seem to be quite adventitious, present to some but not to other spectators when things are described as works of art. "X is a work of art and contains *no* emotion, expression, act of empathy, satisfaction, etc.," is perfectly good sense and may frequently be true. "X is a work of art and . . . was made by no one," or . . . "exists only in the mind and not in any publicly observable thing," or . . . "was made by accident when he spilled the paint on the canvas," in each case of which a normal condition is denied, are also sensible and capable of being true in certain circumstances. None of the criteria of recognition is a defining one, either necessary or sufficient, because we can sometimes assert of something that it is a work of art and go on to deny any one of these conditions, even the one which has traditionally been taken to be the basic, namely, that of being an artifact: Consider, "This piece of driftwood is a lovely piece of sculpture." Thus, to say of anything that it is a work of art is to commit oneself to the presence of *some* of these conditions. One would scarcely describe X as a work of art if X were not an artifact, or a collection of elements sensuously presented in a medium, or a product of human skill, and so on. If none of the conditions were present, if there were no criteria present for recognizing something as a work of art, we would not describe it as one. But, even so, no one of these or any collection of them is either necessary or sufficient.

The elucidation of the descriptive use of "Art" creates little difficulty. But the elucidation of the evaluative use does. For many, especially theorists, "This is a work of art" does more than describe; it also praises. Its conditions of utterance, therefore, include certain preferred properties or characteristics of art. I shall call these "criteria of evaluation." Consider a typical example of this evaluative use, the view according to which to say of something that it is a work of art is to imply that it is a *successful* harmonization of elements. Many of the honorific definitions of art and its sub-concepts are of this form. What is at stake here is that "Art" is construed as an evaluative term which is either identified with its criterion or justified in terms of it. "Art" is defined in terms of its evaluative property, e.g., successful harmonization. On such a view, to say "X is a work of art" is (1) to say something which is taken *to mean* "X is a successful harmonization" (e.g., "Art *is* significant form") or (2) to say something praiseworthy *on the basis* of its successful harmonization. Theorists are never clear whether it is (1) or (2) which is being put forward. Most of them, concerned as they are with this evaluative use, formulate (2), i.e., that feature of art that *makes* it art in the praise-sense, and then go on to state (1), i.e., the definition of "Art" in terms of its art-making feature. And this is clearly to confuse the conditions under which we say something evaluatively with the meaning of what we say. "This is a work of art," said evaluatively, cannot mean "This is a successful harmonization of elements"—except by stipulation—but at most is said in virtue of the art-making property, which is taken as a (the) criterion of "Art," when "Art" is employed to assess. "This is a work of art," used evaluatively, serves to praise and not to affirm the reason why it is said.

The evaluative use of "Art," although distinct from the conditions of its use, relates in a very intimate way to these conditions. For, in every instance of "This is a work of art" (used to praise), what happens is that the criterion of evaluation (e.g., successful harmonization) for the employment of the concept of art is converted into a criterion of recognition. This is why, on its evaluative use, "This is a work of art" implies "This has P," where "P" is some chosen art-making property. Thus, if one chooses to employ "Art" evaluatively, as many do, so that "This is a work of art and not (aesthetically) good" makes no sense, he uses "Art" in such a way that he refuses to *call* anything a work of art unless it embodies his criterion of excellence.

There is nothing wrong with the evaluative use; in fact, there is good reason for using "Art" to praise. But what cannot be maintained is that theories of the evaluative use of "Art" are true and real definitions of the necessary and sufficient properties of art. Instead they are honorific definitions, pure and simple, in which "Art" has been redefined in terms of chosen criteria.

But what makes them—these honorific definitions—so supremely valuable is not their disguised linguistic recommendations; rather it is the *debates* over the reasons for changing the criteria of the concept of art which are built into the definitions. In each of the great theories of art, whether correctly understood as honorific definitions or incorrectly accepted as real definitions, what is of the utmost importance are the reasons proffered in the argument for the respective theory, that is, the reasons given for the chosen or preferred criterion of excellence and evaluation. It is this perennial debate over these criteria of evaluation which makes the history of aesthetic theory the important study it is. The value of each of the theories resides in its attempt to state and to justify certain criteria which are either neglected or distorted by previous theories. Look at the Bell-Fry theory again. Of course, "Art is significant form" cannot be accepted as a true, real definition of art; and most certainly it actually functions in their aesthetics as a redefinition of art in terms of the chosen condition of significant form. But what gives it its aesthetic importance is what lies behind the formula: In an age in which literary and representational elements have become paramount in painting, *return* to the plastic ones since these are indigenous to painting. Thus, the role of the theory is not to define anything but to use the definitional form, almost epigrammatically, to pin-point a crucial recommendation to turn our attention once again to the plastic elements in painting.

Once we, as philosophers, understand this distinction between the formula and what lies behind it, it behooves us to deal generously with the traditional theories of art; because incorporated in every one of them is a debate over and argument for emphasizing or centering upon some particular feature of art which has been neglected or perverted. If we take the aesthetic theories literally, as we have seen, they all fail; but if we reconstrue them, in terms of their function and point, as serious and argued-for recommendations to concentrate on certain criteria of excellence in art, we shall see that aesthetic theory is far from worthless. Indeed, it becomes as central as anything in aesthetics, in our understanding of art, for it teaches us what to look for and how to look at it in art. What is central and must be articulated in all the theories are their debates over the reasons for excellence in art—debates over emotional depth, profound truths, natural beauty, exacti-

tude, freshness of treatment, and so on, as criteria of evaluation—the whole
of which converges on the perennial problem of what makes a work of art
good. To understand the role of aesthetic theory is not to conceive it as definition, logically doomed to failure, but to read it as summaries of seriously
made recommendations to attend in certain ways to certain features of art.

Note on Source. The material quoted in this section is from
Morris Weitz's article "The Role of Theory in Esthetics," published
in *The Journal of Aesthetics and Art Criticism*, Volume XV, 1956.

READING QUESTIONS

1. What is Professor Weitz's purpose in reviewing six "great theories
of art"? Name them. Which had he held at one time?
2. "I plead for the rejection of *this* problem." Namely? Why?
3. Use he makes of Wittgenstein's point about games.
4. "A concept is open if its conditions of application are emendable
and corrigible." (a) Illustrate his point here. (b) Is this concept of
"open" itself open or closed?
5. Why he thinks that the concept of art is an open concept.
6. His point in the contrast between tragedy and extant Greek tragedy.
7. What does he mean by "honorific" definitions of art? What makes
them "so supremely valuable"?
8. Why, and under what condition, we should deal generously with
traditional theories of art.
9. Wherein you find Professor Weitz (a) most, (b) least convincing.

INDEPENDENT STUDY

1. Secure a copy of *Art and Philosophy: Readings in Aesthetics*,
edited by W. E. Kennick. It is divided into seven parts. Mr. Kennick contributes an explanatory essay next to the end of each part,
immediately preceding the "Suggestions for Additional Reading"
at the end of each part. Read Mr. Kennick's explanatory essays as
they come. Is there a "position" worked out? Or is it what, finally,
Mr. Weitz's paper calls for?
2. Turn to page 93 in Mr. Kennick's book of readings. See subheading "On the Problem of Defining the Nature of Art." Track down

the essays listed there, especially Mr. Kennick's own essay "Does Traditional Aesthetics Rest on a Mistake?" Write a paper covering these studies in "Anti-aesthetics."

3. You have read Weitz's paper "The Role of Theory in Aesthetics." Now read Kennick's paper "Does Traditional Aesthetics Rest on a Mistake?" Use both to work out a paper indicating what might be done, comparable to what they do in aesthetics, if you wrote on ethics, or semantics, or epistemology, or philosophy of history.

topic seven
traditional metaphysics

THE PROBLEM STATED

One of the best-known remarks in the history of philosophy is ascribed to the Greek thinker, Thales. He is said to have held that "all things are made of water." On the face of it, this seems both unimportant and false. Why, then its historical importance? Why has Thales been bracketed, along with Copernicus and Darwin, as having initiated a line of thought which marked an epoch in human speculation?

The reason is this. It required, in the first instance, a bold mind to conceive any proposition having the general form "All things are made of . . ."; because if there is one proposition that would appear to be justified by the facts of our everyday experience, it is that all things are not made of any one thing. Multiplicity and variety are the obvious facts about the everyday world. The effort of thought required to break down the testimony of the everyday world must have been considerable, as it certainly was subsequently fruitful.

Thales probably had his reasons. Such apparently diverse things as ice, snow, mist, vapor, steam are all "made of" water, if we use the term loosely. Why not other things too? Whatever his reasons may have been, his remark, once made, continued to re-echo in the minds of generations which came after him. "All things are made of. . . ."

514   In fact, the problem is with us to this day. What are all things

made of? What do we intend by the phrase *made of?* If we brush aside Thales's answer, what do we propose in place of it? Speculations on this question constitute part of the philosophical discipline called metaphysics. That is, metaphysics is, in part, an inquiry into the question of what all things are "made of."

Suppose we consider a miscellaneous collection of things, a clay pipe, a bird's egg, a rainbow, a copy of *Hamlet,* an uprising in Central China, an act of mercy, a cry in the night, a new planet. What are all these things made of? Varying the words, to what common substance are these all reducible? Of what "underlying reality" are they all manifestations? Is this underlying reality itself further reducible?

The notion that the observed multiplicity and variety of the everyday world are reducible to something common and uniform and *not* given as part of the everyday world is not an unreasonable notion. Few persons would care to deny it in principle, much as they might argue over what that something is to which all things are reducible. Granted the propriety of the notion of an ultimate reality, a "real" world in contrast to the "everyday" world, it is necessary to go one step further. In some sense or other, the everyday world is an appearance or a manifestation of the real world. There is the real world, the world as it really is, and there are its appearances, how it appears.

It is then possible to restate our central problem: What is the nature of that ultimate reality, that real world, of which the everyday world is the appearance? Answers to this question vary. If it is held that there is *an* ultimate reality, we have what is called *monism* in metaphysics, the belief that ultimate reality is one in kind. If it is held that there are at least two ultimate realities, we have what is called *dualism* in metaphysics, the belief that ultimate reality is two in kind. If it is held that there are three or more ultimate realities, we have what is called *pluralism* in metaphysics, the belief that ultimate reality is three or more in kind.

Within these classifications others will occur. You and I might agree that monism is a true belief. Our agreement might extend no further. When we came to the question of the nature of this ultimate reality, we might differ. I might claim that it was matter; you might claim that it was mind; a third person might claim that it was neither, but something more ultimate of which both matter and mind are manifestations.

In this topic we are to be concerned with such inquiries. A metaphysical claim is about the nature of ultimate reality. In considering any such claim, it will be helpful to ask, "Is it a form of monism, or dualism, or pluralism? What reasons are given, or may be given, in support of it? What reasons against it? What consequences follow from it? Do these agree with our experience of the everyday world? Or do they make nonsense of it?" Reflection upon the nature of ultimate reality is not the whole of metaphysics, but it is a large part of it. For a beginner in metaphysics, two things are of primary importance: to demand reasons for accepting any claim, and to note consequences that follow from accepting the hypothesis. If a materialist in metaphysics claims that all and only material things are real things ("If X is real, then X is matter"), we should ask him *why* he thinks so; and what follows *from* this metaphysical claim.

The readings and comments that follow help in thinking about this question. There are four sets of them: one from the seventeenth century (Hobbes, materialism) one from the eighteenth century (Berkeley, idealism), and two from the nineteenth century (Schopenhauer, voluntarism; and Comte, positivism). These men have been chosen because they are typical, and because, among them, they provide good argument. Each is convinced of his views and eager to spread them among "all rational minds." Each realizes that he must be prepared to argue his case. There is, among them, no appeal to emotions; at least, not intentionally. They are all, in this respect, "hardheaded rationalists." Here, for the eye that can detect it, is one of man's supreme intellectual sports insofar as he is a "rational" animal. Here are corrosive skepticism, caustic (if obscure) wit, resounding thwacks, closely built arguments, relentless determination to "begin at the beginning" and "think it through," and proud gestures directing attention to "positions established" and "positions overthrown." A taste for metaphysics and a flare for the practice of metaphysics are not widely diffused, but the genuine article, like a love for poetry or painting, is irrepressible once it has become aware of itself.

The readings are in chronological order, but the order exhibits development. Hobbes contributes the claim that all things are made of matter, that matter alone is real; "if X is real, then X is matter." This is monism and materialism, as full-blown as one could wish. The position taken up by Berkeley begins by a deliberate and reasoned-out rejection of Hobbes's materialism. All things, the claim here is, are either mind or objectifications of mind, spirit, *Geist*, and so on. Hobbes's materialism and Berkeley's idealism between them account for much traditional metaphysics. The term *voluntarism*, associated with Schopenhauer, who seems to have been familiar with the claims of both Hobbes and Berkeley, indicates a position somewhat closer to Berkeley than to Hobbes: it covers the claim that neither matter nor mind in the sense of intellect, but *will*, is the ultimate substance of all things. The ultimately real stuff, of which all things are manifestations, to which all things in the world of appearance are "reducible," is will, the power to act, to perform a deed. As

Faust says, *Im Anfang war die Tat,* "in the beginning was the deed." Auguste Comte's positivism proposes an abandonment of metaphysics, a doubt that the question asked by metaphysics is a genuine question ("What, and what only, is finally real, and not appearance reducible to a more basic reality?"), susceptible of a meaningful answer. When Comte's repudiation of the reality question is put that way, the argument moves from speculative metaphysics ("What is it to be *real?*") to critical metaphysics. This latter was not initiated by Comte. Indeed, he desired an end of metaphysics, whether speculative (as in Hobbes, Berkeley, or Schopenhauer) or critical, as in Kant or Collingwood. The transition from speculative to critical metaphysics antedated Comte in Hume and Kant. Critical metaphysics will bring us to our eighth and final Topic.

TRIGGER QUESTIONS

1. Why has speculative metaphysics been a standing invitation to skepticism?
2. Formulate a statement of materialism, making clear this ism is *speculative.*
3. Is materialism, a theory in speculative metaphysics, compatible with (a) empiricism in epistemology, or (b) the verifiability theory in semantics?
4. Contrast materialism with any other position in speculative metaphysics.
5. Is materialism open to either proof or disproof? If not, then what?
6. Why is it sometimes claimed that materialism in speculative metaphysics implies (a) determinism, (b) sensationism, (c) hedonism, (d) atheism, (e) behaviorism, (f) epiphenomenalism, (g) identity theory in philosophy of mind?

SECTION 1. THOMAS HOBBES: IF X IS REAL, THEN X IS MATTER

Biographical Note. Thomas Hobbes was born in England in 1588, the year in which Elizabeth became queen of England, and died in 1679 at the age of ninety-one. The English had their major political revolution between 1641 and 1688. For them this was somewhat comparable to what the Americans had beginning in 1776, the French beginning in 1789, the Russians beginning in 1917, and the Chinese in the years that culminated in 1949. Hobbes was a close student of revolutionary politics and the then recent physical sciences. His life's work was to formulate a conceptual framework, given which a person could assimilate the outcomes of the political and scientific revolutions. He led a long and busy life, interesting in itself and also because of the years through which it was lived. He was educated at Oxford. Thereafter he became tutor and secretary to the Earl of Devonshire. In this capacity he made the acquaintance of Francis Bacon, Ben Jonson, and other literary figures. He published a translation of Thucydides. When his patron died, Hobbes took over the education of his son with whom he made the Grand Tour, making the acquaintance of Galileo, Gassendi, and other scientific luminaries on the Continent. He returned to England to study politics. It was the time of England's civil war against Charles I. Hobbes was Royalist, siding against Cromwell. Circulation of his book, *The Body Politic,* obliged him to leave England and reside in Paris. This time he met Descartes and engaged him in metaphysical controversy. The exiled Prince of Wales, afterwards Charles II, was also in Paris. Hobbes became his tutor. He published again on the subject of politics, this time rousing the wrath of some of the Royalists. He returned to England and enjoyed such peace as obtained under Cromwell's regime, making friends with William Harvey, who discovered the circulation of the blood, with the poet Cowley, and others. Upon the restoration of Charles II to the English throne, Hobbes moved once more to a place in the sun and on the pension list. He was one of the most influential men of his day among persons who were open to ideas. He believed that matter is the ultimate reality; that our sense organs are transformers, not revealers; that man does not have a free will; that all human action is motivated by complete selfishness; that an absolute sovereign is needed, whether in the form of a monarch or a parliament, to insure peace under law; and that religion is a "pill which it is better to swallow without chewing."

The Arguments of the Passages.   The following passages give a simple formulation of metaphysical materialism. From a statement of the essential point, that all is matter moving according to laws, the passages follow Hobbes through the principal turns of his belief. They present a development and, in some cases, a defense of the implications of the fundamental belief. It should be remembered that Hobbes is writing here as a philosopher, not as a scientist. In the strict sense of the word, he was not a scientist, either by temperament or training. He is, where it is relevant, restating or referring to the labors of Copernicus, Kepler, Galileo, Harvey, and the rest. But the point of his writings, in effect, is this: If what such men are finding out, is once accepted without reservation, then over all we are committed to these more comprehensive beliefs.

Think not, courteous reader, that the philosophy which I am going to set in order is that which makes philosophers' stones. It is the natural reason of man, busily flying up and down among the creatures, and bringing back a true report of their order, causes, and effects. Philosophy is therefore the child of the world and your own mind. Like the world, its father, as it was in the beginning, it is a thing confused. If you will be a philosopher in good earnest, let your reason move upon the deep of your own cogitations and experience; those things that lie in confusion must be set in order, distinguished, and stamped everyone with its own name.

Philosophy excludes theology, I mean the doctrine of God. It excludes the doctrine of angels and also such things as are neither bodies nor properties of bodies. It excludes history, natural as well as political, because such knowledge is but experience or authority and not reason. It excludes astrology and all such divinations. It excludes all such knowledge as is acquired by divine inspiration, or revelation, as not derived to us by reason but by some supernatural sense. Lastly it excludes the doctrine of God's worship as being not to be known by the light of natural reason but by the authority of the church.

I am not ignorant how hard a thing it is to weed out of men's minds inveterate opinions that have taken root there, and been confirmed by the authority of eloquent writers; especially since true philosophy rejects the paint and false colors, the ornaments and graces, of language. The first grounds of knowledge are not only not beautiful; they are poor and arid, and, in appearance, deformed. Nevertheless, there being some men who are delighted with truth and strength of reason, I thought I might do well to take these pains for the sake of even those few. I proceed therefore and take my beginning from the definition of philosophy.

With these preliminary observations, Hobbes closes in on his theme:

The subject of philosophy is every body [i.e., piece of matter] of which we can conceive any beginning, which we can compare with other bodies, or which is capable of composition and resolution; that is to say, every body of whose beginning or properties we can have any knowledge.

The definition of body may be this: <u>a body is that which, having no dependence upon our thought</u>, is coincident or coextended with some part of space.

The world—I mean the whole mass of things that are—is corporeal, that is to say, body; and that which is not body is no part of the universe. . . . The universe being the aggregate of all bodies, there is no real part thereof that is not also body.

The basic thesis once stated, Hobbes moves on to a series of implications, propositions that follow from the fundamental position. The first of these is that motion is the one thing that "really" takes place; all else is mere appearance, thrown off, so to speak, by matter in motion.

There can be no cause of motion except in a body contiguous and moved.

Mutation, that is, change, can be nothing but motion of the parts of that body which is changed. We say that that which appears to our senses is otherwise than it appeared formerly. Both appearances are effects produced in the sentient creature; and, if they be different, it is necessary that some part of the agent which was formerly at rest is now moved, and so the mutation consists in the motion; or some part which was formerly moved, is now otherwise moved, and so the mutation consists in this new motion; or which, being formerly moved, is now at rest, and so again mutation is motion.

A second corollary is rigid determinism, that is, the belief that everything happens of necessity, or inevitably.

Whatever effect is produced at any time, the same is produced by a necessary cause. For whatsoever is produced had an entire cause, had all those things which, being supposed, it cannot be understood but that the effect follows; that is, it had a necessary cause. In the same manner, whatsoever effects are hereafter to be produced, shall have a necessary cause, so that all the effects that have been or shall be produced have their necessity in things antecedent.

From this determinism it would follow that, given enough knowledge of the past and present one could predict all future events in the greatest detail. Hobbes is aware of this claim. It has been made, off and on, ever since his time. Better than a century later the French astronomer, LaPlace, wrote:

We ought to regard the present state of the universe as the effect of its antecedent state and as the cause of the state that is to follow. An intelligence, who for a given instant should be acquainted with all the forces by which nature is animated, and with the several positions of the beings composing it, if his intellect were vast enough to submit these data to analysis, would include in one and the same formula the movement of the largest bodies in the universe and those of the lightest atom. Nothing would be uncertain for him, the future as well as the past would be present to his eyes.

Before resuming the elaboration of his views, Hobbes pays lip-service to natural theology:

He that from any effect he seeth come to pass, should reason to the next and immediate cause thereof, and from thence to the cause of that cause, and plunge himself profoundly into the pursuit of causes, shall come at last to this, that there must be, as even the heathen philosophers confessed, one first mover, one first cause of things which is that which men mean by the name of God.

Having disposed of that, Hobbes turns to noting further implications of his materialism. All living organisms, it would follow, are just so many complicated machines:

Seeing that life is but a motion of limbs and organs, why may we not say that all automata (engines that move themselves by springs and wheels as doth a watch) have an artificial life? For what is the heart but a spring, and the nerves but so many strings, and the joints but so many wheels, giving motion to the whole body?

Materialism in metaphysics, he urges, implies sensationism in epistemology; implies, that is, that all knowledge originates in sensations.

The original of men's thoughts is sense, for there is no conception in a man's mind which hath not, totally or by parts, been begotten upon the organs of sense. The rest are derived from that original.

As I said before, whatsoever we conceive, hath been perceived first by sense, either all at once or by parts. A man can have no thought representing anything, not subject to sense.

Imagination is nothing but decaying sense. From whence it followeth that the longer the time is after the sense, the weaker is the imagination.

Imagination being only of those things which have been formerly perceived by sense, it followeth that imagination and memory are but one thing which for divers considerations hath diverse names.

Materialism. Determinism. Mechanism. Sensationism. And now the doctrine of representative perception, that is, the belief that sensations represent but do not reveal the real nature of the external world. Hobbes labors this point at great length.

The cause of sense is the external object which presseth the organ proper to each sense either immediately or mediately. This pressure, by the mediation of the nerves and other strings and membranes, continueth inward and causeth there a reaction or counter-pressure; which endeavor because outward, seemeth to be some matter without. This seeming is that which men call sense; and consisteth, as to the eye, in a light or colored figure; to the ear, in a sound; and so on. All which qualities, called sensible qualities, are, in the object that causeth them only so many several motions of the matter by which it presseth our organs diversely. Neither in us that are pressed, are they anything else but divers motions; for motion produceth nothing but motion. For if these sensible qualities (colors, sounds) were in the object which causeth them, they could not be severed from them as by mirrors and echoes they are.

The cause of perception consisteth in this: When the uttermost part of the organ is pressed, it no sooner yields but the next part within it is pressed also. In this manner the pressure or motion is propagated through all the parts of the organ to the innermost. Also, the pressure of the uttermost part proceedeth from the pressure of some more remote body, and so continually till we come to the object. Sense therefore is some internal motion in the sentient organism, generated by some internal motion of the parts of the object, and propagated through all the media to the innermost part of the organ.

I shall endeavor to make plain these points: that the object wherein color is inherent is not the object seen; that there is nothing without us, really, which we call image or color; that color is but the apparition unto us of the motion, agitation, or change which the object worketh in the brain or some internal substance of the head; that as in vision, so also in the other senses, the subject of their inherence is not the object but the sentient creature.

As a color is not inherent in the object, but an effect thereof upon us, caused by motion in the object, so neither is sound in the thing we hear, but in ourselves. The clapper hath no sound in it, but action, and maketh motion in the internal parts of the bell; so the bell hath motion, and not sound, that imparteth motion to the air; and the air hath motion, but no sound, which it imparteth by the ear and nerve unto the brain; and the brain hath motion, but not sound.

From hence it followeth that whatsoever qualities our senses make us think there be in the world, they be not there, but are seeming and apparitions only; the things that really are in the world without us are those motions by which these seemings are caused. And this is the great deception of sense.

Hobbes is stopped by a problem. If the sensation, say the red color of a cherry, is really so much motion of particles in the observer's head, how can we explain the fact that it appears out there in space, located where the cherry is? As Hobbes asks, "Why doth the sensation appear as something situated without the organ?" His answer is:

Why doth the sensation appear as something situated without the organ? It is thus: There is in the whole organ, by reason of its own internal natural action some reaction against the motion which is propagated from the object to the innermost part of the organ. In the organ there is an endeavor opposite to the endeavor which proceedeth from the object. That endeavor inwards is the last action in the act of sense. Then from the reaction, an idea hath its being, which by reason that the endeavor is now outward, doth always appear as something situated without the organ.

But though all sense be made by reaction, as I have said, it is not necessary that everything that reacteth should have sense. I know there have been philosophers, and those learned men, who have maintained that all bodies are endued with sense. Nor do I see how they can be refuted if the nature of sense be placed in reaction only.

The argument turns from the subjectivity of sensations to the question of desires. These too must be admitted to be merely so much matter in motion.

As that which is really within us, in sensation, is only motion caused by the action of external objects, so that which is really within us in appetite or desire is nothing but motion. But the appearance of that motion we call either pleasure or pain.

When appetites and aversions arise alternately concerning the same thing, so that sometimes we have an appetite to it and sometimes an aversion from it, then the whole sum of desires and aversions is what we call *deliberation*.

In deliberation, the last appetite or aversion, immediately adhering to the act or the omission thereof, is what we call *will*.

If this be the whole story of man's preferences and desires, Hobbes is in a position to make short shrift of any lofty moral idealism. This he proceeds to do:

Moral philosophy is nothing else but the science of what is good and evil in the conversation and society of mankind. Good and evil are names that signify our appetites and aversions; which in different tempers, customs, and doctrines of men, are different, and divers men differ not only in their judgment, on the sense of what is pleasant and unpleasant to the taste, smell, hearing, touch, and sight, but also what is comfortable or disagreeable to reason in the actions of common life. Nay the same man, in divers times differeth from himself and at one time praiseth, that is, calleth good what at another time he dispraiseth, that is, calleth evil.

Every man calleth that which pleaseth him, *good;* and that which displeaseth him, *evil.* Since every man differeth from another in constitution, they differ also from one another concerning the common distinction of good and evil. Nor is there any such thing as absolute goodness considered without relation.

Whatsoever is the object of any man's appetite or desire, that it is which he for his part calleth good; and the object of his hate and aversion, evil. For these words *good* and *evil* are ever used with relation to the person that useth them, there being nothing simply and absolutely so, nor any rule of good and evil to be taken from the nature of objects themselves; but from the man, where there is no commonwealth.

To the commitments thus far, Hobbes adds one more: a categorical denial of man's free will:

I conceive that nothing taketh beginning from itself, but from the action of some other immediate agent without itself. Therefore, when a man hath an appetite or will to something, to which before he had no appetite or will, the cause of his will is not the will itself but something else not in his own disposing.

Neither is the freedom of willing or not willing greater in man than in other living creatures. For where there is appetite, the entire cause thereof hath preceded, and, consequently, the appetite could not choose but follow; that is, hath of necessity followed. Therefore such a liberty as is free from necessity is not to be found in the will.

If by *freedom* we understand the power, not of willing but of doing what we will, then certainly that freedom is to be allowed to both men and animals.

The ordinary definition of a *free agent* is that he is one that when all things are present which are needful to produce an effect, can nevertheless not produce it. This implies a contradiction that is nonsense, being as much as to say the cause of anything may be sufficient and yet the effect shall not follow. There is no such thing as an "agent," which when all things requisite to action are present, can nevertheless forbear to produce it. Or, which is all one, there is no such thing as freedom from necessity.

The essentials of Hobbes's materialism are now before us. The position bristles with difficulties. With unerring instinct Hobbes places his finger upon the one point which, more than any other perhaps, will be disputed. I mean the denial of man's free will. The following passages show Hobbes attempting to defend his determinism against anticipated objections:

To deny necessity is to destroy the power and foreknowledge of God Almighty. For whatsoever God hath purposed to bring to pass by man, or foreseeth shall come to pass, a man might frustrate and make not come to pass if he have freedom from necessity. Then would God foreknow such things as never shall be, and decree such things as shall never come to pass.

Liberty and necessity are consistent: as in the water, that hath not only liberty but a necessity to descend by the channel. So likewise in the actions men voluntarily do; which because they proceed from their will are termed *voluntary*. And yet, because every act of man's will and every desire and inclination proceedeth from some cause, and that from some other cause, in a continual chain, it proceedeth from necessity. To him that could see the connection of those causes, the necessity of all men's voluntary actions would appear manifest.

The necessity of an action doth not make the laws that prohibit it unjust. Whatsoever necessary cause precede an action, yet if the action be forbidden, he that doth it willingly may justly be punished. For instance, suppose the law on pain of death prohibit stealing. Suppose there be a man who by the strength of temptation is necessitated to steal, and is thereupon put to death. Doth not this punishment deter others from theft? Is it not a cause that others steal not? Doth is not frame and make their wills to justice? To make the law is therefore to make a cause of justice, and so to necessitate justice. The intention of the law is not to grieve the delinquent for that which is past and not to be undone; but to make him and others just who might otherwise not be so. It respecteth not the evil act past, but the good to come. But you will say, how is it just to kill one man to amend another, if what were done were necessary? To this I answer: men are justly killed, not because their actions are not necessitated, but because their actions are noxious. We destroy, without being unjust, all that is noxious, both beasts and men.

Repentance is nothing but a glad returning into the right way, after the grief of being out of the way. Even though the cause that made a man go astray were necessary, there is no reason why he should not grieve. So likewise, even though the cause that made a man return into the right way were necessary, there remaineth still the cause of joy. So that I say the necessity of actions taketh away neither of those parts of repentance, neither grief for the error nor joy for the returning.

As for praise and dispraise, they depend not at all on the necessity of the action praised or dispraised. For what is it to praise, but to say a thing is good? Good for me, good for someone else, or good for the commonwealth. What is it to say an act is good, but to say it is as I wish it, or as another wish it, or according to the law of the commonwealth? Can no action please me, or another, or the commonwealth, that should happen of necessity? Doth not praise and dispraise, reward and punishment, make and conform the will to good and evil by example?

Materialism is always with us. It is as old as the records of Western philosophy, having received an elaborate presentation in the fifth century B.C. in the writings—which we now possess only as a few suggestive fragments—of the Greek materialist Democritus, and several centuries later, in the writings of the Roman materialist Lucretius. Our task is to grasp the meaning of materialism and its implications. To recapitulate: It is the belief that reality is moving particles of matter. Its adherents have usually felt committed to certain further claims, as, for example, all events are rigidly predictable; all organisms are only mechanisms; all knowledge, originating in sensations, is knowledge of appearances only, since sensations are entirely subjective; human conduct is strictly determined by antecedent and concomitant events; human motives are essentially egocentric; and the achievement of happiness, in the sense of the satisfaction of desire, is the only finally good thing. These assorted doctrines are not, of course, as logically interdependent as the materialist would have us believe. But they are temperamentally interdependent. They give expression to a mood or a temperament or a frame of mind which is sufficiently widespread to demand a courteous hearing.

Note on Sources. The Hobbes material in this section is quoted, abridged, or paraphrased from the relevant chapters in his *The Elements of Philosophy,* his *Human Nature,* his *Of Liberty and Necessity,* and his *Leviathan.* The Molesworth Edition of Hobbes's English Works was used for these texts.

Reading References. A good small book on Hobbes is by Sir Leslie Stephen. It is in the series *English Men of Letters.* The literature on materialism itself is very large. One can only suggest a few things. A good beginning may be made in T. H. Huxley's volume mentioned already under Descartes, *Method and Results.* The third and fifth essays deal with phases of materialism. Hugh Elliott's *Modern Science and Materialism* is a competent and aggressive presentation of the case. Elliott has the virtue of *caring* whether his reader believes in materialism or does not. Santayana remarked of himself that he was perhaps the sole surviving materialist. The volume *Reason in Science,* in his five-volume treatise *The Life of Reason,* provides a statement of his materialism. It is also to be found in his later book *The Realm of Matter.*

READING QUESTIONS

1. He begins by excluding from philosophy (a) theology, (b) angelology, (c) history, (d) astrology, (e) things known by inspiration or revelation, (f) doctrines of worship. On what principle?
2. Philosophy, then, appeals only to what and talks only about what?
3. He proposes a reductive analysis—"A is nothing but B"—of many things. Change is nothing but what? Organisms are nothing but what? Knowledge is nothing but what? Imagination is nothing but what? Sensation is nothing but what? Will is nothing but what? Good and evil are nothing but what?
4. Why he is led to propose these and similar reductions.
5. Why determinism is a corollary of materialism.
6. "And this is the great deception of sense." What is? What theory leads Hobbes to the conclusion that sense perception is sense deception?
7. Are sense organs best thought of as transformers or revealers?
8. How Hobbes would correlate the distinction between primary and secondary qualities with the distinction between objective and subjective.
9. If you say that sense qualities are secondary and subjective, and that knowledge originates in sense experience, what problem have you set yourself in regard to "matter"?
10. He asks why a sensation—say, color or sound—appears as something situated outside the sense organ. (a) Why this is a problem for him. (b) His explanation.
11. Hobbes's reasons for denying man's free will.
12. How he seeks to get theology on his side in this denial of man's free will.
13. The definition of *liberty* that enables him to say "liberty and necessity are consistent"; and to use the analogy of water in the channel.
14. Why, in connection with his denial of man's free will, Hobbes deals with (a) punishment, (b) repentance, (c) praise and dispraise. How he handles each of these points.

15. If you punish a person for wrongdoing, do you, according to Hobbes, presuppose that the person could have done otherwise?
16. Wherein you find Hobbes (a) most, (b) least convincing.
17. How you would account for the persistence and popularity of materialism?

INDEPENDENT STUDY

1. Read the article on Hobbes by R. S. Peters and on materialism by K. Campbell, both in the *Encyclopedia of Philosophy*. Peters's article can be supplemented by his paperback book *Hobbes* (1956, England). Work out a paper on "Materialism and Hobbes."
2. An educationally valuable project, *Ancient Materialism and Lucretius*, can be worked out on Lucretius's long philosophical poem *On the Nature of Things*. It contains an exposition and defense of materialism.
3. Read *Hobbes*, in the series English Men of Letters, by L. Stephen. Work out a paper on the "General Philosophy of Thomas Hobbes."
4. Refer to the *Contemporary Materialism* part of the bibliography at the end of the Campbell article mentioned in item 1 above. Consult the items listed, until you are in a position to write on "Materialism Since World War II."
5. Familiarize yourself with the movement in the 1960's usually referred to as the identity theory, and associated with the writings of Place, Smart, Armstrong, and others. Give an account of that position. Make clear that it is a "mopping up" phase of recent and contemporary materialism.

SECTION 2. GEORGE BERKELEY: TO BE IS TO BE PERCEIVED BY A PERCEIVER

From Hobbes to Berkeley. It was to be expected that Hobbes's tough-minded materialism would provoke protest and criticism. Throughout the seventeenth and eighteenth centuries, it is not too much to say, materialism was the "specter" that haunted Western metaphysics. Some resorted to the simple expedient of ignoring such views. Some reviled the personal characters of those who held them. Some attacked the premises and disputed the validity of the conclusions that comprised the materialist's position. Among these, in the eighteenth century, was George Berkeley, the founder of modern idealism and one of the shrewdest metaphysicians of modern times.

Biographical Note.   George Berkeley was born in Ireland in 1685, and died in 1753 at the age of sixty-eight. He was educated at the Trinity College, Dublin, where while yet an undergraduate, he conceived the necessity of "refuting atheists and materialists." At the age of twenty-five he published *A Treatise Concerning the Principles of Human Knowledge,* and three years later his *Three Dialogues Between Hylas and Philonous.* These two small volumes, by the youngest and brightest philosophical mind of his generation, contain the statement and defense of his case against materialism and his case for idealism. For a while he was laughed at, as readers of Boswell's *Johnson* will remember. But the scattered ranks of those who had been troubled by the fashionable materialism launched by Hobbes and others in the preceding century soon closed in his support. Shortly after publication, Berkeley visited England and was received into the circle of Addison, Pope, and Steele. He traveled on the continent in various capacities, and on his return was appointed lecturer in divinity and Greek in Trinity College, Dublin. He received a D.D. and was made an ecclesiastical dean. He was promised aid to found a college in Bermuda for training clergymen for the colonies and missionaries for the Indians. He was made, finally, Bishop of Cloyne. He died at Oxford, beloved and respected, if not clearly understood, by all who knew him.

The Argument of the Passages.   Berkeley desires to establish the proposition that reality is spiritual, that a man's mind provides him with a better example of the constituent "stuff" of things than is provided by a lump of matter. This is his idealism. The first step is a critique of materialism. This Berkeley proceeds to construct. He starts from premises the materialists themselves admit (any others would be irrelevant) and seeks to show that their conclusions either (1) are incompatible with these premises, or (2) do not follow from these premises. He then approaches materialism from another angle, seeking this time to explain how materialists have come to hold their "misguided" conclusions. Methodologically this procedure is usable. A communist might apply it to capitalism as the first step in a general statement of the case for communism. A free trader might apply it to protectionism as the first step in a general statement of the case for free trade. A liberal might apply it to conservatism as the first step in a general statement of the case for liberalism. The same remarks are applicable to capitalists, protectionists, and conservatives.

The case against materialism stated, Berkeley moves on to the case for idealism. He formulates a few premises that anyone, he thinks, will admit. From these he seeks to deduce his idealism. He turns then to consider possible objections that might be urged against it before they are made.

The case against materialism stated, the case for idealism stated, the possible objections anticipated, he closes in on what, after all, he considers to be the most important part of the whole business, namely, an elucidation of the implications of his metaphysical idealism, an enumeration of the propositions that are also true if his idealism is true.

The total argument begins as follows:

It is plain that the notion of what is called *matter* or *corporeal substance* involves a contradiction,[1] so much so that I should not think it necessary to spend time exposing its absurdity. But belief in the existence of matter seems to have taken so deep a root in the minds of philosophers, and draws after it so many ill consequences, that I choose rather to be thought prolix and tedious than to omit anything that might conduce to the discovery and extirpation of that prejudice.

The following distinction between primary and secondary qualities and the claim that primary qualities are alone real, whereas secondary qualities are merely subjective, were familiar notions in Berkeley's day.

Some there are who make a distinction between primary and secondary qualities. By *primary qualities* they mean extension, figure, motion, rest, solidity, and number. By *secondary qualities* they mean sensible qualities, as colors, sounds, tastes, and so forth.

Our ideas of secondary qualities they acknowledge not to be the resemblances of anything existing without the mind or unperceived. But they will have our ideas of the primary qualities to be patterns or images of things which exist without the mind in an unthinking substance which they call *matter.* By *matter,* therefore, we are to understand an inert, senseless substance in which extension, figure, and motion do actually exist.

Colors, sounds, heat, cold, and such like secondary qualities, they tell us, are sensations existing in the mind alone, depending on and occasioned by the different size, texture and motion of the minute particles of matter. This they take for an undoubted truth, which they can demonstrate beyond all exception.

By *materialism,* then, Berkeley proposes to mean the belief in an inert, senseless substance possessing primary qualities in its own right but not possessing secondary qualities in the same intimate fashion. His first criticism of this belief is as follows:

But can anyone conceive the extension and motion of a body without any of its secondary qualities? It is not in my power to frame an idea of a body

---

[1] The "contradiction" would seem to be in saying that all knowledge is from sense-data, and at the same time admitting that matter is not a sense-datum. How then do we know it?

extended and moving but I must withal give it some color or other secondary quality which is acknowledged to exist only in the mind. In short, primary qualities abstracted from secondary qualities are inconceivable. Where therefore the secondary qualities are, to wit, in the mind and nowhere else, there must the primary qualities be also.

His second criticism is this:

Great and small, swift and slow, degrees of extension and motion, are allowed to exist only in the mind, being entirely relative, and changing as the frame or position of the sense organs varies. The extension therefore that exists independently of the mind is neither great nor small; the action, neither swift nor slow. That is, they are nothing at all.

His third criticism is this:

Number is entirely a creature of the mind. Even though the other primary qualities be allowed to exist without, it will be evident that the same thing bears a different denomination of number as the mind views it with different respects. Thus the same extension is one, or three, or thirty-six, according as the mind considers it with reference to a yard, a foot, or an inch. Number is so visibly relative and dependent on men's understanding that it is strange anyone should give it an absolute existence without the mind.

His fourth criticism is this:

One argument whereby modern philosophers would prove that secondary qualities do not exist in matter but in our minds may be turned likewise against primary qualities. Thus, it is said that heat and cold are affections only of the mind and not at all qualities of real things; for the same body which appears cold to one hand seems warm to another. Thus, too, it is proved that sweetness is not really in the sapid thing; because, the thing remaining unaltered, the sweetness is changed to bitterness, as in the case of a fever or otherwise vitiated palate.

Now, why may we not as well argue that figure and extension are not real qualities existing in matter? To the same eye at different stations, or to eyes of a different texture at the same station, they appear various. By parity of reasoning, therefore, they cannot be ideas of anything settled and determinate without the mind.

In short, those arguments which are thought to prove that secondary qualities (colors, tastes, etc.) exist only in the mind, may with equal force be brought to prove the same thing of primary qualities (extension, figure, motion, etc.).

His fifth criticism is this:

Suppose it were possible that material substances possessing only primary qualities do exist independent of the mind. Yet how is it possible for us to know this? Either we know it by our senses or by our reason. As for our senses, by them we have knowledge only of our sensations: but they do not inform us that things exist independent of the mind, or unperceived by the mind, like to those which are perceived. This the materialists themselves acknowledge; nay, insist.

It remains, therefore, that, if we have any knowledge at all of material substances, it must be by our reason inferring their existence from what is immediately perceived by sense. But I do not see what reason can induce us to believe in the existence of bodies independent of the mind, from what we perceive, since the very patrons of matter themselves do not pretend there is any necessary connection betwixt them and our ideas.

His sixth criticism is this:

It may be thought easier to explain the production of our sensations by supposing external bodies, rather than otherwise; and so it might be at least probable that there are such things as bodies that excite ideas in our minds. But neither can this be said. For, though we give the materialists their "external bodies," they by their own confession are no nearer knowing how our ideas are produced, since they own themselves unable to comprehend in what manner body can act upon spirit (or mind) or how it could imprint any idea in the mind.

Hence it is evident that the production of ideas or sensations in our minds can be no reason why we should suppose matter or corporeal substances; since their production is acknowledged to remain equally inexplicable with or without this particular supposition. If therefore it were possible for bodies to exist without the mind, yet to hold that they do so must needs be a very precarious opinion. In short, if there were external bodies, it is impossible we should come to know it; and if there were not, we might have the very same reasons to think there were that we have now. Which consideration were enough to make any reasonable person suspect the strength of whatever arguments he may think himself to have, for the existence of external bodies independent of the mind.

His conclusion is this:

It is on this, therefore, that I insist, to wit, that the absolute existence of unthinking things are words without a meaning, or which include a contradiction. This is what I repeat and inculcate, and earnestly recommend to the attentive thoughts of the reader.

He turns now to an exploration of the reasons that may have led men "to suppose the existence of material substance":

It is worth while to reflect on the motives which induced men to suppose the existence of material substance; so that having observed the gradual ceasing and expiration of those motives, we may withdraw the assent that was grounded on them.

First it was thought that the sensible qualities did really exist without the mind. And for this reason it seemed needful to suppose that some unthinking substratum or substance wherein they did exist, since they could not be conceived to exist by themselves.

Then, in time, men being convinced that secondary qualities had no existence without the mind, they stripped this substratum or material substance of those qualities, leaving only the primary ones, which they still conceive to exist without the mind and consequently to stand in need of a material support.

But now, it having been shown that none even of these can possibly exist otherwise than in a spirit or mind which perceives them, it follows that we have no longer any reason to suppose the being of "matter," nay, that it is utterly impossible that there should be any such thing so long as that word is taken to mean an unthinking substratum or substance for qualities wherein they exist without mind. It is an extraordinary instance of the force of prejudice that the mind of man retains so great a fondness, against all the evidence of reason, for a stupid, thoughtless Somewhat as a support of the qualities we perceive.

Thus Berkeley on materialism. One is moved to ponder its effect upon Thomas Hobbes. A smile perhaps, a sharpening of his controversial quill as he prepared to do battle with this newcomer. For Berkeley, having "dethroned" matter, sets about to "enthrone" spirit. His first step is to secure one or two propositions that "any rational man" would admit.

It is evident to anyone who takes a survey of the objects of human knowledge, that they are either ideas imprinted on the senses; or such as are perceived by attending to the passions and operations of the mind; or lastly, ideas formed by help of memory and imagination—compounding, dividing, or merely representing those originally perceived in the aforesaid ways.

As several such ideas are observed to accompany each other, they come to be marked by one name, and so reputed as one thing. Thus a certain color, taste, smell, figure, and consistence having been observed to go together, are accounted one distinct thing, signified by the name *apple*. Other collections of ideas constitute a stone, a tree, a book, and the like.

Besides the ideas or objects of knowledge, there is something which knows or perceives them, and exercises divers operations as willing, imagining, remembering, about them. This perceiving active being I call "mind," "spirit," "soul," or "myself."

The existence of an idea consists in its being perceived. Its *esse* is *percipi*. The table I write on I say "exists"; that is, I see and feel it; and if I were out of my study, I should say it "existed"; meaning that if I was in my study, I might perceive it, or that some other spirit actually does perceive it. There was an odor, that is, it was smelt; there was a sound, that is, it was heard; there was a color or figure, that is, it was perceived by sight or touch. That is all I can understand by these and like expressions. Their *esse* is *percipi*. Nor is it possible they should have any existence out of the minds which perceive them.

All our ideas and sensations are visibly inactive. There is nothing of power or agency included in them. One idea or sensation cannot produce or alter another. The very being of an idea implies passiveness and inertness in it; insomuch that it is impossible for an idea to do anything, or be the cause of anything.

We perceive a continual succession of ideas. Some are excited anew, others are changed or totally disappear. There is therefore some cause of these ideas, whereon they depend, and which produces and changes them.

Having premised the preceding facts, Berkeley proceeds to argue from them:

It is clear, from what hath been said, that this cause cannot itself be any idea or sensation since all such are passive and inert. It must therefore be a substance. But it has been shown that there is no corporeal or material substance. It remains therefore that the cause of our ideas and sensations is an incorporeal active substance, or spirit.

I find I can excite some of my ideas in my mind at pleasure, and vary and shift the scene as oft as I think fit. This making and unmaking of ideas doth very properly denominate the mind active. Thus much is certain and grounded on experience. But when we talk, as do materialists, of unthinking substances producing ideas, we only amuse ourselves with words.

But whatever power I have over some of my ideas, I find that others have not a like dependence on my will. When, for example, I open my eyes in broad daylight, it is not in my power to choose whether I shall see or no, nor to determine what I shall see. It is likewise as to hearing and the other senses. The ideas imprinted on them are not creatures of my will. There is, therefore, some other will or mind or spirit that produces them.

These ideas which I cannot control, these ideas of sense, are more strong, more lively, more distinct than those which I can control. They have, likewise, a steadiness, order, and coherence which belong not to those that are the effects of my will. They speak themselves the products of a Mind more powerful and wise than human minds.

Some truths there are so near and obvious to the human mind that a man need only open his eyes to see them. Such I take this important one to be, namely, that all the choir of heaven and furniture of the earth, in a word, all those bodies which compose the mighty frame of the world, have not any subsistence without a mind; that their being is to be perceived or known; that, consequently, so long as they are not actually perceived by me, or do not exist in my mind or the mind of any other created spirit, they must either have no existence at all or else subsist in the mind of some Eternal Spirit. For it is unintelligible to attribute to any single part of them an existence independent of (perception by a) Spirit.

Until his premises are effectively questioned, or his reasoning from these premises shown to be fallacious, Berkeley may now survey his work with satisfaction. Are there any loopholes? The passages that follow show Berkeley at work on this question.

Before we proceed any farther, it is necessary that we spend some time in answering objections which may probably be made against the principles we have hitherto laid down. In this, if I seem too prolix, I desire I may be excused, since all men do not equally apprehend things of this nature; and I am willing to be understood by every man.

It might be objected:

By the foregoing principles all that is real and substantial in nature is banished out of the world. All things that exist, it will be said, exist only in the mind, that is, are purely notional. What therefore becomes of the sun, moon, and stars? What must we think of houses, rivers, mountains, trees, stones, nay even of our own bodies? Are all these but so many chimeras and illusions?

To this objection he has an answer:

We are not deprived of any one thing in nature. Whatever we see, hear, feel, or any wise conceive or understand remains as secure as ever, and is as real as ever. I do not argue against the existence of any one thing that we can apprehend either by sense or reflection. That the things I see with my eyes and touch with my hands do really exist, I make not the least question. The only thing whose existence I deny is that which philosophers call *matter*. There are minds which will or excite ideas in themselves at pleasure. Other ideas, which they do not so excite, speak themselves the effects of a mind more powerful and wise than human spirits. These latter are said to be more real than the former. In this sense the sun I see is the real sun. In this sense, everything in the world is as much a real being by our principles as by any other. If the word *substance* be taken for a combination of sensible qualities, we cannot be accused of denying its existence.

It sounds harsh to say we eat and drink ideas, and are clothed with ideas. But, in common discourse, the word *idea* is not used to signify the several combinations of sensible qualities which are called *things*. But this concerns not the truth of the proposition, which says no more than that we are fed and clothed with those things which we perceive immediately by our senses. The sensory qualities which, combined, constitute the several sorts of victuals and apparel, have been shown to exist only in the mind that perceives them. This is all that is meant by calling them *ideas*. If you agree that we eat and drink and are clad with the immediate object of sense, which cannot exist unperceived, I shall readily grant that it is more conformable to custom that they should be called *things* rather than *ideas*.

"I will still believe my senses and will never suffer any argument, how plausible soever, to prevail over the certainty of them." Be it so. Assert the evidence of your senses. We are willing to do the same. That what I see, hear, feel, etc., doth exist, I no more doubt of than I do of my own being. But, *I do not see how the testimony of sense can be alleged as a proof for the existence of anything which is not perceived by the senses.* We are not for having any man turn skeptic and doubt his senses.

Again, it might be objected:

From these principles it follows that things are every moment annihilated and created anew. The objects of sense exist only when they are
perceived. The trees are in the garden, the chairs in the parlor, only while
there is someone there to perceive them. Upon shutting my eyes it is all
reduced to nothing, and upon opening them it is again created.

His answer:

It is thought absurd that, upon closing my eyelids, all the visible objects
around me should be reduced to nothing. Yet, is not this what my very critics
and opponents commonly acknowledge when they agree on all hands that
light and color, which are the immediate objects of sight, are mere sensations, mere "subjective states" which exist no longer than they are perceived?
Indeed we hold the objects of sense to be nothing else but ideas which
cannot exist unperceived. Yet we may not hence conclude that they have no
existence except only when they are perceived by us; there may be some
other spirit that perceives them though we do not. It would not follow,
hence, that bodies are annihilated and created every moment, or exist not at
all during the intervals between our perception of them.

It might be objected:

If primary qualities exist only in the mind, it follows that mind is extended, since extension is a primary quality of things.

The answer:

It no more follows that the mind is extended because extension is in it
alone, than that it is red or blue because those qualities exist in it alone and
nowhere else. Yet my opponents admit that secondary qualities exist in the
mind alone; i.e., are "subjective."

It might be objected:

There have been a great many things explained by matter and motion.
Take these away and you destroy the whole atomic theory, and undermine
those principles of mechanics which have been applied with so much success to account for things. In short, whatever advances have been made in
the study of nature, do all proceed on the supposition that "matter" doth
exist.

To which Berkeley replies:

To "explain" things is all one as to show why, upon such and such occasions, we are affected with such and such ideas. But, how "matter"

operates on mind, or produces any idea in it, is what no philosopher will pretend to explain. Of what use is it, therefore? Besides, things are accounted for by figure, motion and other qualities; not by "matter." Such qualities are no more than ideas, and therefore cannot be the cause of anything, since ideas cannot be the cause of anything.

It might be objected:

Does it not seem absurd to take away "natural causes" and ascribe everything to the operation of spirit? To say, not that fire heats or water cools, but that a spirit heats or a spirit cools, etc. Would not a man be deservedly laughed at who should talk after this manner?

To which Berkeley rejoins:

In such things we ought to think with the learned and speak with the vulgar. Those who are convinced of the truth of Copernican astronomy do nevertheless say "the sun rises," and "the sun sets." Yet it doth not. But if such persons affected a contrary style in common talk, it would appear ridiculous. It is the same with our tenets.

It might be objected:

Is not the universal assent of mankind an invincible argument on behalf of matter? Must we suppose the whole world to be mistaken? If so, what cause can be assigned of so widespread and predominant an error?

To which Berkeley responds:

It will perhaps not be found that so many do really believe in the existence of "matter." Strictly, to believe that which involves a contradiction, or has no meaning, is impossible. I admit men act as if the cause of their sensations were some senseless, unthinking being. But, that they clearly apprehend any meaning thereby, that they have formed a settled speculative opinion, is what I am not able to conceive.

Adding, too:

Even though we should grant a notion to be universally and steadfastly held to, yet that is but a weak argument for its truth. A vast number of prejudices and false opinions are everywhere embraced by the unreflecting part of mankind. There was a time when the antipodes and the motion of the earth were looked upon as monstrous absurdities even by men of learning.

It is demanded that we assign a cause of this prejudice that matter exists and is the cause of our sensations. I answer: Men, knowing they perceived several ideas whereof they themselves were not the author, nor depending on their wills, first maintained that those ideas had an existence independent of and external to the mind. But, seeing that the immediate objects of perception do not exist except they are being perceived, they then argued that there are objects, distinct from the colors, etc. immediately perceived by the mind, of which those latter are images or resemblances or effects imprinted on us by those objects. So the notion of an imperceived and unthinking "matter" owes its origin to the consciousness that we are not the authors of our sensations, which must therefore have some cause distinct from our minds upon which they are imprinted.

It might be objected:

You say: Though the ideas themselves do not exist without the mind, yet there may be things like them whereof they are copies or resemblances, which exist without the mind in an unthinking substance.

To which Berkeley counters:

It is indeed an opinion strangely prevailing among men that houses, mountains, rivers, in a word, all sensible objects, have an existence distinct from their being perceived by the understanding. But this principle involves a manifest contradiction. For what are the aforementioned objects but the things we perceive by sense? And what do we perceive besides our own ideas or sensations? Could any of these exist unperceived? There was an odor, that is, it was smelt; there was a sound, that is, it was heard; there was a color or figure, that is, it was perceived by sight or touch. That is all I can understand by these and like expressions. Their *esse* is *percipi*. Nor is it possible they should have any existence out of the minds which perceive them.

An idea can be like nothing but an idea; a color can be like nothing but a color. It is impossible for us to conceive a likeness except only between our ideas.

I ask whether the supposed originals or external things, of which our ideas are pictures or representations, be themselves perceivable or no? If they are, then they are ideas, and we have gained our point. If they are not, I appeal to anyone whether it be sense to say a color is like something which is invisible; to say hard or soft is like something intangible; and so of the rest.

It might be objected:

Let us admit that the notion of "matter" as the cause or support of the perceived qualities of things, is not needed. Yet there may perhaps be some inert, unperceiving substance, as incomprehensible to us as colors to a man born blind; supporting, it may be, qualities of which we know nothing because we have no senses adapted to them, but which, if we had other senses we should know of.

To which Berkeley replies:

If by *matter* you mean the unknown (and unknowable) cause or support of unknown (and unknowable) qualities, I see no point in affirming or denying its existence. I see no advantage in disputing about something we know not what and we know not why.

And adds:

If we had those other senses, they could only furnish us with new ideas or sensations. In which case we should have the same reason against their existing in an unperceiving substance that has been already offered with relation to such qualities as we do perceive: they would exist only in a mind perceiving them. This is true not only of ideas we are acquainted with at present but likewise of all possible ideas whatsoever.

The case is by now almost completed. He has stated and refuted materialism. He has stated and established idealism. He has anticipated and parried every objection that he can imagine. He proceeds to draw some conclusions.

Having posed and met possible objections, we proceed to take a view of our principles with regard to their consequences. After what hath been premised, I think we may lay down the following conclusions.

First: It is plain that men amuse themselves in vain when they inquire for any natural cause distinct from a mind or spirit.

Second: Since the whole creation is the workmanship of a wise and good Agent, it should seem to be in order to employ our thoughts about the final causes, or purposes of things. This not only discovers to us the attributes of the Creator and Sustainer, but may also direct us to the proper uses and applications of things.

Third: The natural immortality of the soul is a necessary consequence of these principles. To assert natural immortality is not to assert that it is incapable of annihilation by the Creator who first gave it being but only that it is not liable to be broken or dissolved by the laws of nature or motion. Bodies are ideas in the mind or soul. The latter is indivisible, incorporeal, unextended, and consequently indissoluble. Changes, decays, dissolutions, which we see in bodies cannot affect a spirit which hath none of their properties. Such a being, a mind or soul or active spirit, is therefore indissoluble by the forces of nature.

Fourth: From what hath been said, it is plain that we cannot know the existence of other minds or spirits otherwise than by their operations or the ideas excited by them in us. I perceive combinations of ideas, and changes thereof, that inform me that there are agents like myself which accompany them and concur in their production. But the knowledge I have of these other spirits or mind is hence indirect; not as is the knowledge of my ideas, but depending on the intervention of ideas by me referred to minds as spirits distinct from myself.

Fifth: Though there be some things (i.e., combinations of sensations) which convince us that human agents are concerned in producing them, yet it is evident that nature, that is, the far greater part of the ideas or sensations perceived by us, is not produced by or dependent on the wills of men. There is therefore some other Spirit that causeth them. But if we consider the regularity, order, and concatenation of natural things, the surprising magnificence, beauty, and perfection of the larger, and the exquisite contrivance of the smaller parts of creation, we shall clearly perceive that the attributes One, Eternal, Infinitely Wise, Good, and Perfect, belong all of them to the aforesaid Spirit, who "works in all" and "by whom all things consist."

Hence it is evident that God is known as certainly and immediately as any other mind or spirit, distinct from ourselves. We may even assert that the existence of God is more evident than the existence of men; because the effects of nature are more numerous and considerable than those ascribed to men. There is not any one mark which denotes a man, or effect produced by him, that does not more strongly evince the being of that Spirit which is the author of nature. A human spirit is not perceived by sense: when we perceive the color, size, etc. of a man, we perceive only sensations or ideas excited in our own minds. These being exhibited to our view in sundry distinct collections, serve to mark out unto us the existence of finite spirits like ourselves. And after the same manner we see God. All the difference is that whereas some one finite and narrow assemblage of ideas denotes a particular human mind, on the other hand wherever we direct our view we perceive manifest tokens of the Divinity, "in whom we live and move and have our being."

It will be objected here that monsters, untimely births, fruits blasted in the blossom, rains falling in desert places, waste, miseries incident to human life, and so on, are evidence that the whole frame of nature is not actuated and superintended by a Spirit of infinite wisdom and goodness. If, that is to say, God is the author of all things, is He not the author of evil and undesirable things? Is this coherent with His infinite wisdom and goodness?

I answer: The very blemishes and defects of nature are not without their use. They make an agreeable variety and augment the beauty of the rest of creation, as shadows in a picture serve to set off the brighter parts.

I add: We do well, before we tax the author of nature with wastefulness, to examine whether such accusation be not the effect of prejudice contracted by our familiarity with impotent and saving mortals. In man, thriftiness with what he cannot easily secure may be wisdom. But, an Omnipotent Spirit can produce everything by a mere fiat. Hence nature's splendid profusion should not be interpreted as wastefulness in the author of nature. Rather is it an evidence of the riches of His power.

I add: As for the pain which is in the world, pursuant to the general laws of nature and the actions of finite imperfect Spirits, this is indispensably necessary to our well-being. We consider some one particular pain and account it an evil. But our view is too narrow. If we enlarge our view, so as to comprehend the various ends, connections, and dependencies of things, we shall be forced to acknowledge that those particular things which, considered in themselves, appear to be evil, have the nature of good when considered in connection with the whole system of beings.

From what hath been said, it will be manifest that it is merely for want of attention and comprehensiveness of mind that there are any atheists or Manichaeans. Little and unreflecting souls may indeed burlesque the works of Providence, the beauty and order whereof they have not the capacity or will not be at the pains to comprehend. But those who are masters of any justness and extent of thought can never sufficiently admire the tracs of wisdom and goodness that shine through the economy of nature.

Since it is downright impossible that a soul pierced and illumined with a thorough sense of the omnipresence, holiness, and justice of that Spirit, should persist in a remorseless violation of His laws, we ought therefore earnestly to meditate on those important matters, that so we may attain conviction without scruple.

For, after all, what deserves the first place in our studies, is the consideration of God and duty; which to promote, was the main drift and design of my labors.

What is to be said of this flight of the metaphysical imagination? A generation later it caught the attention of David Hume. He observed, somewhat tartly, "The speculations of the ingenious Dr. Berkeley—they admit of no refutation, but they produce no conviction," and proceeded to deal with idealism as Berkeley had dealt with materialism, rejecting spiritual substance as Berkeley had rejected material substance. But of that, more later. Meanwhile, one does well to know the argument. It has long served as a kind of rallying point for the like-minded in each generation. He provided an apparently coherent case against the "specter" of materialism. He gave articulation to that perennial temperament that dreads and despises and mistrusts the "appeal to matter." For his premises, others have been substituted. To his conclusions, especially his repudiation of materialism, little of importance or variety has been added.

Note on Sources. The Berkeley material in this section has been quoted, abridged, or paraphrased from his small book *A Treatise Concerning the Principles of Human Knowledge*, Part I. This book, usually referred to as the *Principles*, consists of 156 numbered paragraphs. The order of my quotations, and so on, does not follow the order in Berkeley's book.

Reading References A great number of books and chapters have been written about and against the philosophical position taken up by Berkeley. Mention might be made of four items. The first is a book by T. H. Huxley, *Hume, with Helps to the Study of Berkeley.* The "helps" part of this book is interesting and illuminating, inasmuch as Huxley is ordinarily credited with views that fall short of Berkeley's religiously motivated idealism. The second is a book by John Wild, *George Berkeley, a Study of His Life and Philosophy.* This is a careful and elaborate exposition of Berkeley. The third is the chapter on Berkeley in Mary Whiton Calkins's book *The Persistent Problems of Philosophy.* The fourth is G. E. Moore's well-known essay "The Refutation of Idealism," contained in his book *Philosophical Studies.*

READING QUESTIONS

1. Enumerate the four large steps in Berkeley's argument. Show how that four-step pattern could be used by (a) a socialist, (b) a hedonist, (c) an evolutionist, (d) a fundamentalist, (e) a determinist, (f) an atheist.
2. He begins by reminding his reader of the distinction between primary qualities, which are objective, and secondary qualities, which are subjective. Would a materialist admit this distinction?
3. What sound principle of criticism is illustrated by Berkeley's use of claims admitted by the materialist?
4. State the materialist thesis that Berkeley proposes to criticize.
5. His first claim is that the primary qualities, extension and motion, are intellectual abstractions. What use does he make of that?
6. His second claim is about *degrees* of those primary qualities. State it. Use to which he puts said claim.
7. His third claim is about number. State it. Use to which he puts said claim.
8. His fourth claim is that an argument used to prove that secondary qualities are subjective may be turned against primary qualities. Show.
9. His fifth claim is that even if the materialists' "matter" does exist, we could not know it. Show.
10. It might be at least probable that the materialists' matter exists. Why so? Berkeley's rejoinder.
11. Why it is worthwhile to reflect on the motives that induced men to suppose the existence of material substance. What those motives were.
12. Which of Berkeley's criticisms of materialism you find (a) most, (b) least convincing.
13. We have ideas. Their *"esse est percipi."* What that means. Would a materialist admit it? How Berkeley uses the claim as a step in his argument for idealism.
14. "We have ideas. Their *esse est percipi*. They must have some cause." You take it from there.
15. Why Berkeley's idealism should not be called solipsism.
16. He formulates a number of objections that he thinks will be offered. State each briefly. Which objections strike you as the most telling?
17. Show how he handles each objection.
18. Which objection, or objections, he handles (a) most effectively, (b) least effectively.

542 an introduction to modern philosophy

19. Having criticized materialism, argued for idealism, met objections to idealism, he concludes by drawing five consequences. State each.
20. Why he becomes involved in the problem of evil. How he seeks to dispose of it.
21. Wherein you find Berkeley (a) most, (b) least convincing.

INDEPENDENT STUDY

1. Read the article on Berkeley by H. B. Acton in the *Encyclopedia of Philosophy*. Read as much as you need in Volume II, *The Works of George Berkeley*, edited by A. A. Luce and T. E. Jessup, in order to work out a paper.
2. Read Sections 27 and 135, 136, 137, 138, 139, 140, 141, 142, 143, 144, 145 in Berkeley's *Principles of Human Knowledge*. Those sections will cue you in on a controversy centering on Berkeley's notion of the "I" in "I perceive," "I think," "i will." Study the relevant parts of *Berkeley's Immaterialism*, a commentary on Berkeley's *Principles* by A. A. Luce. Move on to the paperback *New Studies in Berkeley's Philosophy*, edited by W. E. Steinkraus. Read selectively with reference to Berkeley's position on the perceiver in such an expression as "To be is to be perceived *by a perceiver*."
3. Read J. O. Wisdom's book *The Unconscious Origin of Berkeley's Philosophy*. The book is number 47 in the International Psychoanalytical Library edited by E. Jones. If you know enough psychoanalytical theory, do a paper on Wisdom's psychoanalysis of Berkeley.
4. Read G. E. Moore's celebrated essay on Berkeley's idealism: "The Refutation of Idealism." Make sure you know Berkeley's position, and that you follow clearly Moore's critique. Has Moore finished off Berkeley?

SECTION 3. ARTHUR SCHOPENHAUER: THE WORLD AS WILL

From Berkeley to Schopenhauer. It is sometimes argued that metaphysics is a question of temperament. There is a half truth in the claim. What it comes to is something like this: Descartes was a somewhat conventional individual, inclined to safe, middle-of-the-road opinions. This is reflected in his orthodox claims about God, human souls, and matter. Hobbes was a hardheaded, realistically minded individual, inclined to discount flights of imagination and to stick to the "facts." What more natural, then, than his unvarnished materialism? Berkeley was a devout and genial Anglican cleric, inclined to share the pious aspirations enshrined in the institution for which he was a spokesman. Why not an idealism, under these circumstances? Why not the firm conviction that this world is, in the last analysis, but the manifestation of a Supreme Mind? Hume was a canny, skeptically minded Scot, impressed, above everything else, with man's seemingly boundless credulity. What more natural than his carefully reasoned refutation of Descartes, Hobbes, and Berkeley? And so one might continue, seeking to "psychologize" away any claim of metaphysics to rational consideration. There is a flaw in this notion. No explanation in terms of nature and training, of why man believes anything, has any relevance to the question of whether the beliefs are true or false. It is well to raise this point here for two reasons: (1) One's introduction to a variety of alternative metaphysical hypotheses is usually marked by a sense of confusion and a ready ear to the dissolving suggestion that, "After all, it's only a question of temperament." The best reply is that the truth of an opinion has nothing to do with the temperament of the man who holds the opinion. (2) In the case of Arthur Schopenhauer, there is a great tendency to "explain away" his doctrine by reference to his biography. It is known that in life he was bitter, disillusioned, cynical, pessimistic. It is also known that his metaphysical views amount to the claim that the nature of ultimate reality is such as to justify his cynicism and pessimism. The result has sometimes been that persons who reject his metaphysics, with something approaching abhorrence, do so on the ground that "his temperament explains his views." Perhaps it does, but that is not the important point. What one should ask is, "Does the nature of things justify his views?"

Biographical Note. Arthur Schopenhauer was born in Germany in 1788 and died in 1860 at the age of seventy-two. His life was marked by selfishness, suspiciousness, and bitterness. He spent some time in a commercial house before going to the universities at Göttingen, Jena and Berlin. He left his business career in disgust. He berated most of his fellows and teachers at the universities. Upon the death of his father, his mother had moved to Weimar. Schopenhauer followed her, quarreled with her, and took separate lodgings; met Goethe, quarreled with him, and left town to settle a while in Dresden. Here he wrote his great work, *The World as Will and Idea.* As soon as it was published, he left for Italy. There he fumed jealously over the reputation and the gallantries of Lord Byron. He returned to Germany to find his book almost unnoticed. He raged at the obtuseness of his contemporaries and set himself up as a privat-docent at the university in Berlin. Here he was outclassed by the famous Hegel, whom he denounced as a "windbag," and left Berlin for Frankfort. In Frankfort, despite squabbles with persons who shared his rooming house, he spent the remaining years of his life writing brilliant essays on various themes in his own philosophy, compiling a scrapbook of all articles and notices dealing with his work, preparing for a second and third edition of his treatise, and watching his doctrines and fame spread slowly over the Western world.

The Argument of the Passages.   Schopenhauer's metaphysics is called *voluntarism.* It may be contrasted with materialism. It is the belief that will, not matter, is the ultimate reality of which all things are manifestations. Reality is *will,* manifested as nature and present in man. The following passages fall into two groups. The first, given immediately below, without comment, comprises what might be called the *data.* The second sets forth what might be called the *theory.* The first group requires little elucidation. Collectively, they might be inscribed "cynicism and pessimism." They are random reflections on the rottenness of things. As I read him, Schopenhauer would have these disconnected observations on nature and life fall, like so many drops of acid, into the reader's mind, preparing him to understand and appreciate the metaphysical theory which is to fol-low. "See," he seems to say, "see—these are the facts. Think them over. Then, but not until then, I'll give you a theory that will fit them."

Unless suffering is the direct and immediate object of life, our existence must entirely fail of its aim. It is absurd to look upon the enormous amount of pain that abounds everywhere in the world, originating in needs and necessities inseparable from life itself, as serving no purpose, as being the result of mere chance.

Let us consider the human race. Here life presents itself as a task to be performed. Here we see, in great and in small, universal need, ceaseless wars, compulsory activity, extreme exertion of mind and body. Millions united into nations, striving for a common good, each individual on account of his own. But thousands are sacrificed. Now silly delusions, now intriguing politics, excite them to wars. Then sweat and blood must flow to carry out someone's ideas or expiate someone's folly. In peace time it is industry and trade. Inventions work miracles, seas are navigated, delicacies are brought from the ends of the earth, waves engulf thousands. The tumult passes de-scription. And all to what end? To sustain life through a brief span, and then to reproduce and begin again.

From whence did Dante take the materials for his hell but from our ac-tual world? And a very proper hell he was able to make of it. When, on the other hand, he came to describe heaven and its delights, he was confronted with a difficulty, for our world affords no materials for this.

In early youth we are like children in a theater before the curtain is raised, sitting in high spirits and eagerly waiting for the play to begin. It is a blessing we do not know what is actually going to happen . . . the longer you live, the more clearly you feel that life is a disappointment, nay, a cheat.

We are like lambs in a field, disporting under the eye of the butcher who chooses first one and then another. In our good days we are unconscious of the evil which fate may have in store for us—sickness, poverty, mutilation, blindness, insanity, and so on.

It is folly to try to turn this scene of misery into a garden of pleasure. It is folly to aim at joy and pleasure instead of the greatest possible freedom from pain. There is some wisdom in taking a gloomy view of things, in looking upon the world as a kind of hell and in confining one's efforts to securing a little room not too exposed to the fire.

Human life? It is like a drop of water seen through a microscope, teeming with infusoria; or a speck of cheese full of mites invisible to the naked eye. We laugh as they bustle about, and struggle. It is only in the microscope that our life looks so big. It is an almost invisible point, drawn out and magnified by the powerful lenses of time and space.

Unrest is the mark of human existence. We are like a man running down hill who cannot keep on his legs unless he runs on. We are like a pole balanced on the tip of one's finger, or like a planet which would crash into its sun the moment it should cease to hurry on its way.

As far as real physical pleasure is concerned, man is no better off than the brute. The higher possibilities of his brain and nervous system make him sensitive to more and intenser kinds of pleasure, but also to more and intenser kinds of pain. Boredom is a form of suffering unknown to brutes, except perhaps when they are domesticated. Whereas, in man it has become a scourge. Of a truth, need and boredom are the two poles of human life.

In every man there dwells, first and foremost, a colossal egotist who snaps the bands of right and justice with consummate ease. Newspapers show it every day. History shows it on every page. Does not the need of a balance of power in Europe demonstrate it? If it were egotism only, it would be bad enough. But to the egotist in man is joined a fund of hatred, anger, envy, rancor, malice, accumulated like the venom in a serpent's tooth.

I have been reading a book on the condition of the slaves in the southern states. This book constitutes one of the heaviest indictments against the so-called human race. No one can put it down without a feeling of horror. Whatever you may have heard will seem small when you read of how those human devils, those bigoted, church-going, Sabbatarian rascals treated their black brothers whom they had gotten into their clutches.

What is our civilized world but a big masquerade, where you meet knights, priests, soldiers, scholars, lawyers, clergymen, philosophers and so on? But they are not what they pretend to be. They are only masks, and behind the masks, as a rule, you will find moneymakers. It is merchants and moneylenders alone who, in this respect, constitute an honest class.

Formerly faith was the chief support of a throne. Now it is credit. The pope himself is scarcely more concerned over the faithful than over his creditors. In times past it was the guilty debt of the world which was lamented. Now it is the financial debt which arouses dismay. Formerly it was the Last Day which was prophesied. Now it is the great repudiation, the bankruptcy of nations.

Leibnitz, you know, argued that this is the best of all possible worlds. Those who agree with him are optimists. If I could conduct a confirmed optimist through hospitals, infirmaries, operating rooms, asylums; through prisons, torture chambers, and slave kennels; over battlefields, places of execution and sudden death; if I were to open to him all the dark abodes where misery hides from cold curiosity—he might come finally to understand the nature of this "best of all possible worlds."

Nature has appointed that the propagation of the species shall be the business of men who are young, strong, and handsome; so that the species may not degenerate. There is no law older or more powerful than this. Woe to the man who sets up claims and interests that conflict with it; they will be unmercifully crushed at the first serious encounter.

If we contemplate life, we behold a trumoil where most are occupied with want and misery, straining to dodge or ward off its multifarious sorrows. In the midst of this tumult, we see the stealthy glance of two lovers. Why so fearful, so secret? Because—unrealized by them, perhaps—these lovers are traitors who seek to perpetuate whole sordid rounds of want and drudgery which would otherwise come to an end.

If children were brought into the world by an act of pure reason, would human life continue to exist? Are not most of us trapped into life? Would not a man rather have so much sympathy with the coming generation that he would spare it the burden of existence?

Kant speaks much of the dignity of man. I have never seen it. It seems to me that the notion of dignity can be applied to man only in an ironical sense. His will is sinful. His intellect is limited. His body is weak and perishable. How shall a man have dignity whose conception is a crime, whose birth is a penalty, whose life is toil, whose death is a necessity?

Human life must be some kind of mistake. Else why is man a compound of needs and necessities so hard so satisfy? And why, if perchance they should be satisfied, is he thereby abandoned to boredom? This is direct proof that existence has no real value. For what is boredom but the feeling of the emptiness of life? The fact that this most perfect manifestation of life, the human organism, with the infinite cunning and complex working of its machinery, must oscillate between need and boredom and finally fall to dust and extinction, this fact, I say, is eloquent to him who has the mind to understand it.

Disillusion is the mark of old age. By that time the fictions are gone which gave life its charm and spurred on the mind to activity. By that time the splendors of the world have proved themselves null and vain. Its pomp, grandeur, ideals, and enthusiasms are faded. Not till a man has attained his three score years and ten does he quite understand the first verse of Ecclesiastes.

The world and man is something that had better not have been. This may sound strange. But it is in keeping with the facts. And it reminds us of that which is, after all, the most necessary thing in life—the tolerance, patience, regard, love of neighbor, which everyone needs and which everyone owes to his fellow.

You need only look at the way woman is formed to see that she is not meant to undergo great labor either of mind or body. She pays the debt of life not by what she does but by what she suffers: by the pains of childbearing, by caring for the child, by submission to her husband to whom she should be a patient and cheering companion.

That woman is meant by nature to obey may be seen by the fact that every woman who is placed in the unnatural position of complete independence immediately attaches herself to some man by whom she allows herself to be guided and ruled. If she is young, it will be a lover; if she is old, it will be a priest or a lawyer.

The institution of monogamy, and the marriage laws which it entails, bestow upon women an unnatural position of privilege by considering her as the full equivalent of a man, which is by no means the case. Seeing this, men who are shrewd and prudent often scruple to make so great a sacrifice and to acquiesce in so one-sided an arrangement.

The nobler and more perfect a thing is, the later and slower it is to mature. A man reaches the maturity of his reasoning powers hardly before the age of twenty-eight; a woman at eighteen—and then it is only reason of a sort, very niggard in its dimensions.

This weakness of woman's reasoning power explains why she shows more sympathy for the unfortunate than men do; present circumstances have a stronger hold over her, and those concrete things, that lie directly before her eyes, exercise a power which is seldom counteracted to any extent by abstract principles of thought, by fixed rules of conduct, or in general by consideration for the past and the future.

Women are dependent, not upon strength but upon craft. Hence their instinctive capacity for cunning and their inveterate tendency to say what is not true. For as lions are provided with claws and teeth, elephants with boars and tusks, cuttlefish with clouds of inky fluid, so nature has equipped woman with the arts of dissimulation. Therefore a perfectly truthful and straightforward woman is perhaps an impossibility. It may indeed be questioned whether women should be allowed to take an oath in court.

It is only the man whose intellect is clouded by his sexual impulses that could give the name of "fair sex" to that undersized, narrow-shouldered, broad-hipped, short-legged race. For the whole beauty of women is bound up with that impulse.

Nature proceeds with her usual economy. Just as the female ant, after fecundation, loses her wings which are then superfluous, nay, a danger to the business of breeding; so after giving birth to one or two children, a woman generally loses her beauty; probably for similar reasons.

What can you expect of women, when you consider that the most distinguished intellects among them have never produced a single achievement in the fine arts that is really great, genuine, and original? Not even in painting, where mastery of technique is as much within their power as within man's, and where they have diligently cultivated it. The case is not altered by a few partial exceptions. Taken together, women are and remain thorough Philistines and incurable.

There is no proportion between the troubles of life and the gains of life. In the lives of the brute creation, the vanity of life's struggle is easily grasped. The variety and ingenuity of adaptation contrasts sharply with any lasting aim. Only momentary comfort, only fleeting pleasures conditioned and succeeded by want, much suffering, long strife, war of all against all as Hobbes has it, each one a hunter and a hunted, everywhere pressure, need, anxiety, shrieking, howling, and sudden death. And this, *in secula seculorum* or till once again the crust of the planet breaks.

The bulldog ant of Australia affords us a most instructive example. If it is cut in two, a battle begins between the head and the tail. The head seizes the tail with its teeth; the tail defends itself by stinging the head. The battle may last for half an hour, until they die or are dragged off by other ants.

Yunghahn relates that he saw in Java a plain, as far as the eye could reach, entirely covered with skeletons. He took it for a battlefield. They were, however, merely the skeletons of large turtles which come out of the sea to lay their eggs and are then attacked by wild dogs who drag them over onto their backs, strip off the small shell from the stomach, and devour them alive. For this, these turtles are born. Thus life preys upon itself, and in different forms is its own nourishment.

Under the firm crust of the planet dwell powerful forces of nature. Some accident affords them free play. The crust is destroyed, with every living thing on it. The earthquake of Lisbon, the destruction of Pompeii, are only playful hints of what is possible.

The only thing that reconciles me to the Old Testament is the story of the Fall. In my eyes, that is the only metaphysical truth in the book, even though it appears as an allegory. There seems to me no better explanation of our existence than that it is the result of some false step, some sin for which we are paying the penalty.

Vanini, whom his contemporaries burned, finding that easier than refuting him, put the same matter in a very forcible way: "Man is so full of misery that, if it were not contrary to the Christian religion, I should say that evil spirits, if there are any, have passed into human form and are now atoning for their crimes."

Tragedy is the summit of poetical art. The pain and wail of humanity, the triumph of evil, the mastery of chance, the fall of just and innocent, are here presented for us. And in it lies a significant hint of the nature of the world and man: the strife of the will against itself comes here into prominence. It is shown in the sufferings of men due to chance and error, reaching sometimes even the appearance of design. This we are led to see in the noblest works of the tragic muse.

Religious teachers tell us that suicide is cowardice, that only a madman could be guilty of it, and other insipidities of the same kind. Or else they make the nonsensical remark that suicide is wrong, when obviously there is nothing to which every man has a more unassailable title than to his own life and person.

The ancients did not regard the matter in that light. Pliny says "Life is not so desirable as to be protracted at any cost. Whoever you are you are sure to die, even though your life has been full of abomination and crime. The chief remedy for a troubled mind is the feeling that there is no greater blessing than an opportune death; and that every one can avail himself of."

Two Chinamen traveling in Europe paid their first visit to the theater. One of them spent all his time studying the machinery. He succeeded in finding out how it was worked. The other tried to get at the meaning of the piece being presented, in spite of his ignorance of the language. There you have the scientist and the philosopher.

The passages thus far have been expressions of Schopenhauer's pessimism and cynicism. They form a prolegomenon to his metaphysical voluntarism. His general argument is to this effect: Metaphysical voluntarism is the only hypothesis which will account for the many facts upon which I base my cynicism and pessimism. The next four passages set forth his fundamental thesis.

I teach that the inner nature of everything is will.

That which makes itself known to us in the most immediate knowledge as our will is also that which objectifies or manifests itself at different grades in all the phenomena of the world.

If we observe the unceasing impulse with which the waters hurry to the ocean, the persistence with which the magnet turns to the pole, the readiness with which iron flies to the magnet; if we see the crystal take form, the attraction and repulsion of bodies; if we feel how a burden which hampers us by its gravitation toward the earth presses and strains in pursuit of its one tendency—if we note all these things, it requires no great effort of the imagination to recognize in nature what is will in us.

As the magic lantern shows many different pictures made visible by one and the same light, so in all the multifarious phenomena which fill the world, or throng after each other as events, only one will manifests itself, of which everything is the visibility, the objectivity, the manifestation. It is that which is identical in all this variety and change.

To throw his position into bolder relief, Schopenhauer contrasts it with pantheism, the belief that reality is God Himself manifested in everything.

Pantheism is the belief that God is the world—a belief which has always puzzled me. Taking an unprejudiced view of the world as it is, who would regard it as a god? A very ill-advised god, surely, who knows no better than to turn himself into such a world as ours, such a mean, shabby world; there to take the form of countless millions who are fretted and tormented, who live only by preying upon one another. What a pastime for a god!

With the pantheist, I have that One-in-All in common; but my One is not God. I do not go beyond experience, taken in its widest sense; and still less do I fly in the face of the facts which lie before me. The "God" of pantheism is, and must ever remain, an unknown "X." The will, on the other hand, is the one thing known most immediately in experience and therefore exclusively fitted for the explanation of the rest. What is unknown should always be explained by what is better known, not conversely.

The "God" of pantheism manifests himself to unfold his glory. What glory! Apart from the vanity here attributed to him by pantheism, there is immediately created the obligation to sophisticate away the colossal evil of the world. With me, there is none of this. With me alone, the evil of the world is honestly confessed in its whole magnitude. I alone have no need to have recourse to palliatives and sophistries.

From pantheism, he turns to the more orthodox alternative of theism, the belief, namely, that nature is God's handiwork.

There are two things which make it impossible to believe that this world is the successful work of a wise, good and all-powerful Being. The first is the misery which abounds everywhere. The second is the obvious imperfection of its highest product, man, who is a burlesque of what he should be.

In its explanation of the origin of the world—creation by God—Judaism is inferior to any other form of religious doctrine professed by a civilized people. That Jehovah should have created this world of misery and woe, because he enjoyed it, and should then have clapped his hands in praise of his own work, declaring everything to be good—that will not do at all!

I shall be told that my philosophy is comfortless—because I speak the truth. People prefer to be assured that everything the Lord has made is good. Go the the priests, then. Or go to your university professors; they are bound to preach optimism; and it is an easy task to upset their theories.

These matters of contrast noted, he resumes the exposition of his own metaphysical thesis:

That which, in us, pursues its ends by the light of knowledge, strives in nature blindly and dumbly in a one-sided and unchangeable manner. Yet in both cases it may be brought under the conception of will; just as the first dim light of dawn must share the name of sunlight with the rays of full midday.

The lowest grades of the objectification of the will are to be found in those most universal forces of nature which partly appear in all matter, as gravity, impenetrability, and so on, which it is the work of physics and chemistry to discover. They are the simplest modes of its objectification.

The conception of "will" has hitherto been subordinated to the conception of "force." I reverse the matter. I desire that every force in nature be understood in terms of will. This is not mere quibbling. For at the basis of the conception of force, as of all conceptions except will, there lies the sense-perceptual knowledge of the objective world, and the conception is constructed out of this. It is hence an abstraction from what is given in sense-perception. We have no direct experience of "forces" in nature, only of connections and sequences. The conception of will, however, is of all conceptions the one which does not have its origin in sense perception, in ideas of things. It comes from within, and proceeds from our immediate consciousness. If therefore, we refer the conception of will to the conception of force we have referred the better known to the less known.

From inanimate nature, Schopenhauer passes to the world of living things. It, too, is only a higher manifestation of the same underlying will:

Every species of animal is a longing of the will-to-live. For instance, the will is seized with a longing to live in trees, to hang from their branches, to devour their leaves. This longing becomes objectified in the sloth. It can hardly walk, being only adapted for climbing. It is helpless on the ground, agile on trees, looks like moss so as to escape its pursuers.

The will is active in nature where no knowledge guides it. This we see in the instincts and mechanical skills of animals. The ends toward which they strive are to them unknown. The bird of a year old has no idea of eggs for which it builds a nest. The young spider has no idea of the prey for which it spins its first web. Ants, marmots, bees, lay in provision for the winter they have never experienced. Insects deposit their eggs where the coming brood finds future nourishment. The larva of the stag bettle makes the hole in the wood, in which it is to await its metamorphosis, twice as big if it is going to be a male beetle as it would if it were going to be a female beetle—so that there will be room for the horns which no female beetle possessed. Has it knowledge thus in advance? The point is merely this: Knowledge is not necessary to guide will. It acts instinctively at some levels.

The instincts of plants and animals give us the best illustration of what is meant by teleology in nature. An instinct is an action like that which is guided by a purpose, and is yet entirely without purpose. So all constructions of nature resemble that which is guided by an aim, and yet is entirely without it. What we think to be means and end is, in every case, the manifestation of the unity of the one will.

Everywhere in nature pervading this adaptation we see strife. In this we can recognize that variance with itself which is essential to the will. Every grade of objectification fights for the matter of the others. The permanent matter must continually change its form. This strife may be followed through the whole of nature. It is most visible in the animal kingdom. For animals have the whole of the vegetable kingdom for their food, and within the animal kingdom one order is the prey and food of another. Thus the will everywhere preys upon itself and in different forms is its own nourishment.

From the lower forms of animal life, Schopenhauer turns to consider the higher levels at which instinct and impulse are somewhat modified by the emergence of intellect and knowledge.

From grade to grade, yet still without consciousness, as an obscure striving force, the will rises through matter and the vegetable kingdoms to the point at which the individuals in whom it is manifested can no longer receive food through mere movement following upon stimuli. The chances of the individual that is moved merely by stimuli would be too unfavorable. Its food must be sought out and selected. For this purpose movement following upon motive, and therefore consciousness, becomes necessary.

Consciousness, called in at this stage for the conversation of the individual, appears. It is represented by the brain, just as every other effort of the will is represented by an organ. With this new addition, the "world as idea" comes into existence at a stroke, with all its forms and categories, its subject and object, its time and space and causality and multiplicity. The world now shows its second side.

Till now mere will, it becomes now also idea, object to a knowing conscious subject. Up to this point the will followed its tendency in the dark with unerring certainty. But at this grade it kindles for itself a light as a means to an end, as an instrument needed to deal with the throng and complication of its prior manifestations; a need which would have accrued precisely to its highest manifestation.

The hitherto infallible certainty and regularity with which will worked in unorganized and vegetable matter, rested upon the fact that it alone was active in its original nature as blind impulse, as unconscious will, without interruption from a second and entirely different world, the world of perception. But with consciousness, its infallible certainty comes to an end. Animals are thereby exposed to deception and error. They have, however, only ideas arising out of perception. They have no conceptual powers, no reflective powers, and are therefore bound to the present.

This "knowledge without reason" becomes insufficient. When the will has attained to the highest grade of its objectification, the kind of knowledge which arises out of mere perception confined to what is immediately present to the senses, does not suffice. That complicated and many-sided imaginative being, man, with his many needs, exposed to innumerable dangers, must, if he is to exist, be lighted by a double knowledge. A higher power than mere perception must be given him.

With this new power of reasoning, of framing and using abstract conceptions, there has appeared reflection, surveying the past, anticipating the future, deliberation, care, premeditated action, and finally the full and distinct awareness of one's own deliberate volition as such.

With mere knowledge of perception there arose the possibility of illusion and error, by which the previous infallibility of the blind striving of the will was done away with. With the entrance of reasoning powers that certainty and infallibility are almost entirely lost. Instinct diminishes. Deliberation, supposed to supplant everything from physical causation to instinctive reaction, begets irresolution and uncertainty. Errors become widely possible, and in many cases obstruct the will in action.

Thus knowledge, rational as well as sensuous, proceeds originally from the will itself, belongs to the inner being of the higher grades of objectification as an instrument of selection and adaptation, a means of supporting the individual and the species like any other organ. Destined to forward the aims of the will, it remains almost entirely subject to its service. It is so in all brutes and in almost all men.

In all grades of its manifestations, from the lowest inorganic forms to the highest organic forms, the will is controlled by no final goal or aim. It always strives, for striving is its sole nature which no attaining can put to an end.

Therefore it is not capable of any final satisfaction, but only of obstruction. This endless striving, of the will-to-be, the will-to-live, the will-to-conquer, the will-to-reproduce, we see everywhere, and see hindered in many ways. Wherever blocked, we see suffering. So if there be no final aim and no final satisfaction, there are no measure and end of suffering.

We ask: For what purpose does all this torment and agony exist? There is only one consideration that may serve to explain. It is this: The will-to-live, which underlies the whole world of phenomena, must satisfy its cravings by feeding on itself. This it does by forming a graduated scale of phenomena in which one level exists at the expense of another. Note two animals, one of which is engaged in eating the other.

By now man's place in nature has been indicated. Two passages conclude this somewhat evolutionary account.

In the life of man all this appears with greatest distinctness, illumined by the clearest knowledge. As the manifestation of the will rises higher, the suffering becomes more apparent. In the plant there is no sensibility and therefore no pain. In the lowest forms of animal life, a small degree of suffering may be experienced. As the level rises, sensitivity becomes wider and deeper. It appears in a high degree with the complete nervous system of backboned animals, and increases as intelligence develops. Thus, as knowledge increases, as consciousness attains to greater distinctness, pain also increases, and reaches its highest degree in man. And the more intelligent and finely formed a man is, the more pain he is open to.

Every human being is only another short dream of that endless spirit of nature, the persistent will-to-live; only another fleeting form carelessly sketched on an infinite page, and obliterated to make room for new. And every one of these fleeting forms must be paid for with many deep and long-drawn sufferings, and finally with a relentless death. Do you wonder why the sight of a corpse is never funny?

From the vantage point of his metaphysical hypothesis Schopenhauer feels himself in a position to account for the futility, the restlessness, the unhappiness and boredom which mark human life. If mankind is nothing but an objectification of a blindly striving universal will what else could be expected?

Man's appetites are insatiable. Every satisfaction he gets lays the seeds of some new desire. There is hence no end to the wishes of any individual will. Why is this? The reason is simple. Will is the lord of all worlds. Everything is but a manifestation of will. Therefore no one single thing can ever give it satisfaction. Only the totality of things—which is endless.

The basis of all willing and striving is need, deficiency, pain. Thus the nature of man is subject to pain originally and in its essence. If, on the other hand, it lacks objects of desire, a terrible void and boredom comes over it. The man's life swings like a pendulum, backwards and forwards, between uneasiness and boredom. (Hence, in his speculations, after man had transferred all pains to hell, there remained nothing over for heaven but boredom.)

Real boredom is by no means an evil to be lightly esteemed. In the end it depicts on the countenance a real despair. It makes beings who love each other so little as men do, seek each other eagerly. Like its opposite evil, famine in every form, it provokes us to elaborate precautions. People require *panem et circenses*—bread and circuses. As want is the constant scourge of the lower classes, boredom is the lash laid across the back of the fashionable world. In the great middle classes, boredom is represented by Sunday and want by the six weekdays.

Thus, between desiring and attaining, all human life flows on. The wish is, in its nature, uneasiness. The attainment soon begets satiety. The end was only apparent, and possession drives away the charm.

It should be added to this that satisfaction, or what is commonly called *happiness,* is never positive. It is not something original, growing out of itself, so to speak; but must always be the satisfaction of some wish or longing. The wish, the want, the need, the desire, these are the positive things; and these precede, condition, and follow every satisfaction.

The life of every individual, surveyed as a whole, is a tragedy. Here and there in detail, it may have the character of a comedy. The restless irritations of a moment, the needs and vexations of a day, the mishaps and fears of a week, are scenes in a comedy. But the overarching, never-satisfied wishes, the frustrated efforts, the crushed and abandoned hopes, the deep errors of a whole life, with increasing pain or boredom, and death at the close, are always a tragedy. As if the fates would add derision to the miseries of our existence, our life must contain all the ingredients of a tragedy while in detail it will have the foolish look of a comedy.

That happiness is not something positive, that it is merely the satisfaction of some want, to be followed by another or by ennui, finds support in art, that true mirror of the world and life. Every epic and dramatic poem can only represent struggle, effort, fight for happiness; never enduring and complete happiness. It conducts its heroes through a thousand difficulties and dangers to the goal. But, as soon as this is reached, the curtain falls, for now there remains nothing for it to do but show that what lured the hero on as happiness, materialized as disappointment.

Everyone who has awakened from the first dream of youth will realize, if his judgment is not paralyzed, that this world is the kingdom of chance and error, of folly and wickedness. Hence, everything better only struggles through with difficulty. What is noble and wise seldom attains to expression. The absurd and perverse in thought, the dull and tasteless in art, the wicked and deceitful in action, assert a real supremacy broken only by brief interruptions. In vain the sufferer calls on his gods for help. This irremediable evil is only the mirror of the will, of which himself is the objectification.

To me, optimism, when it is not merely the thoughtless verbalizing of those who have nothing but words under their low foreheads, is not merely absurd; it is wicked. It is a bitter mockery of the unspeakable misery of mankind. To me, as the writers of the Gospels, the *world* and *evil* are almost synonymous terms.

Thus far Schopenhauer the metaphysician. Now Schopenhauer the moralist. The latter directs the argument from this point to its despairing conclusion. In our own day Thomas Hardy has expressed in poetry what Schopenhauer, up to this point, has been arguing in prose.

Given this view of things, what is Schopenhauer's message for mankind? It is one of pity and self-mortification. His argument turns to these matters, beginning with an explanation of the origin of humanity's pervasive egoism and selfishness, working around gradually to counsels of despair.

What I have been saying comes to this: In the whole of nature, at all the grades of the objectification of the will, there is a necessary and constant conflict, expressing the inner contradiction of the will with itself. This phenomenon exhibits itself with greater distinctness at the highest level of the will's objectification, namely in man. What I propose now is to trace to its source that egoism which is the starting point of all conflict.

The will everywhere manifests itself in separate individuals. But this separateness does not concern the will as it is in itself. The will itself is present, whole and undivided, in every one of these—as the color red is present, whole and undivided, in any red object—and beholds around it the innumerably repeated images of its own nature. Therefore everyone desires everything for himself, and would destroy whatever would oppose it. Every individual feels himself the center of the world, has a primary and inextinguishable regard for his own existence and well-being.

This disposition, which I call *egoism,* is essential to everything in nature. It is by reason of this primary fact that the inner conflict of the will with itself attains such terrible proportions. Yet this egoism has its being and continuance in that opposition of the microcosm and the macrocosm, in the fact that the objectification of the will has individualization as its form, in the fact that it manifests itself in the same way in innumerable individuals. In the highest grade of consciousness all this appears in its sharpest form.

We see the consequences of this basic fact everywhere in human life, in small things and great. We see its terrible side in the lives of great tyrants and miscreants, and in world-desolating wars. We see its absurd side in conceit, vanity, and minor selfishness. We see it writ large in history, which is the record of struggles ranging from vast armies to pairs of human alley cats. We see it when any mob of men is set free from law and order and restraint. Then that "war of all against all" which Hobbes has described so admirably, shows itself. This is the highest expression of egoism.

This "primary and ineradicable egoism" is the fact upon which Schopenhauer proceeds to build a moral philosophy, an ethics of pity and despair.

Out of this primary and ineradicable egoism arise both misery and wickedness. Do we desire to know what men so constituted, are worth in moral terms? We have only to consider their fate as a race. This is want, wretchedness, affliction, misery, and death. There is a species of eternal justice in it all. In this sense the world is the judgment of the world. Could we lay the misery of the world in one scale of the balance, and the guilt of the world in the other, the needle would point to the center.

I referred to an eternal justice in the scheme of things. To him who has grasped in all of its ramifications the thought which I have been developing, this will be evident. The world, in all its parts, is the manifestation of one will. The will is free. The will is almighty. The world is its mirror. As the will is, so is the world. It alone bears the responsibility for what comes into being.

However, the world does not stand thus revealed to the knowledge of him whose mind is still bound to the service of his will, as it does to him who has risen to an entirely objective contemplation. The vision of the uncultured individual is clouded. He does not see the reality behind the phenomenon in time and space. He sees not the inner unity and identity of things, but only its separated, individualized, disunited, opposed, manifestations. For him pleasure is one thing and pain another. He sees one manifestation of the will live in abundance and ease, while at his door another dies of want and cold. He asks, "Where is Justice?"

But the vision of eternal justice is beyond him. He sees no inner connection. He sees the wicked flourish and the oppressed suffer. He cannot rise above these individual differences. Hence he does not understand the nature of this world's justice. That man only will grasp and comprehend eternal justice who raises himself above particular things, who sees through the individualizations of the real. He alone sees that the difference between him who inflicts suffering and him who bears it, is phenomenal only and concerns not the will as thing-in-itself. The inflicter of suffering and the sufferer are one. If the eyes of both were opened, the inflicter of suffering would see that he lives in all that suffers pain. The sufferer would see that all the wickedness in the world proceeds from that will which constitutes his own nature.

The comprehension of this eternal justice, of the tie that unites the evil of my crime with the evil of your misery, demands the power to rise above the limits of individuality. Therefore it will always remain unattainable by most men.

What I have been arguing is this: Hatred and wickedness are conditioned by egoism, and egoism rests on the entanglement of knowledge in the principle of individuation, in the fact that the will realizes itself in separate individuals.

If this penetration of the principle of individuation, this direct knowledge of the identity of the will in its diverse manifestations, is present in a high degree of distinctness, it will show an influence upon the will of the individual who has achieved this insight. If the veil is lifted from his eyes so that he no longer makes the egotistical distinction between his self and other selves, then he will regard the infinite suffering of all sufferers as his own.

To such a man no suffering is any longer strange. All the miseries of others work upon his mind like his own. It is no longer the changing joy and sorrow of his own person that he has in view. All lies equally near him. He knows the ultimately real, and finds that it consists in a constant passing away, a vain striving, an inward conflict, a continual suffering. Wherever he looks he sees suffering humanity and a world in passage. But all this now lies as near him as his own person lies to the man who is still in bondage to egoism.

The moralist, backed by the metaphysician, is now in a position to ask pointedly, "Why should man, with this knowledge of ultimate reality, accept life on such terms? Why should man be a yea-sayer? Why not a nay-sayer?"

Why should he, now, with this knowledge of ultimate reality, assert this very life through constant acts of will? Knowledge of the nature of the thing-in-itself becomes a quieter of the individual will. The individual will now turns away from life, now shudders at the pleasures in which it once recognized the assertion of life, now attains to voluntary renunciation, resignation, indifference, will-less-ness.

If we compare life to a course which we must run, a path of red-hot coals with here and there a cool spot, then he who is still entangled in the egoistic delusion is consoled by the cool places and sets out to run the course. But he who sees through individualization to the one will which is identical in all is no longer susceptible to such consolation. He sees himself in all places at once, and withdraws. His will turns round, no longer asserts itself, but denies.

This denial of the will by an individual manifestation of it follows the recognition of the real nature of the thing-in-itself. It is the transition from virtue to asceticism. This is to say, when a man has once seen, it no longer suffices for him to love others as himself. There arises within him a horror of that will of which he is himself a manifestation.

Nothing but a manifestation of the will, the individual ceases now to will anything. His body he denies. His health he is indifferent to. His desires he ignores. He desires no gratification of any appetite in any form.

More concretely, what is meant by this exhortation to suppress and deny the will-to-live? Schopenhauer is clear enough about it all. Upon unhappy man he urges a program of chastity, asceticism, self-chastisement, and ultimate starvation:

Voluntary and complete chastity is the first step in asceticism, the first move in the denial of the will-to-live. It denies the assertion of the will which extends beyond the individual's own life. It gives assurance that the life of this body, the will whose manifestation it is, ceases.

Asceticism shows itself further in voluntary and intentional poverty; not only *per accidens* as when possessions are given away to mitigate the sufferings of others, but directly to serve as a constant mortification of the will, so that the satisfaction of desires, the sweet things of life, shall not rouse the will of which a penetrating self-knowledge has conceived a horror.

Asceticism extends further as humility and patience. He who denies the will as it appears in his own person will not resist if another does wrong to him. Suffering, insult, ignominy, he will receive gladly, as the opportunity of learning that he no longer stands behind his will. Patience and meekness will replace impatience and pride and anger.

Asceticism culminates in self-chastisement, fasting, and starvation. By constant privation and suffering he who has seen the nature and source of the evil of life in the will-to-live is able more and more to break down and destroy that manifestation in himself; to crush in himself that which he recognizes and abhors as the source of his own and humanity's misery and wickedness.

When death comes to such a one, it is most welcome. Here it is not, as in the case of others, merely the manifestation of the will that ends in death. The inner nature of the will has long been restrained, denied, crushed. The last slight bond is now broken. For him who ends thus, the world also ends.

With a backward glance over the whole argument of his metaphysics and moral philosophy, Schopenhauer concludes:

What I have described here with feeble tongue and only in general terms, is no philosophical fable. It is the moral of the life of saints and ascetics in all ages and all religions. The inner nature of holiness, self-renunciation, mortification, is here expressed, abstractly and free from mythology, as the denial of the will-to-live, appearing after the complete knowledge of its own nature has become a quieter of all volition.

Before us there is certainly only nothingness. We look with deep and painful longing upon the perfect calm of the spirit which has strangled and subdued the will-to-live. Beside it, the misery and evil of life is thrown into clear contrast. Yet, only when we have recognized the incurable suffering and endless wickedness which follows upon the assertion of the will, and have ordered our days to its denial, do we attain any lasting consolation. To those in whom the will has turned against itself, this world of planets, suns, and milky ways is nothing.

Note on Sources.   The Schopenhauer material in this section is quoted, abridged, or paraphrased from his *World as Will and Idea*, especially Book IV; his Supplements to *The World as Will and Idea*; his *On the Will in Nature*; and his two volumes of miscellaneous essays, *Parerga and Paralipomena*—e.g., "On Women," "On Suicide," "On Pantheism," and so forth.

Reading References.   In a book by R. A. Tsanoff, *The Nature of Evil*, will be found a good, brief account of Schopenhauer's life and thought. Tsanoff writes on a gallery of pessimists, but his tenth and eleventh chapters are on Schopenhauer alone. A book by V. J. McGill, *Schopenhauer: Pessimist and Pagan*, is a popular biographical study. There is an edition of Schopenhauer, by Will Durant, which contains good selections. There is a single-volume collection, *Essays of Schopenhauer*, in which seven small volumes are bound in one. These are more easily read than the selections from *The World as Will and Idea*. Much criticism of Schopenhauer is either narrowly technical, in which case the whole point of the man is somehow overlooked, or is so pious and horror-stricken that one feels that after all there must be something to what Schopenhauer says. An exception to this might be found in the "Pessimism" chapter of Paulsen's *System of Ethics*. A valuable little book, *Thomas Hardy's Universe*, by Ernest Brennecke, will show the way in which Schopenhauer's metaphysics forms a basis upon which Hardy's poems, tales, and novels can be understood.

READING QUESTIONS

1. Berkeley died in 1753. Schopenhauer published in 1819. Just for the record, how much "public strife" marked the years between?
2. What point brings each of the following into the first long group of quotations from Schopenhauer: (a) Dante, (b) children in a theater, (c) the two poles of human life, (d) the southern states, (e) Leibniz, (f) lovers, (g) Kant, (h) Ecclesiastes, (i) woman, (j) monogamy, (k) the bull-dog ant, (l) the wild dogs of Java, (m) Lisbon and Pompeii, (n) the Old Testament, (o) tragedy, (p) suicide, (q) two Chinamen.
3. Use the distinction between "manifested as" and "present in" to state Schopenhauer's metaphysical thesis.
4. Contrast his position with (a) materialism, (b) theism, (c) pantheism.
5. Why intellect succeeds instinct in the hierarchy of being. What happens to the world at that point? What is his "instrumentalist" theory of the intellect?
6. Between what alternatives human life swings. Why happiness is never positive. What he has to say about optimism.
7. What he means by "egoism" in relation to the will. In what sense egoism is an illusion. Illusory or not, however, what consequences follow from this egoism?
8. An all-pervading will. Manifested as separate individual persons. Hence misery and wickedness. Whence, then, the "eternal justice" of it?
9. How the recognition of the illusory character of egoism gives rise to morality. And then to asceticism. With what final outcome?

10. Why Schopenhauer's doctrine of the will is a fitting metaphysical prelude to the Age of Darwin, Marx, and Freud.
11. Wherein you find Schopenhauer (a) most, (b) least convincing.

INDEPENDENT STUDY

1. Read the article on Schopenhauer by P. Gardiner in the *Encyclopedia of Philosophy,* and that by R. Taylor in *A Critical History of Western Philosophy,* edited by D. J. O'Connor; also read the article "Pessimism and Optimism" by L. E. Lolmker in the *Encyclopedia of Philosophy.* Write on Schopenhauer and pessimism.
2. Read the Gardiner and Taylor articles noted above, then the Schopenhauer part of I. Knox, "The Aesthetic Theories of Kant, Hegel and Schopenhauer." Make sure you read the relevant part of Schopenhauer's own *World as Will and Idea.* A paper on the status of art and aesthetics in the philosophy of Schopenhauer.
3. Thomas Hardy's doctrine of the will compared with Schopenhauer's doctrine of the will.
4. An essay on the moral philosophy (the "ethics") of Schopenhauer.

SECTION 4. AUGUSTE COMTE: DOUBTS ABOUT TRADITIONAL METAPHYSICS

From Schopenhauer to Comte. Each century tackles the problem of traditional metaphysics in its own way. The seventeenth century, represented in Hobbes's materialism, differs in method from the eighteenth. The eighteenth, represented by Berkeley's idealism, differs again from the nineteenth century, represented in the writings of Schopenhauer and Auguste Comte. By the 1830's, it seemed unnecessary to reopen the hectic controversies that inspired and followed from earlier attempts to formulate a metaphysics. At least, Comte appears to have felt as much. The picture is altered. Comte approaches philosophy from the point of view of a man who is interested primarily in the range and organization of the various bodies of science. He pins a controversial tag on himself, no doubt; for *positivism,* as will be seen, means "no more metaphysics." But he is inclined to sweep controversy to one side and ask several new leading questions: What common method has the growth of science revealed? What relations, if any, exist among the different sciences? What significance, for general education, may be ascribed to the sciences as a whole? In what fields, if any, may we look for the emergence of new sciences? For these reasons, among others, Comte is perhaps more convincing to one who is either innocent of Hume and Kant or who has lost those peculiar sensibilities that respond to their anxieties and convictions.

Biographical Note. Auguste Comte was born in France in 1798, and died in 1857 at the age of fifty-nine. He showed an early aptitude for mathematics, which he began to teach in Paris. When he was twenty-eight, he embarked on a series of public lectures designed to offer a synoptic account of the principal sciences. These attracted considerable attention; but after the third lecture, his brain temporarily gave way, and he tried to commit suicide. Two years later he had sufficiently recovered to resume his lectures. In 1830 he began the publication of his great survey of the sciences. It was completed in six large volumes and served through several generations as a storehouse of fact and generalization for students in France and abroad. He continued to maintain himself by teaching mathematics and serving as an examiner in that subject. Unfortunately, however, he became embroiled in controversies that caused him to lose a great part of his means of living. The English philosopher J. S. Mill, who had been impressed by the value of Comte's work, was instrumental in securing a considerable sum of money from Comte's admirers in England. This tided him over his immediate difficulties. When this was used up, Comte faced poverty; however, aid came eventually from admirers in France who banded together to provide the lonely polymath with a small income for the rest of his life.

Comte's interest in epistemology was not direct. To get this point as clearly and, at the same time, as sympathetically as possible, we need to recall a bit of French history. Comte wrote for the first generation after Napoleon. The old regime, the epoch of the grand monarchy, formed a remote background. It had been swept away by the French Revolution. Liberal hopes had run high, only to be disappointed by the autocratic domination of Napoleon; and now, following the Congress of Vienna, France had been made over once more into a monarchy under Louis XVIII and Charles X. These drastic changes appear to have inspired Comte with the dream of a new era in which they would no longer be possible. This new era was to be built upon science and the application of science to industry. But, as Comte saw it, several obstacles blocked the path of the new age. They were remnants from the past. They were, more particularly, beliefs or mental sets that still lingered from the Middle Ages, the period of the grand monarchy, the Age of Reason, the French Revolution, and Napoleon. They were beliefs about such matters as God, the soul, ultimate reality, immortality, natural laws, inalienable rights, men of destiny, and so forth. These beliefs, Comte felt, were not only groundless, they were harmful. They had been responsible for continuous tyranny, revolt, suppression, war, and they would continue to be. What the world needed was a riddance of such beliefs, and Comte would supply it under cover of this new term *positivism*, which was to abolish the old loyalties and controversies, to set up the ideal of scientific method and its application to nature in the interests of human welfare.

The Argument of the Passages. Comte begins by elaborating what he calls the *law of the three stages*. This enables him to dispose of metaphysics and theology. He turns then to a statement of his theory of the sciences. The passages tell their own story from that point on:

(1)

In order to understand the true value and character of positivism, we must take a brief general view of the progress of the human mind; for no conception can be understood otherwise than through its history.

From the study of the development of human understanding, in all directions and through all times, the discovery arises of a fundamental law. The law is this: that each of our leading conceptions, each branch of our knowledge, passes through three different theoretical conditions: the theological or fictitious, the metaphysical or abstract, the scientific or positive. This fundamental law should henceforth be, in my opinion, the starting point of all philosophical researches about man and society.

The human mind employs in its progress three methods of philosophizing, the characteristics of which are essentially different and even radically opposed: the theological, the metaphysical, and the scientific. Hence arise three philosophies, or three general systems of thought, each of which excludes the other. The first is the mind's necessary point of departure; the second is merely a state of transition; the third is the mind's fixed and definitive state.

An instance of what Comte means might be the following: In the early stages of man's study of the heavens, he accounted for their motion in terms of various deities. Later he envisaged them as controlled by the force of gravitation. Finally he repudiates explanation in terms of gods and forces and is satisfied to describe the motion in terms of formulae which enable him to locate and predict:

Different departments of our knowledge have passed through the three stages at different rates. The rate depends on the nature of the knowledge in question. Any kind of knowledge reaches the positive stage early in proportion to its generality, simplicity, and independence of other branches of knowledge. Thus astronomy, which is above all made up of facts which are general, simple, and independent of other facts, was the first science to attain the positive stage, then physics, then chemistry, and finally physiology.

In the theological stage, the human mind, seeking the essential nature of things, their first and final causes, supposes all things to be produced by the immediate action of supernatural beings. Here imagination predominates over observation.

A natural and irresistible instinct disposes the human race to adopt theological ideas as its earliest principles of explanation. The personal action exerted by man on other things is, at first, the only kind he is able to understand. He is thus led to conceive, in an analogous way, the action of external bodies on himself and on each other. This is animism. Continued observation leads him to convert this primitive hypothesis into another, less enduring one: that of a "dead" inert nature guided by invisible superhuman agents, distinct and independent of one another. This is polytheism. Continued observation and reflection disposes him gradually to reduce the number of these supernatural agencies until he is led from polytheism to monotheism. The theological system arrived at its highest perfection when it substituted the providential action of a single supreme Being for the varied operations of numerous divinities; when, that is, it passed from polytheism to monotheism.

The entire theological system is based on the supposition that the earth is made for man, and the whole universe made for the earth. Remove this supposition, and the system crumbles. Hence the true astronomical theory, proposed by Copernicus and proved by Kepler, Galileo, and Newton, would alone have sufficed to demolish the theological system. In the light of the fact that our planet, one of the smallest, is in no respect different from the others, revolving like them around the sun, the hypothesis that nature is made for mankind alone so shocks good sense and contradicts fact that it must appear absurd and collapse. With it falls the theological edifice.

In the metaphysical stage, which is only a modification of the first, the mind supposes abstract forces, personified abstractions, inherent in all things and capable of producing them, instead of supernatural beings. What is called the *explanation* of anything is, in this stage, a reference of it to its proper force, principle, or abstraction.

To explain sleep, for example, in terms of what used to be called the *dormitive principle* is to explain observed phenomena by reference to what Comte would call a *metaphysical abstraction*. Many such phrases are to be found strewn through the annals of science and philosophy. Thus Hegel's *reason* or *time-spirit*, Schopenhauer's *will*, Bergson's *élan vital*, Freud's *censor*, the erstwhile *vis viva*, *vis inertia*, and *entelechy* are, I suspect, all instances of what Comte would call *metaphysical abstractions*. His objection to them is that they are attempts to explain the known by the unknown, to postulate something which is not revealed in experience to account for what is revealed in experience.

Even today, after all our advance in positive knowledge, if we try to understand how the fact which we name a cause produces the fact which we name its effect, we should be compelled, as Hume points out, to resort to images similar to those which serve as the basis of primitive human theories. (Cause is a metaphysical notion; regularity of succession is the positive notion.)

The metaphysical system arrived at its last stage when men substituted the one great entity—nature—as the cause of everything.

In the scientific or positive stage the mind has given over the vain search after absolute knowledge; abandoned the quest for knowledge of the origin and destination of the universe, of causes and forces; and applies itself solely to the study of laws, to the study of relations of succession and resemblance. Reasoning and observation, duly combined, are the means of this knowledge. What is now called the *explanation* of anything is the establishment of a connection between it and some general laws, the number of which continually diminishes with the progress of science.

Observation of fact is the only solid basis for human knowledge. Taking this principle in its most rigorous sense, we may say that a proposition which does not admit of being reduced to a simple enunciation of fact, particular or general, can have no real or intelligible sense.

The first characteristic of positivism is that it regards all things as subject to invariable laws. Our business—seeing how vain is any search into what are called causes, either first or final—is to pursue an accurate discovery of those laws, with a view to reducing them to the smallest possible number. The best illustration of this is in the case of the law of gravitation. We say things are explained by it, because it connects an immense variety of facts under one head.

The positive system would attain its ultimate perfection if men could represent all particular facts as instances of one general law, e.g., the law of gravitation.

There is no science, which, having attained to the positive stage, does not bear marks of having passed through the two previous stages. At some earlier period it was composed of metaphysical abstractions; and, further back in its evolution, it took its form from theological conceptions. Our most advanced sciences still bear traces of the earlier stages through which they have passed.

(2)

In mentioning just now the four principal categories of phenomena—the astronomical, the physical, the chemical, the physiological—there was an omission. Nothing was said of social phenomena. These demand a distinct classification, by reason of their importance and difficulty. They are the most complicated and the most dependent on others. Their science, therefore, will be the latest to attain positivity.

This branch of science has not hitherto entered the domain of positive knowledge. Theological and metaphysical conceptions and methods, exploded and abandoned in other departments, are still used in the treatment of social subjects, though the best minds are weary of disputes about "divine rights," "sovereignty of the people," and so on. This is the great, the only, gap to be filled to constitute solid and entire the positive philosophy. This is what men have now most need of.

This once done, the philosophical system of the moderns will be complete. There will then be no phenomena which do not enter into one of the five great categories—astronomical, physical, chemical, physiological, and sociological.

So much, then, for the law of the three stages. For Comte, its principal virtue seems to reside in the fact that it eliminates, at one fell swoop, a whole army of clamorous hypotheses and controversies which constitute a large portion of modern philosophy.

Comte now turns his attention to the question of the classification of the positive sciences. (It should be noted that, as Comte uses it, the term *physiology* has the broader meaning that we extend today to the term *biology*.)

(3)

We propose to classify the fundamental sciences. They are six, as we shall see. We cannot make them less; and most scientists would make them more. To classify the sciences is not so easy as may appear. It always involves something, if not arbitrary, at least artificial; and in so far, it will always involve imperfection. It is perhaps impossible to exhibit the sciences, quite rigorously, in their natural relations and mutual dependence so as to avoid, in some degree, the danger of overlapping.

What we seek to determine is the dependence of scientific studies. Does physics depend upon physiology? Does sociology depend upon chemistry? Dependence among the sciences can result only from dependence among the corresponding phenomena. For a principle in terms of which to classify the sciences, then, we must look to the different orders of phenomena through which science discovers the laws which are her object.

All phenomena may be included within a very few natural categories, so arranged that the study of each may be grounded on the principle laws of the preceding and serve as the basis of the next ensuing. We have now obtained our rule. We proceed next to our classification.

We are first struck by the clear division of all natural phenomena into two classes: inorganic and organic. Each of these two great halves had subdivisions. Inorganic phenomena may be divided into two classes: celestial and terrestrial. Terrestrial inorganic phenomena may be divided into two classes according as we regard bodies in their mechanical or chemical character. Organic phenomena may be divided into two classes: those which relate to the individual and those which relate to groups.

Thus we have five basic sciences in successive dependence: astronomy, physics, chemistry, physiology, and sociology. The first considers the most general, simple, and remote phenomena known to us, and those which affect all others without being affected by them. The last considers the most particular, complex, and nearest phenomena. Between these two the degrees of speciality and complexity are in regular proportion to the place of the respective sciences in the scale exhibited. This we must regard as the true filiation of the sciences.

It is proposed to consolidate the entire body of positive knowledge into one body of homogeneous doctrine. But it must not be supposed that we are proposing to study this vast variety as proceeding from one single law. There is something so chimerical in attempts at explanation in terms of one single law, that it may be as well to repudiate any such notion. Our intellectual resources are too narrow, and the universe too complex, to justify any hope that it will ever be within our power to carry scientific perfection to this last degree of simplicity.

This notion of all phenomena referable to a single law is by no means necessary to the systematic formation of science. The only necessary unity is that of method. And this is already, in great part, attained: The scientific method of thought is the same for all fields of knowledge, however widely they may vary and however irreducible they may be in content.

Comte's meaning is probably this: In the scientific exploration of any field, the method is the same. Initial data are collected, usually in the light of some tentatively held hypothesis; this hypothesis is then assumed to be true, and its consequences or implications deduced; facts subsequently acquired, by observation or experiment, verify the deductions made from the hypothesis. The hypothesis may be with regard to some particular fact or some general law.

The most interesting point in our hierarchical classification is its effect on education, both general and scientific. This is its direct and unquestionable result. No science can be effectually pursued without a competent knowledge of the anterior sciences upon which it depends.

Your competent physicist must have at least a general knowledge of astronomy. Chemists cannot properly understand chemistry without physics and astronomy. Physiologists require some knowledge of chemistry, physics, and astronomy. Above all, students of social science require a general knowledge of the anterior sciences. As such conditions are rarely fulfilled, there is among us, no genuinely rational scientific education. To this may be attributed, in part, the imperfection of even the most important sciences at this day.

In our enumeration of the basic sciences there is one prodigious omission. We have said nothing of mathematics. The omission was intentional, and the reason was the vast importance and unique status of mathematics. It is, however, less a constituent part of the body of positive knowledge than a basis for the whole of that knowledge. It is the most powerful instrument that the human mind can employ in the investigation of the laws of natural phenomena. It must, therefore, hold the first place in the hierarchy of the sciences and be the point of departure for all education in any of the sciences.

From the question of the classification of the sciences, Comte addresses himself to certain advantages which, he thinks, will arise from the unified view which results. It is interesting to note that these include the elimination of logic and the reduction of psychology to behaviorism.

(4)

We have now considered philosophically the articulation of the positive sciences. The order that results is this: mathematics, astronomy, physics, chemistry, physiology, and sociology. We must glance at the principal advantages to be derived from a study of them. Of these advantages, four may be pointed out.

In the *first* place, the study of the positive sciences affords the only rational means of exhibiting the logical laws of the human mind. Looking at all scientific theories as so many great logical facts, it is only by the observation of these facts that we can arrive at the knowledge of logical laws.

Psychology pretends to discover the laws of the human mind by contemplating the mind itself. Such an (introspective) attempt, made in defiance of the physiological study of our intellectual organs, cannot succeed. The mind may observe all phenomena but its own. There can be nothing like scientific observation of mental phenomena except from without, and by another. The observing and observed organ are here the same. In order to observe its activity, your mind must pause from activity; yet it is this very activity that you want to observe. If you cannot pause, you cannot observe; if you do pause, there is nothing to observe. The results of such a method are in proportion to its absurdity.

After two thousand years of psychology, no one proposition is established to the satisfaction of psychologists. To this day they are divided into a multitude of schools, still disputing about the very elements of their doctrine. The psychologists have done some good in keeping up the activity of our understandings when there was no better work for our minds to do.

What we have said with regard to psychology as a positive science applies yet more strikingly to logic, that is, to the "study" of scientific method. Scientific method can be judged of only in action. It cannot be studied apart from the work on which it is employed. Such a study would be dead, could produce nothing of value in the mind which loses time on it. We may talk forever about scientific method, and state it in terms very wise and learned, without knowing half so much about it as the man who has once put it into practice upon a single piece of research. Thus have logicians, by dint of reading the aphorisms of Bacon and the discourses of Descartes mistaken their own dreams for science. We cannot explain the great logical procedures apart from their applications.

In the *second* place, a study of positive science as here conceived will regenerate education. The best minds are agreed that our European education, still essentially theological, metaphysical, and literary, must be superseded by a scientific education conformable to our time and needs.

Everything yet done to this end is inadequate. What is required is an organic conception of the sciences such as positivism presents. The exclusive specializing tendencies of our sciences spoil our teaching. If any student desires to form a conception of science as a whole, he is compelled to go through each department as it is now taught, as if he were to be only an astronomer or only a chemist. The result, be his intellect what it may, is unsatisfactory when what he requires is a general conception of the entire range of positive knowledge.

It is such a general conception of the entire range of the sciences which must henceforth be the permanent basis of all human combinations. It will constitute the mind of future generations. But to this end it is necessary that the sciences, considered as branches from one trunk, should yield us as a whole, their chief methods and results.

In the *third* place, the proposed study of the organically related generalizations of the positive sciences will aid the progress of each separate science. The divisions we establish between the sciences are, though not arbitrary, essentially superficial. The subject of our researches is one; we divide it for convenience, in order to deal more easily with separate problems. But it sometimes happens that we need what we cannot obtain under the present isolation of the sciences, namely a combination of several special points of view. For want of this, important problems wait for their solution.

To go into the past for an example: Descartes' grand conception with regard to analytical geometry, a discovery which has changed the whole face of mathematics, issued from the union of two sciences which had before been separately studied and pursued.

Again, it was undecided whether azote is a simple or a compound body. Almost all chemists held that azote is a simple body. But the illustrious Berzelius, influenced by the physiological observation that animals which receive no azote in their food have as much of it in their tissue as carnivorous animals, was able to throw new light on the question. Thus must physiology unite with chemistry to inform us whether azote is simple or compound, and to institute a new series of researches upon the relation between the composition of living bodies and their mode of alimentation.

In the *fourth* place, philosophy based on the positive sciences offers the only solid basis for that social reorganization which must succeed the critical condition in which even the most civilized nations are now living.

It cannot be necessary to argue that ideas govern the world or throw it into chaos, that all social mechanism rests upon opinions held by the members of society. The great political and moral crisis that societies are now undergoing proceeds from intellectual anarchy. Stability in fundamental principles is the first condition of genuine social order: We witness an utter disagreement on all such matters. Till a certain number of general ideas can be acknowledged as a rallying point for social doctrine, nations will remain in a revolutionary state whatever palliatives may be advised, and their institutions only provisional and makeshift.

But when the necessary agreement on first principles can be obtained, appropriate institutions will issue from them without shock or resistance. It is in this direction that those must look who desire a natural, regular, normal state of society.

Now, the existing disorder is abundantly accounted for by the existence, all at once, of three incompatible philosophies—the theological, the metaphysical, and the positive. Any one of these might alone secure some sort of social order. But while the three coexist, it is impossible for us to understand one another upon any essential point whatever. If this is true, we have only to ascertain which of the philosophies must, in the nature of things, eventually prevail.

Comte's point here might be illustrated by controversies centering in such questions as birth control, sterilization of the subnormal and criminal, and so on. Consider the case of sterilization. A sincere Catholic might oppose the measure as contrary to the will of God; a sincere democrat might oppose it as contrary to the rights of man; a social scientist disregarding both grounds of opposition, might simply argue that offspring born to such parents are likely to prove a needless burden and menace to a society which must, in the end, either support them or imprison them.

This problem, once recognized, cannot remain long unsolved; for all considerations point to a philosophy based on the positive sciences as the one destined to prevail. It alone has been advancing during the course of centuries while others have been declining. The fact is incontestable. Some may deplore it, but none deny it or destroy it, nor neglect it save on pain of being betrayed by illusory speculations.

This general revolution of the human mind is nearly accomplished. We have only to complete the hierarchy of the positive sciences by bringing the facts and problems of society within its comprehension. The preference which almost all minds, from the highest to the commonest, accord to positive knowledge over vague and mystical conceptions, is a pledge of what this philosophy will receive when it is once completed by the addition of a positive social science. When this has been accomplished, its supremacy will be automatic and will establish order throughout society.

Note on Sources.   The Comte material in this section is quoted, abridged, or paraphrased from his treatise *The Positive Philosophy*, Introduction and Chapters I and II.

Reading References.   Comte's influence has been considerable. Many unphilosophically minded scientists are Comteans, in the sense that they would endorse his positivism. Further reading in Comte should be done in those writings in which he sets forth his conception of the new social sciences, the new social order, and the new religion of humanity. John Morley's essay on Comte in one of the volumes of his *Miscellanies* is worthwhile. John Stuart Mill's *Auguste Comte and Positivism*, published shortly after Comte's death, is still an illuminating account and, with respect to what Mill describes as Comte's "later aberrations," a vigorous polemic. The account of Comte in Volume Two of Hoffding's *History of Modern Philosophy* is excellent. The standard work on Comte is by Lucien Lévy-Bruhl.

READING QUESTIONS

1. What Comte means by (a) a theological explanation, (b) a metaphysical explanation, (c) a positive or scientific explanation. Which of these explanations was, or could be, teleological. Why neither of the others could be.
2. His law of the three stages. The three substages of the first main stage. Contrast the last stage of each of the three main stages.
3. Bearing of Copernican astronomy on the first main stage.
4. Basis on which he classifies the six positive sciences. The resulting hierarchy.
5. Bearing on education of the hierarchical classification of the sciences.
6. Why he eliminates (a) logic, (b) psychology from the hierarchy of the positive sciences.
7. The four principal advantages to be derived from the study of the hierarchy of the positive sciences.
8. Show how Hume, Kant, and Comte reach antimetaphysical conclusions from different premises.
9. Comte's positivism provided no place for logic or psychology. Would it have a place for ethics?
10. Wherein you find Comte (a) most, (b) least convincing.

INDEPENDENT STUDY

1. Read the article on Comte by B. Mazlish in the *Encyclopedia of Philosophy*. Follow by reading J. S. Mill's small book *The Positive Philosophy of Auguste Comte*. Base a paper on Mill's critique of Comte.
2. An interesting project can be made out of R. L. Hawkins's two books: (a) *Auguste Comte and the United States*, (b) *Positivism in the United States*. These volumes give an account of Comte's influence in this country down to the Civil War. To enjoy working at

this topic you must have a taste for minor figures and episodes in American intellectual history.

3. Read the article on positivism by S. H. Swinney in Hastings's *Encyclopedia of Religion and Ethics*. Use the article as a basis for further relevant reading on Comte's religious ideas and followers. Supplement the Swinney article by the Comte chapter in Gilson's *Unity of Philosophical Experience*.

topic eight
experience and knowledge

SECTION 1. DAVID HUME: "SHOW ME THE IMPRESSION" [1]

From Locke to Hume. For most readers, during the closing years of the seventeenth and most of the eighteenth century, the problem of knowledge meant John Locke's *Essay Concerning Human Understanding.* His general common-sense tone, his homely appeal to experience, his determination not to be led into unverifiable speculations, all combined to secure for him a wide circle of readers and followers. It was only natural, therefore, that the next stage in the development of epistemological theory should take the form of an attempt to "begin where Locke left off." His position briefly was this: All knowledge may be analyzed into ideas. All ideas come to us from experience. All experience is by way of the senses. This *empiricism,* as it is called, was Locke's contribution to epistemological theory. His successor in these matters, David Hume, wrote for a generation that was familiar with the problem as Locke had stated it, and the appeal to experience as Locke had formulated it. Hume set himself a simple task: to deduce more rigorously the implications of Locke's position.

572   [1] For biographical note see pp. 19–20.

The Argument of the Passages. In a preceding topic we have met Hume as a critic of natural theology. His method there was to show what happens in natural theology if one sticks closely to the terms laid down by traditional speculation in these matters. He applies the same method in epistemology. It is proposed to make an appeal to experience, he writes; let the appeal be made, then, and not abandoned because it is found to lead to inconvenient consequences. The argument of his position is simple and direct. All knowledge may be analyzed into impressions and ideas. All ideas are derived from earlier impressions. We have certain "metaphysical" ideas, such as "matter," "mind," "causal connection," "free will," "the uniformity of nature." These ideas play a large part in human thinking and speculating. In fact, they are the fundamental terms in the modern man's general reflections upon the world about him. What are they worth? From what "impressions" are they derived? What corresponds to them in that actual experience to which Locke proposed to appeal? In each case Hume's answer is "they have no basis in experience." They are unjustifiable knowledge claims, and any speculation which incorporates them is waste of ink and paper. He begins, in the manner of Locke, by explaining that an inquiry into the nature of knowledge is directed toward eliminating as mere speculation all abstruse ideas which clutter up human thinking:

> The only method of freeing learning from abstruse questions is to inquire seriously into the nature of human understanding and show, from an exact analysis of its powers and capacity, that it is by no means fitted for such subjects.

The premises of his theory of knowledge are to be the following:

> We may divide all perceptions into two classes: impressions and ideas. By impressions I mean all our perceptions when we hear, see, feel, love, hate, desire, etc. Ideas are those less lively perceptions of which we are conscious when we reflect on any of those sensations mentioned above.
> All ideas are copies of impressions. . . . Even those ideas which seem most wide of this origin are found, upon a nearer scrutiny to be derived from it. . . . We shall always find that every idea is copied from a similar impression . . . it is impossible for us to think of anything which we have not antecedently felt by our senses.

The test of all ideas is to be "show me the impression":

> When we entertain any suspicion of a philosophical term, we need but inquire from what impression is that supposed idea derived. If it be not possible to assign any, this will serve to confirm our suspicion that it is employed without meaning. . . . By this means we can throw light upon ideas

and render them precise. Produce the impressions or originals from which the ideas are copied.

The first idea to be tested by the appeal to impressions is the now familiar idea of substance or matter:

Some philosophers found much of their reasonings on the distinction of *substance* and *quality*. I would fain ask them whether the idea of substance be derived from impressions of sensations or impressions of reflection. Does it arise from an impression? Point it out to us, that we may know its nature and qualities. But if you cannot point out any such impression, you may be certain you are mistaken when you imagine you have any such idea.

If the impression from which we derive our idea of substance be conveyed to us by our senses, I ask, by which of them? If by the eyes, it must be a color. If by the ears, it must be a sound. If by the palate, it must be a taste. And so of the other senses. But I believe none will assert that substance is either a color, a sound, or a taste.

Is the idea of substance, then, derived from an impression of reflection [i.e., introspection]? But impressions of reflection resolve themselves into our feelings, passions, and emotions, none of which can possibly resemble a substance. We have, therefore, no idea of substance, apart from that of a collection of qualities.

The idea of substance is nothing but a collection of ideas of qualities, united by the imagination and given a particular name by which we are able to recall that collection. The particular qualities which form a substance are commonly referred to an unknown something in which they are supposed to "inhere." This is a fiction.

We may well ask what causes us to believe in the existence of material substance. 'Tis certain there is no question in philosophy more abstruse. By what argument can it be proved that perceptions must be caused by external objects entirely different from them? By an appeal to experience? But here experience is and must be entirely silent. The mind has never anything present to it but its perceptions and cannot possibly have any experience of their connection with objects. The supposition of such a connection is, therefore, without any foundation in reasoning.

Philosophers distinguish betwixt *perceptions* and *objects*. The perceptions are supposed to be caused by the object, and to be interrupted, perishing and different at different times and for different people. The objects are supposed to cause the perceptions, and to be uninterrupted, continuous, and identical. But, however this new view may be esteemed, I assert that there are no principles, either of the understanding or the fancy which lead us to embrace this opinion of the double existence of perceptions and objects.

This hypothesis of the double existence of perceptions and objects has no primary recommendation to reason. The only existences of which we are certain are perceptions. Being immediately present to us by consciousness, they commend our strongest assent, and must be the foundation of all our reasonings. But, as nothing is ever present to the mind but perceptions, it follows that we can never observe any "object," or any connection, causal or otherwise, between perceptions and objects.

The idea of substance as something underlying a set of qualities is unable to produce its credentials. Away with it, then. As Hume remarks of all such ideas, "Commit it to the flames." From material substance he turns to the idea of mental or spiritual substance:

There are some philosophers (e.g., Berkeley) who imagine we are every moment intimately conscious of what we call our *self;* that we feel its existence and its continuance in existence, and are certain of its identity and simplicity.

Unluckily all these positive assertions are contrary to that very experience which is pleaded for them. Have we any idea of a self? From what impression could it be derived? It must be some impression that gives rise to every idea. But self or person is not any one impression. If any impression gives rise to the idea of one's self, that impression must continue to be the same, since one's self is supposed to continue to be the same. But there is no such continuing, constant impression.

For my part, when I enter most intimately into what I call my *self,* I always stumble on some particular perception or other, of heat or cold, light or shade, love or hatred, pain or pleasure, color or sound, etc. I never catch my self, distinct from some such perception.

If anyone thinks he has a different notion of his self, I must confess I can no longer reason with him. He may perceive something simple and continued which he calls his *self;* though I am certain there is no such principle in me.

Setting aside metaphysicians of this kind, I may venture to affirm of the rest of mankind that they are nothing but a bundle or collection of different perceptions which succeed each other with an inconceivable rapidity and are in a perpetual flux and movement. Our eyes cannot turn in their sockets without varying their perceptions. Our thoughts are still more variable. And all our other senses and powers contribute to this change.

The mind (or self) is a kind of theater where perceptions make their appearance, pass, repass, glide away, and mingle in an infinite variety. But there is no simplicity, no one simple thing present or pervading this multiplicity; no identity pervading this change; whatever natural inclination we may have to imagine that there is. The comparison of the theater must not mislead us: it persists, while the actors come and go. Whereas, only the successive perceptions constitute the mind.

The idea of mind or self or Spirit fails to reveal any basis in immediate impressions. That seals its fate. But the question persists: "Why do we entertain such a notion?" It is one thing to show that an idea is a mere fiction. It is another thing to account for its widespread presence in human thinking.

Why do we ascribe an identity amid these successive perceptions, and suppose our selves possessed of an invariable and uninterrupted existence through the whole course of our life? The identity which we ascribe to minds and selves is only a fictitious one, but why do we ascribe it?

Suppose we could see clearly into the mind of another, and observe that succession of perceptions which constitutes his mind. Suppose, too, that he always preserves the memory of a considerable part of past perceptions. It is evident that nothing could more readily contribute to bestowing a relation between these successive perceptions. Would not the frequent placing of these remembered perceptions in the chain of thought convey our imagination more easily from one to another? And so make the whole seem like the continuance of one object?

As memory alone acquaints us with the continuance and extent of a succession of perceptions, it is to be considered, on that account chiefly, as the source of personal identity. Had we no memory, we should never have any notion of that succession of perceptions which constitutes our self or person. But having once acquired this notion from the operation of memory, we can extend the same beyond our memory and come to include times which we have entirely forgot. And so arises the fiction of person and personal identity.

Material substance is gone. Mental substance is gone. Hume turns to the notion of causal connection between events. He is here proposing to invade the citadel of eighteenth-century science, a structure that was believed to rest squarely on the notion of causal connection. Hume's handling of this idea should be observed closely. His first question is, "What do people mean by the idea of causal connection?" His answer is that by causal connection they mean necessary connection; they believe that there is a necessary connection between a cause and its effect. His next question is the inevitable one: "What evidence, open to our senses, have we for believing that there is any necessity in causal connection?" His answer is, "None whatever."

There is no idea in metaphysics more obscure or uncertain than *necessary connection* between cause and effect. We shall try to fix the precise meaning of this term by producing the impressn from which it is copied.

When we look at external objects, and consider the operation of causes, we are never able, in a single instance, to discover a necessary connection; any quality which binds the effect to the cause, and renders the one a necessary consequence of the other. We find only that the effect does, in fact, follow the cause. The impact of one billiard ball upon another is followed by the motion of the second. There is here contiguity in space and time, but nothing to suggest necessary connection.

The scenes of the universe are continually shifting, and one object follows another in an uninterrupted succession. But any "force" or necessary connection pervading the whole machine never discovers itself in any of the sensible qualities of body. We know that heat is a constant attendant of flame. But as to any necessary connection between them, we have no room so much as to conjecture or imagine.

In single instances of causal connection we never, by our utmost scrutiny, discover anything but one event following another. We detect no necessary connection between the cause and its effect. All events seem loose and separate. One event follows another. But we observe no tie between them, beyond contiguity in space and time. They are contiguous, thus; but never connected. As we can have no idea of anything of which we have had no correspondent impression, the conclusion seems to be that we have no idea of necessary connection, and that these words are absolutely without meaning.

We are apt to imagine that we could discover effects from their causes by the mere operation of our reason, without experience. We fancy that, were we brought on a sudden into this world, we could have inferred that one billiard ball would communicate motion to another upon impact; and that we need not have waited for the event, in order to pronounce with certainty concerning it.

Knowledge of this relation arises entirely from experience. We find that particular objects are constantly conjoined with each other. Knowledge of this relation is not, in any instance, attained by reasonings *a priori*. Causes and effects are discoverable by experience, not by reason. Every effect is a distinct event from its cause. It could not, therefore, be discovered in the cause (prior to experience of their conjunction). Without the assistance of observation and experience, we should in vain pretend to determine any single event or infer any cause or effect. A man must be very sagacious who could discover by reasoning that ice is the effect of cold, without being previously acquainted with the operation of these qualities.

Hence no philosopher who is rational and modest has ever pretended to assign the ultimate cause of any natural operation. Ultimate springs and principles (causes) are totally shut off from human curiosity and enquiry.

As in the case of our idea of mind or self, Hume pauses to inquire why we ascribe to the connection between cause and effect something which is not revealed in experience.

Why do we imagine a necessary connection? From observing many constant conjunctions? But what is there in a number of instances which is absent from a single instance? Only this: After a repetition of similar instances the mind is carried by habit, upon the appearance of the cause, to expect the effect. This connection, which we feel in the mind, this customary and habitual transition of the imagination from a cause to its effect, is the impression from which we form the idea of necessary connection. There is nothing further in the case.

When we say a cause is necessarily connected with its effect, we mean, therefore, that they have acquired a connection in our thought: a conclusion which is somewhat extraordinary, but seems founded on sufficient evidence.

Every idea is copied from some impression. In all single instances of causal connection there is nothing that can suggest any idea of necessity. But when many instances have been experienced, we begin to entertain the idea. We then feel a new impression, to wit, a customary transition in our thoughts or imagination between the cause and its effect. This impression is the original of that idea which we seek for. For, as this idea arises from a number of similar instances, it must arise from the circumstance in which the number of instances differ from each single instance. This customary transition is the only circumstance in which they differ.

His rejection of the idea of cause as necessary connection suggests at once that he may be in a position to say something about the longstanding controversy over free will and determinism. That dispute arises because men hold (a) that human acts are caused, and (b) that causes are necessary connections. Hume's claim here is not that he can solve the problem but that he can dissolve it.

The question of man's free will has been long disputed among philosophers. Does man have freedom of will? Or are his acts determined? If motives determine acts, are motives themselves determined? This dispute has been much canvassed on all hands, and has led into such labyrinths of obscure sophistry that a sensible reader inclines to turn a deaf ear to the question, expecting neither instruction nor entertainment. I hope to make it appear that the whole controversy has hitherto turned merely upon words.

We ascribe necessity to matter. The degree and direction of every motion are prescribed with exactness. Do we similarly ascribe necessity to persons? Are the degree and direction of every action prescribed with exactness?

Two circumstances form the whole of the necessity we ascribe to matter: a constant conjunction between cause-events and effect-events, and a consequent inference in our minds from the one to the other. Beyond these two circumstances we have no notion of any necessity in the motion of matter.

Do not these two circumstances take place in the voluntary actions of men? Are not similar motives followed by similar actions? Are there not detectable uniformities in human action? Is it impossible to collect any general observations concerning mankind? Has experience of human affairs, however accurately digested by reflection, no purpose?

The most irregular and unexpected resolutions of men may be accounted for by those who know every particular circumstance of their character and situation. A genial person, contrary to expectation, may give a peevish answer, but he has a toothache or has not dined. Even when, as sometimes happens, an action cannot be accounted for, do we not put it down to our ignorance of relevant details?

Thus it appears that the conjunction between motive and action is as regular and uniform as between cause and effect in any part of nature. In both cases, constant conjunction and inference from one to the other.

Though constant conjunction and customary transition be all that is discoverable between a cause and an effect in nature, men believe they perceive something like a necessary connection. Then, when they consider the operations of their own wills and feel no such necessary connection between motive and action, they suppose there is a difference between the cause-effect relation and the motive-action relation. And are hence led to say that man's will, unlike matter, is free.

But our knowledge of causation, like our knowledge of motivation, is merely of a constant conjunction and a consequent inference in our minds from one to the other. It is the same in both cases. It is different only if it be pretended that the mind can perceive, in the operation of matter, some other connection between cause and effect than has place in the voluntary actions of intelligent beings. It is incumbent on those who pretend thus to make good their assertion. So long as we rashly suppose that we have an idea of some necessity in the operations of external nature, beyond constant conjunction and an habitual inference in our minds; and, at the same time, admit we can find nothing such in the voluntary actions of the mind, we shall continue in confusion.

Thus far Hume has examined the ideas of material substance, of mental substance, of causal connection, of free will. Of each in turn he has asked one question: "Upon what impression, received by the senses, does it rest? From each in turn he has received only silence for an answer. One more idea remains, namely, the idea of a uniformity of nature, the unquestioned premise of all our inductions and generalizations from nature. Why do we believe, so unquestioningly, that the "future will resemble the past"? Why do we argue, for instance, that fire will always melt ice, when our only ground for this belief is the fact that it has done so in the past?

All our conclusions from experience proceed on the supposition that the future will resemble the past. To prove that the future will resemble the past, by arguing from experience, is evidently going in a circle, and taking that for granted which is the very point in question.

As to past experience, it can be allowed to give direct and certain information of those precise objects only, and that precise period of time only, which fell under its cognizance. But why this experience should be extended to future times and other objects, is the question on which I would insist. So to extend it is a process of mind or thought of which I would willingly know the foundation.

Not by an argument from experience can we prove this resemblance of the past to the future, for all such arguments are founded on the supposition of that resemblance. Let the course of things be allowed hitherto ever so regular. That alone, without some new inference, does not prove that for the future it will continue so.

My practice, you say, refutes my doubts. But you mistake the purport of my question. In practice I am satisfied. As a philosopher, who has some share of curiosity, I will not say skepticism, I want to learn the foundation of this inference. No reading, no inquiry, has yet been able to remove my difficulty. Upon what grounds can we argue that the future will resemble the past? Upon what grounds expect similar effects from causes which are similar?

Geometry (or any mathematics), when taken into the assistance of science, is unable to remedy this defect. Every part of applied mathematics proceeds on the supposition that certain laws are established by nature in her operations. Mathematical reasonings are employed to assist experience in the discovery of these laws, or to determine their influence in particular instances. But the discovery of the law itself is owing merely to experience, and all the mathematical reasoning in the world could never lead one step toward the knowledge of it.

In all reasonings from experience, then, there is a step taken by the mind (that the future resembles the past)) which is not supported by any argument. Nevertheless, we take this step. There must therefore be some other principle (than rational or demonstrative argument).

Though none but a fool or madman will ever pretend to dispute the authority of experience, it may surely be allowed a philosopher to have so much curiosity as to examine the principle of human nature which gives authority to experience.

This principle is custom, or habit. Wherever repetition produces a propensity to renew the same act, without being impelled by any reasoning, we say this propensity is the effect of custom or habit. That habit or custom is the ultimate principle of all our conclusions from experiences, seems to be the only hypothesis which explains why we draw from many instances an inference which we are not able to draw from one instance that is in no respect different from them.

All inferences from experience are, therefore, effects of habit or custom, not of reasoning. The conclusions which we draw, based on reasoning, from considering one circle, are the same which we would draw from surveying all circles. But no man, having seen only one body impelled by another, could infer that every other similar body would move after a like impulse.

Custom, then, not reason, is the great guide of human life. It is that principle alone which renders our experience useful to us, and makes us expect, for the future, a similar train of events with those which have appeared in the past. Without the influence of custom, we should be entirely ignorant of every matter of fact beyond what is immediately present to the memory or the senses.

What, then, is the conclusion of the whole matter? A simple one, though, it must be confessed, pretty remote from the common theories of philosophy. All belief concerning matters of fact or real existence, is derived merely from some object present to the memory or the senses, and a customary conjunction between that and some other object. Having found, in many instances, that two kinds of objects have been conjoined (say, flame and heat), the mind is carried by custom to expect the same in the future. This is the whole operation of the mind in all our conclusions concerning matters of fact and existence.

Here, then, is a kind of pre-established harmony between the course of nature and formation of our beliefs. Custom or habit is the principle of human nature by which this correspondence, so necessary to the subsistence of our species and the regulation of our conduct, has been effected. Did not the presence of an object excite in us the ideas of other objects commonly conjoined with it, all human knowledge would be limited to the narrow sphere of our memory and senses. Those who delight in the discovery of purposes in nature have here ample subject to employ their wonder and admiration.

As this operation of the mind, whereby we infer like effects from like causes, is so essential to human life, it is not probable that it could be trusted to the fallacious deductions of our reason, which is slow in its operation and extremely liable to error and mistake. It is more conformable to the ordinary wisdom of nature to secure so necessary an act of the mind by some instinct or mechanical tendency which may be infallible in its operations and independent of all the labored deductions of understanding.

Hume is now at the end of his review:

> By way of conclusion to these reflections on diverse questions: When we run over libraries, persuaded of the principles here expounded, what havoc must we make? If we take in hand any volume, of divinity or metaphysics, for instance, let us ask: Does it contain any reasoning concerning quantity or number? No. Does it contain any experimental (probable) reasoning concerning matter of fact? No. Commit it then to the flames: for it can contain nothing but sophistry and illusion.
>
> I am at first affrighted and confounded with that forlorn solitude in which I am placed by my philosophy, and fancy myself some strange uncouth monster, utterly abandoned and disconsolate. Fain would I run into the crowd for shelter and warmth. I call upon others to join me. But no one will hearken to me. Everyone keeps at a distance, and dreads that storm which beats upon me from every side. I have exposed myself to the enmity of all metaphysicians, logicians, mathematicians, and theologians. Can I wonder at the insults I must suffer? I have declared my disapprobation of their systems. Can I be surprised if they should express a hatred of my ideas and my person? When I look about me, I foresee on every hand, dispute, contradiction, anger, calumny, detraction. When I turn my eye inward, I find only doubt and ignorance. Every step I take is with hesitation; every new reflection makes me dread an error and absurdity in my reasoning.

Note on Sources. The Hume material in this section is quoted, abridged, or paraphrased from his book *An Enquiry Concerning Human Understanding,* particularly Sections 1, 2, 4, 5, 7, 8, and 12. However, since Hume had already, in an earlier book, *A Treatise of Human Nature,* worked over much of the materials in those sections of the *Enquiry,* I have sometimes drawn on corresponding sections of the *Treatise* to replace or supplement passages in the *Enquiry.*

Reading References. It would be advantageous to consult the pages on Hume in B. A. G. Fuller's *History of Philosophy.* They form a section in a chapter on Locke, Berkeley, Hume. The Hume portion should be read straight through. It brings together his critique of natural theology and his theory of knowledge. T. H. Huxley's little book on Hume, recommended elsewhere, is noted again here. Time given to C. W. Hendel's *Studies in the Philosophy of David Hume* will be well spent.

READING QUESTIONS

1. Hume proposes to free learning from abstruse questions. (a) What are the marks of an "abstruse" question? (b) How he proposes to free learning from such questions.
2. He begins by distinguishing between "impressions" and "ideas." What is the distinction here?
3. He then says that all ideas are copies of impressions. Is this an empirical generalization? Does it presuppose in any way that the future will resemble the past?
4. What test does he propose for all ideas? Unless he knows that all ideas do originate in, are copies of, impressions, how good is this test?
5. If he does not know that all ideas originate in, are copies of, impressions, then should his test be worded somehow thus: "If an idea originates in, is a copy of, an impression, then and only then is it to be validated by tracing it to its impression"?
6. Enumerate the "abstruse" ideas to which he applies his proposed test.
7. His criticism of the traditional idea of material substance. His final redefinition of it.
8. His criticism of the traditional idea of the self as a spiritual substance. His final redefinition of it. How he accounts for the traditional, albeit mistaken, idea of the self as a substance.
9. If you criticize or punish a person for wrongdoing, do you presuppose that the person criticized (or punished) is the same person who did the wrong act?
10. His criticism of the traditional idea of a "necessary connection" between a cause and its effect. His final redefinition of it. How he accounts for the traditional, albeit mistaken, idea of causal connection as necessary connection.
11. The impression of "customary transition" is the origin of the idea of "necessary connection." Is there more to the idea of necessary connection than simply constant conjunction? If so, then how did this "more" get there? Do impressions give rise to ideas that contain "more" than the impressions? When they do this, is the result an "abstruse" idea? Has Hume provided for the power in impressions to produce "abstruse" ideas? Toward the end of his account he traces all thinking about matters of fact to the operation of a certain "mechanical tendency." Do we, then, owe our "abstruse" ideas to the presence and operation of this "mechanical" tendency?

12. Which: (a) Constant conjunction is the meaning of causal connection, or (b) constant conjunction is evidence of causal connection.
13. Why, probably, Hume's rejection of the idea of necessary connection between causes and effects jolted some persons more than his rejection of the idea of substance.
14. How he dissolves the traditional problem of free will.
15. When we act we frequently get the impression that we could have done otherwise. Hence our idea that we could have done otherwise. Would Hume deny that we do get this impression? Or that we are therefore entitled to the corresponding idea?
16. When something in "external nature" acts, e.g., a stone rolling down a hill, do *we* get the impression that *it* could have done otherwise? If not, why *should* we have the idea that it could have? If we shouldn't, then are the two cases analogous?
17. His criticism of the traditional idea ("supposition") that the future will resemble the past.
18. He ascribes this traditional idea (that the future will resemble the past) to the operation of a "mechanical tendency." What is a "mechanical" tendency? Are there any tendencies which are not mechanical? Are we to suppose that Hume's efforts to think about thinking, to rid the mind of abstruse questions, is itself simply the working out of a mechanical tendency? If we owe our abstruse ideas to the operation of this mechanical tendency in human thinking, then how are we to know that Hume's own ideas are not themselves abstruse?
19. My practice, you say, refutes my doubts. How so? His rejoinder.
20. Wherein you find Hume (a) most, (b) least convincing.

INDEPENDENT STUDY

1. Read the article on Hume by D. G. C. MacNabb in the *Encyclopedia of Philosophy*. The article offers an overview of pretty much the whole of Hume's philosophy. Pick out one "area," and use one or more of the volumes in the bibliography at the end of the article to work out a paper on the area that you find interesting.
2. Read Sections IV and V in Hume's small book *Enquiry Concerning Human Understanding*. Section IV expounds what Hume refers to as "Skeptical Doubts Concerning the Operations of the Understanding." Section V expounds a "Skeptical Solution of

These Doubts." Make a clearly connected, step-by-step analysis of Hume's claims in these two sections. What is "Skeptical" about the solution?
3. Read and give an account of the papers by R. P. Wolff ("Hume's Theory of Mental Activity") and T. Penelhum ("Hume on Personal Identity") in *Hume,* edited by V. C. Chappell.
4. Read carefully through the somewhat elaborate table of contents in *Studies in the Philosophy of David Hume,* by C. W. Hendel. Choose any four chapters, give them a careful, step-by-step reading. Then write on whatever you find yourself most interested in.

SECTION 2. IMMANUEL KANT: THE A PRIORI AND THE EMPIRICAL

From Hume to Kant.   Locke, it will be remembered, was led to pose the problem of knowledge as a measure of caution. His words indicate this:

If by this inquiry into the nature of the understanding I can discover the powers thereof, how far they reach, to what things they are in any degree proportionate and where they fail us, I suppose it may be of use to prevail with the busy mind of man to be more cautious in meddling with things exceeding its comprehension, to stop when it is at the utmost extent of its tether, and to sit down in a quiet ignorance of those things which, upon examination, are found to be beyond the reach of our capacities.

Nothing could be more straightforward. From an insight into the nature of knowledge, to recognize that some things lie beyond its reach. The hypothesis that Locke advanced was this: All knowledge comes from experience and all experience is by way of the senses.

By the middle of the eighteenth century, in Hume's writings, things had undergone a change. Indeed, it would perhaps be more accurate to say that they had come to something of an impasse. What Hume did, in effect, was to take Locke's appeal to experience and push it to its "logical conclusion." This conclusion was that much of the familiar furniture of man's world was dissolved into a series of question marks. The metaphysical notions of material substance and mental substance were declared to be so much verbiage. No appeal to experience showed any grounds for believing in their existence. The notion of free will went the same way. Only the come-and-go of impressions and ideas remained. The generally accepted notions of cause and uniformity of nature met a like fate; they were mere habits, mere effect of custom. The theological notions of God as first cause and designer were weighed and found wanting. Hume tried, indeed, to undermine the credibility even of mathematics, by arguing, for example, that such geometrical notions as straight line, circle, equal angles, and so on, were "mere notions" to which nothing discoverable in experience could be said to correspond. Hume's own consternation at this reduction of Locke's empiricism was genuine. His words will be recalled:

I am at first affrighted and confounded with that forlorn solitude in which I am placed by my philosophy, and fancy myself some strange uncouth monster, utterly abandoned and disconsolate. Fain would I run into the crowd for shelter and warmth. I call upon others to join me. But no one will hearken to me. Everyone keeps at a distance, and dreads that storm which beats upon me from every side. I have exposed myself to the enmity of all metaphysicians, logicians, mathematicians, and theologians. Can I wonder at the insults I must suffer? I have declared my disapprobation of their systems. Can I be surprised if they should express a hatred of my ideas and my person? When I look about me, I foresee on every hand, dispute, contradiction, anger, calumny, detraction. When I turn my eye inward, I find only doubt and ignorance. Every step I take is with hesitation; every new reflection makes me dread an error and absurdity in my reasoning.

These conclusions, which filled Hume with grave doubts about the whole epistemological enterprise, were meanwhile being reflected upon by the German philosopher, Immanuel Kant. They did not fill his mind with fright and confusion. Their effect was, to quote his well-known words, "to rouse me from my dogmatic slumbers." Where Hume was "affrighted and confounded," Kant was stimulated and enlightened. For he detected an element of irony in the situation. Here was Hume, in the name of a theory of knowledge, denying that there is any knowledge. Knowing that it is the function of a theory to account for that of which it is a theory, not to deny it, Kant was moved to say, in effect, "So much the worse for Hume's theory." If the appeal to experience will not serve as a satisfactory hypothesis, by means of which to account for the fact of knowledge, then so much the worse for the appeal to experience; surely, not so much the worse for knowledge. Hume's conclusions served only to convince Kant that unrelieved empiricism must somehow be mistaken.

That is the first fact to be kept in mind with respect to Kant. There is another fact, equally important. It was this: Kant believed firmly in the existence of God, in the freedom of the will, and the immortality of the soul. But, being also widely read in modern philosophy he knew that his age, the Age of Reason, was unsympathetic with such convictions. The age was willing, in theory, that a man should entertain these convictions as a matter of faith. But it would not in practice let it go at that. It was inclined to challenge, even to ridicule, such faith. It urged an appeal to reason, confident that in such an appeal faith would come off second best. Everything was to be tried at the "bar of reason." Kant's answer to all this was to carry the war into the enemies' country. He determined to put reason itself on trial. To this end he wrote his large and epoch-making treatise *Critique of Pure Reason.*

Kant's handling of the problem of knowledge was motivated, then, by these two considerations. First, a theory of knowledge was required to replace the empiricism of Hume. Second, a theory of knowledge was required to deflate the appeal to reason that was placing obstacles in the way of ventures of faith. What Kant proposed was this: to replace the appeal to experience and the appeal to reason by a critical analysis of the function of reason in experience.

Biographical Note. Immanuel Kant was born in Germany in 1724 and died in 1804 at the age of seventy-nine. His parents were members of a German sect known as Pietists. This meant that he was associated from infancy with persons of a devout turn of mind. This devotion to the "fundamentalism" of his parents did not outlast his adolescence, but it was succeeded by an equally rigorous adherence to the fundamentals of morality. His early education was intended to direct his thoughts toward the church. University years directed them along more secular lines. He graduated in classics, mathematics, science, and philosophy. At the age of thirty-one he became a privatdocent in the University at Königsberg. Here, for fifteen years, he provided coaching in mathematics, physics, physical geography, logic, and metaphysics. During these years he was gradually awakened to the dilemmas of the modern mind. He took his mathematics and his natural sciences with great seriousness; he found, on the one hand, that the kind of world to which they pointed was "incompatible" with his belief in God, free will, immortality, and the supremacy of a high-minded morality; and he found, on the other, that the unquestioned appeal to experience among progressive minds cast doubts on the reliability of mathematics and the sciences. This was not the only respect in which the "modern mind" was at sixes and sevens with itself. In the fields of theology and metaphysics, confusion reigned. In the name of reason there were claims and counterclaims; theism, atheism, skepticism with respect to Deity; dualism, materialism, idealism, skepticism, with respect to the nature of ultimate reality. All these eddies and cross-currents met in the mind of this young man whose business was to provide instruction in science and philosophy. The thought that gradually took shape in his speculations was this: The modern mind appears to be divided against itself. Used in one field, it has provided us with the beauties and achievements of mathematics and science; used in another field, it has created endless confusion in which unverifiable speculation is met with unverifiable denial. He looked into his own mind and found two unshakable convictions; on the one hand, mathematics and the sciences must be "saved" from the skeptics; on the other, the normal beliefs of a conscientious and God-fearing soul must be "saved" from both the sciences and the skeptics. As these various dilemmas clarified themselves, he saw his task: What was required, apparently, was an examination of the human mind itself. His thoughts began to shape themselves along these lines. He was, at the age of forty-six, appointed to the chair of philosophy in his university. In his inaugural address he communicated to his fellow professors his intention to devote himself to a critical analysis of the mind's power to know. For the next eleven years he did just that, and in 1781, at the age of fifty-seven, published his long-awaited *Critique of Pure Reason*.

The Argument of the Passages. Kant's problem, in its general outlines, was clear enough. The question was where to begin. He found a starting point in the distinction between *a priori* and *a posteriori* knowledge. Both he held to be undoubted facts, but the current appeal to experience would account only for the latter; the former it either ignored or sought to deny. This point gave Kant the opening he required. It is time to let him speak for himself. As the passages begin, he is reflecting upon metaphysics. As his thoughts move around, he hits upon the distinction between *a priori* and *a posteriori* knowledge.

My object is to persuade all those who think metaphysics worth studying, to pause, and, neglecting everything that has been done, to propose the preliminary question: Is metaphysics possible?

How does it come about that metaphysics, unlike other sciences, cannot obtain universal and permanent recognition? It seems almost ridiculous that, while every other science is continually advancing, we should, in metaphysics, move constantly around on the same spot without gaining a single step. We do not find men, confident of their ability to shine in other sciences, venturing their reputation here. And so its followers have melted away.

Time was when metaphysics held a royal place among all the sciences. If the will were taken for the deed, the importance of her subject matter might well have secured her that place of honor. But at present it is the fashion to despise her; and like Hecuba, she languishes forsaken and alone. Time was when her rule was despotic. But intestinal war and anarchy broke out. The skeptics, a kind of nomad tribe, despising all settled cultivation of her lands, broke up all civil society. Fortunately their number was small; they could not prevent the old settlers from returning to till the ground afresh. But the old settlers returning had no fixed plan or agreement. At present there reign in metaphysics weariness and indifference, the mother of chaos and night. Near-reforms, ill-applied study, have rendered her counsels dark, confused, and useless.

It is vain, however, to assume a kind of artificial indifference with respect to inquiries to which human nature cannot be indifferent. Nay, even
those who pretend indifference, if they think at all, fall back inevitably into
those very metaphysical dogmas which they profess to despise.

Nevertheless, this widespread indifference to metaphysics is worth attention and consideration. It is, clearly, not the result of carelessness but of
matured judgment. Our age will no longer rest satisfied with the mere appearance of knowledge in these matters. Its patience has run out. This fact
constitutes a powerful challenge, a powerful appeal to reason to undertake
anew the most difficult of her duties, to institute a court of appeal which,
while it will protect her own rights, will dismiss all groundless claims. This
court of appeal is no other than a critique of pure reason.

By a *critique of pure reason* I do not mean a criticism of books and systems. I mean a critical analysis of the power of reason itself, touching that
whole class of knowledge which it may strive after unassisted by experience.
This must decide the questions: Is metaphysics possible or impossible?

Since the origin of metaphysics nothing has ever happened which was
more decisive to its fate than the attack made upon it by David Hume. He
started from a single, but important concept, namely causal connection. He
challenged reason, which pretends to have given birth to this idea, to tell
him by what right she thinks anything to be so constituted that it is necessarily connected with something else; for that is the meaning of causal connection. He demonstrated, beyond refutation, that it is impossible for us to see
why, in consequence of the existence or occurrence of one thing, another
thing must necessarily exist or occur also.

Hence he inferred that reason was deluded with reference to this conception of causal connection; that she erroneously considered it one of her
children; that, in reality, it was nothing but a bastard child of imagination
impregnated by experience; that a subjective necessity of habit was mistaken for an objective necessity arising from insight. I frankly confess, the
suggestion of David Hume was the very thing which, many years ago first interrupted my dogmatic slumber, and gave my investigations in the field of
speculative philosophy quite a new direction.

Hume's question was not whether the conception of causal connection
was right, useful, even indispensable for our knowledge of nature. This he
had never doubted. His question was whether that conception could be
thought, by reason, *a priori;* whether it thus possessed an inner truth, independent of all experience. That was Hume's problem. It was, as we see, a
question concerning the origin of the conception, not its indispensability.

I tried whether Hume's objection could not be put in a general form, and
soon found that the conception of causal connection was by no means the
only idea by which the understanding thinks the connection of things *a
priori.*

It may be advisable to interrupt the movement of Kant's thought
at this point. He has already used this fundamental term *a priori*
twice. He is going to explain what it means, give an illustration of its
use, and contrast it with *a posteriori.* The entire argument of his

position revolves around this idea. It may therefore be well to try to fix its meaning for ourselves. If we say that some fact is known, or can be known, *a priori*, we mean that it is known or can be known in advance of experience of it. Thus, we might say, "I don't know whether there are any triangles on the far side of the moon; but if there are, I can say *a priori* that the sum of their interior angles will equal two right angles." Or, we might say, "I don't know whether a slave economy was the cause of the fall of the Roman Empire, but I can say *a priori* that there was a cause." Or, we might say, "I don't know whether there are two chairs in the next room, and two in the hall; but if there are, I can say *a priori* that they will add up to four chairs." Or, we might say, "I don't know what happened either before or after I ate my dinner, but I can say *a priori* that something happened both before and after." These illustrations could be extended indefinitely. As Kant will indicate, the problem which they present is this: How does it happen that we can know certain sorts of facts *a priori*?

It is a question worth investigating, whether there exists any knowledge independent of experience and all sense impressions. Such knowledge is called *a priori* and is distinguished from *a posteriori* knowledge which has its sources in experience. That there is genuine *a priori* knowledge, that we can advance independent of all experience, is shown by the brilliant example of mathematics.

This term *a priori* requires closer definition. People are wont to say, even with regard to knowledge derived from experience, that we have it or might have it *a priori*. They mean we might derive it from a general rule. Thus, of one who undermines the foundations of his house, they would say he might have known *a priori* that it would tumble down; know it, that is, from the general rule that unsupported bodies fall. But this general rule has itself been derived from experience. Whoever knows this general rule had first to learn it from experience. He could not have known this entirely *a priori*. (This Hume has shown.) In what follows, we shall use the term more strictly. We shall understand by *a priori* that which is absolutely independent of all experience, and not of this or that experience only. Opposed to this is *a posteriori* or empirical knowledge, such as is derived from experience.

Experience tells us what is, but not that it must necessarily be as it is. It therefore never gives us any necessary, *a priori*, knowledge. Experience never imparts to its judgments any strict universality, but only relative universality (by means of induction) so that we ought always to say, "so far as we have experienced, there is no exception to this or that rule." Necessity and universality are criteria of the *a priori*. If, therefore, a judgment is thought with strict universality and necessity so that no exception is admitted as possible, it cannot have been derived from experience.

We have here a mystery. We must discover the ground of *a priori* judgments. We must understand the conditions which render them possible. The real problem is contained in the question: How is *a priori* knowledge possible? That metaphysics has hitherto remained in so vacillating a condition of ignorance and contradiction is due entirely to the fact that this problem has been ignored.

David Hume, who among all philosophers approached nearest to this problem, arrived at the conclusion that *a priori* knowledge is impossible. According to his reasoning everything we call metaphysics would turn out to be mere delusion. But if he had grasped clearly the problem of the *a priori* he would never have thought of an assertion which destroys all metaphysics, because he would have seen that, according to such an argument, neither was mathematics possible (since it contains *a priori* judgments). And from such an assertion his good sense would probably have saved him.

It is to be noted that our problem is not: Are *a priori* judgments possible? For there are enough of them to hand, of undoubted certainty, that we need not argue for their possibility. (What is actual must be possible.) We must inquire into the grounds of the possibility of their existence. The proper problem, upon which all depends, when expressed precisely is this: How are *a priori* propositions possible?

It again seems advisable to break in upon Kant's meditations. He is saying things that cut deep. He began by admitting a sort of bankruptcy on all hands in matters philosophical. He added, however, that no philosopher worth his salt would therefore feel justified in crying quits. He realized that Hume had been an important factor, despite his negative conclusions. He wants, above all, a toe-hold, some fact upon which he can take a stand. His eye catches sight of this apparently neglected distinction between *a priori* knowledge and *a posteriori* knowledge. He fastens on this, realizing that this may have important implications. He sees, also, that the fact of the *a priori* raises a problem. The *a priori* is a fact. The problem is how to account for it.

Although all our knowledge begins *with* experience, it does not follow that it arises entirely *from* experience. For it is quite possible that our empirical knowledge is a compound of that which we receive through impressions and that which our own faculty of knowing (incited by impressions) supplies from itself—a supplement to impressions which we do not distinguish from that raw material (i.e., impressions) until long practice has roused our attention and rendered us capable of separating one from the other.

Hitherto it has been supposed that all our knowledge must conform to the objects, but, under that supposition, all attempts to establish any knowledge about them *a priori* have come to nothing.

The experiment therefore ought to be made, whether we should not succeed better by assuming that objects must conform to our forms of knowledge. For this would agree better with the required possibility of an *a priori* knowledge of objects; that is, with the possibility of settling something about those objects before they are given us in experience.

We have here the same case as with the first thought of Copernicus. Not

being able to explain the movements of the heavenly body so long as he assumed that the stars moved around the spectator, he tried assuming the spectator to be turning around and the stars to be at rest. A similar experiment
may be tried in metaphysics, so far as our knowledge of objects is concerned.
If our knowledge has to conform to the nature of objects, I do not see how
we could know anything *a priori*. But if the object of knowledge has to conform to the constitution of our power of knowing, I can very well conceive
the possibilities of such *a priori* knowledge.

If Copernicus had not dared, by an hypothesis which contradicted the
senses, to seek the observed movements in the spectator instead of in the
heavenly bodies, the laws of planetary motion would have remained for ever
undiscovered. I propose my own view, which has so many analogies with
the Copernican hypothesis, as, at first, an hypothesis only.

Kant's argument at this point becomes too complicated for
reproduction in quotation. For that reason, the next passages are
mere descriptions of his argument, not selections or paraphrases
from his *Critique*. Thus far, what he has been saying comes to this:
Metaphysical speculation is in disrepute. Hume's criticism seems to
have put an end to it. His conclusions followed from his dogma that
all knowledge comes from experience. Since, on this premise, he
could not account for *a priori* knowledge, he denied it. But a theory
of knowledge that issues in a denial of knowledge is a poor theory. *A
priori* knowledge is a fact to be accounted for, not an illusion to be
denied. Since the appeal to experience has failed, something else
must be tried. A new theory of knowledge is required to account for
the fact of *a priori* knowledge. Kant's hypothesis is this: That knowledge is a joint product of mind and external world, arising in experience. This hypothesis raises the following question: If knowledge is
a joint product of mind and external world, then what part of the joint
product is contributed by the mind? Kant answers by distinguishing
between the form and the content of knowledge. The form of knowledge is contributed by the mind. The content is contributed by the
external world. In the production of knowledge the mind acts to impose form on content supplied by the external world. This leads to a
new problem: If knowledge is a joint product of mind and world, and
mind's contribution is the form, can these formal elements in knowledge be isolated and analyzed? What, in other words, is the form that
mind contributes?

Kant answers by distinguishing between perceptual, conceptual,
and speculative knowledge. To our perceptual knowledge, mind
contributes the forms of space and time. These Kant calls *forms of
sensibility*. To our conceptual knowledge mind contributes the forms
of quantity, quality, relation, and modality. These, when further analyzed, he calls *categories of understanding*. To our speculative
knowledge, mind contributes the forms of self, universe, and God.

These he calls *ideas of reason.* I shall refer to them as *forms of speculation.* Space and time are forms of perception, not things perceived. Things are always perceived spread-out-and-strung-along,
are always perceived in a background-foreground and a before-and-
after setting. This invariable spatial and temporal character is the
form of all perceptual knowledge. On Kant's hypothesis, it is due to
the "diffracting" action of mind or consciousness. Except as forms of
consciousness, these words have no meaning. They are forms of
awareness, not things of which we are aware. In Kant's words, space
and time are "empirically real, but transcendentally ideal," that is,
real in experience but otherwise only ideal. Quotations are here possible once more:

> Space does not represent any property of things in themselves, nor does
> it represent them in their relation to one another. . . . Space is nothing but
> the form of all appearances of outer sense. It is the subjective condition of
> sensibility under which alone outer perception is possible for us.
>
> Since the capacity to be affected by objects must precede all perceptions
> of these objects, it can readily be understood how the form of all appear-
> ances (i.e., space) can be given prior to all perceptions, and so exist in the
> mind *a priori;* and how, as a pure intuition, in which all objects must be de-
> termined, it can contain, prior to all experiences, principles which determine
> the relations of these objects. It is, therefore, solely from the human stand-
> point that we can speak of space, of extended things. If we depart from the
> subjective, the representation of space stands for nothing whatsoever.
>
> This predicate (i.e., space) can be ascribed to things only insofar as they
> appear to us; that is, to objects of sensibility. Since, however, we cannot treat
> the special conditions of sensibility as conditions of the possibility of things,
> but only of their appearances, we can indeed say that space comprehends all
> things that appear to us as external, but not all things in themselves. For we
> cannot judge in regard to the perceptions of other kinds of thinking beings,
> whether they are bound by the same conditions as limit us.
>
> The proposition that all things are side by side in space is valid under
> the limitation that these things are viewed as objects of our perception. Our
> exposition claims the reality, the objective validity, of space in respect of
> whatever can be presented us; but also, at the same time, the ideality of
> space in respect of things when they are considered in themselves, that is,
> without regard to the constitution of our sensibility.
>
> We assert, then, the empirical reality of space, as regards all possible
> outer experience, and, at the same time, its transcendental ideality, i.e., that
> it is nothing at all, immediately we withdraw the said condition, namely lim-
> itation to possible experience, and look upon it as something that underlies
> things in themselves.
>
> The transcendental conception of appearances in space is a critical re-
> minder that nothing perceived in space is a thing in itself; that space is not a
> form inhering in things in themselves as their intrinsic property; that objects
> in themselves are nothing but mere representations of our sensibility, the
> form of which is space. The true correlate of sensibility, the thing in itself, is

not known, and cannot be known, through these representations; and in experience no question is ever asked in regard to it.

Kant's remarks on the status of time, which parallel, roughly, his remarks on the status of space, may be quoted in part:

Time is not an empirical conception that has been derived from any experience. For neither coexistence nor succession (the two modes of time) would ever have come within our perception, if the representation of time were not presupposed as underlying them *a priori.*

Time is not something which exists of itself or inheres in things. Were it a determination (i.e., property) of things in themselves, it could not be known *a priori.* But such *a priori* knowledge is quite possible if time is nothing but the subjective condition under which alone perception can take place in us. For, that being so, this form of intuition can be represented prior to the objects and therefore *a priori.*

Time is a purely subjective condition of our human perception, and, in itself, apart from the subject, is nothing. . . . What we are maintaining is the empirical reality of time, its objective validity of all objects which allow of ever being given to our senses. Since our perception is always sensible (i.e., by the senses), no object can ever be given to us in experience which does not conform to the condition of time. On the other hand, we deny to time any claim to absolute reality; that is to say, we deny that it belongs to things absolutely, as their condition or property independently of any reference to the form of our perception. Properties that belong to things in themselves can never be given to us through the senses. This, then, is what constitutes the ideality of time.

What we mean by the *ideality of time* is this: If we abstract from the subjective conditions of sensuous perception, time is nothing, and cannot be ascribed to the objects in themselves apart from their relation to our perception, neither in the way of subsistence nor of inherence.

By *categories* Kant means such forms of understanding things as unity and plurality, substance and quality, cause and effect, and so on. He enumerates twelve. The number is not as important as his recognition that conceptual knowledge has form as well as content, and his hypothesis that the form is the mind's contribution. Thus, to consider one of these categories, causation is a form of understanding, not a reality in its own right. When a drop in temperature causes the water to freeze, there are not three things, namely, dropping temperature, freezing water, and a cause connecting the two. Rather, there are two things understood in terms of a category. Our understanding of anything involves many such categories. Kant's point is the simple, but revolutionary, suggestion that categories of understanding are not objects of knowledge but forms of knowledge; not things known but ways of knowing. Our understanding of things given in experience is conditioned by the categories in terms of which our minds work. These categories are forms of understanding what is given in experience; they are, themselves, not given in experience.

Speculation is the attempt to carry understanding beyond the limits of experience. Since the categories are only forms to which experience gives content, any such attempt is doomed to fail. To use a common expression, it can never be anything more than "mere speculation." Kant notes, and condemns, three forms of speculation, three ways in which the mind perennially seeks to transcend the limits of experience.

The first of these is the attempt to speculate on the nature of the mind itself, to seek to understand the nature of that which contributes form to knowledge. Beyond detecting the forms, we cannot go. The mind itself is outside of experience. It is itself never given in experience. It can never be content for its own forms. The attempt to formulate a rational psychology, that is, to gain an understanding of the mind, soul, self, ego, is, on Kant's theory of knowledge, to attempt the impossible. We cannot pierce beyond the stream of consciousness, to a knowledge of the factors that make it to be the kind of thing it is. That there is a mind, beyond the stream of consciousness, Kant is prepared to argue, as against Hume. His reason for refusing to stop short with Hume is simple. The latter, it will be recalled, "reduced" mind to a succession of awarenesses. To this Kant has a rejoinder. The fact to be accounted for, he points out, is not a succession of awarenesses, but an awareness of succession. If that which is aware passed with the awareness, there could be no awareness of succession. But there is precisely this, namely, awareness of succession.

The second attempt to extend knowledge beyond experience, is to speculate on the nature of the whole of things, beyond what is given piecemeal in experience. The attempt to formulate a rational cosmology, that is, to extend the categories beyond experience is to attempt the impossible. The mind's categories are valid only within experience. As the universe comes within the grasp of experience, it becomes understood in terms of the categories. Beyond that, as in the case of rational psychology, is "mere speculation."

The third attempt to extend knowledge beyond experience is to speculate on the nature of God. For reasons that will appear later, Kant believed in the existence of God, but he is prepared to argue that such belief is not to be confused with knowledge. To attempt to formulate a rational theology, that is, to know God as we know things that fall within our experience, is to attempt the impossible. Kant reiterates and extends Hume's destructive criticism of the grounds for theism. Like rational psychology and rational cosmology, rational theology is "mere speculation." A quotation from Kant is possible here:

Human reason begins with principles which, in the course of experience it must follow. With these again, according to the necessities of its nature, it rises higher and higher to more remote conditions. Thus it becomes involved in darkness and contradictions. It may conclude that errors must be lurking somewhere, but it is unable to discover them because the principles which it follows go beyond all limits of experience and so beyond all experimental verification. Metaphysics is the battlefield of these endless controversies.

Kant contrasts the forms of sensibility and the categories of understanding with these three ideas or forms of speculation. The two former are constitutive of knowledge. That is, within the limits of experience, they enter into and contribute to genuine knowledge. The latter, however, are merely regulative. This distinction between constitutive and regulative forms of knowledge is important. The ideas of self, cosmos, and God are regulative goals toward which knowledge moves but to which it never attains.

Kant's distinction between *phenomena* and *noumena*, between things as known and things-in-themselves, follows as a corollary from this general theory of knowledge. It arises thus: Knowledge is a joint product of mind and external world arising in experience. There are here two contributing factors: the mind and external world. The latter "appears" through the forms and categories of the former. The word *phenomena* is derived from a Greek word meaning "that which appears." Hence reality as known is appearance, is phenomenal, is to be contrasted with reality as it is, which is noumenal. As Kant sweepingly remarks, "We only know phenomena."

We are now in a position to return to the one basic fact which this elaborate theory was invoked to account for, namely, *a priori* knowledge. Our *a priori* knowledge is formal only, and arises out of the dual origin of knowledge. We know *a priori* that things perceived will be perceived as spread-out-and-strung-along. We know *a priori* that things will be understood as effects of causes. We know *a priori* that things will be understood as qualities inhering in substances. We know *a priori* that things will be understood in terms of part–whole relations. And so on through the categories. But this knowledge is purely formal. We do not know *a priori* what the content of future experiences will be. We know that it will exhibit the various forms referred to, because, by hypothesis, knowledge is a joint product of mind-imposed forms filled with experience-given content. Thus did Kant "answer" Hume. At this point we can resume quoting directly from his writings.

I must, therefore, even before objects are given me in experience, presuppose the "rules of the understanding," or the "principles of knowledge" as existing within me *a priori*. These rules are expressed in *a priori* concepts to which all objects of experience must necessarily conform and to which they must agree. By thus changing our point of view, the possibility of *a priori* knowledge can well be explained.

After a superficial view of this work, it may seem that its results are negative only, warning us against venturing beyond the limits of experience. Such is no doubt its primary use. But its results are seen to be positive, when we perceive that it leads inevitably to a narrowing, a limiting, of the employment of reason; to the impossibility of going by it beyond the frontier of possible experience.

But thus and thus alone can we cut away the very root of materialism, idealism, skepticism, fatalism, atheism, fanaticism, and superstition. If governments ever think proper to interfere with the affairs of the learned, it would be consistent with their wise regard for science and society, to favor the freedom of such a criticism as can establish the labors of reason on a firm footing.

To deny that this service, setting limits to the speculative use of reason, is a positive advantage, would be the same as to deny that the police confer any positive advantage on us in preventing that violence which citizens have to fear from citizens. The police protection enables each to pursue his vocation in peace and security. The critique of reason does as much for the powers of the mind.

To illustrate this, let us suppose that the necessary distinction, established in our critique, between things as phenomena and things-in-themselves, had not been made. In that case the principle of causality, and with it the mechanical interpretation of nature, would apply to all things and not to their appearances only. I should then not be able to say of one and the same thing, for instance, the human soul, that it is both free and subject to necessity, without involving myself in a contradiction.

If, however, we may legitimately take an object in two senses, namely, as phenomenon and as thing-in-itself; and if the principle of causality applies to things only as phenomena and not as noumena, then we can, without any contradiction, think one and the same thing when phenomenal as necessarily conforming to the principle of causality and so far not free, and yet, in itself not subject to that principle and therefore free.

Suppose morality necessarily presupposed freedom of the will while speculative reason had proved that such freedom cannot even be thought. In such case freedom, and with it morality, would have to make room for the mechanical interpretation of nature. But our critique has revealed our inevitable ignorance of things-in-themselves, has limited our knowledge to mere phenomena. So, as morality requires only that freedom should not entail a contradiction, there is no reason why freedom should be denied to the will, considered as thing-in-itself, merely because it must be denied to it as phenomenon. The doctrine of morality may well hold its place, and the doctrine of nature too; which would have been impossible without our theory of the nature and limitations of knowledge.

If I cannot deprive speculative reason of its pretensions to transcendent insight, I cannot even assume freedom of will, not even in the interests of morality. I had, therefore, to remove the possibility of knowledge of what lies beyond experience, in order to make room for faith. This question of free will is but one of many which derive positive advantage from the limitations imposed by my theory of knowledge, on the speculative reach of pure reason beyond experience.

Let any reader who finds these inquiries obscure consider that not every one is bound to study metaphysics; that many minds will succeed very well in the exact sciences more closely allied to practical experience while they cannot succeed in investigations dealing exclusively with abstract conceptions. In such cases men should apply their talents to other subjects.

Thus Kant on the problem of knowledge in his *Critique of Pure Reason*. His ideas here are closely connected with the ideas that he was to put into his second *Critique*. The latter was directed toward a clarification and defense of his convictions in ethics.

Note on Sources. The Kant material in this section is quoted, abridged, or paraphrased from his *Critique of Pure Reason*, particularly from the preface to the first edition, the preface to the second edition, and the introduction. In the present volume that carries you to page 591. Kant's argument, at that point, becomes too complicated for anything but a brief outline summary (pp. 591–595). The material on space and time is derived from the Transcendental Aesthetic (*Critique of Pure Reason*, immediately following the introduction). Pages 593–595 again give only a brief outline summary of Kant's doctrines about the categories and the forms of speculation. Then, by way of conclusion, pages 596–597 give further material from Kant's prefaces and introduction to his *Critique*.

Reading References. It has been said that more books have been written on Shakespeare, Goethe, and Kant than on any three other persons. Kant is a perennially attractive figure. Anyone who is familiar with the main turns of modern philosophy can feel the tug that his ideas exert even when had at second hand. The account of Kant to be found in Will Durant's *Story of Philosophy* is for beginners. For those who desire to go a little further, the chapters on Kant in Collingwood's *Metaphysics* are recommended.

READING QUESTIONS

1. Why Kant felt that Hume's philosophical investigations were important.

2. What Kant means by *a priori* knowledge. Give an example. The problem such knowledge raised for him.

3. What was Kant's "Copernican" revolution in philosophy? Why he proposed it. What was revolutionary about it? What was "Copernican" about it?

4. Knowledge, he says, is a joint product. What factors combine to produce it? Problem raised by this "joint-product" conception of knowledge.

5. How close to Kant do you come in Leibniz' remark: *"Nihil est in intellectu quod non primus erat in sensu; nisi intellectus ipse."*

6. Kant's distinction between form and content. How related to his distinction between *a priori* and *a posteriori*.

7. What he means by (a) the forms of sensibility, (b) the categories of understanding, (c) the ideas of reason.

8. Use the notion of either cause or substance to explain what Kant means by calling them categories.

9. How he uses his theory of the "Ideas" to liquidate (a) rational psychology, (b) rational cosmology, (c) rational theology.

10. Point of his distinction between constitutive and regulative.

11. What is the point of his distinction between phenomena and noumena? To what use would he put it?

12. Explanatory comment on: "We only know phenomena."

13. Explanatory comment on his policeman analogy.

14. He says he wanted to make room for faith (a) Why? (b) How?

15. Many persons have boggled at Kant's notion of *noumenal* objects. Why, do you suppose?

INDEPENDENT STUDY

1. Read the account of Collingwood's theory of "absolute presuppositions in Section 4 of this Topic. Then read Collingwood's account of Kant in his (Collingwood's) book *Metaphysics*. Tell what Collingwood says about Kant, relating it to Collingwood's own position.

2. Read the prefatory essay that Kant wrote for the first edition of his *Critique;* and for his *Prolegomena to Every Future Metaphysic;* and for the second edition of his *Critique*. Read also the introductory essay that he wrote for the second edition of his *Critique*. In these essays Kant explains why he wrote the *Critique*. Give an account of Kant's intentions.

SECTION 3. A. J. AYER: THE VERIFIABILITY Like Comte, others·
THEORY OF MEANING

From Kant to Ayer.   Our first author in this topic, David Hume, proposed *impression* as a catch-all term for present experience. Your present experience is providing you with a direct impression of this, that, and the other "object of experience." From these impressions come your *ideas*. To validate any idea his proposal was "Show me the impression." The outcome of this proposal was a considerable amount of high-level skepticism. Many of our most prestigious "ideas" (for example, the idea of God, of necessary connection, of free will, of immortality, of substance, and so on) appear to lack any such basis in "experience," in the sense of direct impressions. Hume proposed that all such "baseless" ideas be "committed to the flames," thus ridding European learning of "abstruse ideas." In traditional language the outcome was the liquidation of all claims to possess any "metaphysical knowledge."

This collapse of "empiricism" ("show me the impression") into skepticism over the entire range of "metaphysical" claims to be knowledge, roused Kant from his dogmatic slumber. He proposed a new task for metaphysics, in performing which it would regain a hold on the life of the mind. The task was to arrive at a systematic and orderly knowledge of what he called *synthetic a priori* ideas or principles; to show the role that they played in the derivation of knowledge from experience. Such ideas or principles were *"a ratione priori";* that is, from reason prior to experience. His usual example was "Every event has a cause." This is not an empirical generalization from experience of events having causes. It is presupposition laid down in advance of experience enabling us to use experience to support the claim that *A* is the cause of event *B*. It thus makes the appeal to experience possible as a source of empirical knowledge. That these *a priori* principles are not empirically derived by us from experience, but are presupposed by us as a necessary condition for deriving knowledge from experience, he called his "Corpernican revolution in philosophy."

In a manner of speaking, this was Kant's "answer" to Hume. It did not restore traditional metaphysics in the sense in which Hume had called that into question. But what it did do was to restore a lively interest in *"a priori"* ideas, and to give them a kind and degree of importance in the life of the mind that Hume and the Humeans found objectionable indeed. Any "committed" empiricist, any "loyal" follower of Hume, looked for the day when Kant's work on behalf of "synthetic *a priori* principles" would be undone, and his "critical metaphysics" shown to be baseless pretension. This counterattack has been attempted by twentieth-century *positivism*. It will be found supplying dynamic motivation in the philosophical writings of A. J. Ayer, whose *verifiability theory of meaning* has been widely entertained as a possible basis upon which to discredit Kant and restore Hume to his slightly altered but still rightful throne. Hence it has come to pass in our day that "metaphysics" has encountered more than skepticism. It has met with repudiation; and the repudiation has been based, not on the grounds that metaphysics is doubtable or doubtful, but on the grounds that it is meaningless. This is more radical than skepticism. It is one thing to say, "I doubt the truth of your claim. I am skeptical about it"; it is another to say, "The question whether your claim is true or false, probable or improbable, does not arise, because your claim is meaningless." If a person utters what sounds like a meaningful statement, you might say, "I doubt that"; but if you suspect that you were mistaken in thinking that it was a meaningful statement, that, in fact, it was so much meaningless jargon, you would not say, "I doubt that." You would say, "Talk sense if you want me to believe or doubt or deny what you say." This is to go beyond skepticism. The thesis "Metaphysical statements are meaningless" is more radical than the thesis "Metaphysical statements are doubtable, or doubtful, or false." This is not itself metaphysics. It is a thesis about metaphysics. Let us refer to it as antimetaphysics. The anti-metaphysician does not have doubts *in* metaphysics. He has doubts *about* metaphysics.

Biographical Note. Alfred Jules Ayer was born in 1910. He was educated at Eton and Oxford. For fourteen years (1932–1946) he held teaching, research, and administrative positions in Oxford colleges. For thirteen years (1946–1959) he was Grote Professor in philosophy in the University of London. In 1959 he was appointed Wykeham Professor of philosophy in Oxford University. His best-known book, *Language, Truth and Logic,* proposing an extended critique of metaphysics and related modes of thinking, was published in 1936. Professor Ayer has done as much as anyone to secure a wide and sympathetic hearing for antimetaphysics in the English-speaking world. He writes with clarity and vigor and great personal conviction. This makes him interesting and persuasive. "He that is not with me is against me" sounds through his lively pages. His writings have done more than stimulate; they have challenged. Many persons relish metaphysics. Professor Ayer has given them a bad conscience, or stirred them to indignation. This was all to the good. It made the years between the two world wars memorable. One of the great debates in philosophy was metaphysics versus antimetaphysics. Ayer's book *Language, Truth and Logic* and Collingwood's book *An Essay on Metaphysics* are excellent handlings, pro and con, of this issue.

Ayer's Antimetaphysics. Professor Ayer has published several books and a great number of papers. His doubts about metaphysics, his campaign against it, will be found in many of these. But two items in particular let you in on the argument—namely, "Demonstration of the Impossibility of Metaphysics," published in 1934 in the English philosophical journal *Mind;* and "The Elimination of Metaphysics," published in 1936 as Chapter I of his book *Language, Truth and Logic.* These, you might say, are antimetaphysics in the grand manner. As the titles indicate, Professor Ayer does not pull his philosophical punches.

His purpose is the same in both papers, namely to evict metaphysics from the mansion of philosophy. The 1934 paper aims to demonstrate that metaphysics is impossible. The 1936 paper aims to eliminate metaphysics. In either case, whether eliminated or shown to be impossible, metaphysics is in for a rough time.

He proposes to achieve this purpose by showing that metaphysics is meaningless. This will show that it is impossible. Now, how do you show that discourse is meaningless? Professor Ayer suggests that you need a criterion of meaning, of meaningfulness. This will enable you to settle the question. If discourse satisfies the criterion, then it is meaningful; if not, then not. What then is the criterion of meaning? How do you get at it? Professor Ayer outlines a procedure.

First, you take cases that everyone agrees are meaningful, and cases that everyone agrees are meaningless. These are "given," that is, you do not choose them by having the criterion of meaning and finding that they do or do not satisfy it. You get them first. Then you ask what it is the meaningful statements have in common, by virtue of which they are meaningful; and what it is the meaningless statements lack, by virtue of which they are meaningless. This gives you the criterion of meaning. An analogy might help. Suppose you want the criterion of rightness, satisfying which you judge an act right. You take cases which everyone agrees are right, and cases which everyone agrees are wrong. These are "given"; that is, you do not choose them by having a criterion of rightness and finding that they do or do not satisfy it. You get them first. Then you ask what it is the right acts have in common, by virtue of which they are right; and what it is the wrong acts lack, by virtue of which they are wrong. This gives you the criterion of rightness. You would proceed similarly if you wanted to get at the criterion for judging whether something is or is not a work of art.

Thus far, then, you have statements whose meaningfulness is not doubtful, statements whose meaninglessness is not doubtful, and the criterion of meaning that the first cases satisfy and the second cases do not. At this point you consider what Professor Ayer calls "doubtful" cases. These would be statements about which you would not be sure, at first glance, whether they were meaningful or meaningless. You apply your criterion to these cases. If they fail to satisfy it, they are meaningless, nonsensical; and out they go. (See *Mind*, p. 345, Vol. 43, 1934.)

So much for procedure. When Professor Ayer followed this procedure, what criterion of meaning did he arrive at? Having ascertained it, he gave it a name: the Verifiability Criterion of Meaning. But we need more than the name. What is the criterion so designated? Here the going is more difficult. Professor Ayer spends many pages in an attempt to find words which will enable him to state the criterion satisfactorily. We will not follow him through the details of this search.

Perhaps this will suffice: he discovers that all unquestionably meaningful statements may be divided into two groups. The first consists of those statements that you would verify or refute by an appeal to experience, an appeal to "observation statements." This verification or refutation would be either direct or indirect. For example, "My neighbor's house is colored green" would be verified directly, by confronting the statement with the experienced fact of the green color of the house. However, "There was a tree there before he cut it down and built his house where the tree stood," or "There are mountains on the far side of the moon," could not be verified directly. The tree is no longer there; and you can't see the other side of the moon. Direct confrontation of statement with experienced fact is not possible. In such cases you show that the statements about the tree and the mountains can be *inferred* from some *other* statements that can be verified directly. In this way the statements about the tree and the mountains are said to be verified indirectly.

To put all this negatively, you would not satisfy yourself of their truth or falsity, probability or improbability, by merely reflecting on their meaning. Their truth or falsity does not stare up at you from their meaning alone. If I say, "There are mountains on the far side of the moon," you do not verify or refute my statement by merely reflecting on its meaning. From a knowledge of its meaning alone you do not get a knowledge of its truth or falsity. Evidence for such statements is not obtained by reflecting on their meaning. This is sometimes expressed in popular speech by saying that they are not their own evidence, are not "self-evident." Professor Ayer calls such statements "empirical." Empirical statements are those that can be verified or refuted either directly or indirectly by an appeal to experience.

The second group stands in sharp contrast. It consists of those statements that you would verify or refute by an appeal to their meaning alone. You would see that they were true or false by reflecting on their meaning. Nothing further would be relevant. To put it negatively, you would not settle their truth or falsity by an appeal, direct or indirect, to any "observation statements." If I say, "All fathers are parents," or, "All circles have equal radii," you do not "check" on these statements by investigating examples of fathers or circles. You reflect on the meaning of what is said and that settles it. From a knowledge of their meaning alone you can arrive at a knowledge of their truth or falsity. Here "evidence" is obtained by reflecting on their meaning. This is sometimes expressed in popular speech by saying that they are, or contain, their own evidence, are "self-evident." Professor Ayer calls such statements "tautologies," or "analytic."

His claim is that all unquestionably meaningful statements are either empirical or tautological, empirical or analytic. The basis for this division is the way in which you would go about to verify or refute them. If they are meaningful, they are verifiable or refutable in either of the two ways explained above; and conversely, if they are verifiable or refutable in either of those two ways, they are meaningful. Since Professor Ayer concedes no third way in which any meaningful statement can be verified or refuted, he speaks of their verifiability, or the mode of their verifiability, as the criterion of their meaningfulness. Further, it will be found that no unquestionably meaningless statement can be verified or refuted in either of these two ways; and, conversely, that any statement that cannot be verified or refuted in either of these two ways, is unquestionably meaningless. This is the Verifiability Criterion of Meaning, and its derivation from admittedly meaningful and meaningless statements. As suggested above, it might as a theory in semantics, be compared, *mutatis mutandis*, to a theory in ethics, for example the Utility Criterion of Rightness, and its derivation from admittedly right and wrong acts.

At this point the argument, now possessed of a criterion of meaning, turns from admittedly meaningful and meaningless statements to doubtful cases. Their fate is to be settled by seeing whether they satisfy the Verifiability Criterion of Meaning in either of its modes; that is, by seeing whether they are empirical or tautological. Professor Ayer closes in on metaphysics. Give him any statement from metaphysics and he puts it to the question, Is it empirical or tautological? Is its claim to be true directly or indirectly, supported or supportable by any fact of experience? Is it claimed to be true because self-evident, true by virtue of its meaning alone?" If so, either way, it is meaningful; if not, it is meaningless.

Once the chips are down, Professor Ayer extends no quarter. The stakes are high and he plays for keeps. His purpose is to exhibit the bankruptcy of traditional metaphysics, to remove metaphysics from philosophy. One metaphysical claim after another is audited and declared bankrupt. This is his "demonstration that metaphysics is impossible," his "elimination of metaphysics" from philosophy. If any so-called metaphysical claim satisfies the criterion, that is, makes sense, is found to be meaningful, it is not declared bankrupt but it is ordered out of philosophy on the grounds that it belongs in some empirical science or in mathematics or in formal logic. By the time Professor Ayer is finished he has, by one or the other of these arguments, emptied philosophy of metaphysics. It is thrown out either on the grounds that it is meaningless or on the grounds that it is not philosophy.

Professor Ayer did not stop at metaphysics. He used the same criterion and the same argument to demonstrate the impossibility, the semantic bankruptcy, of theology, ethics, aesthetics, and much traditional philosophical psychology. As with metaphysics, their claims were tested, found meaningless, and thrown out of philosophy; or found meaningful, therefore empirical or analytic, and declared part of some inductive or deductive science. Their traditional problems and propositions were written off as pseudo-problems and pseudo-propositions, which hustled them into bankruptcy; or they were unmasked as bonafide scientific problems and propositions masquerading as philosophy. In either case they were eliminated from philosophy. All that was left was semantics and logic. Semantics stayed because the Verifiability Criterion of Meaning was needed to initiate these evictions. Logic stayed because its propositions were found to be analytic and hence meaningful.

It seems to me that anyone who has the interests of philosophy at heart will feel grateful to Professor Ayer and the "logical positivists." At least they stirred things up. They made a bonfire of much old lumber. They thinned out the traffic in vague, obscure, and pretentious thinking. They forced those interested in philosophy to put up or shut up. And these things were all to the good.

It would be misleading to suggest that Professor Ayer and the friends of "logical positivism" had things all their own way. In these matters it is possible to win the battles and yet lose the war. The attack raised some valuable questions.

1. Consider, for example, the procedure, described by Professor Ayer in his 1934 paper, for arriving at criteria, in his case the criterion of meaning. You start with positive and negative cases agreed to without benefit of the criterion. Everything hinges on that. This places a premium on knowing what you are talking about before beginning to philosophize about it. If there is serious disagreement about the cases, there is no way to derive the criterion. And you cannot use the criterion to enforce agreement about the cases. If there is

serious disagreement about the cases, all you can do is establish "party lines." You cannot arrive at a knowledge of the criterion that would enable you to rise above such party lines. What is the status of this knowledge which precedes the derivation of the criterion? Is it "above the battle"?

2. Again, consider the statement of a criterion once it has been arrived at. Let it be the criterion of meaning: "a proposition is meaningful, if and only if . . ." and finish it any way you have to. The completed statement is itself meaningful. No one would want it that a statement of the criterion of meaning was itself meaningless. Therefore the statement itself is either empirical or tautological. If it is empirical, then it does not belong in philosophy, but in some empirical science. If it is a tautology ("all fathers are parents," "all circles have equal radii," and so on) then it is "true by definition," to use one of Professor Ayer's expressions. But what is the status of definitions? If they are "arbitrary," you cannot use them to enforce agreement. If they are not arbitrary, what constrains them? [2]

3. One of Professor Ayer's older contemporaries, Professor G. E. Moore, had argued in his *Principia Ethica* that the basic concept in ethics, "good," is indefinable. There is no logically prior concept that you can use to arrive at a definition of "good." Given "good" as indefinable you can use it to define other ethical concepts, for example, right. Now you have here the notion of a basic concept and the thesis that it is indefinable. Does this apply in semantics? If not, why not? If so, is it indefinable? If not, why not? If so, can you use the criterion of meaning, as Professor Ayer proposes, to arrive at a definition of meaning? If so, the "structural analogy" between ethics and semantics does not hold. If not, what is the distinction between and relation between a criterion and a definition?

4. Professor Ayer's elimination of metaphysics requires that metaphysical statements be subject to verification; that the notion of verification should apply to them; and that if it doesn't, the trouble lies with metaphysical statements and not with verification. This is to say that every meaningful statement is either empirical or tautological. Is this true? Are there no meaningful statements which are nei-

---

[2] The friends of the Verifiability Criterion of Meaning have sought to side-step this objection by saying that the verbal formulation of the criterion is itself not a statement, not a proposition, therefore neither true nor false. Instead, they say it is a "proposal" or an "imperative." You don't verify or refute proposals or commands; you act on them or refuse to act on them. Therefore they are not amenable, not answerable, to the Verifiability Criterion of Meaning. They are not meaningful by virtue of satisfying it. It applies only to statements, propositions. However, proposals, commands, petitions, imperatives and the like *are* meaningful. So, this postpones the agony by leaving unsettled the question of the criterion by which proposals, and so on, are to be declared meaningful or meaningless.

ther empirical nor tautological? How about the statement itself? How about such statements as the following: (a) "Every proposition is either true or false." (b) "No true proposition is inconsistent with any other true proposition." (c) "Every event has a cause." (d) "Miracles never happen." (e) "Same cause, same effect." (f) "Matter does not cease to exist." (g) "No surface is both red all over and green all over." (h) "Change occurs according to law." (i) "In the last analysis you always do what you want to do." (j) "Space and time are infinite." (k) "*I ought to* implies *I can.*" (l) "If nothing is necessary, then nothing is probable." (m) "A liar and a thief ought to change his ways." (n) "If H_1 accounts for more facts than any other H, then it is probably true."

5. Verifying and refuting are activities. Are there any principles and presuppositions operative in these activities? If not, why not? If so, then their status is crucial. They make these activities possible. Remove them, and the activities do not get under way. Now, assuming that there are such principles and presuppositions, are they subject to the Verifiability Criterion of Meaning? Are they either empirical or tautological? If so, there is no problem. But suppose they are neither empirical nor tautological. Then the Verifiability Criterion does not cover them. Are they, then, meaningless? Must one say that principles and presuppositions which are operative in "getting to know," in verifying and refuting, are themselves meaningless? The alternative would be to say that they are meaningful, but that in their case some *other* criterion of meaning is involved. Now (a) What is this other criterion? (b) If there is *this* exception to the Verifiability Criterion, can we be sure that there are no other exceptions? How?

Consider this second alternative further. It opens up the possibility that there are principles and presuppositions operating in knowing, proving, refuting, which are not themselves candidates for verification. They make verification possible. Therefore the question "Can they themselves be verified?" does not arise. What principles and presuppositions are thus operative in the activities called getting to know, verifying, refuting, and the like? Let the job of metaphysics be to run them down. Call them "ultimate" or "absolute" to indicate the difference between their status and the status of the empirical statements whose discovery or verification or refutation they make possible. They are operative in verifications, but are not themselves verifiable. They enter into the verification. Then you could say that the task of metaphysics is to ascertain the "ultimate" or "absolute" principles and presuppositions of empirical knowledge. And metaphysics would be back in business again.

The following passage is quoted from Professor Ayer's article "Demonstration of the Impossibility of Metaphysics":

The views expressed in this paper are not original. The work of Wittgenstein inspired it. The arguments which it contains are for the most part such as have been used by writers in *Erkenntnis*, notably by Moritz Schlick in his *Positivismus und Realismus* and Rudolf Carnap in his *Überwindung der Metaphysik durch logische Analyse der Sprache*. But some may find my presentation of them the clearer. And I hope to convince others by whom the work of Wittgenstein and the Viennese school has so far been ignored or misunderstood.

Definition of Metaphysics

My purpose is to prove that any attempt to describe the nature or even to assert the existence of something lying beyond the reach of empirical observation must consist in the enunciation of pseudo-propositions, a pseudo-proposition being a series of words that may seem to have the structure of a sentence but is in fact meaningless. I call this a demonstration of the impossibility of metaphysics because I define a metaphysical enquiry as an enquiry into the nature of the reality underlying or transcending the phenomena which the special sciences are content to study. Accordingly if I succeed in showing that even to ask whether there is a reality underlying the world of phenomena is to formulate a bogus question, so that any assertion about the existence or nature of such a reality is a piece of nonsense, I shall have demonstrated the impossibility of metaphysics in the sense in which I am using the term. If anyone considers this an arbitrary definition, let him refer to any work which he would call metaphysical, and consider how it differs from an enquiry in one of the special sciences. He will find, not that the authors are merely using different means to derive from the same empirical premises the same sort of knowledge, but that they are seeking totally different types of knowledge. The metaphysician is concerned with a reality transcending the phenomena about which the scientist makes his generalisations. The metaphysician rejects the methods of the scientist, not because he believes them to be unfruitful in the field in which the scientist operates, but because he believes that by his own metaphysical methods he will be able to obtain knowledge in his own metaphysical field. It will be shown in this paper not that the metaphysician ought to use scientific methods to attain his end, but that the end itself is vain. Whatever form of reasoning he employs, he succeeds in saying nothing.

Comparison with Kant's Procedure

That the speculative reason falls into self-contradiction when it ventures out beyond the limits of experience is a proposition maintained by Kant. But by his formulation of the matter he is committed to a view different from that which will here be maintained. For he implies that there is a transcendent reality, but the constitution of our speculative reason is such that we cannot hope to gain knowledge of it: he should therefore find no absurdity in imagining that some other being, say a god, had knowledge of it, even though the existence of such a being could not be proved. Whereas on our view to say that there is or that there is not a transcendent reality is to utter a pseudo-proposition, a word-series empty of logical content: and no supposition about the knowledge of a higher reality possessed by a higher being is for us even a significant hypothesis. The difference between the two views is best expressed by saying that while Kant attempted to show that there were certain problems which the speculative reason was in virtue of its own nature incapable of solving, our aim is to show that these are not genuine problems.

No criticism of Kant's transcendental philosophy will be undertaken in this paper. But the method by which we demonstrate the impossibility of metaphysics, in the sense in which Kant too held it to be impossible, serves also to show that no knowledge is both synthetic and *a priori*. And this is enough to prove the impossibility of metaphysics, in the special sense which Kant reserved for the term, though it in no way discredits the excellent pieces of philosophical analysis which the *Critique of Pure Reason* contains.

Formulation of a Criterion of Significance

The method of achieving these results lies in the provision of a criterion by which the genuineness of all *prima facie* propositions may be tested. Having laid down the conditions which must be fulfilled by whatever is to be a significant proposition, we shall find that the propositions of metaphysics fail to satisfy the conditions and are therefore meaningless.

What is it, then, that we are asking when we ask what is the meaning of a proposition? I say "ask the meaning of a proposition" rather than "ask the meaning of a concept," because questions about the meaning of concepts reduce themselves to questions about the meanings of propositions. To discover the meaning of a concept we form its corresponding primary proposition, i.e., the simplest proposition in which it can significantly occur, and attempt to analyse this. I repeat "what is it that we are asking when we ask what is the meaning of a proposition?" There are various ways in which the correct answer can be formulated. One is to say that we are asking what are the propositions to which the proposition in question is reducible. For instance, if "being an amphisbæna" means "being a serpent with a head at both ends," then the proposition "X is an amphisbæna" is reducible to (or derivable from) the propositions "X is a serpent" and "X has a head at either end of its body." These propositions are in turn reducible to others until we reach the elementary propositions which are not descriptive at all but ostensive. When the analysis reaches its furthest point the meaning of the proposition can no longer be defined in terms of other propositions but only pointed to or shown. It is to this process that those philosophers refer who say that philosophy is an activity and not a doctrine.

Alternatively the procedure of definition may be described by saying that to give the meaning of a proposition is to give the conditions under which it would be true and those under which it would be false. I understand a proposition if I know what observations I must make in order to establish its truth or falsity. This may be more succinctly expressed by saying that I understand a proposition when I know what facts would verify it. To indicate the situation which verifies a proposition is to indicate what the proposition means.

Application of the Criterion

Let us assume that some one says of my cat that it is corylous. I fail to understand him and enquire what circumstances would make it true to say that the cat was corylous. He replies "its having blue eyes." I conclude that in the sense in which he uses the word corylous "X is corylous" means "X has blue eyes." If he says that, although the fact that my cat has blue eyes and no other fact makes it true to say that it is corylous, nevertheless he means by "corylous" something more than "blue-eyed," we may infer that the use of the word "corylous" has for him a certain emotional value which is absent when he merely says "blue-eyed." But so long as its having blue eyes is all that is necessary to establish the truth of the proposition that something is corylous, and its having eyes of another colour all that is necessary to establish its falsehood, then "having blue eyes" is all that "being corylous" means.

In the case when something is called corylous and no description or indication can be given of the situation which verifies the proposition, we must conclude that the assertion is meaningless. If the speaker protests that he does mean something, but nothing that mere observation can establish, we allow that he has certain feelings which are in some way connected with the emission of the sound "corylous": and it may be a matter of interest to us that he should express these feelings. But he does not thereby make any assertion about the world. He utters a succession of words, but they do not form a genuine proposition. His sentence may provide good evidence of his feelings. In itself it has no sense.

So in every case where we have a series of words which seems to be a good grammatical sentence, and we wish to discover whether it really makes sense—i.e., whether it expresses a genuine proposition—we must consider what are the circumstances in which the proposition apparently expressed would be called true or false: what difference in the world its truth or falsity would entail. And if those who have uttered it or profess to understand it are unable to describe what in the world would be different, if it were true or false, or in any way to show how it could be verified, then we must conclude that nothing has been asserted. The series of words in question does not express a genuine proposition at all, but is as much a piece of nonsense as "the moon is the square root of three" or "Lenin or coffee how." The difference is merely that in some cases where a very slight transformation of the phrase, say the alteration of a single word, would turn it into a propositional sign, its senselessness is harder to detect.

Meaninglessness of Every Metaphysical Assertion

In this way it can quickly be shown that any metaphysical assertion is nonsensical. It is not necessary to take a list of metaphysical terms such as the Absolute, the Unconditioned, the Ego, and so forth, and prove each of them to be meaningless: for it follows from the task metaphysics sets itself that all its assertions must be nonsense. For it is the aim of metaphysics to describe a reality lying beyond experience, and therefore any proposition which would be verified by empirical observation is *ipso facto* not metaphysical. But what no observation could verify is not a proposition. The fundamental postulate of metaphysics "There is a super- (or hinter-) phenomenal reality" is itself not a proposition. For there is no observation or series of observations we could conceivably make by which its truth or falsehood would be determined. It may seem to be a proposition, having the sensible form of a proposition. But nothing is asserted by it.

An example may make this clearer. The old conflict between Idealism and Realism is a fine instance of an illusory problem. Let us assume that a picture is unearthed, and that the finder suggests that it was painted by Goya. There are definite means of settling this question. The critics examine the picture and consider what points of resemblance it has to other works of Goya. They see if there is any contemporary or subsequent reference to the existence of such a work—and so on. Suppose now that two of the experts have also read philosophy and raise a further point of dispute. One says that the picture is a collection of ideas (his own or God's): the other that its colours are objectively real. What possible means have they of settling this question? Can either of them indicate any circumstances in which to the question "are those colours a collection of ideas?" or to the question "are those colours objective sensibilia?" the answer "yes" or "no" could be given? If they cannot then no such questions arise. And plainly they cannot. If it is raining now outside my window my observations are different from what they would be if it were fine. I assert that it rains and my proposition is verifiable. I can indicate the situation by which its truth or falsity is established. But if I ask "is the rain real or ideal?" this is a question which no observations enable me to answer. It is accordingly not a genuine question at all.

It is advisable here to remove a possible source of misunderstanding. I am not maintaining that if we wish to discover whether in a *prima facie* proposition anything is really being asserted, we must consider whether what seems to be asserted is practically verifiable. As Professor Schlick has pointed out, it makes perfectly good sense to say "there is a mountain 10,000 feet high on the other side of the moon," although this is a proposition which through practical disabilities we are not and may never be in a position to verify. But it is in principle verifiable. We know what sort of observations would verify or falsify it. If we got to the other side of the moon we should know how to settle the question. But the assertions of metaphysics are in principle unverifiable. We may take up any position in space and time that our imagination allows us to accupy, no observation that we can make therefrom makes it even probable in the least degree that any answer to a metaphysical question is correct. And therefore we conclude that there are no such questions.

Metaphysical Assertions Not Hypotheses

So the conclusion is not that metaphysical assertions are uncertain or arbitrary or even false, but that they are nonsensical. They are not hypotheses, in the sense in which general propositions of law are hypotheses. It is true that assertions of such general propositions are not assertions of fact in the way that assertions of singular propositions are assertions of fact. To that extent they are in no better case than metaphysical assertions. But variable hypotheticals (general propositions of law) make sense in a way in which metaphysical assertions do not. For a hypothesis has grounds. A certain sequence of events occurs and a hypothesis is formulated to account for it—i.e., on the strength of the hypothesis, when we make one such observation, we assume that we shall be able to make the others. It is the essence of a hypothesis that it admits of being used. In fact, the meaning of such general propositions is defined by reference to the situations in which they serve as rules for predictions, just as their truth is defined by reference to the accuracy of the predictions to which believing them gives rise. A so-called hypothesis which is not relevant to any situation is not a hypothesis at all. As a general proposition it is senseless. Now there is no situation in which belief in a metaphysical proposition bridges past and potential observations, in the way in which my belief in the poisonousness of arsenic connects my observation of a man's swallowing it with my expectation that he will shortly die. Therefore metaphysical propositions are not hypotheses. For they account for nothing.

READING QUESTIONS

1. Use Descartes or Hobbes or Berkeley or Schopenhauer, to illustrate what it is about traditional metaphysics that invites skepticism.
2. What is a "criterion of meaning"? Why Professor Ayer is interested in formulating one. How he goes about to do so. What criterion of meaning resulted.
3. Elucidate the phrase "The Verifiability Theory of Meaning." In what sense is it, as a theory in semantics, comparable to a theory in ethics, e.g., utilitarianism?
4. How would you distinguish between these two statements: (a) Every father is a parent. (b) Every father is happy.
5. How Professor Ayers uses the Verifiability Theory of Meaning, a doctrine in semantics, to eliminate all doctrines in metaphysics.
6. Point here: "If there is a disagreement about the cases."
7. Point here: "The statement itself is either empirical or tautological."
8. Point here: "A basic concept and the thesis that it is indefinable."

9. Point of the (a–n) statements on page 606.
10. Point here: The status of principles and presuppositions operative in such activities as getting to know, verifying, refuting, and so on.
11. How the demand that metaphysical statements be confirmable leads to Professor Collingwood's notion of pseudo-metaphysics (see p. 618).
12. Point of Professor Ayer's contrast between himself and Kant.
13. Professor Ayer: "Metaphysical Assertions (are) not Hypotheses." (a) Why not? (b) What then are they?
14. Wherein you find Professor Ayer (a) most, (b) least convincing.

INDEPENDENT STUDY

1. Read the chapter on the *a priori* in Ayer's *Language, Truth and Logic*. Supplement it by anything else he has written on that topic. Compare and contrast Ayer's position with Hume and Kant.
2. Read the brief article on Ayer by D. J. O'Connor in the *Encyclopedia of Philosophy*. Then read the articles "Positivism" by N. Abbagnano and "Logical Positivism" by J. Passmore in the same encyclopedia. Using these three articles, together with anything you have read by Ayer, work out a paper on his position.
3. Read Chapters 6 and 7 of Ayer's *Language, Truth and Logic*. These chapters give his criticisms of ethics and theology and some positions in philosophical psychology. They will extend your knowledge of his thinking beyond his criticism of metaphysics. Work out a paper on the rationale of his claims in these two chapters.

SECTION 4. R. G. COLLINGWOOD: SCIENCE HAS PRESUPPOSITIONS

From Ayer to Collingwood. Ayer's book *Language, Truth and Logic,* was published in 1936. He aimed to continue the empiricism of Hume, providing it with the benefits of European positivism, especially German and Austrian in the twentieth century. The book became a text, not to say something of a scripture, for much Anglo-American philosophizing during the years before World War II.

Like Hume in his *Treatise* and *Enquiry,* Ayer argued for the elimination ("commit it to the flames") of metaphysics. It will be recalled that Hume's attack on metaphysics roused Kant from his dogmatic slumber, goading him into writing his *Critique* and *Pro-legomena*, in which he argued for a redefinition and reconstitution of metaphysics along lines intended to provide it with a new lease on life. The Kantian "critical metaphysics" was to work out a systematic and orderly account of the role of synthetic *a priori* principles (e.g., "Every event has a cause") in the scientific thinking of animals rational in Sense Two.

Something comparable to Kant's response to Hume is to be found in Collingwood's response to Ayer. Collingwood's book *Essay on Metaphysics* was published in 1940. It proposed a Kant-like alternative to the then lively positivism for which Ayer's book was a symbol. In it he argued for a redefinition and reconstitution of metaphysics along lines intended to provide it with a new lease on life. The Collingwoodian "critical metaphysics" was to work out a systematic and orderly account of absolute presuppositions ("Every event has a cause") in the scientific thinking of rational animals.

Biographical Note. R. G. Collingwood was born in England in 1889, and died in 1943 at the age of fifty-four. Professor T. M. Knox, concludes his memorial paper for the British Academy with the statement: ". . . his was the most original and constructive mind in English philosophy since Bradley." Collingwood was educated at Eton and Oxford. He became a fellow and tutor of Pembroke College at Oxford in 1912. He served with the Admiralty Intelligence during World War I, and returned to his college when the war was over. In 1934 he was appointed Waynflete Professor of Metaphysical Philosophy to succeed J. A. Smith, and was elected a Fellow of the British Academy. In 1938 he received an Honorary L.L.D. from St. Andrews University in Scotland. He retired in 1941. His most important philosophical books were *Speculum Mentis* (1924), *An Essay on Philosophical Method* (1933), *The Principles of Art* (1937), *An Autobiography* (1939), *An Essay on Metaphysics* (1940), *The New Leviathan* (1942), *The Idea of Nature* (1945), and *The Idea of History* (1946). These books provide ample support for Professor Knox's remark about Collingwood's place in English philosophy since Bradley.

The Argument of the Passages. The following passages are taken from Collingwood's book *An Essay on Metaphysics.* The thesis of the book is that scientific thinking, thinking productive of science, rests upon presuppositions which are not themselves pieces of scientific knowledge. The title is intended to suggest that the term *metaphysics* be reserved for the name of the activity whereby a knowing mind diagnoses—analyzes out—its science-producing presuppositions. Since these presuppositions cannot be verified or refuted, they are never known to be either true or false. They are never proved or disproved. When presupposed, however, they make proof possible. Collingwood calls them "absolute presuppositions," and his book deals with the role which such presuppositions play in the activity called "getting to know." To try to prove an absolute presupposition is to treat it as a hypothesis. This is to mistake its character in relation to knowledge. Ferretting out absolute presuppositions Collingwood calls "metaphysics"; trying to prove them, once they have been tracked down, he calls "pseudo-metaphysics," and warns against it as the besetting mistake of empiricism or positivism when it seeks to promote presuppositions into knowledge, or, seeks to abandon them when it finds that such promoting is not possible. His book on these matters is an interesting alternative to Professor Ayer's *Language, Truth and Logic*. It is related to that lively book in something the same way that Kant's *Critique* and *Prolegomena* were related to Hume's *Treatise* and *Inquiry*. Collingwood's absolute presuppositions invite comparison with Kant's synthetic *a priori* propositions.

Scientific Thinking

In proportion as a man is thinking scientifically, when he makes a statement, he knows that his statement is the answer to a question and knows what the question is. To ask questions, knowing that you are asking them, is the first stage in high-grade thinking.

Has Presuppositions

Whenever anybody states a thought there are more thoughts in his mind than are expressed in his statement. Among these, some stand in a peculiar relation to the thought he has stated: they are its presuppositions.

One can make presuppositions without knowing it, and without knowing what presuppositions one is making.

In low-grade or unscientific thinking we hardly know that we are making any presuppositions at all.

Every question involves a presupposition from which it "arises." This presupposition in turn has other presuppositions, which are thus indirectly presupposed by the question. Unless this presupposition were made, the question to which it is logically prior could not be logically asked.

Some of These Are "Absolute"

A presupposition is either relative or absolute. By a relative presupposition I mean one which stands to one question as its presupposition and to another question as its answer.

To question a presupposition, to demand that it be "verified," is to demand that a question be asked to which the affirmative answer would be that presupposition itself. To verify the presupposition that my measuring-tape is accurate is to ask a question admitting of the answer "the tape is accurate." Hence to speak of verifying a presupposition involves supposing that it is a relative presupposition.

An absolute presupposition is one which stands, relatively to all questions to which it is related, as a presupposition, never as an answer. Thus if you asked a pathologist about a certain disease "What is the cause of the event E which sometimes happens in this disease?" he would reply "The cause of E is C. That was established by So-and-so." You might go on to ask: "I suppose before So-and-so found out what the cause of E was, he was quite sure it has a cause?" The answer would be "Quite sure, of course." If you now say "Why?" he will probably answer, "Because everything that happens has a cause." If you ask "But how do you know that everything that happens has a cause?" he will probably blow up right in your face, because you have put your finger on one of his absolute presuppositions, and people are apt to be ticklish in their absolute presuppositions. But if he keeps his temper and gives you a civil and candid answer, it will be to the following effect: "That is a thing we take for granted in my job. We don't question it. We don't try to verify it. It isn't a thing anybody has discovered, like microbes or the circulation of the blood." He is telling you that it is an absolute presupposition of the science he pursues.

An absolute presupposition is not a "dodge," and people who "start" a new one do not start it because they "like" to start it. People are not ordinarily aware of their absolute presuppositions, and are not, therefore, aware of changes in them; such a change, therefore, cannot be a matter of choice. Nor is there anything superficial or frivolous about it. It is the most radical change a man can undergo, and entails the abandonment of all his most firmly established habits and standards for thought and action.

Why do such changes happen? Briefly, because the absolute presuppositions of any given society, at any given phase of its history, form a structure which is subject to "strains" of greater or less intensity, which are "taken up" in various ways, but never annihilated. If the strains are too great, the structure collapses and is replaced by another, which will be a modification of the old with the destructive strain removed; a modification not consciously devised but created by a process of unconscious thought.

Peculiar Status of Absolute Presuppositions

Absolute presuppositions are not verifiable. This does not mean that we should like to verify them but are not able to; it means that the idea of verification is an idea which does not apply to them; because, to speak of verifying a presupposition involves supposing that it is a relative presupposition.

The distinction between truth and falsehood does not apply to absolute presuppositions. Putting the same point differently: absolute presuppositions are never propounded; they are presupposed. To be propounded is not their business; their business is to be presupposed. The scientist's business, as we shall see, is not to propound them but to propound the proposition that this or that one of them is presupposed.

We do not acquire absolute presuppositions by arguing; on the contrary, unless we have them already, arguing is impossible to us. Nor can we change them by arguing; unless they remained constant all our arguments would fall to pieces. We cannot confirm ourselves in them by "proving" them; proof depends on them, not they on proof.

Absolute presuppositions are not "derived from experience," but are catalytic agents which the mind must bring out of its own resources to the manipulation of what is called "experience" and conversion of it into science.

An absolute presupposition cannot be undermined by the verdict of "experience," because it is the yard-stick by which "experience" is judged.

Metaphysics Is the Study of Such Presuppositions

There are absolute presuppositions. The analysis which detects them I call metaphysical analysis.

Metaphysics is the science which deals with the presuppositions underlying science.

The business of metaphysics is to reveal the absolute presuppositions that are involved in any given piece of thinking. The general class of study to which metaphysics belongs is thus the study of thought. Metaphysics is one branch of the science of thought.

There are two things you can do with absolute presuppositions. One of them is what the scientist does, and the other what the metaphysician does. You can presuppose them, which is what the scientist does; or you can find out what they are, which is what the metaphysician does. I mean finding out what absolute presuppositions are in fact made.

Metaphysics arises out of the pursuit of knowledge. That pursuit, science, involves disentangling the presuppositions of our thought. This again involves discovering that some of them are relative presuppositions which have to be justified, and that others are absolute presuppositions which neither stand in need of justification nor can in fact be justified. A person who has made this discovery is already a metaphysician.

Science and metaphysics are inextricably united, stand or fall together. The birth of science, the establishment of orderly thinking, is also the birth of metaphysics. As long as either lives the other lives; if either dies the other must die with it.

Metaphysical analysis, the discovery that certain presuppositions are absolute, is an integral part of scientific work. In the interests of science it is necessary that the work of metaphysics should be done.

Physics has become a science by obtaining a firm grasp on its own presuppositions, asking questions that arose from them, and devising experiments by which these should be answered.

It is important for every one who either thinks scientifically, or profits by the fruits of other peoples' scientific thinking, that the work of metaphysics should be done, and well done.

People do not need to analyse their thoughts very deeply in order to find out that there are a good many things they take for granted. Further analysis, however, is needed to settle the question whether the things are taken relatively for granted or absolutely for granted. It might seem that the question should be an easy one to answer, because presupposing is a thing people do in their minds, and the distinction between presupposing relatively and presupposing absolutely is a distinction between two ways of doing it, so that a man need only be ordinarily intelligent and truthful, one might think, to give an accurate answer to the question which of them he is doing.

But it is not quite so simple as that. To begin with, people may have a motive for deceiving themselves and each other. In modern Europe absolute presuppositions are unfashionable. The smart thing is to deny their existence. Even people who regard this as a silly fashion may be so far influenced by it as to weaken at the critical moment when every available ounce of determination is needed in order to decide whether a given presupposition is absolute or relative; and may allow a kind of mass-suggestion to decide them in favour of its being relative.

It is only by analysis that any one can come to know either that he is making absolute presuppositions or what absolute presuppositions he is making. Such analysis may in certain cases proceed in the following manner. If the inquirer can find a person to experiment upon who is well trained in a certain type of scientific work, intelligent and earnest in his devotion to it, and unaccustomed to metaphysics, let him probe into various presuppositions that his "subject" has been taught to make in the course of his scientific education, and invite him to justify each or to abandon it. If the "inquirer" is skilful and the "subject" the right kind of man, these invitations will be contemplated with equanimity, and even with interest, so long as relative presuppositions are concerned. But when an absolute presupposition is touched, the invitation will be rejected, even with a certain degree of violence.

The rejection is a symptom that the "subject," cooperating with the work of analysis, has come to see that the presupposition he is being asked to justify or abandon is an absolute presupposition; and the violence with which it is expressed is a symptom that he feels the importance of this absolute presupposition for the kind of work to which he is devoted. This is what I called being "ticklish in one's absolute presuppositions." This ticklishness is a sign of intellectual health combined with a low degree of analytical skill. A man who is ticklish in that way is a man who knows, "instinctively" as they say, that absolute presuppositions do not need justification.

This is a precarious method, because the qualifications it demands in the "subject" are too delicate. As soon as the "subject" understands what is going on he will lose the ticklishness on which his value depends. The only altogether satisfactory method is for the analyst to experiment on himself; because this is the only case in which familiarity with the experiments will make the subject more valuable, instead of less. But it demands great resolution, and the temptation to cheat is stronger than one would expect. The purpose of the experiments is to find out what absolute presuppositions are made. Presuppositions are brought to light, and about each the question is raised and settled whether it is relative or absolute.

It is a mistake to fancy that by investigating the truth of their absolute presuppositions a metaphysician could show that one school of science was fundamentally right and another fundamentally wrong.

Some persons think there are two things you can do with absolute presuppositions: presuppose them, which is what the ordinary scientist does with them; or find out whether they are true or false, which is what the metaphysician does with them. I deny this. The second thing cannot be done. To inquire into the truth of a presupposition is to assume that it is a relative presupposition. Such a phrase as "inquiry into the truth of an absolute presupposition" is nonsense.

I distinguish between metaphysics and pseudo-metaphysics. Pseudo-metaphysics will ask such questions as this, where AP stands for any absolute presupposition: Is AP true? Upon what evidence is AP accepted? How can we demonstrate AP? What right have we to presuppose it if we can't? Answers to questions like these are neither metaphysical truths nor metaphysical errors. They are nonsense: the kind of nonsense which comes of thinking that what is absolutely presupposed must be either true or false. That kind of nonsense I call pseudo-metaphysics. Let the distinction between metaphysics and pseudo-metaphysics be firmly grasped. Let it be understood that the business of metaphysics is to find out what absolute presuppositions have actually been made by various persons at various times in doing various pieces of scientific thinking.

Metaphysics Is an Historical Investigation

All metaphysical questions are historical questions, and all metaphysical propositions are historical propositions.

Metaphysics is the attempt to find out what absolute presuppositions have been made by this or that person or group of persons, on this or that occasion or group of occasions, in the course of this or that piece of scientific thinking. Arising out of this, it will consider (for example) whether absolute presuppositions are made singly or in groups, and if the latter, how the groups are organized; whether different absolute presuppositions are made by different individuals or races or nations or classes; or on occasions when different things are being thought about; or whether the same have been made *semper, ubique, ab omnibus.* And so on.

The metaphysician is not confined to one single constellation of absolute presuppositions. He has before him an indefinite number of them. He can study the presuppositions of European science at any phase in its history for which he has evidence. He can study the presuppositions of Arabic science, of Indian science, of Chinese science; again in all their phases, so far as he can find evidence for them. He can study the presuppositions of the science practised by "primitive" and "prehistoric" peoples. All these are his proper work; not an historical background for his work, but his work itself.

When he has some knowledge about several different constellations of absolute presuppositions, he can compare them. This has its uses. It can convince the metaphysician that there are no "eternal" or "crucial" or "central" problems in metaphysics. It will rid him of the parish-pump idea that the metaphysical problems of his own generation, or, more likely, the one next before his own, are the problems that all metaphysicians have been worrying about. It will give him a hint of the way in which different sets of absolute presuppositions correspond not only with differences in the structure of what is generally called scientific thought but with differences in the entire fabric of civilization.

Reflections on Positivism

Positivism is the doctrine that the only valid method of attaining knowledge is the method used in the natural sciences, and hence that no knowledge is genuine unless it either is natural science or resembles natural science in method.

Positivists say that scientific thought has no presuppositions.

They never discovered that there were such things as absolute presuppositions. Presuppositions they misunderstood as general propositions about matters of fact, advanced upon credit and awaiting verification. This would do at a pinch as an account of relative presuppositions, in whose case verification is a word that has meaning. As an account of absolute presuppositions, which are neither in need of verification nor susceptible of it, the description of them as generalizations is nonsensical.

The positivist says either of two things about an absolute presupposition. (1) He describes it as a generalization about matters of fact; and consequently maintains that by observing facts one could hope to verify it. Indeed, it must have been arrived at by observing facts; for here it is; and there was no other way in which that could have been arrived at. Heads I win. (2) He says that it was not arrived at by observing facts, for it was not a record of observations; and that, since there was no other way in which it could have been arrived at, it had not been arrived at; consequently, although it looks like a significant statement, it could not be one; it is just a piece of nonsense. Tails you lose.

They take absolute presuppositions and play "heads I win" with them, in order to exhibit them as generalizations from observed facts. Their reason for playing "heads I win" with them, arises from the fact that, having constituted themselves philosophical patrons of natural science, they thought themselves bound to justify any presuppositions which natural science thought fit to make. "Metaphysics," said Bradley, "is the finding of bad reasons for what we believe upon instinct." If I understand this epigram correctly, it is an accurate description of what the positivist does when he attempts to justify some absolute presupposition inductively. What Bradley seems to be saying is this: "Why we believe things of that kind I do not know. Let us give this ignorance a name by saying that we believe them upon instinct; meaning that it is not because we see reason to believe them. Metaphysics is the attempt to find reasons for these beliefs. Experience shows that the reasons thus found are always bad ones."

It is not the business of metaphysics to find reasons for "what we believe upon instinct," to raise the presuppositions of ordinary scientific thinking to the level of ascertained and demonstrated truths.

The positivistic mistake about metaphysics is the mistake of thinking that metaphysics is the attempt to justify by appeal to observed facts the absolute presuppositions of our thought. This attempt is bound to fail because absolute presuppositions cannot stand as the answers to questions, and therefore the question whether they are justifiable, which in effect is identical with the question whether they are true, is a question that cannot logically arise. To ask it is the hall-mark of pseudo-metaphysics.

If metaphysics were an attempt to provide empirical justification for the presuppositions of science, it might prove detrimental to science itself, not by its success but by its failure; for when the discovery was made that no justification of this kind is to be had, the belief that it is nevertheless necessary might lead to the false conclusion that the whole fabric of scientific thought is rotten at the core.

It is a characteristic of modern European civilization that metaphysics is habitually frowned upon and the existence of absolute presuppositions denied. If this denial ever achieves the eradication of metaphysics, the eradication of science and civilization will be accomplished at the same time.

The result of thinking systematically according to any given set of presuppositions is the creation of science. The result of thinking systematically about what presuppositions are actually in use is the creation of metaphysics. The result of simply presupposing our presuppositions, clinging to them by a sheer act of faith, whether or not we know what they are, whether or not we work out their consequences, is the creation of a religion.

Note on Sources. The above materials are quoted, with an occasional abridgment or paraphrase, from Collingwood's book *An Essay on Metaphysics.* The passages are almost all from Part I and Part II of that book.

Reading References. Collingwood, like Plato and William James and a small number of other writers on philosophy, is a joy to read. The student is recommended, therefore, to secure a copy of *An Essay on Metaphysics* and read for himself as much as he will. Collingwood conceives of philosophy, in general, as the activity whereby a mind gets to know the principles and presuppositions which are operative in its thinking and acting. Thus *An Essay on Metaphysics* does this for the activity called "getting to know." His *Principles of Art* does this for the activity whereby an artist produces, or "creates," a work of art. His *The New Leviathan* does this for man considered as a political animal. His *The Idea of History* does it for the activity by which the historian produces some history—i.e., seeks to make the past intelligible. His *Autobiography* contains an account of the activities and experiences which led him to entertain and elaborate this conception of the activity called philosophizing.

READING QUESTIONS

1. His distinction between absolute and relative presuppositions.
2. Do absolute presuppositions change? If so, why?
3. He says they are neither true nor false. Why not?
4. His distinction between metaphysics and pseudo-metaphysics.
5. His distinction between what the scientist does and what the metaphysician does.
6. "Science and metaphysics stand or fall together." How so?
7. Why people are "ticklish" in their presuppositions.
8. Sense in which "metaphysics" is a historical science, according to Collingwood.
9. Sense in which positivists play "heads I win" and "tails you lose" with absolute presuppositions. Why they do this.
10. His distinction here: (a) science, (b) metaphysics, (c) religion.
11. Wherein you find Collingwood (a) most, (b) least convincing.

INDEPENDENT STUDY

1. The four sections in this Topic have been used to suggest that the relation of eighteenth-century empiricism, as represented in Hume, to eighteenth-century "critical metaphysics," as represented in Kant, is analogous to the relation of twentieth-century positivism, as represented in Ayer, to twentieth-century "critical metaphysics," as represented in Collingwood. Write an essay attacking or defending this suggested analogy.
2. Read the brief article on Collingwood by A. Donagan in the *Encyclopedia of Philosophy*. Then read Collingwood's *Autobiography* in which he gives an account of his philosophical thinking down to 1938. Write a paper on one or more essential components in Collingwood's position as of that time. The *Essay on Metaphysics* was not published until 1940. Do you see any indications that it is on its way?
3. Take the claim that every event has a cause. Track down half-a-dozen essays dealing with the status of this claim. Use them to arrive at a statement of what you think yourself.
4. Read Thomas Kuhn's book *The Structure of Scientific Revolution*. Give an account of what he says, making clear any point or points where his claims resemble Collingwood's account of absolution presuppositions in relation to the science of an epoch.

index

623